A GAZETTEER OF VIRGINIA AND WEST VIRGINIA

By
HENRY GANNETT

Two Volumes in One

CLEARFIELD

Reprinted for
Clearfield Company, Inc. by
Genealogical Publishing Co., Inc.
Baltimore, Maryland
1994, 1998, 2002

Originally published: Washington, D.C., 1904
as *A Gazetteer of Virginia*,
U.S. Geological Survey, Bulletin No. 232
and *A Gazetteer of West Virginia*,
U.S. Geological Survey, Bulletin No. 233
Reprinted: Two volumes in one
Genealogical Publishing Co., Inc.
Baltimore, 1975, 1980
From a volume in the Enoch Pratt Free Library
Baltimore, Maryland
Library of Congress Catalogue Card Number 74-21655
International Standard Book Number 0-8063-0657-2
Made in the United States of America

| 58TH CONGRESS, | HOUSE OF REPRESENTATIVES. | DOCUMENT |
| 2d Session. | | No. 727. |

Bulletin No. 232   Series F, Geography, 40

DEPARTMENT OF THE INTERIOR
UNITED STATES GEOLOGICAL SURVEY
CHARLES D. WALCOTT, DIRECTOR

A

GAZETTEER OF VIRGINIA

BY

HENRY GANNETT

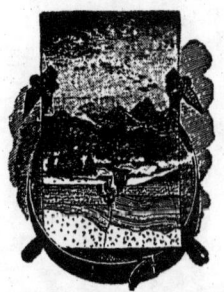

LETTER OF TRANSMITTAL.

DEPARTMENT OF THE INTERIOR,
UNITED STATES GEOLOGICAL SURVEY,
Washington, D. C., March 9, 1904.

SIR: I have the honor to transmit herewith, for publication as a bulletin, a gazetteer of Virginia.

Very respectfully,

HENRY GANNETT,
Geographer.

Hon. CHARLES D. WALCOTT,
Director United States Geological Survey.

A GAZETTEER OF VIRGINIA.

By Henry Gannett.

GENERAL DESCRIPTION OF THE STATE.

Virginia is one of the easternmost States of the Union. It lies on the Atlantic seaboard between latitudes 36° 30' and 39° 30' and longitudes 75° and 84°. Its limits are very irregular, except on the south, and even there the boundary, though nominally a parallel of latitude, is actually by no means such a line.

From the Atlantic Ocean, just above the parallel of 38°, the boundary crosses the peninsula known as the Eastern Shore, which separates Chesapeake Bay from the Atlantic, in a direction south of west. Then, after a sinuous course among islands fringing the west coast of this peninsula, it crosses Chesapeake Bay to a point on the south side of the mouth of Potomac River. It follows the south bank of the Potomac at low-water line up to Harpers Ferry, where the river cuts through the Blue Ridge. Here the boundary leaves the river and makes a generally southwest course, with several jogs to the northwest, to a point near the head of the Tug Fork of the Big Sandy. From this point it follows a fairly constant southwest course, most of the way along the summit of Pine Mountain, to Cumberland Gap. Here it turns sharply to the east along a parallel which was originally intended to be 36° 30' north latitude. The line in reality, however, is from 2 to 6 minutes north of that parallel. This general eastern course it follows to the Atlantic coast.

Virginia was one of the original thirteen States. It adopted the Constitution on June 25, 1788. As admitted it comprised not only its present area but West Virginia and Kentucky. Kentucky was set off and admitted as an independent State June 1, 1792. During the civil war the counties forming what is now the State of West Virginia were admitted to the Union as an independent State, the admission taking effect June 19, 1863.

In 1791 the State ceded to the General Government a tract of country lying south of the Potomac and forming what is now the county of Alexandria, Va., as a portion of the District of Columbia, but in 1846

5

Congress re-ceded this area to the State. The gross area of Virginia as at present constituted is 42,450 square miles, of which 40,125 is land area, the remainder consisting of land-locked bays and harbors, Drummond Lake, and rivers.

The topography is varied. Along the coast and extending for a varying distance inland the surface is low, being in few places over 200 feet above tide, and along the immediate coast much of the land is marshy. The rivers in this part of the State have the form of estuaries, are broad, with little current, and all streams of any magnitude are tidal. This region, commonly known as the Coastal Plain, is covered with soft Cretaceous and Tertiary rocks. Within it, in the southeast corner of the State, is the great Dismal Swamp, reaching an elevation nowhere more than 22 feet above mean sea level, and it is an almost impassable jungle of canebrake. In its center and upon its highest ground is Drummond Lake, an area of water 5 square miles in extent, without affluents, but drained by two or three artificial ditches.

The Coastal Plain is terminated on the west by what is called the "fall line." This is in the narrow zone in which the granitic rocks lying to the west pass below tide level. Over this fall line the streams from the Potomac to the south boundary of the State pass in a succession of rapids or falls due to the ledges of hard rock in the stream beds. This line is crossed by the Potomac at Georgetown, by the Rappahannock at Fredericksburg, and by the James at Richmond. The mills at Manchester, opposite Richmond on the James, are run by water power from the rapids at this point.

Above the fall line is what is known as the Piedmont Plateau, a region in the main composed of metamorphic rocks, largely granite and allied rocks. This region is higher than the Coastal Plain, and the relief increases westward. The gorges of the streams become deeper and occasional short ridges appear, outliers of the Blue Ridge.

The Blue Ridge is the principal eastern range of the Appalachian Mountain system. It is crossed by the Potomac at Harpers Ferry, and from that point it extends southwestward, crossing the south boundary of the State in longitude 80° 50'. At Harpers Ferry it has a height of about 1,200 feet, but it increases southwestward, reaching 3,374 feet in Mount Marshall, 4,031 feet in Stonyman, and 4,001 feet in the Peaks of Otter. Farther southwest it has a plateau-like character, with a steep descent to the southeast and a gentle slope to the northwest. It is cut through by several streams, as stated above—by the Potomac at Harpers Ferry, and by the James and the Roanoke.

West of the Blue Ridge lies the Appalachian Valley, whose northern part is drained toward the northeast by the Shenandoah, a branch of the Potomac, farther south by the headwaters of the James and the

Roanoke, by New River, one of the principal sources of the Kanawha, which flows northwestward to the Ohio, and by the various branches of the Holston, which is one of the chief sources of Tennessee River. This valley is composed of many smaller valleys, separated by narrow, sinuous ridges, trending in the general direction of the main valley. These ridges are cut through at frequent intervals by streams, which thus pass from one secondary valley to another.

The highest point in the State is Mount Rogers, on the Blue Ridge, near the southern boundary.

The average elevation of the State above sea level is 950 feet. The areas between different zones of altitude are as follows:

Areas in Virginia at different altitudes.

	Square miles.
0 to 100 feet	9,700
100 to 500 feet	10,500
500 to 1,000 feet	5,950
1,000 to 1,500 feet	4,700
1,500 to 2,000 feet	4,200
2,000 to 3,000 feet	6,800
3,000 to 4,000 feet	600

The principal rivers of the State, after the Potomac, which can scarcely be said to belong to it, although it serves as an important means of communication and drains a considerable area, are the Rappahannock, the James, which is navigable nearly to Richmond, and the Roanoke, which is partly within the State, but is not navigable within its limits. The coast is everywhere low, that facing the Atlantic is sandy, and much of it is bordered by sand bars. The principal ports are Norfolk and Newport News, both with good harbors opening upon the foot of Chesapeake Bay.

Virginia lies within the temperate zone, in the region of the prevailing westerly winds. The mean annual temperature ranges from 50° in the northern and western or mountainous parts to 60° in the Coastal Plain and the Piedmont region. The annual rainfall, which is fairly well distributed through the year, ranges from 40 to 60 inches, most of the Coastal Plain and the Piedmont region having a rainfall between 45 and 50 inches, while in the mountains the precipitation is considerably greater.

Virginia was originally forested over nearly all of its area, but through clearing the land for cultivation and the cutting of timber for various economic purposes the amount of merchantable timber remaining is comparatively small. No estimate of it has, however, been made.

Virginia was one of the first States of the Union to be settled, and at the time of the first census, taken in 1790, it had a population of nearly three-fourths of a million, being at that time the most populous of all the States. The following table shows the population at each census and the rate of increase:

Population of Virginia at each census since 1790.

Year.	Population.	Increase.
		Per cent.
1790	747,610	....
1800	880,200	17.7
1810	974,600	10.7
1820	1,065,366	9.3
1830	1,211,405	13.7
1840	1,239,797	2.3
1850	1,421,661	14.7
1860	1,596,318	12.3
1870	1,225,163	a 23.3
1880	1,512,565	23.5
1890	1,655,980	9.5
1900	1,854,184	12

a Decrease, due to the loss of West Virginia.

The population is given for the State as it existed at the time of the census—that is, up to 1860 it included West Virginia, while since that time it includes only what is now within its limits. The rate of increase, however, has been computed upon the population which existed within the present limits of the State. In 1900, with a population of 1,854,184, it was the seventeenth State in number of inhabitants. Of the total population, only 14.6 per cent were found in cities having a population of 8,000 or more, and the remaining 85.4 per cent, or about six-sevenths of all the inhabitants, are classed under this definition as rural. This proportion of rural population is much greater than that of the country at large.

There are ten cities in the State each having a population exceeding 8,000. They are as follows:

Population of cities in Virginia having more than 8,000 inhabitants.

Richmond	85,050
Norfolk	46,624
Petersburg	21,810
Roanoke	21,495
Newport News	19,635
Lynchburg	18,891
Portsmouth	17,427
Danville	16,520
Alexandria	14,528
Manchester	9,715

The above cities are independent of county government.

The State is divided into 100 counties. These with their areas and populations will be found in the general alphabetical list following.

In 1900 the population was very nearly equally divided between the sexes, the males constituting 49.9 per cent and the females 50.1 per cent. As to color, the proportions are 64.3 per cent white and 35.6 per cent colored. The colored are practically all negroes, as the number of Chinese, Japanese, and Indians is trifling. The white race increased in the decade between 1890 and 1900 at the rate of 16.9 per cent, while the negroes increased at the rate of only 4 per cent, owing to a movement of the negro population away from the State, probably southward. The population is nearly all of native birth, there being 99 per cent born in the United States and 1 per cent born abroad.

Of the total number of persons 10 years of age or more 22.9 per cent were unable to read, the most of them being negroes. Of the whites 10 years of age and over, only 11.1 per cent were illiterate. Of persons of school age—that is, between 5 and 20 years, 42 per cent attended school.

The total number of persons engaged in gainful occupations was 48.6 per cent of the entire population 10 years of age and over; that is to say, of this class, nearly one-half were engaged in gainful occupations. Of this class of wage-earners 45.3 per cent were engaged in agriculture, 3.2 per cent in professional pursuits, 23.6 per cent in domestic and other personal service, 11.2 per cent in trade and transportation, and 16.7 per cent in manufactures and mining. It thus appears that agriculture is the principal occupation of the people of the State, the number engaged in it being nearly one-half of all the wage-earners, and nearly twice as great as the number engaged in any other pursuit.

Virginia is preeminently an agricultural State, although it has some manufactures of importance. In 1900 the number of farms was 167,886, of which 73.3 per cent, or nearly three-fourths, were occupied by white farmers, while the remainder, 26.7 per cent, were occupied by negroes. As to tenure, 69.3 per cent, or nearly seven-tenths, of the farms in the State were owned by their occupants, 9.9 per cent were rented for a cash rental, and 20.8 per cent were rented for a share of the products. A much larger proportion of the negro farmers were tenants than of the white farmers, and as a rule the negro tenants pay their rent by a share of the product.

The total area of farms was 19,907,883 acres. The average size of farms was 118.6 acres, being considerably less than the average of the United States. The total amount of improved land was 10,094,805 acres, or little more than one-half the total area of farms, and 39.3 per cent of the total area of the State; in other words, about two-fifths of the State was under cultivation.

The value of all farm property was $323,515,997. This includes the

the value of the lands, buildings, live stock, implements, machinery, etc.—in short, the total farming capital. The average of this per farm was $1,927. The total value of the products of the farms was $86,548,545. This is between 26 and 27 per cent of the farming capital.

The following table shows the number of different classes of live stock upon farms in the State:

Live stock in Virginia.

Neat cattle	825,512
Horses	298,522
Mules	47,474
Sheep	692,929
Swine	946,443

The following table shows the amount of the principal agricultural products:

Statistics of agricultural products in Virginia.

Dairy products	dollars	7,000,000
Corn	bushels	1,910,000
Wheat	do	927,266
Oats	do	275,394
Hay	tons	612,962
Tobacco	pounds	122,884,900

In the product of tobacco this State is exceeded only by Kentucky and North Carolina, and the excess of the product of the latter State over Virginia is but trifling.

As a manufacturing State, Virginia does not take high rank, but with her rich deposits of excellent coking coal and of iron, it is probable that manufacturing will greatly increase in future years. General statistics of the manufacturing industry in 1900 are set forth in the following table:

Statistics of manufacturing in Virginia.

Manufacturing capital		$103,670,988
Wage-earners	number	72,702
Wages		$22,445,720
Materials		$74,851,757
Products		$132,172,910

The above gross product of manufactures was made up in part of the following items:

Principal classes of manufactures in Virginia in 1900.

Cars, etc	$6,277,279
Flour	12,687,267
Iron and steel	8,341,888
Lumber	12,137,177
Lumber planing mills	2,686,898
All textiles	3,282,583
Cotton goods	2,655,002

Tobacco	$21,278,266
Fertilizers	3,415,850
Foundry and machine-shop products	4,833,137
Leather	4,716,920

The above are the leading manufacturing products of the State and include three-fifths of all the manufactures.

In 1902 the State included 3,832 miles of railway, or 9.55 miles for each 100 square miles, and 19.98 miles for each 10,000 inhabitants. The railways of the State are, in the main, included in the five following systems: Southern, Chesapeake and Ohio, Atlantic Coast Line, Norfolk and Western, and Baltimore and Ohio.

The principal mineral products are coal and iron ore, both of which are found chiefly in the southwestern mountainous portion of the State. The coal production in 1901 was 2,725,873 short tons, and the amount of coke produced was 907,130 short tons. In the States of Virginia and West Virginia there were produced in the same year 925,394 long tons of iron ore. The production of Virginia can not be given separately. There were smelted within the State of Virginia in that year 448,662 long tons of pig iron. Besides the above, 4,275 tons of manganese ore were mined.

GAZETTEER.

Aaron; post village in Carroll County.
Aaron; creek, small right-hand branch of Dan River in Halifax County.
Abbie; post village in Carroll County.
Abbott; post village in Craig County.
Abbs; valley in Tazewell County.
Abbyville; post village in Mecklenburg County.
Abell; post village in Charlotte County.
Abercorn; post village in Amelia County.
Abert; post village in Bedford County on the Chesapeake and Ohio Railway.
Abilene; post village in Charlotte County.
Abingdon; county seat of Washington County, on the Norfolk and Western and the Virginia-Carolina railroads. Altitude, 2,057 feet. Population, 1,306.
Abner Knob; summit in Montgomery County. Elevation, 2,838 feet.
Abraham; post village in Floyd County.
Abrams; creek, a small left-hand tributary to North Fork of Holston River, which rises in Washington County.
Abrams; creek, a small left-hand tributary of Shenandoah River in Frederick County.
Abrams Falls; post village in Washington County.
Abrams Mount; summit in Rockingham County.
Acadia; village in Lee County.
Accakeek; creek, a small right-hand tributary to Potomac River in Stafford County.
Accomac; county, situated on the eastern shore of Chesapeake Bay. The surface is low and level, and much of it, especially near the coast on either side, is marshy. It is but little elevated above tide. The area is 478 square miles. Population, 32,570—white, 20,743; negro, 11,825; foreign born, 65. County seat, Accomac. The mean magnetic declination in 1900 was 4° 35'. The mean annual rainfall is 40 to 50 inches, and the temperature 55° to 60°. The county is traversed by the New York, Philadelphia and Norfolk Railroad.
Accomac; county seat of Accomac County.
Accotink; post village in Fairfax County on the Washington Southern Railroad.
Accotink; creek, a small right-hand tributary of Potomac River in Fairfax County.
Accotink; bay, an arm of Potomac River in Fairfax County.
Achilles; post village in Gloucester County.
Acorn; post village in Halifax County.
Acteon; post village in Prince Edward County.
Ada; post village in Fauquier County.
Adamsgrove; post village in Southampton County on the Southern Railway.
Adams; peak in South Mountain. Elevation, 2,990.
Adelphia; post village in Scott County.
Aden; post village in Prince William County.
Adial; post village in Nelson County.

Adlai; post village in Augusta County.
Admant; post village in Lee County.
Adner; post village in Gloucester County.
Adney; gap in Blue Ridge, Franklin County.
Adonis; post village in Halifax County.
Adria; post village in Tazewell County.
Adriance; post village in Cumberland County.
Advance Mills; post village in Albemarle County.
Adwolf; village in Smyth County.
Afton; post village in Nelson County on the Chesapeake and Ohio Railway. Elevation, 1,407 feet.
Agee; post village in Nelson County.
Agnewville; post village in Prince William County.
Aguste; post village in Isle of Wight County.
Ahala; post village in Orange County.
Aid; post village in Caroline County.
Aidyl; post village in Southampton County.
Aiken; swamp in Chesterfield County on James River.
Aily; post village in Dickenson County.
Airfield; post village in Southampton County.
Airmont; post village in Loudoun County.
Airpoint; post village in Roanoke County.
Aittlers; run, a small left-hand tributary to Shenandoah River in Frederick County.
Aivland; post village in Sussex County.
Ajax; post village in Pittsylvania County on the Southern Railway.
Alanthus; post village in Culpeper County.
Albano; post village in Orange County.
Albemarle; county, situated in the central part of the State in the Piedmont region and extends on the west to the summit of the Blue Ridge, there having an altitude in the summits of 3,000 feet. The county is traversed by a number of short ridges parallel to the Blue Ridge. In altitude its surface ranges from 300 to 3,000 feet. The area is 755 square miles. Population, 28,473—white, 18,135; negro, 10,337; foreign born, 214. Court-house located in Charlottesville. The mean magnetic declination in 1900 was 3°. The mean annual rainfall is 40 to 50 inches, and the temperature 55° to 60°. The county is traversed by the Chesapeake and Ohio and the Southern railways.
Albemarle and Chesapeake; canal, extending from the mouth of Southern Branch of Elizabeth River to North Landing River in Norfolk County.
Alberene; post village in Albemarle County on the Chesapeake and Ohio Railway.
Albin; post village in Frederick County.
Albro; creek, a small right-hand branch of James River in Chesterfield County.
Alchie; post village in Halifax County.
Alcoma; post village in Buckingham County.
Alden; post village in King George County.
Alderman; post village in Floyd County.
Aldie; post village in Loudoun County.
Alean; post village in Franklin County.
Alexandria; county, situated in the eastern part of the State along Potomac River, opposite the District of Columbia. It has a rolling surface, ranging from sea level to 400 feet. The chief city within its limits is Alexandria, formerly the county seat, but now independent in government. Area, 32 square miles. Population, 6,430—white, 3,963; negro, 2,467; foreign born, 294. County seat, Fort Myer. The mean magnetic declination in 1900 was 4° 30′. The mean annual rainfall is 40 to 50 inches, and the temperature 55°.

Alexandria; city, independent, with a population of 14,528, on the Baltimore and Ohio, the Chesapeake and Ohio, the Southern, the Washington, Alexandria and Mount Vernon Electric, and the Washington Southern railroads.
Alex; run, a small right-hand tributary of James River in Botetourt County.
Alfonso; post village in Lancaster County.
Alfred; post village in Albemarle County.
Alfred; fork, a small right-hand branch of Knox Creek in Buchanan County.
Algoma; village in Franklin County.
Alhambra; post village in Nelson County.
Alleghany; county, situated in the western part of the State in the Appalachian Valley. The surface consists of a close alternation of sandstone ridges and limestone valleys. It is drained by numerous small streams of James River. Area, 452 square miles. Population, 16,330—white, 12,315; negro, 4,013; foreign born, 168. County seat, Covington. The mean magnetic declination in 1900 was 1° 45'. The mean annual rainfall is 50 to 60 inches, and the temperature 50° to 60°. The county is traversed by the Chesapeake and Ohio Railway.
Alleghany; tunnel in Alleghany Mountains on the State line in Greenbriar and Alleghany counties. Altitude, 2,068 feet.
Alleghany Spring; post village in Montgomery County.
Alleghany Station; post village in Alleghany County on the Chesapeake and Ohio Railway. Altitude, 2,056 feet.
Allegheny Front; the eastern escarpment of the Allegheny Plateau, traversing Virginia, West Virginia, Maryland, and Pennsylvania. Elevation in Virginia ranges from 2,000 to 4,000 feet.
Allen; creek, a small left-hand branch of James River in Amherst and Nelson counties.
Allen; mountains in Greene County. Elevation, 1,000 to 1,500 feet.
Allenscreek; post village in Amherst County on the Chesapeake and Ohio Railway.
Allenslevel; post village in Buckingham County.
Alley; post village in Scott County.
Alliance; post village in Surry County.
Allisonia; post village in Pulaski County on the Norfolk and Western Railway.
Allmondsville; post village in Gloucester County.
Allwood; post village in Amherst County.
Alma; post village in Page County.
Almagro; post village in Pittsylvania County.
Almond; village in Rockingham County.
Alone; post village in Rockbridge County.
Alonzaville; post village in Shenandoah County.
Alpha; post village in Buckingham County on the Chesapeake and Ohio Railway.
Alphin; post village in Rockbridge County.
Alrich; post village in Spottsylvania County on the Potomac, Fredericksburg and Piedmont Railroad.
Althea; post village in Campbell County.
Alto; post village in Amherst County.
Alton; post village in Halifax County on the Southern Railway.
Altoona; mines in Pulaski County.
Alumine; post village in Franklin County on the Norfolk and Western Railway. Altitude, 881 feet.
Alumridge; post village in Floyd County.
Alum; springs in Rockbridge County.
Alumwells; post village in Washington County.
Alvah; post village in Henry County.
Alvarado; post village in Washington County.

Amaryllis; post village in Louisa County.
Ambar; post village in King George County.
Amburg; post village in Middlesex County.
Amelia; county, situated in the central part of the State in the Piedmont region. It has an undulating surface, ranging in altitude from 300 to 500 feet. Area, 355 square miles. Population, 9,037—white, 3,052; negro, 5,985; foreign born, 50. County seat, Amelia. The mean magnetic declination in 1900 was 3° 15′. The mean annual rainfall is 40 to 50 inches, and the temperature 55° to 60°. The county is traversed by the Southern Railway.
Amelia; county seat of Amelia County on the Southern Railway. Altitude, 361 feet.
Amherst; county, situated in the central part of the State in the Piedmont region, its western boundary being the summit of the Blue Ridge. Its surface is somewhat broken by short ridges and isolated summits, outliers of the Blue Ridge. It is drained by James River. The altitude ranges from 500 feet up to 3,000 in the summits of the Blue Ridge. Area, 464 square miles. Population, 17,864—white, 10,807; negro, 7,057; foreign born, 70. County seat, Amherst. The mean magnetic declination in 1900 was 3° 10′. The mean annual rainfall is 40 to 50 inches, and the temperature 50° to 60°. The county is traversed by the Southern and the Chesapeake and Ohio railways.
Amherst; county seat of Amherst County on the Southern Railway. Altitude, 629 feet.
Amicus; post village in Greene County.
Amissville; post village in Rappahannock County.
Ammon; post village in Amelia County.
Amos; creek, a small tributary to Copper Creek in Scott County.
Amos; post village in Floyd County.
Amsterdam; post village in Botetourt County.
Amy; post village in Amherst County.
Ancella; post village in Grayson County.
Anchor; post village in Surry County.
Anderson; post village in Augusta County on the Big Stony Railway.
Andersonville; post village in Buckingham County.
Andrews; post village in Spottsylvania County.
Angels Rest; mountain in Giles County. Elevation, 3,600 feet.
Angola; creek, a small left-hand branch of Appomattox River in Cumberland County.
Angola; post village in Cumberland County.
Ann; post village in Lee County.
Annandale; post village in Fairfax County.
Annex; post village in Augusta County.
Anstelle; post village in Botetourt County.
Ante; post village in Brunswick County.
Antelope, post village in Rockingham County.
Anthony Knobs; summits in Botetourt County. Elevation, 1,500 to 2,500 feet.
Anthony Mill; creek, a small left-hand tributary to Roanoke River in Bedford County.
Anthony; ferry over Roanoke River in Pittsylvania County.
Anthony; ford in Roanoke River in Franklin County.
Antioch; post village in Fluvanna County on Farmville and Powhatan Railroad. Altitude, 487 feet.
Antlers; post village in Mecklenburg County.
Appalachia; post village in Wise County on the Interstate and the Louisville and Nashville railroads.
Appleberry; mountains in Albemarle County. Elevation, 1,000 to 1,500 feet.

Applegrove; post village in Louisa County.
Apple Orchard; summits in Botetourt County.
Appold; post village in Botetourt County.
Appomattox; county, situated in the southern part of the State in the Piedmont region. It has an undulating surface, with an altitude ranging from 400 to 800 feet. It is drained by James and Roanoke rivers; area, 342 square miles. Population, 9,662—white, 5,731; negro, 3,931; foreign born, 15. County seat, West Appomattox. The mean magnetic declination in 1900 was 2° 30′. The mean annual rainfall is 50 to 60 inches, and the temperature 55° to 60°. The county is traversed by the Norfolk and Western Railway.
Appomattox; post village in Appomattox County on the Norfolk and Western Railway. Altitude, 825 feet.
Appomattox; river which heads in the Piedmont region and flows in a sinuous eastward course to its junction with the James. Length, 130 miles; navigable to Petersburg.
Aqua; post village in Rockbridge County.
Aquia; creek, a small right-hand branch of Potomac River in Stafford County.
Aral; post village in Carroll County.
Ararat; post village in Patrick County.
Ararat; river, a left-hand branch of Yadkin River, rising in Patrick County.
Arborhill; post village in Augusta County.
Arbutus; post village in Grayson County.
Arcanum; post village in Buckingham County.
Archer Knob; summit in North Mountain.
Archie; post village in Culpeper County.
Arch Mills; post village in Botetourt County.
Arco; post village in Warren County.
Arcola; post village in Loudoun County.
Arcturus; village in Fairfax County on the Washington, Alexandria and Mount Vernon Electric Railway.
Ark; post village in Gloucester County.
Arkton; village in Rockingham County.
Arlington; post village in Alexandria County on the Washington, Alexandria and Mount Vernon Electric Railway.
Armel; post village in Frederick County.
Armstrong; post village in Bath County.
Arnold; creek, a small right-hand branch of James River in Rockbridge County.
Arnold; valley in the southern part of Rockbridge County.
Arringdale; post village in Southampton County on the Southern Railway.
Arrington; post village in Nelson County on the Southern Railway. Altitude, 692 feet.
Arritts; post village in Alleghany County.
Arthur; marshy creek tributary to Rowanty Creek, a swamp in Dinwiddie County.
Artrip; post village in Russell County on the Norfolk and Western Railway. Altitude, 1,560 feet.
Arvonia; post village in Buckingham County on the Chesapeake and Ohio Railway.
Asberrys; post village in Tazewell County.
Ashburn; post village in Loudoun County.
Ashby; gap in the Blue Ridge in Clarke County.
Ashby; post village in Cumberland County on the Norfolk and Western Railway. Altitude, 597 feet.
Ashcake; post village in Hanover County on the Chesapeake and Ohio Railway. Altitude, 199 feet.
Ash Camp; creek, a small left-hand tributary to Roanoke River in Charlotte County.

Ashgrove; post village in Fairfax County.
Ash Hollow; run, a small left-hand tributary to Shenandoah River in Frederick County.
Ashland; town in Hanover County on the Richmond, Fredericksburg and Potomac Railroad. Population, 1,147. Altitude, 221 feet.
Ashton; creek, a small right-hand tributary to James River in Chesterfield County.
Aspenview; post village in Brunswick County.
Aspenwall; post village in Charlotte County.
Assamoosick; creek, a left-hand branch of Nottoway River in southeast Virginia.
Assamoosick; post village in Southampton County.
Assawoman; post village in Accomac County.
Athlone; village in Rockingham County.
Athos; post village in Orange County.
Atkins; post village in Smyth County on the Norfolk and Western Railway. Altitude, 2,279 feet.
Atlantic; post village in Accomac County.
Atlas; post village in Pittsylvania County.
Atlee; post village in Hanover County on the Chesapeake and Ohio Railway. Altitude, 202 feet.
Atoka; post village in Fauquier County.
Attoway; post village in Smyth County.
Auburn; post village in Fauquier County.
Auburn Mills; post village in Hanover County.
Augusta; county, situated in the western part of the State in the Appalachian Valley, its eastern boundary being the summit of the Blue Ridge; its surface is undulating and but little broken. It is drained mainly northward into branches of Shenandoah River. The altitude ranges from 1,200 to 4,500 feet in Elliott Knob. Area, 1,012 square miles. Population, 32,370—whites, 26,670; negro, 5,700; foreign born, 107. County seat, Staunton. The mean magnetic declination in 1900 was 2° 15'. The mean annual rainfall is 50 to 60 inches, and the temperature 50 to 55°. The county is traversed by the Baltimore and Ohio, the Chesapeake and Ohio, and the Norfolk and Western railroads.
Augusta Springs; post village in Augusta County on the Chesapeake and Ohio Railway.
Augusta White Sulphur; springs in Augusta County.
Austin; creek, a small right-hand tributary to James River in Buckingham County.
Austin; run, a small right-hand tributary to Potomac River in Stafford County.
Austinville; post village in Wythe County on the Norfolk and Western Railway.
Autumn; post village in Scott County.
Avalon; post village in Northumberland County.
Averett; post village in Mecklenburg County.
Avis; post village in Augusta County.
Avon; post village in Nelson County.
Axtell; post village in Buckingham County on the Danville and Western Railway.
Axton; post village in Henry County on the Danville and Western Railway. Altitude, 1,020 feet.
Ayers; post village in Scott County.
Aylett; post village in King William County.
Aylmer; post village in Nelson County.
Azen; post village in Washington County.
Bachelors Hall; post village in Pittsylvania County.
Back; bay, a lagoon on the southeast coast, separated from the Atlantic Ocean by a sand bar.

Bull. 232—04——2

Back; creek, a small left-hand tributary to Goose Creek in Campbell County.
Back; creek, a small right-hand branch of Jackson River in Highland County.
Back; creek, a left-hand tributary of James River in Bath and Highland counties.
Back; creek, a small left-hand tributary to James River in Rockbridge County.
Back; creek, a small right-hand tributary to James River in Botetourt County.
Back; creek, a small right-hand branch of Potomac River in Frederick County, Va., and Berkeley County, W. Va.
Back; creek, a small right-hand tributary to Roanoke River in Roanoke County.
Back; creek, a right-hand branch of Roanoke River in Roanoke County.
Back; creek, a small left-hand tributary to Shenandoah River in Augusta County.
Back; creek, a small right-hand tributary to Shenandoah River in Augusta County.
Back; run, a small left-hand branch of James River in Rockbridge County.
Backbay: post village in Princess Anne County on the Norfolk and Southern Railroad.
Backbone; post village in Alleghany County on the Chesapeake and Ohio Railway. Altitude, 1,670 feet.
Back Creek; mountains in Botetourt County. Elevation, 2,000 feet.
Back Creek; mountains in Highland and Bath counties. Elevation, 2,000 to 4,000 feet.
Bacon; post village in James City County.
Bacons Castle; post village in Surry County.
Baffle; post village in Southampton County.
Bagby; post village in Caroline County.
Bagleys Mills; post village in Lunenburg County.
Bailey; creek, a small left-hand branch of James River in Henrico County.
Bailey; creek, a small right-hand tributary to James River in Prince George County.
Bailey; post village in Tazewell County on the Chesapeake and Ohio Railway. Altitude, 2,600 feet.
Bailey; mountain in Nelson County.
Bailey Crossroads; post village in Fairfax County.
Baileyville; post village in Charlotte County.
Baker; creek, a small left-hand tributary to Shenandoah River in Augusta County.
Baker; mountain in Prince Edward County.
Baker Mines; post village in Carroll County.
Bakers Mill; village in Rockingham County.
Balcony Falls; post village in Rockbridge County on the Chesapeake and Ohio Railway. Altitude, 712 feet.
Bald; mountain in Craig County. Elevation, 1,500 to 2,500 feet.
Bald; mountain ridge in Augusta County. Elevation, 3,000 to 4,000 feet.
Bald Knob; summit in Amherst County.
Bald Knob; summit in Appomattox County.
Bald Knob; summit in Augusta County. Elevation, 4,410 feet.
Bald Knob; summit in Franklin County. Elevation, 1,421 feet.
Bald Knob; summit in Salt Pond Mountain in Giles County. Elevation, 4,348 feet.
Bald Knob; summit in Warm Spring Mountain. Elevation, 4,245 feet.
Baldwin; ridge in Fauquier County. Elevation, 500 feet.
Baldwin Station; post village in Botetourt County on the Chesapeake and Ohio Railway. Altitude, 970 feet.
Bales; post village in Lee County.
Balham; post village in Goochland County.
Ball; mountain in Nelson County.
Ballard; post village in Patrick County.
Ballinger; creek, a small left-hand tributary to James River in Fluvanna County.

Ballinger; creek, a small left-hand branch of James River in Albemarle County.
Ball Room; mountain in Nelson County.
Ballston; post village in Alexandria County.
Ballsville; post village in Powhatan County on the Farmville and Powhatan Railroad. Altitude, 397 feet.
Balty; post village in Caroline County.
Banco; post village in Madison County.
Bandana; post village in Hanover County.
Bandy; post village in Tazewell County.
Bane; post village in Giles County.
Banister; left-hand branch of Dan River in Pittsylvania and Halifax counties.
Banister; post village in Pittsylvania County on the Norfolk and Western Railway. Altitude, 364 feet.
Banks; mountain in Madison County.
Banks; post village in Essex County.
Banks Mountain; summit in Amherst County. Elevation, 2,000 feet.
Banner; post village in Wise County.
Baptist; valley in Tazewell County.
Baptist Valley; post village in Tazewell County.
Barb; post village in Shenandoah County.
Barbers; creek, a small right-hand tributary to Jackson River in Craig County.
Barbett; creek, a small right-hand tributary to New River in Carroll County.
Barbett Knob; summit in Carroll County. Elevation, 3,034 feet.
Barboursville; post village in Orange County on the Southern Railway.
Barcroft; post village in Alexandria County on the Southern Railway.
Barden; run, a small right-hand tributary to James River in Botetourt County.
Bare; mountain, summit in Augusta County.
Barhamsville; post village in New Kent County.
Bark Camp; small right-hand branch of New River in Pulaski County.
Barker Mill; pond in Hanover County on Elder Creek.
Barley; post village in Greenesville County.
Barlow; village in Lee County.
Barnesville; post village in Charlotte County.
Barnett; village in Russell County.
Barnhardt; creek, a small right-hand branch of Roanoke River in Roanoke County.
Barque; post village in Campbell County.
Barrel; point of land in Isle of Wight County, extending into James River.
Barrenridge; post village in Augusta County.
Barren Springs; post village in Wythe County on the Norfolk and Western Railway. Altitude, 1,908 feet.
Barrmoor; post village in Smyth County.
Barrows Mill; village in Henry County.
Barrows Store; post village in Brunswick County.
Bartee; post village in Norfolk County.
Barterbrook; post village in Augusta County.
Barton Heights; town in Henrico County. Population, 763.
Basham; post village in Floyd County.
Basic City; town in Augusta County on the Chesapeake and Ohio and the Norfolk and Western railways. Population, 1,270.
Baskerville; post village in Mecklenburg County on the Southern Railway.
Bass; creek, a small left-hand branch of Appomattox River in Chesterfield County.
Basses; post village in Halifax County.
Bassetts; post village in Henry County on the Norfolk and Western Railway. Altitude, 740 feet.

Bassil; post village in Patrick County.
Bateman; post village in Patrick County.
Batesville; post village in Albemarle County.
Bath; county, situated in the western part of the State in the Appalachian Valley. Its surface consists of an alternation of sandstone ridges and limestone valleys. It is drained by branches of James River. The altitude ranges from 1,100 up to 4,000 feet. Area, 548 square miles. Population, 5,595—white, 4,589; negro, 1,006; foreign born, 66. County seat, Warm Springs. The mean magnetic declination in 1900 was 2° 15′. The mean annual rainfall is 50 to 60 inches, and the temperature 50° to 55°. The county is traversed by the Chesapeake and Ohio Railway.
Batna; post village in Culpeper County.
Batt; post village in Gloucester County.
Batten; post village in Isle of Wight County.
Battersea; canal in Dinwiddie County extending along Appomattox River.
Battery; post village in Essex County.
Battery; creek, a small right-hand branch of James River in Bedford County.
Batterypark; post village in Isle of Wight County.
Battle; run, a small right-hand tributary to Rappahannock River in Rappahannock County.
Battle; mountains in Rappahannock County. Elevation, 1,000 feet.
Battlehill; post village in Roanoke County.
Bay; post village in Floyd County.
Bayard; post village in Warren County.
Bayford; post village in Northampton County.
Baylor; post village in Grayson County.
Baynesville; post village in Westmoreland County.
Bayon; post village in Halifax County.
Bayport; post village in Middlesex County.
Bays Mill; creek, a small left-hand tributary to Shenandoah River in Augusta County.
Bayview; post village in Northampton County.
Baywood; post village in Grayson County.
Beach; post village in Chesterfield County on the Farmville and Powhatan Railroad. Altitude, 283 feet.
Beachem; run, a small right-hand tributary to Chickahominy River in Henrico County.
Beachland; post village in Surry County.
Beacon Quarter; branch, a small left-hand tributary to James River in Henrico County.
Beagle; gap in the Blue Ridge in Augusta County.
Beahm; post village in Page County.
Bealeton; post village in Fauquier County on the Southern Railway. Altitude, 290 feet.
Beamer Knob; summit in Carroll County. Elevation, 3,400 feet.
Beamon; post village in Nansemond County on the Southern Railway.
Bean; branch, a small right-hand tributary to Potomac River in Fauquier County.
Bear; creek, a small left-hand tributary to Guest River in Wise County.
Bear; creek, a small right-hand branch of Middle Fork of Holston River in Smyth County.
Bear; creek, a small left-hand tributary to Roanoke River in Campbell County.
Bear; mountain in Amherst County. Elevation, 1,500 feet.
Bear; mountain in Augusta County. Elevation, 2,500 feet.
Bear; mountain in Highland County.

Beard; mountains in Bath County. Elevation, 1,500 to 2,500 feet.
Bear Garden; creek, a small right-hand branch of James River in Buckingham County.
Bear Garden; run, a small right-hand tributary to Potomac River in Frederick County.
Bear Lithia; post village in Rockingham County.
Bear Pen; small left-hand branch of Pigeon Creek in Wise County.
Beartown; mountain in Russell County. Elevation, 4,710 feet.
Bearwallow; mountain in Buchanan County. Altitude, 3,170 feet.
Bearwallow; post village in Buchanan County.
Bear Wallow; run, a small right-hand tributary to James River in Botetourt County.
Beauford; post village in Floyd County.
Beautiful; run, a small left-hand tributary to Rapidan River in Madison County.
Beaver; branch, a small right-hand tributary to New River in Grayson County.
Beaver; small right-hand branch of Cripple Creek in Wythe County.
Beaver; creek, a left-hand tributary to Dan River in Henry County.
Beaver; creek, a small left-hand tributary to James River in Amherst County.
Beaver; creek, a small right-hand branch of James River in Campbell County.
Beaver; creek, a small right-hand tributary to New River in Grayson and Carroll counties.
Beaver; creek, a small left-hand branch of North Fork of Holston River in Smyth County.
Beaver; creek, a small left-hand tributary to Shenandoah River in Rockingham County.
Beaver; fork, a small tributary to Botetourt River in Tazewell County.
Beaverdam; post village in Hanover County on the Chesapeake and Ohio Railway. Altitude, 282 feet.
Beaverdam; creek, a small right-hand tributary to Potomac River in Loudoun County.
Beaverdam; creek, a small left-hand branch of Chickahominy River in Hanover County.
Beaverdam; creek, a small left-hand branch of James River in Goochland County.
Beaverdam; creek, a small left-hand tributary to James River in Louisa County.
Beaverdam; creek, a small right-hand tributary to New River in Carroll County.
Beaverdam; creek, a small right-hand tributary to New River in Floyd County.
Beaverdam; creek, a small left-hand tributary to New River in Wythe County.
Beaverdam; creek, a small left-hand tributary to Powell River in Wise County.
Beaverdam; creek, a small left-hand branch of Roanoke River in Bedford County.
Beaverdam; creek, a small left-hand tributary to South Fork of Holston River in Washington County.
Beaverdam; creek, a small left-hand tributary to York River in Hanover County.
Beaverdam Mills; post village in Hanover County.
Beaverpond; branch, a small left-hand tributary to Roanoke River in Campbell County.
Beaverpond; creek, a small left-hand tributary to Nottoway River in Dinwiddie County.
Beaverpond; creek, a small right-hand tributary to Appomattox River in Amelia County.
Beaverpond; post village in Amelia County.
Beazley; ford across Ducker Creek in Buckingham County.
Beazley; post village in Essex County.
Beck; post village in Prince Edward County.
Beckham; post village in Appomattox County.
Beckner; gap in Catawba Mountains, caused by Mason Creek, in Roanoke County.

Beck Ridge; mountains extending from Washington County, Va., into Sullivan County, Tenn.

Becky; creek, a small right-hand branch of Roanoke River in Franklin County.

Bedford; county, situated in the southern part of the State in the upper part of the Piedmont region, and consisting of a rolling and somewhat broken country, with numerous short ridges, which are outliers of the Blue Ridge, in the upper part of the county. It is drained by Roanoke River and its tributaries. The altitude ranges from 600 up to 4,000 feet in the Peaks of Otter, which forms the northwestern limit of the county. Area, 729 square miles. Population, 30,356— white, 20,617; negro, 9,739; foreign born, 71. County seat, Bedford City. The mean magnetic declination in 1900 was 2°. The mean annual rainfall is 50 to 60 inches, and the temperature 55° to 60°. The county is traversed by the Norfolk and Western Railway.

Bedford City; county seat of Bedford County on the Norfolk and Western Railway. Population, 2,416.

Bedford Springs; post village in Campbell County.

Bee; small right-hand branch of Slate Creek in Buchanan County.

Bee; post village in Dickenson County.

Beech; creek, a small left-hand tributary to Dry Fork, rising in Tazewell County.

Beech Lick Knob; summit in Rockingham County. Elevation, 3,000 feet.

Beechnut; post village in Mecklenburg County.

Beechspring; village in Lee County.

Beechtree; creek, a small right-hand branch of Roanoke River in Pittsylvania County.

Beesville; post village in Buckingham County.

Behams; gap in the Blue Ridge in Rappahannock County.

Belamar; post village in Hanover County.

Beldor; post village in Rockingham County.

Belfast Mills; post village in Russell County.

Belfield; post village in Greenesville County.

Belgrade; post village in Shenandoah County.

Belinda; post village in Accomac County.

Bell; creek, a small right-hand tributary to Appomattox River in Prince Edward County.

Bellamy; post village in Scott County.

Bellbranch; post village in Buckingham County.

Belle; small island in James River in Henrico County.

Belle Coe; creek, a small left-hand tributary to James River in Rockbridge County.

Belle Hampton; post village in Pulaski County.

Bellehaven; town in Accomac County. Population, 331.

Bellevue; post village in Bedford County on the Norfolk and Western Railway. Altitude, 848 feet.

Bellfair Mills; post village in Stafford County.

Bells; post village in Bedford County.

Bells Crossroads; post village in Louisa County.

Bells Valley; post village in Rockbridge County on the Chesapeake and Ohio Railway. Altitude, 1,507 feet.

Belmont; bay, an arm of Potomac River extending into Prince William and Fairfax counties.

Belmont; post village in Spottsylvania County.

Belona; post village in Powhatan County on the Farmville and Powhatan Railroad. Altitude, 368 feet.

Belroi; post village in Gloucester County.

Belsches; post village in Sussex County.

Ben; post village in Alleghany County.
Bena; post village in Gloucester County.
Benbow; post village in Tazewell County.
Bend; ford across Roanoke River in Roanoke County.
Bend; post village in Louisa County.
Benges; small right-hand branch of Powell River in Wise County.
Benges; gap in Little Stone Mountain made by Benges Branch.
Benhams; post village in Washington County on the Virginia and Southwestern Railway.
Benhur; post village in Lee County on the Louisville and Nashville Railroad.
Bennettcreek; post village in Nansemond County.
Bennetts Mill; post village in Montgomery County.
Benns Church; post village in Isle of Wight County.
Bens; branch, a small right-hand tributary to Jackson River in Alleghany County.
Bensons; run, a small left-hand tributary to James River in Highland County.
Bent; creek, a small right-hand branch of Appomattox River in Amelia County.
Bent; creek, a small right-hand branch of James River in Appomattox County.
Bent; mountain in Floyd County.
Bent; mountains in Roanoke County.
Bentcreek; post village in Appomattox County.
Bentley; branch, a small left-hand tributary to New River in Pulaski County.
Bent Mountain; post village in Roanoke County.
Bentonville; post village in Warren County on the Norfolk and Western Railway. Altitude, 729 feet.
Berea; post village in Stafford County.
Berkeley; town in Norfolk County on the Norfolk and Southern Railroad. Population, 4,988.
Berlin; post village in Southampton County.
Bermuda Hundred; post village in Chesterfield County.
Bernard; creek, a small right-hand branch of James River in Powhatan County.
Berringer; mountain in Montgomery County.
Berry; creek, a small right-hand tributary to New River in Floyd County.
Berryman; post village in Surry County.
Berrys; post village in Clarke County.
Berryville; town and county seat of Clarke County on the Norfolk and Western Railway. Altitude, 968 feet. Population, 938.
Bertha; post village in Wythe County on the Norfolk and Western Railway.
Berthaville; post village in King George County.
Berton; post village in Giles County on the Norfolk and Western Railway. Altitude, 1,655 feet.
Bess; post village in Alleghany County.
Bessemer; post village in Botetourt County on the Chesapeake and Ohio Railway.
Bestland; post village in Essex County.
Bethel Academy; post village in Fauquier County.
Betsey; branch, a small right-hand tributary to Levisa Fork in Buchanan County.
Betsey Bell; summit in Augusta County. Elevation, 1,500 feet.
Betty; creek, a small right-hand branch of Roanoke River in Franklin County.
Beulahville; post village in King William County.
Beverly; post village in Pittsylvania County.
Bevi; creek, a small left-hand tributary to Shenandoah River in Augusta County.
Bevils; bridge across Appomattox River from Chesterfield into Amelia County.
Bibb; post village in Louisa County on the Norfolk and Western Railway.
Bible; run, a small right-hand tributary to Shenandoah River in Rockingham County.

Bickley Mill; post village in Russell County.
Big; branch, a small right-hand tributary to Jackson River in Craig County.
Big; branch, a small right-hand tributary to Levisa Fork in Buchanan County.
Big; small right-hand branch of New River in Carroll County.
Big; branch, a small right-hand tributary to North Fork of Holston River, rising in Scott County.
Big; small right-hand branch of Clinch River rising in Russell County.
Big; creek, a small right-hand tributary to Clinch River in Tazewell County.
Big; island on James River in Amherst County.
Big; run, a small right-hand tributary to New River in Floyd County.
Big; run, a small right-hand branch of Shenandoah River in Rockingham County.
Big; tunnel, in Montgomery County on the Norfolk and Western Railway.
Big Bundy; creek, a small right-hand tributary to North Fork of Powell River.
Big Cedar; creek, a left-hand branch of Clinch River, rising in Russell County.
Big Cobbler; mountains in Fauquier County. Elevation, 1,000 to 1,500 feet.
Big Cranberry; creek, a small right-hand tributary to New River in Carroll County.
Bigcreek; post village in Tazewell County.
Bigcut; post village in Scott County.
Big Fork Ridge; mountains in Buchanan County. Elevation, 2,500 feet.
Big Fox; creek, a small right-hand tributary to Russell Fork, rising in Buchanan County.
Biggs; mountain in Botetourt and Rockbridge counties.
Biggs; run, a small right-hand tributary to James River in Botetourt County.
Bighill; post village in Lee County on the Chesapeake and Ohio Railway.
Big Hollow; small right-hand branch of Levisa Fork in Buchanan County.
Big Hound; creek, a small right-hand tributary to Nottoway River in Lunenburg County.
Big House Mountain; summit in Rockbridge County. Elevation, 3,612 feet.
Big Indian; run, a small right-hand tributary to Rappahannock River in Culpeper County.
Big Island; post village in Bedford County on the Chesapeake and Ohio Railway. Altitude, 596 feet.
Big Laurel; run, a small left-hand tributary to Shenandoah River in Rockingham County.
Big Levels; summits in the Blue Ridge in Augusta County.
Big Lick Draft; small right-hand tributary to Jackson River in Bath County.
Big Licking; creek, a small left-hand branch of James River in Goochland County.
Big Moccasin; creek, a left-hand tributary to Clinch River, rising in Russell County.
Big Moccasin; creek, a small right-hand branch of North Fork of Holston River in Scott County.
Big Nottoway; river, a head branch of Nottoway River, rising in Lunenburg County and forming the boundary between Nottoway and Lunenburg counties.
Big Otter; creek, a left-hand branch of Roanoke River, formed by North and South forks, in Bedford County.
Big Piney; mountains in Amherst County. Elevation, 1,000 to 2,000 feet.
Big Prator; creek, a small left-hand branch of Levisa Fork, rising in Buchanan County.
Big Reed Island; creek, a right-hand branch of New River in Carroll County.
Big Ridge; mountain in Bland County. Elevation, 3,000 to 4,000 feet.
Big Ridge; mountains in Augusta County.
Big Ridge; mountains in Scott County.
Bigriver; post village in Augusta County.
Bigrock; post village in Buchanan County.

Big Shuffle; branch, a small left-hand tributary to New River in Pulaski County.
Big Spring; small right-hand branch of Walker Creek in Giles County.
Big Spy; summit in the Blue Ridge in Augusta County.
Big Stone; gap in Little Stone Mountain, made by Powell River, in Wise County.
Bigstone Gap; town in Wise County on the Louisville and Nashville and the Virginia and Southwestern railroads. Altitude, 1,966 feet. Population, 1,617.
Big Stone Ridge; mountains in Tazewell County.
Big Tom; creek, a small right-hand tributary to Clinch River, rising in Wise County.
Big Town Hill; creek, a small right-hand branch of Clinch River in Tazewell County.
Bigtunnel; post village in Montgomery County.
Bill Young; branch, a small right-hand tributary to Levisa Fork in Buchanan County.
Bill Young; gap in Keen Mountain in Buchanan County.
Binfords; post village in Brunswick County.
Binns Hall; post village in Charles City County.
Birch; post village in Halifax County.
Birchen; creek, a small left-hand tributary to Nottoway River in Nottoway County.
Birchleaf; post village in Dickenson County.
Birds; branch, a small left-hand tributary to Roanoke River in Charlotte County.
Birdsnest; post village in Northampton County on the New York, Philadelphia and Norfolk Railroad.
Birdsong; post village in Sussex County.
Birdwood; post village in Albemarle County.
Biscoe; post village in King and Queen County.
Bishops; creek, a small left-hand tributary to Roanoke River in Campbell County.
Black; creek, a small right-hand tributary to James River in Roanoke County.
Black; creek, a small right-hand branch of Powell River in Wise County.
Blackberry; village in Henry County.
Blackey; fork, a small left-hand fork of Knox Creek in Buchanan County.
Black Oak; mountains in Shenandoah County.
Black Oak Ridge; mountains in Bath, Rockbridge, and Augusta counties. Elevation, 2,000 feet.
Blackridge; post village in Mecklenburg County.
Blackrock Springs; post village in Augusta County.
Blacks; gap in North Mountains in Botetourt County.
Blacksburg; town in Montgomery County. Population, 768. Altitude, 2,170 feet.
Blackstone; town in Nottoway County on the Norfolk and Western Railway. Population, 585.
Blackwalnut; post village in Halifax County.
Blackwater; creek, a small right-hand branch of Clinch River in Lee County, Va., and Hancock County, Tenn.
Blackwater; ford across Roanoke River in Roanoke County.
Blackwater; post village in Lee County.
Blackwater; river, a small left-hand tributary to Staunton River, formed by North and South forks.
Blackwater; river, a right-hand branch of Roanoke River in Franklin County.
Blackwater; river, a small right-hand branch of North Landing River in Norfolk County.
Blackwater; river of southeast Virginia, one of the sources of Chowan River.
Blackwater; swamp in Prince George County.
Blackwells; post village in Northumberland County.
Blair; ferry in New River in Grayson County.
Blairs; post village in Prince George County on the Norfolk and Western Railway.

Blakes; post village in Mathews County.
Blanche; post village in Dickenson County.
Bland; county, located in the western part of the State in the Appalachian Valley. Its surface consists of an alternation of short parallel ridges and valleys. The elevation ranges from 2,000 up to nearly 4,000 feet above sea level. Area, 352 square miles. Population, 5,497—white, 5,285; negro, 212; foreign born, 6. County seat, Bland. The mean magnetic declination in 1900 was 1°. The mean annual rainfall is 50 to 60 inches, and the temperature 50° to 55°.
Bland; county seat of Bland County.
Bland; creek, a small right-hand tributary to Appomattox River in Nottoway County.
Blankenship; village in Lee County.
Blantons; post village in Caroline County on the Chesapeake and Ohio Railway.
Bleak; post village in Fauquier County.
Blenheim; post village in Albemarle County.
Blickville; post village in Dinwiddie County.
Bliss; post village in Frederick County.
Bloom; post village in Frederick County on the Southern Railway.
Bloomer; post village in Scott County.
Bloomfield; post village in Loudoun County.
Bloomtown; post village in Accomac County on the New York, Philadelphia and Norfolk Railroad.
Blossom Hill; post village in Princess Anne County.
Blount; village in Bedford County.
Bloxom; post village in Accomac County on the New York, Philadelphia and Norfolk Railroad.
Blue; run, a small right-hand tributary to Rappahannock River in Orange County.
Bluegrass; post village in Russell County.
Bluemont; post village in Loudoun County.
Blue Ridge Springs; post village in Botetourt County on the Norfolk and Western Railway.
Bluespring; creek, a small right-hand tributary to James River in Alleghany County.
Bluespring; run, a small right-hand tributary to Jackson River in Alleghany County.
Bluespring Run; post village in Alleghany County.
Bluestone; post village in Tazewell County on the Norfolk and Western Railway.
Bluestone; river, rising in Tazewell County, Va., and flowing northeast into New River in Summers County, W. Va.
Bluff; creek, a small left-hand tributary to James River in Amherst County.
Bluff; run, a small right-hand tributary to Mattapony River in Spottsylvania County.
Bluff City; post village in Giles County.
Bluff; mountain in Amherst County. Elevation, 3,350 feet.
Bluff Spur; mountains in Wise County.
Boards; mountain in Bedford County. Elevation, 1,515 feet.
Boatswain; creek, a small left-hand branch of Chickahominy River in Hanover County.
Boaz; post village in Nelson County.
Boaz Mountains; summits in Albemarle County. Elevation, 1,500 to 2,000 feet.
Bobs; post village in Isle of Wight County.
Bocock; post village in Campbell County on the Norfolk and Western Railway. Altitude, 782 feet.
Bodley; post village in Augusta County.
Bodycamp; creek, a small left-hand tributary to Roanoke River in Bedford County.

Bodycamp; post village in Bedford County.
Boer; post village in Lancaster County.
Boggs; post village in Accomac County.
Bohannon; post village in Mathews County.
Bolar; post village in Bath County.
Bold; branch, a small left-hand tributary to Roanoke River in Bedford County.
Bold Knob; summit in Rockingham County.
Boler; mountains in Bath County. Elevation, 2,000 to 3,000 feet.
Bolington; post village in Loudoun County.
Bolling; post village in Buckingham County.
Bolt; post village in Carroll County.
Bolton; village in Russell County.
Bonair; post village in Chesterfield County on the Southern Railway.
Bonbrook; creek, a small right-hand tributary to James River in Cumberland County.
Bonbrook; post village in Franklin County.
Bond; town in Wise County. Population, 295.
Boner; mountain in Warm Spring Mountain, Bath County.
Bonnie; brook, a small left-hand branch of Shenandoah River in Rockingham County.
Bonney; cove in Back Bay in Princess Anne County.
Bonney; post village in Princess Anne County.
Bonsacks; post village in Roanoke County on the Norfolk and Western Railway.
Bonton; post village in Bedford County.
Bony; run, a small right-hand branch of South Fork of Roanoke River in Montgomery County.
Booker; post village in Sussex County.
Boone; run, a small left-hand branch of Shenandoah River in Rockingham County.
Boone Mill; post village in Franklin County on the Norfolk and Western Railway. Altitude, 1,113 feet.
Boonesville; post village in Albemarle County.
Boonsboro; post village in Bedford County.
Boons Path; post village in Lee County.
Booth Knob; summit in Floyd County.
Borden; post village in Shenandoah County.
Bore Auger; creek, a small left-hand tributary to Roanoke River in Bedford County.
Borneo; post village in Greene County.
Borthwick; post village in Dinwiddie County.
Boston; post village in Culpeper County on the Southern Railway. Altitude, 325 feet.
Boswell; post village in Cumberland County on the Chesapeake and Ohio Railway.
Botetourt; county, situated in the western part of the State in the Appalachian Valley, its southern boundary being the Blue Ridge. Its surface consists of narrow parallel ridges separated by limestone valleys. It is traversed by James River. The altitude ranges from 800 to 4,000 feet. Area, 548 square miles. Population, 17,161—white, 13,284; negro, 3,877; foreign born, 47. County seat, Fincastle. The mean magnetic declination in 1900 was 1° 45′. The mean annual rainfall is 50 to 60 inches, and the temperature 50° to 55°. The county is traversed by the Chesapeake and Ohio and the Norfolk and Western railways.
Botetourt; post village in Botetourt County.
Botetourt; springs in Roanoke County.
Bottom; creek, a small right-hand tributary to Roanoke River in Roanoke County.
Boulevard; post village in New Kent County.
Bowden; post village in Halifax County.

Bowers; post village in Southampton County.
Bowershill; post village in Norfolk County on the Seaboard Air Line Railway.
Bowlecamp; creek, a small left-hand branch of Pond River in Wise County.
Bowlers Wharf; post village in Essex County.
Bowles; post village in Clarke County.
Bowling; post village in Tazewell County on the Baltimore and Ohio Railroad.
Bowling Green; county seat of Caroline County. Population, 458.
Bowling Green Ridge; mountains in Wythe County. Elevation, 3,000 feet.
Bowmans; post village in Shenandoah County on the Southern Railway.
Boxelder; post village in Nansemond County.
Boxwood; post village in Henry County on the Danville and Western Railway.
Boyce; post village in Clarke County on the Norfolk and Western Railway. Altitude, 472 feet.
Boyd Tavern; post village in Albermarle County.
Boydton; county seat of Mecklenburg County on the Southern Railway. Population, 527.
Boyers Ferry; post village in Grayson County.
Boykins; town in Southampton County on the Seaboard Air Line Railway. Population, 224.
Bracey; post village in Mecklenburg County on the Seaboard Air Line Railway.
Bracket; post village in Hanover County.
Bradley Mill; bridge across Swift Creek in Chesterfield County.
Bradleys Store; post village in Charles City County.
Bradshaw; creek, a small left-hand branch of North Fork of Roanoke River in Roanoke and Montgomery counties.
Bradshaw; post village in Roanoke county on the Norfolk and Western Railway.
Brake; small right-hand branch of Roanoke River in Montgomery County.
Branchville; post village in Southampton County on the Seaboard Air Line Railway.
Brand; small right-hand branch of Cripple Creek in Wythe County.
Brand; post village in Page County on the Chesapeake and Ohio Railway. Altitude, 1,330 feet.
Brander; bridge across Swift Creek in Chesterfield County.
Brandon; post village in Prince George County.
Brandy Station; post village in Culpeper County on the Southern Railway.
Brandywine; post village in Caroline County.
Brattans; mountains in Rockbridge County. Elevation, 2,000 to 2,500 feet.
Brays; post village in Essex County.
Breeze; post village in Pittsylvania County.
Bremo; creek, a small left-hand branch of James River in Fluvanna County.
Bremobluff; post village in Fluvanna County.
Brents; point on Potomac River in King George County.
Brentsville; post village in Prince William County.
Brewster; post village in Russell County.
Brian; post village in Louisa County.
Briar Patch; mountains in Grayson County. Elevation, 3,000 to 3,650 feet.
Brickhaven; post village in Alexandria County.
Brick Store; village in Lee County.
Bridge; cove in Back Bay in Princess Anne County.
Bridges; post village in Gloucester County.
Bridgetown; post village in Northampton County.
Bridgewater; town in Rockingham County. Population, 384.
Bridle; creek, a small right-hand branch of New River in Grayson County.
Bridlecreek; post village in Grayson County.

Brierfield; post village in Bedford County.
Brierhook; post village in Buckingham County.
Briery; branch, a small left-hand tributary to Shenandoah River in Rockingham County.
Briery; creek, a small right-hand branch of Appomattox River in Prince Edward County.
Briery; post village in Prince Edward County.
Briery; run, a small left-hand tributary to James River in Albemarle and Fluvanna counties.
Briery Branch; gap in Narrow Back Mountains, caused by Briery Branch, in Rockingham County.
Briery Branch; wind gap in Shenandoah Mountains on the State line in Rockingham County, Va., and Pendleton County, W. Va.
Briery Branch Knob; summit in Shenandoah Mountains on the State line between Virginia and West Virginia.
Briggs; post village in Clarke County on the Norfolk and Western Railway.
Brighton; post village in Northampton County.
Brights; post village in Pittsylvania County.
Brightwood; post village in Madison County.
Brink; post village in Greenesville County.
Brio; post village in Carroll County.
Bristersburg; post village in Fauquier County.
Bristol; city situated in Washington County, but independent in government; on the Holston Valley, the Norfolk and Western, the Southern, and the Virginia and Southwestern railways. Population, 4,579.
Bristow; post village in Prince William County on the Southern Railway.
Britain; post village in Loudoun County.
Broad; bay near eastern coast in Princess Anne County.
Broad; creek, a small right-hand tributary to James River in Rockbridge County.
Broad; ford in Holston River in Smyth County.
Broad; run, a right-hand branch of Potomac River in Prince William County.
Broad; run, a small left-hand tributary to Shenandoah River in Augusta County.
Broad; run, a small right-hand tributary to Potomac River in Fauquier County.
Broad; run, a small right-hand tributary to James River in Craig County.
Broad; run, a small right-hand branch of Potomac River in Loudoun County.
Broadcreek; post village in Princess Anne County.
Broaddus; post village in Nelson County.
Broadford; post village in Smyth County.
Broad Hollow; creek, a small left-hand branch of Walker Creek in Giles County.
Broad Rock; small right-hand branch of James River in Chesterfield County.
Broad Run; mountains in Craig County. Elevation, 1,500 to 2,000 feet.
Broadrun; post village in Fauquier County on the Southern Railway.
Broadshoals; ford across Little River in Montgomery County.
Broadshoals; post village in Floyd County.
Broadwater; post village in Northampton County.
Broadway; town in Rockingham County on the Southern Railway. Population, 400.
Brock; run, a small right-hand branch of Chickahominy River in Henrico County.
Brockett; post village in Shenandoah County.
Brockroad; post village in Spottsylvania County on the Potomac, Fredericksburg and Piedmont Railroad.
Brocks; gap in Little North Mountain, caused by the North Fork of Shenandoah River.
Brodnax; post village in Brunswick County.

Brokenburg; post village in Spottsylvania County.
Bromley; creek, a small right-hand branch of North Fork of Holston River in Washington County.
Bronze; post village in Carroll County.
Brooke; post village in Stafford County on the Richmond, Fredericksburg and Potomac Railroad.
Brookewood; post village in Augusta County.
Brookhill; post village in Henrico County.
Brookings; post village in Goochland County.
Brooklyn; village in Halifax County.
Brookneal; post village in Campbell County on the Norfolk and Western Railway.
Brooks; run, a small right-hand tributary to Rappahannock River in Culpeper County.
Brooks; ford in Blackwater River in Franklin County.
Brookvale; post village in Lancaster County.
Brosville; post village in Pittsylvania County.
Brothers; post village in Patrick County.
Brow; post village in Pittsylvania County.
Brown; gap in the Blue Ridge in Rockingham County.
Brown; mountain ridge in Augusta County.
Brownallen; post village in Buckingham County.
Brown Mountain; summit in Campbell County.
Browns; creek, a small left-hand tributary to James River in Amherst County.
Browns; landing on James River in Buckingham County.
Browns; mountain in Amherst County. Elevation, 2,000 to 2,500 feet.
Browns; peak in Wythe County. Elevation, 3,000 to 3,500 feet.
Browns Store; post village in Northumberland County.
Brownsburg; post village in Rockbridge County.
Browns Cove; post village in Albemarle County.
Browntown; post village in Warren County.
Bruce; village in Rockingham County on the Atlantic Coast Line Railroad.
Brucetown; post village in Frederick County.
Bruceville; post village in Lunenburg County.
Brughs Mill; post village in Botetourt County.
Bruington; post village in King and Queen County.
Brumley; creek, a small right-hand branch of North Fork of Holston River, rising in Washington County.
Brumley Gap; post village in Washington County.
Brunswick; county, situated in the southern part of the State in the eastern edge of the Piedmont region; it has a rolling surface, and is of slight elevation. Area, 529 square miles. Population, 18,217—white, 7,375; negro, 10,842; foreign born, 21. County seat, Lawrenceville. The mean magnetic declination in 1900 was 3° 15′ W. The mean annual rainfall is 40 to 50 inches, and the temperature 55 to 60°. The county is traversed by the Southern and the Seaboard Air Line railways.
Brush; creek, a small left-hand branch of New River in Carroll County.
Brush; creek, a small right-hand branch of Little River in Montgomery County.
Brush; creek, a small right-hand branch of New River in Grayson County.
Brush; creek, a small right-hand tributary to Potomac River in Frederick County.
Brush; post village in Grayson County.
Brushy; mountain ridge in the western part of the State with an elevation of 2,000 to 3,000 feet.
Brushy; mountain in Rockbridge, Bath, and Alleghany counties. Elevation, 1,500 to 3,500 feet.

Brushy; mountain in Pittsylvania County. Elevation, 1,000 feet.
Brushy; mountain in Rockbridge County. Elevation, 2,000 feet.
Brushy; run, a small right-hand tributary to James River in Botetourt County.
Brushy Hills; summits in Rockbridge County. Elevation, 1,500 feet.
Brushy Mountain; summit in Fauquier County. Elevation, 750 to 1,000 feet.
Brutus; post village in Pittsylvania County.
Bryant; post village in Nelson County.
Bryant; ridge in Botetourt County. Elevation, 1,500 to 2,000 feet.
Brydie; post village in Lunenburg County.
Buchanan; county, situated in the western part of the State on the Alleghany Plateau, and is deeply dissected. It is drained by Levisa Fork of Big Sandy River. The altitude ranges from 1,000 to 3,700 feet at the summit. Area, 492 square miles. Population, 9,692—white, 9,687; foreign born, 4; and negro, 5. County seat, Grundy. The mean magnetic declination in 1900 was 30′. The mean annual rainfall 50 to 60 inches, and the temperature 50 to 55°.
Buchanan; town in Botetourt County on the Chesapeake and Ohio and the Norfolk and Western railways. Altitude, 834 feet; population, 716.
Buck; branch, a small left-hand tributary to Roanoke River in Appomattox County.
Buck; creek, a small right-hand tributary to James River in Appomattox County.
Buck; creek, a small left-hand tributary to James River in Nelson County.
Buck; creek, a small left-hand branch of Powell River in Lee County.
Buck; creek, a small right-hand tributary to Shenandoah River in Augusta County.
Buck; mountain in Amherst County.
Buck; mountain in Augusta County.
Buck; mountain in Roanoke County. Elevation, 1,992 feet.
Buck; mountains in Albemarle County. Elevation, 1,000 feet.
Buck; mountains in Grayson County. Elevation, 4,680 feet.
Buck; mountains in Rappahannock County. Elevation, 1,000 feet.
Buck; run, a small left-hand tributary to Rappahannock River in Rappahannock County.
Buckeye; mountains in Giles County. Elevation, 2,000 to 2,500 feet.
Buckhall; post village in Prince William County.
Buck Hill; summit in Highland County,
Buck Hill; summit in Shenandoah County. Elevation, 1,500 feet.
Buckhorn; creek, a small right-hand tributary to New River in Carroll County.
Buckhorn; mountains in Tazewell, Giles, and Bland counties. Elevation 2,500 to 3,500 feet.
Buckhorn; post village in Nansemond County.
Buckingham; county, situated in the central part of the State in the Piedmont region on James River, which forms its southern boundary. Its surface is in the most part undulating, rising from 300 feet on James River to 1,500 feet in Spear Mountain, in the western part of the county. Area, 552 square miles. Population, 15,266—white, 7,415; negro, 7,851; foreign born, 65. County seat, Buckingham. The mean magnetic declination in 1900 was 3°. The mean annual rainfall is 40 to 50 inches, and the temperature 55° to 60°. The county is traversed by the Southern Railway.
Buckingham; county seat of Buckingham County. Altitude, 550 feet.
Buck Island; creek, a small left-hand tributary to James River in Albemarle County.
Buckland; post village in Prince William County.
Buckman; run, a small right-hand tributary to Jackson River in Highland County.
Buck Mountain; creek, a small left-hand tributary to James River in Albemarle County.
Buck Mountain; creek, a small left-hand branch of James River in Nelson County.
Buckners Station; post village in Louisa County on the Chesapeake and Ohio Railway.

Buckskin; creek, a small right-hand tributary to Appomattox River in Amelia County.
Buckton; post village in Warren County on the Southern Railway.
Bucu; post village in Dickinson County.
Buddle; post village in Wythe County.
Buell; post village in Norfolk County.
Buena; post village in Culpeper County.
Buenavista; city in Rockbridge County, but independent in government; population, 2,388; on the Chesapeake and Ohio and the Norfolk and Western railways.
Buff; branch, a small right-hand branch of Roanoke River in Franklin County.
Buffalo; branch, a small left-hand tributary to Shenandoah River in Augusta County.
Buffalo; creek, a small right-hand branch of Appomattox River in Prince Edward County.
Buffalo; creek, a small left-hand tributary to James River in Rockbridge County.
Buffalo; creek, a small left-hand tributary to James River in Nelson County.
Buffalo; creek, a small right-hand tributary to James River in Rockbridge County.
Buffalo; creek, a small right-hand branch of Roanoke River in Halifax County.
Buffalo; creek, a small left-hand tributary to Roanoke River in Bedford and Campbell counties.
Buffalo; creek, a small left-hand tributary to Roanoke River in Botetourt County.
Buffalo; ford over the North Fork of Holston River in Russell County.
Buffalo; gap, a small right-hand tributary to James River in Buchanan County.
Buffalo; gap in Little North Mountains, caused by Buffalo Branch, in Augusta County.
Buffalo; hill in Augusta County.
Buffalo; river, a left-hand tributary of James River, formed by North and South forks, in Amherst and Nelson counties.
Buffaloforge; post village in Rockbridge County on the Norfolk and Western Railway. Altitude, 752 feet.
Buffalo Gap; post village in Augusta County on the Chesapeake and Ohio Railway. Altitude, 1,882 feet.
Buffalo Junction; post village in Mecklenburg County on the Southern Railway.
Buffalo Lithia Springs; post village in Mecklenburg County on the Southern Railway.
Buffalo Mills; post village in Rockbridge County.
Buffalo Ridge; mountains in Amherst and Nelson counties. Elevation, 1,000 feet.
Buffalo Ridge; post village in Patrick County.
Buffalo Springs; station on James River in Nelson County on the Chesapeake and Ohio Railway.
Buffalo Station; post village in Nelson County.
Bula; post village in Goochland County.
Bull; creek, a small right-hand branch of Clinch River, rising in Wise County.
Bull; creek, a small left-hand branch of Levisa Fork, rising in Buchanan County.
Bull; run, a small right-hand tributary to Potomac River in Fairfax County.
Bull; run, a small right-hand tributary to Roanoke River in Franklin County.
Bullbegger; post village in Accomac County.
Bull Pasture; mountains in Highland County. Elevation, 2,500 to 3,000 feet.
Bull Run; mountains in Fauquier and Prince William counties. Elevation, 750 to 1,000 feet.
Bullrun; post village in Fairfax County.
Bumpass; post village in Louisa County on the Chesapeake and Ohio Railway.
Bundick; post village in Northumberland County.
Bunkerhill; post village in Bedford County.
Bunker Hill; summit in Franklin County.

Burdens; run, a small left-hand tributary to James River in Rockbridge County.
Burger; branch, a small left-hand tributary to Roanoke River in Campbell County.
Burgess; post village in Dinwiddie County on the Seaboard Air Line Railway.
Burgess Store; post village in Northumberland County.
Burke Garden; an elliptical valley drained by Wolf Creek into New River.
Burkes Garden; post village in Tazewell County on the Norfolk and Western Railway.
Burkes Station; post village in Fairfax County on the Southern Railway.
Burketown; post village in Augusta County.
Burkeville; town in Nottoway County. Population, 510.
Burkfork; post village in Floyd County.
Burks; fork, a small right-hand tributary to New River in Floyd and Carroll counties.
Burks; run, a small right-hand branch of New River in Pulaski County.
Burnleys; post village in Albemarle County on the Southern Railway.
Burns; creek, a small right-hand branch of Guest River in Wise County.
Burns Knob; summit in Rockingham County.
Burnsville; post village in Bath County.
Burnt Chestnut; branch, a small right-hand tributary to Levisa Fork in Buchanan County.
Burrhill; post village in Orange County.
Burrowsville; post village in Prince George County.
Burton; creek, a small right-hand tributary to James River in Campbell County.
Burton; post village in King and Queen County on the Chesapeake and Ohio Railway.
Burtons Creek; post village in Campbell County.
Burts; post village in Sussex County.
Burwellville; village in Pittsylvania County.
Bush; small creek in Princess Anne County, emptying into Willoughby Bay.
Bush; post village in Brunswick County.
Bush; river, a small right-hand branch of Appomattox River in Prince Edward County.
Bush Ford; branch, a small left-hand tributary to Roanoke River in Charlotte County.
Bushpark; post village in Cumberland County.
Bushy; mountains in Wythe County. Elevation, 2,500 to 3,000 feet.
Bushy; post village in Middlesex County.
Butcher; creek, a small left-hand tributary to Powell River in Wise County.
Butler; mountain in Nelson County.
Butt; mountains in Giles County. Elevation, 2,500 to 4,195 feet.
Butterwood; creek, a small left-hand branch of Appomattox River in Powhatan County.
Butterwood; creek, a small left-hand tributary to Nottoway River in Dinwiddie County.
Butterwood; creek, a small left-hand tributary to Roanoke River in Charlotte County.
Butterworth; bridge in Dinwiddie County.
Button; creek, a small left-hand tributary to Roanoke River in Campbell County.
Butylo; post village in Middlesex County.
Buzzard Roost; summit in Lee County. Elevation, 3,000 feet.
Byars; creek, a small left-hand branch of Middle Holston River in Smyth County.
Bybee; post village in Fluvanna County.
Byrd; creek, a small left-hand branch of James River in Fluvanna County.
Byrdton; post village in Northumberland County.

Bull. 232—04——3

Byrdville; post village in Pittsylvania County.
Cabell; village in Carroll County.
Cabin; post village in Grayson County.
Cabin; run, a small right-hand tributary to Shenandoah River in Warren County.
Cabinpoint; post village in Surry County.
Cahas; mountains in Franklin County. Elevation, 1,500 to 3,000 feet.
Cahas Knob; summit in Franklin County.
Ca Ira; post village in Cumberland County.
Caldwell; mountains in Botetourt County. Elevation, 1,500 to 2,500 feet.
Caledonia; post village in Goochland County.
Calfee; ford over New River in Pulaski County.
Calf Pasture; river, a small left-hand tributary to James River in Augusta and Rockbridge counties.
Calicorock; post village in Franklin County.
Callaghan; post village in Alleghany County on the Chesapeake and Ohio Railway. Altitude, 428 feet.
Callands; post village in Pittsylvania County.
Callao; post village in Northumberland County.
Callaville; post village in Brunswick County.
Callaway; post village in Franklin County.
Callihan; creek, a small right-hand branch of Powell River in Wise County.
Calno; post village in King William County.
Calvary; post village in Shenandoah County.
Calverton; post village in Fauquier County on the Chesapeake and Ohio and the Southern railways.
Cambria; post village in Montgomery County.
Camden; creek, a small left-hand tributary to James River in Rockingham County.
Camden; gap in Amherst County between Richardson and Cedar mountains.
Camel; post village in Carroll County.
Cameron; post village in Scott County.
Cameron; run, a small right-hand branch of Potomac River in Fairfax County.
Camm; post village in Buckingham County.
Camp; post village in Smyth County.
Camp; branch, a small right-hand tributary to Jackson River in Craig County.
Camp; creek, a small right-hand tributary to Roanoke River in Floyd County.
Camp; small creek rising and sinking in Lee County.
Camp; creek, a small right-hand tributary to New River in Floyd County.
Camp; fork, a small right-hand tributary to New River in Carroll and Floyd counties.
Camp; mountain in Rockbridge County.
Campbell; branch, a small left-hand tributary to Clinch River, rising in Russell County.
Campbell; county, in the southern part of the State in the Piedmont region. Its surface is undulating and somewhat broken in the southern part by short ridges, outliers of the Blue Ridge. The southern part is drained by the Roanoke and the northern part by the James. The altitude ranges from a little less than 500 feet up to 1,500 feet. Area, 554 square miles. Population, 23,256—white, 13,641; negro, 9,615; foreign born, 136. County seat, Rustburg. The mean magnetic declination in 1900 was 2° 10'. The mean annual rainfall is 50 to 60 inches, and the temperature 55° to 60°. The county is traversed by the Southern and the Norfolk and Western railways.
Campbell; post village in Albermarle County on the Chesapeake and Ohio Railway.
Campbells; small left-hand branch of North Fork of Holston River in Smyth County.

Campbells; run, a small right-hand tributary to Rappahannock River in Culpeper County.
Campcreek; post village in Floyd County.
Camp Rock; summit in Scott County. Elevation, 4,000 feet.
Cana; post village in Carroll County.
Cane; creek, a right-hand branch of Powell River in Lee County.
Caney; fork, a small right-hand branch of Clinch River, rising in Russell County.
Cannon; creek, a small left-hand tributary to James River in Henrico County.
Canon; post village in Carroll County.
Canova; post village in Prince William County.
Canterburg; post village in Frederick County.
Cap; post village in Carroll County.
Cape Charles; town in Northampton County on the New York, Philadelphia and Norfolk Railroad. Population, 1,040.
Capeville; post village in Northampton County.
Capola; mountain in Shenandoah County.
Caponroad; post village in Shenandoah County on the Baltimore and Ohio Railroad.
Cappahosic; post village in Gloucester County.
Capron; post village in Southampton County on the Southern Railway.
Captain; post village in Craig County.
Card; post village in Buchanan County.
Cardinal; post village in Mathews County.
Cardinal; summit in Amherst County.
Cardwell; post village in Goochland County.
Caret; post village in Essex County.
Carlock; creek, a small right-hand branch of Middle Fork of Holston River in Smyth County.
Carloover; post village in Bath County.
Carltons Store; post village in King and Queen County.
Carmel; post village in Shenandoah County.
Carnation; post village in King George County.
Carne; creek, a small right-hand tributary to James River in Alleghany County.
Caroline; county, situated in the central part of the State on the Atlantic plain. It has a rolling surface, and is but little elevated above sea level. Area, 562 square miles. Population, 16,709—white, 7,667; negro, 9,042; foreign born, 50. County seat, Bowling Green. The mean magnetic declination in 1900 was 3° 55′. The mean annual rainfall is 40 to 50 inches, and the temperature 55° to 60°. The county is traversed by the Richmond, Fredericksburg and Potomac Railroad.
Carrico; post village in Culpeper County.
Carrie; post village in Dickenson County.
Carroll; county, situated in the southern part of the State. It is limited on the south by the summit of the Blue Ridge, on the west by New River, and on the north and east by arbitrary lines. Its surface is an elevated, undulated plateau, drained by many streams to New River. The altitude ranges from 2,000 to 3,600 feet above sea level. Area, 445 square miles. Population, 19,303—white, 18,964; negro, 339; foreign-born, 11. County seat, Hillsville. The mean magnetic declination in 1900 was 1°. The mean annual rainfall is 50 to 60 inches, and the temperature 50° to 55°. The county is traversed by the Norfolk and Western Railway.
Carroll Sulphur; springs in Carroll County.
Carrollton; post village in Isle of Wight County.
Carrs; mountain in Madison County. Elevation, 1,300 feet.
Carrsville; post village in Isle of Wight County on the Seaboard Air Line Railway.

Carsley; post village in Surry County.
Carson; post village in Prince George County.
Carsonville; post village in Grayson County.
Carter; ferry over Clinch River in Scott County.
Carter; mountains in Albemarle County. Elevation, 500 to 1,500 feet.
Carter; run, a small left-hand branch of Rappahannock River in Fauquier County.
Carters Bridge; post village in Albemarle County.
Carters Island; ford over Roanoke River in Bedford County.
Carters Island; post village in Bedford County.
Carters Mills; post village in Patrick County.
Cartersville; post village in Cumberland County.
Carters Wharf; post village in Richmond County.
Carterton; post village in Russell County on the Norfolk and Western Railway. Altitude, 1,495 feet.
Carthage; post village in Floyd County.
Cartmill; gap in the northern part of Purgatory Mountains, caused by Purgatory Creek.
Cartwrights Wharf; post village in Nansemond County.
Carvins; cove in Tinker Mountains drained by Carvins Creek in Botetourt County.
Carvins; creek, a small left-hand tributary to Roanoke River in Botetourt County.
Carysbrook; post village in Fluvanna County.
Casanova; post village in Fauquier County on the Southern Railway.
Cascade; post village in Pittsylvania County on Danville and Western Railway.
Casco; post village in Hanover County.
Cash; post village in Gloucester County.
Cashville; post village in Accomac County.
Caskie; post village in Nelson County on the Chesapeake and Ohio Railway.
Cassel; post village in Patrick County.
Castlecraig; post village in Campbell County.
Castleman; ferry over Shenandoah River in Clarke County.
Castlemans Ferry; post village in Clarke County.
Castle Rock; summit in Albemarle County.
Castleton; post village in Rappahannock County.
Castlewood; post village in Russell County on the Norfolk and Western Railway. Altitude, 1477 feet.
Cast Steel; run, a small right-hand tributary to Jackson River in Alleghany County.
Catalpa; post village in Culpeper County.
Catawba; creek, a small right-hand tributary to James River in Roanoke County.
Catawba; creek, a small right-hand branch of James River in Botetourt County, formed by North and South forks.
Catawba; mountains in Roanoke County. Elevation, 2,000 to 2,906 feet.
Catawba; post village in Roanoke County.
Catharines; branch, a small left-hand tributary to North Fork of Holston River, rising in Washington County.
Catharpin; post village in Prince William County.
Catharpin; run, a small right-hand tributary to Mattapony River in Spottsylvania County.
Catharpin; run, a small right-hand tributary to Potomac River in Prince William County.
Cathay; village in Augusta County.
Catlett; post village in Fauquier County on the Southern Railway.
Catoctin; creek, a small right-hand branch of Potomac River formed by two forks, North and South, in Loudoun County.
Catoctin; mountains in Loudoun County. Elevation, 500 feet.

Catron; post village in Wythe County.
Cattail; branch, a small right-hand tributary to James River in Dinwiddie County.
Cattail; run, a small right-hand tributary to Potomac River in Fauquier County.
Cauthornville; post village in King and Queen County.
Cave; mountain in Wythe County. Elevation, 2,500 feet.
Cave Hill; summit in Augusta County.
Cave Spring; branch, a small right-hand tributary to Roanoke River in Roanoke County.
Cavespring; post village in Roanoke County.
Cavitt; creek, a small right-hand branch of Clinch River, rising in Tazewell County.
Caylor; post village in Lee County.
Cedar; creek, a small left-hand tributary to Clinch River, rising in Russell County.
Cedar; creek, a small right-hand branch of James River in Rockbridge County.
Cedar; creek, a small left-hand tributary to James River in Bath County.
Cedar; creek, a small right-hand branch of Middle Holston River in Washington County.
Cedar; creek, a small left-hand branch of North Fork of Holston River in Smyth County.
Cedar; creek, a small left-hand branch of Shenandoah River in Frederick and Warren counties.
Cedar; creek, a small left-hand tributary to Shenandoah River in Shenandoah County.
Cedar; mountain in Amherst County.
Cedar; run, a small left-hand tributary to New River in Wythe County.
Cedar; run, a small right-hand tributary to Potomac River in Prince William and Fauquier counties.
Cedar; run; a small right-hand tributary to Potomac River in Fauquier County.
Cedar; run, a small right-hand tributary to Rappahannock River in Culpeper County.
Cedar; run, a small left-hand tributary to Shenandoah River in Rockingham County.
Cedar; small island in Back Bay in Princess Anne County.
Cedar; small point of land in Isle of Wight County, extending into James River.
Cedarbluff; post village in Tazewell County on the Norfolk and Western Railway. Altitude, 1,988 feet.
Cedar Forest; post village in Pittsylvania County.
Cedargrove; post village in Frederick County.
Cedar Ridge; mountains in Botetourt County. Elevation, 1,500 feet.
Cedar Springs; post village in Wythe County.
Cedarville; post village in Warren County on the Norfolk and Western Railway. Altitude, 566 feet.
Cedon; post village in Caroline County.
Cellar; creek, a small right-hand tributary to Appomattox River in Nottoway County.
Cellar; mountain in Augusta County. Elevation, 2,500 feet.
Centenary; post village in Buckingham County.
Centercross; post village in Essex County.
Center Mills; post village in Montgomery County.
Centerville; post village in Fairfax County.
Centralia; post village in Chesterfield County.
Central Lovely; mountain in Pulaski County. Elevation, 1,785 feet.
Centralplains; post village in Fluvanna County.
Centralpoint; post village in Caroline County.
Cephas; post village in Mecklenburg County.
Ceres; post village in Bland County.

Chaffin; bluff in Henrico County.
Chaffin; post village in Halifax County.
Chalk; mountains in Albemarle County.
Chalk; run, a small left-hand tributary to James River in Rockbridge County.
Chalklevel; post village in Pittsylvania County.
Chalk Mine; mountain in Rockbridge County. Elevation, 2,960 feet.
Chamberlains Bed; small left-hand tributary to Nottoway River in Dinwiddie County.
Chambersville; post village in Frederick County.
Chamblissburg; post village in Bedford County.
Champlain; post village in Essex County.
Chance; post village in Essex County.
Chandler; mountain in Campbell County. Altitude, 1,405 feet.
Chandler: post village in Lee County.
Chaney; small right-hand branch of Cripple Creek in Wythe County.
Chaneys; post village in Pittsylvania County.
Chantilly; post village in Fairfax County.
Chap; post village in Appomattox County.
Charity; post village in Patrick County.
Charlemont; post village in Bedford County, lying between the James and Appomattox rivers, just above their junction, but on the Atlantic plain. The surface is low and rolling, but little elevated above tide.
Charles; cape, point of land in Northampton County, the northern point at the entrance to Chesapeake Bay.
Charles City; county, situated in the eastern part of the State. Area 183 square miles. Population, 5,040—white, 1,344; negro, 3,696; foreign born, 15. County seat, Charles City. The mean magnetic declination in 1900 was 3° 45′. The mean annual rainfall is 40 to 50 inches, and the mean annual temperature 55° to 60°. The county is traversed by the Chesapeake and Ohio Railway.
Charles City; county seat of Charles City County.
Charlie Hope; post village in Brunswick County.
Charlotte; county, situated in the southern part of the State in the Piedmont region. Its surface presents but little relief, ranging from 300 to 500 feet above sea level. Area 479 square miles. Population, 15,343—white, 6,798; negro, 8,545; foreign born, 37. County seat, Charlotte. The mean magnetic declination in 1900 was 2° 45′. The mean annual rainfall is 50 to 60 inches, and the temperature 55° to 60°. The county is traversed by the Southern Railway.
Charlotte; county seat of Charlotte County.
Charlottesville; city, located in Albemarle County on the Chesapeake and Ohio and the Southern railways. It is independent in government, and has a population of 6,449. It contains the court-house.
Chase; village in Mecklenburg County on the Southern Railway. Population, 542.
Chase Wharf; post village in Lancaster County.
Chatham; county seat of Pittsylvania County on the Southern Railway. Altitude, 624 feet. Population, 918.
Chatham Hill; post village in Smyth County.
Chatmoss; post village in Henry County on the Danville and Western Railway.
Chatterton; post village in King George County.
Cheapside; post village in Northampton County.
Cheatwood; post village in Appomattox County.
Check; post village in Floyd County.
Cheese; creek, a small, left-hand tributary to Roanoke River in Campbell County.
Chells; ford over Roanoke River in Pittsylvania County.
Cherriton; post village in Northampton County.

Cherry; village in Norfolk County.
Cherrydale; post village in Alexandria County.
Cherrygrove; post village in Rockingham County.
Cherrystone; post village in Northampton County.
Chesapeake; largest bay on the Atlantic coast. It stretches northward from Capes Charles and Henry at its entrance for 175 miles, with an average breadth of from 25 to 30 miles, and is navigable to its head by vessels of considerable draft. It penetrates the States of Virginia and Maryland. Into it flow many rivers, especially from the west, the largest of which are the Potomac, Rappahannock, York, and James. Upon its west are the important cities of Baltimore, Newport News, and Norfolk.
Chesapeake; post village in Northampton County.
Chesconnessex; post village in Accomac County.
Chester; gap in the Blue Ridge. Altitude, 1,320 feet.
Chester; post village in Chesterfield County, on the Atlantic Coast Line, the Farmville and Powhatan, and the Seaboard Air Line railroads.
Chesterbrook; post village in Fairfax County.
Chesterfield; county, situated in the central part of the State in the Piedmont region, the boundary upon the north being in part the Appomattox River. The surface is undulating or rolling, elevated 200 or 300 feet above sea level. Area, 484 square miles. Population, 18,804—white, 11,105; negro, 7,699; foreign born, 361. County seat, Chesterfield. The mean magnetic declination in 1900 was 3° 30′. The mean annual rainfall is 40 to 50 inches, and the temperature 55° to 60°. The county is traversed by the Atlantic Coast Line, the Seaboard Air Line, the Farmville and Powhatan, and the Southern railroads.
Chesterfield; county seat of Chesterfield County.
Chestnut; creek, a right-hand branch of New River in Carroll County.
Chestnut; creek, a right-hand tributary to Roanoke River in Franklin County.
Chestnut; post village in Amherst County.
Chestnutfork; post village in Bedford County.
Chestnut Level; summit in Alleghany Front, in Bath County.
Chestnut Lick; small right-hand tributary to Potomac River in Prince William County.
Chestnut Mountain; summit in Botetourt County. Elevation, 2,000 to 2,500 feet.
Chestnut Ridge; mountains in Amherst County. Elevation, 2,000 to 3,000 feet.
Chestnut Ridge; mountains in Augusta County.
Chestnut Ridge; mountains in Bath County. Elevation, 2,000 to 3,000 feet.
Chestnut Ridge; mountains in Bland County.
Chestnut Ridge; mountains in Rockingham County. Elevation, 1,500 feet.
Chestnut Ridge; mountains in Scott County.
Chestnut Ridge; mountains in Smyth and Wythe counties. Elevation, 2,500 feet.
Chestnut Ridge; mountains in Tazewell and Bland counties. Elevation, 3,000 to 4,000 feet.
Chestnut Ridge; mountains in Washington County.
Chestnut Ridge; summit in Rockingham County.
Chickahominy; river, heading in the eastern edge of the Piedmont region and flowing southeast, joining James River a short distance above its mouth.
Childress; post village in Montgomery County.
Chilesburg; post village in Caroline County.
Chilhowie; small right-hand branch of Middle Fork of Holston River in Smyth County.
Chilhowie; post village in Smyth County on the Norfolk and Western Railway.
Chiltons; post village in Westmoreland County.
Chimney; branch, a small right-hand tributary to New River in Pulaski County.

Chimney; run, a small left-hand tributary to James River in Bath County.
Chimney Rock; fork, a small right-hand tributary to Clinch River in Scott County.
Chincoteague Island; post village in Accomac County.
Chisel Knob; summit in Carroll County. Elevation, 3,663.
Chisleys; run, a small right-hand tributary to Jackson River in Alleghany County.
Chopawamsic; creek, a small right-hand branch of Potomac River in Prince William and Stafford counties.
Chrisman; post village in Rockingham County.
Christian; creek, a small tributary to Shenandoah River in Augusta County.
Christiansburg; county seat of Montgomery County on the Norfolk and Western Railway. Altitude, 2,007 feet. Population, 659.
Christie; post village in Halifax County on the Southern Railway.
Christopher; creek, a small left-hand tributary to York River in Louisa County.
Chub, post village in Sussex County.
Chuckatuck; post village in Nansemond County.
Chuckatuck Island; small creek emptying into James River in Nansemond County.
Chula Depot; post village in Amelia County on the Southern Railway.
Chum; post village in Carroll County.
Church; small right-hand branch of Slate Creek in Buchanan County.
Church; ford in Clinch River in Scott County.
Church; run, a small right-hand tributary to York River in Orange County.
Churchland; post village in Norfolk County on the Atlantic Coast Line Railroad.
Church Road; post village in Dinwiddie County on the Norfolk and Western Railway.
Church Rock; summit in North Mountain.
Church View; post village in Middlesex County.
Churchville; post village in Augusta County.
Churchwood; post village in Pulaski County.
Cifax; post village in Bedford County.
Cisco; post village in Mecklenburg County.
Cismont; post village in Albemarle County.
Citypoint; post village in Prince George County on the Norfolk and Western Railway.
Claiborne; post village in Amherst County.
Claudville; post village in Patrick County.
Clapboard; creek, a small right-hand branch of New River in Pulaski County.
Clare; post village in Augusta County.
Claremont; village in Surry County on the Southern Railway. Population, 565.
Claresville; post village in Greenesville County.
Clark; mountains in Orange County. Elevation, 500 to 1,000 feet.
Clarke; county, situated in the northern part of the State in the Shenandoah Valley, the eastern boundary being the crest of the Blue Ridge. The surface is mainly level, but in the eastern part are the heavy spurs of the Blue Ridge. Area, 189 square miles. Population, 7,927—whites, 5,695; negro, 2,231; foreign born, 29. County seat, Berryville. The mean magnetic declination in 1900 was 4°. The mean annual rainfall is 50 to 60 inches, and the temperature 50° to 55°. The county is traversed by the Norfolk and Western Railway.
Clarkes; creek, a small left-hand tributary to Yadkin River in Patrick County.
Clarkes Gap; post village in Loudoun County on the Southern Railway. Altitude, 578 feet.
Clarks; creek, a small left-hand tributary to James River in Amherst County.
Clarkson; post village in Culpeper County.
Clarksville; town in Mecklenburg County on the Southern Railway. Population, 723

Clarkton; post village in Halifax County on the Norfolk and Western Railway.
Clary; post village in Shenandoah County.
Claudville; post village in Patrick County.
Clay; small right-hand branch of Roanoke River in Pittsylvania County.
Claybank; post village in Gloucester County.
Clayce; post village in Floyd County.
Claypool; post village in Nelson County.
Clays Mills; post village in Halifax County.
Clayville; post village in Powhatan County on the Southern Railway.
Clear; creek, a small right-hand branch of New River in Wythe and Carroll counties.
Clear; creek, a small right-hand branch of Great River in Wise County.
Clear; creek, a small right-hand tributary to Beaver Creek, rising in Washington County.
Clear; fork, a tributary to Wolf Creek, rising in Tazewell County.
Clear; fork, a small right-hand branch of New River in Grayson County.
Clearbrook; post village in Frederick County on the Cumberland Valley Railroad.
Clearfork; post village in Bland County.
Cleave Knob; mountains in Wythe County. Elevation, 2,500 feet.
Cleghorn; valley in Smyth County.
Clems Branch; post village in Grayson County.
Clendening; creek, a small right-hand branch of New River in Giles County.
Cleopus; post village in Nansemond County.
Cleveland; post village in Russell County on the Norfolk and Western Railway. Altitude, 1,425 feet.
Clevilas; post village in Bedford County.
Clide; village in Russell County.
Cliff Mills; post village in Fauquier County.
Clifford; post village in Amherst County.
Clift; post village in Alleghany County.
Clifton Forge; town in Alleghany County on the Chesapeake and Ohio Railway. Altitude, 1,052 feet. Population, 3,212.
Clifton Station; post village in Fairfax County on the Southern Railway.
Clinch; mountain ridge extending from Grainger County, Tenn., to Tazewell County, Va. Maximum height, 4,274 feet.
Clinch; post village in Scott County.
Clinch; river, rising in Tazewell County, Va., flowing southwest into Kingston County, Tenn., and discharging into Tennessee River.
Clinchport; town in Scott County, on the Virginia and Southwestern Railway. Population, 183.
Clinton; post village in Cumberland County.
Clintwood; county seat of Dickenson County. Population, 255.
Clio; post village in Floyd County.
Clip; village in Washington County.
Clito; post village in Grayson County.
Clover; creek, a small left-hand tributary to Roanoke River in Bedford County.
Clover; hollow, a small right-hand tributary to New River in Craig and Giles counties.
Clover; town in Halifax County on the Southern Railway. Population, 400.
Clovercreek; post village in Highland County.
Cloverdale; post village in Botetourt County on the Norfolk and Western Railway. Altitude, 1,122 feet.
Cloyds; mountains in Pulaski County. Elevation, 2,000 to 2,500 feet.
Clung; post village in Carroll County.
Coakley; post village in Stafford County.

Coal; creek, a small right-hand branch of Clinch River in Tazewell County.
Coal; run, a small right-hand tributary to Bluestone River in Tazewell County.
Coal; run, a small left-hand tributary to Shenandoah River in Augusta County.
Coalcreek; post village in Carroll County.
Coal Hill; post village in Henrico County.
Coan; post village in Northumberland County.
Coates; post village in Louisa County.
Cobbler; mountains in Bath County.
Cobbs Creek; post village in Mathews County.
Cobbs Mount; summit in Bedford County. Elevation, 1,410 feet.
Cobham; post village in Albemarle County on the Chesapeake and Ohio Railway.
Coby Knob; summit in Grayson County.
Cochran; post village in Brunswick County on the Seaboard Air Line Railway.
Cockpit; point on Potomac River in Prince William County.
Coddyshore; post village in Sussex County.
Cody; post village in Halifax County.
Coeburn; town in Wise County on the Norfolk and Western Railway. Altitude, 1,982 feet. Population, 295.
Coffee; creek, a small left-hand tributary to James River in Amherst County.
Coffee; post village in Bedford County.
Cohoke; post village in King William County.
Coke; post village in Gloucester County.
Coldharbor; village in Hanover County.
Cold Sulphur Springs; post village in Rockbridge County.
Cole; creek, a small right-hand tributary to New River in Carroll County.
Colemans Falls; post village in Bedford County on the Chesapeake and Ohio Railway.
Cole Mountain; summit in Amherst County.
Coles; creek, a small right-hand tributary to Roanoke River in Franklin County.
Coles Ferry; post village in Charlotte County.
Coles Knob; summit in Floyd County. Elevation, 2,903 feet.
Coles Knob; summit in Franklin County.
Coles Point; post village in Westmoreland County.
Colesville; post village in Patrick County.
Colina; post village in Dinwiddie County.
Colleen; post village in Nelson County.
College Park; post village in Campbell County.
Colley; post village in Dickenson County.
Collier; creek, a small right-hand tributary to James River in Rockbridge County.
Collierstown; post village in Rockbridge County.
Collins Mill; post village in Grayson County.
Collinsville; post village in Frederick County.
Collison Ridge; mountains in Bath County. Elevation, 2,000 to 2,500 feet.
Cologne; post village in King and Queen County.
Colonial Beach; town in Westmoreland County. Population, 453.
Colosse; post village in Isle of Wight County.
Columbia; town in Fluvanna County on the Chesapeake and Ohio Railway. Population, 216.
Columbia Furnace; post village in Shenandoah County.
Columbian Grove; post village in Lunenburg County.
Colvin Run; post village in Fairfax County.
Comans Well; post village in Sussex County.
Comb Point; summit in Russell County. Elevation, 2,000 feet.
Comer Rock; summit in Iron Mountains. Elevation, 4,113 feet.

Comers Rock; post village in Grayson County.
Comet; post village in Isle of Wight County.
Comfort; post village in Lee County.
Como; village in Henry County.
Comorn; post village in King George County.
Compton; post village in Page County on the Norfolk and Western Railway.
Concord Depot; post village in Campbell County on the Norfolk and Western Railway. Altitude, 833 feet.
Cone; mountains in Nelson County.
Conicville; post village in Shenandoah County.
Conklin; post village in Loudoun County.
Conley; post village in Southampton County.
Conrad; ferry across Potomac River in Loudoun County.
Conrads Mills; post village in Middlesex County.
Consent; post village in Patrick County.
Contra; post village in King and Queen County.
Contrary; creek, a small left-hand tributary to York River in Louisa County.
Contrary; creek, a small right-hand branch of Levisa Fork in Buchanan County.
Converse; post village in Norfolk County.
Conway; river, a small right-hand tributary to Rappahannock River in Greene County.
Cook; post village in Carroll County.
Cooks; creek, a small left-hand tributary to York River in Orange County.
Cooks; run, a small left-hand tributary to South Fork of Roanoke River in Montgomery County.
Coolwell; post village in Amherst County.
Coonseye; post village in Wise County.
Coonsville; post village in Bedford County.
Cooper; post village in Middlesex County.
Cootes Store; post village in Rockingham County.
Copeland; post village in Nansemond County on the Southern Railway.
Copper; creek, a small left-hand tributary to Clinch River, rising in Russell County.
Copper; ridge, in Russell and Scott counties, extending northeast and southwest. Elevation, 2,000 to 2,500 feet.
Copperhill; post village in Floyd County.
Copper Valley; post village in Floyd County.
Corbet; post village in Scott County.
Corbin; post village in Caroline County.
Cordova; post village in Culpeper County.
Corinth; post village in Wythe County.
Corleyville; post village in Roanoke County.
Cornland; post village in Norfolk County.
Cornsville; post village in Scott County.
Cornwall; post village in Rockbridge County on the Norfolk and Western Railway.
Cosby; post village in Orange County.
Cotman; post village in Henrico County.
Cotopaxi; post village in Augusta County on the Norfolk and Western Railway.
Coulson; post village in Carroll County.
Council; post village in Buchanan County.
Counts; village in Russell County.
Co rt House; creek, a small left-hand tributary to James River in Goochland County.
Courtland; county seat of Southampton County on the Southern Railway. Population, 288.

Cove; creek, a small left-hand branch of Cripple Creek in Wythe County.
Cove; creek, a small left-hand branch of North Fork of Holston River, rising in Washington County.
Cove; creek, a small left-hand tributary to James River in Albemarle and Nelson counties.
Cove; creek, a small right-hand branch of Clinch River in Scott County.
Cove; creek, a small right-hand branch of North Fork of Holston River in Smyth County.
Cove; creek, a small right-hand tributary to Jackson River in Alleghany County
Cove; creek, a small right-hand tributary to Wolf Creek in Tazewell County.
Cove; mountains in Craig and Roanoke counties. Elevation, 2,500 to 3,000 feet.
Cove; run, a small right-hand tributary to Jackson River in Alleghany County.
Cove; run, a small left-hand tributary to Shenandoah River in Shenandoah County.
Covecreek; post village in Tazewell County.
Cove Mountain; summit in Rockingham County. Elevation, 2,000 feet.
Cove Ridge; mountains in Scott County. Elevation, 2,000 feet.
Covesville; post village in Albemarle County on the Southern Railway. Altitude, 804 feet.
Coveton; post village in Wythe County.
Covington; river, a small right-hand tributary to Rappahannock River in Rappahannock County.
Covington; county seat of Alleghany County on the Chesapeake and Ohio Railway. Population, 2,950. Altitude, 1,245 feet.
Cowan; small branch of Sinking Creek in Scott County.
Cowan; small right-hand branch of Opossum Creek in Scott County.
Cowans Depot; post village in Rockingham County.
Cowans Mills; post village in Montgomery County.
Cowardin; post village in Bath County.
Cowardin; run, a small left-hand tributary to James River in Bath County.
Cowart; post village in Northumberland County.
Cowpasture; river, a small left-hand branch of James River in Bath County.
Cowpasture; river, a left-hand tributary to James River in Highland County.
Cox; small right-hand branch of North Fork of Clinch River in Scott County.
Cox; creek, a small left-hand branch of North Fork of Holston River in Smyth County.
Cox; creek, a small right-hand tributary to North Fork of Powell River.
Cox; ferry across New River in Pulaski County.
Cox; ford over New River.
Cox; post village in Lee County.
Cox Knob; summit in Botetourt County. Elevation, 3,525 feet.
Coyners; mountain in Botetourt County. Elevation, 1,500 feet.
Coyners Springs; post village in Botetourt County.
Crab; creek, a small right-hand branch of New River in Pulaski County.
Crab; creek, a small right-hand tributary to New River in Grayson County.
Crab; post village in Gloucester County.
Crab; run, a small left-hand tributary to James River in Highland County.
Crabbottom; post village in Highland County.
Crabneck; post village in York County.
Crab Orchard; creek, a small right-hand tributary to Walker Creek, rising in Bland County.
Crab Orchard; creek, small right-hand branch of North Fork of Powell River.
Crab Orchard; creek, a small left-hand tributary to Roanoke River in Bedford County.
Crab Orchard; post village in Lee County.

Crabtree; falls in a branch of South Fork of Tye River in Nelson County.
Craddock; creek, a small left-hand branch of Roanoke River in Bedford County.
Craddockville; post village in Accomac County.
Craft; ferry over Clinch River in Scott County.
Crafts; ford in Blackwater River in Franklin County.
Cragged; branch, a small left-hand tributary to Roanoke River in Bedford County.
Craig; county, situated in the western part of the State in the Appalachian Valley. Area, 351 square miles. Its surface consists of an alternation of parallel ridges, trending northeast and southwest, separated by limestone valleys, and is drained by branches of James River. The altitude ranges from 1,200 to 3,600 feet above sea level. Population, 4,293—white, 4,032; negro, 261; foreign born, 9. County seat, Newcastle. The mean magnetic declination in 1900 was 1° 10′. The mean annual rainfall is 50 to 60 inches, and the temperature 50° to 55°. The county is traversed by the Chesapeake and Ohio Railway.
Craig; creek, a right-hand tributary to Jackson River in Craig County.
Craig; creek, a right-hand tributary to James River in Craig and Montgomery counties.
Craig City; post village in Craig County.
Craig Healing; springs in Craig County.
Craigs Creek; post village in Craig County.
Craigs Mills; village in Washington County.
Craigsville; post village in Augusta County on the Chesapeake and Ohio Railway. Altitude, 1,515 feet.
Cranberry; creek, a small right-hand tributary to New River in Carroll County.
Crandon; post village in Bland County.
Cranes Nest; creek, a small left-hand tributary to Russell Fork, rising in Dickenson County.
Cranes Nest; post village in Wise County.
Craney; island in Elizabeth River.
Craney; island in James River in Norfolk County.
Crank; post village in Louisa County on the Chesapeake and Ohio Railway.
Crawford; gap in Tobacco Row Mountain in Amherst County.
Crawford; mountains in Augusta County. Elevation, 2,500 to 3,500 feet.
Crawford Draft; small tributary to Shenandoah River in Augusta County.
Crawford Ridge; mountains in Montgomery and Roanoke counties.
Crayon; post village in Mecklenburg County.
Creeds; post village in Princess Anne County.
Cremona; post village in Cumberland County.
Creola; post village in Grayson County.
Cressy; creek, a small left-hand branch of South Fork of Holston River in Smyth County.
Crest; post village in Stafford County.
Creswell; village in Russell County.
Crewe; town in Nottoway County on the Norfolk and Western Railway. Population, 1,329.
Crichton; post village in Brunswick County.
Cricket Hill; post village in Mathews County.
Criders; post village in Rockingham County.
Criglersville; post village in Madison County.
Crimora Station; post village in Augusta County on the Norfolk and Western Railway. Altitude, 1,239 feet.
Cripple; creek, a left-hand branch of New River in Wythe County.
Cripple; creek, a right-hand branch of New River, rising in Smyth County.
Cripple Creek; post village in Wythe County on the Norfolk and Western Railway.

Crittenden; post village in Nansemond County.
Critz; post village in Patrick County on the Danville and Western Railway.
Croaker; post village in James City County.
Crockett; cove in Big Stone Ridge in Tazewell County.
Crockett Depot; post village in Wythe County on the Norfolk and Western Railway. Altitude, 2,327 feet.
Crockett Springs; post village in Montgomery County.
Crofton; post village in Fluvanna County.
Cromwells; run, a small right-hand tributary to Potomac River in Fauquier County.
Crooked; branch, a small right-hand tributary to James River in Chesterfield County.
Crooked; creek, a small right-hand tributary to Nottoway River in Lunenburg County.
Crooked; creek, a right-hand branch of New River in Carroll County.
Crooked; run, a small right-hand branch of Potomac River in Fauquier County.
Crooked; run, a small right-hand tributary to James River in Botetourt County.
Crooked; run, a small right-hand tributary to Roanoke River in Franklin County.
Crooked; run, a small right-hand tributary to Rappahannock River bordering on Culpeper and Madison counties.
Crookedrun; post village in Culpeper County.
Crosby; post village in Campbell County.
Cross Junction; post village in Frederick County.
Crosskeys; post village in Rockingham County.
Crossroads; post village in Halifax County.
Crouch; post village in King and Queen County.
Crow; run, a small right-hand tributary to Jackson River in Alleghany County.
Crowell; gap, in the Blue Ridge in Franklin County.
Crowspring; village in Chesterfield County.
Croxton; post village in Caroline County.
Crozet; post village in Albemarle County on the Chesapeake and Ohio Railway. Altitude, 718 feet.
Cruise; post village in Patrick County.
Crump; creek, a small right-hand branch of Pamunkey River in Hanover County.
Crump; post village in Amelia County.
Crums; post village in Clarke County.
Crush; run, a small right-hand tributary to James River in Botetourt County.
Crystal; post village in Bedford County.
Crystalhill; post village in Halifax County on the Norfolk and Western Railway. Altitude, 547 feet.
Cub; creek, a small left-hand tributary to Roanoke River in Appomattox and Charlotte counties.
Cub; creek, a small right-hand tributary to York River in Louisa County.
Cub; run, a small left-hand branch of Shenandoah River in Rockingham County.
Cub; run, a small left-hand tributary to James River in Nelson County.
Cub; run, a small right-hand tributary to Potomac River in Fairfax County.
Cub; run, a small right-hand tributary to Shenandoah River in Page County.
Cubcreek; post village in Charlotte County.
Cuckoo; post village in Louisa County.
Culpeper; county, situated in the eastern part of the State in the Piedmont region. It has a rolling surface, broken here and there by short ridges. The altitude is only a few hundred feet above the sea. Area, 399 square miles. Population, 14,123—white, 8,069; negro, 6,053; foreign born, 59. County seat, Culpeper. The mean magnetic declination in 1900 was 3° 55'. The mean annual rainfall is 40 to 50 inches, and the temperature 50° to 60°. The county is traversed by the Chesapeake and Ohio and the Southern railways.

Culpeper; county seat of Culpeper County on the Chesapeake and Ohio and the Southern railways. Population, 1,618.

Cumberland; county, situated in the central part of the State in the Piedmont region. It is drained by James River, which flows along its southern boundary. Willis River, a branch of the James, crosses it from southwest to northeast. Altitude, 200 to 500 feet. Area, 297 square miles. Population, 8,996—white, 2,791; negro, 6,205; foreign born, 16. County seat, Cumberland. The mean magnetic declination in 1900 was 3° 15′. The mean annual rainfall is 40 to 50 inches, and the temperature is 55° to 60°. The county is traversed by the Farmville and Powhatan and the Norfolk and Western railroads.

Cumberland; county seat of Cumberland County on the Farmville and Powhatan Railroad.

Cumberland; gap in the Cumberland Mountains at the southwestern corner of State. Altitude, 1,600 feet.

Cumberland; mountains in the southwestern part of Lee County, forming the boundary line between Kentucky and Virginia. Elevation, 2,500 to 3,000 feet.

Cumbow; village in Lee County.

Cumnor; post village in King and Queen County.

Cunningham; creek, a small left-hand tributary to James River in Fluvanna County.

Cunningham; creek, a small right-hand tributary to Appomattox River in Prince Edward County.

Curdsville; post village in Buckingham County.

Curles; neck of land formed by a bend in the James River in Henrico County.

Curlew; post village in Spottsylvania County.

Currin; post village in Montgomery County.

Curtis; post village in Bedford County.

Curve; post village in Giles County on the Norfolk and Western Railway.

Cuscowilla; post village in Mecklenburg County.

Cutalong; post village in Louisa County.

Cut Banks; ford across Appomattox River in Buckingham County.

Cutler; post village in Caroline County.

Cuzco; post village in Louisa County.

Cynthia; village in Lee County.

Cypress Chapel; post village in Nansemond County

Dabneys; post village in Louisa County.

Daggers; post village in Botetourt County.

Dahlia; post village in Greenesville County.

Daisy; post village in King and Queen County.

Dalbys; post village in Northampton County.

Dale; mountain in Rockbridge County.

Dale Enterprise; post village in Rockingham County. Altitude, 1,350 feet.

Daleville; post village in Botetourt County.

Dalzell; post village in Campbell County.

Damascus; post village in Washington County.

Damon; post village in Albemarle County.

Dan; small right-hand branch of Knox Creek in Buchanan County.

Dan; river of North Carolina and Virginia, one of the two main branches of Roanoke River. It heads in northwestern North Carolina and flows in a generally northeast course to its junction with the Roanoke in Halifax County, Va.; mean discharge, 3,026 cubic feet per second. It is navigable to Madison, N. C.

Daniels; run, a small left-hand tributary to Staunton River in Franklin County.

Danieltown; post village in Brunswick County.

Danripple; post village in Halifax County.

Danton; post village in Orange County.
Danville; city, independent in government, located on Dan River in Pittsylvania County on the Danville and Western and the Southern railways. Population, 16,520.
Darden; post village in Isle of Wight County.
Dark; run, a small right-hand branch of Roanoke River in Montgomery County.
Darlington Heights; post village in Prince Edward County.
Dartha; post village in Wise County.
Darvills; post village in Dinwiddie County.
Darwin; post village in Dickenson County.
Dash; post village in New Kent County.
Daugherty; post village in Accomac County.
Davenport; post village in Buchanan County.
David; creek, a small right-hand branch of James River in Appomattox and Buckingham counties.
Davids; run, a small right-hand tributary to James River in Botetourt County.
Davis; branch, a small left-hand tributary to James River in Amherst County.
Davis; creek, a small left-hand branch of North Fork of Holston River in Smyth County.
Davis Knob; summit in Grayson County. Elevation, 3,020.
Davis Mills; post village in Bedford County.
Davis Wharf; post village in Accomac County.
Dawn; post village in Caroline County.
Dawson; creek, a small right-hand branch of Appomattox River in Amelia County.
Dawson; summit in Nelson County.
Dawsonville; post village in Greene County.
Daysville; post village in Loudoun County.
Dayton; town in Rockingham County on the Chesapeake and Western Railway. Population, 425.
Dean; creek, a small right-hand branch of New River, rising in Wythe County.
Deane; post village in Nansemond County on the Norfolk and Carolina Railroad.
Dearborn; post village in Amherst County.
Deatonsville; post village in Amelia County.
Debusk; post village in Dickenson County.
De Bust; ford of Powell River in Lee County.
Deep; creek, a left-hand tributary to Elizabeth River in Norfolk County.
Deep; creek, a small left-hand tributary to Appomattox River in Chesterfield County.
Deep; creek, a small right-hand tributary to Appomattox River in Nottoway County.
Deep; creek, a small right-hand branch of Appomattox River in Amelia County.
Deep; creek, a small right-hand branch of James River in Powhatan County.
Deep; creek, a small right-hand tributary to York River in Louisa County.
Deep; run, a small left-hand branch of Rappahannock River in Fauquier and Stafford counties.
Deep; run, a small left-hand tributary to James River in Henrico County.
Deep; run, a small right-hand tributary to Rappahannock River in Madison County.
Deep; run, a small right-hand branch of the Rappahannock River in Spottsylvania County.
Deep; run, a small right-hand branch of Shenandoah River in Rockingham County.
Deepcreek; post village in Norfolk County.
Deep Water; creek, a small right-hand tributary to New River in Floyd and Carroll counties.
Deep Water; fork, small left-hand tributary to New River in Carroll County.

Deerfield; post village in Augusta County.
Deer Head; summit in Shenandoah County.
Deerrock; post village in Nelson County.
Deerwood; ford across Roanoke River in Pittsylvania County.
Dehaven; post village in Frederick County.
Dejarnette; post village in Caroline County.
Delaplane; post village in Fauquier County on the Southern Railway.
Delaware; post village in Southampon County on the Seaboard Air Line Railway.
Delay; post village in Bedford County.
Delclisur; post village in Lee County.
Delila; post village in Halifax County.
Dell; post village in Grayson County.
Delos; post village in Caroline County.
Delton; post village in Pulaski County on the Norfolk and Western Railway.
Democrat; post village in Lee County.
Demonet; post village in Clarke County.
Denaro; post village in Amelia County.
Denbigh; county seat of Warwick County.
Dendron; post village in Surry County on the Surry, Sussex and Southampton Railway.
Denmark; post village in Rockbridge County.
Denniston; post village in Halifax County on the Norfolk and Western and the Southern railways.
Denton Valley; creek, a small left-hand branch of South Fork of Holston River in Washington County.
Derby; post village in Prince George County.
Desert; sand desert along the eastern coast of Princess Anne County.
Desha; post village in Essex County.
Design; village in Pittsylvania County.
Deskin; mountains in Tazewell County. Elevation, 2,500 feet.
Deskins; post village in Buchanan County.
Detrick; post village in Shenandoah County.
Devil; fork, a small right-hand tributary to Clinch River in Scott County.
Devils; creek, a small left-hand branch of Knox Creek, rising in Buchanan County.
Devils Hole; mountains in Shenandoah County.
Devils Knob; summit in the Blue Ridge in Nelson County.
Dew; post village in Middlesex County.
Dewey; post village in Wise County.
Dewitt; post village in Dinwiddie County on the Seaboard Air Line Railway.
Dexter; post village in Russell County.
Dial Rock; summit in Buckhorn Mountains.
Diamondgrove; post village in Brunswick County.
Diana Mills; post village in Buckingham County.
Diascond; post village in James City County on the Chesapeake and Ohio Railway.
Dick; branch, a small right-hand tributary to Potomac River in Prince William County.
Dick; creek, a small tributary to Dry Fork in Tazewell County.
Dicken; branch, a small right-hand tributary to New River in Carroll County.
Dickens; post village in Goochland County.
Dickensonville; village in Russell County.
Dickerson; ford of Powell River in Lee County.
Dickey; creek, a small left-hand branch of South Fork of Holston River in Smyth County.
Dickey; hill in Warren County. Elevation, 1,500 to 2,000 feet.

Dickenson; county, located in the western part of the State in the Alleghany Plateau, here deeply dissected. It is drained by Russell Fork of Big Sandy River. The altitude ranges from 1,000 to 3,000 feet above sea level. Area, 297 square miles. Population, 7,747—all white. County seat, Clintwood. The mean magnetic declination in 1900 was 15′. The mean annual rainfall is 50 to 60 inches, and the temperature 50° to 55°.

Dickinson; post village in Franklin County on the Chesapeake and Ohio Railway.

Dicks; creek, a small right-hand tributary to James River in Craig County.

Dido; post village in King George County.

Difficult; run, a small right-hand branch of Potomac River in Fairfax County.

Difficult; run, a small left-hand tributary to Roanoke River in Bedford County.

Difficult; village in Fairfax County.

Diggs; post village in Mathews County.

Dilbeck; post village in Shenandoah County.

Dillon; village in Henry County on the Chesapeake and Ohio Railway.

Dillons Mills, post village in Franklin County.

Dillwyn; post village in Buckingham County on the Chesapeake and Ohio Railway. Altitude, 645 feet.

Dingley; post village in Northampton County.

Dinguid; post village in Campbell County.

Dinwiddie; county, situated in the central part of the State in the Piedmont region, the boundary on the north being in part the Appomattox River. The surface is undulating or rolling. Elevation, 200 or 300 feet above sea level. Area, 521 square miles. Population, 15,374—white, 5,874; negro, 9,500; foreign born, 119. County seat, Dinwiddie. The mean magnetic declination in 1900 was 3° 20′. The mean annual rainfall is 40 to 50 inches, and the temperature 55° to 60°. The county is traversed by the Seaboard Air Line, the Atlantic Coast Line, and the Norfolk and Western railroads.

Dinwiddie; county seat of Dinwiddie County on the Seaboard Air Line Railway.

Dipsey; post village in Carroll County.

Dismal; creek, a right-hand tributary to Walker Creek, rising in Giles County.

Dismal; creek, a small right-hand branch of Levisa Fork, rising in Buchanan County.

Dismal; mountain in Amherst County.

Dismal; swamp lying mainly in southeast Virginia, but partly in North Carolina. Its extent is rather indefinite, as its limits can not be sharply defined. Its highest point is 22 feet above sea. It is in part covered with a cypress forest and in part by canebrakes. It is traversed by the Dismal Swamp canal and by numerous smaller ditches. Near the summit is Drummond Lake.

Dismal Swamp; canal, running southward through the Dismal Swamp from Deep Creek to Albemarle Sound. It is accompanied throughout by a wagon road.

Dismal Swamp; post village in Norfolk County.

Dispatch; post village in Powhatan County on the Southern Railway.

Disputanta; post village in Prince George County on the Norfolk and Western Railway.

Diston; post village in Dinwiddie County.

Ditchley; post village in Fairfax County on the Southern Railway.

Dividing; branch, a small left-hand tributary to Roanoke River in Charlotte County.

Dividing Spring; creek, a small right-hand tributary to Roanoke River in Roanoke County.

Dixie; post village in Mathews County.

Dixon; branch, a small right-hand tributary to New River in Carroll County.

Dixon; ford in New River in Carroll County.

Dixondale; post village in Gloucester County.

Dixon Ridge; summit in Rockingham County.

Doak; post village in Tazewell County.
Dobyn; post village in Patrick County.
Dodds; post village in Stafford County.
Doddville; post village in Fauquier County.
Dodson; post village in Patrick County.
Doe; creek, a small right-hand branch of New River in Giles County.
Doe; mountains in Giles County. Elevation, 2,500 to 3,500 feet.
Doe Branch; creek, a small left-hand branch of Appomattox River in Cumberland County.
Doehill; post village in Highland County.
Doe Hollow; gap in Buckhorn Mountains.
Dog e; creek, a small right-hand tributary to Potomac River in Fairfax County.
Dogue; post village in King George County.
Dolphin; post village in Brunswick County.
Dominion; village in Halifax County.
Domino; post village in Lee County.
Donald; summit in Rockbridge County.
Donaldsburg; post village in Rockbridge County.
Dongola; post village in Louisa County.
Dooley; post village in Wise County on the Norfolk and Western Railway.
Dooms; post village in Augusta County on the Norfolk and Western Railway.
Dorcas; post village in Augusta County.
Dorchester; post village in Wise County.
Dormer; post village in Carroll County.
Dorrill; run, a small right-hand tributary to Potomac River in Prince William and Fauquier counties.
Dorset; post village in Powhatan County on the Southern Railway.
Dory; post village in Southampton County on the Surry, Sussex and Southampton Railway.
Doswell; post village in Hanover County on the Chesapeake and Ohio and the Richmond, Fredericksburg and Potomac railroads.
Dot; post village in Lee County.
Double; bridges across Meherrin River in Lunenburg County.
Doublebridge; post village in Lunenburg County.
Double Top; mountain in Madison County. Elevation, 3,000 feet.
Douglas; village in Lee County.
Dover; creek, a small left-hand branch of James River in Goochland County.
Dover; post village in Loudoun County.
Dover Mines; post village in Goochland County.
Dovesville; post village in Rockingham County.
Downings; post village in Richmond County.
Doyles; river, a small left-hand tributary to James River in Albemarle County.
Doylesville; post village in Albemarle County.
Dragonville; post village in King and Queen County.
Drake; branch, a small left-hand branch of North Fork of Clinch River in Scott County.
Drakes Branch; post village in Charlotte County.
Dranesville; post village in Fairfax County.
Draper; mountains in Pulaski County. Elevation, 2,500 to 3,000 feet.
Draper; mountains in Wythe and Pulaski counties. Elevation, 2,000 to 3,000 feet.
Draper; post village in Pulaski County on the Norfolk and Western Railway. Altitude, 2,040 feet.
Drapersville; post village in Mecklenburg County.
Dreaming; creek, a small right-hand branch of James River in Campbell County.

Dreka; post village in Accomac County.
Drenn; post village in Carroll County.
Drewry; bluff in Chesterfield County.
Drewrys Bluff; post village in Chesterfield County on the Atlantic Coast Line Railroad.
Drewryville; post village in Southampton County on the Southern Railway.
Driver; post village in Nansemond County.
Drum; marshy point extending into Back Bay in Princess Anne County.
Drummon; post village in Craig County.
Drummond; lake in Nansemond and Norfolk counties. Elevation above sea level, 22 feet.
Drummond Hill; summits in Botetourt and Rockbridge counties.
Dry; branch, a small left-hand tributary to James River in Augusta County.
Dry; branch, a small left-hand tributary to Powell River in Lee County.
Dry; branch, a small left-hand tributary to Shenandoah River in Augusta County.
Dry; branch, a small right-hand tributary to James River in Botetourt County.
Dry; small left-hand branch of Cripple Creek in Wythe County.
Dry; small left-hand branch of New River in Pulaski County.
Dry; small left-hand branch of North Fork of Holston River in Smyth County.
Dry; small right-hand branch of Roanoke River in Roanoke County.
Dry; creek, a small left-hand branch of Appomattox River in Cumberland County.
Dry; creek, a small left-hand tributary to Appomattox River in Chesterfield County.
Dry; creek, a small right-hand branch of North Fork of Clinch River in Scott County.
Dry; creek, a small right-hand tributary to Nottoway River in Lunenburg County.
Dry; fork, a small right-hand tributary to Clinch River in Scott County.
Dry; fork, a small right-hand tributary to Clinch River in Tazewell County.
Dry; fork, a small right-hand tributary to North Fork of Shenandoah River in Rockingham County.
Dry; fork, a small right-hand tributary to Wolf Creek in Bland County.
Dry; river, a small left-hand tributary to Shenandoah River in Rockingham County.
Dry; run, a small left-hand tributary to James River in Alleghany County.
Dry; run, a small left-hand tributary to James River in Montgomery County.
Dry; run, a small left-hand tributary to North Fork of Roanoke River.
Dry; run, a small left-hand tributary to Shenandoah River in Rockingham County.
Dry; run, a small right-hand tributary to Shenandoah River in Page County.
Dry; run, a small right-hand tributary to Shenandoah River in Rockingham County.
Dry Branch; gap in North Mountains in Augusta County.
Dry Branch; post village in Pulaski County on the Norfolk and Western Railway.
Drybridge; post village in Chesterfield County on the Southern Railway.
Dryburg; post village in Halifax County.
Dryden; post village in Lee County on the Louisville and Nashville Railroad.
Dryfork; post village in Pittsylvania County on the Southern Railway. Altitude, 624 feet.
Dry Mountain; summit in Campbell County. Elevation, 770 feet.
Dry Pond; mountains in Wythe and Carroll counties. Elevation, 2,500 feet.
Dry Tripe; small right-hand branch of Slate Creek in Buchanan County.
Dublin; post village in Pulaski County on the Norfolk and Western Railway. Altitude, 2,058 feet.
Ducat; post village in King George County.
Duck; run, a small left-hand tributary to Shenandoah River in Frederick County.
Ducker; creek, a small left-hand branch of Appomattox River in Buckingham County.
Duckinghoe; creek, a small left-hand tributary to York River in Louisa County.

Duet; post village in Madison County.
Duffield; town in Scott County. Population, 98.
Dugspur; post village in Carroll County.
Dugwell; village in Franklin County.
Duke; post village in Louisa County.
Dulany; post village in Floyd County.
Dulce; post village in Albemarle County.
Dumbarton; post village in Henrico County.
Dumfries; town in Prince William County. Population, 160.
Dump; creek, a small right-hand tributary to Clinch River, rising in Russell County.
Dumpcreek; post village in Russell County.
Dun; post village in Sussex County.
Dunavant; post village in Spottsylvania County.
Dunbrooke; post village in Essex County.
Duncan Knob; summit in Jack Mountain in Bath County.
Duncans; post village in Floyd County.
Duncans Mills; post village in Scott County.
Dundee; post village in Bedford County.
Dundore; mountains in Rockingham County. Elevation, 2,500 to 3,000 feet.
Dungannon; post village in Scott County.
Dunlap; creek, a right-hand branch of Jackson River in Alleghany County.
Dunlap; post village in Alleghany County on the Atlantic Coast Line Railroad.
Dunn Loring; post village in Fairfax County.
Dunnsville; post village in Essex County.
Dunreath; post village in Louisa County.
Duprees; post village in Charlotte County.
Durand; post village in Greenesville County on the Southern Railway.
Durmid; post village in Campbell County on the Norfolk and Western and the Southern railways. Altitude, 681 feet.
Dutch; post village in Amelia County.
Dutch Gap; canal across the neck of James River in Henrico County.
Dutchman; branch, a small right-hand tributary to New River in Carroll County.
Dutoy; creek, a small right-hand branch of James River in Powhatan County.
Duty; post village in Dickinson County.
Dwale; post village in Dickinson County.
Dwight; post village in Buchanan County on the Norfolk and Western Railway.
Dwina; post village in Wise County.
Dyer Store; post village in Henry County.
Eaglerock; post village in Botetourt County on the Chesapeake and Ohio Railway. Altitude, 936 feet.
Eagle Rock; summit in Botetourt County.
Eakin; post village in Craig County.
Eanes Crossroads; post village in Brunswick County.
Earlehurst; post village in Alleghany County.
Earls; post village in Amelia County.
Early; post village in Carroll County.
Earlygrove; post village in Scott County.
Earlysville; post village in Albemarle County.
Earnest; post village in York County.
East; branch, a small left-hand tributary to Roanoke River in Charlotte County.
East; branch, a small right-hand tributary to Jackson River in Highland County.
East; fork, a small right-hand tributary to New River in Carroll and Grayson counties.
Eastend; post village in Alexandria County.

Eastham; post village in Albemarle County.
East Leake; post village in Goochland County.
East Lexington; post village in Rockbridge County on the Baltimore and Ohio and the Chesapeake and Ohio railroads.
East Radford; post village in Montgomery County on the Norfolk and Western Railway.
East River; mountains in Giles and Tazewell counties, extending northeast and southwest, bordering on Bland County, Va., and Mercer County, W. Va. Elevation, 3,000 to 4,000 feet.
East Stone Gap; town in Wise County. Population, 349.
Eastview; post village in Floyd County.
Eastville; county seat of Northampton County on New York, Philadelphia and Norfolk Railroad. Population, 313.
Ebony; post village in Brunswick County.
Echols; ferry over North River, near Glasgow, in Rockbridge County.
Eckington; post village in Culpeper County.
Eddy; post village in Franklin County.
Edenburg; post village in Shenandoah County on the Baltimore and Ohio Railroad. Altitude, 845 feet.
Edgar; post village in Caroline County.
Edgehill; post village in King George County.
Edgerton; post village in Brunswick County.
Edgewater; post village in Grayson County.
Edgewood; post village in Henry County.
Edinburg; town in Shenandoah County on the Southern Railway. Population, 512.
Edith; post village in Shenandoah County.
Edmunds Store; post village in Brunswick County.
Edna; post village in King and Queen County.
Edom; post village in Rockingham County.
Edward Knob; summit in Carroll County.
Effna; post village in Bland County.
Effy; post village in Wythe County.
Eggbornsville; post village in Culpeper County.
Eggleston; post village in Giles County on the Norfolk and Western Railway. Altitude, 1,644 feet.
Eggleston; springs in Giles County near New River.
Egmont; post village in Mecklenburg County.
Ego; post village in Floyd County.
Eheart; post village in Orange County.
Ela; village in Scott County.
Elamsville; post village in Patrick County.
Elba; post village in Pittsylvania County on the Richmond, Fredericksburg and Potomac Railroad.
Elbow; post village in Powhatan County.
Elder; creek, a small left-hand branch of Chickahominy River in Hanover County.
Eldridges Mill; post village in Buckingham County.
Elect; village in Pittsylvania County.
Eliber Spring; branch, a small right-hand tributary to James River in Craig County.
Elijah; post village in Patrick County.
Elizabeth; river, an estuary in southeast Virginia formed by the junction of its eastern, southern, and western branches, and opening into Hampton Roads; forms the harbor of Norfolk.

Elizabeth City; county, situated in the eastern part of the State in the Atlantic plain north of James River and upon the west shore of Chesapeake Bay. It is low and level. Area, 50 square miles. Population, 19,460—white, 10,757; negro, 8,582; foreign born, 1,909. County seat, Hampton. The mean magnetic declination in 1900 was 3° 55′. The mean annual rainfall is 40 to 50 inches, and the temperature 55° to 60°. The county is traversed by the Chesapeake and Ohio Railway.

Elk; creek, a small left-hand tributary to Roanoke River in Bedford County.
Elk; creek, a small left-hand tributary to York River in Louisa County.
Elk; creek, a small right-hand branch of New River in Grayson County.
Elk; run, a small left-hand branch of Rapidan River in Madison County.
Elk; run, a small left-hand tributary to Shenandoah River in Augusta County.
Elk; run, a small right-hand tributary to Potomac River in Fauquier County.
Elkcreek; post village in Grayson County.
Elk Garden; post village in Russell County.
Elk Garden Ridge; mountains in Russell County. Elevation, 2,500 to 3,000 feet.
Elkhill; post village in Goochland County on the Chesapeake and Ohio Railway.
Elkhorn; small right-hand branch of New River in Carroll County.
Elk Horn; mountain in Augusta County.
Elk Knob; summit in Wise County. Elevation, 2,500 feet.
Elk Lick; small right-hand tributary to Potomac River in Loudoun County.
Elko; post village in Henrico County on the Chesapeake and Ohio Railway.
Elk Pond; mountains in Rockbridge County.
Elkrun; post village in Fauquier County.
Elkspur; post village in Carroll County.
Elk Spur; ridge in Carroll County.
Elkton; post village in Rockingham County on the Chesapeake Western and the North Western railways. Altitude, 955 feet.
Elkwood; post village in Culpeper County on the Southern Railway.
Ellendale; post village in Smyth County.
Ellerson; post village in Hanover County on the Chesapeake and Ohio Railway.
Ellett; post village in Montgomery County.
Elliott; creek, a small left-hand tributary to South Fork of Roanoke River in Montgomery County.
Elliott Knob; summit of North Mountain in Augusta County. Elevation, 4,473 feet.
Ellis; fork, a small right-hand tributary to Appomattox River in Nottoway County.
Ellis; post village in Grayson County.
Elliston; post village in Montgomery County on the Norfolk and Western Railway.
Ellisville; post village in Louisa County.
Elmeria; post village in Rockbridge County.
Elmington; post village in Nelson County on the Southern Railway. Altitude, 632 feet.
Elmo; post village in Halifax County.
Elmont; post village in Hanover County.
Elms; post village in Sussex County.
Elm Wood; creek, a small, right-hand branch of Rappahannock River in Essex County.
Elmwood; village in Henry County.
Elon; post village in Amherst County.
Elota; post village in Carroll County.
Elsie; post village in Amherst County.
Elvan; post village in Loudoun County.
Elway; post village in Russell County.

Elwood; post village in Nansemond County.
Ely; creek, a small left-hand tributary to Stone Creek in Lee County.
Emaus; post village in Bedford County.
Embrey; post village in Fauquier County.
Emmerton; post village in Richmond County.
Emmetts; post village in Hanover County.
Emory; post village in Washington County on the Norfolk and Western Railway. Altitude, 2,094 feet.
Emporia; county seat of Greensville County on the Atlantic Coast Line and the Southern railroads. Population, 3,819.
Enchanted; creek, a small left-hand tributary to James River in Amherst County.
Endicott; post village in Franklin County.
Enfield; post village in King William County.
England Ridge; mountains in Amherst County.
Engleman; post village in Rockbridge County.
English; post village in Franklin County.
Enoch; creek, a small left-hand tributary to Roanoke River in Bedford County.
Enoch; post village in Middlesex County.
Enoch Knob; summit in Carroll County. Altitude, 3,022 feet.
Enon; post village in Goochland County.
Enonville; post village in Buckingham County.
Enterprise; post village in Southampton County.
Entray; creek, a small left-hand tributary to Roanoke River in Campbell County.
Eona; post village in Carroll County.
Epes; post village in Lunenburg County.
Ephesus; post village in Bedford County.
Epling; post village in Giles County.
Epperly; post village in Floyd County.
Epperly Knob; summit in Floyd County.
Eppes; bridge across Appomattox River between Chesterfield and Amelia counties.
Eppes; creek, a small left-hand branch of James River in Charles City County.
Eppes; island in Charles City County.
Epps; creek, a small left-hand tributary to James River in Albemarle County.
Epworth; post village in King William County.
Era; post village in Dinwiddie County.
Erald; post village in Greene County.
Erica; post village in Westmoreland County.
Erin Shades; post village in Henrico County.
Ernest; post village in Tazewell County.
Esmont; post village in Albemarle County on the Chesapeake and Ohio Railway.
Essex; county, situated in the eastern part of the State in the Atlantic plain, bordering on Rappahannock River on the south side. The surface is low and level. Area, 277 square miles. Population, 9,701—white, 3,576; negro, 6,125; foreign born, 10. County seat, Tappahannock. The mean magnetic declination in 1900 was 4° 15'. The mean annual rainfall is 40 to 50 inches, and the temperature 55° to 60°.
Essie; post village in Pulaski County.
Esto; post village in Henry County.
Ethel; post village in Richmond County.
Etlan; post village in Madison County.
Etna Mills; post village in King William County.
Etter; post village in Wythe County.
Ettricks; post village in Chesterfield County.
Eubon; post village in Lunenburg County.

Eulalia; post village in Franklin County.
Eura; post village in Page County.
Eureka Mills; post village in Charlotte County.
Evans Wharf; post village in Accomac County.
Everets; post village in Nansemond County.
Evergreen; post village in Appomattox County on the Norfolk and Western Railway. Altitude, 730 feet.
Evergreen Mills; post village in Loudoun County.
Everona; post village in Orange County.
Evington; post village in Campbell County on the Southern Railway. Altitude, 724 feet.
Evol; post village in Campbell County.
Ewell; post village in James City County.
Ewing; mountains between Wythe and Carroll counties.
Ewing; post village in Lee County on the Louisville and Nashville Railroad.
Exit; post village in Nansemond County.
Exmore; post village in Northampton County on the New York, Philadelphia and Norfolk Railroad.
Experiment; post village in Amherst County.
Ezell; post village in Brunswick County.
Fabers Mills; post village in Nelson County on the Southern Railway. Altitude, 550 feet.
Fagg; post village in Montgomery County.
Fairfax; county, situated in the northeastern part of the State in the Piedmont region, bordering on the south bank of Potomac River. Its surface is undulating. Area, 433 square miles. Population, 18,580—white, 13,576; negro, 5,003; foreign born, 413. County seat, Fairfax. The mean magnetic declination in 1900 was 5° 10'. The mean annual rainfall is 40 to 50 inches, and the temperature 55°. The county is traversed by the Chesapeake and Ohio, the Southern, the Richmond, Frederick and Potomac, and the Arlington and Roundhill Branch railroads.
Fairfax; county seat of Fairfax County on the Chesapeake and Ohio and the Southern railways. Population, 373.
Fairfield; post village in Rockbridge County on the Baltimore and Ohio Railroad. Altitude, 519 feet.
Fairoaks; post village in Accomac County on the Southern Railway.
Fairport; post village in Northumberland County.
Fairview; post village in Scott County.
Fairy; post village in Grayson County.
Faith; post village in Buckingham County.
Falcon; village in Floyd County.
Falding; falls in Spring Creek, in Alleghany County.
Fall; run, a small left-hand branch of Rappahannock River in Stafford County.
Fallcreek Depot; post village in Pittsylvania County on the Southern Railway. Altitude, 535 feet.
Fall Hollow; branch, a small right-hand tributary to Jackson River in Alleghany County.
Falling; creek, a small left-hand branch of Roanoke River in Bedford County.
Falling; creek, a small right-hand tributary to Appomattox River in Prince Edward County.
Falling; creek, a small right-hand branch of James River in Chesterfield County.
Falling; creek, a small right-hand tributary to James River in Chesterfield County.
Falling; river, a small left-hand tributary to Roanoke River in Campbell County.
Falling; run, a small left-hand tributary to James River in Rockbridge County.

Falling Spring; run, a small left-hand tributary to Shenandoah River in Augusta County.
Fallingwater; creek, a small right-hand tributary to James River in Botetourt County.
Falls; creek, a small right-hand tributary to Nottoway River in Lunenburg County.
Falls; run, a small left-hand branch of Rappahannock River in Stafford County.
Falls Church; town in Fairfax County on the Southern Railway. Population, 1,007.
Falls Hill; creek, a small left-hand branch of North Fork of Holston River, rising in Washington County.
Falls Mills; post village in Tazewell County on the Norfolk and Western Railway. Altitude, 2,323 feet.
Fallville; post village in Grayson County.
Falmouth; post village in Stafford County.
False; cape on sand bar on the Atlantic coast in Princess Anne County. A life-saving station is located there.
Fan; mountains in Albemarle County. Elevation, 1,000 to 1,500 feet.
Fancy; gap in mountains in Patrick County.
Fancygap; post village in Carroll County.
Fancyhill; post village in Rockbridge County.
Fanshaw; post village in Hanover County.
Fantine; post village in Pittsylvania County.
Fariston; post village in Charlotte County.
Farland; post village in Roanoke County.
Farmer; mountains in Carroll County. Elevation, 2,500 feet.
Farmers Fork; post village in Richmond County.
Farmville; county seat of Prince Edward County on the Farmville and Powhatan and the Norfolk and Western railroads. Population, 2,471.
Farnham; post village in Richmond County.
Farr; post village in Fairfax County.
Farrar; island, surrounded by James River and the Dutch Gap canal.
Farrington; post village in Hanover County.
Farris; village in Washington County.
Fauquier; county, situated in the northern part of the State in the Piedmont region, with the summit of the Blue Ridge as its northwestern boundary. The southern part has a rolling surface, breaking up in the northern part into short ridges and the spurs of the Blue Ridge. The altitude ranges from 200 to 3,000 feet. Area, 676 square miles. Population, 23,374—white, 15,074; negro, 8,298; foreign born, 175. County seat, Warrenton. The mean magnetic declination in 1900 was 3° 45'. The mean annual rainfall is 40 to 50 inches, and the temperature 50° to 55°. The county is traversed by the Southern Railway.
Fauquier Springs; post village in Fauquier County.
Favonia; post village in Wythe County.
Favor; post village in King and Queen County.
Fawcett; gap in Little North Mountains.
Fawcettgap; post village in Frederick County.
Fawn; small left-hand branch of Straight Creek in Lee County.
Faye; post village in Prince Edward County.
Feedstone; mountains in Rockingham County. Elevation, 3,500 feet.
Felden; post village in Prince Edward County.
Felicia; post village in Franklin County.
Felt Knob; summit in Carroll County. Elevation, 3,216 feet.
Felts; post village in Southampton County.
Fentriss; post village in Norfolk County.

Fergusonville; post village in Nottoway County.
Fergussons Wharf; post village in Isle of Wight County.
Fernalda; post village in Wise County.
Ferrol; post village in Augusta County on the Chesapeake and Ohio Railway. Altitude, 1,810 feet.
Ferrum; post village in Franklin County on the Norfolk and Western Railway. Altitude, 1,237 feet.
Festoon; post village in Dickenson County.
Fetzer; gap in Little North Mountain in Shenandoah County.
Fiddler; creek, a small left-hand tributary to Roanoke River in Bedford County.
Fido; post village in Scott County.
Fiery; run, a small left-hand tributary to Rappahannock River in Rappahannock County.
Fields; post village in Mecklenburg County.
Fife; post village in Goochland County.
Fifteen Mile; creek, a small right-hand branch of South Fork of Holston River in Washington County.
Fig; post village in Lee County.
Fighting; creek, a small left-hand branch of Appomattox River in Powhatan County.
Figsboro; post village in Henry County.
Fincastle; county seat of Botetourt County. Population, 652. Altitude, 1,250 feet.
Finchley; post village in Mecklenburg County on the Southern Railway.
Findlay; mountains in Nelson County. Elevation, 1,000 feet.
Fine; creek, a small right-hand branch of James River in Powhatan County.
Finecreek Mills; post village in Powhatan County.
Finley; creek, a small left-hand branch of North Fork of Holston River in Washington County.
Finley; post village in Grayson County.
Finney; post village in Accomac County on the Norfolk and Western Railway.
Finneys Siding; post village in Russell County.
Finneywood; post village in Mecklenburg County on the Southern Railway.
First; mountains in Page County. Elevation, 1,500 to 2,000 feet.
Fisher; small right-hand branch of Cripple Creek in Wythe County.
Fisherman; post village in Lancaster County.
Fishers; gap in the Blue Ridge, caused by Robertson River, in Madison County.
Fishers Hill; post village in Shenandoah County on the Southern Railway.
Fishersville; post village in Augusta County on the Chesapeake and Ohio Railway. Altitude, 1,320 feet.
Fishing; creek, a small right-hand branch of Roanoke River in Campbell County.
Fishing; point in Isle of Wight County, extending into James River.
Fish Pond; creek, a small left-hand tributary to Appomattox River in Appomattox County.
Fitchetts; post village in Mathews County.
Fitzhugh; post village in Brunswick County.
Fiveforks; post village in Prince Edward County.
Fiveoaks; post village in Tazewell County on the Norfolk and Western Railway. Altitude, 2,468 feet.
Flag; rocks in Warm Spring Mountain in Bath County.
Flagpond; post village in Scott County.
Flanagans Mills; post village in Cumberland County.
Flat; creek, a small left-hand tributary to Roanoke River in Campbell County.
Flat; creek, a small right-hand tributary to Appomattox River in Nottoway County.
Flat; run, a small right-hand tributary to Rappahannock River in Orange County.

Flatridge; post village in Grayson County.
Flat Rock; creek, a small right-hand tributary to Clinch River in Russell County.
Flatrock; post village in Scott County on the Farmville and Powhatan Railroad.
Flatrun; post village in Orange County.
Flat Top; mountains in Bland and Giles counties. Elevation, 2,000 to 3,500 feet.
Flat Top; summit in the central part of Bedford County. Elevation, 1,978 feet.
Flat Top; summit in the Peaks of Otter Mountains in the northern part of Bedford County. Elevation, 4,000.
Flatwoods; branch, a small left-hand tributary to Roanoke River.
Flatwoods; post village in Scott County.
Flax; post village in Dinwiddie County.
Fleenors; post village in Washington County.
Fleet; post village in Washington County.
Flem; post village in Patrick County..
Fleming; mountain in Bedford County. Elevation, 2,000 feet.
Fletcher; post village in Greene County.
Flint; post village in Floyd County.
Flint; run, a small right-hand tributary to Shenandoah River in Warren County.
Flinthill; post village in Rappahannock County.
Flint Hill; summit in Franklin County.
Floris; post village in Fairfax County.
Floyd; county, situated in the southern part of the State upon a summit of the Blue Ridge, here having the form of a plateau with the escarpment to the southeast. The surface consists of an undulating and broken country, drained by South Fork of Roanoke River. The altitude ranges from 2,000 to over 3,000 feet above sea level. Area, 383 square miles. Population, 15,388—white, 14,313; negro, 1,075; foreign born, 4. County seat, Floyd. The mean magnetic declination in 1900 was 4° 45'. The mean annual rainfall is 50 to 60 inches, and the temperature 50° to 55°.
Floyd; county seat of Floyd County. Population, 402.
Flumen; post village in Rockbridge County.
Fluvanna; county, situated in the central part of the State in the Piedmont region. It is traversed by Ravanna River, while the James forms its southern boundary. The surface is undulating; it is elevated 250 to 500 feet above sea level. Area, 289 square miles. Population, 9,050—white, 5,039; negro, 4,011; foreign born, 18. County seat, Palmyra. The mean magnetic declination in 1900 was 3°. The mean annual rainfall is 40 to 50 inches, and the temperature 55° to 60°. The county is traversed by the Chesapeake and Ohio Railway.
Fly; post village in Halifax County.
Fodder House; summit in Black Creek Mountains in Bath County.
Folly Mills; post village in Augusta County on the Baltimore and Ohio Railroad.
Foneswood; post village in Westmoreland County.
Fontella; post village in Bedford County.
Forbes; post village in Buckingham County.
Ford; bridge across Chickahominy River in Hanover County.
Ford; post village in Dinwiddie County on the Norfolk and Western Railway.
Fore; mountains in Alleghany County. Elevation, 2,500 feet.
Foremans; run, a small left-hand tributary to Shenandoah River in Frederick County.
Foremost; run, a small left-hand tributary to York River in Spottsylvania County.
Fores Store; post village in Appomattox County.
Forestburg; post village in Prince William County.
Forest Depot; post village in Bedford County on the Norfolk and Western Railway and the Baltimore and Ohio railroads. Altitude, 863 feet.

Foresthill; post village in Brunswick County.
Forestville; post village in Shenandoah County on the Southern Railway.
Forge; post village in Dinwiddie County.
Fork; mountains in Giles County. Elevation, 2,500 to 4,000 feet.
Fork; mountains in Greene County. Elevation, 2,000 to 3,000 feet.
Forkland; post village in Nottoway County.
Fork Mountain; summit in Amherst County. Elevation, 2,000 to 2,500 feet.
Forks of Buffalo; post village in Amherst County.
Forksville; post village in Mecklenburg County.
Fork Union; post village in Fluvanna County.
Formosa; post village in Charlotte County.
Fort; valley between Massanutten, Powells, and Three Top mountains.
Fort Blackmore; post village in Scott County.
Fort Defiance; post village in Augusta County on the Baltimore and Ohio Railroad. Altitude, 1,247 feet.
Fort Hoover; village in Rockingham County.
Fort Lee; post village in Henrico County on the Chesapeake and Ohio Railway.
Fort Lewis; mountains in Roanoke County. Elevation, 1,500 to 3,800 feet.
Fort Lewis; post village in Bath County.
Fort Mitchell; post village in Lunenburg County.
Fort Monroe; military post in Elizabeth City County, at Old Point Comfort, on Hampton Roads, opposite Norfolk.
Fort Myer; military post and county seat in Alexandria County on the Washington, Alexandria and Mount Vernon Electric Railway.
Foster; post village in Mathews County.
Foster Knob; summit in Bedford County. Elevation, 2,576 feet.
Fosters Falls; post village in Wythe County on the Norfolk and Western Railway. Altitude, 1,960 feet.
Fostoria; post village in Alexandria County on the Southern Railway.
Fountains; creek, a small right-hand branch of Meherrin River in the southeastern part of the State.
Four Mile; run, a small right-hand branch of Potomac River in Alexandria County.
Fowler; village in Washington County.
Fowlers; small left-hand branch of North Fork of Holston River, rising in Scott County.
Fox; creek, a small right-hand branch of New River in Grayson County.
Fox; post village in Grayson County.
Fox Knob; summit in Grayson County. Elevation, 3,500 feet.
Francisco; post village in Craig County.
Francis Mill; creek, a small left-hand branch of Cripple Creek in Wythe County.
Frank; branch, a small left-hand tributary to Appomattox River in Chesterfield County.
Frank; branch, a small right-hand tributary to James River in Chesterfield County.
Franklin; county, situated in the southern part of the State in the upper portion of the Piedmont plain, including the escarpment of the ridge. The altitude ranges from 1,000 to 3,500 feet. Area, 690 square miles. Population, 25,953—white, 20,005; negro, 5,947; foreign born, 4. County seat, Rockymount. The mean magnetic declination in 1900 was 1° 45′. The mean annual rainfall is 50 to 60 inches, and the temperature 55° to 60°. The county is traversed by the Norfolk and Western and the Southern railways.
Franklin; creek, a small left-hand branch of James River in Amherst County.
Franklin; town in Southampton County on the Seaboard Air Line and the Southern railways. Population, 1,143.

Franklin City; post village in Accomac County on the Philadelphia, Baltimore and Washington Railroad.
Franktown; post village in Northampton County.
Fray; post village in Madison County.
Fred; post village in Floyd County.
Frederick; county, situated in the northern part of the State in the Appalachian Valley; its surface is mainly a rolling plain, but intersected by a number of minor ridges, separated by limestone valleys; the altitude ranges from 500 to 2,500 feet, that elevation being found on the Great North Mountain and in the western part of the county. Area, 425 square miles. Population, 13,239—white 12,486; negro, 753; foreign born, 84. County seat, Winchester. The mean magnetic declination in 1900 was 4°. The mean annual rainfall is 50 to 60 inches, and the temperature 50° to 55°. The county is traversed by the Baltimore and Ohio and the Cumberland Valley railroads.
Fredericksburg; city in Spottsylvania County, but independent in government, on the Potomac, Fredericksburg and Piedmont and the Richmond, Fredericksburg and Potomac railroads. Population, 5,068.
Fredericks Hall; post village in Louisa County on the Chesapeake and Ohio Railway.
Freeda; post village in Pulaski County.
Freedom Hill; summit in Fairfax County.
Freeling; post village in Dickinson County.
Freeman; post village in Brunswick County on the Chesapeake and Ohio Railway.
Freemason; run, a small left-hand tributary to Shenandoah River in Augusta County.
Freeport; post village in Gloucester County.
Freeshade; post village in Middlesex County.
Freestone; point on Potomac River in Prince William County.
Free Union; post village in Albemarle County.
French Hay; post village in Hanover County.
Fresh; pond in eastern part of Princess Anne County.
Freshwater; post village in Nelson County.
Friar; post village in Amherst County.
Friar; summit in Amherst County.
Fridley; gap in Massanutten Mountain.
Friedens; village in Rockingham County.
Friendship; post village in Washington County.
Friends Mission; post village in Patrick County.
Fries; post village in Grayson County on the Norfolk and Western Railway.
Fritts; village in Lee County.
Front Royal; county seat of Warren County on the Norfolk and Western and the Southern railways. Altitude, 546 feet. Population, 1,005.
Frost; post village in Rappahannock County.
Fruitley; post village in Albemarle County.
Fry; post village in Henry County.
Fryingpan; creek, a small left-hand branch of Russell Fork, rising in Dickenson County.
Fugates Hill; post village in Russell County.
Fulks Run; post village in Rockingham County.
Fullhardt Knob; summit in Botetourt County. Elevation, 2,329 feet.
Fultz; river, a small right-hand tributary to Shenandoah River in Page County.
Funt; creek, a small right-hand branch of Russell Fork, rising in Buchanan County.
Furnace; post village in Rockingham County on the Potomac, Fredericksburg and Piedmont Railroad.

Furnace; branch, a small left-hand tributary to Shenandoah River in Frederick County.
Furnace; branch, a small right-hand tributary to James River in Botetourt County.
Gage; post village in Floyd County.
Gainesboro; post village in Frederick County.
Gaines Crossroads; post village in Rappahannock County.
Gaines Mill; pond at head of Powhite Creek, a small left-hand branch of Chickahominy River in Hanover County.
Gainesville; post village in Prince William County on the Southern Railway.
Gala; post village in Botetourt County on the Chesapeake and Ohio Railway. Altitude, 936 feet.
Galfred; gap, caused by a left-hand tributary to James River in Alleghany Front Mountains in Highland County.
Galts Mills; post village in Amherst County.
Galveston; post village in Pittsylvania County on the Southern Railway.
Gambette; post village in Carroll County on the Norfolk and Western Railway.
Gambrill; post village in Fairfax County.
Gap; mountains in Giles County. Elevation, 2,000 to 2,500 feet.
Gap; run, a small right-hand branch of Potomac River in Fauquier County.
Gap; run, a small right-hand tributary to Potomac River in Frederick County.
Gap; run, a small right-hand branch of Shenandoah River in Rockingham County.
Gaprun; post village in Frederick County.
Gap Store; post village in Tazewell County.
Garden; fork, a small left-hand branch of Levisa Fork, rising in Buchanan County.
Garden; mountains in Tazewell and Bland counties. Elevation, 3,000 to 4,000 feet.
Gardenia; post village in Prince Edward County.
Garden Mountain; summit in Botetourt County.
Gardners; post village in Russell County on the Norfolk and Western Railway.
Garfield; post village in Fairfax County.
Gargatha; post village in Accomac County.
Garnard; small right-hand branch of Roanoke River in Roanoke County.
Garners; creek, a small left-hand tributary to Yadkin River, rising in Patrick County.
Garrett; creek, a small left-hand branch of North Fork of Holston River, rising in Washington County.
Garrett; post village in Buckingham County.
Garrison; ford in New River in Grayson County.
Garrisonville; post village in Stafford County.
Garth; post village in Albemarle County.
Gary; post village in Lunenburg County.
Garysville; post village in Prince George County.
Gasburg; post village in Brunswick County.
Gaskins; post village in Greenesville County.
Gaspards; creek, a small left-hand branch of North Fork of Holston River, rising in Washington County.
Gate City; county seat of Scott County on the Virginia and Southwestern Railway. Population, 521.
Gatewood; post village in Spottsylvania County.
Gatlion; branch, a small left-hand tributary to James River in Montgomery County.
Gayle; post village in Scott County.
Gaylord; post village in Clarke County.
Gays; post village in Louisa County.
Gayton; post village in Henrico County.
Gee; post village in Prince George County.

Genito; creek, a small left-hand branch of James River in Goochland County.
Genito; post village in Powhatan County.
Genoa; post village in Rockingham County.
George; creek, a small left-hand tributary to Russell Fork, rising in Dickenson County.
George; creek, a small right-hand branch of Pound River, rising in Dickenson County.
Georgel; post village in Wise County.
Georges; run, a small left-hand branch of South Fork of Roanoke River in Montgomery County.
Georges Mill; post village in Loudoun County.
Gera; post village in King George County.
German; river, a small right-hand tributary to Shenandoah River in Rockingham County.
German; river, a small left-hand tributary to Shenandoah River in Rockingham County.
Germania; ford across Rapidan River in Culpeper County.
German Ridge; mountains in Madison County. Elevation, 1,000 to 1,500 feet.
Gertie; post village in Norfolk County.
Getz; post village in Shenandoah County.
Gholsonville; post village in Brunswick County.
Gibson Hill; summit in Augusta County.
Gibson Knob; summit in Carroll County. Elevation, 3,036.
Gibson Station; post village in Lee County on the Chesapeake and Ohio Railway.
Gibsonville; post village in Russell County.
Gidsville; post village in Amherst County.
Giffraff; post village in Charlotte County.
Gig; post village in Lunenburg County.
Giles; county, situated in the western part of the State in the Appalachian Valley. Its surface consists of sandstone ridges separated by limestone valleys. It is crossed by New River and drained by that stream and its tributaries. The altitude ranges from 1,500 to 4,400 feet above sea level. Area, 349 square miles. Population, 10,793—white, 9,994; negro, 799; foreign born, 22. County seat, Pearisburg. The mean magnetic declination in 1900 was 2° 55'. The mean annual rainfall is 50 to 60 inches, and the temperature 50° to 55°. The county is traversed by the Norfolk and Western and the Big Stony railways.
Gillaspie; post village in Bedford County on the Norfolk and Western Railway. Altitude, 2,254 feet.
Gilliamsville; post village in Buckingham County.
Gillis; creek, a small left-hand branch of James River in Henrico County.
Gills; creek, a small head branch of Meherrin River, rising in Charlotte County.
Gills; creek, a small right-hand tributary to Roanoke River in Franklin County.
Gills; post village in Amelia County on the Southern Railway.
Gilman; post village in Hanover County.
Gilmerton; post village in Norfolk County on the Norfolk and Western Railway.
Gilmores Mills; post village in Rockbridge County on the Chesapeake and Ohio Railway.
Gin; creek, a small left-hand branch of Straight Creek in Lee County.
Glade; creek, a small left-hand tributary to New River in Wythe County.
Glade; creek, a small left-hand tributary to Roanoke River in Roanoke and Botetourt counties.
Glade; creek, a small right-hand tributary to New River in Carroll County.
Gladehill; post village in Franklin County on the Southern Railway.
Gladesboro; post village in Carroll County.
Glade Spring; town in Washington County on the Norfolk and Western Railway. Altitude, 2,074 feet. Population, 304.

Gladeville; town in Wise County on the Norfolk and Western and the Virginia and Kentucky railways. Altitude, 2,474 feet. Population, 511.
Gladstone; post village in Nelson County on the Chesapeake and Ohio Railway.
Glady; fork, a small right-hand tributary to New River in Grayson County.
Glady; run, a small right-hand tributary to Mattapony River in Spottsylvania County.
Gladys; post village in Campbell County on the Norfolk and Western Railway. Altitude, 770 feet.
Glasgow; post village in Rockbridge County on the Chesapeake and Ohio and the Norfolk and Western railways.
Glass; post village in Gloucester County.
Glenallen; post village in Henrico County on the Richmond, Fredericksburg and Potomac Railroad. Altitude, 855 feet.
Glenbrook; post village in Fairfax County.
Glencarlyn; post village in Alexandria County on the Southern Railway.
Glendale; post village in Henrico County.
Glendower; post village in Albemarle County.
Glendoyle; post village in Dinwiddie County.
Glenfall; post village in Appomattox County.
Glenford; post village in Washington County.
Glenland; post village in Pittsylvania County.
Glenlyn; post village in Giles County on the Norfolk and Western Railway. Altitude, 1,520 feet.
Glenmore; post village in Buckingham County.
Glenns; post village in Gloucester County.
Glenora; post village in Spottsylvania County.
Glenvar; post village in Roanoke County on the Norfolk and Western Railway.
Glen Wilton; post village in Botetourt County on the Chesapeake and Ohio Railway.
Globe; post village in King William County.
Glory; post village in Madison County.
Gloucester; county, situated in the eastern part of the State on the Atlantic plain on the north side of York River, at its mouth, and the west side of Chesapeake Bay; it is but little elevated above tide. Area, 253 square miles. Population, 12,832—white, 6,224; negro, 6,608; foreign born, 14. County seat, Gloucester. The mean magnetic declination in 1900 was 4°. The mean annual rainfall is 40 to 50 inches, and the temperature 55° to 60°.
Gloucester; county seat of Gloucester County.
Gloucester Point; post village in Gloucester County.
Glove; post village in Lunenburg County.
Goblintown; post village in Patrick County.
Goby; post village in King George County.
Godfrey; post village in Culpeper County.
Goffs; post village in Bedford County.
Gogginsville; village in Franklin County.
Golansville; post village in Caroline County.
Golddale; post village in Orange County.
Golden Spring; post village in Buchanan County.
Goldenvale; creek, a small right-hand branch of Rappahannock River in Caroline County.
Goldhill; post village in Buckingham County. Altitude, 540 feet.
Gold Mine; creek, a small left-hand tributary to York River in Louisa County.
Goldvein; post village in Fauquier County.
Gondola; post village in Buckingham County.

Goochland; county, situated in the central part of the State in the Piedmont region. It is drained by James River, which forms its southern boundary. The altitude ranges from 200 to 400 feet. Area, 296 square miles. Population, 9,519—white, 3,961; negro, 5,558; foreign born, 30. County seat, Goochland. The mean magnetic declination in 1900 was 3° 15′. The mean annual rainfall is 40 to 50 inches, and the temperature 55° to 60°. The county is traversed by the Chesapeake and Ohio Railway.

Goochland; county seat of Goochland County.
Goodall; post village in Hanover County.
Goode; bridge across Appomattox River between Chesterfield and Amelia counties.
Goode; creek, a small left-hand branch of Appomattox River in Chesterfield County.
Goode; creek, a small right-hand branch of James River in Chesterfield County.
Goodes; post village in Bedford County on the Norfolk and Western Railway.
Goodes Ferry; post village in Mecklenburg County.
Goodloes; post village in Spottsylvania County.
Goodman; post village in Roanoke County.
Goods Mills; post village in Rockingham County.
Goods Mountain; summit in Rockingham County.
Goodview; post village in Bedford County.
Goodwin; bridge across Stoney Creek in Dinwiddie County.
Goodwin; post village in Spottsylvania County.
Goodwins; ferry across New River in Giles County.
Goodwins Ferry; post village in Giles County.
Goodwynsville; post village in Dinwiddie County.
Gooneys; creek, a small right-hand tributary to Shenandoah River in Warren County.
Goose; creek, a left-hand branch of Roanoke River, formed by two forks, North and South, in Bedford County.
Goose; creek, a right-hand branch of Potomac River in Loudoun County.
Goose; creek, a small right-hand tributary to Potomac River in Rappahannock County.
Goose; creek, a small right-hand tributary to Potomac River in Fauquier and Loudoun counties.
Goose; creek, a small right-hand tributary to Shenandoah River in Augusta County.
Gordonsville; town in Orange County on the Chesapeake and Ohio Railway. Population, 603.
Gore; post village in Frederick County.
Goshen; town in Rockbridge County on the Chesapeake and Ohio and the Rockbridge Alum Springs and Victoria and Western railroads. Altitude, 1,410 feet. Population, 253.
Goshen Bridge; post village in Rockbridge County.
Gossan; post village in Carroll County.
Gouldin; post village in Hanover County.
Grace; post village in Princess Anne County.
Gracepoint; post village in Lancaster County.
Grady; fork, a small left-hand fork of Mountain Fork in Scott County.
Grady; post village in Pittsylvania County.
Grafton; post village in York County.
Graham; branch, a small right-hand tributary to New River in Wythe County.
Graham; creek, a small left-hand tributary to James River in Amherst County.
Graham; town in Tazewell County on the Norfolk and Western Railway. Altitude, 2,387 feet. Population, 1,554.
Grahams Forge; post village in Wythe County. Altitude, 2,387 feet.

Grangeville; post village in Accomac County.
Granite; post village in Chesterfield County on the Chesapeake and Ohio and the Southern railways.
Granite Springs; post village in Spottsylvania County.
Grannys; run, a small right-hand tributary to James River in Craig County.
Grant; post village in Grayson County.
Grantland; post village in Henrico County on the Chesapeake and Ohio Railway.
Grape; post village in Accomac County.
Grapefield; post village in Bland County.
Grapelawn; village in Nelson County.
Grape Vine; bridge across the Chickahominy River in Hanover County.
Grassfield; post village in Norfolk County.
Grassland; post village in Orange County.
Grassy; creek, a small left-hand tributary to Clinch River, rising in Russell County.
Grassy; creek, a small right-hand branch of Roanoke River in North Carolina and southern Virginia.
Grassy; creek, a small right-hand branch of Levisa Fork in Buchanan County.
Grassy; creek, a small right-hand tributary to New River in Carroll County.
Grassy Hill; summit in Franklin County. Elevation, 1,968 feet.
Grassy; mount in Rockbridge County.
Grattan Hill; summit in Rockingham County. Elevation, 1,500 feet.
Gratton; post village in Tazewell County.
Gravelhill; post village in Buckingham County.
Gravelly; small right-hand branch of Roanoke River in Pittsylvania and Franklin counties.
Gravelly; run, a small left-hand tributary to Nottoway River in Dinwiddie County.
Gravelly; run, a small right-hand branch of Rowanty Creek in Dinwiddie County.
Gravel Spring; post village in Frederick County.
Graves Mill; post village in Madison County.
Gray; small right-hand branch of Maiden Spring Creek, a tributary to Clinch River, in Tazewell County.
Gray; post village in Sussex County.
Grays; a small right-hand branch of Cripple Creek in Wythe County.
Grayson; county, situated in the southern part of the State along the North Carolina boundary. It is bounded on the north by Iron Mountain. Its surface is broken, and it is drained by New River. The altitude ranges from 3,000 to over 4,000 feet. Area, 438 square miles. Population, 16,853—white, 15,894; negro, 959; foreign born, 7. County seat, Independence. The mean magnetic declination in 1900 was 15′. The mean annual rainfall is 50 to 60 inches, and the temperature 50° to 55°.
Grayson· post village in Carroll County on the Norfolk and Western Railway.
Graysville; post village in Floyd County.
Greasy; creek, a small right-hand tributary to New River in Floyd and Carroll counties.
Great; run, a small left-hand branch of Rappahannock River in Fauquier County.
Great; branch, a small right-hand tributary to James River in Chesterfield County.
Great; run, a small right-hand tributary to Rappahannock River in Madison County.
Greatbridge; post village in Norfolk County.
Greatfalls; post village in Fairfax County.
Great Knobs; summits in Washington County along the bank of Holston River.
Great Narrows; passage between Marshy Islands connecting North and Back bays in Princess Anne County.
Great North; mountain on west side of Shenandoah Valley. Elevation, 2,000 to 4,000 feet.

Greek; post village in Grayson County.
Green; creek, a small left-hand branch of Appomatox River in Cumberland County.
Green; creek, a small left-hand tributary to James River in Albemarle County.
Green; marshy point on North Landing River in Princess Anne County.
Green; mountain in Bedford County. Elevation, 1,500 to 1,747 feet.
Green; mountain in Page County.
Green; mountains in Albemarle County. Elevation, 500 feet.
Greenbackville; post village in Accomac County.
Greenbay; post village in Prince Edward County on the Southern Railway. Altitude, 589 feet.
Greenbrier; fork, a small right-hand tributary to Russell Fork, rising in Buchanan County.
Greencove; post village in Washington County.
Green Cove; small left-hand branch of White Top Creek, tributary to South Fork of Holston River, cutting into Stone Mountain.
Greendal ; creek, a small left-hand branch of North Fork of Holston River, rising in Washington County.
Greendale; post village in Washington County.
Greendun; post village in Halifax County.
Greene; county, situated in the central part of the State in the Piedmont region, stretching from the Rapidan River to the summit of the Blue Ridge. The southeastern part of the county is undulating, while the remainder is occupied by heavy spurs of the Blue Ridge. The altitude is from 500 feet at Rapidan River to 2,400 feet at High Knob on the Blue Ridge. Area is 150 square miles. Population, 6,214—white, 4,783; negro, 1,431; foreign born, 2. County seat, Stanardsville. The mean magnetic declination in 1900 was 3°. The mean annual rainfall is 50 inches, and the temperature 50° to 55°.
Greenesville; county, located in the southern part of the State on the Atlantic plain, bordering on North Carolina. It has a rolling surface, and but little elevated above the sea. Area is 288 square miles. Population, 9,758—white, 3,402; negro, 6,356; foreign born, 51. County seat, Emporia. The mean magnetic declination in 1900 was 3° 15'. The mean annual rainfall is 40 to 50 inches, and the temperature 55° to 60°. The county is traversed by the Atlantic Coast Line and the Southern railroads.
Greenfield; post village in Nelson County.
Green Hill; ferry across Roanoke River in Halifax County.
Green Hill; mountains in Rockbridge County.
Greenlaws Wharf; post village in King George County.
Greenlee; post village in Rockbridge County on the Chesapeake and Ohio Railway.
Greenmount; post village in Rockingham County.
Green Mountain; summit in Albemarle County.
Greenplains; post village in Greenesville County on the Southern Railway.
Green Ridge; mountains in Botetourt County. Elevation, 1,500 to 2,453 feet.
Green Sea; marsh forming a part of Dismal Swamp.
Green Spring; run, a small right-hand tributary to Potomac River in Frederick County.
Greens Knob; summit in Bedford County. Elevation, 2,563 feet.
Greenspring Depot; post village in Louisia County on the Chesapeake and Ohio Railway. Altitude, 529 feet.
Green Valley; post village in Bath County.
Greenville; post village in Augusta County on the Baltimore and Ohio and the Norfolk and Western railroads. Altitude, 1,547 feet.
Greenway; post village in Nelson County on the Chesapeake and Ohio Railway.
Greenwich; post village in Prince William County on the Norfolk and Southern Railroad.

Greenwood Depot; post village in Albemarle County on the Chesapeake and Ohio Railway.
Greers; ford across Roanoke River in Bedford County.
Greyburn; post village in Buckingham County.
Greystone; village in Henry County.
Gridley; post village in Shenandoah County.
Griffinsburg; post village in Culpeper County.
Griffith; post village in Bath County on the Chesapeake and Ohio Railway.
Griffith Knob; summit in Bland County. Altitude, 3,773 feet.
Grigsby; post village in King George County.
Grimes; creek, a small right-hand branch of Roanoke River in Franklin County.
Grimes; post village in Frederick County.
Grimstead; post village in Mathews County.
Grindall; creek, a small right-hand branch of James River in Chesterfield County.
Grinels; post village in Middlesex County.
Grindstone; mountains in Page County. Elevation, 1,500 to 2,500 feet.
Grindstone; summit in Augusta County.
Grizzard; post village in Sussex County on the Southern Railway.
Grizzle; post village in Dickenson County.
Grose; creek, a small left-hand branch of South Fork of Holston River in Washington County.
Groseclose; post village in Smyth County.
Grosses; post village in Smyth County.
Grotons; post village in Accomac County.
Grottoes; post village in Rockingham County on the Norfolk and Western Railway.
Grove; post village in York County on the Chesapeake and Ohio Railway.
Grovehill; post village in Page County on the Norfolk and Western Railway. Altitude, 963 feet.
Grundy; county seat of Buchanan County. Population, 200. Altitude, 1,065 feet.
Guess; fork, a small right-hand branch of Knox Creek, rising in Buchanan County.
Guest; river, a small right-hand branch of Clinch River, rising in Wise County.
Guilford; post village in Accomac County on the Southern Railway.
Guinea; mountains in Giles County.
Guinea Mills; post village in Cumberland County.
Guineys; post village in Caroline County.
Gulley Mountain; summit in Botetourt County.
Gumspring; post village in Louisa County.
Gun Mountain; summit in Amherst County.
Gunshill; post village in Dinwiddie County.
Gunston; post village in Fairfax County.
Gunston Cove; an arm of the Potomac River, in the southern part of Fairfax County, into which enter Accotink and Pohick bays.
Guy; post village in Mecklenburg County.
Guynn; post village in Mathews County.
Guys; run, a small left-hand tributary to James River in Bath and Rockbridge counties.
Gwathmey; station in Hanover County, on the Richmond, Fredericksburg and Potomac Railroad.
Gypsum; post village in Smyth County on the Norfolk and Western Railway.
Gypsy; post village in Mecklenburg County.
Haddonfield; post village in Wise County.
Hadens; post village in Botetourt County on the Chesapeake and Ohio Railway.
Hadensville; post village in Goochland County.
Hadlock; post village in Northampton County.
Hagan; post village in Lee County on the Louisville and Nashville Railroad.

Hagood; post village in Patrick County.
Hague; post village in Westmoreland County.
Haislets; creek, a small right-hand tributary to James River in Rockbridge County.
Hale; branch, a small right-hand tributary to Levisa Fork in Buchanan County.
Haleford; post village in Franklin County.
Hales; bridge across Roanoke River in Franklin County.
Hales; creek, a small left-hand branch of Roanoke River in Bedford County.
Hales Mill; post village in Scott County.
Halfway; post village in Fauquier County.
Halifax; county, located on the southern boundary of the State, the northern and eastern boundaries following the Roanoke River. It is situated in the Piedmont region, and its surface is undulating, with little relief. The altitude rises from about 300 feet to 600 feet above sea level. Area, 806 square miles. Population, 37,197—white, 17,922; negro, 19,275; foreign born, 102. County seat, Houston. The mean magnetic declination in 1900 was 2° 15'. The mean annual rainfall is 50 to 60 inches, and the temperature 55° to 60°. The county is traversed by the Norfolk and Western and the Southern railways.
Hallieford; post village in Mathews County.
Hallowing; point on Potomac River in Fairfax County.
Hallsboro; post village in Chesterfield County on the Southern Railway.
Hallwood; post village in Accomac County on the New York, Philadelphia and Norfolk Railroad.
Halsteads Point; post village in York County.
Hamburg; post village in Shenandoah County.
Hamilton; town in Loudoun County on the Southern Railway. Population, 364.
Hamilton Draft; small left-hand tributary to James River in Augusta County.
Hamilton Knob; summit in Draper Mountains. Elevation, 3,163.
Hammet; post village in Bedford County.
Hampden Sidney; post village in Prince Edward County.
Hampstead; post village in King George County.
Hampton; county seat of Elizabeth City County on the Chesapeake and Ohio Railway.
Hampton Roads; harbor at mouth of James River, by which the latter is connected with Chesapeake Bay. It lies between Newport News and Fort Monroe on the north and the shore about Norfolk Harbor on the south.
Handsom; post village in Southampton County on the Seaboard Air Line Railway.
Handy; village in Franklin County.
Hanford; post village in Mecklenburg County.
Hanger; post village in Buchanan County.
Hanging Rock; summit in Potts Mountain. Elevation, 3,000 feet.
Hangmans; run, a small right-hand branch of Shenandoah River in Rockingham County.
Hank; branch, a small right-hand tributary to New River in Carroll County.
Hankey; mountains in Augusta County. Elevation, 3,000 feet.
Hanna; post village in Wise County.
Hanover; county, situated in the central part of the State lying in part in the Piedmont region and in part on the Atlantic plain. It is traversed by South Anna River, North Anna River forming its northern boundary. The altitude ranges from 100 to 300 feet above sea level. Area, 478 square miles. Population, 17,618—white, 9,696; negro, 7,898; foreign born, 72. County seat, Hanover. The mean magnetic declination in 1900 was 3° 30'. The mean annual rainfall is 40 to 50 inches, and the temperature 55° to 60°. The county is traversed by the Chesapeake and Ohio and the Richmond, Fredenck and Potomac railroads.
Hanover; county seat of Hanover County on the Chesapeake and Ohio Railway.
Hansonville; post village in Russell County. Altitude, 2,175 feet.

Happy; creek, a small right-hand branch of Shenandoah River in Warren County.
Happy Creek; post village in Warren County on the Southern Railway. Altitude, 790 feet.
Haran; post village in Roanoke County.
Harborton; post village in Accomac County.
Hardenburg; post village in Spottsylvania County.
Hardesty; post village in Warren County.
Hardie; post village in Henry County.
Hardware; post village in Fluvanna County on the Chesapeake and Ohio Railway.
Hardware; river, a small left-hand tributary to James River in Albemarle County, formed by North and South forks.
Hardy; creek, a small right-hand tributary to New River in Carroll County.
Hardy; creek, a small right-hand tributary to Powell River in Lee County.
Hardy; run, a small right-hand tributary to Jackson River in Alleghany County.
Hardys Ford; post village in Franklin County.
Hargrove; creek, a small left-hand tributary to James River in Nelson County.
Harkening Hill; summit in the Blue Ridge in Botetourt County. Altitude, 3,878 feet.
Harless; post village in Montgomery County.
Harman; post village in Tazewell County on the Baltimore and Ohio Railroad.
Harmon; branch, a small right-hand tributary to Jackson River in Alleghany County.
Harmony; small left-hand branch of New River in Pulaski County.
Harmony; post village in Halifax County.
Harmony Village; post village in Middlesex County.
Harpers Home; post village in Brunswick County.
Harrell; post village in Nansemond County.
Harris; small left-hand branch of Roanoke River in Bedford County.
Harris; creek, a small left-hand tributary to James River in Albemarle County.
Harris; post village in Louisa County.
Harris Creek; post village in Amherst County.
Harrison; creek, a small right-hand tributary to James River in Dinwiddie County.
Harrisonburg; county seat of Rockingham County on the Baltimore and Ohio, the Chesapeake Western, and the Southern railroads. Altitude, 1,338 feet. Population, 3,521.
Harriston; post village in Augusta County on the Norfolk and Western Railway.
Harrisville; post village in Shenandoah County.
Harry; branch, a small right-hand tributary to Levisa Fork in Buchanan County.
Harshberger; gap in Massanutten Mountain in Rockingham County.
Hartsock; post village in Scott County.
Hartwood; post village in Stafford County.
Harvest; village in Lee County.
Hervey Mills; post village in Warren County.
Haste; post village in Franklin County.
Hat; creek, a small left-hand tributary to James River in Nelson County.
Hat; creek, a small left-hand tributary to Roanoke River in Campbell County.
Hat; post village in Shenandoah County.
Hatcher; creek, a small right-hand tributary to James River in Buckingham County.
Hatcher; post village in Cumberland County.
Hatcher; run, a small branch of Rowanty Creek in Dinwiddie County.
Hatcher; run, a small left-hand tributary to Nottoway River in Dinwiddie County.
Hatcreek; post village in Campbell County.
Hatfield; creek, a small right-hand branch of Roanoke River in Franklin County.
Hatton, post village in Albemarle County on the Chesapeake and Ohio Railway.
Haught; post village in Franklin County.

Haw; branch, small right-hand tributary to Appomattox River in Amelia County.
Haw; small right-hand branch of New River in Pulaski County.
Hawk; post village in Cumberland County on the Farmville and Powhatan Railroad.
Hawkins; creek, a small left-hand tributary to York River in Louisa County.
Hawkins; run, a small left-hand tributary to Nottoway River in Dinwiddie County.
Hawkinstown; post village in Shenandoah County.
Hawks Bill; creek, a small right-hand branch of Shenandoah River in Rockingham County.
Hawksbill; creek, a small right-hand tributary to Shenandoah River in Page County.
Hawks Bill; summit in the Blue Ridge in Madison County. Elevation, 4,066 feet.
Hawlin; post village in Rappahannock County.
Hay; run, a small right-hand tributary to Roanoke River in Franklin County.
Haycock; post village in Floyd County.
Hayes Store; post village in Gloucester County.
Hayfield; post village in Frederick County.
Haymakertown; post village in Botetourt County.
Haymarket; post village in Prince William County on the Southern Railway.
Haynesville; post village in Richmond County.
Hays; creek, a small right-hand tributary to James River in Alleghany County.
Hays; creek, a small right-hand tributary to Jackson River in Alleghany County.
Hays; creek, a small left-hand tributary to James River in Rockbridge County.
Haysi; post village in Dickinson County.
Hayter; gap in Clinch Mountains in Washington County.
Haywood; post village in Madison County.
Hazel; river, a small right-hand tributary to Rappahannock River in Rappahannock and Culpeper counties.
Hazel; run, a small right-hand branch of Rappahannock River in Spottsylvania County.
Hazelspring; post village in Washington County.
Headforemost; mountain in Bedford County. Elevation, 3,773 feet.
Headquarters; post village in Shenandoah County.
Headwaters; post village in Highland County.
Healing Springs; post village in Bath County.
Heard; summit in Albemarle County.
Hearing; post village in Norfolk County.
Heathsville; county seat of Northumberland County.
Hebron; post village in Dinwiddie County.
Heiskell; post village in Frederick County.
Helena; post village in Bedford County on the Virginia-Carolina Railway.
Hell; creek, a bayou tributary to Back Bay in Princess Anne County.
Helm Mountain; summit in Nelson County.
Helms; post village in Franklin County.
Helton; creek, a small left-hand branch of New River, rising in Grayson County.
Hematite; post village in Alleghany County on the Chesapeake and Ohio Railway.
Hemp-patch; mount in Roanoke County.
Hendricks Store; post village in Bedford County.
Henrico; county situated in the central part of the State, lying in part in the Piedmont region and in part on the Atlantic plain, its southern boundary being formed by James River. The altitude ranges from 100 to 300 feet above sea level. Area, 273 square miles. Population, 30,062—white, 17,246; negro, 12,816; foreign born, 815. County seat, Richmond. The mean magnetic declination in 1900 was 3°. The mean annual rainfall is 40 to 50 inches, and the temperature 55° to 60°. The county is traversed by the Atlantic Coast Line, the Chesapeake and Ohio, the Richmond, Frederick and Potomac, the Seaboard Air Line, and the Southern railroads.

Henry; cape, point of land in Princess Anne County, the southern point at the entrance to Chesapeake Bay.

Henry; county, situated in the southern part of the State in the Piedmont region. It has a rolling, broken surface. Area, 425 square miles. Population, 19,265—white, 10,881; negro, 8,383; foreign born, 16. County seat, Martinsville. The mean magnetic declination in 1900 was 1° 45′. The mean annual rainfall is 50 to 60 inches, and the mean annual temperature 55° to 60°. The county is traversed by the Danville and Western and the Norfolk and Western railways.

Hepners; post village in Shenandoah County.

Hera; post village in Nottoway County.

Herald; post village in Wise County.

Herbert; post village in Princess Anne County.

Hermitage; post village in Augusta County on the Seaboard Air Line Railway.

Hernando: post village in Franklin County.

Herndon; town in Fairfax County. Population, 692.

Herring; canal in Norfolk County, connecting Dismal Swamp Canal with the Southern Branch of Elizabeth River.

Hewlett; post village in Hanover County.

Hick; creek, a small left-hand branch of Middle Fork of Holston River in Smyth County.

Hickman; village in Franklin County.

Hickory; creek, a small left-hand tributary to James River in Nelson County.

Hickory; creek, a small left-hand tributary to York River in Louisa County.

Hickory; post village in Norfolk County.

Hickorygrove; post village in Prince William County.

Hicks Store; post village in Spottsylvania County.

Hicksville; post village in Bland County.

Hicks Wharf; post village in Mathews County.

Higgins; post village in Grayson County.

High; bridge across Appomattox River between Prince Edward and Cumberland counties.

High Cock; summit in Bedford County.

Highco Mountain; summit in the Blue Ridge. Elevation, 2,880 feet.

Highgate; post village in Surry County.

Highhill; post village in Halifax County.

High Knob; summit in the Blue Ridge in Rockingham County.

High Knob; summit in Wise County. Elevation, 4,188 feet.

High Knob; summit in Warren County. Elevation, 2,385 feet.

Highland; county, situated in the northwestern part of the State in the Appalachian Valley. The surface consists of an alternation of sandstone ridges and limestone valleys, drained by tributaries to James River. Altitude ranges from 1,800 up to over 4,000 feet. Area, 407 square miles. Population, 5,647—white, 5,269; negro, 378; foreign born, 5. County seat, Monterey. The mean magnetic declination in 1900 was 2° 30′. The mean annual rainfall is 50 to 60 inches, and the temperature 45° to 50°.

Highland Springs; post village in Henrico County.

Highpeak; post village in Franklin County.

High Point; summit in Bath County. Altitude, 3,318 feet.

High Point; summit in Sugar Run Mountain. Elevation, 3,910 feet.

High Rock; summit in Walker Mountain. Elevation, 3,837 feet.

High Rocks; summits in Wythe County. Elevation from 3,000 to 3,660 feet.

High Top; summit in Montgomery County. Elevation, 2,690 feet.

Hightown; post village in Highland County.

Hilda; post village in Sussex County on the Southern Railway.

Hildebrand; post village in Augusta County.

Hillandale; post village in Charlotte County.
Hillcroft; post village in Charlotte County.
Hillgrove; post village in Pittsylvania County.
Hills; creek, a small left-hand tributary to Roanoke River in Campbell County.
Hillsboro; town in Loudoun County. Population, 131.
Hill Station; post village in Scott County.
Hillsville; county seat of Carroll County. Altitude, 2,570 feet.
Hilo; post village in Augusta County.
Hilton; ford of North Fork of Holston River, near Fido, in Scott County.
Hiltons; post village in Scott County on the Virginia and Southwestern Railway.
Hinckle; post village in Frederick County.
Hines; small left-hand branch of Clinch River in Tazewell County.
Hinesville; post village in Pittsylvania County.
Hinnom; post village in Westmoreland County.
Hinton; post village in Rockingham County.
Hitch; post village in Fauquier County.
Hitchcock; post village in Greenesville County.
Hitesburg; post village in Halifax County.
Hively; post village in Bath County.
Hixburg; post village in Appomattox County.
Hoadly; post village in Prince William County.
Hobson; post village in Nansemond County.
Hockman; post village in Tazewell County on the Norfolk and Western Railway.
Hodges Draft; small left-hand tributary to James River in Augusta County.
Hodges Ferry; post village in Norfolk County on the Southern Railway.
Hog; creek, a small left-hand tributary to James River in Albemarle County.
Hog Back; mountains in Loudoun County. Elevation, 500 feet.
Hog Back; summit in Little North Mountain. Elevation, 3,000 feet.
Hoges Store; post village in Giles County.
Hog Pen Mountain; summit in Rockingham County. Elevation, 2,000 feet.
Hogthief; creek, a small right-hand branch of Middle Holston River in Washington County.
Hogtrough; creek, a small left-hand branch of South Fork of Holston River in Smyth County.
Hogue; creek, a small right-hand tributary to Potomac River in Frederick County.
Holcombs Rock; post village in Bedford County on the Chesapeake and Ohio Railway. Altitude, 563 feet.
Holdcroft; post village in Charles City County.
Holiday; creek, a small left-hand branch of Appomattox River in Appomattox County.
Holladay; post village in Spottsylvania County.
Holland; town in Nansemond County on the Southern Railway. Population, 133.
Hollins; post village in Roanoke County on the Norfolk and Western Railway.
Hollow; run, a small left-hand tributary to Shenandoah River in Shenandoah County.
Holly; creek, a small left-hand tributary to Russell Fork, rising in Dickenson County.
Holly; post village in Chesterfield County.
Hollybrook; post village in Bland County.
Hollydale; post village in Lunenburg County.
Hollywood; post village in Appomattox County.
Holmans; creek, a small left-hand tributary to Shenandoah River in Shenandoah County.
Holmes; run, a small right-hand tributary to Potomac River in Fairfax County.
Holmhead; post village in Fluvanna County.

Holstein Mills; village in Smyth County.
Holston; mountains in Washington County. Elevation, 2,000 to 3,000 feet.
Holston; post village in Washington County on the Norfolk and Western Railway.
Holston; river formed by three forks in Wythe County, and flowing southwest into Tennessee River. Drainage area, 3,790 square miles; discharge, 1,000 cubic feet per second.
Holston Bridge; post village in Scott County.
Holts; branch, a small right-hand tributary to James River in Appomattox County.
Homade; post village in Dickinson County.
Home; creek, a small right-hand branch of Levisa Fork, rising in Buchanan County.
Homeland; post village in Culpeper County.
Homer; post village in Russell County.
Homeville; post village in Sussex County.
Homewood; post village in Surry County.
Honaker; small left-hand branch of New River in Pulaski County.
Honaker; town in Russell County on the Norfolk and Western Railway. Altitude, 1,900 feet. Population, 295.
Hone Quarry; mountains in Rockingham County.
Hone Quarry; run, a small left-hand tributary to Shenandoah River in Rockingham County.
Honeyville; post village in Page County.
Hood; post village in Madison County.
Hooes; post village in King George County.
Hoover; post village in Rockingham County.
Hoover Camp; small right-hand branch of Knox Creek in Buchanan County.
Hopeful; post village in Louisa County.
Hope Mills; village in Page County.
Hopeside; post village in Northumberland County.
Hopeton; post village in Accomac County.
Hopeville; post village in Greensville County.
Hopkins; creek, a small left-hand tributary to Roanoke River in Bedford County.
Hopkins; post village in Accomac County.
Hoppen; run, a small left-hand branch of Rappahannock River in Fauquier County.
Hopper; village in Henry County.
Hopyard; post village in King George County.
Horeb; post village in Bedford County.
Horn; ford in Back Creek, a right-hand tributary to Roanoke River in Roanoke County.
Horners; post village in Westmoreland County.
Horns; small left-hand branch of Cripple Creek in Wythe and Smyth counties.
Horntown; post village in Accomac County.
Horse; mountains in Alleghany County. Elevation, 2,000 to 2,500 feet.
Horseleys; creek, a small left-hand tributary to James River in Amherst County.
Horse Pasture; post village in Henry County.
Horsepen; cove in Big Stone Ridge in Tazewell County.
Horsepen; creek, a small left-hand tributary to Nottoway River in Nottoway County.
Horsepen; creek, a small right-hand tributary to Appomattox River in Amelia County.
Horsepen; post village in Tazewell County.
Horsepen; small right-hand branch of Appomattox River in Amelia County.
Horse Pen Mountain; summit in the western part of Bedford County.
Horseshoe; mountains in Nelson County. Elevation, 1,500 to 2,000 feet.
Horse Swamp; creek, a small right-hand branch of Chickahominy River in Henrico County.
Horsey; post village in Accomac County.

Hortons; summit in Scott County.
Hortons Summit; post village in Scott County on the Virginia and Southwestern Railroad.
Hot Springs; post village in Bath County on the Chesapeake and Ohio Railway. Altitude, 2,195 feet.
Hough; creek, a small left-hand branch of Rappahannock River in King George County.
House and Barn; mountain in Russell County. Altitude, 3,450 feet.
Houston; county seat of Halifax County on the Norfolk and Western Railway. Altitude, 1,345 feet. Population, 687.
Howard; creek, a small right-hand tributary to York River in Hanover County.
Howards; ferry over New River in Pulaski County.
Howardsville; post village in Albemarle County on the Chesapeake and Ohio Railway.
Howell; post village in Patrick County.
Howells; gap in Weaver Knob.
Howertons; post village in Essex County.
Howerys; post village in Floyd County.
Howlett; post village in Appomattox County.
Hubard; post village in Buckingham County on the Chesapeake and Ohio Railway.
Hubbard; run, a small right-hand branch of Rappahannock River in Culpeper County.
Hubbard Springs; post village in Lee County on the Chesapeake and Ohio Railway.
Huckleberry Mountain; summit in Rockingham County.
Huddle; creek, a small right-hand branch of Cripple Creek in Wythe County.
Huddleston; post village in Alleghany County.
Hudgins; post village in Mathews County.
Hudson; creek, a small left-hand tributary to Shenandoah River in Augusta County.
Hudson; creek, a small right-hand tributary to York River in Louisa County.
Hudson Mill; post village in Culpeper County.
Huffman; post village in Craig County.
Huffman Knob; summit in Carroll County.
Huffville; post village in Floyd County.
Hugh; post village in Charlotte County.
Hughart; run, a small left-hand tributary to James River in Augusta County.
Hughes; creek, a small right-hand branch of Jackson River in Bath County.
Hughes; creek, a small right-hand tributary to James River in Bath County.
Hughes; river, a small right-hand tributary to Rappahannock River in Rappahannock County.
Hughes River; post village in Rappahannock County.
Hughesville; post village in Loudoun County.
Huguenot; post village in Powhatan County.
Huguenot; springs in Powhatan County.
Hull; post village in Highland Country.
Hume; post village in Fauquier County.
Humpback; summit in Nelson County. Elevation, 3,645 feet.
Hundley Springs; post village in Appomattox County.
Hungary; creek, a small right-hand tributary to Chickahominy River in Henrico County.
Hungary Town; summit in Lunenburg County. Elevation, 490 feet.
Hungry; run, a small right-hand tributary to Potomac River in Loudoun County.
Hungry Hollow; creek, a small right-hand tributary to Middle Fork of Holston River.

Hungry Mother; creek, a small right-hand branch of Middle Fork of Holston River in Smyth County.
Hunter; gap in Powell Mountain in Lee County.
Hunter; valley lying between Stone Mountain and Chestnut Ridge in Scott County.
Hunter Hall; post village in Franklin County.
Hunters Lodge; post village in Fluvanna County.
Hunters Mills; post village in Fairfax County.
Hunting; creek, a small left-hand tributary to Roanoke River in Bedford County.
Hunting; creek, a small right-hand branch of James River in Bedford County.
Hunting; run, a small right-hand tributary to Rappahannock River in Spottsylvania County.
Hunting Camp; creek, a small left-hand tributary to Wolf Creek, rising in Bland County.
Hunts; creek, a small right-hand tributary to James River in Buckingham County.
Huon; post village in Louisa County.
Hupp; village in Rockingham County.
Hurley; post village in Buchanan County.
Hurricane; branch, a small right-hand tributary to Levisa Fork in Buchanan County.
Hurricane; small left-hand branch of Nottoway River in Nottoway County.
Hurricane; creek, a small right-hand tributary to Russell Fork, rising in Buchanan County.
Hurricane; fork, a small right-hand tributary to Clinch River, rising in Russell County;
Hurt; post village in Pittsylvania County on the Southern Railway.
Hurtsville; post village in Appomattox County.
Hutchison Rock; summit in Clinch Mountain. Altitude, 4,724 feet.
Hutton; creek, a small left-hand branch of Middle Fork of Holston River in Smyth County.
Huttons; small right-hand branch of Middle Fork of Holston River in Washington County.
Hyacinth; post village in Northumberland County.
Hybla; post village in King William County.
Hyco; post village in Halifax County.
Hycootee; small right-hand branch of Dan River in Halifax County.
Hydraulic; post village in Albemarle County.
Hylas; post village in Hanover County.
Hyters Gap; post village in Washington County.
Iberis; post village in Lancaster County.
Ibex; post village in Dickenson County.
Ida; post village in Page County.
Ideal; post village in Caroline County.
Idem; post village in Amherst County.
Igo; post village in King George County.
Ilda; village in Fairfax County.
Inca; post village in Mecklenburg County.
Inch; branch, a small right-hand tributary to Shenandoah River in Augusta County.
Independence; county seat of Grayson County.
Independent Hill; post village in Prince William County.
Index; post village in King George County.
Indian; creek, a small left-hand branch of Pound River in Wise County.
Indian; creek, a small left-hand tributary to James River in Amherst County.
Indian; creek, a small right-hand branch of Clinch River, rising in Tazewell County.

Indian, creek, a small right-hand branch of Powell River, rising in Lee County and flowing south into Powell River.
Indian; creek, a small right-hand branch of Roanoke River in Franklin County.
Indian; creek, a small right-hand branch of Russell Fork, rising in Dickenson County.
Indian; creek, a small right-hand tributary to New River, rising in Floyd County.
Indian; creek, a small right-hand tributary to York River in Louisa County.
Indiancreek; post village in Norfolk County.
Indian Draft; small left-hand tributary to James River in Bath County.
Indian Draft; small right-hand branch of Jackson River in Alleghany County.
Indianneck; post village in King and Queen County.
Indian Ridge; mountains in Floyd and Carroll counties. Elevation, 3,000 feet.
Indianrock; post village in Botetourt County.
Indiantown; post village in Orange County.
Indian Valley; post village in Floyd County.
Indika; post village in Isle of Wight County.
Inez; post village in Louisa County.
Inge; post village in Lunenburg County.
Ingle; post village in Pulaski County.
Ingles; ferry over New River in Pulaski County.
Ingles; mountains in Pulaski County.
Ingram; post village in Halifax County.
Inlet; post village in Culpeper County on the Southern Railway.
Inman; post village in Wise County on the Virginia and Southwestern Railway.
Ino; post village in King and Queen County.
Interior; post village in Giles County on the Big Stony Railway.
Invermay; post village in Mecklenburg County.
Ionia; post village in Dinwiddie County.
Iraville; post village in Essex County.
Irby; post village in Nottoway County.
Irene; post village in Loudoun County.
Irisburg; post village in Henry County.
Irish; creek, a small left-hand tributary to James River in Rockbridge County.
Irish; gap in South Mountains, caused by Irish Creek, in Rockbridge County.
Irishcreek; post village in Rockbridge County.
Iron; mountain in Alleghany County.
Iron; mountains extending from Washington County to Wythe County. Elevation, 3,000 to 4,000 feet.
Iron Gate; gap in Patch Mountains, through which flows Jackson River, in Alleghany County.
Irongate; town in Alleghany County on the Chesapeake and Ohio Railway. Altitude, 1,019 feet. Population, 392.
Iron Hill; springs in Alleghany County.
Ironside; village in Henry County.
Irvey Notch; gap in Garden Mountain in Botetourt County.
Irvington; post village in Lancaster County.
Irwin; post village in Goochland County on the Chesapeake and Ohio Railway.
Isaac; creek, a small right-hand tributary to Potomac River in Frederick County.
Isaac; post village in Southampton County.
Isabel; post village in Culpeper County.
Isham; post village in Lunenburg County.
Isis; post village in Scott County.
Island; creek, a small left-hand tributary to Roanoke River in Bedford County.

Island; creek, a small right-hand tributary to New River in Carroll County.
Island; ford of Jackson River in Alleghany County.
Island; post village in Goochland County.
Islandford; post village in Rockingham County.
Isle of Wight; county, situated in the southeastern part of the State, fronting on the south bank of James River near its mouth. The surface is level and but little elevated above tide. Area, 352 square miles. Population, 13,102—white 6,833; negro, 6,268; foreign born, 35. County seat, Isle of Wight. The mean magnetic declination in 1900 was 3° 45′. The mean annual rainfall is 40 to 50 inches, and the temperature 55° to 60°. The county is traversed by the Norfolk and Western and the Seaboard and Roanoke railways.
Isle of Wight; county seat of Isle of Wight County.
Israel Mountain; summit in Albemarle County. Elevation, 1,000 feet.
Issequena; post village in Goochland County.
Itata; post village in Surry County.
Ivanhoe; post village in Wythe County on the Norfolk and Western Railway.
Ivondale; post village in Richmond County.
Ivor; post village in Southampton County on the Norfolk and Western Railway.
Ivy; creek, a small left-hand tributary to James River in Nelson County.
Ivy; creek, a small right-hand branch of James River in Bedford and Campbell counties.
Ivy Depot; post village in Albemarle County on the Chesapeake and Ohio Railway. Altitude 545 feet.
Ivyview; post village in Halifax County.
Jack; mountains in Highland County, extending into Pendleton County, W. Va. Elevation, 3,500 to 4,000 feet.
Jacks; branch, a small left-hand tributary to Nottoway River in Nottoway County.
Jacks Hill; summit in Nelson County.
Jacks Mill; post village in Floyd County.
Jackson; ferry in New River at Jackson in Wythe County.
Jackson; post village in Louisa County on the Chesapeake and Ohio Railway. Altitude, 845 feet.
Jackson; river, a head branch of James River, which has its source in North Mountain and flows in a generally southward course to its junction with the James.
Jacksondale; post village in Princess Anne County on the Norfolk and Southern Railroad.
Jacobsville, post village in Pittsylvania County.
Jadwyn; post village in Shenandoah County.
Jamaica; post village in Middlesex County.
James; river, formed by two forks, North and South, which head in North Mountain on the west side of the valley of Virginia, and crossing the Valley in a circuitous course passes the Blue Ridge through a gap a few miles above Lynchburg, thence in a generally easterly course it flows into Chesapeake Bay through Hampton Roads; drainage area, 9,684 square miles; mean discharge, 1,854 (Buchanan, Va.); navigable to Richmond.
James City; county, situated on the Atlantic plain between York and James rivers, in the eastern part of the State. The surface is low and level, and little elevated. Area, 159 square miles. Population, 3,688—white, 1,346; negro, 2,342; foreign born, 58. County seat, Williamsburg. The mean magnetic declination in 1900 was 3° 45′. The mean annual rainfall is 40 to 50 inches, and the temperature 55° to 60°. The county is traversed by the Chesapeake and Ohio Railway.
James River; post village in Amherst County.

James Store; post village in Gloucester County.
Jamestown; bridge across Appomattox River between Prince Edward and Cumberland counties.
Jamestown; post village in James City County.
Jamesville; post village in Northampton County.
Jane; post village in Dickenson County.
Jap; post village in Lee County.
Jar; post village in Buckingham County.
Jarman; gap in the Blue Ridge in Augusta County.
Jarratt; post village in Sussex County.
Jasper; post village in Lee County on the Virginia and Southwestern Railway.
Jasper Mountain; summit in Pittsylvania County. Elevation, 1,000 feet.
Jefferson; post village in Powhatan County.
Jeffersonton; post village in Culpeper County.
Jeffress; post village in Mecklenburg County on the Southern Railway.
Jeffries; branch, a small right-hand tributary to Potomac River in Loudoun County.
Jeffs; post village in York County.
Jelico; post village in Buchanan County.
Jenkings; branch, a small left-hand tributary to Shenandoah River in Augusta County.
Jenkins; gap in Crawford Mountain, caused by Jenkins Branch, in Augusta County.
Jenkins Bridge; post village in Accomac County.
Jennings; creek, a small right-hand tributary to James River in Botetourt County.
Jennings Gap; post village in Augusta County.
Jennings Mountain; summit in Amherst County.
Jennings Ordinary; post village in Nottoway County.
Jeremiah; run, a small right-hand tributary to Shenandoah River in Page County.
Jericho; canal connecting Drummond Lake with Suffolk in Nansemond and Norfolk counties.
Jerkemtight; creek, a small left-hand tributary to James River in Bath County.
Jerome; post village in Shenandoah County.
Jerry; run, a small right-hand tributary to Jackson River in Alleghany County.
Jesses Mill; creek, a small left-hand branch of Clinch River, rising in Russell County.
Jeter; post village in Bedford County.
Jetersville; post village in Amelia County on the Southern Railway.
Jetts; creek, a small left-hand branch of King George County.
Jetts; post village in Greenesville County.
Jewell Ridge; mountains in Buchanan County.
Jimbo; post village in Bedford County.
Joe; creek, a small left-hand tributary to James River in Nelson County.
Joe; post village in Buchanan County.
Joel; small right-hand branch of Slate Creek in Buchanan County.
Joel; village in Franklin County.
Joes; creek, a small left-hand tributary to Shenandoah River in Rockingham County.
John; creek, a small right-hand tributary to Chickahominy River in Henrico County.
John; village in Russell County.
John; run, a small right-hand tributary to Shenandoah River in Augusta County.
Johns; creek, a right-hand tributary to James River in Craig County.
Johns; creek, a small right-hand tributary to Jackson River in Craig County.
Johns; run, a small right-hand tributary to Jackson River in Alleghany County.
Johns Creek; mountains in Giles and Craig counties. Elevation, 3,000 to 3,500 feet.
Johnson; creek, a small left-hand tributary to Yadkin River in Patrick County.
Johnson; creek, a small left-hand tributary to Roanoke River in Campbell County.
Johnson; post village in Scott County.

Johnson; run, a small right-hand tributary to Potomac River in Frederick County.
Johnson Creek; post village in Patrick County.
Johnson Mountain; summit in Bedford County. Altitude, 1,375 feet.
Johnsons Springs; post village in Goochland County.
Jonas; run, a small right-hand tributary to Rappahannock River in Culpeper County.
Jones; small right-hand branch of Opossum Creek in Scott County.
Jones; creek, a small right-hand branch of James River in Powhatan County.
Jones; creek, a small right-hand branch of North Fork of Powell River in Lee County.
Jones; fork, a small right-hand tributary to Levisa Fork in Buchanan County.
Jones; neck of land nearly inclosed by a bend in James River in Chesterfield County.
Jones; post village in Halifax County.
Jonesboro; post village in Brunswick County.
Jones Hole; small swamp in Prince George and Sussex counties.
Jonesville; county seat of Lee County.
Jonican; branch, a small left-hand tributary to James River in Charlotte and Appomattox counties.
Joplin; post village in Wise County.
Jordan; river, a small right-hand tributary to Rappahannock River in Rappahannock County.
Jordan Springs; post village in Frederick County.
Jordans Store; post village in Powhatan County.
Jorgensen; post village in Lunenburg County.
Joseph; post village in Pittsylvania County.
Joshua; creek, a small right-hand tributary to James River in Buckingham County.
Joyceville; post village in Mecklenburg County.
Judd; branch, a small right-hand tributary to Appomattox River in Amelia County.
Judd; post village in Brunswick County.
Judge; post village in Dickenson County.
Judith; creek, a small right-hand branch of James River in Bedford County.
Jump; mountains in Rockbridge County. Elevation, 2,500 feet.
Jump; post village in Rockbridge County.
Jumping; run, a small left-hand branch of Roanoke River in Bedford County.
Jump Rock; summit in Rockbridge County. Elevation, 3,190 feet.
Junta; village in Franklin County.
Just; post village in Lee County.
Justisville; post village in Accomac County.
Ka; post village in Scott County.
Kadesh; village in Pittsylvania County.
Kara; post village in Lunenburg County.
Karl; post village in Appomattox County.
Kasey; post village in Bedford County.
Kate; creek, a small left-hand tributary to Roanoke River in Bedford County.
Katie; small right-hand branch of Maiden Spring Creek, a tributary to Clinch River, rising in Tazewell County.
Kays; run, a small left-hand branch of Rappahannock River in King George County.
Keats; post village in Mecklenburg County.
Keeling; post village in Pittsylvania County.
Keen; mountains in Buchanan County. Elevation, 2,500 feet.
Keene; post village in Albemarle County.
Keezletown; post village in Rockingham County on the Chesapeake Western Railway.

Keller; post village in Accomac County on the New York, Philadelphia and Norfolk Railroad.
Kelley; mountains in Augusta County. Elevation, 2,000 to 3,000 feet.
Kellys Ford; post village in Culpeper County.
Kelso; village in Bedford County.
Kempis; post village in Amelia County.
Kempsville; post village in Princess Anne County on the Norfolk and Southern Railroad.
Kendallgrove; post village in Northampton County on the New York, Philadelphia and Norfolk Railroad.
Kenmore; post village in Fairfax County.
Kennedy; creek, a small right-hand tributary to Shenandoah River in Augusta County.
Kennett; post village in Franklin County.
Kent; branch, a small left-hand tributary to James River in Fluvanna County.
Kent Ridge; mountains in Russell and Tazewell counties. Elevation, 2,500 feet.
Kents Store; post village in Fluvanna County.
Kentuck; post village in Pittsylvania County.
Kenwood; station in Hanover County on the Richmond, Fredericksburg, and Potomac Railroad.
Kepheart; run, a small left-hand tributary to Shenandoah River in Rockingham County.
Kerfoot; post village in Fauquier County.
Kerns; mountains in Shenandoah County. Elevation, 1,500 to 3,000 feet.
Kernstown; post village in Frederick County on the Baltimore and Ohio Railroad. Altitude, 744 feet.
Kerrs; creek, a small left-hand tributary to James River in Rockbridge County.
Kerrs Creek; post village in Rockbridge County.
Keswick; post village in Albemarle County on the Chesapeake and Ohio Railway.
Ketron; post village in Washington County.
Kettle; run, a small right-hand tributary to Potomac River in Prince William County.
Kew; post village in Campbell County.
Keysville; town in Charlotte County on the Southern Railway. Altitude, 628 feet. Population, 82.
Kibler; post village in Patrick County.
Kidd; post village in Albemarle County.
Kilmarnock; post village in Lancaster County.
Kimball; post village in Page County on the Norfolk and Western Railway. Altitude, 892 feet.
Kimballton; post village in Giles County on the Big Stony Railway.
Kimberling; creek, a small left-hand branch of Walker Creek in Bland County.
Kimberling; creek, a small right-hand tributary to Walker Creek, rising in Bland County.
Kimberling; post village in Bland County.
Kimberling; springs in Bland County.
Kinderwood; post village in Lunenburg County.
Kindrick; post village in Grayson County.
King and Queen; county, situated in the central part of the State on the Atlantic plain. The surface is level and but little elevated above tide. Area, 336 square miles. Population, 9,265—white, 4,006; negro, 5,259; foreign born, 2. County seat, King and Queen. The mean magnetic declination in 1900 was 4°. The mean annual rainfall is 45 to 50 inches, and the temperature 55° to 60°.
King and Queen; county seat of King and Queen County.

King George; county, situated in the eastern part of the State, lying on the south side of Potomac River on the Atlantic plain. The surface is rolling and but little elevated above tide. Area, 183 square miles. Population, 6,918—white, 3,596; negro, 3,322; foreign born, 22. County seat, King George. The mean magnetic declination in 1900 was 4° 15′. The mean annual rainfall is 40 to 50 inches, and the temperature 55° to 60°.
King George; county seat of King George County.
Kings Hill; summit in Augusta County.
Kingsland; creek, a small right-hand branch of James River in Chesterfield County.
Kings Mill; post village in Washington County.
King William; county, situated in the central part of the State on the Atlantic plain. It has a level surface, but little elevated. Area, 246 square miles. Population, 8,380—white, 3,266; negro, 4,962; foreign born, 35. County seat, King William. The mean magnetic declination in 1900 was 3° 36′. The mean annual rainfall is 40 to 50 inches, and the temperature 55° to 60°. The county is traversed by the Southern Railway.
King William; county seat of King William County.
Kinsale; post village in Westmoreland County.
Kinser; creek, a small left-hand branch of Cripple Creek in Wythe County.
Kiosk; post village in Lee County.
Kipling; post village in Grayson County.
Kiracofe; post village in Augusta County.
Kirk; post village in Lee County.
Knightly; post village in Augusta County.
Knob; fork, a small right-hand branch of New River in Grayson County.
Knob; post village in Tazewell County.
Knob; summit in Botetourt County.
Knob; summit in Rockbridge County. Elevation, 2,000 feet.
Knolls; post village in Campbell County.
Knopf; post village in Caroline County.
Koiners Store; post village in Augusta County.
Kola; post village in Patrick County.
Kopp; post village in Prince William County.
Korea; post village in Culpeper County.
Koskoo; post village in Southampton County.
Kountz; post village in Page County.
Kruger; post village in Prince George County.
Kunath; post village in Lunenburg County.
Kyle; village in Botetourt County.
Laban; post village in Mathews County.
Lacey Spring; post village in Rockingham County.
Lackey; post village in York County.
Laconia; post village in Charlotte County.
Lacrosse; post village in Mecklenburg County on the Seaboard Air Line and the Southern railways.
Lacy; post village in Pittsylvania County.
Ladd; village in Augusta County.
Lafayette; post village in Montgomery County on the Potomac, Fredericksburg and Piedmont Railroad.
Lagrange; post village in Culpeper County on the Chesapeake and Ohio Railway. Altitude, 1,618 feet.
Lahore; post village in Orange County.
Laird; post village in Dinwiddie County.
Laird Knob; summit in Massanutten Mountain.

Lakeview; post village in Clarke County.
Lakota; post village in Culpeper County.
Lamb; creek, a small left-hand branch of Rappahannock River in King George County.
Lamb; post village in Greene County.
Lambert; post village in Mecklenburg County.
Lambsburg; post village in Carroll County.
Lamont; post village in Smyth County.
Lancaster; county, situated in the eastern part of the State on the north side of Rappahannock River and on the north and west shores of Chesapeake Bay. Its surface is level, and but little elevated above tide. Area, 137 square miles. Population, 8,949—white, 4,058; negro, 4,891; foreign born, 25. County seat, Lancaster. The mean magnetic declination in 1900 was 4° 30′. The mean annual rainfall is 40 to 50 inches, and the temperature 55° to 60°.
Lancaster; county seat of Lancaster County.
Lance; post village in Stafford County.
Land; post village in Princess Anne County on the Norfolk and Southern Railroad.
Landis; post village in Augusta County.
Landmark; post village in Fauquier County.
Land of Promise; post village in Princess Anne County.
Landsdown; post village in Prince William County.
Lanesville; post village in King William County.
Laneview; post village in Essex County.
Lanexa; post village in New Kent County on the Chesapeake and Ohio Railway.
Langley; post village in Fairfax County.
Lantana; post village in Goochland County.
Lantz Mills; post village in Shenandoah County.
Lapsley; run, a small right-hand tributary to James River in Botetourt County.
Lara; post village in Northumberland County.
Lasley; post village in Louisa County.
Lassiter; post village in Goochland County.
Latona; village in Rockingham County.
Laughon; village in Bedford County.
Laurel; branch, a small right-hand tributary to Jackson River in Alleghany County.
Laurel; small right-hand branch of Knox Creek in Buchanan County.
Laurel; creek, a small left-hand tributary to South Fork of Holston River in Washington County.
Laurel; creek, a small left-hand tributary to Wolf Creek, rising in Bland County.
Laurel; creek, a small right-hand tributary to Roanoke River in Roanoke County.
Laurel; creek, a small right-hand tributary to New River, rising in Floyd County and flowing into Pulaski County.
Laurel; creek, a small right-hand tributary to James River in Alleghany County.
Laurel; creek, a small right-hand branch of Wolf Creek in Bland County.
Laurel; small creek tributary to North Fork of Holston River, rising in Tazewell County.
Laurel; creek, a small tributary to Bluestone River in Tazewell County.
Laurel; creek, a small right-hand branch of North Fork of Holston River, rising in Tazewell County.
Laurel; fork, a small left-hand branch of North Fork of Potomac River in Highland County.
Laurel; fork, a small right-hand tributary to Clinch River in Scott County.
Laurel; fork, a small right-hand tributary to Dry Fork, rising in Tazewell County.
Laurel; fork, a small right-hand tributary to New River in Carroll County.
Laurel; fork, a small right-hand branch of Pigeon Creek in Wise County.

Laurel; run, a small left-hand tributary to James River in Rockbridge County.
Laurelfork; post village in Carroll County.
Laurelgrove; post village in Pittsylvania County.
Laurelhill; post village in Augusta County.
Laurel Hollow; branch, a small right-hand branch of Little Walker Creek in Pulaski County.
Laurel Mills; post village in Rappahannock County.
Laurel Ridge; mountains in Montgomery County.
Laurel Shorts; creek, a small right-hand tributary to New River in Carroll County.
Lawford; post village in Buckingham County.
Lawrenceville; county seat of Brunswick County on the Southern Railway. Population, 760.
Lawton; post village in Giles County.
Lawyers; post village in Campbell County.
Layman; post village in Craig County.
Layton; post village in Essex County.
Leader; post village in Chesterfield County.
Leaf; post village in Scott County.
Leah; post village in Floyd County.
Leaksville; post village in Page County on the Danville and Western Railway.
Leatherwood; post village in Henry County.
Leavells; post village in Spottsylvania County on the Atlantic and Danville Railroad.
Lebanon; county seat of Russell County. Population, 325. Altitude, 2,131 feet.
Lebanon Church; post village in Shenandoah County.
Leck; post village in Dickenson County.
Leda; post village in Halifax County.
Ledbetter; creek, a small left-hand branch of Meherrin River in Lunenburg County.
Lee; county, situated in the southwestern part of the State, having for its northern boundary the escarpment of the Cumberland Plateau, which here forms the State line with Kentucky. Its southern line is the boundary of Tennessee. Its surface consists mainly in an alternation of short parallel ridges of sandstone and narrow valleys filled with limestone. It is drained by Powell River. Area, 433 square miles. Population, 19,856—white, 19,116; negro, 740; foreign born, 17. County seat, Jonesville. The mean annual rainfall is 50 to 60 inches, and the temperature 50° to 55°. The county is traversed by the Louisville and Nashville Railroad.
Lee; creek, a small right-hand tributary to Appomattox River in Nottoway County.
Lee; creek, a small right-hand tributary to James River in Botetourt County.
Lee; post village in Goochland County on the Chesapeake and Ohio Railway.
Leeds; post village in Amherst County.
Leedstown; post village in Westmoreland County.
Leehall; post village in Warwick County on the Chesapeake and Ohio Railway.
Lee Mill; pond in Prince George County at the mouth of Warwick Swamp.
Leeland; post village in Stafford County.
Leemont; post village in Accomac County.
Lee Mountain; summit in Botetourt County.
Leesburg; county seat of Loudoun County on the Southern Railway. Population, 1,513.
Lees Mills; post village in Washington County.
Leesville; post village in Campbell County.
Left Crab Orchard; creek, a small right-hand tributary to North Fork of Powell River.
Legato; post village in Fairfax County.
Legg; post village in Wise County on the Interstate Railroad.

Leigh; mountain in Prince Edward County. Elevation, 715 feet.
Leighs; post village in Fairfax County.
Leithton; post village in Loudoun County.
Lelia; post village in Floyd County.
Lemar; post village in Franklin County.
Lemons; run, a small left-hand tributary to Roanoke River in Botetourt County.
Lenah; post village in Loudoun County.
Lennie; village in Lee County.
Lennig; post village in Halifax County.
Lenore; post village in Frederick County.
Lent; post village in Caroline County.
Leon; post village in Madison County.
Leonis; village in Fluvanna County.
Leplo; village in Washington County.
Leslie; post village in Roanoke County.
Lester Manor; post village in King William County on the Southern Railway.
Lesters; post village in Montgomery County.
Letcher; post village in Bath County.
Levelrun; post village in Pittsylvania County.
Levisa Fork; river, tributary to Ohio River, formed by two forks, North and South, in Buchanan County, and flowing northwest into the Big Sandy.
Levy; post village in Loudoun County.
Lew; post village in Frederick County.
Lewinsville; post village in Fairfax County.
Lewis; creek, a small left-hand tributary to Shenandoah River in Augusta County.
Lewis; creek, a small right hand tributary to Clinch River in Russell County.
Lewis; run, a small left-hand branch of Shenandoah River in Clarke County.
Lewisetta; post village in Northumberland County.
Lewiston; post village in Spottsylvania County.
Lexington; county seat of Rockbridge County on the Chesapeake and Ohio and the Baltimore and Ohio railroads. Altitude, 946 feet. Population, 3,203.
Libbie; post village in Lee County.
Liberty Furnace; post village in Shenandoah County.
Liberty Hill; small branch of Maiden Spring Creek tributary to Clinch River in Tazewell County.
Liberty Hill; summit in Tazewell County.
Liberty Mills; post village in Orange County.
Lick; branch, a small right-hand tributary to James River in Craig County.
Lick; branch, a small left-hand tributary to Roanoke River in Bedford County.
Lick; small right-hand branch of Knox Creek in Buchanan County.
Lick; creek, a small right-hand branch of Clinch River, rising in Russell Fork.
Lick; creek, a small right-hand tributary to Roanoke River in Floyd County.
Lick; creek, a small right-hand tributary to New River in Montgomery County.
Lick; creek, a small left-hand branch of Russell Fork, rising in Dickenson County.
Lick; creek, a small right-hand branch of Russell Fork, rising in Buchanan County.
Lick; creek, a small right-hand tributary to North Fork of Holston River, rising in Bland County.
Lick; mountain in Bedford County. Elevation, 1,839 feet.
Lick; mountain in Craig County.
Lick; mountains in Alleghany County. Elevation, 2,000 to 2,990 feet.
Lick; mountains in Wythe County. Elevation, 2,500 to 3,000 feet.
Lick; run, a small left-hand tributary to Roanoke River in Bedford County.
Lick; run, a small left-hand tributary to Shenandoah River in Frederick County.
Licking; post village in Goochland County.

Licking; creek, a small right-hand tributary to James River in Chesterfield County.
Licking; run, a small right-hand tributary to Potomac River in Fauquier County.
Lickinghole; creek, a small left-hand branch of Chickahominy River in Hanover County.
Lickinghole; creek, a small left-hand tributary to James River in Albemarle County.
Lick Log; branch, a small right-hand tributary to Jackson River in Alleghany County.
Lick Run; ferry across Jackson River at Lick Run in Botetourt County.
Lickrun; post village in Botetourt County on the Chesapeake and Ohio Railway. Altitude, 1,019 feet.
Lieutenant; creek, a small right-hand tributary to James River in Dinwiddie County.
Lightfoot; post village in York County.
Lignite; post village in Botetourt County.
Lignum; post village in Culpeper County.
Lilburn; post village in Powhatan County.
Lilian; post village in Northumberland County.
Lilly; village in Rockingham County.
Limeton; post village in Warren County.
Limstrong; post village in Prince William County.
Lina; post village in Dinwiddie County.
Lincoln; post village in Loudoun County.
Lincolnia; post village in Fairfax County.
Lindell; post village in Washington County.
Linden; post village in Warren County on the Southern Railway. Altitude, 916 feet.
Lindsay; post village in Albemarle County on the Chesapeake and Ohio Railway.
Lindward; post village in Charlotte County.
Link; post village in Norfolk County.
Linkhorn; bay, a lagoon in Princess Anne County, separated from the Atlantic Ocean by a sand bar.
Linkous; ferry over New River in Pulaski County.
Linn Camp; creek, a small right-hand branch of Levisa Fork, rising in Buchanan County.
Linnville; creek, a small left-hand tributary to Shenandoah River in Rockingham County.
Linnville; post village in Rockingham County on the Southern Railway. Altitude, 1,242 feet.
Lipps; post village in Wise County.
Lipscomb; post village in Augusta County on the Norfolk and Western Railway.
Lipses; run, a small right-hand tributary to James River in Botetourt County.
Lisbon; post village in Bedford County.
Lithia; post village in Botetourt County on the Norfolk and Western Railway. Altitude, 965 feet.
Little; creek, a small right-hand tributary to Appomattox River in Amelia and Nottoway counties.
Little; small creek in Princess Anne County.
Little; creek, a small branch of Wolf Creek in Tazewell County.
Little; creek, a small right-hand tributary to Roanoke River in Franklin County.
Little; mountain in Craig County. Elevation, 2,000 feet.
Little; mountains in Bath County. Elevation, 2,000 to 3,000 feet.
Little; mountains in Franklin County.
Little; mountains in Highland County. Elevation, 3,000 to 4,000 feet.

Little; river, a small left-hand tributary to Shenandoah River in Augusta County.
Little; river, a left-hand tributary to York River in Hanover County.
Little; river, a right-hand tributary to New River rising in Floyd County.
Little; river, a right-hand branch of New River in Montgomery County.
Little; river, a small right-hand tributary to Potomac River in Fauquier County.
Little; summit in Back Creek Mountain in Bath County.
Little Back; creek, a small right-hand tributary to Roanoke River in Roanoke County.
Little Back; creek, a small left-hand tributary to James River in Bath County.
Little Bear; creek, a small right-hand tributary to Shenandoah River in Rockingham County.
Little Beaver; creek, a small right-hand branch of James River in Campbell County.
Little Bottom; creek, a small right-hand tributary to Roanoke River in Roanoke County.
Little Briery; creek, a small right-hand tributary to Appomattox River in Prince Edward County.
Little Brush; creek, a small left-hand tributary to New River in Carroll County.
Little Brushy; mountains in Smyth County. Elevation, 2,500 feet.
Little Buffalo; creek, a small right-hand branch of Appomattox River in Prince Edward County.
Little Bull; run, a small right-hand tributary to Roanoke River in Franklin County.
Little Byrd; creek, a small left-hand tributary to James River in Goochland County.
Little Calf Pasture; river, a small left-hand tributary to James River in Rockbridge and Augusta counties.
Little Camp; mountain in Rockbridge County. Elevation, 2,000 to 3,000 feet.
Little Cast Steel; run, a small right-hand tributary to Jackson River in Alleghany County.
Little Catawba; creek, a small right-hand tributary to James River in Botetourt County.
Little Cattail; creek, a small left-hand tributary to Nottoway River in Dinwiddie County.
Little Cattail; creek, a small right-hand branch of Rowanty Creek.
Little Cedar; creek, a small left-hand tributary to Clinch River, rising in Russell County.
Little Cobbler; mountains in Fauquier County. Elevation, 750 to 1,000 feet.
Little Cranberry; creek, a small right-hand tributary to New River in Carroll County.
Little Falling; river, a small left-hand tributary to Roanoke River in Campbell County.
Little Fox; creek, a small right-hand tributary to New River in Grayson County.
Little Fox; creek, a small right-hand tributary to Russell Fork, rising in Buchanan County.
Little George; creek, a small right-hand branch of James River in Buckingham County.
Little Guinea; creek, a small left-hand branch of Appomattox River in Cumberland County.
Little Hound; creek, a small right-hand tributary to Nottoway River in Lunenburg County.
Little House Mountain; summit in Rockbridge County. Elevation, 3,410 feet.
Little Hunting; creek, a small right-hand branch of Potomac River in Fairfax County.

Little Indian; creek, a small left-hand tributary to Clinch River, rising in Russell County.
Little Indian; creek, a small right-hand tributary to New River in Floyd County.
Little Indian; run, a small right-hand tributary to Rappahannock River in Culpeper County.
Little Isaac; creek, a small right-hand tributary to Potomac River in Frederick County.
Little Laurel; creek, a small right-hand tributary to New River in Pulaski County.
Little Lickinghole; creek, a small left-hand tributary to James River in Goochland County.
Little Lynville; creek, a small right-hand tributary to Roanoke River in Franklin County.
Little Mack; creek, a small right-hand tributary to New River in Pulaski County.
Little Mare; mountains in Bath County.
Little Mary; creek, a small left-hand tributary to James River in Rockbridge County.
Little Middle; mountains in Bath and Alleghany counties.
Little Mill; creek, a small right-hand branch of Clinch River in Russell County.
Little Mountain; summit in Franklin County.
Little Narrows; passage between islands in Back Bay, Princess Anne County.
Little North; mountains in Augusta, Rockbridge, Shenandoah, and Frederick counties. Elevation, 2,000 to 3,000 feet.
Little Nottoway; river, a small left-hand branch of Nottoway River in Nottoway County.
Little Ogle; creek, a small right-hand tributary to Jackson River in Alleghany County.
Little Opossum; creek, a small right-hand branch of James River in Campbell County.
Little Oregon; creek, a small right-hand tributary to James River in Craig County.
Little Otter; river, a small left-hand tributary to Roanoke River, formed by two forks, North and South, in Bedford County.
Little Passage; creek, a small left-hand tributary to Shenandoah River in Shenandoah County.
Little Patterson; creek, a small right-hand tributary to James River in Botetourt County.
Little Piney; small left-hand tributary to James River in Amherst County.
Little Piney; mountains in Bath County.
Little Plymouth; post village in King and Queen County.
Little Prator; creek, a small left-hand branch of Levisa Fork, rising in Buchanan County.
Little Priest; summit in Nelson County.
Little Reed Island; creek, a right-hand tributary to New River in Carroll County.
Little Ridge; mountains in Botetourt County.
Little River; post village in Floyd County on the Chesapeake and Ohio Railway.
Little Roanoke; creek, a small left-hand branch of Roanoke River in Charlotte County.
Little Sandy; creek, a small right-hand tributary to Appomattox River in Prince Edward County.
Little Seneca; river, a small left-hand tributary to Roanoke River in Campbell County.
Little Sluice; mountains in Shenandoah County. Elevation, 2,000 feet.
Little Snake; creek, a small right-hand tributary to New River in Carroll County.
Little Spy; summit in the Blue Ridge in Augusta County.
Little Stone; gap in Little Stone Mountain in Wise County.

Little Stone; mountains in Wise County.
Little Stone Ridge; mountains in Tazewell County. Elevation, 3,000 feet.
Little Stony; creek, a small left-hand tributary to Roanoke River in Bedford County.
Little Stony; creek, a small left-hand tributary to Shenandoah River in Shenandoah County.
Little Stony; creek, a small right-hand branch of New River in Giles County.
Little Straightstone; creek, a small right-hand tributary to Roanoke River in Pittsylvania County.
Little Tom; creek, a small right-hand tributary to Clinch River, rising in Wise County.
Littleton; post village in Sussex County.
Little Town Hill; creek, a small right-hand tributary to Clinch River in Tazewell County.
Little Tumbling; creek, a small right-hand branch of North Fork of Holston River in Smyth County.
Little Walker; creek, a small right-hand branch of Walker Creek in Pulaski County.
Little Walker; creek, a small left-hand branch of Walker Creek, rising in Bland County.
Little Walker; mountains in Pulaski, Wythe, and Bland counties. Elevation, 2,000 to 3,000 feet.
Little Willis; river, a small right-hand tributary to James River in Buckingham and Cumberland counties.
Litwalton; post village in Lancaster County.
Lively; post village in Lancaster County.
Livingston; creek, a small left-hand branch of North Fork of Holston River, rising in Washington County.
Lloyds; post village in Essex County.
Lobelia; post village in Franklin County.
Lochleven; post village in Lunenburg County.
Locker; post village in Rockbridge County.
Locket; creek, a small right-hand tributary to Appomattox River in Prince Edward County.
Lockhart; post village in Albemarle County.
Locklies; post village in Middlesex County.
Loco; post village in Sussex County.
Locust; creek, a small left-hand tributary to York River in Louisa County.
Locust; creek, a small right-hand tributary to Roanoke River in Botetourt County.
Locustcreek; post village in Louisa County.
Locustdale; post village in Madison County.
Locustgrove; post village in Orange County.
Locusthill; post village in Middlesex County.
Locustlane; post village in Scott County.
Locustmount; post village in Accomac County.
Locustville; post village in Accomac County.
Lodge; post village in Northumberland County.
Lodi; post village in Washington County.
Lodore; post village in Amelia County.
Loftis; post village in Halifax County.
Lofton; post village in Augusta County on the Norfolk and Western Railway. Altitude, 1,782 feet.
Logan; creek, a small left-hand branch of North Fork of Holston River in Washington County.

Logan; post village in Spottsylvania County.
Lois; post village in Fauquier County.
Lola; post village in Pittsylvania County.
Londonbridge; post village in Princess Anne County on the Norfolk and Southern Railroad.
Lone Buck; small left-hand branch of James River in Amherst County.
Lonecedar; post village in Patrick County.
Lone Fountain; post village in Augusta County.
Lonegum; village in Bedford County.
Loneoak; post village in Henry County.
Lonepine; post village in Bedford County.
Lone Tree; summit in Blue Ridge in Augusta County. Elevation, 3,180 feet.
Long; branch, a small left-hand tributary to Nottoway River in Nottoway County.
Long; small left-hand branch of Nottoway River in Nottoway County.
Long; branch, a small right-hand tributary to Levisa Fork in Buchanan County.
Long; branch, a small right-hand tributary to Potomac River in Fairfax County.
Long; island in Roanoke River in Pittsylvania County.
Long; marshy island in Back Bay in Princess Anne County.
Long; mountains in Campbell County. Elevation, 1,000 feet.
Long; post village in Page County.
Long; run, a small right-hand tributary to James River in Botetourt County.
Longcreek; post village in Louisa County.
Long Dale; mines in North Mountains in Alleghany County.
Longdale; post village in Alleghany County on the Chesapeake and Ohio Railway. Altitude, 1,166 feet.
Long Drive; mountains in Augusta County. Elevation, 2,500 feet.
Longfield; post village in Lee County.
Longglade; post village in Augusta County.
Long Glade; run, a small left-hand tributary to Shenandoah River in Augusta County.
Longhollow; post village in Smyth County.
Long Meadow; creek, a small tributary to Shenandoah River in Augusta County.
Long Mountain; post village in Amherst County.
Long Mountain; summit in Amherst County.
Long Ridge; summit in Page County.
Longs Gap; post village in Grayson County.
Longs Shop; post village in Montgomery County.
Longspur; post village in Bland County.
Longview; post village in Isle of Wight County.
Longwood; post village in Rockbridge County.
Lookout; mountains in Augusta County. Elevation, 2,000 to 2,500 feet.
Looney; creek, a small right-hand branch of Levisa Fork, rising in Buchanan County.
Looney; creek, a small right-hand tributary to Powell River in Wise County.
Looney; post village in Craig County.
Looneys Mill; creek, a small right-hand tributary to James River in Botetourt County.
Loop; summit in Rockbridge County. Elevation, 2,500 feet.
Loretto; post village in Essex County.
Lorne; post village in Caroline County
Lorraine; post village in Henrico County on the Chesapeake and Ohio Railway.
Lorton Valley; post village in Fairfax County.
Lost; creek, a small right-hand branch of Guest River in Wise County.
Lost; mountains in Roanoke County. Elevation, 2,000 feet.

Lost; mountains in Fauquier County. Elevation, 750 feet.
Lost Mountain; summit in Madison County.
Lot; post village in Middlesex County.
Lots; gap in Mays Mountain.
Lottie; post village in Rappahannock County.
Lottsburg; post village in Northumberland County.
Lotus; post village in Wise County.
Loudoun; county, situated in the northern part of the State in the Piedmont region, the western boundary being the summit of the Blue Ridge and northern and eastern boundaries being Potomac River. The surface is mainly rolling, and it is traversed by the Catoctin Mountain, Short Hill, and the eastern slopes of the Blue Ridge. Most of its area lies below the 500-foot level. Area, 519 square miles. Population, 21,948—white, 16,079; negro, 5,868; foreign born, 101. County seat, Leesburg. The mean magnetic declination in 1900 was 3° 15′. The mean annual rainfall is 40 to 50 inches, and the temperature 50° to 55°. The county is traversed by the Southern Railway.
Loudoun Heights; summit in the Blue Ridge on the south side of Harpers Ferry Gap.
Louisa; county, situated in the central part of the State in the Piedmont region. It has an undulating surface, and lies but a few hundred feet above sea level. Area, 529 square miles. Population, 16,517—white, 7,896; negro, 8,621; foreign born, 49. County seat, Louisa. The mean magnetic declination in 1900 was 3° 35′. The mean annual rainfall is 40 to 50 inches, and the temperature 55° to 60°. The county is traversed by the Chesapeake and Ohio Railway.
Louisa; county seat of Louisa County on the Chesapeake and Ohio Railway. Population, 261.
Loup; creek, a small left-hand tributary to Clinch River in Russell County.
Louse; creek, a small left-hand tributary to Roanoke River in Charlotte County.
Love; post village in Nelson County.
Love; run, a small right-hand tributary to Shenandoah River in Augusta County.
Lovelady; creek, a small right-hand branch of North Fork of Clinch River in Lee County.
Lovelady; creek, a small left-hand tributary to James River in Amherst County.
Lovelady; gap in Powell Mountain, made by Lovelady Creek, in Lee County.
Lovelady Mountain; summit in Amherst County.
Lovels; creek, a small left-hand tributary to Yadkin River in Patrick County.
Love Mills; village in Washington County.
Lovett; point on Elizabeth River in Norfolk County.
Lovettsville; town in Loudoun County. Population, 97.
Lovingston; county seat of Nelson County.
Low; gap in Grayson County.
Low; gap in Sandy Ridge Mountains in Russell County.
Lower; gap in Back Creek Mountains, made by Back Creek, a left-hand tributary to James River in Highland County.
Lower Field; small right-hand branch of Slate Creek in Buchanan County.
Lowesville; post village in Amherst County.
Lowland, post village in Washington County.
Lowmoor; post village in Alleghany County on the Chesapeake and Ohio Railway. Altitude, 1,156 feet.
Lowry; post village in Bedford County on the Norfolk and Western Railway. Altitude, 779 feet.
Loyalty; post village in Loudoun County.
Lucia; post village in Henry County.
Luckets; post village in Loudoun County.
Lula; post village in Charlotte County.

Luma; village in Washington County.
Lumberton; post village in Sussex County.
Lundy; post village in Grayson County.
Lunenburg; county, situated in the southern part of the State in the Piedmont region. It has an undulating surface with an altitude of from 300 to 500 feet above sea level. Area, 471 square miles. Population, 11,705—white, 5,133; negro, 6,572; foreign born, 122; county seat Lunenburg. The mean magnetic declination in 1900 was 3°. The mean annual rainfall is 50 inches, and the temperature 55° to 60°. The county is traversed by the Seaboard Air Line and the Southern railways.
Lunenberg; county seat of Lunenburg County.
Lunette; post village in Loudoun County.
Lunsford; post village in Cumberland County.
Luray; county seat of Page County on the Norfolk and Western Railway. Altitude, 819 feet. Population, 1,147.
Lurich; post village in Giles County on the Norfolk and Western Railway. Altitude, 1,526 feet.
Luster; fork, a small left-hand branch of Knox Creek, rising in Buchanan County.
Lux; post village in Dinwiddie County.
Lydia; post village in Greene County.
Lyells; post village in Richmond County.
Lylevue; post village in Botetourt County.
Lynch; creek, a small left-hand tributary to James River in Nelson County.
Lynch; river, a small left-hand tributary to James River in Greene and Albemarle counties.
Lynchburg; city, independent in government, situated in Campbell County, on the Chesapeake and Ohio, the Norfolk and Western, and the Southern railways. Altitude, 524 feet. Population, 18,891.
Lynchburg; mines in the western part of the Blue Ridge in Botetourt County.
Lynch Station; post village in Campbell County on the Seaboard Air Line Railway.
Lyndhurst; post village in Augusta County on the Norfolk and Western Railway. Altitude, 1,337 feet.
Lynhams; post village in Northumberland County.
Lynne Camp; branch, a small right-hand tributary to Levisa Fork in Buchanan County.
Lynn Haven; inlet, a passage through the bordering sand bar on the southeast coast.
Lynnhaven; post village in Princess Anne County on the Norfolk and Western Railway.
Lynn Haven; river, rising in Princess Anne County and flowing north through Lynn Haven Inlet into Chesapeake Bay.
Lynn Haven; roads, a harbor at the mouth of Lynn Haven River, by which it is connected with Chesapeake Bay, in Princess Anne County.
Lynnville; creek, a small right-hand branch of Roanoke River in Franklin County.
Lynnville; ford in Roanoke River in Franklin County.
Lynville; mountains in Bedford County. Elevation, 1,500 to 2,000 feet.
Lynnwood; post village in Rockingham County.
Lyon; gap in Walker Mountains in Smyth County.
Lytton; ford in Powell River in Lee County.
Mableton; post village in Hanover County.
MacAfee Knob; summit in Catawba Mountains in Roanoke County. Elevation, 3,201 feet.
Macanie; post village in Shenandoah County.
McClellan; post village in Isle of Wight County.
McClung; post village in Bath County.

McClung Ridge; mountains in Bath County.
McClure; fork, a small left-hand branch of Russell Fork, rising in Dickenson County.
McConnell; post village in Scott County on the Norfolk and Western Railway.
Maccrady; post village in Smyth County.
McDaniel; small left-hand branch of North Fork of Holston River in Smyth County.
McDonalds Mill; post village in Montgomery County.
McDowell; town in Highland County. Population, 136.
McDuff; post village in Caroline County.
Maceo; post village in Dinwiddie County.
Maces Spring; post village in Scott County.
McFalls; branch, a small right-hand tributary to James River in Botetourt County.
McFalls; mountain in Bedford County. Elevation, 2,426 feet.
McFarlands; post village in Lunenburg County.
McGaheysville; post village in Rockingham County on the Chesapeake Western Railway.
McGavock; river, a small left-hand tributary to New River in Wythe County.
McGehees; post village in Fluvanna County.
McGrady; creek, a small right-hand branch of North Fork of Holston River in Smyth County.
McGraw; gap in Alleghany County caused by Smyth Creek.
McHenry; creek, a small left-hand tributary to North Fork of Holston River in Washington County.
McHenry; post village in Spottsylvania County.
Machipongo; post village in Northampton County on the New York, Philadelphia and Norfolk Railroad.
Machodoc; creek, a small right-hand branch of Potomac River in King George County.
Machodoc; post village in Westmoreland County.
McHolt; post village in Halifax County.
McInturf; gap in Short Mountain in Shenandoah County.
McIvors; station in Amherst County on the Richmond and Danville Railway. Altitude, 704 feet.
Mack; creek, a small right-hand branch of New River in Pulaski County.
Mack; mountains in Pulaski and Floyd counties. Elevation, 2,000 to 3,404 feet.
Mackalls Hill; summit in Fairfax County.
MacKeever; ferry over Roanoke River in Fairfax County.
McKenney; post village in Dinwiddie County on the Seaboard Air Line Railroad.
Mackie; post village in Norfolk County.
McKinley; post village in Augusta County.
MacMullen; post village in Green County on the Norfolk and Western Railway.
Macon; post village in Powhatan County on the Farmville and Powhatan Railroad.
MacRaes; post village in Cumberland County on the Farmville and Powhatan Railroad.
McVeigh; ford of Roanoke River in Bedford County.
Madcap; creek, a small right-hand tributary to Roanoke River in Franklin County.
Maddux; post village in Nottoway County.
Madison; county, situated in the northern part of the State in the Piedmont region. Its southeastern part is rolling with a few isolated summits, while the western part is made up of heavy spurs of the Blue Ridge. The elevation ranges from 300 to 4,000 feet, the latter being in the Blue Ridge summits. Area, 336 square miles. Population, 10,216—white, 6,695; negro, 3,521; foreign born, 6. County seat, Madison. The mean magnetic declination in 1900 was 3° 30′. The mean annual rainfall is 50 to 55 inches, and the temperature 50°.

Madison; county seat of Madison County on the Chesapeake and Ohio Railway.
Madison; run, a small right-hand branch of Shenandoah River in Rockingham County.
Madison Mill; branch, a small left-hand tributary to Roanoke River in Charlotte County.
Madison Mills; post village in Madison County.
Madison Run; post village in Orange County.
Madisonville; post village in Charlotte County.
Madrid; post village in Augusta County.
Mad Sheep; summit in Alleghany Front in Bath County.
Mad Tom; summit in Alleghany Front in Bath County.
Maggie; post village in Craig County.
Maggoty; creek, a small left-hand tributary to Staunton River in Franklin County.
Maggoty; gap in the western part of the Blue Ridge, caused by a small branch of Back Creek, in Roanoke County.
Maggoty; small right-hand tributary to Roanoke River in Franklin County.
Magnet; post village in Isle of Wight County.
Magnolia; post village in Nansemond County.
Magruder; post village in York County.
Mahala; post village in Loudoun County.
Mahoney; post village in Bland County.
Maiden; branch, a small left-hand tributary to North Fork of Holston River in Washington County.
Maidens; post village in Goochland County on the Chesapeake and Ohio Railway.
Maiden Spring; creek, a left-hand tributary to Clinch River, rising in Tazewell County.
Main Top Mountain; summit in Nelson County.
Major; post village in Grayson County on the Chesapeake and Ohio Railway.
Mallory; branch, a small left-hand tributary to Nottoway River in Nottoway County.
Mallory; post village in Louisa County.
Mallorys; creek, a small right-hand branch of James River in Buckingham County.
Mallow; post village in Alleghany County on the Pennsylvania Railroad.
Malone; bridge across Rowanty Creek in Dinwiddie County.
Malva; post village in Mecklenburg County.
Malvern Hill; post village in Henrico County.
Manassas; gap in the Blue Ridge in Warren County.
Manassas; county seat of Prince William County on the Chesapeake and Ohio and the Southern railways. Population, 817.
Manchester; city in Chesterfield County, but independent in government; on the Atlantic Coast Line, Seaboard Air Line, and the Southern railroads. Population, 9,715.
Manchester; run, a small right-hand branch of James River in Prince George County.
Maness; post village in Scott County.
Mangohick; post village in King William County.
Manila; post village in Franklin County.
Mannboro; post village in Amelia County.
Manquin; post village in King William County.
Manry; post village in Southampton County.
Mansfield; post village in Louisa County.
Mansion; village in Campbell County.
Mantapike; post village in King and Queen County.
Manteo; post village in Buckingham County.

Manteo; station in Nelson County on the Chesapeake and Ohio Railway.
Maple; branch, a small right-hand tributary to New River in Pulaski County.
Maple; post village in Botetourt County.
Maplegrove; post village in Westmoreland County.
Mapleton; post village in Princess Anne County.
Maplewood; post village in Amelia County on the Southern Railway.
Mappsburg; post village in Accomac County on the New York, Philadelphia and Norfolk Railroad.
Mappsville; post village in Accomac County.
Marble Valley; post village in Augusta County.
Marengo; post village in Mecklenburg County.
Marganna; post village in Culpeper County,
Marion; county seat of Smyth County on the Norfolk and Western Railway. Altitude, 2,124 feet. Population, 2,045.
Marionville; post village in Northampton County.
Markham; post village in Fauquier County on the Southern Railway. Altitude, 552 feet.
Marksville; post village in Page County on the Norfolk and Western Railway. Altitude, 1,063 feet.
Marl; post village in Prince George County.
Marlboro; point on Potomac River in Stafford County.
Marlboro; post village in Frederick County.
Marlbrook; post village in Rockbridge County on the Norfolk and Western Railway. Altitude, 1,162 feet.
Marlbrook; run, a small left-hand tributary to James River in Rockbridge County.
Marmion; post village in Rockbridge County.
Marmora; post village in Dinwiddie County.
Marrowbone; creek, a small left-hand tributary to Roanoke River in Appomattox County.
Marrowbone; creek, a small right-hand tributary to Appomattox River in Prince Edward County.
Marsh; run, a small left-hand branch of Rappahannock River in Fauquier County.
Marshall; creek, a small left-hand tributary to Appomatox River in Chesterfield County.
Marshall; post village in Fauquier County on the Southern Railway.
Marshall; run, a small left-hand tributary to Shenandoah River in Rockingham County.
Marsh Market; post village in Accomac County.
Martin; branch, a small left-hand tributary to Roanoke River in Charlotte County.
Martin; creek, a right-hand branch of Powell River in Lee County.
Martin; creek, a small left-hand tributary to Roanoke River in Appomattox County.
Martin; village in Henry County.
Martins Store; post village in Halifax County.
Martinsville; county seat of Henry County; on the Danville and Western and the Norfolk and Western railways. Altitude, 934 feet. Population, 2,384.
Marumsco; creek, a small right-hand branch of Potomac River in Prince William County.
Marye; a post village in Spottsylvania County.
Mary Gray; summit in Augusta County.
Marysville; post village in Campbell County. Altitude, 525 feet.
Maryus; post village in Gloucester County.
Masada; post village in Washington County.
Mascot; post village in King and Queen County.
Mason; creek, a small left-hand branch of Roanoke River in Roanoke County.

Mason; creek, a small right-hand tributary to Roanoke River in Roanoke County.
Mason; creek in Princess Anne County emptying into Willoughby Bay.
Mason; island in Potomac River in Loudoun County.
Mason Cove; small branch of Mason Creek tributary to Roanoke River in Roanoke County.
Mason Knob; summit in Roanoke County. Elevation, 3,217 feet.
Masons Depot; post village in Sussex County on the Southern Railway.
Masons Store; county seat of Russell County.
Massanetta Springs; village in Rockingham County.
Massanutten; mountains in the Shenandoah Valley between the forks of Shenandoah River. Elevation, 1,500 to 2,500 feet.
Massanutton; post village in Page County.
Massaponax; river, a small right-hand branch of Rappahannock River in Spottsylvania County.
Massaponax; post village in Spottsylvania County.
Massey; post village in Accomac County.
Massie Mountain; summit in Nelson County.
Massies Mill; post village in Nelson County.
Masters; post village in Alleghany County.
Mat; river, a small right-hand tributary to Mattaponi River in Spottsylvania County.
Mathews; county, situated in the eastern part of the State on the west coast of Chesapeake Bay. The surface is level and but little elevated above the sea. Area, 92 square miles. Population, 8,239—white, 5,844; negro, 2,395; foreign-born, 13. County seat, Mathews. The mean magnetic declination in 1900 was 4° 57′. The mean annual rainfall is 40 to 50 inches, and the temperature 55° to 60°.
Mathews; creek, a small right-hand tributary to James River in Buckingham County.
Mathews; county seat of Mathews County.
Mathias Point; post village in King George County.
Matilda; post village in Bedford County.
Matoaca; post village in Chesterfield County on the Chesapeake and Ohio Railway.
Matta; river, a small right-hand branch of Mattaponi River in Caroline County.
Mattaponi; river, heading in the Piedmont region and flowing southeast to its junction with the Pamunkey to form York River; navigable to Mundy Bridge, a distance of 55 miles.
Mattoax; post village in Amelia County on the Southern Railway.
Mattox; creek, a small right-hand branch of Potomac River in Westmoreland and King George counties.
Matts; creek, a small right-hand branch of James River in Bedford County.
Mauck; post village in Page County.
Maurertown; post village in Shenandoah County on the Baltimore and Ohio Railroad. Altitude, 788 feet.
Mauzy; village in Rockingham County.
Max; post village in Carroll County.
Max Meadows; post village in Wythe County on the Norfolk and Western Railway. Altitude, 2,015 feet.
Maxwell; post village in Tazewell County, on the Norfolk and Western Railway. Altitude, 2,356 feet.
Maxwelton; post village in Halifax County.
May; creek, a small left-hand branch of James River in Nelson County.
Mayberry; post village in Patrick County.
Maybrook; post village in Giles County.
Mayland; village in Rockingham County.

Mayo; post village in Halifax County.
Mayoforge; village in Patrick County.
Mays; mountain in Wythe County. Elevation, 2,500 to 2,849 feet.
Maywood; post village in Craig County.
Meade; post village in Essex County.
Meadow; small right-hand branch of Potomac River in Stafford County.
Meadow; bridge across Chickahominy River in Hanover County.
Meadow; creek, a small right-hand tributary to James River in Buckingham County.
Meadow; creek, a small right-hand tributary to James River in Craig County.
Meadow; creek, a small right-hand tributary to New River in Montgomery County.
Meadow; fork, a small right-hand fork of Straight Creek in Lee County.
Meadow; run, a small right-hand tributary to New River in Floyd County.
Meadow; run, a small left-hand tributary to James River in Highland County.
Meadowcreek; post village in Grayson County.
Meadowdale; post village in Highland County.
Meadow Mills; post village in Frederick County.
Meadows of Dan; post village in Patrick County.
Meadow Station; post village in Henrico County.
Meadowview; post village in Washington County on the Norfolk and Western Railway. Altitude, 2,138 feet.
Meadowville; post village in Chesterfield County.
Meadville; post village in Halifax County.
Mears; post village in Accomac County.
Mearsville; post village in Accomac County.
Mecca; post village in Pulaski County.
Mechanicsburg; town in Bland County. Population, 113.
Mechanicsville; post village in Loudoun County.
Mechum; creek, a small left-hand tributary to James River in Albemarle and Fluvanna counties.
Mechumps; creek, a small right-hand branch of Pamunkey River.
Mechum River; post village in Albemarle County on the Chesapeake and Ohio Railway.
Mecklenburg; county, situated in the southern part of the State in the eastern part of the Piedmont region, bordering the North Carolina line. It has a rolling surface, and elevated only about 300 to 500 feet. Area, 640 square miles. Population, 26,551—white, 10,353; negro, 16,198; foreign born, 64. County seat, Boydton. The mean magnetic declination in 1900 was 3°. The mean annual rainfall is 50 to 60 inches, and the temperature 55° to 60°. The county is traversed by the Seaboard Air Line and the Southern railways.
Medina; village in Washington County.
Medley; village in Roanoke County.
Medlock; post village in Louisa County.
Meetinghouse; small left-hand branch of Slate Creek in Buchanan County.
Meetze; post village in Fauquier County on the Southern Railway.
Meherrin; post village in Lunenburg County on the Southern Railway. Altitude, 589 feet.
Meherrin; river, a head branch of Chowan River in southeastern part of the State.
Melfa; post village in Accomac County on the New York, Philadelphia and Norfolk Railroad.
Melita; post village in Buckingham County.
Melrose; village in Rockingham County.
Meltons; post village in Louisa County on the Chesapeake and Ohio Railway. Altitude, 519 feet.

Menchville; post village in Warwick County on the Chesapeake and Ohio Railway.
Mendota; post village in Washington County on the Virginia and Southwestern Railway.
Menla; post village in Pittsylvania County.
Mentow; post village in Bedford County.
Mercerville; post village in Louisa County.
Meredithville; post village in Brunswick County.
Meridian; post village in Dinwiddie County.
Meriwether; post village in Pittsylvania County.
Merrifield; post village in Fairfax County.
Merrimac; post village in Culpeper County.
Merrypoint; post village in Lancaster County.
Messick; post village in York County.
Messongo; post village in Accomac County.
Metomkin; point on Potomac River in King George County.
Metomkin; post village in Accomac County.
Meyerhoeffers Store; village in Rockingham County.
Meyrick; village in Bedford County.
Michaux; post village in Powhatan County.
Middle; creek, a small right-hand tributary to James River in Craig and Botetourt counties.
Middle; creek, a small right-hand branch of Clinch River in Tazewell County.
Middle; mountain in Craig County.
Middle; mountain in Rockbridge County.
Middle; mountains in Augusta County.
Middle; mountains in Highland County. Elevation, 3,500 to 4,000 feet.
Middle; mountains in Page County. Elevation, 2,000 to 2,500 feet.
Middle; river, a branch of Shenandoah River in Augusta County.
Middle; river, a small right-hand tributary to Potomac River in Fairfax County.
Middle; run, a small right-hand tributary to Rappahannock River in Greene County.
Middlebrook; post village in Augusta County.
Middleburg; town in Loudoun County. Population, 296.
Middle Elk; creek, a small right-hand branch of Knox Creek, rising in Buchanan County.
Middle Fox; creek, a small right-hand tributary to New River in Grayson County.
Middle Ridge; mountains in Franklin County.
Middlesex; county, situated in the eastern part of the State on the south side of Rappahannock River, and extending to the west shore of Chesapeake Bay. The surface is level and but little elevated. Area, 156 square miles. Population, 8,220—white, 3,684; negro, 4,536; foreign born, 6. County seat, Saluda. The mean magnetic declination in 1900 was 4° 15′. The mean annual rainfall is 40 to 50 inches, and the temperature 55° to 60°.
Middletown; town in Frederick County on the Baltimore and Ohio Railroad. Altitude, 660 feet. Population, 423.
Midland; post village in Fauquier County on the Southern Railway.
Midlothian; post village in Chesterfield County on the Southern Railway.
Midvale; post village in Rockbridge County on the Norfolk and Western Railway.
Midway; post village in Halifax County.
Midway; small right-hand tributary to Levisa Fork in Buchanan County.
Midway Mills; post village in Nelson County on the Chesapeake and Ohio Railway.
Mike; post village in Campbell County.
Mila; post village in Northumberland County.
Mile; run, a small right-hand branch of Shenandoah River in Rockingham County.

Milford; post village in Caroline County on the Richmond, Fredericksburg and Piedmont Railroad.
Mill; small right-hand branch of Roanoke River in Roanoke County.
Mill; small branch of Walker Creek in Giles County.
Mill; branch, a small left-hand tributary to Roanoke River in Bedford County.
Mill; small right-hand branch of Powell River in Wise County.
Mill; branch, a small right-hand tributary to Levisa Fork in Buchanan County.
Mill; creek, a small left-hand branch of North Fork of Holston River in Smyth County.
Mill; creek, a small left-hand branch of South Fork of Holston River in Washington County.
Mill; creek, a small left-hand tributary to Clinch River, rising in Scott County.
Mill; creek, a small right-hand tributary to New River in Montgomery County.
Mill; creek, a small right-hand branch of Wolf Creek, a tributary to New River in Giles County.
Mill; creek, a small right-hand branch of Guest River in Wise County.
Mill; creek, a small right-hand branch of Rappahannock River in Caroline County.
Mill; creek, a small left-hand tributary to James River in Amherst and Rockbridge counties.
Mill; creek, a small right-hand branch of Roanoke River in Pittsylvania County.
Mill; creek, a small right-hand branch of Powell River in Lee County.
Mill; creek, a small right-hand tributary to Jackson River in Craig County.
Mill; creek, a small left-hand branch of Shenandoah River in Rockingham County.
Mill; creek, a small left-hand branch of James River in Botetourt County.
Mill; creek, a small right-hand tributary to James River in Botetourt County.
Mill; creek, a small right-hand tributary to Roanoke River in Franklin County.
Mill; creek, a small right-hand branch of Clinch River in Tazewell and Russell counties.
Mill; creek, a small right-hand tributary to Shenandoah River in Page County.
Mill; gap in Little Mountains caused by East Branch, a left-hand tributary to James River, in Highland County.
Mill; mountains in Bath, Rockbridge, and Alleghany counties. Elevation, 2,000 feet.
Mill; post village in Carroll County.
Mill; run, a small right-hand tributary to Jackson River in Alleghany County.
Mill or North Buckskin; creek, a small right-hand tributary to Appomattox River in Amelia County.
Millbank; post village in Prince Edward County.
Millboro; post village in Bath County on the Chesapeake and Ohio Railway. Altitude, 1,680 feet.
Millboro Spring; post village in Bath County.
Millburn; post village in Buckingham County.
Milldale; post village in Warren County.
Millenbeck; post village in Lancaster County.
Miller; branch, a small right-hand tributary to Jackson River in Alleghany County.
Miller; creek, a small left-hand tributary to New River in Wythe County.
Miller; creek, a small right-hand tributary to Appomattox River in Prince Edward County.
Miller; run, a small right-hand branch of James River in Buckingham County.
Millers; cove in Roanoke County.
Millers; creek, a small right-hand tributary to New River in Wythe County.
Millers; ford in Roanoke River in Pittsylvania County.
Millers; mountain in Bedford County. Elevation, 1,413 feet.
Millers Knob; summit in Rockingham County.

Millers Tavern; post village in Essex County.
Millgap; post village in Highland County.
Millington; post village in Albemarle County.
Mill Mountain; summit in Roanoke County. Elevation, 1,721 feet.
Mill Mountain; summit on State line in Shenandoah County, extending into Hardy County, W. Va.
Mill Ridge; mountains in Alleghany County. Elevation, 2,000 to 2,500 feet.
Mills; creek, a small right hand tributary to Shenandoah River in Augusta County.
Mills; mountains in Botetourt and Roanoke counties. Elevation, 1,500 to 2,806 feet.
Millstone; small right-hand branch of Clinch River in Tazewell County.
Millwood; post village in Clarke County on the Baltimore and Ohio Railroad.
Milnesville; post village in Augusta County.
Milt; post village in Lee County.
Mine; creek, a small right-hand tributary to New River in Carroll County.
Mine; mountain in Rockingham County. Elevation, 2,500 feet.
Mine; run, a small right-hand tributary to Rappahannock River in Orange County.
Minebank; post village in Frederick County.
Mineral; post village in Louisa County.
Minerun; post village in Orange County.
Minerva; post village in Carroll County.
Mingo; village in Franklin County.
Mink Hill; sand hill in Princess Anne County near the eastern coast.
Minneola; post village in Pittsylvania County.
Minnieville; post village in Prince William County.
Minor; post village in Essex County.
Mint Spring; post village in Augusta County on the Baltimore and Ohio Railroad.
Miona; post village in Accomac County.
Mirafork; post village in Floyd County.
Miry; run, a small right-hand branch of Appomattox River in Dinwiddie County.
Miskimon; post village in Northumberland County.
Mitchell Knob; summit in Carroll County. Altitude, 3,240 feet.
Mitchells; post village in Culpeper County on the Southern Railway.
Mizphia; post village in Lunenburg County.
Moab; village in Washington County.
Mobjack; post village in Mathews County.
Moccasin Ridge; mountains in Scott and Russell counties. Elevation, 2,500 feet
Model; village in Rockingham County.
Modest; creek, a small right-hand tributary to Nottoway River in Lunenburg County.
Modesttown; post village in Accomac County.
Modoc; village in Henry County.
Moffats Creek; post village in Augusta County.
Moffet; post village in Halifax County on the Southern Railway.
Moffets; creek, a small left-hand tributary to James River in Rockbridge and Augusta counties.
Moffett; run, a small left-hand tributary to Shenandoah River in Augusta County.
Mohawk; creek, a small right-hand branch of James River in Powhatan County.
Mohea; post village in Warwick County.
Mohemenco; post village in Powhatan County.
Mole; hill in Rockingham County.
Molina; post village in Warren County.
Moll; creek, a small left-hand tributary to Clinch River, rising in Russell County.
Molley; creek, a small left-hand tributary to Roanoke River in Campbell County.
Molusk; post village in Lancaster County.
Monarat; post village in Carroll County.

Monasco; mountain in Nelson County.
Monaskon; post village in Lancaster County.
Monday; post village in Floyd County.
Moneta; post village in Bedford County.
Monitor; post village in Amherst County.
Monmouth; post village in Rockbridge County.
Monrovia; post village in Orange County.
Montague; post village in Essex County.
Montebello; post village in Nelson County.
Monteithville; post village in Stafford County.
Monterey; county seat of Highland County. Population, 246. Altitude, 3,008 feet.
Monterey; mountains in Highland County. Elevation, 3,000 to 3,500 feet.
Montevideo; post village in Rockingham County on the Chesapeake Western Railway.
Montezuma; village in Rockingham County.
Montfort; village in Orange County.
Montgomery; county, situated in the western part of the State in the Appalachian Valley. Its surface consists in part of undulating country with some parallel ridges and valleys separating them. It is drained by Roanoke River. The altitude ranges from 1,200 to 3,000 feet. Area, 394 square miles. Population, 15,852—white, 12,927; negro, 2,925; foreign born, 37. County seat Christiansburg. The mean magnetic declination in 1900 was 1° 30'. The mean annual rainfall is 50 to 60 inches, and the temperature 50° to 55°. The county is traversed by the Norfolk and Western Railway.
Montgomery; post village in Washington County on the Norfolk and Western Railway. Altitude, 1,990 feet.
Montgomery Knob; summit in Rich Patch Mountains in Alleghany County. Elevation, 2,000 to 2,500 feet.
Montgomery Springs; post village in Montgomery County.
Montpelier; post village in Hanover County on the Southern Railway.
Montross; county seat of Westmoreland County.
Montvale; post village in Bedford County on the Norfolk and Western Railway.
Moody; post village in Hanover County.
Moomaw; village in Roanoke County.
Moore; small right-hand branch of Beaver Creek, rising in Washington County.
Moore; creek, a small left-hand tributary to James River in Albemarle County.
Moore; creek, a small right-hand tributary to James River in Rockbridge and Powhatan counties.
Moores Mill; post village in Henry County.
Moores Store; post village in Shenandoah County.
Moorings; post village in Surry County on the Surry, Sussex and Southampton Railroad.
Moormans; river, a small left-hand tributary to James River in Albemarle County.
Moormans River; post village in Albemarle County.
Moran; post village in Lancaster County on the Norfolk and Western Railway.
Moreland; gap in Short Mountains, caused by Gap Creek, in Shenandoah County.
Morgan; post village in Scott County.
Morly Mountain; summit in Amherst County.
Morris; hill in Alleghany County.
Morris Church; post village in Campbell County.
Morris Knob; summit in Tazewell County. Elevation, 4,510 feet.
Morrison; post village in Warwick County.
Morrisonville; post village in Loudoun County.

Morrisville; post village in Fauquier County.
Mortons; ford of Rapidan River in Culpeper County.
Morven; post village in Amelia County.
Mosby; post village in Fauquier County.
Moscow; post village in Augusta County.
Moseley; post village in Buckingham County on the Farmville and Powhatan and the Southern railroads.
Moseley Mountain; summit in Bedford County. Elevation, 1,268 feet.
Moseleys Junction; post village in Powhatan County on the Farmville and Powhatan Railroad.
Mossing Ford; post village in Charlotte County.
Mossneck; post village in Caroline County.
Mossy; creek, a small left-hand tributary to Shenandoah River in Augusta County.
Mossy; run, a small right-hand tributary to Jackson River in Alleghany County.
Mossycreek; post village in Augusta County on the Chesapeake Western Railway.
Motleys; post village in Pittsylvania County on the Southern Railway.
Mount; creek, a small right-hand branch of Rappahannock River in Caroline County.
Mount; post village in Stafford County.
Mountain; branch, a small left-hand tributary of James River in Rockbridge County.
Mountain; branch, a small left-hand tributary to Roanoke River in Appomattox County.
Mountain; creek, a small right-hand tributary to Appomatox River in Prince Edward County.
Mountain; fork, a small right-hand tributary to Clinch River in Scott County.
Mountain; lake in Giles County.
Mountain; run, a small left-hand tributary to Shenandoah River in Augusta County.
Mountain; run, a small right-hand tributary to Rappahannock River in Culpeper County.
Mountain; run, a small right-hand tributary to Rappahannock River in Orange County.
Mountain Falls; post village in Frederick County.
Mountaingap; post village in Loudoun County.
Mountaingrove; post village in Bath County.
Mountain Lake; post village in Giles County.
Mountain Road; post village in Halifax County.
Mountain Valley; post village in Henry County.
Mountainview; post village in Stafford County.
Mountairy; post village in Pittsylvania County.
Mount Alto; summit in Albemarle County.
Mount Athos; post village in Campbell County.
Mount Carmel; post village in Halifax County.
Mountcastle; post village in New Kent County on the Chesapeake and Ohio Railway.
Mount Clifton; village in Shenandoah County.
Mount Clinton; post village in Rockingham County.
Mount Crawford; town in Rockingham County on the Baltimore and Ohio Railroad. Altitude, 1,171 feet. Population, 330.
Mountcross; post village in Pittsylvania County.
Mount Erin; summit in Fairfax County.
Mountfair; post village in Albemarle County.
Mount Field; branch, a small right-hand tributary to Roanoke River in Pittsylvania County.
Mount Gilead; post village in Loudoun County.

Mount Holly; post village in Westmoreland County.

Mount Jackson; town in Shenandoah County on the Southern and the Baltimore and Ohio railroads. Altitude, 916 feet. Population, 472.

Mount Landing; post village in Essex County.

Mount Laurel; post village in Halifax County.

Mount Leigh; post village in Prince Edward County.

Mount Meridian; post village in Augusta County.

Mount Olive; post village in Shenandoah County.

Mount Pleasant; post village in Spottsylvania County on the Baltimore and Potomac Railroad.

Mount Pleasant; summit in Amherst County. Elevation, 4,098 feet.

Mount Sidney; town in Augusta County on the Baltimore and Ohio Railroad. Altitude, 1,258 feet. Population, 197.

Mount Solon; post village in Augusta County.

Mount Vernon on the Potomac; post village in Fairfax County on the Washington, Alexandria and Mount Vernon Electric Railway.

Mountville; post village in Loudoun County.

Mount Vinco; post village in Buckingham County.

Mount Williams; post village in Frederick County.

Mount Zion; post village in Campbell County.

Mouth of Wilson; post village in Grayson County.

Muckross; post village in Mecklenburg County.

Mud; creek, a small left-hand branch of Powell River in Lee County.

Mud; creek, a small right-hand tributary to Appomattox River in Prince Edward County.

Mud; fork, a small left-hand tributary to New River, rising in Grayson County.

Mud; fork, a small tributary to Bluestone River in Tazewell County.

Mud; run, a small left-hand tributary to James River in Amherst County.

Muddy; small creek emptying into North Bay in Princess Anne County.

Muddy; creek, a small left-hand branch of North Fork of Holston River, rising in Washington County.

Muddy; creek, a small left-hand branch of Rappahannock County.

Muddy; creek, a small left-hand tributary to Shenandoah River in Rockingham County.

Muddy; creek, a small right-hand tributary to James River in Buckingham County.

Muddy; creek, a small right-hand branch of James River in Powhatan and Cumberland counties.

Muddy; run, a small left-hand tributary to James River in Bath County.

Muddy; run, a small right-hand tributary to Rappahannock River in Culpeper County.

Mud Hole; gap in Three Top Mountains, caused by Little Passage Creek.

Mud Lick; creek, a small right-hand branch of Clinch River in Tazewell County.

Mud Lick; creek, a small right-hand branch of Roanoke River in Roanoke County.

Mud Lick; creek, a small right-hand tributary to Powell River in Wise County.

Mulberry; creek, a small left-hand tributary to Roanoke River in Appomattox County.

Mulberry Island; post village in Warwick County.

Mulch; post village in Richmond County.

Mullin; small right-hand branch of Slate Creek in Buchanan County.

Mumpower; village in Washington County.

Munden; post village in Princess Anne County on the Norfolk and Southern Railroad.

Mundy Point; post village in Northumberland County.

Mundys; post village in Amherst County.

Munford; post village in Botetourt County.

Munson Hill; summit in Fairfax County.

Murat; post village in Rockbridge County.
Murray; gap in western part of the Blue Ridge, caused by a small branch of Back Creek, in Roanoke County.
Murray Knob; summit in Franklin County.
Murrill; gap between Taylors and McFalls mountains in Bedford County.
Murtleville; post village in Stafford County.
Muse; post village in Augusta County.
Museville; post village in Pittsylvania County.
Musselman; post village in Stafford County.
Myndus; post village in Nelson County.
Myra; fork, a small right-hand tributary to New River in Floyd County.
Myron; post village in Prince William County.
Myrtle; post village in Nansemond County on the Norfolk and Western Railway.
Nace; post village in Botetourt County.
Naffs; post village in Franklin County.
Nahor; post village in Fluvanna County.
Nain; post village in Frederick County.
Naked; creek, a small left-hand tributary to Shenandoah River in Augusta County.
Naked; creek, a small right-hand branch of Shenandoah River between Page and Rockingham counties.
Naked; mountain in Nelson County.
Naked; mountain in Fauquier County. Elevation, 750 to 1,250 feet.
Nameless; post village in Campbell County.
Namozine; creek, a small right-hand branch of Appomattox River between Amelia and Dinwiddie counties.
Namozine; post village in Amelia County.
Nandua; post village in Accomac County.
Nansemond; county, situated in the southeastern part of the State on the Atlantic plain. It includes the western portion of the great Dismal Swamp with the bluffs and high ground bordering on the west. The high parts of the county consist of undulating country, rarely exceeding 100 feet in altitude. Area, 393 square miles. Population, 23,078—white, 10,115; negro, 12,962; foreign born, 88. County seat, Suffolk. The mean magnetic declination in 1900 was 3° 27.5'. The mean annual rainfall is 40 to 50 inches, and the temperature 55 to 60°. The county is traversed by the Atlantic Coast Line, the Norfolk and Western, the Seaboard Air Line, the Suffolk and Carolina, the Seaboard and Roanoke, and the Southern railroads.
Nansemond; river, heading in the Atlantic plain and flowing northeast into James River just above its mouth. It is navigable to Town Point.
Naola; post village in Amherst County.
Naples; post village in Highland County.
Napoleon; village in Chesterfield County.
Naptha; post village in Brunswick County.
Narcott; post village in Floyd County.
Narrow; creek, a small right-hand tributary to Roanoke River in Roanoke County.
Narrow Back; mountains in Rockingham and Augusta counties. Elevation, 2,000 to 2,500 feet.
Narrow Passage; creek, a small left-hand tributary to Shenandoah River in Shenandoah County.
Narrows; post village in Giles County on the New River, Holston and Western and the Norfolk and Western railroads. Altitude, 1,547 feet.
Narseal; post village in Amherst County.
Naruna; post village in Campbell County on the Norfolk and Western Railway. Altitude, 646 feet.
Nasbie; post village in Dickenson County.

Nash; post village in Nelson County on the Farmville and Powhatan Railroad.
Nasons; post village in Orange County.
Nassawadox; post village in Northampton County on the New York, Philadelphia and Norfolk Railroad.
Nasturtium; post village in Floyd County.
Natal; post village in Pittsylvania County.
Nathalie; post village in Halifax County on the Norfolk and Western Railway. Altitude, 510 feet.
National Soldiers Home; post village in Elizabeth City County.
Nat Lick; branch, a small left-hand tributary to New River in Pulaski County.
Natural Bridge; post village in Rockbridge County on the Norfolk and Western and the Chesapeake and Ohio railways. Altitude, 736 feet.
Navy; post village in Fairfax County.
Nawney; small creek emptying into Back Bay in Princess Anne County.
Naylors; post village in Richmond County.
Neabsco Mills; post village in Prince William County on the Baltimore and Potomac Railroad.
Neals; creek, a small right-hand tributary to Appomattox River in Amelia County.
Neapsco; creek, a small right-hand branch of Potomac River in Prince William County.
Neathery; post village in Halifax County.
Nebletts; post village in Lunenburg County.
Nebo; post village in Smyth County.
Neck; creek, a small left-hand branch of New River in Pulaski County.
Neck; post village in Culpeper County.
Need; post village in Franklin County.
Neenah; post village in Westmoreland County.
Neersville; post village in Loudoun County.
Negro; post village in Hanover County.
Negro; run, a small left-hand tributary to York River, forming the boundary line between Orange and Louisa counties.
Negroarm; post village in Powhatan County on the Farmville and Powhatan Railroad. Altitude, 2,136 feet.
Neill; post village in King George County.
Nellysford; post village in Nelson County.
Nelson; county, situated in the central part of the State in the upper part of the Piedmont region, its western boundary being the summit of the Blue Ridge. The eastern part has a rolling surface, and the western part is greatly broken by short ridges, outliers of the Blue Ridge. It is drained by James River. The altitude varies from a few hundred feet up to 4,000 feet in the Blue Ridge summit. Area, 472 square miles. Population, 16,075—white, 10,403; negro, 5,672; foreign born, 39. County seat, Lovingston. The mean magnetic declination in 1900 was 2° 30′. The mean annual rainfall is 50 inches, and the temperature 55°. The county is traversed by the Southern and the Chesapeake and Ohio railways.
Nelson; ferry across Pamunkey River in Hanover County.
Nelson; fork, a small right-hand tributary to James River in Buckingham County.
Nelson; post village in Mecklenburg County on the Southern Railway.
Nelsonia; post village in Accomac County.
Nest; post village in Gloucester County.
Nester; post village in Carroll County.
Nethers; post village in Madison County.
Netta; post village in Brunswick County.
Nettle; creek, a small left-hand tributary to James River in Rockbridge County.
Nettle; mountains in Rockbridge County.

Nettleridge; post village in Patrick County.
Neva; village in Franklin County.
New; bridge across Chickahominy River in Hanover County.
New; river, formed by junction of North and South forks in Ashe County, N. C., flows north through Carroll, Wythe, Pulaski, and Giles counties, Va., into Kanawha River in Fayette County, W. Va.
New Baltimore; post village in Fauquier County.
Newbern; town in Pulaski County. Population, 152.
New Canton; post village in Buckingham County on the Chesapeake and Ohio Railway.
Newcastle; town and county seat in Craig County on the Chesapeake and Ohio Railway. Population, 299.
New Church; post village in Accomac County.
Newfound; river, a small right-hand tributary to York River in Hanover County.
New Glasgow; post village in Amherst County on the Southern Railway. Altitude, 714 feet.
New Hampden; post village in Highland County.
New Hope; town in Augusta County on the Potomac, Fredericksburg and Piedmont Railroad. Population, 124.
Newington; post village in Fairfax County.
New Kent; county, situated in the eastern part of the State on the Atlantic plain, between York and James rivers. The surface is low and level. Area, 233 square miles. Population, 4,865—white, 1,660; negro, 3,204; foreign born, 10. County seat, New Kent. The mean magnetic declination in 1900 was 4°. The mean annual rainfall is 40 to 50 inches, and the temperature 55° to 60°. The county is traversed by the Chesapeake and Ohio and the Southern railways.
New Kent; county seat of New Kent County.
Newland; post village in Richmond County.
New London; post village in Caroline County.
Newman Ridge; mountains in the southeastern part of Lee County, extending southwest into Tennessee.
Newmans; post village in Hanover County on the Chesapeake and Ohio Railway.
Newmarket; town in Shenandoah County on the Southern Railway. Population, 684.
New Plymouth; post village in Lunenburg County.
Newpoint; post village in Mathews County.
Newport; post village in Giles County.
Newport News; city in Warwick County, but independent in government. Population, 19,635. It has a large shipbuilding plant and much commerce.
Newriver Depot; post village in Pulaski County on the Norfolk and Western Railway. Altitude, 1,768 feet.
News Ferry; post village in Halifax County on the Southern Railway.
Newsoms; post village in Southampton County on the Seaboard Air Line Railway.
New Store; post village in Buckingham County.
Newton; creek, a small right-hand branch of Eastern Branch of Elizabeth River in Princess Anne County.
Newtown; post village in King and Queen County.
New Upton; post village in Gloucester County.
Newville; post village in Prince George County.
Nibbs; creek, a small right-hand tributary to Appomattox River in Amelia County.
Nicholls Knob; summit in Alleghany County. Elevation, 3,573 feet.
Nichols; small right-hand branch of Potomac River in Fairfax County.
Nick; post village in Albemarle County.
Nickelsville; post village in Scott County.
Nigger; creek, a small right-hand branch of James River in Buckingham County.

Nigger Head; summit in Nelson County.
Nigh Way; small right-hand branch of Slate Creek in Buchanan County.
Nile; post village in Prince Edward County.
Nimmo; post village in Princess Anne County.
Nimrod Hall; post village in Bath County.
Nindes Store; post village in King George County.
Nine Mile Spur; mountains in Wise County.
Nineveh; post village in Warren County.
Nininger; village in Bedford County.
Noble; village in Wythe County.
Noel; post village in Hanover County on the Chesapeake and Ohio Railway.
Nogo; post village in Lunenburg County.
Nokesville; post village in Prince William County on the Southern Railway.
Nokomis; post village in Northumberland County.
Nola; post village in Franklin County.
Noland; post village in Halifax County.
Nominygrove; post village in Westmoreland County.
Non Intervention; post village in Lunenburg County.
Nono; post village in Lunenburg County.
Nooning; creek, a small left-hand branch of Appomattox River in Chesterfield County.
Nordick; village in Washington County.
Nordyke; creek, a small left-hand branch of North Fork of Holston River, rising in Washington County.
Norfolk; city in Norfolk County, but independent in government, on the Atlantic Coast Line, the Chesapeake and Ohio, the New York, Philadelphia and Norfolk, the Norfolk and Southern, the Norfolk and Western, the Seaboard Air Line, and the Southern railroads. Population, 46,624.
Norfolk; county, situated in the southeastern part of the State. It consists entirely of lowland, most of it marshy, and includes the greater portion of the great Dismal Swamp. Little of the county has an altitude above sea exceeding 20 feet. Area, 425 square miles. Population, 50,780—white, 19,113; negro, 31,600; foreign born, 772. County seat, Portsmouth. The mean magnetic declination in 1900 was 4° 7.5'. The mean annual rainfall is 40 to 50 inches, and the temperature 55° to 60°. The county is traversed by the Atlantic Coast Line, the Seaboard and Roanoke, the Chesapeake and Ohio, the New York, Philadelphia and Norfolk, the Seaboard Air Line, the Southern, and the Norfolk and Western railroads.
Norma; post village in Westmoreland County.
Norman; post village in Culpeper County.
Norris; post village in Fauquier County.
Norris; run, a small right-hand branch of New River in Pulaski County.
North; bay, a lagoon on the southeastern coast separated from the Atlantic Ocean by a sand bar in Princess Anne County.
North; creek, a small right-hand tributary to James River in Appomattox and Botetourt counties.
North; mountains in Craig and Botetourt counties. Elevation, 2,000 to 3,000 feet.
North; mountains in Rockbridge and Alleghany counties. Elevation, 1,500 to 3,000 feet.
North; post village in Mathews County.
North; river, a left-hand branch of James River in Rockbridge County. The mean discharge at Glasgow is 985 cubic feet per second.
North; river, a left-hand branch of Shenandoah River in Augusta County. The mean discharge at Port Republic is 970½ cubic feet per second.

North; run, a small right-hand tributary to Chickahominy River in Henrico County.

Northampton; county, situated on the eastern peninsula of Virginia, extending into its southern end at Cape Charles. Its surface is low and level with much marshy land upon either side. Area, 232 square miles. Population, 13,770—white, 6,141; negro, 7,627; foreign born, 81. County seat, Eastville. The mean magnetic declination in 1900 was 4° 17.5′. The mean annual rainfall is 40 to 50 inches, and the temperature 55° to 60°. The county is traversed by the New York, Philadelphia and Norfolk Railroad.

North Anna; river, a small left-hand tributary to York River, forming the boundary between Orange, Louisa, and Spottsylvania counties.

Northbranch; post village in Grayson County.

North Business; creek, a small left-hand tributary to Walker Creek in Giles and Bland counties.

North East; creek, a left-hand tributary to York River in Spottsylvania County.

Northfork; post village in Loudoun County.

North Garden; post village in Albemarle County on the Southern Railway. Altitude, 634 feet.

North Landing; post village in Princess Anne County.

North Landing; river, rising in Princess Anne County and flowing south into Currituck Sound, North Carolina.

North River; gap between Narrow Back and Lookout mountains, caused by North River, in Augusta County.

North River; post village in Rockingham County.

North Shady; branch, a small right-hand tributary to New River in Floyd County.

Northside; town in Henrico County. Population, 584.

North Tazewell; town in Tazewell County. Population, 320.

Northumberland; county, situated in the eastern part of the State on the Atlantic plain, bordering Chesapeake Bay on the south side of the Potomac. Its surface is level and but little elevated above tide. Area, 235 square miles. Population, 9,846—white, 5,680; negro, 4,166; foreign born, 80. County seat, Heathsville. The mean magnetic declination in 1900 was 4° 30′. The mean annual rainfall is 40 to 50 inches, and the temperature 55° to 60°.

Northview; post village in Mecklenburg County.

Northwest; canal connecting Dismal Swamp Canal with Northwest River in Norfolk County.

North West; marshy river rising in Norfolk County and flowing into Currituck Sound, North Carolina.

Northwest; post village in Norfolk County on the Norfolk and Southern Railroad.

Norton; town in Wise County on the Louisville and Nashville and the Norfolk and Western railroads, and the Wise Terminal Company. Altitude, 2,133 feet. Population, 654.

Nortonsville; post village in Albemarle County.

Norvello; post village in Mecklenburg County.

Norwood; post village in Nelson County on the Chesapeake and Ohio Railway.

Nottoway; county, situated in the central part of the State in the Piedmont region. It has an undulating surface. Altitude, 200 to 500 feet. Area, 304 square miles. Population, 12,366—white, 4,966; negro, 7,400; foreign born, 75. County seat, Nottoway. The mean magnetic declination in 1900 was 3° 35′. The mean annual rainfall is 40 to 50 inches, and the temperature 55° to 60°. The county is traversed by the Norfolk and Western and the Southern railways.

Nottoway; county seat in Nottoway County on the Norfolk and Western Railway.

Nottoway; river of southeast Virginia; one of the sources of Chowan River.

Novum; post village in Madison County.

Nowlins Mill; post village in Franklin County.

Nuckols; post village in Buckingham County.
Nunley; post village in Russell County.
Nunn; post village in Mecklenburg County.
Nurneysville; post village in Nansemond County.
Nurseries; post village in Lee County.
Nutbush; post village in Lunenburg County.
Nutters; mountains in Craig County. Elevation, 2,000 to 2,500 feet.
Nuttree; creek, a small left-hand tributary to Appomattox River in Chesterfield County.
Nuttree; post village in Chesterfield County.
Nuttsville; post village in Lancaster County.
Ny; river, a small branch of Mattapony River in Spottsylvania and Caroline counties.
Nye; cove, in East River Mountain caused by Cove Creek.
Oak; post village in New Kent County.
Oakdale; post village in Rockbridge County.
Oakforest; post village in Cumberland County.
Oakgrove; post village in Westmoreland County.
Oakhall; post village in Accomac County on the New York, Philadelphia and Norfolk Railroad.
Oakland; post village in Louisa County.
Oaklette; post village in Norfolk County.
Oaklevel; village in Henry County.
Oakley; post village in Mecklenburg County.
Oak Mountain; branch, a small left-hand tributary to Roanoke River in Bedford County.
Oakpark; post village in Madison County.
Oakridge; post village in Nelson County on the Southern Railway.
Oakton; post village in Fairfax County.
Oaktree; post village in York County.
Oakview; post village in Mecklenburg County.
Oakville; post village in Appomattox County.
Oakwood; village in Rockingham County.
Oatlands; post village in Loudoun County.
Obey; creek, a small left-hand tributary to Clinch River in Scott County.
Ocala; post village in Carroll County.
Occoquan; creek, a small right-hand branch of Potomac River in Prince William County.
Occoquan; town in Prince William County on the Washington Southern Railway. Population, 297.
Occupacia; creek, a small right-hand branch of Rappahannock River in Essex County.
Occupacia; post village in Essex County.
Oceana; post village in Princess Anne County on the Norfolk and Western Railway.
Oceanview; post village in Norfolk County.
Ochre; post village in Chesterfield County on the Farmville and Powhatan Railroad.
Ocoonita; post village in Lee County on the Louisville and Nashville Railroad.
Ocran; post village in Lancaster County.
Octagon; post village in Brunswick County.
Octavia; post village in Buckingham County.
Offley; post village in Hanover County.
Ogburn; post village in Mecklenburg County.
Ogden; post village in Roanoke County.

Ogle; creek, a small right-hand tributary to Jackson River in Alleghany County.
Oglesby; small right-hand branch of New River in Grayson County.
Oilville; post village in Goochland County.
Oklahoma; post village in Carroll County.
Oldchurch; post village in Hanover County.
Oldenplace; post village in Dinwiddie County.
Oldfield; post village in Charles City County.
Oldhams; post village in Westmoreland County.
Old Mount Airy; summit in Wythe County. Elevation, 2,500 feet.
Old Town; creek, a small right-hand tributary to James River in Chesterfield County.
Oldtown; post village in Grayson County. Altitude, 2,485 feet.
Old Woman; creek, a small right-hand tributary to Roanoke River in Pittsylvania County.
Olesko; post village in Cumberland County.
Olga; post village in Amelia County.
Olinger; gap in Stone Mountain made by Powell River.
Olinger; post village in Lee County on the Louisville and Nashville Railroad.
Olive; post village in Culpeper County.
Oliver; mountains in Alleghany County. Elevation, 2,500 to 3,500 feet.
Oliver; post village in Hanover County.
Oliveville; post village in Nottoway County.
Ollie; post village in Alleghany County.
Olo; post village in Lunenburg County.
Olympia; post village in Smyth County.
Oma; post village in Culpeper County.
Omega; post village in Halifax County.
Omohundro; post village in Buckingham County.
Onan; post village in Nelson County.
Onancock; town in Accomac County. Population, 938.
Onawan; village in Rockingham County.
O'Neal; post village in Floyd County.
Oneida; branch, a small right-hand tributary to Wolf Creek in Tazewell County.
One Mile; creek, a small left-hand tributary to James River in Henrico County.
Onion Mountain; summit in Bedford County. Elevation, 3,828 feet.
Onley; post village in Accomac County on the New York, Philadelphia and Norfolk Railroad.
Ontario; post village in Charlotte County on the Southern Railway.
Onville; post village in Stafford County.
Opal; post village in Fauquier County.
Open; fork, a small left-hand tributary to Russell Fork, rising in Dickenson County.
Opequon; creek, a left-hand branch of Shenandoah River in Clarke and Berkeley counties.
Opequon; post village in Frederick County.
Ophelia; post village in Northumberland County.
Opie; post village in Mecklenburg County.
Opossum; small right-hand branch of North Fork of Holston River, rising in Hawkins County, Tenn.
Opossum; creek, a small right-hand branch of James River in Campbell County.
Opossum Hollow; small left-hand tributary to New River in Pulaski County.
Ora; post village in Washington County.
Oradell; post village in Grayson County.
Oral Oaks; post village in Lunenburg County.
Oranda; post village in Shenandoah County.

Orange; county, situated in the central part of the State in the Piedmont region. It has a rolling surface broken only by a few ridges, outliers of the Blue Ridge. The altitude ranges from 200 to 300 feet up to 1,200 feet. Area, 349 square miles. Population, 12,571—white, 7,050; negro, 5,519; foreign born, 60; county seat, Orange. The mean magnetic declination in 1900 was 3° 35′. The mean annual rainfall is 40 to 50 inches, and the temperature 55° to 60°. The county is traversed by the Chesapeake and Ohio, the Potomac, Frederick and Piedmont, and the Southern railroads.

Orange; county seat of Orange County on the Chesapeake and Ohio, the Potomac, Fredericksburg and Piedmont, and the Southern railroads. Altitude, 506 feet. Population, 536.

Orb; post village in Lunenburg County.
Orbit; post village in Isle of Wight County.
Orchid; post village in Louisa County.
Ordsburg; post village in Brunswick County.
Ordway; post village in Carroll County.
Orebank; post village in Buckingham County.
Ore Bank Mountains; summits in Botetourt County.
Oreton; post village in Wise County on the Virginia and Southwestern Railway.
Orgainsville; post village in Mecklenburg County.
Orion; post village in Greenesville County.
Oriskany; post village in Botetourt County on the Chesapeake and Ohio Railway.
Orkney Springs; post village in Shenandoah County.
Orlando; post village in Prince William County.
Orlean; post village in Fauquier County.
Oronoco; post village in Amherst County.
Orrix; post village in Bedford County.
Ortis; post village in Albemarle County.
Osage; post village in Patrick County.
Osborn; small left-hand branch of Slate Creek in Buchanan County.
Osborn; ford in Scott County.
Osborns Gap; post village in Dickenson County.
Osceola; village in Washington County.
Oscer; village in Floyd County.
Oslins; post village in Buckingham County.
Osso; post village in King George County.
Othma; post village in Goochland County.
Otho; post village in Floyd County.
Otter; branch, a small left-hand tributary to Appomattox River in Chesterfield County.
Otter; creek, a small left-hand tributary to James River in Amherst County.
Otter; river, a left-hand tributary to Roanoke River, formed by two forks, North and South, in Bedford and Campbell counties.
Otterdale; post village in Chesterfield County.
Otterhill; village in Bedford County.
Otter River; post village in Campbell County on the Southern Railway. Altitude, 665 feet.
Otterview; post village in Bedford County.
Ottobine; post village in Rockingham County.
Ottoman; post village in Lancaster County.
Otway; post village in Nelson County.
Oty; post village in Montgomery County.
Oven Top; summit in Rappahannock County.

Overall; post village in Page County on the Norfolk and Western Railway. Altitude, 659 feet.
Overall; run, a small right-hand tributary to Shenandoah River in Page County.
Overland; post village in Mecklenburg County.
Overly; post village in Prince Edward County.
Overton; post village in Albemarle County.
Owens; creek, a small left-hand branch of James River in Nelson County.
Owens; creek, a small right-hand tributary to York River in Louisa County.
Owens; post village in King George County on the Southern Railway.
Owenton; post village in King and Queen County.
Owl; creek, a small right-hand branch of Meherrin River in Lunenburg County.
Owl; small creek in Princess Anne County, emptying into Atlantic Ocean through Rudy Inlet.
Owl; run, a small right-hand tributary to Potomac River in Fauquier County.
Oxalis; post village in King and Queen County.
Ozeana; post village in Essex County.
Paces; post village in Halifax County on the Southern Railway.
Paddy; creek, a small left-hand tributary to James River in Albemarle County.
Paddy; mountains in Frederick County, which extend into Shenandoah County, W. Va. Elevation, 2,500 feet.
Paddy; run, a small left-hand tributary to Shenandoah River in Frederick County.
Pads; creek, a small left-hand tributary to James River in Bath County.
Paeonian Springs; post village in Loudoun County on the Southern Railway.
Page; county, situated in the northwestern part of the State. It includes the valley of the South Fork of the Shenandoah, extending from the summit of Massanutten Mountain on the west to that of the Blue Ridge on the east. The altitude ranges from 600 feet along the Shenandoah to 4,000 feet on Stony Man and Hawks Bill summits of the Blue Ridge. Area is 317 square miles. Population, 13,794—white, 12,354; negro, 1,440; foreign born, 31. County seat, Luray. The mean magnetic declination in 1900 was 3° 50′. The mean annual rainfall is 50 to 60 inches, and the temperature 50° to 55°. The county is traversed by the Norfolk and Western Railway.
Page Mountain; summit in Amherst County.
Paige; post village in Caroline County.
Paine; run, a small right-hand tributary to Shenandoah River in Augusta County.
Paineville; post village in Amelia County.
Paintbank; post village in Craig County.
Painter; creek, a small left-hand branch of New River in Carroll County.
Painter; post village in Accomac County.
Paint Lick; mountains in Tazewell County. Elevation, 2,500 to 3,500 feet.
Paintlick; post village in Tazewell County.
Palace; post village in Dickenson County.
Palestine; post village in Washington County.
Palls; post village in King William County.
Palmer; post village in Lancaster County.
Palmer Springs; post village in Mecklenburg County.
Palmetto; post village in Patrick County.
Palmyra; county seat of Fluvanna County.
Paloalto; post village in Highland County.
Pampa; post village in Gloucester County.
Pamplin City; post village in Appomattox County on the Norfolk and Western Railway. Altitude, 679 feet.
Pamunky; post village in Orange County.

Pamunkey; river heading in the Piedmont region and flowing southeast to its junction with the Mattaponi, forming York River.
Pamunsend; creek, a small right-hand tributary to Rappahannock River in Caroline County.
Panther; creek, a small right-hand tributary to New River in Carroll County.
Panther; gap in Mill Mountains, caused by a creek in Bath County. Altitude, 1,594 feet.
Panther; mountain in Rockbridge County.
Panther; summit in Amherst County. Elevation, 1,500 to 2,000 feet.
Panther Mountain; summit in Botetourt County.
Panther Ridge; mountains in Alleghany County. Elevation, 2,000 to 2,500 feet.
Paris; mountains in Montgomery County. Elevation, 1,500 to 3,000 feet.
Paris; post village in Fauquier County.
Parishville; post village in Frederick County.
Parites; post village in Madison County.
Park; post village in Grayson County.
Parker; post village in Spottsylvania County on the Potomac, Fredericksburg and Piedmont Railroad.
Parkins Mill; post village in Frederick County.
Parksley; post village in Accomac County on the New York, Philadelphia and Norfolk Railroad.
Parnassus; post village in Augusta County.
Parr; post village in Botetourt County on the Chesapeake and Ohio Railway.
Parridge; run, a small left-hand branch of James River in Amherst County.
Parrotts; post village in Albemarle County.
Parsells; post village in Franklin County.
Partlow; post village in Spottsylvania County.
Pass; run, a small right-hand tributary to Shenandoah River in Page County.
Passage; creek, a small left-hand tributary to Shenandoah River in Shenandoah and Page counties.
Passapatanzy; post village in King George County.
Passing; post village in Caroline County.
Pastoria; post village in Accomac County.
Patch; creek, a small right-hand tributary to Powell River in Wise County.
Path Ridge; mountains in Rockingham County.
Patrick; county, which lies along the southern boundary of the State, its northwestern boundary being the summit of the Blue Ridge escarpment. Its surface is rolling and broken, with a steep rise upon the southwest. Area, 489 square miles. Population, 15,403—white, 13,779; negro, 1,624. County seat, Stuart. The mean magnetic declination in 1900 was 1° 30′. The mean annual rainfall is 50 to 60 inches, and the temperature 55° to 60°. The county is traversed by the Danville and Western Railway.
Patrick Springs; post village in Patrick County on the Danville and Western Railway. Altitude, 1,305 feet.
Patterson; creek, a small right-hand tributary to James River in Botetourt County.
Patterson; mountains in Botetourt County. Elevation, 1,500 to 2,000 feet.
Patterson; post village in Wythe County on the Norfolk and Western Railway. Altitude, 1,132 feet.
Patti; post village in Franklin County.
Pattonsville; post village in Scott County. Altitude, 1,710 feet.
Paulington; village in Rockingham County.
Paul Mountain; summit in Amherst County. Elevation, 1,500 feet.
Pauls; creek, a small left-hand tributary to Yadkin River in Patrick County.

Pauls Crossroads; post village in Essex County.
Paw Paw; creek, a left-hand branch of Knox Creek, formed by two forks, Left and Right, in Buchanan County.
Pax; post village in Floyd County.
Paxon; post village in Loudoun County.
Payne; creek, a small right-hand tributary to James River in Buckingham and Cumberland counties.
Paynes; post village in Fluvanna County on the Chesapeake and Ohio Railway.
Peach Bottom; creek, a small right-hand branch of New River in Grayson County.
Peach Bottom; post village in Grayson County.
Peach Grove Hill; summit in Fairfax County.
Peak; creek, a small left-hand branch of New River, rising in Wythe County.
Peak; summit in Blue Ridge in Rappahannock County. Elevation, 2,953 feet.
Peak; summit in Massanutten Mountains in Rockingham County.
Peak; summit in Bedford County. Elevation, 3,875 feet.
Peak; summit in Tazewell County. Elevation, 4,230 feet.
Peak Creek Knob; summit in Draper Mountains. Elevation, 3,374 feet.
Peakes Turnout; post village in Hanover County.
Peaks of Otter; mountains in Bedford County. Elevation, 1,500 to 4,000 feet
Peaksville; post village in Bedford County.
Peanut; post village in Sussex County.
Pearch; post village in Bedford County on the Chesapeake and Ohio Railway.
Pearis; mountains in Giles County. Elevation, 2,000 to 3,500 feet.
Pearisburg; town and county seat of Giles County. Population, 464.
Peatross; post village in Pittsylvania County.
Peavine Mountain; summit in Nelson County.
Peck; post village in Carroll County.
Peddler; creek, a small left-hand tributary to Roanoke River in Bedford County.
Pedlar; gap in Amherst County.
Pedlar; river, a small left-hand branch of James River in Amherst County.
Pedlar Hills; mountains in Montgomery County. Elevation, 1,500 to 2,000 feet.
Pedlar Mills; post village in Amherst County.
Pedlars; creek, a small left-hand tributary to Roanoke River in Bedford County.
Pedro; post village in Essex County.
Peeds; post village in Westmoreland County.
Peers; post village in Goochland County.
Pellitory; point extending into Back Bay in Princess Anne County.
Pelton; post village in Shenandoah County.
Pemberton; post village in Goochland County on the Chesapeake and Ohio Railway.
Pembroke; post village in Giles County on the Norfolk and Western Railway. Altitude, 1,618 feet.
Pender; post village in Fairfax County.
Pendletons; post village in Louisa County on the Chesapeake and Ohio Railway
Penhook; post village in Franklin County on the Southern Railway.
Penicks; post village in Bedford County.
Penlan; post village in Buckingham County on the Chesapeake and Ohio Railway.
Penn; small right-hand branch of Cripple Creek in Wythe County.
Pennington; gap made by the North Fork of Powell River in Stone Mountains.
Pennington Gap; town in Lee County on the Louisville and Nashville Railroad. Population, 399.
Penn Laird; post village in Rockingham County on the Chesapeake Western Railway.
Penny; post village in Mathews County.

Penola; post village in Caroline County on the Potomac, Fredericksburg and Piedmont Railroad.
Penrith; post village in Cumberland County.
Penrose; post village in Augusta County.
Peola Mills; post village in Madison County.
Peppers; ferry over New River in Pulaski County.
Pera; post village in Amherst County.
Perdue; post village in Montgomery County on the Farmville and Powhatan Railroad.
Perkinsville; post village in Goochland County
Pernello; post village in Franklin County.
Perriwinkle; branch, a small right-hand tributary to New River in Carroll and Pulaski counties.
Perrows; post village in Campbell County.
Perrowville; post village in Bedford County.
Perry; creek, a small left-hand tributary to James River in Albemarle County.
Perry; mountain in Nelson County.
Perth; post village in Halifax County.
Peter; creek, a small left-hand branch of Roanoke River in Roanoke County.
Peters; creek, a small right-hand branch of James River in Bedford County.
Peters; creek, a small left-hand tributary to Roanoke River in Roanoke County.
Peters; mountains in Giles County. Elevation, 2,500 to 3,000 feet.
Peters Creek; post village in Patrick County.
Petersburg; city, situated in Dinwiddie County, but independent in government, on the Atlantic Coast Line, the Norfolk and Western, and the Seaboard Air Line railroads. Population, 21,810.
Peters Hill; summit in Craig County. Elevation, 2,000 feet.
Peters Ridge; mountains in Alleghany County.
Petites; gap in Blue Ridge in Bedford County.
Petunia; village in Wythe County.
Peytonsburg; post village in Pittsylvania County.
Phelps; branch, a small right-hand tributary to James River in Appomattox County.
Phillipa; small left-hand branch of Middle Fork of Holston River in Smyth County.
Phillips; post village in Floyd County on the Virginia and Southwestern Railway.
Phillis; post village in Mecklenburg County.
Philomont; post village in Loudoun County.
Philpott; post village in Henry County.
Phoebus; town in Elizabeth City County on the Chesapeake and Ohio Railway. Population, 2,094.
Phone; post village in Goochland County.
Pianketank; river, heading in Essex County and flowing southeast to Chesapeake Bay.
Pickaway; post village in Pittsylvania County.
Piedmont; post village in Bedford County.
Pig; point of land in Nansemond County, extending into James River.
Pig; river, a right-hand tributary to Roanoke River in Pittsylvania County.
Pig; run, a small left-hand tributary to James River in Bath County.
Pigeon; creek, a small right-hand branch of Powell River.
Pigeon; run, a small left-hand tributary to York River in Spottsylvania County.
Pigg; river, a right-hand branch of Roanoke River in Pittsylvania County.
Pig Nut; mountains in Fauquier County. Elevation, 750 to 1,000 feet.
Pig River; post village in Franklin County.
Pike; post village in Chesterfield County.

Pike Knob; summit in Carroll County. Elevation, 3,200 feet.
Pilkinton; post village in Powhatan County.
Pilot; mountains in Montgomery County. Elevation, 2,000 to 2,500 feet.
Pilot; post village in Montgomery County.
Pilot Knob; summit in Grayson County. Elevation, 3,021 feet.
Pilot Mountain; summit in Appomattox County.
Pilot Mountain; summit in Bedford County.
Pimmit; run, a small right-hand branch of Potomac River in Fairfax County.
Pinckney; post village in Highland County.
Pine; branch, a small right-hand tributary to New River in Carroll County.
Pine, fork, a small right-hand tributary to New River in Carroll and Floyd counties.
Pine; mountains in Botetourt and Rockbridge counties. Elevation, 1,500 to 2,500 feet.
Pine; mountains in Washington County. Elevation, 1,500 to 2,000 feet.
Pine; mountains in the southern part of Scott County, extending into Hawkins County, Tenn.
Pine; post village in Pulaski County.
Pine; run, a small left-hand branch of New River in Wythe and Pulaski counties.
Pineapple; post village in Spottsylvania County.
Pine Ridge; mountains in Botetourt County. Elevation, 1,500 feet.
Pine Ridge; mountains in Frederick County. Elevation, 1,000 feet.
Pine Ridge; mountains in Wythe County. Elevation, 2,500 feet.
Pine Ridge; summits in Augusta County.
Pinero; post village in Gloucester County.
Pine Spur; gap in the Blue Ridge in Franklin County.
Pine Swamp; creek, a small left-hand tributary to New River, rising in Grayson County.
Pinetop; post village in Orange County.
Pinetta; post village in Gloucester County.
Pineview; post village in Fauquier County.
Piney; creek, a small left-hand tributary to James River in Albemarle County.
Piney; mountains in Bath County.
Piney; mountains in Bedford County. Elevation, 2,000 feet.
Piney; mountains in Craig County.
Piney; river, a small left-hand tributary to James River between Nelson and Amherst counties.
Piney; run, a small right-hand branch of Potomac River in Loudoun County.
Piney Knob; summit in Rockbridge County.
Piney Mountain; summit in Amherst County.
Piney Mountain; summit in Appomattox County.
Piney Mountain; summit in Page County. Elevation, 1,500 feet.
Pinnacle; post village in Carroll County.
Pinnacle; summit in Cumberland Mountains in Lee County. Elevation, 2,500 feet.
Pinner; point on Elizabeth River in Norfolk County.
Pinners; post village in Norfolk County.
Pinopolis; post village in Southampton County.
Piper; gap in Carroll County.
Piper; gap in mountains in Patrick County.
Pipers Gap, post village in Carroll County.
Pisgah; post village in Tazewell County on the Norfolk and Western Railway. Altitude, 2,344 feet.
Pistol; small left-hand branch of Levisa Fork in Buchanan County.
Pittston; post village in Pittsylvania County.

Pittsville; post village in Pittsylvania County on the Southern Railway.
Pittsylvania; county, situated in the southern part of the State on the Atlantic plain, the northern limit being Roanoke River. The surface is undulating. The altitude ranges from 4,000 to 1,200 feet. Area, 986 square miles. Population, 46,894—white, 25,605; negro, 21,289; foreign born, 63. County seat, Chatham. The mean magnetic declination in 1900 was 1° 47.5'. The mean annual rainfall is 50 to 60 inches, and the temperature 55° to 60°. The county is traversed by the Southern, the Danville and Western, and the Norfolk and Western railways.
Pizarro; post village in Floyd County.
Plainview; post village in King and Queen County.
Plank Cabin; creek, a small left-hand tributary to Clinch River in Scott County.
Plantersville; post village in Lunenburg County.
Plasterburg; post village in Smyth County.
Plasterco; post village in Washington County.
Plato; post village in Halifax County.
Pleasantgrove; post village in Lunenburg County.
Pleasanthill; post village in Tazewell County.
Pleasantridge; post village in Princess Anne County on the Norfolk and Southern Railroad.
Pleasantshade; post village in Greenesville County on the Southern Railway.
Pleasant Valley; post village in Loudoun County on the Baltimore and Ohio Railroad. Altitude, 1,248 feet.
Pleasantview; post village in Amherst County.
Pleasure House; creek, a small left-hand branch of Lynn Haven River in Princess Anne County.
Pluck; post village in King George County.
Plum; branch, a small left-hand tributary to Roanoke River in Campbell County.
Plum; creek, a small left-hand branch of Clinch River in Tazewell County.
Plum; creek, a small right-hand branch of New River, rising in Montgomery County.
Plumbranch; post village in Campbell County.
Plumpoint; post village in New Kent County.
Plymale; post village in Bedford County.
Po; river, a small right-hand branch of Mattaponi River in Spottsylvania and Caroline counties.
Poages Mill; post village in Roanoke County.
Poague; run, a small left-hand tributary to James River in Rockbridge County.
Pocahontas; town in Tazewell County on the Norfolk and Western Railway. Altitude, 2,320 feet. Population, 2,789.
Poco; village in Shenandoah County.
Pocoshock; creek, a small right-hand tributary to James River in Chesterfield County.
Poge Mill; creek, a small left-hand branch of South Fork of Holston River in Washington County.
Pohick; bay, an arm of the Potomac River, extending into Fairfax County.
Pohick; run, a small right-hand tributary to Potomac River in Fairfax County.
Poindexter; post village in Louisa County.
Point Eastern; post village in Caroline County.
Point Lookout; mountains in Grayson County. Elevation, 3,000 to 4,623 feet.
Point Pleasant; post village in Bland County on the Pittsburg, Shawmut and Northern Railroad.
Point Truth; post village in Russell County.
Pole Cat; creek, a small left-hand tributary to New River in Wythe County.
Polegreen; post village in Hanover County.
Pollard; post village in Amelia County.

Polo; post village in King and Queen County.
Pond; gap in Little North Mountains in Augusta County. Altitude, 1,682 feet.
Pond; mountain in Smyth County. Elevation, 2,500 to 3,000 feet.
Pond; mountains in Fauquier County. Elevation, 1,500 to 2,500 feet.
Pond; run, a small right-hand tributary to Shenandoah River in Augusta County.
Pondgap; post village in Augusta County.
Pond Hill; summit in Montgomery County.
Poney; creek, a small right-hand branch of Pamunkey River in Hanover County.
Pons; post village in Isle of Wight County.
Pony; summits in Culpeper County. Elevation, 500 to 750 feet.
Poo; run, a small right-hand tributary to James River in Dinwiddie County.
Poole; post village in Brunswick County on the Norfolk and Ocean View Railroad.
Poolville; post village in Halifax County.
Poor; mountain in Roanoke and Montgomery counties. Elevation, 2,500 to 3,900 feet.
Poor; valley in Tazewell County.
Poor; valley lying along Clinch Mountain in Scott and Washington counties.
Poor; valley lying between Poor Valley Ridge and Stone Mountain in Lee County.
Poore; small right-hand branch of New River in Carroll County.
Poor Valley Ridge; mountains extending northeast and southwest in Lee County.
Pope; post village in Southampton County, on the Southern Railway.
Pope Knob; summit in Carroll County. Elevation, 3,039 feet.
Popham; run, a small right-hand tributary to Rappahannock River in Madison County.
Poplar; branch, a small right-hand tributary to New River in Montgomery County.
Poplar; creek, a small left-hand branch of Levisa Fork, rising in Buchanan County.
Poplar; post village in Nelson County.
Poplar Camp; creek, a small right-hand tributary to New River in Wythe and Carroll counties.
Poplar Camp; mountains in Carroll and Wythe counties. Elevation, 2,500 to 3,161 feet.
Poplarhill; post village in Giles County.
Poplar Knob; summit in Carroll County, Elevation, 3,166 feet.
Poplarmount; post village in Greenesville County.
Poquoson; post village in York County.
Porpoise; point projecting into Back Bay in Princess Anne County.
Port; post village in Madison County.
Port Conway; post village in King George County.
Porter; ferry over New River in Wythe County.
Porterfield; run, a small right-hand tributary to Shenandoah River in Augusta County.
Porters; mountains in Botetourt and Bedford counties. Elevation, 1,500 to 2,000 feet.
Port Haywood; post village in Mathews County.
Port Norfolk; post village in Norfolk County on the Atlantic Coast Line Railroad.
Port Republic; post village in Rockingham County.
Port Royal; town in Caroline County on the Norfolk and Western Railway. Altitude, 1,093 feet. Population, 193.
Portsmouth; county seat of Norfolk County, but independent in government, on the Atlantic Coast Line, the Chesapeake and Ohio, the New York, Philadelphia and Norfolk, and the Seaboard Air Line railroads. Population, 17,427.
Port Walthall; post village in Chesterfield County.
Posey; post village in Floyd County.
Possum; small creek in Hanover County.

Possum; run, a small left-hand tributary to James River in Rockbridge County.
Possum Jaw; creek, a small right-hand branch of North Fork of Holston River in Smyth County.
Postoak; post village in Spottsylvania County.
Potato; post village in Grayson County.
Potato; run, a small right-hand tributary to Rappahannock River in Culpeper County.
Potato Hill; summit in Amherst County. Elevation, 1,000 feet.
Potato Hill; summit in Wise County.
Poteet; ford of Powell River in Lee County.
Potomac; creek, a small right-hand branch of Potomac River in Stafford County.
Potomac; post village in Prince William County.
Potomac; river of Maryland, Virginia, and West Virginia. It heads in West Virginia, in North and South branches. The North Branch rises near the Fairfax Stone, the southwestern point of Maryland, and flows northeast to Cumberland, where it turns to a southeastern course. A few miles farther down it is joined by the South Branch, and at Harpers Ferry, where it cuts through the Blue Ridge, by the Shenandoah; thence the river flows in a generally southeasterly course to its mouth in Chesapeake Bay at Point Lookout. The area of its drainage basin is 14,479 square miles, including the Shenandoah. It is navigable to Little Falls, in the District of Columbia.
Potomac Mills; post village in Westmoreland County.
Potts; creek, a right-hand branch of Jackson River in Alleghany County.
Potts; mountains in Craig and Alleghany counties. Elevation, 2,500 to 3,822 feet.
Potts; post village in Amherst County.
Potts Creek; post village in Alleghany County.
Poulson; post village in Accomac County.
Pound; gap in Pine Mountains in Wise County.
Pound; post village in Wise County.
Pound; river, a left-hand branch of Russell Fork, rising in Wise County.
Pounding Mill; creek, a small left-hand branch of Clinch River in Tazewell County.
Pound Mill; creek, a small left-hand branch of Knox Creek, rising in Buchanan County.
Pounding Mill; creek, a small left-hand tributary to James River in Alleghany County.
Pounding Mill; post village in Tazewell County on the Norfolk and Western Railway. Altitude, 2,140 feet.
Poverty; creek, a small right-hand tributary to New River in Pulaski and Montgomery counties.
Poverty; post village in Highland County.
Powcan; post village in King and Queen County.
Powell; gap in the Blue Ridge in Rockingham County.
Powell; gap in the Blue Ridge, caused by McFalls Branch, in Botetourt County. Altitude 1,906 feet.
Powell; mountains, extending from the southern part of Wise County along the boundary line of Scott and Lee counties into Hancock County, Tenn.
Powell; river, rising in Wise County and flowing southwest through Lee County into Tennessee, where it flows into Clinch River. It is formed by two forks, North and South.
Powell Mountain; summit in Nelson County.
Powells; creek, a small right-hand branch of Potomac River in Prince William County.
Powells; mountains in Shenandoah County.
Powellton; post village in Brunswick County.
Powers; post village in Clarke County.

Powhatan; county, situated in the central part of the State in the Piedmont region. It is drained by James River, which flows along its southern boundary. The altitude ranges from 200 to 400 feet. Area, 284 square miles. Population, 6,824—white, 2,343; negro, 4,481; foreign born, 43. County seat, Powhatan. The mean magnetic declination in 1900 was 3° 35'. The mean annual rainfall is 40 to 5C inches, and the temperature 55° to 60°. The county is traversed by the Farmville and Powhatan Railroad.

Powhatan; county seat of Powhatan County on the Farmville and Powhatan Railroad.

Powhite; creek, a small left-hand branch of Chickahominy River in Hanover County.

Powhite; creek, a small right-hand branch of James River in Chesterfield County.

Prater; creek, a small right-hand branch of Roanoke River in Franklin County.

Prater; post village in Buchanan County.

Pratts; post village in Madison County.

Preacher; creek, a small right-hand tributary to Powell River in Wise County.

Preacher; post village in Wise County on the Interstate Railroad.

Prease; village in Bedford County.

Preston; post village in Henry County on the Danville and Western Railroad. Altitude, 930 feet.

Preston Knob; summit in Franklin County. Elevation, 1,331 feet.

Pretlow; post village in Southampton County.

Pretty; creek, a small left-hand branch of James River in Botetourt County.

Price; mountains in Montgomery County. Elevation, 2,000 feet.

Prices; ford of Jackson River in Botetourt County.

Prices; mountains in Botetourt County. Elevation, 2,000 to 2,500 feet.

Prices Fork; post village in Montgomery County.

Priddys; post village in Albemarle County.

Pridemore; village in Lee County.

Priest; summit in Nelson County. Elevation, 4,080 feet.

Prillamans; post village in Franklin County.

Prince; post village in King and Queen County.

Prince Edward; county, situated in the central part of the State in the Piedmont region. The surface is undulating and the altitude ranges from 300 to 600 feet. Area, 345 square miles. Population, 15,045—white, 5,276; negro, 9,769; foreign born, 117. County seat, Farmville. The mean magnetic declination in 1900 was 3°. The mean annual rainfall is 50 inches, and the temperature 55° to 60°. The county is traversed by the Southern, the Farmville and Powhatan, and the Norfolk and Western railroads.

Prince George; county, situated in the central part of the State on the Atlantic plain. It has a rolling surface with much marsh along the streams. The altitude ranges in the highest points to about 200 feet. Area, 302 square miles. Population, 7,752—white, 2,886; negro, 4,858; foreign born, 282. County seat, Prince George. The mean magnetic declination in 1900 was 3° 30'. The mean annual rainfall is 40 to 50 inches, and the temperature 55° to 60°. The county is traversed by the Norfolk and Western and the Atlantic Coast Line railroads.

Prince George; county seat of Prince George County.

Princess Anne: county, situated in the southeastern part of the State. It borders on the Atlantic Ocean and North Carolina, lying east of the great Dismal Swamp. It contains much marsh land, and on the whole lies very low, little of it exceeding 20 to 25 feet above sea level. Area, 285 square miles. Population, 11,192—white, 5,505; negro, 5,687; foreign born, 74. County seat, Princess Anne. The mean magnetic declination in 1900 was 4° 15'. The mean annual rainfall is 50 to 60 inches, and the temperature 55° to 60°. The county is traversed by the Norfolk and Southern and the Virginia Beach railroads.

Princess Anne; county seat of Princess Anne County on the Norfolk and Southern Railroad.

Prince William; county, situated in the eastern part of the State in the Piedmont region. It has an undulating surface, rising in the western edge to the summit of the Blue Ridge, which forms the boundary. Most of the area of the county lies between 200 and 500 feet in altitude. Area, 353 square miles. Population, 11,112—white, 8,240; negro, 2,871; foreign born, 167. County seat, Manassas. The mean magnetic declination in 1900 was 4°. The mean annual rainfall is 45 to 50 inches, and the temperature 55° to 60°. The county is traversed by the Chesapeake and Ohio, the Southern, and the Richmond, Fredericksburg and Potomac railroads.

Printz Mill; post village in Page County.

Prise House Mountain; summit in Botetourt County.

Proffit; post village in Albemarle County on the Southern Railway.

Progress; village in Franklin County.

Prospect; post village in Prince Edward County on the Norfolk and Western Railway. Altitude, 573 feet.

Prospect Dale; post village in Giles County.

Prospect Hill; post village in Fairfax County.

Providence Forge; post village in New Kent County on the Chesapeake and Ohio Railway.

Pruntys; village in Henry County.

Pryor; post village in Amherst County.

Puckell; creek, a small left-hand branch of Straight Creek in Lee County.

Puckett; post village in Patrick County.

Pughs; post village in Norfolk County on the Atlantic Coast Line Railroad.

Pughs; run, a small left-hand tributary to Shenandoah River in Shenandoah County.

Pughs Run; post village in Shenandoah County.

Pulaski; county, situated in the western part of the State in the Appalachian Valley. It is limited on the east by New River, the northwest by Walker Mountain, and on the southwest by an arbitrary line. Its surface is undulating, with a few northeast and southwest ridges separated by valleys. The altitude ranges from 1,700 to 3,000 feet. Area, 338 square miles. Population, 14,609—white, 11,372; negro, 3,237; foreign born, 88. County seat, Pulaski City. The mean magnetic declination in 1900 was 1° 15′. The mean annual rainfall is 50 to 60 inches, and the temperature 50° to 55°. The county is traversed by the Norfolk and Western Railway.

Pulaski City; county seat of Pulaski County on the Norfolk and Western Railway. Altitude, 1,904 feet. Population, 2,813.

Pullens; post village in Pittsylvania County.

Pulliam; branch, a small left-hand tributary to Roanoke River in Campbell County.

Punch Bowl Mountain; summit in the Blue Ridge.

Pungo; ferry over North Landing River between Norfolk and Princess Anne counties.

Pungo; post village in Princess Anne County on the Norfolk and Southern Railroad.

Pungoteague; post village in Accomac County.

Purcellville; post village in Loudoun County on the Southern Railway. Altitude, 553 feet.

Purchase; post village in Scott County.

Purchase Ridge; mountains in Scott County.

Purgatory; creek, a small left-hand branch of James River in Botetourt County.

Purgatory; mountains in Botetourt County. Elevation, 1,500 to 2,500 feet.

Purity; village in Franklin County.

Purvis; gap in Nelson County.

Push; post village in Mecklenburg County.

Putneys; post village in Prince Edward County.

Quail; post village in Louisa County.
Quantico; creek, a small right-hand branch of Potomac River in Prince William County.
Queensberry Knob; summit in Carroll County. Elevation, 2,935 feet.
Queens Knob; summit in Wythe County. Elevation, 3,000 to 3,204 feet.
Quicksburg; post village in Shenandoah County on the Southern Railway.
Quillin; post village in Norfolk County.
Quinby; post village in Accomac County.
Quinque; post village in Greene County.
Quinton; post village in New Kent County on the Southern Railway.
Quoit: post village in Floyd County.
Rabat; post village in Halifax County.
Raccoon; creek, a small left-hand tributary to James River in Fluvanna County.
Raccoon; run, a small left-hand tributary to Shenandoah River in Rockingham County.
Raccoon Ford; post village in Culpeper County.
Race; fork, a small left-hand branch of Knox Creek, rising in Buchanan County.
Radcliffe; post village in Mecklenburg County.
Radford; small right-hand branch of New River, rising in Pulaski County.
Radford; city in Montgomery County, but independent in government, on the Norfolk and Western Railway. Altitude, 1,773 feet. Population, 3,344.
Radford Furnace; post village in Pulaski County.
Radfords; ford in Roanoke River, Franklin County.
Radiant; post village in Madison County.
Ragged; marshy island in Back Bay in Princess Anne County.
Ragged; mountains in Albemarle County. Elevation. 1,000 to 1,500 feet.
Ragged; mountains in Madison County. Elevation, 2,000 to 3,000 feet.
Ragged; summit in Brattans Mountain, Rockbridge County.
Rainbow; post village in Rockingham County.
Raines; post village in Cumberland County on the Farmville and Powhatan Railroad. Altitude, 524 feet.
Rainey; pond in the eastern part of Princess Anne County.
Rainswood; post village in Northumberland County.
Rallings; run, a small left-hand branch of James River in Amherst County.
Ramble; post village in Halifax County.
Ramsey; gap in Great North Mountains in Rockbridge County.
Ramsey Draft; small left-hand tributary to James River in Augusta County.
Ramsey Mountain; summit in Augusta County.
Ranch; post village in Orange County.
Randolph; creek, a small right-hand tributary to James River in Buckingham County.
Randolph; post village in Charlotte County on the Southern Railway.
Rangeley; village in Henry County.
Ransons; post village in Buckingham County.
Raphine; post village in Rockbridge County on the Baltimore and Ohio Railroad.
Rapidan; post village in Culpeper County.
Rapidan; river, a right-hand branch of Rappahannock River, forming the boundary between Greene and Orange counties on one side, and Madison and Culpeper on the other.
Rappahannock; county, situated in the northern part of the State in the Piedmont region, the western boundary being the summit of the Blue Ridge. In the eastern part its surface is rolling, becoming broken in the west by short ridges, outlayers of the Blue Ridge and by the heavy spurs of that range. The elevation ranges from 300 up to 3,500 feet in the summits of the Blue Ridge. Area, 264 square miles. Population, 8,843—white, 6,121; negro, 2,722; foreign born, 6; county seat, Washington. The mean magnetic declination in 1900 was 4° 05'. The mean annual rainfall is 50 to 60 inches, and the temperature 50° to 55°.

Rappahannock; river, which heads in the Blue Ridge in Fauquier County and flows southeast to Chesapeake Bay. It is navigable to Fredericksburg.
Rappahannock Academy; post village in Caroline County.
Rapps Mill; post village in Rockbridge County.
Rasnake; post village in Russell County.
Rat Hole; mountains in Botetourt County.
Rattle; creek, a small left-hand tributary to North Fork of Holston River in Washington County.
Rattlesnake; branch, a small left-hand tributary to Roanoke River in Campbell County.
Rattlesnake; mountains in Rappahannock County. Elevation, 1,500 feet.
Raven; post village in Tazewell County on the Norfolk and Western Railway.
Ravens Nest; post village in Washington County.
Rawley Springs; post village in Rockingham County.
Ray; post village in Pittsylvania County.
Ray; fork, a small tributary to Dry Fork, rising in Tazewell County.
Raynor; post village in Isle of Wight County.
Reads Wharf; post village in Northampton County.
Readus; village in Shenandoah County.
Reams; post village in Dinwiddie County on the Atlantic Coast Line Railroad.
Reardon; post village in Charlotte County.
Reba; post village in Bedford County.
Rectortown; post village in Fauquier County on the Southern Railway.
Rectory; post village in Stafford County.
Redbank; post village in Halifax County.
Redbluff; post village in Wythe County.
Red Bud; run, a small left-hand tributary to Shenandoah River in Frederick County.
Redeye; post village in Pittsylvania County.
Redhill; post village in Albemarle County on the Southern Railway. Altitude, 626 feet.
Redhouse; post village in Charlotte County.
Reding; post village in Goochland County.
Rediviva; post village in Rappahannock County.
Red Mills; post village in Rockbridge County.
Redmonds; village in Albemarle County.
Redoak; post village in Charlotte County.
Redoak Knob; small summit in Highland County.
Red Oak Mountain; summits in Fauquier County. Elevation, 750 to 1,000 feet.
Red Rock; summit in Washington County. Elevation, 4,456 feet.
Redwood; post village in Franklin County on the Southern Railway.
Reed; creek, a left-hand branch of New River in Wythe County.
Reed; creek, a small right-hand tributary to North Fork of Powell River in Lee County.
Reed; creek, a right-hand branch of New River rising in Wythe County.
Reed; creek, a small right-hand branch of James River in Bedford County.
Reedcreek; village in Henry County.
Reed Island; post village in Pulaski County on the Norfolk and Western Railway. Altitude, 1,886 feet.
Reeds; gap in the Blue Ridge in Nelson County.
Reedville; post village in Northumberland County.
Reedy; creek, a small left-hand tributary to Nottoway River in Dinwiddie County.
Reedy; creek, a small left-hand tributary to Roanoke River in Appomattox County.
Reedy; creek, a small right-hand branch of James River in Chesterfield County.

Reedy; post village in Lunenburg County.
Reeses; post village in Charlotte County.
Regent; post village in Middlesex County.
Regulus; village in Henry County.
Rehoboth; post village in Lunenburg County.
Rehoboth Church; post village in Lancaster County.
Rei; post village in Washington County.
Reliance; post village in Warren County.
Relief; post village in Frederick County.
Remington; town in Fauquier County on the Southern Railway. Population, 198.
Renan; post village in Pittsylvania County.
Renie; post village in Amherst County.
Renoville; post village in Princess Anne County.
Repton; post village in Nelson County.
Republican Grove; post village in Halifax County.
Rescue; post village in Isle of Wight County.
Residence; post village in Halifax County.
Rest; post village in Frederick County.
Return; post village in Caroline County.
Retz; post village in Mathews County.
Reusens; post village in Campbell County on the Chesapeake and Ohio Railway.
Reva; post village in Culpeper County.
Rex; post village in Carroll County.
Rexburg; post village in Essex County.
Reynolds; creek, a small right-hand tributary to James River in Cumberland County.
Reynolds Store; post village in Frederick County.
Rhoadesville; post village in Orange County.
Ribbon; post village in Louisa County.
Rice; creek, a small right-hand tributary to Appomattox River in Prince Edward County.
Rice Depot; post village in Prince Edward County on the Norfolk and Western Railway.
Riceville; post village in Pittsylvania County.
Rich; creek, a small right-hand branch of New River in Giles County.
Rich; mountains in Tazewell and Bland counties. Elevation, 2,500 to 3,000 feet.
Rich; valley in Washington County.
Richards; ford of Rappahannock River in Stafford County.
Richardson; post village in Carroll County.
Richardson Mountain; summit in Amherst County.
Richardsville; post village in Culpeper County.
Rich Hill; mountains in Giles County.
Rich Hill; summits in Rockbridge County.
Rich Hill; summit in Botetourt County.
Richland; mountains in Rockingham County.
Richlands; town in Tazewell County on the Norfolk and Western Railway. Altitude, 1,926 feet. Population, 475.
Richmond; county, situated in the eastern part of the State on the Atlantic plain near the coast, and borders on Rappahannock River on the north. The surface is rolling; elevation, about 200 feet above tide. Area, 188 square miles. Population, 7,088—white, 4,159; negro, 2,929; foreign born, 28. County seat, Warsaw. The mean magnetic declination in 1900 was 4° 15′. The mean annual rainfall is 40 to 50 inches, and the temperature 55° to 60°.

Richmond; county seat of Henrico County and capital of the State. It is on the Atlantic Coast Line, the Chesapeake and Ohio, the Richmond, Fredericksburg and Potomac, the Seaboard Air Line, and the Southern railroads. Independent in government. Population, 85,050.

Rich Mountain; summit in Carroll County. Elevation, 3,551.

Rich Patch; mountains in Alleghany and Botetourt counties. Elevation, 1,500 to 3,500 feet.

Richpatch; post village in Alleghany County.

Rich Valley; post village in Smyth County.

Ridge; run, a small left-hand tributary to York River in Orange County.

Ridgemont; post village in Bedford County.

Ridgeway; town in Henry County on the Norfolk and Western Railway. Altitude, 819 feet. Population, 332.

Rifton; post village in Floyd County.

Riles; run, a small left-hand tributary to Shenandoah River in Shenandoah County.

Rileyville; post village in Page County on the Norfolk and Western Railway. Altitude, 923 feet.

Riner; post village in Montgomery County.

Ringgold; post village in Pittsylvania County on the Southern Railway.

Rinkerton; post village in Shenandoah County.

Rio; post village in Albemarle County on the Southern Railway.

Riovista; post village in Henrico County on the Chesapeake and Ohio Railway.

Ripley Mills; post village in Craig County.

Ripplemead; post village in Giles County on the Norfolk and Western Railway. Altitude, 1,603 feet.

Ripraps; post village in Elizabeth City County.

Ripshin; creek, a small right-hand branch of New River in Gray County.

Ritchieville; post village in Dinwiddie County.

Rival; post village in Buckingham County.

Rivanna; post village in Albemarle County on the Chesapeake and Ohio Railway.

Rivanna; river, a small left-hand tributary to James River, formed by two forks, North and South, in Albemarle County.

Riven; rocks in Jack Mountain, Highland County.

Riven Rock; mountains in Rockingham County. Elevation, 2,500 feet.

Riverdale; post village in Southampton County.

River Knobs; summits in Scott County.

River Knobs; summits in Washington County.

Rivermont; post village in Franklin County.

Riverside; post village in Rockbridge County on the Norfolk and Western Railway. Altitude, 935 feet.

Riversidepark; post village in Fairfax County on the Washington, Alexandria and Mount Vernon Electric Railway.

Riverton; post village in Warren County on the Norfolk and Western and the Southern railways.

Riverville; post village in Amherst County.

Rives; post village in Prince George County.

Rixeyville; post village in Culpeper County.

Roach; river, a small left-hand tributary to James River in Greene County.

Roadside; post village in Rockingham County.

Roague; run, a small left-hand tributary to Shenandoah River in Augusta County.

Roanes; post village in Gloucester County.

Roanoke; river of Virginia and North Carolina, heading in the Valley of Virginia and largely in Roanoke County. It flows in a generally southeast course to its mouth in Albemarle Sound in North Carolina. From the mouth of its principal branch, Dan River, to the point near its source, it is commonly known as Staunton River. It is navigable to the fall line at Weldon, N. C. The mean discharge is 506 cubic feet per second; drainage area, 9,237 square miles.

Roanoke; county, situated in the western part of the State on the summit of the Blue Ridge, there having the form of a broad plateau with an escarpment facing the east. Its surface is broken with many parallel ridges, turning northeast and southwest, and limestone valleys. It is drained by Roanoke River. The altitude ranges from 900 up to 3,500 feet above sea level. Area, 297 square miles. Population, 15,837—white, 11,991; negro, 3,845; foreign born, 48. County seat, Salem. The mean magnetic declination in 1900 was 1° 30′. The mean annual rainfall is 50 to 60 inches, and the temperature 50° to 55°. The county is traversed by the Norfolk and Western Railway.

Roanoke; city in Roanoke County, independent in government, on the Norfolk and Western Railway. Population, 21,495. Altitude, 907 feet.

Roaring; fork, a small right-hand tributary to Powell River in Wise County.

Roaring; fork, a small tributary to North Fork of Holston River in Tazewell County.

Roaring; run, a small left-hand branch of James River in Botetourt County.

Roaring; run, a small right-hand tributary to James River in Botetourt County.

Roaring Falls; mountains in Wythe County.

Roaring Run; village in Botetourt County.

Rob; post village in Botetourt County.

Roberta; post village in Franklin County.

Roberts; creek, a small left-hand branch of North Fork of Holston River, rising in Scott County.

Roberts; mountains in Nelson County.

Robertson; river, a small right-hand tributary to Rappahannock River in Madison County.

Robertson; run, a small right-hand tributary to Mattaponi River in Spottsylvania County.

Robertsons; post village in Bedford County.

Robinett; post village in Scott County.

Robinson; gap in Blue Ridge in Rockbridge County.

Robinson; river, a small right-hand tributary to Rappahannock River in Madison County.

Robinsons; branch, a small left-hand tributary to James River in Rockbridge County.

Robious; post village in Chesterfield County on the Southern Railway.

Rochelle; post village in Madison County.

Rock; creek, a small right-hand tributary to New River in Carroll County.

Rock; creek, a small right-hand tributary to James River in Cumberland County.

Rock; island in James River in Buckingham County.

Rockbridge; county, situated in the western part of the State in the Appalachian Valley, the eastern boundary being the summit of the Blue Ridge. The surface in the eastern part is broken by many short ridges and isolated summits. It is drained by South River and a branch of the James. The altitude ranges from 800 up to 3,500 feet. Area, 593 square miles. Population, 21,799—white, 17,715; negro, 4,084; foreign born, 57. County seat, Lexington. The mean magnetic declination in 1900 was 1° 40′. The mean annual rainfall is 50 to 60 inches, and the temperature 50° to 55°. The county is traversed by the Chesapeake and Ohio, the Baltimore and Ohio, and the Norfolk and Western railroads.

Rockbridge Alum Springs; post village in Rockbridge County on the Rockbridge Alum Springs and Virginia and Western Railroad.

Rockbridge Baths; post village in Rockbridge County.

Rockcastle; creek, a small left-hand tributary to Roanoke River in Bedford County.

Rockcastle; post village in Goochland County on the Chesapeake and Ohio Railway.

Rockdale; creek, a small right-hand branch of James River in Chesterfield County.

Rockdell; post village in Russell County.

Rock Enon Springs; post village in Frederick County.
Rock Fish; gap in the Blue Ridge in Augusta County on the Southern Railway.
Rockfish; river, a left-hand branch of James River in Nelson County.
Rockfish; run, a small left-hand branch of James River in Fluvanna County.
Rockfish Depot; post village in Nelson County.
Rockford; post village in Stafford County.
Rockhouse; post village in Russell County.
Rockingham; county, situated in the northwestern part of the State in the Appalachian Valley, its eastern boundary being through most of its course the summit of the Blue Ridge. The surface is rolling, with the exception of the slopes of the Blue Ridge and Massanutten Mountain. The altitude ranges from a little less than a few thousand feet up to 3,500 feet in the Blue Ridge summits. Area, 870 square miles. Population, 33,527—white, 30,893; negro, 2,632; foreign born, 100. County seat, Harrisonburg. The mean magnetic declination in 1900 was 2° 45'. The mean annual rainfall is 50 to 60 inches, and the temperature 50° to 55°. The county is traversed by the Baltimore and Ohio, the Chesapeake Western, the Southern, and the Norfolk and Western railroads.
Rockingham; post village in Rockingham County.
Rock Island; post village in Buckingham County.
Rock Island; run, a small right-hand branch of James River in Buckingham County.
Rock Lick; branch, a small right-hand branch of Levisa Fork in Buchanan County.
Rock Lick; creek, a small right-hand branch of Levisa Fork, rising in Buchanan County.
Rocks; summit in Nelson County. Elevation, 3,210 feet.
Rock Spring; small right-hand branch of New River in Pulaski County.
Rockville; post village in Hanover County.
Rocky; branch, a small left-hand tributary to James River in Bath County.
Rocky; branch, a small right-hand tributary to Chickahominy River in Henrico County.
Rocky; ford in Goose Creek in Bedford County.
Rocky; fork, a small left-hand tributary to Guest River in Wise County.
Rocky; gap between Rich and Wolf Creek mountains, caused by a left-hand branch of Wolf Creek.
Rocky; river, a small left-hand tributary to James River in Albemarle County.
Rocky; run, a small left-hand branch of James River in Botetourt County.
Rocky; run, a small left-hand tributary to Appomattox River in Appomattox County.
Rocky; run, a small left-hand tributary to Shenandoah River in Rockingham County.
Rockygap; post village in Bland County.
Rocky Hollow; small left-hand branch of Cripple Creek in Wythe County.
Rocky Mount; county seat of Franklin County on the Norfolk and Western and the Southern railways. Population, 612. Altitude, 1,132 feet.
Rocky Mount; turnpike in Bedford County.
Rocky Mountain; summit in Rockbridge County. Elevation, 4,010 feet.
Rockypoint; post village in Botetourt County on the Chesapeake and Ohio Railway.
Rocky Ridge; summit in Black Creek Mountains in Bath County.
Rocky Row; mountains in Amherst County. Elevation, 1,500 to 2,000 feet.
Rocky Row; run, a small left-hand branch of James River in Amherst County.
Rockyrun; post village in Orange County.
Rodden; post village in Halifax County.
Rodes; post village in Bedford County.
Rodophil; post village in Amelia County.
Rogers; mountain between Grayson and Smyth counties.

Rogers; post village in Montgomery County.
Rolla; post village in Augusta County.
Rolling Hill; post village in Charlotte County.
Rollins Fork; post village in King George County.
Roma; post village in Bedford County.
Roman; post village in Augusta County.
Rondabush; post village in Greene County.
Rondo; post village in Pittsylvania County.
Roop; village in Montgomery County.
Rorer Mines; village in Roanoke County on the Norfolk and Western Railway.
Rorrer; post village in Carroll County.
Rosa; post village in Halifax County.
Rose; run, a small left-hand branch of South Fork of Roanoke River in Montgomery County.
Rose Bower; post village in Appomattox County.
Rosebrook; post village in Greene County.
Rosedale; post village in Russell County.
Rosehill; post village in Lee County on the Louisville and Nashville Railroad.
Roseland; post village in Nelson County.
Rose Mills; post village in Nelson County.
Rosena; post village in Albemarle County.
Rosenbaum; creek, a small left-hand branch of South Fork of Holston River in Washington County.
Rosenberger; post village in Frederick County.
Roseville; post village in Stafford County.
Rosewood; post village in Pittsylvania County.
Rosier; creek, a small right-hand branch of Potomac River in King George County.
Rosita; post village in King George County.
Rosslyn; post village in Alexandria County on the Philadelphia, Baltimore and Washington and the Washington, Alexandria and Mount Vernon railroads.
Rough; creek, a small left-hand tributary to Roanoke River in Charlotte County.
Rough; creek, a small branch of Appomattox River in Appomattox County.
Rough; mountains in Bath County. Elevation, 1,500 to 2,500 feet.
Rough; post village in Bedford County.
Roughcreek; post village in Charlotte County.
Round; mountain in Bland County. Elevation, 2,500 to 3,500 feet.
Round Hill; summit in Augusta County.
Round Hill; summit in Frederick County.
Round Hill; summit in Roanoke County.
Round Hill; summit in Rockingham County. Elevation, 1,500 feet.
Round Hill; town in Loudoun County on the Southern Railway. Altitude, 558 feet.
Round Mountain; summit in Amherst County. Elevation, 1,000 feet.
Round Mountain; summit in Botetourt County.
Round Top; summit of the Blue Ridge in Nelson and Amherst counties. Elevation, 3,430 feet.
Rouss; post village in Scott County.
Routts; post village in Fauquier County.
Rowanta; post village in Dinwiddie County.
Rowanty; creek, a left-hand branch of Nottoway River in southeast Virginia.
Roxbury; post village in Charles City County on the Chesapeake and Ohio Railway.
Roxie; post village in Smyth County.
Roxton; post village in Lunenburg County.
Royville; post village in Loudoun County.
Ruark; post village in Middlesex County.

Rubermont; post village in Lunenburg County.
Rucker; run, a small left-hand tributary to James River in Nelson County.
Ruckers; creek, a small left-hand tributary to James River in Amherst County.
Ruckers; gap in Bath County.
Ruckersville; post village in Greene County.
Ruckles; gap in Massanutten Mount.
Ruddle Mountain; summit on border of Roanoke and Bedford counties.
Rudder; post village in Sussex County.
Rudy; inlet, a narrow passage through the bordering sand bar on the southeast coast.
Rue; post village in Accomac County.
Ruel; post village in Hanover County.
Ruffins; post village in Surry County.
Rugby; post village in Grayson County.
Rumford; post village in King William County.
Ruralbower; post village in Greenesville County.
Rural Home; post village in Grayson County.
Rural Retreat; post village in Wythe County on the Norfolk and Western Railway. Altitude, 2,500 feet.
Rush; creek, a small left-hand branch of South Fork of Holston River in Washington County.
Rush; river, a small right-hand tributary to Rappahannock River in Rappahannock County.
Rushville; post village in Rockingham County.
Ruskin; post village in Tazewell County.
Russell; county, situated in the southwestern part of the State, mainly in the Appalachian Valley. It is drained by the Clinch River on the north. The county extends to the summit of the Alleghany front. It has an altitude of 3,700 feet, while that of Clinch River at the lowest point is about 1,400 feet above sea level. Area, 563 square miles. Population, 18,031—white, 17,267; negro, 764; foreign born, 8. County seat, Lebanon. The mean magnetic declination in 1900 was 1° 15′. The mean annual rainfall is 50 to 60 inches, and the temperature 50° to 55°. The county is traversed by the Norfolk and Western Railway.
Russell; creek, a small right-hand branch of Clinch River, rising in Dickenson County.
Russell; post village in Floyd County.
Russell Prator; small right-hand branch of Russell Fork, rising in Buchanan County.
Russell Rock; summit in Augustia County.
Russian; creek, a small left-hand fork of Clinch River, rising in Russell County.
Rustburg; county seat of Campbell County on the Norfolk and Western Railway. Altitude, 872 feet.
Ruth; post village in Madison County.
Rutherford; creek, a small left-hand branch of Cripple Creek in Wythe County.
Rutherglen; post village in Caroline County on the Richmond, Fredericksburg and Potomac Railroad.
Ruthville; post village in Charles City County.
Rutledges; creek, a small left-hand tributary to James River in Amherst County.
Rutman; branch, a small left-hand tributary to Roanoke River in Botetourt County.
Rux; post village in Brunswick County.
Ryan; post village in Loudoun County.
Ryecove; post village in Scott County.
Rye Valley; post village in Smyth County.
Ryland; post village in Culpeper County.

Sabot Island; post village in Goochland County.
Saddle; creek, a small right-hand branch of New River in Grayson County.
Saddle; post village in Grayson County.
Saffolds; post village in Mecklenburg County
Sago; post village in Pittsylvania County.
St. Brides; post village in Norfolk County on the Norfolk and Western Railway.
St. Clair; creek, a small left-hand branch of South Fork of Holston River in Smyth County.
St. Clair Bottom; village in Smyth County on the Norfolk and Western Railway. Altitude, 2,444 feet.
St. Davids Church; post village in Shenandoah County.
St. Elmo; post village in Alexandria County on the Washington, Alexandria and Mount Vernon Electric Railway.
St. Just; post village in Orange County.
St. Luke; post village in Shenandoah County.
St. Mary; river, a small left-hand tributary to James River in Augusta County.
St. Paul; post village in Wise County on the Norfolk and Western Railway. Altitude, 1,486 feet.
St. Stephens Church; post village in King and Queen County.
Salem; county seat of Roanoke County on the Norfolk and Western and the Southern railways. Altitude, 1,006 feet. Population, 3,412.
Salisbury Furnace; post village in Botetourt County on the Chesapeake and Ohio Railway. Altitude, 894 feet.
Sallee; creek, a small right-hand tributary to James River in Powhatan County.
Sallings Mountain; summits in Rockbridge County.
Salt; creek, a small left-hand tributary to James River in Amherst County.
Salt; pond in the eastern part of Princess Anne County.
Saltcreek; post village in Amherst County.
Saltpetre Cave; post village in Botetourt County on the Chesapeake and Ohio Railway. Altitude, 892 feet.
Salt Pond; mountains in Giles County. Elevation, 3,000 to 4,000 feet.
Saltville; town in Smyth County on the Norfolk and Western Railway. Altitude, 1,739 feet. Population, 1,051.
Saluda; county seat of Middlesex County.
Sambo; post village in Patrick County.
Samos; post village in Middlesex County.
Sampson; post village in Augusta County on the Norfolk and Western Railway.
Sampsons Wharf; post village in Northumberland County.
Sanco; post village in Prince Edward County.
Sand; mountains in Wythe County. Elevation, 2,500 feet.
Sand Bank; mountains in Botetourt County. Elevation, 2,500 feet.
Sand Bridge; locality in Princess Anne County.
Sandidges; post village in Amherst County.
Sandoval; post village in Culpeper County.
Sands; post village in Southampton County.
Sandstone Ridge; mountains in Roanoke County.
Sandy; point on Belmont Bay in Fairfax County.
Sandy; post village in Rappahannock County.
Sandy; river, a left-hand branch of Dan River in Pittsylvania County.
Sandy; river, a small right-hand tributary to Appomattox River in Prince Edward County.
Sandy; run, a small right-hand tributary to Potomac River in Prince William County.
Sandy Bottom; post village in Middlesex County.

Sandyford; post village in Bedford County.
Sandyhook; post village in Goochland County.
Sandy Level; post village in Pittsylvania County.
Sandy Ridge; mountains extending along the boundary line of Russell, Tazewell, and Buchanan counties.
Sandy Ridge; mountains in Wise and Dickenson counties. Elevation, 2,000 to 2,500 feet.
Sandy River; post village in Pittsylvania County.
Sanford; post village in Accomac County.
Sang Camp; fork, a small right-hand tributary to Levisa Fork in Buchanan County.
Sangerville; post village in Augusta County.
Santamo; post village in Buchanan County.
Santiago; post village in Page County.
Santos; post village in Floyd County.
Sanville; post village in Henry County.
Sappony; branch, a small left-hand branch of Appomattox River in Chesterfield County.
Saratoga; post village in Scott County.
Sassafras; post village in Gloucester County.
Sassin; post village in Pulaski County.
Saumsville; post village in Shenandoah County.
Saunders; post village in Nansemond County on the Suffolk and Carolina Railway.
Savage Crossing; post village in Nansemond County.
Savageville; post village in Accomac County.
Savannah; post village in Alleghany County.
Savedge; post village in Surry County on the Southern Railway.
Saw Mill; run, a small left-hand tributary to Shenandoah River in Augusta County.
Saw Mill Ridge; summit in Augusta County.
Saxe; post village in Charlotte County on the Southern Railway.
Saxis; post village in Accomac County.
Sayersville; post village in Tazewell County.
Saylers; creek, a small right-hand branch of Appomattox River in Prince Edward County.
Scaffold; run, a small right-hand tributary to Jackson River in Highland County.
Scheffer; gap in Little North Mountain in Shenandoah County.
School; post village in Henrico County.
Schoolhouse; branch, a small right-hand tributary to James River in Botetourt County.
Schuyler; post village in Nelson County.
Scotland; post village in Surry County on the Surry, Sussex and Southampton Railway.
Scott; county, situated in the southwestern part of the State. Its area consists of an alternation of narrow ridges and valleys, trending northeast and southwest. It is drained by the Clinch and the North Fork of Holston River. The altitude ranges from 1,200 to 4,000 feet. Area, 535 square miles. Population, 22,694—white, 22,067; negro, 627; foreign born, 9. County seat, Gate City. The mean annual rainfall is 50 to 60 inches, and the temperature 50° to 55°. The county is traversed by the Virginia and Southwestern Railway.
Scott; creek, a small left-hand branch of Elizabeth River in Norfolk County.
Scotts; ford of Middle River in Rockingham County.
Scotts; run, a small right-hand branch of Potomac River in Fairfax County.
Scottsburg; post village in Halifax County on the Southern Railway.
Scotts Crossroads; post village in Mecklenburg County.
Scottsford; village in Rockingham County.
Scotts Mountain; summit in Amherst County.

Scottsville; town in Albemarle County on the Chesapeake and Ohio Railway. Altitude, 275 feet. Population, 1,248.
Scrabble; post village in Rappahannock County.
Screamerville; post village in Spottsylvania County on the Potomac, Fredericksburg and Piedmont Railroad.
Scruggs; post village in Franklin County.
Scurff Mountain; summit in Botetourt County.
Sealston; post village in King George County.
Seaview; post village in Northampton County.
Sebrell; post village in Southampton County.
Second; small left-hand branch of Appomattox River in Chesterfield County.
Second; mountain in Rockingham County. Elevation, 2,000 to 2,500 feet.
Second Swamp; small right-hand tributary to James River in Prince George County.
Sedalia; post village in Bedford County.
Seddon; town in Bland County. Population, 240.
Seibert; run, a small right-hand tributary to Jackson River in Highland County.
Selden; post village in Gloucester County on the Chesapeake and Ohio Railway.
Self; village in Henry County.
Sells; village in Grayson County.
Selma; post village in Alleghany County.
Selone; post village in Fauquier County.
Seneca; river, a small left-hand branch of Roanoke River in Campbell County.
Sentinel; post village in Warren County.
Seven Fountains; post village in Shenandoah County.
Seven Islands; post village in Fluvanna County.
Seven Mile; ford of Middle Fork of Holston River in Smyth County.
Seven Mile; mountains in Craig County. Elevation, 2,000 to 2,500 feet.
Sevenmile Ford; post village in Smyth County.
Severn; post village in Gloucester County.
Seville; post village in Madison County.
Sewall; point of land, in Princess Anne County, extending into James River.
Sewells Point; post village in Norfolk County.
Sewish; creek, a small left-hand tributary to Meherrin River in Lunenburg County.
Sexton; post village in Surry County.
Shacklefords; post village in King and Queen County.
Shacklet; post village in Stafford County.
Shack Mills; post village in Buchanan County.
Shadwell; post village in Albermarle County on the Chesapeake and Ohio Railway.
Shadygrove; post village in Franklin County.
Shadyside; post village in Northampton County.
Shafer; creek, a right-hand branch of Powell River in Lee County.
Shafer; ford of Powell River in Lee County.
Shafter; post village in Albemarle County.
Shako; post village in Goochland County.
Shallow; ford of Roanoke River in Franklin County.
Shamrock; post village in Grayson County.
Shanghai; post village in King and Queen County.
Shanklin; post village in Bath County.
Shannon Hill; post village in Goochland County.
Shanty Hollow; small left-hand tributary to James River in Alleghany County.
Sharps; branch, a small right-hand tributary to Holston River, rising in Scott County.
Sharps; creek, a small right-hand tributary to James River in Buckingham County.
Sharps; post village in Richmond County.
Shaws; fork, a small left-hand tributary to James River in Highland County.

Shaws Ridge; mountains in Highland County, extending into Pendleton County, W. Va. Elevation, 2,500 feet.
Shaws Store; post village in Mecklenburg County.
Shawsville; post village in Montgomery County on the Norfolk and Western Railway. Altitude, 1,473 feet.
Shawver Mill; post village in Tazewell County.
Sheep; creek, a small left-hand tributary to Roanoke River in Bedford County.
Sheep; run, a small left-hand tributary to James River in Rockbridge County.
Sheetz; mountain in Boutetourt County.
Sheldries; creek, a small right-hand branch of James River in Buckingham County.
Shelfar; post village in Louisa County.
Shell; marshy point, in Princess Anne County, projecting into Back Bay.
Shell; post village in Mathews County.
Shellville; village in Montgomery County.
Shelton; post village in Nelson County.
Shenandoah; county, situated in the northwestern part of the State in the Appalachian Valley, there known as the Valley of the Shenandoah, extending from the Massanutten Mountain on the east to North Mountain, the State line, on the west. The surface is in the main undulating, diversified by a few parallel ridges. The altitude ranges from 600 feet up to 3,000 feet. Area, 486 square miles. Population, 20,253—white, 19,604; negro, 649; foreign born, 58. County seat, Woodstock. The mean magnetic declination in 1900 was 3° 50′. The mean annual rainfall is 50 to 60 inches, and the temperature 50° to 55°. The county is traversed by the Southern and the Baltimore and Ohio railroads.
Shenandoah; mountains in Highland and Bath counties. Elevation, 2,000 to 3,500 feet.
Shenandoah; river of Virginia and West Virginia; a right-hand branch of the Potomac, which heads in two large branches, North and South forks, in Augusta and Rockingham counties, and flows northeast to its junction with the Potomac at Harpers Ferry. The drainage area is 3,009 square miles.
Shenandoah; town in Page County on the Norfolk and Western Railway. Population, 1,220.
Shenandoah Alum Springs; post village in Shenandoah County.
Shendun; town in Rockingham County. Population, 381.
Sheppards; post village in Buckingham County on the Southern Railway.
Sherando; post village in Augusta County.
Sherwill; village in Campbell County.
Sherwood; post village in Rockbridge County on the Chesapeake and Ohio Railway.
Sheva; post village in Pittsylvania County.
Shields; gap in Nelson County.
Shiloh; post village in King George County.
Shirkey Mill; branch, a small right-hand tributary to James River in Botetourt County.
Shirley; post village in Charles City County.
Shockes; creek, a small left-hand tributary to Roanoke River in Bedford County.
Shockeysville; post village in Frederick County.
Shockoe; creek, a small left-hand tributary to James River in Henrico County.
Shockoe; post village in Pittsylvania County.
Shooting Creek; post village in Franklin County.
Shores; post village in Fluvanna County on the Chesapeake and Ohio Railway.
Short; mountain in Tazewell County. Elevation, 1,300 to 4,000 feet.
Short; mountains in Bath County.
Short; mountains in Shenandoah County. Elevation, 1,000 to 2,500 feet.
Short Hill; mountains in Loudoun County. Elevation, 1,000 feet.
Short Hills; mountains in Rockbridge County. Elevation, 2,000 to 2,565 feet.

Shorts Creek; post village in Carroll County.
Shortsville; post village in Washington County.
Shoulder; run, a small left-hand tributary to Roanoke River in Bedford County.
Shoulders Hill; post village in Nansemond County on the Southern Railway.
Shoult; creek, a small left-hand branch of North Fork of Holston River in Washington County.
Showalter; post village in Floyd County on the Baltimore and Ohio Railroad.
Shraders; post village in Tazewell County.
Shrouds; creek, a small right-hand branch of New River, rising in Pulaski County.
Shuff; post village in Patrick County.
Shuler; post village in Page County.
Shumansville; post village in Caroline County.
Siddons; post village in Mecklenburg County.
Sideburn; post village in Fairfax County on the Southern Railway.
Sideling Hill; mountains in Bath, Rockbridge, and Augusta counties. Elevation, 2,000 to 2,500 feet.
Sideway; post village in Rockbridge County.
Sidna; post village in Carroll County.
Sigma; post village in Princess Anne County.
Signpine; post village in Gloucester County.
Silcott Springs; post village in Loudoun County.
Silentdell; post village Botetourt County.
Siler; post village in Frederick County.
Silva; post village in Accomac County.
Silverton; post village in Southampton County.
Simeon; post village in Albemarle County
Simmonds; gap in Franklin County.
Simmons; gap in the Blue Ridge in Rockingham County.
Simmonsville; post village in Craig County.
Simonson; post village in Richmond County.
Simpson; creek, a small left-hand tributary to James River in Alleghany County.
Simpsons; post village in Floyd County on the Norfolk and Western Railway. Altitude, 665 feet.
Sims; post village in Goochland County.
Sinai; post village in Halifax County.
Singer; post village in Roanoke County on the Norfolk and Western Railway.
Singerglen; town in Rockingham County. Population, 108.
Singville; post village in Amelia County.
Sinking; creek, a small creek in Scott and Russell counties.
Sinking; creek, a right-hand branch of New River in Craig and Giles counties.
Sinking; creek, a small left-hand tributary to James River in Bath and Botetourt counties.
Sinking Creek; post village in Craig County.
Sinnickson; post village in Accomac County.
Sister Knob; summit in Bath County.
Sitlington; post village in Bath County.
Skeetrock; post village in Dickenson County.
Skidmore; fork, a small left-hand tributary to Shenandoah River in Augusta County.
Skidmore; run, a small left-hand tributary to Shenandoah River in Rockingham County.
Skinker; neck of land in Caroline County bounded by Rappahannock River.
Skinnels; creek, a small left-hand tributary to Roanoke River in Bedford County.
Skinquarter; creek, a small left-hand branch of Appomattox River on the border line between Powhatan and Chesterfield counties.

Skinquarter; post village in Chesterfield County on the Farmville and Powhatan Railroad.
Skippers; post village in Greenesville County.
Skipwith; post village in Mecklenburg County on the Southern Railway.
Sky; village in Rockingham County.
Skyland; post village in Page County.
Skyron; post village in King William County.
Slate; creek, a right-hand branch of Levisa Fork, rising in Buchanan County.
Slate; post village in Floyd County.
Slate; river, a small right-hand branch of James River in Buckingham County.
Slate; run, a small right-hand tributary to Potomac River in Prince William County.
Slate; springs in Rockingham County.
Slate Mills; post village in Rappahannock County.
Slate River Mills; post village in Buckingham County.
Slatesville; village in Pittsylvania County.
Slaughter; post village in Nelson County.
Sleepy; creek, a small right-hand tributary to Potomac River, formed by two forks, North and South, in Frederick County.
Slemp; creek, a small right-hand branch of South Fork of Holston River in Smyth County.
Slemp; post village in Lee County.
Slings; gap in the Blue Ridge in Franklin County.
Slings; gap in the Blue Ridge in Roanoke County.
Slusser; post village in Montgomery County.
Smacks; creek, a small right-hand branch of Appomattox River in Amelia County.
Smart; post village in Floyd County.
Smilax; post village in Mecklenburg County.
Smith; creek, a small left-hand tributary to James River in Alleghany and Augusta counties.
Smith; creek, a small left-hand tributary to North Fork of Holston River, rising in Washington County.
Smith; creek, a small left-hand tributary to Shenandoah River in Shenandoah County.
Smith; ford of Blackwater River in Franklin County.
Smith; mountains in Pittsylvania County. Elevation, 1,500 to 2,043 feet.
Smith; post village in Floyd County on the Chesapeake and Ohio Railway.
Smith; river, a large left-hand branch of Dan River in Patrick and Henry counties.
Smithcreek; post village in Washington County.
Smithfield; town in Isle of Wight County. Population, 1,225.
Smithland; post village in Albemarle County.
Smith Ridge; mountains in Roanoke County. Elevation, 1,500 feet.
Smith Ridge; summit in Roanoke County.
Smiths Crossroads; post village in Mecklenburg County.
Smithville; town in Charlotte County. Population, 96. Altitude, 1,150 feet.
Smoky Ordinary; post village in Brunswick County.
Smoots; post village in Caroline County.
Smyrna; post village in Bedford County.
Smyth; county, situated in the southwestern part of the State in the Appalachian Valley, and includes much of the headwaters of Holston River. Its surface is an alternation of narrow ridges and limestone valleys. The altitude ranges from 1,700 up to 4,000 feet. Area, 444 square miles. Population, 17,121—white, 15,950; negro, 1,170; foreign born, 60. County seat, Marion. The mean magnetic declination in 1900 was 1°. The mean annual rainfall is 50 to 60 inches, and the temperature 50 to 55°. The county is traversed by the Norfolk and Western Railway.

Smythers; post village in Carroll County.
Snail Creek; river, a small tributary to Nottoway River in Lunenburg County.
Snake; creek, a small right-hand tributary to New River in Carroll County.
Snake; run, a small right-hand tributary to Jackson River in Alleghany County.
Snakecreek; post village in Carroll County.
Snake Hollow; summit in Rockingham County.
Snake Run Ridge; mountains in Alleghany County. Elevation, 3,000 feet.
Snapp; post village in Tazewell County.
Snead; post village in Franklin County.
Sneads Spring; small left-hand tributary to Nottoway River in Nottoway County.
Snell; post village in Spottsylvania County.
Snelson; post village in Hanover County.
Snickers; gap in the Blue Ridge, Loudoun County.
Snidows; ferry over New River in Giles County.
Snow; creek, a small right-hand branch of James River in Bedford County.
Snowcreek; post village in Franklin County.
Snowden; post village in Amherst County.
Snowflake; post village in Scott County.
Snowville; post village in Pulaski County.
Snyder; post village in Augusta County.
Soapstone; post village in Pittsylvania County.
Soap Stone; quarry in Albemarle County.
Soles; post village in Mathews County.
Solomons; creek, a small right-hand branch of James River in Powhatan County.
Solomons; village in Henrico County.
Somerset; post village in Orange County on the Southern Railway.
Somerton; post village in Nansemond County.
Somerville; post village in Fauquier County.
Sontag; post village in Franklin County.
Soudan; post village in Mecklenburg County on the Southern Railway.
Sounding Knob; summit in Jack Mountains in Highland County.
South; small right-hand branch of Potomac River in Highland County.
South; mountains in Rockbridge County. Elevation, 1,500 to 2,500 feet.
South; river, a left-hand tributary to James River in Rockbridge County.
South; river, a right-hand branch of Shenandoah River in Augusta County. The mean discharge at Port Republic is 331¼ cubic feet per second.
South; river, a small right-hand branch of Mattaponi River in Caroline County.
South; run, a small right-hand tributary to Potomac River in Prince William and Fauquier counties.
South; run, a small right-hand branch of Potomac River in Fairfax County.
Southampton; county, situated in the southern part of the State on the Atlantic plain, bordering the North Carolina line. Its surface is level and but 100 or 200 feet above tide. Area, 609 square miles. Population, 22,848—white, 9,165; negro, 13,683; foreign born, 22. County seat, Courtland. The mean magnetic declination in 1900 was 3° 30'. The mean annual rainfall is 40 to 50 inches, and the temperature 55° to 60°. The county is traversed by the Southern and the Seaboard and Roanoke railways.
South Anna; river, a right-hand tributary to York River in Louisa County.
South Boston; town in Halifax County on the Norfolk and Western and the Southern railways. Population, 1,851.
South Hill; post village in Mecklenburg County on the Southern Railway.
South Norfolk; post village in Norfolk County.
South Quay; post village in Nansemond County.
South Western; mountains in Albemarle County. Elevation, 500 to 1,500 feet.

Sowego; post village in Fauquier County.
Sowers; post village in Floyd County.
Space; post village in Bedford County.
Spainville; post village in Nottoway County.
Spanish Oaks; village in Appomattox County.
Sparkling Springs; post village in Rockingham County.
Sparta; post village in Caroline County.
Spear; mountains in Buckingham County. Elevation, 1,000 to 1,500 feet.
Spear Mount; summit in Spear Mountain. Elevation, 1,500 feet.
Speedwell; post village in Wythe County.
Speer; ferry over Clinch River, at Speer Ferry town, in Scott County.
Speers Ferry; post village in Scott Couuty,
Spencer; post village in Henry County on the Danville and Western Railway. Altitude, 855 feet.
Sperryville; post village in Rappahannock County.
Spitler; post village in Augusta County on the Norfolk and Western Railroad.
Sponge; post village in Scott County.
Sport; post village in Augusta County.
Spotcash; post village in Brunswick County.
Spottsville; post village in Surry County.
Spottswood; post village in Augusta County on the Baltimore and Ohio Railroad.
Spottsylvania; county situated in the central part of the State, mainly in the Piedmont region. It has a rolling surface. The elevation is only 200 or 300 feet above sea level. Area, 401 square miles. Population, 9,239—white, 5,353; negro, 3,886; foreign born, 65. County seat, Spottsylvania. The mean magnetic declination in 1900 was 3° 45'. The mean annual rainfall is 40 to 50 inches, and the temperature 55° to 60°. The county is traversed by the Richmond, Fredericksburg and Potomac and the Southern railroads.
Spottsylvania; county seat of Spottsylvania County.
Spout; run, a small left-hand branch of Shenandoah River in Clarke County.
Spout; run, a small right-hand branch of Potomac River in Alexandria County.
Spoutsprings; post village in Appomattox County on the Norfolk and Western Railway. Altitude, 827 feet.
Spratts; post village in Smyth County.
Spring; branch, a small left-hand tributary to James River in Bath County.
Spring; creek, a small left-hand tributary to James River in Alleghany County.
Spring; creek, a small left-hand branch of Meherrin River in Lunenburg County.
Spring; creek, a small right-hand tributary to Appomattox River in Prince Edward County.
Spring; creek, a small right-hand branch of South Fork of Holston River, rising in Washington County.
Springcreek; post village in Rockingham County on the Chesapeake Western Railway.
Spring Garden; post village in Pittsylvania County.
Springgrove; post village in Surry County.
Springman; post village in Fairfax County.
Spring Mills; post village in Appomattox County.
Springvale; post village in Fairfax County.
Springvalley; post village in Grayson County.
Springville; post village in Tazewell County.
Springwood; post village in Botetourt County on the Chesapeake and Ohio Railway.
Sprouts; run, a small right-hand branch of James River in Botetourt County.
Spruce; run, a small right-hand branch of New River in Giles County.

Spruce Pine; branch, a small right-hand tributary to Levisa Fork in Buchanan County.
Spruce Run; mountains in Giles County. Elevation, 2,000 to 3,000 feet.
Spur; branch, a small right-hand tributary to Walker Creek in Wythe County.
Spurgeon; post village in Louisa County.
Spy; run, a small left-hand tributary to James River in Augusta County.
Spy Rock; summit in Nelson County. Altitude, 3,797 feet.
Squire; small left-hand branch of Slate Creek in Buchanan County.
Stafford; county, situated in the eastern part of the State in the Piedmont region. It has an undulating surface, rising in the western edge and summit of the Blue Ridge, which forms the boundary. Most of the area of the county lies between 200 and 500 feet in altitude, and covers 285 square miles. Population, 8,097—white, 6,489; negro, 1,608; foreign born, 33. County seat, Stafford. The mean magnetic declination in 1900 was 3° 50'. The mean annual rainfall is 40 to 50 inches, and the temperature 55° to 60°. The county is traversed by the Richmond, Fredericksburg and Potomac Railroad.
Stafford; county seat of Stafford County.
Stafford Store; post village in Stafford County.
Staffordsville; post village in Giles County.
Stage Junction; post village in Fluvanna County.
Staley; creek, a small left-hand branch of Middle Fork of Holston River in Smyth County.
Stanardsville; county seat of Greene County.
Standifords; creek, a small right-hand tributary to Roanoke River in Franklin County.
Stanley; post village in Henry County on the Norfolk and Western Railway.
Stanleyton; post village in Page County. Altitude, 1,064 feet.
Stanopher; village in Franklin County.
Stanton; creek, a small right-hand tributary to New River in Carroll County.
Stapleton Mills; post village in Amherst County on the Chesapeake and Ohio Railway.
Star; post village in Carroll County.
Starkey; post village in Patrick County on the Norfolk and Western Railway. Altitude, 1,124 feet.
Star Tannery; post village in Frederick County.
State Line; small right-hand branch of Levisa Fork, rising in Buchanan County.
Staunton; city, situated in Augusta County, but independent in government, although it contains the court-house, on the Chesapeake and Ohio and the Baltimore and Ohio railroads. Altitude 1,366 feet. Population, 7,289.
Staunton; creek, a small right-hand branch of Clinch River.
Staunton; river. See Roanoke River.
Stearnes; post village in Fluvanna County.
Stebbins; post village in Halifax County.
Steeleburg; post village in Tazewell County.
Steeles Tavern; post village in Augusta County.
Steffler; run, a small left-hand branch of Middle Fork of Holston River in Smyth County.
Stella; post village in Patrick County on the Danville and Western Railway.
Stephens; run, a small left-hand tributary to Shenandoah River in Frederick and Warren counties.
Stephens City; town in Frederick County on the Baltimore and Ohio Railroad. Population, 490.
Stephenson; post village in Frederick County on the Baltimore and Ohio Railroad. Altitude, 499 feet.
Sterling; post village in Loudoun County on the Southern Railway.

Sterling Knob; summit in Nelson County.
Stevensburg; post village in Culpeper County.
Stevensville; post village in King and Queen County.
Stewarts; creek, a small left-hand tributary to Yadkin River in Patrick County.
Stewarts Knob; summit in Roanoke County. Elevation, 2,472 feet.
Stewartsville; post village in Bedford County.
Stickleyville; post village in Lee County. Altitude, 1,589 feet.
Stile; post village in Scott County.
Stillhouse; small right-hand branch of North Fork of Holston River in Smyth County.
Stillhouse; small left-hand branch of New River in Grayson County.
Still House; branch, a small left-hand tributary to James River in Alleghany County.
Still House; run, a small right-hand branch of Shenandoah River in Rockingham County.
Stinson; post village in Russell County.
Stith; post village in Halifax County.
Stock; creek, a small right-hand branch of Appomattox River in Amelia County.
Stock; creek, a small right-hand branch of Clinch River in Scott County.
Stocker Knob; summit in Lee County. Elevation, 2,500 feet.
Stockton; fork, a small left-hand tributary to James River in Albemarle County.
Stocton; post village in Henry County.
Stoddert; post village in Cumberland County.
Stokes; post village in Goochland County on the Chesapeake and Ohio Railway.
Stokesland; post village in Pittsylvania County on the Danville and Western and the Southern railways.
Stone; creek, a small right-hand tributary to North Fork of Powell River.
Stone; mountains of Lee, Wise, Russell, and Scott counties.
Stonebridge; post village in Clarke County.
Stone Coal; small right-hand branch of Powell River in Wise County.
Stone Coal; creek, a small right-hand tributary to James River in Botetourt County.
Stonega; post village in Wise County on the Interstate Railroad.
Stonehouse; creek, a small left-hand tributary to James River in Amherst County.
Stoneleigh; post village in Fairfax County.
Stone Mountain; creek, a small right-hand tributary to New River in Carroll County.
Stone Mountain; post village in Carroll County.
Stone Mountain; summit in Bedford County. Elevation, 1,144 feet.
Stonewall; creek, a small right-hand branch of James River in Appomattox County.
Stonewall; post village in Augusta County.
Stoney; creek in Dinwiddie County.
Stoney; run, a small right-hand tributary to Shenandoah River in Page County.
Stony; creek, a left-hand branch of Nottoway River in southeast Virginia.
Stony; creek, a small left-hand tributary to South Fork of Roanoke River in Montgomery County.
Stony; creek, a small left-hand tributary to Shenandoah River in Shenandoah County.
Stony; creek, a small left-hand tributary to Roanoke River in Bedford County.
Stony; creek, a small right-hand branch of Clinch River in Scott County.
Stony; creek, a small right-hand branch of New River in Giles County.
Stony; run, a small left-hand branch of Chickahominy River in Hanover County.
Stony; run, a small left-hand branch of Shenandoah River in Rockingham County.
Stony; run, a small left-hand tributary to Shenandoah River in Augusta County.
Stony; run, a small right-hand tributary to Shenandoah River in Augusta County.

Stony; run, a small right-hand tributary to Shenandoah River in Page County.
Stony Battle; creek, a small right-hand tributary to James River in Botetourt County.
Stonycreek; post village in Sussex County on the Atlantic Coast Line Railroad.
Stonycross; post village in Mecklenburg County.
Stony Man; post village in Page County.
Stony Man; summit of the Blue Ridge in Madison County. Elevation, 4,031 feet.
Stonypoint; post village in Albemarle County.
Stonypoint Mills; post village in Cumberland County.
Stop; post village in Carroll County.
Stormont; post village in Middlesex County.
Stout; small right-hand branch of New River in Grayson County.
Stovall; post village in Halifax County.
Stovalls; creek, a small left-hand branch of James River in Amherst County.
Stover; post village in Augusta River.
Stowersville; post village in Bland County.
Straight; creek, a small left-hand branch of Stone Creek in Lee County.
Straight; creek, a small right-hand tributary to Clinch River in Scott County.
Straight; creek, a small right-hand tributary to Potomac River in Highland County.
Straight; fork, a small branch of North Fork of Potomac River in Highland County.
Straightstone; creek, a small right-hand branch of Roanoke River in Pittsylvania County.
Straightstone; post village in Pittsylvania County.
Stralia; post village in Alleghany County.
Strasburg; town in Shenandoah County on the Southern Railway. Altitude, 637 feet. Population, 690.
Stratford; post village in Westmoreland County.
Stratton; post village in Dickenson County.
Streets; post village in Middlesex County.
Strole; post village in Page County.
Strom; post village in Botetourt County.
Stroubles; creek, a small right-hand branch of New River in Montgomery and Pulaski counties.
Stuart; run, a small left-hand tributary to James River in Highland and Bath counties.
Stuart; county seat of Patrick County on the Danville and Western Railway. Altitude, 1,188 feet. Population, 371.
Stuart Mountain; summit in Lick Mountain in Wythe County.
Stuarts Draft; post village in Augusta County on the Norfolk and Western Railway. Altitude, 1,385 feet.
Stubbs; post village in Spottsylvania County.
Studley; post village in Hanover County.
Stuffle; run, a small branch of Reed Creek, rising in Wythe County.
Stull; run, a small right-hand tributary to Shenandoah River in Augusta County.
Stump; post village in Washington County.
Sturgeon; creek, a small left-hand branch of North Fork of Holston River in Washington County.
Sturgeon Point; post village in Charles City County.
Sturgeonville; post village in Brunswick County.
Suanee; creek, a small branch of Appomattox River in Appomattox County.
Subletts; post village in Powhatan County.
Success; post village in Warren County on the Norfolk and Western Railway.
Suck; creek, a small left-hand tributary to Roanoke River in Campbell County.
Suck; mountains in Bedford County. Elevation, 1,500 to 2,160 feet.

Sudley Springs; post village in Prince William County.

Suffolk; county seat of Nansemond County on the Atlantic Coast Line, the Norfolk and Western, the Seaboard Air Line, the Suffolk and Caroline, and the Southern railroads. Population, 3,827.

Sugar; creek, a small right-hand tributary to James River in Rockbridge County.

Sugar; run, a small left-hand branch of Walker Creek, in Giles County.

Sugar; run, a small right-hand branch of Cripple Creek in Wythe County.

Sugar; run, a small right-hand tributary to New River in Pulaski County.

Sugar; run, a small right-hand tributary to Powell River in Lee County.

Sugar; run, a small right-hand tributary to Roanoke River in Floyd County.

Sugargrove; post village in Smyth County.

Sugarland; run, a small right-hand branch of Potomac River in Loudoun County.

Sugar Loaf; summit in Augusta County. Elevation, 2,000 feet.

Sugar Loaf; summit in Botetourt County. Altitude, 2,393 feet.

Sugar Loaf; summit in Nelson County.

Sugar Loaf; summit in Roanoke County. Elevation, 2,000 feet.

Sugar Ridge; small left-hand branch of New River in Carroll County.

Sugar Run; mountains in Giles County. Elevation, 1,000 to 3,910 feet.

Sulphur Mines; post village in Louisa County.

Sulphur Ridge; spur from Prices Mountain in Botetourt County.

Summerdean; village in Augusta County.

Summerduck; post village in Fauquier County.

Summerduck; run, a small right-hand tributary to Rappahannock River in Culpeper County.

Summerfield; post village in Grayson County.

Summers; post village in Rockbridge County.

Summit; post village in Spottsylvania County on the Richmond, Fredericksburg and Potomac Railroad.

Sunbeam; post village in Southampton County.

Sunlight; post village in Spottsylvania County.

Sunnybank; post village in Northumberland County.

Sunnyside; post village in Cumberland County on the Farmville and Powhatan Railroad.

Sunrise; post village in Bath County.

Supin Lick; mountains in Shenandoah and Rockbridge counties. Elevation, 1,500 to 2,000 feet.

Supply; post village in Essex County.

Surber; post village in Botetourt County on the Chesapeake and Ohio Railway.

Surry; county, situated in the southeastern part of the State on the Atlantic plain. It lies on the south side of James River, at the mouth of Appomattox River. The surface is but little elevated above tide. Area, 292 square miles. Population, 8,469—white, 3,286; negro, 5,183; foreign born, 72. County seat, Surry. The mean magnetic declination in 1900 was 3° 45′. The mean annual rainfall is 40 to 50 inches, and the temperature 55° to 60°. The county is traversed by the Surry, Sussex and Southampton, and the Southern railways.

Surry; county seat of Surry County on the Surry, Sussex and Southampton Railway.

Susan; post village in Mathews County.

Susong; small right-hand branch of Beaver Creek, rising in Washington County.

Sussex; county, situated in the southern part of the State on the Atlantic plain. It has a level surface but little elevated above tide. Area, 490 square miles. Population, 12,082—white, 4,121; negro, 7,961; foreign born, 84. County seat, Sussex. The mean magnetic declination in 1900 was 3° 30′. The mean annual rainfall is 40 to 50 inches, and the temperature 55° to 60°. The county is traversed by the Southern, the Atlantic Coast Line, the Norfolk and Western, and the Surry, Sussex and Southampton railroads.

GAZETTEER OF VIRGINIA. 143

Sussex; county seat of Sussex County.
Sutherland; post village in Dinwiddie County.
Sutherlin; post village in Pittsylvania County on the Southern Railway.
Sutton; post village in Buckingham County.
Swamp; post village in Fauquier County.
Swans; post village in Amherst County.
Swansboro; post village in Chesterfield County.
Swansonville; post village in Pittsylvania County.
Sweathouse; creek, a small right-hand tributary to Appomattox River in Amelia County.
Sweet Chalybeate; post village in Alleghany County.
Sweet Chalybeate; spring in Alleghany County.
Sweet Hall; post village in King William County on the Southern Railway.
Sweet Spring; creek, a small right-hand tributary to Jackson River in Alleghany County.
Sweet Spring; run, a small left-hand branch of South Fork of Roanoke River in Montgomery County.
Sweet Springs; mountains in Alleghany County. Elevation, 2,000 to 3,500 feet.
Swepson; post village in Mecklenburg County.
Swetnam; post village in Fairfax County.
Swift; creek, a small left-hand branch of Appomattox River in Chesterfield County.
Swift; creek, a small right-hand tributary to James River in Chesterfield County.
Swift; run, a small left-hand tributary to James River in Greene County.
Swift; run, a small right-hand tributary to Shenandoah River in Rockingham County.
Swiftrun; post village in Rockingham County.
Swoope; post village in Augusta County on the Chesapeake and Ohio Railway. Altitude, 1,650 feet.
Sword; creek, a small right-hand tributary to Clinch River in Russell County.
Swordscreek; post village in Russell County on the Norfolk and Western Railway. Altitude, 1,861 feet.
Swover; creek, a small left-hand tributary to Shenandoah River in Shenandoah County.
Sycamore; creek, a small right-hand tributary to Roanoke River in Pittsylvania County.
Sycamore Station; post village in Pittsylvania County.
Sycoline; creek, a small right-hand tributary to Potomac River in Loudoun County.
Sycoline; post village in Loudoun County.
Sydney; post village in Montgomery County.
Sydnorsville; post village in Franklin County.
Sylvatus; post village in Carroll County.
Symms; gap in Peters Mountain in Giles County.
Syria; post village in Madison County.
Ta; river, a small right-hand branch of Mattaponi River in Spottsylvania County.
Tabb; post village in York County.
Tabor; post village in Washington County.
Tabscott; post village in Goochland County.
Taccio; village in Franklin County.
Tackett Mills; post village in Stafford County.
Tacoma; town in Wise County on the Norfolk and Western Railway. Altitude, 1,990 feet. Population, 247.
Taggart; post village in Buckingham County.
Talley; creek, a small right-hand tributary to York River.
Talleysville; post village in New Kent County.

Tally; post village in Cumberland County.
Talmash; post village in Giles County.
Talpa; post village in Prince George County.
Tamarack Ridge; mountains in Highland County
Tamesa; post village in Franklin County.
Tampico; post village in York County.
Tamworth; post village in Cumberland County.
Tangier; post village in Accomac County.
Tanner; branch, a small right-hand tributary to Appomattox River in Amelia County.
Tanner; creek, a tidal stream or estuary flowing into Hampton Roads in Princess Anne County.
Tanner; point of land extending into Tanner Creek where it empties into James River.
Tannerscreek; post village in Norfolk County.
Tannersville; post village in Tazewell County.
Tanny; post village in Mecklenburg County.
Tanyard; branch, a small left-hand tributary to Roanoke River in Charlotte County.
Tan Yard; village in Henry County.
Tappahannock; county seat of Essex County. Population, 554.
Taranto; post village in Augusta County.
Tardy; branch, a small left-hand tributary to Roanoke River in Campbell County.
Tarlac; post village in Floyd County.
Taro; post village in Charlotte County.
Tarpon; post village in Dickenson County.
Tarrys Mill; post village in Mecklenburg County.
Tasley; post village in Accomac County on the New York, Philadelphia and Norfolk Railroad.
Tasso; post village in Wise County.
Tate; post village in Montgomery County on the Virginia and Southwestern Railway.
Tattle; small left-hand branch of Middle Fork of Holston River in Smyth County.
Tatum; post village in Orange County.
Taylor; creek, a small left-hand tributary to James River in Nelson County.
Taylors; creek, a small right-hand tributary to York River in Louisa and Hanover counties.
Taylors; mountains in Bedford County. Elevation, 1,500 to 2,555 feet.
Taylorsburg; village in Henry County,
Taylors Store; post village in Franklin County.
Taylorstown; post village in Loudoun County.
Taylorsville; post village in Hanover County on the Richmond, Fredericksburg and Potomac Railroad.
Tazewell; county, situated in the western part of the State in the Appalachian Valley. Its surface consists of an alternation of narrow ridges and valleys, drained in the main by Clinch River. On the north it extends into the Alleghany plateau, including a portion of the upper waters of the Tug Fork of Big Sandy. Area, 557 square miles. Population, 23,384—white, 19,802; negro, 3,582; foreign born, 410. County seat, Tazewell. The mean magnetic declination in 1900 was 1° 45'. The mean annual rainfall is 50 to 60 inches, and the temperature 50° to 55°. The county is traversed by the Norfolk and Western Railway.
Tazewell; county seat of Tazewell County on the Norfolk and Western Railway. Altitude, 2,372 feet. Population, 1,096.
Tea; mountains in Shenandoah County. Elevation, 2,000 feet.
Tear Wallet; creek, a small left-hand branch of Appomattox River in Cumberland County.

Teck; post village in King William County.
Tell; post village in Pittsylvania County.
Temperanceville; post village in Accomac County.
Tempest; post village in Lunenburg County.
Templeman Crossroads; post village in Westmoreland County.
Templeton; branch, a small left-hand tributary to Clinch River in Scott County.
Templeton; post village in Prince George County on the Chesapeake and Ohio Railway.
Tenth Legion; village in Rockingham County.
Terrapin; creek, a small left-hand tributary to Roanoke River in Bedford County.
Terrapin; mountain in the Blue Ridge, Bedford County.
Terryl; post village in Halifax County.
Terrys Fork; post village in Floyd County.
Terryville; post village in Charlotte County.
Tettington; post village in Charles City County.
Thalia; post village in Princess Anne County on the Norfolk and Southern Railroad.
Thaxton; post village in Bedford County on the Norfolk and Western Railway. Altitude, 950 feet.
The Falls; post village in Nottoway County,
The Hollow; post village in Patrick County.
Thelma; post village in Louisa County.
Theological Seminary; post village in Fairfax County.
The Plains; post village in Fauquier County.
Thessalia; post village in Giles County.
Theta; post village in Campbell County.
Third; branch, a small left-hand tributary to Appomattox River in Chesterfield County.
Thomasburg; post village in Brunswick County.
Thompson; creek, a small left-hand tributary to James River in Amherst County.
Thompson; creek, a small right-hand branch of Clinch River in Russell County.
Thompson; valley in Tazewell County.
Thompsons Crossroads; post village in Louisa County.
Thompson Springs; creek, a small left-hand tributary to James River in Bath County.
Thompson Valley; post village in Tazewell County.
Thorn; creek, a small right-hand branch of Cripple Creek in Wythe County.
Thornburg; post village in Spottsylvania County.
Thorne; ferry in New River, Wythe County.
Thornhill; post village in Orange County.
Thornton; gap in the Blue Ridge in Rappahannock County. Elevation, 2,279 feet.
Thornton; river, a small right-hand tributary to Rappahannock River in Rappahannock County.
Thorny; branch, a small right-hand tributary to Jackson River in Alleghany County.
Thorofare; gap between Pond and Bull Run mountains.
Thoroughfare; gap in Nelson County.
Thoroughfare; mountains in Madison County. Elevation, 1,000 feet.
Thoroughfare; post village in Prince William County on the Southern Railway.
Three; creek, a right-hand branch of Nottoway River in southeastern Virginia.
Three Mile; mountains in Shenandoah County. Elevation, 1,500 feet.
Three Ridges; summits in Nelson County.
Three Square; post village in Goochland County.
Three Top; mountains in Shenandoah County. Elevation, 1,000 to 1,500 feet.
Throck; post village in Prince Edward County.

Thumb; run, a small left-hand branch of Rappahannock River in Fauquier County.
Thunder Hill; summit in Botetourt County.
Thurman; post village in Bedford County.
Tibitha; post village in Northumberland County.
Tice; post village in Carroll County.
Tidwells; post village in Westmoreland County.
Tilda; post village in Lee County.
Tilson; gap in Walker Mountain in Wythe County.
Tilson Mill; post village in Bland County.
Tim; post village in Patrick County.
Timber; creek, a left-hand branch of Roanoke River in Botetourt and Roanoke counties.
Timberridge; post village in Rockbridge County on the Baltimore and Ohio Railroad.
Timber Ridge; mountains in Augusta County. Elevation, 2,500 to 3,000 feet.
Timber Ridge; mountains in Botetourt County. Elevation, 1,500 feet.
Timber Ridge; mountains in Frederick County, Va., and Morgan County, W. Va.
Timbertree; creek, a small right-hand tributary to Holston River, rising in Scott County.
Timberville; town in Rockingham County on the Southern Railway. Altitude, 1,018 feet. Population, 173.
Timbo; post village in Bedford County.
Timothy; post village in Craig County.
Timsberry; creek, a small right-hand tributary to James River in Chesterfield County.
Tindall; post village in Floyd County.
Tinker; mountains in Botetourt County. Elevation, 1,500 to 3,029 feet.
Tinkerknob; post village in Botetourt County.
Tinkling; post village in Lunenburg County.
Tin Pot; run, a small left-hand branch of Rappahannock River in Fauquier County.
Tipton; post village in Carroll County on the Norfolk and Western Railway.
Tiptop; post village in Tazewell County on the Norfolk and Western Railway. Altitude, 2,754 feet.
Titus; post village in Appomattox County.
Toad; run, a small left-hand tributary to James River in Rockbridge County.
Toad; run, a small right-hand tributary to James River in Rockbridge County.
Toano; post village in James City County on the Chesapeake and Ohio Railway.
Tobacco; creek, a small right-hand branch of Rappahannock River in Caroline County.
Tobacco; post village in Brunswick County.
Tobacco Row; mountains in Amherst County. Elevation 1,000 to 3,000 feet.
Tobacco Row; summit in Tobacco Row Mountains; a station in triangulation of the United States Coast and Geodetic Survey. Elevation, 2,938 feet.
Tobaccoville; post village in Powhatan County on the Farmville and Powhatan Railroad.
Tobax; post village in Patrick County.
Toga; post village in Buckingham County.
Toka; village in Halifax County.
Tola; post village in Charlotte County.
Tolers; ferry over Roanoke River in Pittsylvania County.
Toluca; post village in Stafford County.
Tomahawk; creek, a small left-hand tributary to Appomattox River in Chesterfield County.
Tomahawk; creek, a small right-hand tributary to James River in Campbell County.
Tomahawk; mountain in Rockingham County.

Tomahawk; village in Pittsylvania County.
Tombs; post village in Lancaster County.
Toms; creek, a small right-hand branch of New River in Pulaski, Montgomery, and Franklin counties.
Tomsbrook; post village in Shenandoah County on the Southern Railway. Altitude, 745 feet.
Toms Brook; small left-hand tributary to Shenandoah River in Shenandoah County.
Tongue Quarter; creek, a small right-hand tributary to James River in Buckingham County.
Tool; creek, a small left-hand branch of North Fork of Holston River in Washington County.
Tooters; creek, a small left-hand branch of James River in Albemarle County.
Topeco; post village in Floyd County.
Tophet; post village in Fairfax County.
Topnot; post village in Shenandoah County.
Topping; post village in Middlesex County.
Torega; post village in Botetourt County.
Torry; mountains in Augusta County.
Tory Knob; summit in Bedford County. Elevation, 2,280 feet.
Toshes; post village in Pittsylvania County on the Southern Railway.
Totaro; post village in Brunswick County.
Totopotomoy; creek, a small right-hand tributary to Pamunkey River in Hanover County.
Towell; village in Lee County.
Tower Hill; mountains in Bath County. Elevation, 2,000 to 3,000 feet.
Towerhill; post village in Appomattox County.
Tower Mountain; summit in Albemarle County. Elevation, 1,000 feet.
Town; small left-hand branch of Clinch River in Tazewell County.
Town; small right-hand branch of New River in Grayson County.
Town; branch, a small right-hand tributary to James River in Botetourt County.
Town; creek, a small right-hand tributary to Walker Creek, rising in Bland County.
Town; creek, a small right-hand branch of Guest River in Wise County.
Town; point on Elizabeth River in Norfolk County.
Town; run, a small right-hand tributary to Potomac River in Fauquier County.
Townsend; post village in Northampton County.
Trace; branch, a small left-hand tributary to Levisa Fork in Buchanan County.
Tract; fork, a small left-hand tributary to New River in Pulaski County.
Tract; mountains in Wythe and Pulaski counties. Elevation 2,500 to 3,000 feet.
Trade; post village in Amelia County.
Traders; post village in Mathews County.
Traffic; post village in Lunenburg County.
Trapp; post village in Loudoun County.
Travis; post village in Prince Edward County.
Trayfoot; mountain in the Blue Ridge in Rockingham County.
Treakles; post village in Lancaster County.
Tredway; post village in Prince Edward County.
Trelow; village in Pittsylvania County.
Trenholm; post village in Powhatan County.
Trenton Mills; post village in Cumberland County.
Trevilians; post village in Louisa County on the Chesapeake and Ohio Railway. Altitude, 523 feet.
Triangle; post village in Nottoway County.
Trice; post village in Louisa County on the Chesapeake and Ohio Railway. Altitude, 1,816 feet.
Triford; post village in Rockbridge County.

Trigg; post village in Giles County on the Norfolk and Western Railway.
Trilby; post village in Northumberland County.
Trimble; mountains in Augusta County.
Trimble; post village in Highland County.
Trinity; post village in Botetourt County.
Triplet; post village in Brunswick County on the Southern Railway.
Trix; post village in Lunenburg County.
Trone; post village in Frederick County.
Troublesome; creek, a small left-hand branch of Clinch River in Scott County.
Troublesome; creek, a small left-hand tributary to Roanoke River in Campbell County.
Troublesome; creek, a small right-hand tributary to James River in Buckingham County.
Trough; run, a small left-hand tributary to Roanoke River in Bedford County.
Trout; creek, a small right-hand tributary to James River in Roanoke County.
Troutdale; post village in Grayson County.
Troutville; post village in Botetourt County.
Trower; post village in Accomac County.
Trueblue; post village in Orange County.
Truhart; post village in King and Queen County.
Truitt; post village in Dinwiddie County.
Truxillo; post village in Amelia County.
Tuan; post village in Stafford County.
Tuckahoe; creek, a small left-hand tributary to James River in Henrico County.
Tuckahoe; post village in Henrico County on the Chesapeake and Ohio Railway.
Tucker; post village in Buckingham County on the Norfolk and Western Railway.
Tuckerhill; post village in Westmoreland County.
Tug; post village in Grayson County.
Tuggles Gap; post village in Patrick County.
Tulip; post village in Frederick County.
Tumbez; village in Russell County.
Tumbling; creek, a small right-hand branch of North Fork of Holston River in Washington County.
Tunis; post village in Rockingham County.
Tunstall; post village in New Kent County on the Southern Railway.
Turbeville; post village in Halifax County.
Turk; gap in the Blue Ridge in Augusta County.
Turk Mountain; summit in Augusta County.
Turk Mountain; summit in Nelson County.
Turkey; run, a small left-hand tributary to Shenandoah River in Frederick County.
Turkey; run, a small right-hand tributary of Potomac iver in Fauquier County.
Turkey Cock; branch, a small left-hand tributary to Roanoke River in Charlotte County.
Turkey Cock; run, a small right-hand tributary to Potomac River in Fairfax County.
Turkeycove; post village in Lee County.
Turkey Egg; creek, a small left-hand tributary to Nottoway River in Dinwiddie County.
Turkey Island; creek, a small left-hand branch of James River in Henrico County.
Turkey Mountain; summit in Amherst County. Elevation, 1,500 feet.
Turkey Mountain; summit in Greene County. Elevation, 1,500 feet.
Turman; post village in Floyd County.
Turnbull; post village in Fauquier County.
Turner; post village in Brunswick County.

Turners; ford of Roanoke River in Bedford County.
Turners; ford of Roanoke River in Franklin County.
Turnip; creek, a small left-hand tributary to Roanoke River in Charlotte County.
Turpin; creek, a small right-hand tributary to James River in Buckingham County.
Turtlerock; post village in Floyd County.
Tuscarora; creek, a small right-hand tributary to Potomac River in Loudoun County.
Tuscola; post village in Dickenson County.
Tusekiah; creek, a small left-hand branch of Meherrin River in Lunenburg County.
Tussocky; creek, a small right-hand tributary to James River in Campbell County.
Twedys; post village in Campbell County.
Twelve O'clock Knob; summit in Roanoke County. Elevation, 2,707 feet.
Twin; small left-hand branch of Slate Creek in Buchanan County.
Two Mile; run, a small right-hand branch of Shenandoah River in Rockingham County.
Twymans Mill; post village in Madison County.
Twymans Store; post village in Spottsylvania County.
Tye; river, a small left-hand branch of James River formed by North and South forks in Nelson County.
Tye River; gap in the Blue Ridge in Nelson County.
Tye River Depot; post village in Nelson County on the Southern Railway. Altitude, 548 feet.
Tygers; creek, a small right-hand tributary to Jackson River in Alleghany County.
Tylers; post village in Hanover County.
Tyro; post village in Nelson County.
Uggal; post village in Southampton County.
Ula; post village in King and Queen County.
Ullainee; post village in Essex County.
Unaka; post village in Tazewell County.
Union; creek, a small right-hand tributary to James River in Rockbridge County.
Unionhall; post village in Franklin County.
Unionlevel; post village in Mecklenburg County on the Southern Railway.
Union Mills; post village in Fluvanna County.
Unionville; post village in Orange County on the Potomac, Fredericksburg and Piedmont Railroad. Altitude, 500 feet.
Unison; post village in Loudoun County.
Unity; post village in Southampton County.
Uno; post village in Madison County.
Upper Elk; creek, a small right-hand branch of Knox Creek, rising in Buchanan County.
Upper Rockhouse; small right-hand branch of Slate Creek, a tributary to Levisa Fork, in Buchanan County.
Upperville; town in Fauquier County. Population, 376.
Upper Zion; post village in Caroline County.
Upright; post village in Essex County.
Upton Hill; summit in Fairfax County.
Urbanna; post village in Middlesex County.
Ursus; post village in Grayson County.
Utt; post village in Carroll County.
Vale; post village in Fairfax County.
Valentine; creek, a small right-hand branch of Roanoke River in Pittsylvania County.
Valentines; post village in Brunswick County.
Valeria; post village in Nansemond County.

Valley; creek, a small left-hand tributary to South Fork of Holston River in Washington County.
Valley; creek, a small left-hand tributary to Clinch River, rising in Scott County.
Valley Center; post village in Highland County.
Valleycreek; post village in Scott County.
Valley Mills; post village in Augusta County.
Van; post village in Lee County.
Vanburen Furnace; post village in Shenandoah County.
Vance; post village in Pittsylvania County.
Vancluse; gold mine in Spottsylvania County.
Vanderpool; gap between Monterey and Back Creek mountains, caused by a tributary to James River.
Vanderpool; post village in Highland County.
Vandola; post village in Pittsylvania County.
Vanlear; post village in Augusta County.
Varallo; post village in Patrick County.
Vareo; post village in Louisa County.
Variety Mills; post village in Nelson County.
Variety Springs; post village in Augusta County on the Chesapeake and Ohio Railway.
Varinagrove; village in Henrico County.
Varst; post village in Madison County.
Vaucluse; post village in Frederick County on the Baltimore and Ohio Railroad.
Vaughn; post village in Floyd County.
Vaughns; creek, a small right-hand tributary to Appomattox River, between Prince Edward and Appomattox counties.
Vaught; small left-hand branch of Middle Fork of Holston River in Smyth County.
Vawters Store; post village in Louisa County.
Veach; post village in Lee County.
Venable; creek, a small left-hand tributary to James River in Fluvanna County.
Venables; bridge across Appomattox River, between Prince Edward and Buckingham counties.
Venner; post village in Prince Edward County.
Venrick; run, a small branch of Reed Creek in Wythe County.
Venter; post village in King William County.
Vera; post village in Appomattox County.
Verano; post village in Patrick County.
Verbena; post village in Page County.
Verdant; post village in Lee County.
Verdierville; post village in Orange County on the Potomac, Fredericksburg and Piedmont Railroad. Altitude, 514 feet.
Verdon; post village in Hanover County on the Chesapeake and Ohio Railway.
Vermilion; post village in Appomattox County.
Verna; post village in Southampton County.
Vernonhill; post village in Halifax County.
Vernon Mills; post village in Fauquier County.
Vesta; post village in Patrick County.
Vestal; post village in Washington County.
Vesuvius; post village in Rockbridge County on the Norfolk and Western Railway. Altitude, 1,417 feet.
Vicar Switch; post village in Montgomery County.
Vick; post village in Floyd County.
Vicksville; post village in Southampton County.
Victoria; mines in Rockbridge County.
Vienna; town in Fairfax County on the Southern Railway. Population, 317.

Viewtown; post village in Rappahannock County.
View Tree; mountains in Fauquier County. Elevation, 500 to 750 feet.
Vigor; post village in Louisa County.
Villa; post village in Franklin County.
Village; post village in Northumberland County.
Vilna; post village in Highland County.
Vincent Store; post village in Charlotte County.
Vine; post village in Princess Anne County.
Vinita; post village in Goochland County on the Chesapeake and Ohio Railway.
Vinton; town in Roanoke County on the Norfolk and Western Railway. Altitude, 910 feet. Population, 1,438.
Virgilina; town in Halifax County on the Southern Railway. Population, 200.
Virginia Beach; resort on the Atlantic coast in Princess Anne County on the Norfolk and Southern Railroad.
Virginia City; post village in Wise County on the Norfolk and Western Railway.
Vivian; post village in King George County.
Void; post village in Mecklenburg County.
Volens; post village in Halifax County.
Volney; post village in Grayson County.
Vontay; post village in Hanover County.
Vulcan; post village in Orange County.
Wachapreague; post village in Accomac County.
Waddy; post village in Spottsylvania County.
Wades; post village in Bedford County.
Wadesville; post village in Clarke County.
Waidsboro; post village in Franklin County on the Norfolk and Western Railway. Altitude, 1,260 feet.
Wainwright; post village in Grayson County.
Wake; post village in Middlesex County.
Wakefield Station; post village in Sussex County on the Norfolk and Western Railway.
Wakema; post village in King William County.
Walcot; post village in Floyd County.
Waldelock; post village in Hanover County.
Waldrop; post village in Louisa County.
Walker; creek, a right-hand tributary to New River, rising in Bland County and flowing northeast into New River.
Walker; creek, a small left-hand tributary to James River in Augusta County.
Walker; creek, a small tributary to Middle Fork of Holston River in Smyth County.
Walker; ford of James River in Amherst County.
Walker; mountains in Bath County. Elevation, 2,000 to 2,500 feet.
Walker; mountains extending from Washington to Bland counties. Elevation, 2,500 to 4,000 feet.
Walkerford; post village in Amherst County on the Chesapeake and Ohio Railway.
Walkers; creek, a small left-hand tributary to James River in Rockbridge County.
Walkers; mountains in Bath and Augusta counties. Elevation, 2,500 to 3,000 feet.
Walkers; post village in New Kent County on the Chesapeake and Ohio Railway.
Walkerton; post village in King and Queen County.
Wallace; branch, a small left-hand tributary to Roanoke River in Charlotte County.
Wallace; creek, a small right-hand branch of Appomattox River in Dinwiddie County.
Wallace; post village in Washington County on the Norfolk and Western Railway. Altitude, 1,880 feet.
Wallaceton; post village in Norfolk County.
Wallen; creek, a small left-hand branch of Powell River in Lee County,

Wallen Ridge; mountains in Lee County.
Wallens Ridge; mountains in the southeastern part of Lee County, extending southwest into Tennessee.
Wallers; post village in Henry County on the Norfolk and Western Railway. Altitude, 730 feet.
Walls Bridge; post village in Surry County.
Walnut; branch, a small left-hand tributary to James River in Albemarle County.
Walnuthill; post village in Lee County.
Walthall Store; post village in Brunswick County.
Walton; fork, a small right-hand tributary to James River in Buckingham County.
Walton Furnace; post village in Wythe County.
Waltons Store; post village in Louisa County.
Wampler; small right-hand branch of Cripple Creek in Wythe County.
Wampler; post village in Dickenson County.
Wan; post village in Gloucester County.
Waqua; post village in Brunswick County.
Ward; small right-hand branch of Cripple Creek in Wythe County.
Ward; cove in Tazewell County.
Wardgap; post village in Carroll County.
Wards; fork, a small left-hand tributary to Roanoke River in Charlotte County.
Wardsfork Mills; post village in Charlotte County.
Wards Mill; branch, a small right-hand tributary to New River in Carroll County.
Wards Mill; post village in Carroll County.
Wards Road; ferry over Roanoke River in Pittsylvania County.
Wardtown; post village in Northampton County.
Ware; creek, a small right-hand branch of Rappahannock River in Caroline County.
Warehouse; post village in Mathews County.
Wareneck; post village in Gloucester County.
Wares Wharf; post village in Essex County.
Warfield; post village in Brunswick County on the Seaboard Air Line Railway.
Warminster; post village in Nelson County on the Chesapeake and Ohio Railway.
Warm Spring; mountains in Alleghany and Bath counties. Elevation, 2,000 to 4,000 feet.
Warm Spring; run, a small left-hand tributary to James River in Bath County.
Warm Springs; county seat of Bath County.
Warner; post village in Middlesex County.
Warren; county, situated in the northern part of the State and including a part of the Shenandoah Valley, its eastern boundary being the summit of the Blue Ridge. The surface consists in part of a level valley, and in part of the heavy spurs of the Blue Ridge; the altitude ranges from 500 to 3,300 feet upon the Blue Ridge. Area, 226 square miles. Population, 8,837—white, 7,372; negro, 1,463; foreign born, 40. County seat, Front Royal. The mean magnetic declination in 1900 was 3° 30′. The mean annual rainfall is 50 to 60 inches, and the temperature 50° to 55°. The county is traversed by the Norfolk and Western and the Southern railways.
Warren; post village in Albemarle County on the Chesapeake and Ohio Railway.
Warrenton; county seat of Fauquier County on the Southern Railway. Population, 1,627.
Warsaw; county seat of Richmond County.
Warwick; county, situated in the eastern part of the State on the north bank of James River on the Atlantic plain. The surface is low and level, and but little elevated above tide. Area, 85 square miles. Population, 4,888—white, 1,159; negro, 3,729; foreign born, 82. County seat, Denbigh. The mean magnetic declination in 1900 was 4°. The mean annual rainfall is 40 to 50 inches, and the temperature 55° to 60°. The county is traversed by the Chesapeake and Ohio Railway.

Warwick; run, a small right-hand tributary to Jackson River in Highland County.
Warwick Ridge; mountains in Bath County. Elevation, 2,500 to 3,000 feet.
Warwick Swamp; small right-hand tributary to James River in Prince George County.
Washikee; post village in Greenesville County.
Washington; county, situated in the southwestern part of the State. It is drained by the three main forks of Holston River, and its surface consists mainly of the valley through which they flow, limited on the north by Clinch Mountain. The altitude ranges from 1,600 to 4,000 feet above sea level. Area, 605 square miles. Population, 28,995—white, 26,433; negro, 2,555; foreign born, 33. County seat, Abingdon. The main annual rainfall is 50 to 60 inches, and the temperature 50° to 55°. The county is traversed by the Norfolk and Western and the Virginia and Southwestern railways.
Washington; county seat of Rappahannock County. Population, 300.
Washington; point on the eastern branch of Elizabeth River in Norfolk County.
Waskey Mills; post village in Botetourt County.
Wasp; post village in Carroll County.
Wat; post village in Culpeper County.
Watauga; post village in Washington County on the Virginia-Carolina Railway.
Watch; run, a small right-hand tributary to James River in Chesterfield County.
Waterfall; post village in Prince William County.
Waterford; town in Loudoun County. Population, 383.
Waterlick; post village in Warren County on the Southern Railway. Altitude, 550 feet.
Waterloo; post village in Culpeper County on the Washington Southern Railway.
Wateroak; post village in Princess Anne County.
Waterview; post village in Middlesex County.
Waterway; post village in Princess Anne County.
Watery; mountains in Fauquier County. Elevation, 750 to 1,000 feet.
Watkins; post village in Halifax County on the Southern Railway.
Watson; creek, a small right-hand tributary to Appomattox River in Nottoway County.
Watson; post village in Loudoun County.
Wattsboro; post village in Lunenburg County.
Wattsville; post village in Accomac County.
Waugh; post village in Bedford County on the Chesapeake and Ohio Railway.
Waughes; ford of James River in Amherst County.
Wauk; point in Princess Anne County, extending into North Landing River.
Waverly; town in Sussex County on the Norfolk and Western and the Southern railways. Population, 493.
Waxpool; post village in Loudoun County.
Way; post village in Amherst County.
Waycross; post village in Highland County.
Wayland; post village in Scott County.
Waynesboro; town in Augusta County on the Chesapeake and Ohio Railway. Altitude, 1,295 feet. Population, 856.
Weal; post village in Pittsylvania County.
Wealthia; post village in Buckingham County.
Weaver Knob; summit in Bedford County. Elevation, 2,615 feet.
Weavers; creek, a small right-hand branch of Clinch River, rising in Russell County.
Webb; post village in Carroll County.
Webb Mill; creek, a small left-hand tributary to Appomattox River in Appomattox County.
Webbs; ford of Roanoke River in Bedford County.
Weddle; post village in Floyd County.

Wedstone; creek, a small left-hand branch of South Fork of Holston River in Smyth County.
Weedonville; post village in King George County.
Weems; post village in Lancaster County.
Welbourne; post village in Loudoun County.
Welchburg; post village in Scott County.
Welches; run, a small left-hand tributary to Roanoke River in Botetourt County.
Welchs; post village in Caroline County.
Welcome; post village in King George County.
Wellford; post village in Richmond County.
Wellington; post village in Prince William County on the Southern Railway.
Wellville; post village in Nottoway County on the Norfolk and Western Railway.
Wellwater; post village in Buckingham County.
Welsh; summit in Nelson County.
Wenonda; post village in Pittsylvania County.
Wert; post village in Appomattox County.
Wesson; post village in Lee County.
West; fork, a small right-hand tributary to New River in Grayson and Wythe counties.
West; mountain in Rockingham County. Elevation, 2,500 feet.
West; run, a small left-hand tributary to Shenandoah River in Frederick and Warren counties.
West Appomattox; county seat of Appomattox County.
West Augusta; post village in Augusta County.
Westboro; post village in Dinwiddie County.
West Clifton Forge; town in Alleghany County. Population, 367.
Westend; post village in Fairfax County.
Westhope; post village in Sussex County.
Westland; post village in Lancaster County.
West Lynchburg; post village in Campbell County.
Westmoreland; county, situated in the eastern part of the State on the Atlantic plain, fronting upon the Potomac. The surface is but little elevated above tide. It rises in the interior to altitudes of 100 feet or more. Area, 245 square miles. Population, 9,243—white, 4,381; negro, 4,861; foreign born, 37. County seat, Montross. The mean magnetic declination in 1900 was 4° 30′. The mean annual rainfall is 40 to 50 inches, and the temperature 55° to 60°.
West Norfolk; post village in Norfolk County on the Southern Railway.
Westover; post village in Charles City County.
West Point; town in King William County. Population, 1,307.
Westview; post village in Goochland County.
Westwood; post village in Hanover County.
Wetsels; post village in Greene County.
Weyanoke; post village in Charles City County.
Weyers Cave; post village in Augusta County on the Baltimore and Ohio Railroad. Altitude, 1,152 feet.
Whaleyville; post village in Nansemond County.
Whealton; post village in Lancaster County.
Wheatfield; post village in Shenandoah County.
Wheatland; post village in Loudoun County.
Wheeler Mountain; summit in Pittsylvania County. Elevation, 1,000 feet.
Whetstone; creek, a small left-hand tributary to Nottoway River in Nottoway County.
Whipping; creek, a small left-hand branch of Roanoke River in Campbell County.

Whipponock; creek, a small right-hand branch of Appomattox River in Dinwiddie County.
Whiskey; creek, a small left-hand tributary to Shenandoah River in Augusta County.
Whispering; creek, a small right-hand tributary to James River in Buckingham County.
Whistle; creek, a small left-hand tributary to James River in Rockbridge County.
Whit; post village in Clarke County.
Whitacre; post village in Frederick County.
Whiteforge; post village in Scott County.
Whitegate; post village in Giles County.
Whitehall; post village in Frederick County on the Chesapeake and Ohio Railway.
Whitehouse; small left-hand branch of South Fork of Roanoke River in Montgomery County.
Whitehouse; post village in New Kent County on the Southern Railway.
Whitemarsh; post village in Gloucester County.
White Oak; creek, a small left-hand branch of North Fork of Holston River in Smyth County.
Whiteoak; creek, a small left-hand tributary to Nottoway River in Dinwiddie County.
White Oak; creek, a small right-hand tributary to York River.
White Oak; run, a small right-hand tributary to Rappahannock River in Madison County.
Whiteplains; post village in Brunswick County.
Whitepoint; post village in Westmoreland County.
Whitepost; post village in Clarke County on the Norfolk and Western Railway.
White Rock; gap in Rich Patch Mountain caused by Cane Creek in Alleghany County.
White Rock; mountains in Smyth County. Elevation, 3,000 to 4,000 feet.
Whiterock; post village in Bedford County.
White Rock Mountain; summit in Rockbridge County.
White Rocks; summit on the southwestern edge of Mill Mountains. Altitude, 4,548 feet.
Whites; gap in the Blue Ridge in Amherst County.
Whites; post village in Caroline County.
Whites; run, a small left-hand tributary to James River in Rockbridge County.
Whiteshoals; post village in Lee County.
Whitesides; run, a small left-hand tributary to James River in Rockbridge County.
Whitestone; post village in Lancaster County.
White Top; creek, a left-hand tributary to South Fork of Holston River in Washington and Smyth counties.
Whitetop; post village in Grayson County. Altitude, 5,530 feet.
Whitley; small right-hand branch of Walker Creek, rising in Giles County.
Whitley; post village in Isle of Wight County.
Whitley; fork, a small right-hand tributary to Powell River in Wise County.
Whitlock; post village in Halifax County.
Whitmell; post village in Pittsylvania County.
Whitney; island of James River in Appomattox County.
Whittles Depot; post village in Pittsylvania County on the Southern Railway. Altitude, 812 feet.
Whittles Mills; post village in Lunenburg County.
Wickliffe; post village in Clarke County.
Wicomico; post village in Gloucester County.

Wicomico Church; post village in Northumberland County.
Widewater; post village in Stafford County on the Richmond, Fredericksburg and Potomac Railroad.
Widner; creek, a small left-hand branch of South Fork of Holston River in Washington County.
Wiedman; post village in Surry County.
Wiehle; town in Fairfax County on the Southern Railway. Population, 51.
Wier; post village in Highland County.
Wiggington Knob; summit in Bedford County. Elevation, 2,461 feet.
Wightman; post village in Mecklenburg County.
Wilburn; bridge across Appomattox River from Buckingham to Prince Edward County.
Wilburn; post village in Lunenburg County.
Wildcat; summit in Wise County.
Wild Cat Knob; summit in Bedford County. Elevation, 2,000 feet.
Wild Cat Mountain; summit in Botetourt County.
Wilderness; post village in Orange County.
Wilderness; run, a small right-hand tributary to Rappahannock River in Spottsylvania County.
Wildway; post village in Appomattox County.
Wiles; village in Pittsylvania County.
Wilhoit; post village in Albemarle County.
Wilkie Ridge; summit in Rockbridge County.
Willard; post village in Loudoun County.
Willcox Wharf; post village in Charles City County.
Williamsburg; county seat of James City County, but independent in government. Population, 2,044.
Williams Mills; post village in Lunenburg County.
Williamsville; post village in Bath County.
Williams Wharf; post village in Mathews County.
Willis; post village in Floyd County.
Willis; run, a right-hand branch of James River in Buckingham and Cumberland counties.
Willis Mountain; summit in Buckingham County. Elevation, 1,159 feet.
Willoughby; bay on the coast north of Norfolk from Hampton Roads in Princess Anne County.
Willoughby Beach; post village in Norfolk County.
Willoughby Spit; point of sand dividing Willoughby Bay from Chesapeake Bay in Princess Anne County.
Willow; village in Amherst County.
Willowbrook; post village in Louisa County.
Willowspring; post village in Russell County.
Wilmington; post village in Fluvanna County.
Wilson; creek, a small left-hand tributary to James River in Alleghany, Bath, and Highland counties.
Wilson; creek, a small right-hand branch of New River in Grayson County.
Wilson; creek, a small right-hand tributary to James River in Botetourt County.
Wilson Falls; run, a small left-hand tributary to James River in Rockbridge County.
Wilsons; post village in Dinwiddie County.
Wilton; post village in Middlesex County on the Chesapeake and Ohio Railway. Altitude, 996 feet.
Winchester; county seat of Frederick County, but independent in government. Population, 5,161.

Winder; post village in Wise County on the Baltimore and Ohio Railroad. Altitude, 717 feet.
Windsor Station; post village in Isle of Wight County on the Norfolk and Western Railway.
Windy; gap of the Blue Ridge in Franklin County.
Windy; post village in Amherst County.
Wine; post village in Shenandoah County.
Winfall; post village in Campbell County on the Norfolk and Western Railway. Altitude, 848 feet.
Winfrey; post village in Culpeper County.
Wingfield Mountain; summit in Bedford County. Elevation, 1,299 feet.
Wingina; post village in Nelson County on the Chesapeake and Ohio Railway.
Wingo; post village in Giles County.
Winnecum; creek, a small right-hand tributary to Appomattox River in Nottoway County.
Winnie; post village in Nottoway County.
Winston; post village in Culpeper County on the Southern Railway.
Winterham; post village in Amelia County.
Winterpock; creek, a small left-hand branch of Appomattox River in Chesterfield County.
Winterpock; post village in Chesterfield County on the Farmville and Powhatan Railroad.
Winticomack; creek, a small right-hand branch of Appomattox River in Amelia County.
Wirtz; post village in Franklin County on the Norfolk and Western Railway.
Wise; county, situated in the southwestern part of the State. Its area consists in part of an alternation of narrow ridges and valleys, while the northern part lies on the Alleghany plateau, which is here deeply dissected into ridges and gorges. It is drained mainly by Powell River. Area, 413 square miles. Population, 19,653—white, 17,688; negro, 1,965; foreign born, 393. County seat, Wise. The mean annual rainfall is 50 to 60 inches, and the temperature 50° to 55°. The county is traversed by the Norfolk and Western and the Interstate railways.
Wise; county seat of Wise County on the Virginia and Kentucky Railroad.
Wiseville; post village in Chesterfield County.
Wishart; post village in Accomac County.
Witcher Knob; summit in Carroll County. Elevation, 2,500 to 2,912 feet.
Witchers; creek, a small left-hand branch of Roanoke River in Bedford County.
Wittens Mills; post village in Tazewell County on the Norfolk and Western Railway.
Witts; post village in Nelson County.
Woburn; post village in Mecklenburg County.
Wolf; branch, a small right-hand tributary to New River in Carroll County.
Wolf; creek, a small left-hand branch of Roanoke River in Roanoke and Bedford counties.
Wolf; creek, a right-hand branch of New River, rising in Bland County.
Wolf; creek, a small right-hand branch of New River, rising in Tazewell County and flowing northeast to where it empties into New River.
Wolf; creek, a small right-hand tributary to South Fork of Holston River in Washington County.
Wolf; run, a small left-hand tributary to North Fork of Holston River, rising in Washington County.
Wolf Creek; mountains in Giles and Bland counties. Elevation, 2,000 to 3,000 feet.
Wolfglade; post village in Carroll County.
Wolfpen; small left-hand branch of Slate Creek in Buchanan County.
Wolf Pen; branch, a small left-hand tributary to Walker Creek in Bland County.

Wolf Pen; branch, a small right-hand tributary to Walker Creek, rising in Bland County.
Wolf Ridge; mountains in Rockingham and Augusta counties.
Wolfrun; post village in Washington County.
Wolftown; post village in Madison County.
Wolftrap; post village in Halifax County on the Southern Railway.
Wolf Trap Shoal; run, a small right-hand tributary to Potomac River in Fairfax County.
Woltz; post village in Carroll County.
Wood; post village in Scott County.
Woodbridge; post village in Prince William County
Woodburn; post village in Loudoun County.
Woodend; post village in Lunenburg County.
Woodford; post village in Caroline County.
Woodlawn; post village in Carroll County.
Woodridge; post village in Albemarle County.
Woods; run, a small left-hand tributary to James River in Rockbridge County.
Woods Crossroads; post village in Gloucester County.
Woods Mountain; summit in Buckingham County
Woods Mountain; summit in Nelson County.
Woodstock; gap between Three Top and Powells mountains in Shenandoah County.
Woodstock; county seat of Shenandoah County on the Baltimore and Ohio Railroad. Altitude, 820 feet. Population, 1,069.
Woodview; post village in Brunswick County.
Woodville; post village in Rappahannock County.
Woody; creek, a small right-hand tributary to Appomattox River in Nottoway County.
Woolsey; post village in Prince William County.
Woolwine; post village in Patrick County.
Worlds; post village in Pittsylvania County.
Worrells; post village in Southampton County.
Worsham; post village in Prince Edward County.
Wreck Island; creek, a small right-hand tributary to James River in Appomattox County.
Wren; post village in Charlotte County on the Southern Railway.
Wright Valley; creek, a small tributary to Bluestone River in Tazewell County.
Wyatt; post village in Franklin County.
Wyche; post village in Brunswick County.
Wylies; run, a small right-hand tributary to Jackson River in Alleghany County.
Wylliesburg; post village in Charlotte County.
Wyndham; post village in Powhatan County.
Wysor; post village in Pulaski County.
Wythe; county, situated in the southwestern part of the State in the Appalachian Valley. It is limited on the south by Iron Mountain and on the north by Walker Mountain. It is drained by Reed and Cripple creeks, tributaries to New River. The surface consists of an alternation of narrow ridges and valleys, constituting a part of the Appalachian Valley. Area, 474 square miles. Population, 20,437—white, 17,653; negro, 2,783; foreign born, 108. County seat, Wytheville. The mean magnetic declination in 1900 was 1°. The mean annual rainfall is 50 to 60 inches, and the temperature 50° to 55°. The county is traversed by the Norfolk and Western Railway.
Wytheville; county seat of Wythe County on the Norfolk and Western Railway. Altitude, 2,230 feet. Population, 3,003.
Yact; post village in Grayson County.

Yak; post village in Pittsylvania County.
Yale; post village in Sussex County on the Southern Railway.
Yancey; post village in Rockingham County on the Norfolk and Western Railway.
Yancey Mills; post village in Albemarle County.
Yards; post village in Tazewell County.
Yellow; creek, a small left-hand branch of Guest River in Wise County.
Yellow; right-hand branch of Powell River in Lee County.
Yellowbranch; post village in Campbell County.
Yellow Mountain; summit in Roanoke County. Elevation, 2,191 feet.
Yellow Sulphur Springs; post village in Montgomery County.
Yokum; village in Lee County.
York; county, situated in the eastern part of the State on the south side of York River at its mouth, and on the west shore of Chesapeake Bay. It is level and but little elevated. Area, 124 square miles. Population, 7,482—white, 3,401; negro, 4,081; foreign born, 42. County seat, Yorktown. The mean magnetic declination in 1900 was 4°. The mean annual rainfall is 40 to 50 inches, and the temperature 55° to 60°. The county is traversed by the Chesapeake and Ohio Railway.
York; river, which heads in two forks, known as the Mattaponi and Pamunkey, which have their sources in the Piedmont region. They unite at Westpoint, which is commonly regarded as the head of York River. Below this point it has the aspect of a tidal estuary. It flows into Chesapeake Bay below Yorktown. It is navigable to the forks.
Yorktown; county seat of York County. Population, 151.
Yost; post village in Bath County.
Youngs; post village in Spottsylvania County on the Norfolk and Western Railway. Altitude, 1, 301 feet.
Yuma; post village in Scott County.
Za; post village in Orange County.
Zacata; post village in Westmoreland County.
Zack; post village in Rockbridge County.
Zanoni; post village in Gloucester County.
Zanto; post village in Louisa County.
Zaza; post village in Essex County.
Zenda; post village in Rockingham County.
Zenobia; post village in Washington County.
Zepp; post village in Shenandoah County.
Zero; post village in Brunswick County.
Zetta; post village in Augusta County.
Zingara; post village in Brunswick County.
Zion; post village in Louisa County.
Zion Mills; post village in Lee County.
Zions Hill; village in Botetourt County.
Zoar; post village in Chesterfield County.
Zollman; post village in Rockbridge County.
Zulla; post village in Fauquier County.
Zuni; post village in Isle of Wight County on the Norfolk and Western Railway.

58TH CONGRESS, } HOUSE OF REPRESENTATIVES. { DOCUMENT
2d Session. No. 728.

Bulletin No. 233   Series F, Geography, 41

DEPARTMENT OF THE INTERIOR

UNITED STATES GEOLOGICAL SURVEY

CHARLES D. WALCOTT, DIRECTOR

A

GAZETTEER OF WEST VIRGINIA

BY

HENRY GANNETT

LETTER OF TRANSMITTAL.

DEPARTMENT OF THE INTERIOR,
UNITED STATES GEOLOGICAL SURVEY,
Washington, D. C., March 9, 1904.

SIR: I have the honor to transmit herewith, for publication as a bulletin, a gazetteer of West Virginia.

Very respectfully,

HENRY GANNETT,
Geographer.

Hon. CHARLES D. WALCOTT,
Director United States Geological Survey.

A GAZETTEER OF WEST VIRGINIA.

By Henry Gannett.

GENERAL DESCRIPTION OF THE STATE.

The State of West Virginia was cut off from Virginia during the civil war and was admitted to the Union on June 19, 1863. As originally constituted it consisted of 48 counties; subsequently, in 1866, it was enlarged by the addition of two counties, Berkeley and Jefferson, which were also detached from Virginia.

The boundaries of the State are in the highest degree irregular. Starting at Potomac River at Harpers Ferry, the line follows the south bank of the Potomac to the Fairfax Stone, which was set to mark the headwaters of the North Branch of Potomac River; from this stone the line runs due north to Mason and Dixon's line, i. e., the southern boundary of Pennsylvania; thence it follows this line west to the southwest corner of that State, in approximate latitude 39° 43½' and longitude 80° 31', and from that corner north along the western boundary of Pennsylvania until the line intersects Ohio River; from this point the boundary runs southwest down the Ohio, on the northwestern bank, to the mouth of Big Sandy River. The Big Sandy and Tug Fork nearly to its head then form the boundary. Thence the line follows a very irregular course, turning east and northeast, but with frequent breaks in direction as it coincides with the irregular boundaries of the counties which were set off to form the State.

The topographic features of West Virginia are simple. Nearly all the area of the State consists of a greatly dissected plateau which slopes from a crest line near the eastern boundary in a northwesterly direction to Big Sandy and Ohio rivers. Ohio River at the mouth of the Big Sandy, which is the lowest part of the State with the exception of the territory surrounding Harpers Ferry, has an altitude of about 500 feet, and the plateau level along the Ohio is 200 or 300 feet higher. From this level, which may be taken as the base of the plateau, the land rises to the northeast, and along the Allegheny Front has an average altitude of perhaps 4,000 feet. The streams of this plateau have cut deep gorges, and in most parts of it are so numerous that the plateau is reduced to an alternation of sharp ridges and deep, narrow canyons.

The principal rivers are the Ohio, which borders the State on the west and which is navigable throughout the portion bordering the boundary; the Big Sandy, which is navigable for small craft up to the junction of Tug and Levisa forks; the Guyandot; the Kanawha, which is navigable nearly to the falls above Charleston; the Little Kanawha; and the Monongahela. All of these are tributaries of the Ohio, and head in the plateau, with the exception of Kanawha River, the main branch of which, known as New River, heads in northwestern North Carolina and cuts a gorge throughout the entire breadth of the plateau in its course to the Ohio.

The mean altitude of the State above sea level is estimated at 1,500 feet. The areas within certain zones of altitude are as follows:

Areas in West Virginia at different altitudes.

	Square miles.
500–1,000	7,900
1,000–1,500	6,000
1,500–2,000	4,200
2,000–3,000	5,280
3,000–4,000	1,200
4,000–5,000	200

The gross area of the State—that is, including all bodies of water as well as land—is 24,780 square miles. The land area, after deducting the river surface, is 24,645 square miles.

The first census of population and industries of the State was taken in 1870. The following table shows the population at that and at each subsequent census, with the rate of increase:

Census of West Virginia at each census since 1870.

Year.	Population.	Rate of increase.
		Per cent.
1870	442,014	....
1880	618,457	39.9
1890	762,794	23.3
1900	958,800	25.7

In 1900 the population was essentially of a rural character, as there were only four cities which had more than 8,000 inhabitants each, namely, Wheeling, Huntington, Parkersburg, and Charleston. The combined population of these four cities was only 73,603, or 8 per cent of the total population of the State, while in the United States at large one-third of all the people live in cities of this class.

The average number of persons to a family was 5.1, a number exceeded by Texas only, in which there were 5.2 persons to a family.

Males were largely in excess of females, the proportion being 521 males to 479 females. This condition is unusual in the eastern part of the country, there being no other State east of the Mississippi in which the proportion of males is as large as in West Virginia. Another unusual feature is represented by the race distribution. Out of every 1,000 persons 955 were white and but 45 colored, while in the District of Columbia and Maryland the proportion of negroes is vastly greater. The proportion of foreign born was also very small; out of 1,000 persons 977 were born in the United States and only 23 in foreign countries. Of all the States of the Union, West Virginia has the largest proportion of native white inhabitants; out of every thousand inhabitants no fewer than 922 were whites born in the United States. There are States having a smaller proportion of foreign blood, but those States, like Mississippi, have a large proportion of negroes.

Persons more than 10 years of age who were unable to read and write comprised 11.4 per cent of all the inhabitants of the State, 10.3 per cent being white inhabitants, and 32.3 per cent being negroes.

Of the whole number of inhabitants of the State over 10 years of age, 46.4 per cent were engaged in gainful occupations. Of this number, nearly one-half, or 46.6 per cent, were engaged in agricultural pursuits, 3.6 per cent in professions, 17.3 per cent in domestic and other personal service, 11.7 per cent in trade and transportation, and 20.8 per cent in manufactures and mining.

Agriculture is the principal industry of the State. In 1900 there were 92,874 farms. Of these, nearly four-fifths, or 78.2 per cent, were owned by their occupiers, the remainder being rented either for a money rental or for a share of the proceeds, the latter plan being the one most in vogue. The total area in farms amounted to 10,654,513 acres. Of this, a little more than half, 5,498,981 acres, was under cultivation; this is 51.6 per cent of the entire farm area and 34.9 per cent, or more than a third, of the whole area of the State. The average size of the farms was 114.7 acres, considerably less than the average of the United States. The total value of the farms, including land, buildings, implements, and live stock—in short, the entire farm capital—was $203,907,349, an average per farm of $2,196.

The following table shows the distribution of the value among the different items:

Value of farm lands, buildings, and accessories in West Virginia.

Land	$134,269,110
Buildings	34,026,560
Implements	5,040,420
Live stock	30,571,259

The farm products had a value of $44,768,979, an average value per farm of $482. This was 22 per cent of the whole amount of farming capital. The following table shows the divisions of live stock and farm products:

Statistics of live stock and farm products in West Virginia.

Cattle	639,782	Wheat............bushels..	4,326,150
Horses	185,188	Oats................do....	1,833,840
Mules	11,354	Potatoes.............do....	2,245,821
Sheep	968,843	Hay.................tons..	644,535
Swine	442,844	Tobacco...........pounds..	3,087,140
Corn ....bushels..	16,610,730	Dairy produce..............	$5,088,153

Although primarily a farming State, West Virginia has a considerable number of manufactures and they are rapidly increasing in importance. These manufactures are mainly in the narrow strip in the north lying between Pennsylvania and Ohio River, in and about Wheeling.

The total number of manufacturing establishments in the State was 4,418. They had a capital of $55,904,238, employed 33,272 hands, and paid $12,969,237 in wages. Raw materials cost $43,006,880, and the products had a gross value of $74,838,330. The following table gives the principal articles of manufacture, with the value of the products:

Statistics of principal manufactures in West Virginia.

Steam railway cars	$2,943,557
Clay products	1,541,239
Coke	3,529,241
Flour	5,541,353
Foundry products	1,401,852
Glass	1,871,795
Iron and steel	16,514,212
Lumber	10,612,837
Leather	3,210,753

In mineral products West Virginia takes high rank, especially in coal, petroleum, and natural gas. The coal produced in 1901 amounted to 24,068,402 short tons, and was exceeded only by Pennsylvania and Illinois. In making coke from its coal it was exceeded by Pennsylvania only, the amount produced being 2,283,700 short tons. Its petroleum production was 14,177,126 barrels, which was exceeded only by Pennsylvania and Ohio. Its natural gas had a value of $3,954,472. Coal, petroleum, and natural gas are found in various places throughout the State. Indeed, most of the plateau seems to be underlain with coal, and within this area petroleum and natural gas may exist.

Of iron ore Virginia and West Virginia together produced 925,394 long tons, and West Virginia smelted 166,597 long tons.

Originally West Virginia was entirely covered by dense forests. In the higher country these were largely coniferous. In Pocahontas

County, above the crest of the Allegheny Plateau, are found extensive tracts covered with white pine similar to that of New England and the Lake States. Farther down the slopes the hard woods become relatively more abundant, and the coniferous species disappear near Ohio River. In the lower portions of the State, near Ohio River, these forests have been largely cut away to make way for cultivation of the soil and to supply needed lumber, but in the eastern part there are vast tracts still untouched by lumbermen. It is estimated that timber still covers not less than 18,400 square miles, or 73 per cent of the area of the State, and that the State still contains not far from 35,000,000,000 feet B. M. In 1900 the Census reported that a little over half a billion feet were cut for lumber purposes, besides that used for firewood, fence posts, etc.

GAZETTEER.

Aaron; branch, a very small right-hand tributary to Kanawha River in Kanawha County.

Aaron; creek, a small right-hand tributary to Guyandot River, a branch of Ohio River, in Lincoln County.

Aaron; creek, a left-hand branch of Deckers Creek in Monongalia County.

Aaron; fork, a small right-hand branch of Little Sandy Creek, a tributary to Elk River, in Kanawha County.

Aarons; post village in Kanawha County.

Abb Camp; branch, a small right-hand tributary to Clear Fork, a branch of Tug Fork of Big Sandy River, in McDowell County.

Abbot; creek, a right-hand branch of Fifteenmile Fork of Cabin Creek, a tributary to Kanawha River, in Kanawha County.

Abbott; branch, a small left-hand tributary to Big Ugly Creek, a branch of Guyandot River, in Lincoln County.

Abbott; post village in Upshur County.

Aberdeen; post village in Lewis County.

Abram; creek, a right-hand tributary to North Fork of Potomac River in Mineral and Grant counties.

Absalom; run, a small left-hand tributary to Right Fork of Steer Creek in Gilmer County.

Academy; post village in Pocahontas County.

Acme; post village in Kanawah County on the Chesapeake and Ohio Railway.

Acord; branch, a small left-hand tributary to Laurel Branch, a tributary to Clear Fork of Guyandot River, in Wyoming County.

Ada; post village in Mercer County on the Norfolk and Western Railway and on East River. Altitude, 2,225 feet.

Adairs; run, a small left-hand tributary to New River in Mercer County.

Adaline; post village in Marshall County.

Adam; post village in Calhoun County.

Adamston; post village in Harrison County.

Adkin; post village in Wyoming County.

Adkin; branch, a very small right-hand tributary to Tug Fork of Big Sandy River in McDowell County.

Adkins; branch, a small right-hand tributary to Beech Fork of Twelvepole Creek, a branch of Ohio River, in Wayne County.

Adkins; branch, a small right-hand tributary to Dunloup Creek, a branch of New River, in Fayette County.

Adkins; fork, a small left-hand branch of Rich Creek, a tributary to East Fork of Twelvepole Creek, in Wayne County.

Adkins; fork, a very small left-hand tributary to Clear Fork of Guyandot River in Wyoming County.

Adkins; fork, a very small left-hand tributary to Spruce Fork of Little Coal River in Logan County.

Adlai; post village in Pleasants County.
Adley; branch, a small right-hand tributary to Dry Fork, a branch of Tug Fork of Big Sandy River, in McDowell County.
Adolph; post village in Randolph County.
Adonijah; fork, a left-hand branch of Big Sycamore Creek, a tributary to Elk River, in Clay County.
Adonis; post village in Tyler County.
Advent; post village in Jackson County.
Afton; post village in Preston County.
Akron; post village in Tyler County.
Alam; village in Greenbrier County on Meadow River.
Alaska; post village in Mineral County.
Alaska; station in Fayette County on the Chesapeake and Ohio Railway and on New River.
Albatross; post village in Putnam County.
Albert; post village in Tucker County on the Virginia and Southwestern Railway.
Albion; Post village in Nicholas County.
Albright; post village in Preston County.
Alderson; branch, a very small right-hand tributary to Winding Gulf, a branch of Guyandot River, in Raleigh County.
Alderson; county seat of Monroe County on the Chesapeake and Ohio Railway. Altitude, 1,548 feet. Population, 518.
Aldrich; branch, a small right-hand tributary to Cranberry River in Webster County.
Aldrich; fork, an indirect left-hand tributary to Dry Fork, a branch of Tug Fork of Big Sandy River, in McDowell County.
Aleck; run, a small left-hand tributury to Right Fork of Buckhannon River in Upshur County.
Alexander; post village in Upshur County.
Alfred; post village in Gilmer County on the Baltimore and Ohio Railroad.
Algeria; post village in Pleasants County.
Algoma; village in McDowell County, on the Norfolk and Western Railroad.
Alice; post village in Gilmer County.
Alkires Mills; post village in Lewis County.
Allegheny Front; the escarpment of the Allegheny Plateau in Pendleton, Grant, and Mineral counties. Elevation, 2,000 to 4,500 feet.
Allegheny Plateau; westernmost member of the Appalachian system, extending as a greatly dissected plateau through southern New York, Pennsylvania, and Maryland, occupying the greater part of West Virginia, and, under the name of Cumberland Plateau, extending across eastern Kentucky and middle Tennessee into northern Alabama.
Allen; creek, a small right-hand tributary to Guyandot River in Raleigh and Wyoming counties.
Allen; creek, a small left-hand branch of Birch River, a tributary to Elk River, in Webster and Nicholas counties.
Allen Knob; summit in Greenbrier County. Altitude, 3,704 feet.
Allensville; post village in Berkeley County.
Alliance; post village in Harrison County.
Alma; post village in Tyler County.
Alpena; post village in Randolph County.
Alpha; post village in Doddridge County.
Alta; post village in Greenbrier County.
Altizer; post village in Calhoun County.

Alton; post village in Upshur County on the Baltimore and Ohio Railroad. Altitude, 1,813 feet.
Alum; creek, a small right-hand tributary to Tug Fork of Big Sandy River in Mingo County.
Alum; creek, a small right-hand tributary to Coal River, a branch of Kanawha River, in Kanawha County.
Alumbridge; post village in Lewis County.
Alvaro; post village in Kanawha County.
Alvon; post village in Greenbrier County.
Alvy; post village in Tyler County.
Amblersburg; post village in Preston County on the Baltimore and Ohio Railroad.
Amboy; post village in Preston County.
Ambrosia; post village in Mason County on the Ohio Central Lines Railroad.
Amma; post village in Roane County.
Amos; fork, a small right-hand branch of Old Lick Creek, a tributary to Holly River, in Webster County.
Amos; post village in Marion County.
Amos; run, a small right-hand branch of Laurel Creek, a tributary to Elk River. in Webster County.
Amos; run, a small creek in Webster County.
Anchor; post village in Boone County.
Andy; post village in Wetzel County.
Angel; fork, a small left-hand tributary to Coal River in Kanawha and Putnam counties.
Angel; post village in Kanawha County.
Angerona; post village in Jackson County on the Baltimore and Ohio Railroad.
Anglin; creek, a small right-hand branch of Meadow River, tributary to Gauley River, in Nicholas County.
Anita; village in Marion County.
Ann; run, a right-hand branch of Simpson Creek in Harrison County.
Annamoriah; post village in Calhoun County.
Ansted; town in Fayette County on a branch of the Chesapeake and Ohio Railway. Altitude, 1,225 feet. Population, 1,090.
Anthem; post village in Wetzel County.
Anthony; creek, a small left-hand tributary to Birch River, a branch of Elk River, in Nicholas County.
Anthony; creek, a left-hand tributary to Greenbrier River in Greenbrier County.
Anthony; post village in Greenbrier County on the Chesapeake and Ohio Railway.
Antioch; post village in Mineral County.
Apgah; post village in Kanawha County.
Applegrove; post village in Mason County on the Baltimore and Ohio Railroad.
Aracoma; town in Logan County. Population, 444.
Arbovale; post village in Pocahontas County.
Arbuckle; creek, a small left-hand tributary to New River in Fayette County.
Arbuckle; post village in Mason County on the Ohio Central Lines.
Arbutus; post village in Kanawha County.
Arca; post village in Wirt County.
Arches; post village in Wetzel County.
Arden; post village in Barbour County on the Baltimore and Ohio Railroad.
Arkansas; branch, a very small right-hand branch of Right Fork of Twelvepole Creek, a tributary to Ohio River, in Wayne County.
Arlee; post village in Mason County.
Arlington; post village in Upshur County on the Norfolk and Western Railway.

Armour; creek, a small right-hand tributary to Kanawha River in Kanawha and Putnam counties.
Armstrong; creek, a left-hand tributary to Kanawha River in Fayette County.
Arnettsville; post village in Monongalia County.
Arnold; post village in Lewis County on the Baltimore and Ohio Railroad.
Arnoldsburg; post village in Calhoun County.
Arroyo; post village in Hancock County on the Pittsburg, Cincinnati, Chicago and St. Louis Railway.
Arthur; post village in Grant County.
Arvilla; post village in Pleasants County.
Asbury; post village in Greenbrier County.
Ash; branch, a small right-hand tributary to Paint Creek, a branch of Kanawha River, in Kanawha and Fayette counties.
Ash; fork, a small right-hand branch of Twentymile Creek, a tributary to Gauley River, in Nicholas and Clay counties.
Ash; post village in Mason County.
Ashbridge; branch, a small right-hand tributary to Salt Lick Fork of Little Kanawha River in Braxton County.
Ash Camp; run, a right-hand branch of Long Drain in Wetzel County.
Ashland; post village in McDowell County.
Ashley; post village in Doddridge County on the Norfolk and Western Railway.
Ashton; post village in Mason County on the Baltimore and Ohio Railroad.
Aspinwall; post village in Lewis County.
Assurance; post village in Monroe County.
Astor; post village in Taylor County.
Athens; post village in Mercer County.
Atkinsville; post village in Raleigh County.
Atlas; post village in Upshur County.
Atwood; post village in Tyler County.
Auburn; post village in Ritchie County.
Audra; post village in Barbour County.
Augusta; post village in Hampshire County.
Aurora; post village in Preston County on the Baltimore and Ohio Railroad.
Austen; post village in Preston County on the Baltimore and Ohio Railroad.
Auvil; post village in Tucker County.
Avon; post village in Doddridge County.
Avondale; post village in McDowell County on the Baltimore and Ohio Railroad.
Ayers; post village in Calhoun County.
Back; creek, a right-hand branch of the Potomac River in Berkeley County.
Back; creek, a small right-hand branch of Indian Creek, a tributary to New River, in Monroe County.
Back; creek, a small left-hand branch to Second Creek, a branch of Greenbrier River, in Monroe County.
Back Allegheny; mountain at head of Shavers Fork of Cheat River in Randolph, Pocahontas, and Greenbrier counties.
Backbone Knob; summit in Logan County.
Back Fork; mountain in Webster and Randolph counties.
Back Fork of Elk; right-hand branch of Elk River in Webster and Randolph counties.
Backus; post village in Fayette County.
Baden; post village in Mason County.
Badway; branch, a small left-hand tributary to Spice Creek, a branch of Tug Fork of Big Sandy River, in McDowell County.

Bailey; branch, a very small left-hand tributary to Indian Creek, a branch of Guyandot River, in Wyoming County.
Bailey; branch, a very small right-hand tributary to Winding Gulf, a branch of Guyandot River, in Raleigh County.
Bailey; branch, a very small right-hand tributary to Pocotaligo River, a branch of Kanawha River, in Putnam County.
Baileysville; post village in Wyoming County.
Baker; fork, a small left-hand branch of Elk Twomile Creek, a tributary to Elk River, in Kanawha County.
Baker; fork, a small left-hand tributary to Elk River in Braxton County.
Baker; post village in Hardy County on the Norfolk and Western Railway.
Bakers; run, a left-hand tributary to Lost River in Hardy County.
Bakerton; post village in Jefferson County on the Baltimore and Ohio Railroad.
Balderson; post village in Wood County.
Bald Knob; summit in Boone County.
Bald Knob; summit in Harris County. Elevation, 1,552 feet.
Bald Knob; summit in Lewis County.
Bald Knob; summit in the eastern part of Pocahontas County on the Virginia State line. Altitude, 4,242 feet.
Baldknob; post village in Boone County.
Baldwin; branch, a small left-hand tributary to Pinnacle Creek, a branch of Guyandot River, in Wyoming County.
Baldwin; post village in Gilmer County.
Ball; creek, a right-hand branch of Tanner Fork of Little Kanawha River in Gilmer County.
Ball; creek, a small left-hand branch of Charley Creek, a tributary to Mud River, in Cabell County.
Ballard; fork, a small left-hand tributary to Horse Creek, a branch of Little Coal River, in Boone County.
Ballard; fork, a small right-hand tributary to Mud River, a branch of Guyandot River, in Boone County.
Ballard; post village in Monroe County.
Ballengee; post village in Summers County.
Balls; post village in Marshall County.
Balser; mountain, a summit in Pocahontas County.
Baltimore, run, a small lett-hand tributary to Back Fork of Elk River in Webster County.
Bancroft; post village in Putnam County.
Bank; post village in Pendleton County.
Bank Camp; branch, a small right-hand tributary to Left Fork of Mud River, a branch of Guyandot River, in Lincoln County.
Bannen; post village in Marshall County.
Bannock Shoal; run, a small right-hand tributary to Williams River in Webster and Pocahontas counties.
Bans; branch, a very small left-hand tributary to Clear Fork, a branch of Guyandot River, in Wyoming County.
Barbecue; fork, a left-hand branch of Grass Run in Gilmer County.
Barbecue; run, a small right-hand branch of Maul Creek in Braxton County.
Barbour; county, situated in the northern part of the State, in the Alleghany Plateau, here not greatly dissected; it is drained by tributaries to the Monongahela. Area, 393 square miles. Population, 14,198—white, 13,390; negro, 808; foreign born, 230. County seat, Philippi. The mean magnetic declination in 1900 was 3°. The mean annual rainfall is 50 inches, and the mean annual temperature 45° to 50°. The county is traversed by the Baltimore and Ohio Railroad.

Barboursville; town in Cabell County on the Chesapeake and Ohio Railway. Altitude, 578 feet. Population, 429.
Bardane; post village in Jefferson County.
Bargers Springs; post village in Summers County.
Barker; creek, a left-hand tributary to Guyandot River in Wyoming County.
Barker Ridge; mountains in Wyoming County.
Barn; post village in Mercer County.
Barn; run, a small left-hand tributary to Right Fork of Steer Creek in Gilmer County.
Barnes Mills; post village in Hampshire County.
Barnett; run, a right-hand branch of Wheeling Creek in Marshall County.
Barns Creek; right-hand branch of Mud River in Lincoln County.
Barnum; post village in Mineral County on the West Virginia Central and Pittsburg Railway.
Barrackville; post village in Marion County on the Baltimore and Ohio Railroad. Altitude, 901 feet.
Barren; branch, a small right-hand tributary to Dunloup Creek, a branch of New River, in Fayette County.
Barren; creek, a small right-hand tributary to Elk River, a branch of Kanawha River, in Kanawha County.
Barren She; creek, a small right-hand tributary to Dry Fork, a branch of Tug Fork of Big Sandy River, in McDowell County.
Barren She; mountain, a summit in Nicholas County. Elevation, 3,000 feet.
Barren She; run, a small right-hand tributary to North Fork of Cherry River in Nicholas County.
Barren She; run, a small left-hand branch of Buffalo Creek, a tributary to Elk River, in Clay County.
Bartholomew; fork, a left-hand branch of Buffalo Creek in Marion County.
Bartlett; creek, a small right-hand tributary to Dry Fork, a branch of Tug Fork of Big Sandy River in McDowell County.
Bartley; post village in Wyoming County.
Barton Knob; summit of Cheat Mountain in Randolph County.
Bartram; post village in Wayne County.
Basin; post village in Wyoming County.
Basnett; village in Marion County.
Bat; run, a left-hand tributary of Fish Creek in Wetzel County.
Batoff; creek, a small left-hand branch of Piney Creek, a tributary to New River, in Raleigh County.
Battern; fork, a small left-hand branch of East Fork of Twelvepole Creek, a tributary to Ohio River, in Wayne County.
Battle; run, a right-hand branch of Little Wheeling Creek in Ohio County.
Bauffman Knob; summit between Elk and Gauley rivers in Webster County.
Bayard; town in Grant County on North Fork of Potomac River and on the West Virginia Central and Pittsburg Railway. Population, 540. Altitude, 3,150 feet.
Bayards Knob; summit in Randolph County. Altitude, 4,150 feet.
Bays; fork, a small left-hand branch of Middle Fork of Davis Creek, tributary to Kanawha River, in Kanawha County.
Bays; post village in Fayette County.
Beach; fork, a right-hand branch of Twelvepole Creek in Wayne County.
Beach Lick; run, a small right-hand tributary to South Fork of Cherry River in Greenbrier County.
Bealls Mills; post village in Lewis County.
Bean Camp; creek, a small right-hand branch of Marrowbone Creek, a tributary to Tug Fork of Chattarawha River, in Logan County.

Bear; branch, a small right-hand tributary to Mud River, a branch of Guyandot River, in Lincoln County.
Bear; branch, a very small right-hand tributary to Laurel Branch, a tributary to Clear Fork of Guyandot River, in Wyoming County.
Bear; branch, a very small right-hand branch of Blue Creek, a tributary to Elk River, in Kanawha County.
Bear; branch, a small left-hand tributary to Horse Creek, a branch of Little Coal River, in Lincoln County.
Bear; creek, a small right-hand tributary to Guyandot River, a branch of Ohio River, in Lincoln County.
Bear; creek, a left-hand tributary to North Fork of Cherry River in Greenbrier County.
Bear; mountain, a summit near the eastern border of Pocahontas County.
Bear; run, a small right-hand tributary to Little Birch River in Braxton County.
Bear; run, a small left-hand tributary to Elk River in Braxton County.
Bear; run, a small left-hand tributary to Little Kanawha River in Gilmer County.
Bear; run, a small right-hand tributary to Oil Creek in Lewis County.
Bear; run, a right-hand tributary to South Fork of Fishing Creek in Wetzel County.
Bear Camp; run, a small left-hand branch of Left Fork of Buckhannon River in Randolph and Upshur counties.
Beard; post village in Pocahontas County on the Chesapeake and Ohio Railway.
Bearden Knob; summit of Brown Mountain in Tucker County.
Beards; fork, a right-hand branch of Loop Creek, a tributary to Kanawha River in Fayette County.
Bear Garden; fork, a small right-hand tributary to Salt Lick Fork of Little Kanawha River in Braxton County.
Bear Garden Knobs; summits in Greenbrier County, one of which reaches an altitude of 3,262 feet.
Bearhole; fork, a small right-hand tributary to Guyandot River in Wyoming County.
Bear Knob; summit in Randolph County.
Bear Pen; branch, a small right-hand branch of Rock Camp Fork of Twentymile Creek, a tributary to Gauley River in Nicholas and Clay counties.
Bear Run; fork, a small right-hand branch of Lilly Fork of Buffalo Creek, a tributary to Elk River, in Clay and Nicholas counties.
Bear Spring; branch, a small left-hand tributary to Huff Creek, a branch of Guyandot River, in Wyoming County.
Bearsville; post village in Tyler County.
Beartown; branch, a small left-hand tributary to Dry Fork, a branch of Tug Fork of Big Sandy River, in McDowell County.
Beartown; fork, a small right-hand tributary to Pinnacle Creek, a branch of Guyandot River, in Wyoming County.
Beartown Ridge; mountains in Wyoming County.
Bearwallow; branch, a very small right-hand tributary to North Fork of Elkhorn Creek in McDowell County.
Bear Wallow; branch, a small right-hand tributary to Dingus Run, a branch of Guyandot River, in Logan County.
Bear Wallow; hill in McDowell County. Altitude, 3,170 feet.
Bear Wallow; run, a small right-hand tributary to Back Fork of Elk River in Webster and Randolph counties.
Bear Wallow Knob; summit in Fayette County. Altitude, 2,460 feet.
Bear Wallow Knob; summit in Greenbrier County. Elevation, 4,030 feet.
Bear Wallow Ridge; mountains in Wyoming County.
Beatrice; post village in Ritchie County.
Beatysville; post village in Jackson County.

Beauty; post village in Fayette County.

Beaver; branch, a very small left-hand tributary to Guyandot River in Wyoming County.

Beaver; creek, a small left-hand tributary to Greenbrier River in Pocahontas County.

Beaver; creek, a small right-hand tributary to Meadow River in Greenbrier County.

Beaver; creek, a right-hand branch of Black Water River in Tucker County.

Beaver; creek, a right-hand tributary to Piney Creek, a branch of New River, in Raleigh County.

Beaver; creek, a small right-hand tributary to Valley River in Randolph and Barbour counties.

Beaver; creek, a small left-hand tributary to Valley River in Randolph County.

Beaver; post village in Nicholas County on the Chesapeake and Ohio Railway.

Beaver; run, a small right-hand tributary to Holly River in Webster County.

Beaver; run, a small right-hand tributary to Patterson Creek, a branch of North Branch of Potomac River, in Mineral County.

Beaver; run, a small right-hand tributary to Gauley River in Webster County.

Beaver Dam Ridge; short spur of Black Mountain in Pocahontas County.

Beaver Lick; mountain, long narrow ridge, lying east of Greenbrier River in Greenbrier and Pocahontas counties. Elevation, 2,500 to 3,500 feet.

Beaver Pond; branch, a small left-hand tributary to Pond Fork of Little Coal River in Boone County.

Bebee; post village in Wetzel County.

Beccas; creek, a small right-hand tributary to Valley River in Randolph County.

Beckley; county seat of Raleigh County. Population, 342. Altitude, 2,300 feet.

Beckwith; post village in Fayette County on Laurel Creek.

Becky; run, a small left-hand tributary to South Fork of Cherry River in Greenbrier County.

Bedington; post village in Berkeley County on the Cumberland Valley Railroad.

Bee; branch, a very small left-hand tributary to Indian Creek, a branch of Guyandot River, in Wyoming County.

Bee; branch, a very small right-hand tributary to Clear Fork, a branch of Guyandot River, in Wyoming County.

Bee; branch, a very small right-hand tributary to Tug Fork of Big Sandy River in McDowell County.

Bee; branch, a small right-hand tributary to Sand Lick Creek, a branch of Marsh Fork of Coal River, in Raleigh County.

Bee; run, a small left-hand tributary to Cranberry River in Webster and Nicholas counties.

Bee; run, a very small right-hand tributary to Elk River in Braxton County.

Bee; run, a left-hand branch of Cheat River in Preston County.

Bee; post village in Putnam County.

Beech; branch, a very small left-hand tributary to Guyandot River, a branch of Ohio River, in Logan County.

Beech; branch, a very small right-hand tributary to Big Huff Creek, a branch of Guyandot River, in Logan and Wyoming counties.

Beech; creek, a small right-hand branch of Tug Fork of Chattarawha River, a tributary to Ohio River, in Logan County.

Beech; creek, a small left-hand branch of Spruce Fork of Little Coal River in Logan County.

Beech; fork, a small left-hand tributary to Birch River, a branch of Elk River, in Nicholas and Webster counties.

Beech; fork, a right-hand branch of Shaver Fork in Braxton County.

Beech; fork, a large right-hand tributary to Twelvepole Creek, a branch of Ohio River, in Wayne County.

Beech; fork, a small right-hand branch of Lilly Fork of Buffalo Creek, a tributary to Elk River, in Clay and Nicholas counties.

Beech; mountain, a short spur from Rich Mountain in Randolph and Nicholas counties.

Beech; post village in Calhoun County.

Beech; run, a small left-hand branch of Big Laurel Creek, a tributary to Cherry River, in Greenbrier County.

Beech; run, a right-hand head fork of Left Fork of Buchannon River in Randolph County.

Beechcreek; post village in Mingo County on the Norfolk and Western Railway. Altitude, 1,019 feet.

Beech Flat Knob; summit in Randolph County.

Beechgrove; post village in Ritchie County on the Baltimore and Ohio Railroad.

Beechhill; post village in Mason County,

Beech Knob; summit in Greenbrier County. Altitude, 4,161 feet.

Beech Lick; run, a right-hand branch of Pyles Fork of Buffalo Creek in Marion County.

Beechwood; post village in Monongalia County on the Baltimore and Ohio Railroad.

Beechy; branch, a small left-hand tributary to East Fork of Twelvepole Creek, a branch of Ohio River, in Wayne County.

Beechy; fork, a small left-hand branch of Fuqua Creek, a tributary to Coal River, in Lincoln County.

Bee Knob; summit in Braxton County.

Bee Knob; summit in Greenbrier County.

Bee Knob; summit in Randolph County.

Bee Knob; summit in Webster County. Altitude, 3,280 feet.

Beelers Station; post village in Marshall County.

Bee Lick Knob; summit in Fayette County. Altitude, 3,118 feet.

Bee Tree; branch, a small left-hand tributary to Devils Fork, a branch of Guyandot River, in Raleigh County.

Bee Tree; run, a small left-hand tributary to Back Fork of Elk River in Randolph County.

Bee Tree Ridge; short spur from Frank Mountain in Pocahontas County.

Behler; post village in Monongalia County.

Belcher; branch, a very small right-hand tributary to Tug River in McDowell County.

Belcher; branch, a very small left-hand tributary to Tug Fork of Big Sandy River in McDowell County.

Belcher; branch, a small left-hand tributary to Pinnacle Creek, a branch of Guyandot River, in Wyoming County.

Belfont; post village in Braxton County.

Belgrove; post village in Jackson County.

Belington; town in Barbour County on the Baltimore and Ohio, the Belington and Beaver Creek, the Roaring Creek and Belington, and the West Virginia Central and Pittsburg railroads. Population, 430.

Bell; creek, a right-hand branch of Twenty Mile Creek, a tributary to Gauley River, in Nicholas, Fayette, and Kanawha counties.

Belle; post village in Kanawha County.

Belleville; post village in Wood County on the Baltimore and Ohio Railroad.

Bellton; post village in Marshall County on the Baltimore and Ohio Railroad.

Belmont; post village in Pleasants County on the Baltimore and Ohio Railroad.

Belva; post village in Nicholas County on the Chesapeake and Ohio Railway.
Ben; creek, a small right-hand branch of Tug Fork of Big Sandy River in Mingo County.
Ben; run, a small left-hand tributary to Indian Fork in Lewis County.
Ben; run, a small left-hand tributary to Elk River, a large branch of Kanawha River, in Clay County.
Ben; run, a small right-hand tributary to Elk River in Braxton County.
Bend; branch, a very small right-hand tributary to Spruce Fork of Little Coal River in Logan County.
Bend; branch, a small left-hand branch of Dunloup Creek, a tributary to New River, in Fayette County.
Bender; run, a small left-hand tributary to left fork of Steer Creek in Braxton County.
Bendolph; village in Marion County.
Ben Lomond; post village in Mason County on the Baltimore and Ohio Railroad.
Bennett; fork, a small indirect right-hand tributary to Pond Fork of Little Coal River, a branch of Coal River, in Boone County.
Bennett; post village in Gilmer County.
Benson; post village in Harrison County.
Bent; creek, a very small left-hand branch of Marrowbone Creek, a tributary to Tug Fork of Chattarawha River, in Logan County.
Bent Mountain; ridge in Mercer County.
Bentons Ferry; post village in Marion County on the Baltimore and Ohio Railroad. Altitude, 883 feet.
Benwood; city in Marshall County, on the Baltimore and Ohio and the Pittsburg, Cincinnati, Chicago and St. Louis railroads. Altitude, 645 feet. Population, 4,511.
Berea; post village in Ritchie County.
Bergoo; fork, a left-hand tributary to Elk River in Webster and Randolph counties.
Bergoo; post village in Webster County.
Berkeley; county situated in the northeastern part of the State, limited on the north by the Potomac; the surface consists in the main of a rolling valley traversed by Little North and Sleepy Creek mountains. Area, 257 square miles. Population, 19,469—white, 17,704; negro, 1,765; foreign born, 237. County seat, Martinsburg. The mean magnetic declination in 1900 was 4° 25'. The mean annual rainfall is 40 to 50 inches, and the mean annual temperature 50° to 55°. The county is traversed by the Baltimore and Ohio and the Cumberland Valley railroads.
Berkeley; run, a left-hand branch of Tygart Valley River in Taylor County.
Berkeley Springs; county seat of Morgan County on the Baltimore and Ohio Railroad. Population, 781.
Berlin; post village in Lewis County.
Bernards Town; post village in Webster County.
Bernie; post village in Lincoln County.
Berry; branch, a very small right-hand tributary to Mud River, a branch of Guyandot River, in Lincoln County.
Berry; branch, a small left-hand tributary to Winding Gulf, a branch of Guyandot River in Raleigh County.
Berry; run, a left-hand tributary of Berkeley Run in Taylor County.
Berryburg; post village in Barbour County on the Baltimore and Ohio Railroad.
Bert; post village in Tyler County.
Bethany; village in Brooke County. Population, 245.
Bethel; post village in Mercer County.
Betsy; run, a right-hand branch of North Fork of Fishing Creek in Wetzel County.
Beury; post village in Fayette County on the Chesapeake and Ohio Railway.

Beverage Knob; summit in Upshur County.
Beverly; town in Randolph County on the West Virginia Central and Pittsburg Railway. Altitude, 2,250 feet. Population, 464.
Bias; branch, a very small right-hand tributary to Spruce Fork of Little Coal River in Boone County.
Bible Knob; summit in Pendleton County.
Bicketts Knob; summit in Monroe County. Altitude, 3,327 feet.
Bickle Knob; summit in Randolph County. Altitude, 4,020 feet.
Big; branch, a small right-hand tributary to Cranberry River in Webster County.
Big; branch, a very small right-hand branch of West Fork of Twelvepole Creek, a tributary to Ohio River, in Wayne County.
Big; branch, a very small right-hand tributary to Dry Fork, a branch of Tug Fork of Big Sandy River, in McDowell County.
Big; branch, a small right-hand tributary to Wide Mouth Creek, a branch of Bluestone River, in Mercer County.
Big; branch, a very small right-hand tributary to Elkhorn Creek, a branch of Tug Fork of Big Sandy River, in McDowell County.
Big; branch, a very small right-hand tributary to Guyandot River in Mingo County.
Big; branch, a small left-hand tributary to Spruce Fork of Little Coal River in Boone County.
Big; branch, a very small left-hand tributary to Middle Fork of Mud River, a branch of Guyandot River in Lincoln County.
Big; branch, a small left-hand tributary to Lilly Fork of Buffalo Creek, a branch of Elk River, in Clay County.
Big; branch, a small left-hand tributary to Second Creek, a branch of Greenbrier River, in Monroe County.
Big; branch, a small left-hand tributary to Clear Fork, a branch of Tug Fork of Big Sandy River, in McDowell County.
Big; branch, a very small left-hand tributary to Guyandot River in Wyoming County.
Big; creek, a small left-hand branch of Big Hart Creek, a tributary to Guyandot River, in Lincoln County.
Big; creek, a very small left-hand branch of Twelvepole Creek, a tributary to Ohio River, in Wayne County.
Big; creek, a left-hand branch of Trace Fork of Mud River in Lincoln and Putnam counties.
Big; creek, a left-hand tributary to Mud River, a branch of Guyandot River, in Lincoln County.
Big; creek, a very small right-hand tributary to Greenbrier River in Summers County.
Big; creek, a small right-hand branch of Guyandot River, a tributary to Ohio River, in Logan County.
Big; creek, an indirect right-hand tributary to Dry Fork, a branch of Tug Fork of Big Sandy River, in McDowell County.
Big; creek, a small right-hand tributary to Gauley River, a branch of Kanawha River, in Fayette County.
Big; fork, a left-hand branch of Strange Creek in Braxton County.
Big; fork, a very small left-hand tributary to Gilbert Creek, a branch of Guyandot River, in Mingo County.
Big; mountain, a short ridge between Laurel Creek and Little Laurel Creek in Nicholas County.
Big; mountain, a ridge west of South Branch of Potomac River in Pendleton County. Elevation, 2,000 to 2,500 feet.
Big; run, a left-hand tributary to North Fork of Potomac River in Pendleton County.

Big; run, a small left-hand tributary to Elk River in Webster and Randolph counties.
Big; run, a small indirect left-hand tributary to West Fork of Monongahela River in Lewis County.
Big; run, a small left-hand tributary to Buckhannon River in Upshur County.
Big; run, a left-hand tributary to Thorn Run, a branch of South Branch of Potomac River, in Pendleton County.
Big; run, a small left-hand tributary to Red Creek in Randolph County.
Big; run, a small left-hand tributary to Gauley River, entering it between Miller Ridge and Hamrick Ridge, in Webster County.
Big; run, a small left-hand tributary to Elk River in Webster County.
Big; run, a small left-hand tributary to Dry Fork of Cheat River in Tucker County.
Big; run, a small left-hand tributary to Spruce Run, a small branch of Cheat River, in Preston County.
Big; run, a small right-hand tributary to Shavers Fork of Cheat River in southeastern part of Randolph County.
Big; run, a small right-hand tributary to East Fork of Greenbrier River in Pocahontas County.
Big; run, a small right-hand branch of Laurel Fork, a tributary to Back Fork of Holly River, in Webster County.
Big; run, a right-hand tributary to North Fork of Fishing Creek in Wetzel County.
Big; run, a small right-hand tributary to Elk River in Webster County.
Big; run, a left-hand branch of Little Kanawha River in Gilmer County.
Big; run, a small right-hand tributary to Valley River in Randolph County.
Big; run, a left-hand branch of Pyles Creek in Marion County.
Big; run, a left-hand branch of Leading Creek in Gilmer County.
Big; run, a small right-hand tributary to South Branch of Potomac River in Hampshire County.
Big; run, a small right-hand tributary to Elk River in Braxton County.
Bigbattle; post village in Doddridge County.
Big Beechy; creek, a very small left-hand tributary to Elk River in Clay County.
Big Beechy; run, a small left-hand tributary to Williams River in Webster County.
Bigbend; post village in Calhoun County on the Chesapeake and Ohio Railway.
Big Briery Knob; summit in Nicholas County. Altitude, 3,738 feet.
Big Buffalo; creek, a small left-hand tributary to Elk River in Braxton County.
Big Buffalo; creek, a left-hand tributary to Cheat River in Preston County.
Big Clear; creek, a right-hand branch of Meadow River in Greenbrier County.
Big Clear; mountain, a curved range in Greenbrier County. Elevation, 3,000 to 4,000 feet.
Big Clear Creek; village in Greenbrier County.
Big Coal; river, a large, left-hand branch of Kanawha River.
Big Cove; run, a small right-hand tributary to Valley River in Barbour County.
Big Cub; branch, a very small left-hand tributary to Tug Fork of Big Sandy River in McDowell County.
Big Cub; creek, a small right-hand tributary to Guyandot River in Wyoming County.
Big Ditch; run, a small right-hand tributary to Gauley River in Webster County.
Big Draft; small right-hand tributary to Anthonys Creek, a branch of Greenbrier River, in Greenbrier County.
Big Elk; run, a small left-hand tributary to Coal River, a branch of Kanawha River, in Raleigh County.
Big Hart; creek, a small left-hand branch of Guyandot River, a tributary to Ohio River, in Lincoln County.
Big Hollow; short right-hand tributary to Kanawha River in Kanawha County.

Big Huff; creek, a right-hand branch of Guyandotte River in Logan and Wyoming counties.
Big Isaac; post village in Doddridge County.
Big Jarrell; fork, a left-hand branch of Hopkins Fork, a tributary to Coal River, in Boone County.
Big Jenny; branch, a small right-hand tributary to Tug Fork of Big Sandy River in McDowell County.
Big Jonathan; run, a small left-hand tributary to Cheat River in Tucker County.
Big Knob; summit in Clay County.
Big Knob; summit in Greenbrier County.
Big Knob; summit in Kanawha County. Altitude, 1,487 feet.
Big Laurel; branch, a small right-hand tributary to Beaver Creek, a branch of Piney Creek, in Raleigh County.
Big Laurel; creek, a small left-hand tributary to Gauley River in Webster County.
Big Laurel; creek, a left-hand tributary to Cherry River, a branch of Gauley River, in Nicholas and Greenbrier counties.
Big Laurel; creek, a small right-hand branch of Kiah Fork of Twelvepole Creek in Wayne County.
Big Laurel; creek, a right-hand tributary to Elk River, a branch of Kanawha River, in Clay County.
Big Laurel; run, a left-hand tributary to Valley River in Randolph County.
Big Laurel; run, a small left-hand branch of Blue Creek, a tributary to Elk River, in Kanawha County.
Biglick; branch, a very small left-hand tributary to Gilbert Creek, a branch of Guyandot River, in Mingo County.
Big Lynn; creek, a small left-hand branch of East Fork of Twelvepole Creek, a tributary to Ohio River, in Wayne County.
Big Moses; post village in Tyler County.
Big Otter; post village in Clay County.
Big Paw Paw; creek, left-hand branch of Monongahela River, in Mineral County.
Big Ridge; mountains in Raleigh County.
Big Ridge; broken mountainous range in Greenbrier County. Elevation, 2,500 to 3,000 feet.
Big Ridge; mountains in Wyoming County.
Big Ridge; short spur in Pocahontas County. Elevation, 2,500 to 3,000 feet.
Big Ridge; short spur in Hardy County. Elevation, 2,000 feet.
Big Right; fork, a small left-hand branch of Loop Creek, a tributary to Kanawha River, in Fayette County.
Big Rock; summit in Fayette County. Altitude, 2,538 feet.
Big Rock; summit in Peters Mountain in Monroe County.
Big Rocky; run, a small right-hand tributary to South Fork of Cherry River in Greenbrier County.
Big Run; gap in hills in Webster County.
Big Sandy; creek, a right-hand tributary to Elk River, a large branch of Kanawha River, in Kanawha County.
Big Sandy; post village in McDowell County.
Big Sandy; river, a large left-hand branch of Ohio River. It turns in the crest of the Alleghany Plateau and flows nearly northwest to its mouth at Catlettsburg, forming through most of its course the boundary line between West Virginia and Kentucky. Drainage area, 4,050 square miles. It is navigable the entire length. Sometimes called the Chatterawha.
Big Sang Kill; very small left-hand branch of Right Fork of Twelvepole Creek, a tributary to Ohio River, in Logan County.
Big Sewell; knob of Big Sewell Mountain in Fayette County.

Big Sewell; mountain, a short, curved ridge in Fayette County. Elevation, 3,000 to 3,500 feet.
Big Spring; fork, a right-hand head fork of Elk River in Pocahontas County.
Bigsprings; post village in Calhoun County.
Big Spruce Knob; summit in Pocahontas County. Altitude, 4,652 feet.
Big Staunch; branch, a small right-hand tributary to Dry Fork, a branch of Tug Fork of Big Sandy River, in McDowell County.
Big Sulphur; creek, a small right-hand branch of Big Ugly Creek, a tributary to Guyandot River, in Lincoln County.
Big Sycamore; creek, a left-hand tributary to Elk River in Clay County.
Big Top; summit in the central part of Pocahontas County.
Big Twomile; creek, a small left-hand tributary to Mud River, a branch of Guyandot River, in Cabell County.
Big Ugly; creek, a right-hand tributary to Guyandot River, a branch of Ohio River, in Lincoln and Boone counties.
Big Whitestick; creek, a small left-hand tributary to Piney Creek, a branch of New River, in Raleigh County.
Big Wolf Knob; summit on boundary line between Lincoln and Logan counties.
Bill; branch, a very small right-hand tributary to Guyandot River in Wyoming and Logan counties.
Bill; creek, a small left-hand tributary to Kanawha River in Putnam County.
Bill; fork, a small right-hand tributary to O'Brien Fork in Braxton County.
Billie; branch, a very small left-hand branch of Blue Creek, a tributary to Elk River, in Kanawha County.
Bills; creek, a small left-hand tributary to Sugar Creek, an indirect tributary to Valley River, in Barbour County.
Billy; branch, a very small right-hand tributary to West Fork of Twelvepole Creek, a branch of Ohio River, in Wayne County.
Billy; branch, a very small right-hand tributary to Middle Fork of Mud River in Lincoln County.
Binola; post village in Wood County.
Birch; fork, a right-hand tributary to Marsh Fork, a left-hand head fork of Coal River, in Raleigh County.
Birch; river, a left-hand branch of Elk River in Braxton and Nicholas counties.
Birch Pen; run, a small right-hand tributary to Laurel Fork of Holly River in Webster County.
Birch River; post village in Nicholas County.
Birch Root; run, a small left-hand branch of Big Buffalo Creek in Preston County.
Bird; post village in Tyler County.
Bird; run, a small left-hand tributary to Knapp Creek, a branch of Greenbrier River, in Pocahontas County.
Bird Knob; summit in Clay County. Altitude, 1,880 feet.
Bishop; branch, a very small left-hand tributary to Paint Creek, a branch of Kanawha River, in Fayette County.
Bishop Knob; summit in Webster County.
Bismarck; post village in Grant County, situated along the Allegany Front. Altitude, 2,863 feet.
Black; fork, a small left-hand branch of Cabin Creek, a tributary to Guyandot River, in Wyoming County.
Black; mountain, a summit in Pocahontas County.
Black; run, a right-hand head fork of Laurel Fork of Cheat River in Randolph County.
Black; run, a small right-hand tributary to North Fork of Greenbrier River in Pocahontas County.

Blackbird Knob; summit in Tucker County.
Blackburn; branch, a small right-hand tributary to Sand Lick Creek, a branch of Marsh Fork of Coal River, in Raleigh County.
Black Lick; creek, a small right-hand tributary to Bluestone River in Mercer County.
Black Lick; creek, a small right-hand tributary to Little Skin Creek in Lewis County.
Black Oak; mountain in Mercer County.
Blacksville; town in Monongalia on the Chesapeake and Ohio Railway. Population, 180.
Black Water; river, a right-hand branch of Dry Fork of Cheat River in Tucker County.
Blaine; island in Kanawha River, near Charleston in Kanawha County.
Blaine; post village in Mineral County on the West Virginia Central and Pittsburg Railway. Altitude, 1,689 feet.
Blake; branch, a left-hand branch of Smithers Creek, a tributary to Kanawha River, in Fayette County.
Blake; creek, a small right-hand tributary to Kanawha River in Putnam and Kanawha counties.
Blake; fork, a left-hand branch of Lynn Camp Run in Wetzel County.
Blaker Mills; post village in Greenbrier County.
Bland; run, a right-hand branch of Church Fork of Fish Creek in Wetzel County.
Blandville; post village in Doddridge County.
Blayney; run, a left-hand tributary of Castleman Run in Ohio County.
Blaze; branch, a small right-hand tributary to Dunloup Creek, a branch of New River, in Raleigh and Fayette counties.
Blaze; fork, a small left-hand tributary to the right-hand head fork of Grassy Creek in Webster County.
Blenn; run, a left-hand branch of Little Fishing Creek in Wetzel County.
Blennerhassett; post village in Wood County on the Baltimore and Ohio Railroad.
Bletcher; branch, a left-hand branch of Mud River in Cabell County.
Blizzard; run, a small right-hand tributary to South Fork of Cherry River in Greenbrier County.
Bloomery; post village in Hampshire County. Altitude, 700 feet.
Bloomington; post village in Roane County.
Blown Timber; fork, a right-hand tributary to Crooked Fork in Braxton County.
Blue; creek, a left-hand tributary to Elk River in Kanawha and Clay counties.
Blue; post village in Tyler County.
Bluecreek; post village in Kanawha County on the Charleston, Clendennin and Sutton Railroad.
Bluefield; city in Mercer County on the Norfolk and Western Railway. Altitude, 2,557 feet. Population, 4,644.
Blue Knob; branch, a small left-hand tributary to South Fork of Cherry River in Greenbrier County.
Blue Knob; creek, a small right-hand tributary to Elk River, a large branch of Kanawha River, in Clay County.
Blue Knob; summit in Greenbrier County.
Blue Knob; summit in Lincoln County.
Blue Knob; summit in Pocahontas County. Altitude, 4,368 feet.
Blue Knob; summit in Randolph County.
Blue Ridge; mountains, the easternmost ridge of the Appalachian System, with the exception of a few short outliers. It extends from Maryland, southwestward to the southern boundary of the State. From Harpers Ferry, where it is cut through by the Potomac in a water gap, and where it has an altitude of from

1,000 to 1,200 feet, it runs southwestward, increasing rapidly in altitude until at Stony Man, near Luray, and the Peaks of Otter, near Lynchburg, it has an altitude of 4,000 feet. James and Roanoke rivers, which head in the valley behind the ridge, have cut deep gaps in it. In the southern part of the State it changes from a ridge to a plateau with an escarpment facing southeast, and in this form enters North Carolina.

Blue Spring; post village in Randolph County.

Bluestone; river, a left-hand branch of New River.

Blue Sulphur Springs; post village in Greenbrier County on the Chesapeake and Ohio Railway. Altitude, 598 feet.

Bluff; fork, a small left-hand branch of Devils Fork, a tributary to Guyandot River, in Raleigh County.

Bluff; post village in Mercer County.

Blundon; post village in Kanawha County.

Board; branch, a very small right-hand tributary to Indian Creek, a branch of Guyandot River, in Wyoming County.

Board; post village in Mason County.

Board Tree; branch, a very small left-hand tributary to Blue Creek, a branch of Elk River, in Kanawha County.

Board Tree; branch, a small right-hand tributary to Twentymile Creek, a branch of Gauley River, in Nicholas County.

Board Tree; gap in Nicholas County, caused by Board Tree Branch in Nicholas County.

Board Tree; post village in Marshall County on the Baltimore and Ohio Railroad.

Boar Knob; summit in Braxton County. Elevation, 1,466 feet.

Boaz; post village in Wood County.

Bob; run, a small left-hand tributary to Elk River in Webster County.

Bobby; creek, a small right-hand branch of Big Ugly Creek, a tributary to Guyandot River, in Lincoln County.

Bob Peak; summit in the central part of Upshur County.

Bob Ross; branch, a very small left-hand tributary to Beech Fork of Twelvepole Creek, a branch of Ohio River, in Wayne County.

Bobs Ridge; short spur between Greenbrier and Alleghany mountains in Greenbrier County. Elevation, 2,000 to 2,500 feet.

Boggs; fork, a small left-hand tributary to Lower Sleith Fork in Braxton County.

Boggs; post village in Webster County on the Baltimore and Ohio Railroad.

Boggs; run, a left-hand tributary to Spring Creek, a branch of Greenbrier River, in Greenbrier County.

Boggs; run, a left-hand branch of Ohio River in Marshall County.

Boggs Knob; summit in Greenbrier County.

Boggs Knob; summit in Fayette County. Altitude, 3,600 feet.

Bois; post village in Webster County.

Bolair; post village in Webster County.

Bolivar; town in Jefferson County. Population, 781.

Bond; creek, a small left-hand tributary to Ohio River in Ritchie County.

Bone Town; gap at mouth of Robinson Creek at its junction with Buffalo Creek, in Clay County.

Booher; post village in Tyler County.

Boomer; branch, a very small right-hand tributary to Kanawha River, in Fayette County.

Boomer; post village in Fayette County on the Ohio Central Lines.

Boone; county, situated in the southern part of the State, on the Allegheny Plateau. It is here deeply dissected. It is drained by Coal and Little Coal rivers. Area, 512 square miles. Population, 8,194—white, 8,059; negro, 135; foreign born, 7.

County seat, Madison. The mean magnetic declination in 1900 was 1°. The mean annual rainfall is 50 to 60 inches, and the mean annual temperature 50° to 55°.

Boone; post village in Fayette County.

Booths; creek, a right-hand branch of West Fork River in Marion County.

Boothsville; post village in Marion County.

Booton; branch, a small right-hand tributary to Beech Fork of Twelvepole Creek, a branch of Ohio River, in Wayne County.

Booton; creek, a very small left-hand tributary to Guyandot River, a branch of Ohio River, in Cabell County.

Boreman; post village in Wood County.

Borland; post village in Pleasants County.

Botkins Ridge; spur in Pendleton County.

Bottom; creek, a small right-hand tributary to Elkhorn Creek, a branch of Tug Fork of Big Sandy River in McDowell County.

Bowen; creek, a right-hand branch of Beech Fork of Twelvepole Creek in Wayne County.

Bowen; post village in Wayne County.

Bowers; creek, a small right-hand branch of Beech Fork of Twelvepole Creek, a branch of Ohio River, in Wayne County.

Bowlby; post village in Monongalia County.

Box; post village in Pendleton County.

Boyd; branch, a very small left-hand tributary to Clear Fork of Coal River in Raleigh County.

Boyd; branch, a very small right-hand tributary to Paint Creek, a branch of Kanawha River, in Fayette County.

Boyer; fork, a small right-hand branch of Piney Creek, a tributary to New River, in Raleigh County.

Boyer; post village in Pocahontas County.

Boyer; run, a small right-hand tributary to Cedar Creek in Braxton County.

Brackin; creek, a small left-hand branch of Meadow River, a tributary to Gauley River, in Fayette County.

Bradford; branch, a very small left-hand tributary to Kanawha River in Kanawha County.

Bradford; post village in Randolph County.

Bradshaw; creek, a left-hand tributary to Dry Fork, a branch of Tug Fork of Big Sandy River in McDowell County.

Bradshaw; creek, a small right-hand branch of Indian Creek, a tributary to New River, in Summers County.

Bradshaw; post village in McDowell County, situated on Bradshaw Creek.

Bradshaw Hill; a knob of Gauley Mountain in Randolph County.

Brady; fork, a left-hand branch of Grass Lick and tributary to Left Fork of Steer Creek in Braxton County.

Brady; post village in Pocahontas County.

Bragg; branch, a small right-hand tributary to Tommy Creek, a head fork of Guyandot River, in Raleigh County.

Bragg; fork, a small right-hand branch of Horse Creek, a tributary to Little Coal River, in Boone County.

Bragg Knob; summit in Clay County. Elevation, 1,674 feet.

Braines; creek, a right-hand branch of Raccoon Creek, a tributary to Valley River, in Preston County.

Brake; run, a small right-hand tributary to South Fork of Potomac River in Hardy County.

Bramwell; town in Mercer County on the Norfolk and Western Railway and on Bluestone River. Altitude, 2,247 feet. Population, 825.
Branch; mountain, a short ridge in Hardy County. Elevation, 1,500 to 2,500 feet.
Branch; post village in Pendleton County.
Brandonville; town in Preston County. Population, 68.
Brandywine; post village in Pendleton County.
Brant; creek, a very small right-hand tributary to Peters Creek, a branch of Gauley River, in Nicholas County.
Braxton; county, situated in the central part of the State on the Allegheny Plateau. It is here deeply dissected. It is traversed and drained by Little Kanawha and Elk rivers. Area, 541 square miles. Population, 18,904—white, 18,717; negro, 187; foreign born, 53. County seat, Sutton. The mean magnetic declination in 1900 was 2°. The mean annual rainfall is 40 to 50 inches, and the mean annual temperature 50° to 55°. The county is traversed by the Baltimore and Ohio Railroad.
Breading; post village in Mingo County.
Breckenridge; creek, a small left-hand tributary to Marsh Fork of Coal River in Raleigh County.
Breeden; creek, a very small left-hand branch of Right Fork of Twelvepole Creek, a tributary to Ohio River, in Logan County.
Bridge; branch, a very small right-hand branch of Laurel Fork, a tributary to Clear Fork of Guyandot River, in Wyoming County.
Bridgeport; town in Harrison County on the Baltimore and Ohio Railroad. Altitude, 979 feet. Population, 464.
Brier; creek, a left-hand tributary to Indian Creek, a branch of Guyandot River, in Wyoming County.
Brier; creek, a right-hand tributary to Coal River, a branch of Kanawha River, in Kanawha County.
Brier; post village in Wyoming County.
Brier Patch; mountain, a peak in the Allegheny Mountains in Randolph County. Altitude, 4,480 feet.
Briery; run, a small right-hand tributary to South Fork of Cherry River in Greenbrier County.
Briery Knob; summit in Nicholas County. Altitude, 1,850 feet.
Briery Knob; summit in Pocahontas County. Elevation, 4,534 feet.
Brierylick; run, a right-hand tributary of Right Fork of Steer Creek in Gilmer County.
Briery Ridge; short spur in Webster County, north of Gauley River.
Brighton; post village in Mason County.
Brillian; post village in Putnam County.
Brink; post village in Marion County.
Briscoe; post village in Wood County.
Bristol; post village in Harrison County on the Baltimore and Ohio Railroad.
Brittain; post village in Taylor County.
Broad; branch, a small left-hand tributary to Big Ugly Creek, a branch of Guyandot River, in Lincoln County.
Broad; run, a small right-hand tributary to Elk River, a branch of Kanawha River, in Kanawha County.
Broad; run, a small right-hand branch of Wolf Creek, a tributary to Greenbrier River, in Monroe County.
Brock; run, a small right-hand branch of Holly River, a tributary to Elk River, in Braxton County.
Brook; branch, a very small left-hand tributary to Guyandot River in Wyoming County.

Brook; creek, a left-hand tributary to Laurel Creek in Webster County.

Brook; run, a small right-hand tributary to Middle Fork of Tygarts Valley River in Randolph County.

Brooke; county, situated in the northern part of the State, in the Panhandle, bordering on Ohio River. Area, 97 square miles. Population, 7,219—white, 7,079; negro, 139, foreign born, 335. County seat, Wellsburg. The mean magnetic declination in 1900 was 3°. The mean annual rainfall is 40 inches, and the mean annual temperature 50° to 55°. The county is traversed by the Pittsburg, Cincinnati, Chicago and St. Louis Railway.

Brooklin; town in Raleigh County on the Chesapeake and Ohio Railway. Population, 632.

Brooks; branch, a very small right-hand tributary to New River in Summers County.

Brooks; post village in Summers County on the Chesapeake and Ohio Railway.

Brooks; run, a very small left-hand branch of Big Laurel Creek, a tributary to Cherry River, in Greenbrier County.

Brookside; post village in Preston County.

Broom; branch, a small left-hand branch of Alum Creek; a tributary to Coal River, in Kanawha County.

Broomfield; post village in Marion County.

Brosius; post village in Morgan County.

Brown; creek, a small right-hand tributary to Tug Fork of Big Sandy River in McDowell County.

Brown; creek, a small right-hand tributary to Big Clear Creek, a branch of Meadow River, in Greenbrier County.

Brown; mountain, a broken mountainous country in Tucker County. Elevation, 3,500 feet.

Brown; post village in Harrison County on the Baltimore and Ohio Railroad.

Brown; run, a left-hand tributary to North Fork of Dunkard Creek in Monongalia County.

Brown; run, a right-hand branch of Fish Creek in Wetzel County.

Browning; fork, a left-hand tributary to Gilbert Creek, a branch of Guyandot River, in Mingo County.

Browns; branch, a very small right-hand branch of Indian Creek, a tributary to New River, in Monroe County.

Browns; branch, a small right-hand tributary to West Fork, a branch of Pond Fork of Little Coal River, in Boone County.

Browns; creek, a small right-hand branch of Knapp Creek, a tributary to Greenbrier River, in Pocahontas County.

Browns; creek, a left-hand tributary to Coal River, a branch of Kanawha River, in Kanawha County.

Browns; knob in Taylor County.

Browns; mountain, a ridge in Pocahontas County between Browns and Knapp creeks. Elevation, 2,500 to 3,000 feet.

Browns; run, a left-hand tributary to the Ohio River in Marshall County.

Browns; run, a right-hand tributary to Little Wheeling Creek in Ohio County.

Bruce; village in Nicholas County.

Bruceton Mills; town in Preston County. Population, 80.

Bruffs; fork, a head fork of Big Sandy Creek in Preston and Barbour counties.

Brush; creek, a small left-hand branch of Coal River, a tributary to Kanawha River, in Boone County.

Brush; creek, a small left-hand tributary to Mud River, a branch of Guyandot River, in Cabell County.

Brush; creek, a right-hand tributary to Bluestone River in Mercer County. It rises in Stony Ridge.
Brush; creek, a small right-hand tributary to New River in Monroe County.
Brush; fork, a small left-hand tributary to Buckhannon River in Upshur County.
Brush; fork, a small left-hand tributary to Cedar Creek in Gilmer and Braxton counties.
Brush; run, a very small right-hand branch of Cedar Creek in Braxton County.
Brush; run, a right-hand branch of Indian Fork in Lewis County.
Brush; run, a right-hand branch of Lost Run in Taylor County.
Brush; run, a left-hand branch of Pyles Fork of Buffalo Creek in Marion County.
Brush; run, a right-hand branch of Buffalo Creek in Marion County.
Brush; run, a left-hand branch of Fishing Creek in Wetzel County.
Brush Camp Low Place; gap at the head of Leatherwood Fork, a left-hand branch of Elk River, in Randolph County.
Brush Fence; run, a small right-hand tributary to Gauley River in Webster County.
Brushfork; post village in Mercer County.
Brushy; branch, a very small right-hand tributary to Paint Creek, a branch of Kanawha River, in Kanawha County.
Brushy; branch, a very small left-hand tributary to Gilbert Creek, a branch of Guyandot River, in Mingo County.
Brushy; creek, a small left-hand branch of East Fork of Twelvepole Creek, a tributary to Ohio River, in Wayne County.
Brushy; creek, a small right-hand tributary to Seneca, a branch of North Fork of Potomac River, in Pendleton County.
Brushy; fork, a small left-hand branch of Huff Creek, a tributary to Guyandot River, in Wyoming County.
Brushy; fork, a small left-hand branch of Peters Cave Fork of Horse Creek, a tributary to Little Coal River, in Lincoln County.
Brushy; fork, a left-hand tributary to Strange Creek in Nicholas County.
Brushy; fork, a small right-hand branch of Muddlety Creek, a tributary to Gauley River, in Nicholas County.
Brushy; fork, a small right-hand tributary to Teter Creek, a branch of Valley River, in Barbour County. It rises in Laurel Hills.
Brushy; fork, a small right-hand tributary to Bluestone River in Mercer County.
Brushy; fork, a small right-hand tributary to Elk River in Braxton County.
Brushy; fork, a right-hand branch of Dunkard Creek in Monongalia County.
Brushy; fork, a small right-hand tributary to Spruce Fork of Little Coal River in Logan County.
Brushy; mountain, a short ridge in Greenbrier and Pocahontas counties. Elevation, 3,000 feet.
Brushy; run, a left-hand branch of Lunice Creek, tributary to South Branch of Potomac River, in Grant County.
Brushy; run, a name applied to the upper course of North Mill Creek, a right-hand tributary to South Branch of Potomac River, in Pendleton and Grant counties.
Brushy Flat; spur from Big Knob in Greenbrier County.
Brushfork; post village in Mercer County.
Brushy Knob; summit in Lincoln County.
Brushy Knobs; summit in Preston County.
Brushy Meadow; creek, an indirect right-hand tributary to Gauley River in Nicholas and Greenbrier counties.
Brushy Ridge; short, narrow range in Greenbrier County. Elevation, 2,500 feet.
Brushyrun; post village in Pendleton County.

Bryan; post village in Mason County.

Buck; creek, a small right-hand tributary to Greenbrier River in Pocahontas County.

Buck; fork, a small left-hand branch of Big Hart Creek, a tributary to Guyandot River, in Logan County.

Buck; fork, a right-hand head fork of Sand Creek, a tributary to Guyandot River, in Lincoln County.

Buck; fork, a small right-hand tributary to Dry Fork, a branch of Tug Fork of Big Sandy River, in McDowell County.

Buck; mountain, a short ridge in Hardy County.

Buck; post village in Summers County.

Buck; run, a very small right-hand tributary to Elk River in Braxton County.

Buck; run, a right-hand tributary to Right Fork of Simpson Run in Taylor County.

Buck; run, a right-hand tributary to South Fork of Fishing Creek in Wetzel County.

Buckeye; branch, a very small left-hand tributary to Gauley River in Webster County.

Buckeye; creek, a small left-hand tributary to Elk River in Braxton County.

Buckeye; fork, a head fork of Little Skin Creek in Lewis County.

Buckeye; post village in Pocahontas County on the Chesapeake and Ohio Railway.

Buck Garden; branch, a small right-hand tributary to Peter Creek, a branch of Gauley River, in Nicholas County.

Buckhannon; county seat of Upshur County on the Baltimore and Ohio Railroad. Altitude, 1,500 feet. Population, 1,589.

Buckhannon; mountain, a broken, mountainous ridge in the western part of Lewis County.

Buckhannon; river, a large left-hand branch of Tygarts Valley River in Upshur, Barbour, and Randolph counties.

Buckhorn; fork, a left-hand branch of Little Sycamore Creek, a tributary to Elk River in Clay County.

Buckhorn; post village in Preston County.

Buck Knob; summit in Greenbrier County.

Buck Knob; summit in Pocahontas County. Altitude, 4,356 feet.

Buckles; branch, a small right-hand tributary to Twenty Mile Creek, a branch of Gauley River, in Fayette County.

Buckley; mountain, a short ridge east of Greenbrier River in Pocahontas County. Elevation, 3,000 feet.

Buck Lick; small right-hand tributary to Gauley River, a large branch of Kanawha River, in Nicholas County.

Buck Lick; run, a left-hand tributary to Spruce Run, a small branch of Cheat River, in Preston County.

Buena; post village in Tucker County.

Buffalo; creek, a very small left-hand branch of Guyandot River, a tributary to Ohio River, in Logan County.

Buffalo; creek, a small left-hand branch of Little Huff Creek, a tributary to Guyandot River, in Wyoming County.

Buffalo; creek, a small left-hand tributary to Mud River, a branch of Guyandot River, in Lincoln County.

Buffalo; creek, a right-hand branch of Guyandot River in Logan County.

Buffalo; creek, a very small right-hand tributary to New River in Fayette and Summers counties.

Buffalo; creek, a very small right-hand branch of Tug Fork of Big Sandy River, a tributary to Ohio River in Logan County.

Buffalo; creek, a small right-hand tributary to North Branch of Potomac River in Grant County.

Buffalo; creek, a left-hand tributary to Elk River, a large branch of Kanawha River, in Clay County.

Buffalo; creek, a right-hand branch of Little Kanawha River in Braxton County.
Buffalo; creek, a small left-hand branch of Ohio River, rising in Pennsylvania and flowing west through Brooke County into Ohio River.
Buffalo; fork, a left-hand tributary to East Fork of Greenbrier River in Pocahontas County.
Buffalo; fork, a right-hand branch of Smithers Creek, a tributary to Kanawha River, in Kanawha County.
Buffalo; fork, a small right-hand branch of Hughes Creek, a tributary to Kanawha River, in Kanawha County.
Buffalo; fork, a small right-hand tributary to Clear Fork of Coal River in Raleigh County.
Buffalo; run, a left-hand branch of Right Fork of Middle Fork of Little Kanawha River in Webster County.
Buffalo; run, a small left-hand branch of Deer Creek, a tributary to North Fork of Greenbrier River, in Pocahontas County.
Buffalo; run, a small right-hand tributary to Cheat River in Preston County.
Buffalo; run, a left-hand branch of South Fork of Fishing Creek in Wetzel County.
Buffalo; village in Putnam County on the Ohio Central Lines. Population, 364.
Buffalo Bull Knob; summit in Webster County.
Buffalo Hills; short ridge west of South Branch of Potomac River in Pendletor County. Elevation, 2,000 to 2,500 feet.
Buffalolick; post village in Roane County.
Buffalo Lick; very small left-hand tributary to Elk River in Kanawha County.
Buffalo Ridge; summit in Marthas Ridge in Pocahontas County.
Buffington; run, a right-hand branch of Cheat River in Preston County.
Buffs; branch, a left-hand branch of Hurricane Creek, a tributary to Kanawha River, in Putnam County.
Bula; post village in Monongalia County.
Bull; creek, a small left-hand tributary to Pond Fork of Little Coal River in Boone County.
Bull; creek, a small left-hand tributary to Tug Fork of Big Sandy River in McDowell County.
Bull; creek, a small left-hand tributary to Ohio River in Wood County.
Bull; creek, a small right-hand tributary to Coal River, a branch of Kanawha River, in Boone County.
Bull; creek, a very small right-hand branch of Tug Fork of Big Sandy River, a tributary to Ohio River, in Wayne County.
Bull; run, a left-hand branch of Cheat River in Preston County.
Bull; run, a left-hand branch of Wheeling Creek in Marshall County.
Bull; run; a left-hand branch of French Creek in Upshur County.
Bull; run, a small left-hand tributary to Cheat River in Tucker County.
Bull; run, a right-hand tributary to Cedar Creek in Gilmer County.
Bull Fork; run, a left-hand branch of Little Kanawha River in Braxton County.
Bull Lick; branch, a small right-hand branch of Kelly Creek, a tributary to Kanawha River, in Kanawha County.
Bullrun; post village in Preston County.
Bullskin; branch, a small right-hand branch of Little Sandy Creek, a tributary to Elk River, in Kanawha County.
Bulltown; post village in Braxton County.
Bumble Bee; run, a small left-hand tributary to South Fork of Cherry River in Greenbrier County.
Bungers; post village in Greenbrier County.
Bunkerhill; post village in Berkeley County on the Cumberland Valley Railroad.

Bunners; post village in Marion County.
Burch; post village in Mingo County.
Burchfield; post village in Wetzel County.
Burdett; post village in Putnam County.
Burditt; creek, a small right-hand tributary to Gauley River in Greenbrier County.
Burk; creek, a very small right-hand tributary to Elkhorn Creek in McDowell County.
Burker; run, a right-hand branch of North Fork of Fishing Creek in Wetzel County.
Burkes; creek, a very small left-hand tributary to Elk River in Kanawha County.
Burlington; post village in Mineral County. Altitude, 800 feet.
Burner; mountain, a short ridge at the head of Greenbrier River in Pocahontas County.
Burner; run, a left-hand branch of Fish Creek in Wetzel County.
Burning Rock; triangulation station in Wyoming County.
Burning Spring; branch, a very small right-hand tributary to Kanawha River in Kanawha County.
Burning Springs; post village in Wirt County.
Burns; run, a small left-hand tributary to Salt Lick Fork of Little Kanawha River in Braxton County.
Burnside; branch, a very small tributary of Coal River, in Boone County.
Burnsville; post village in Braxton County on the Baltimore and Ohio Railroad. Altitude, 758 feet.
Burnt; fork, a small right-hand branch of Slab Fork, a tributary to Guyandot River, in Raleigh County.
Burnt Bottom; branch, a very small right-hand tributary to Pinnacle Creek, a branch of Guyandot River, in Wyoming County.
Burnt Cabin; branch, a small right-hand tributary to Laurel Fork, a branch of Spruce Fork of Little Coal River, in Boone County.
Burnt Cabin; run, a right-hand branch of Tygart Valley River in Marion County.
Burnt Camp; branch, a very small right-hand tributary to Pond Fork of Little Coal River in Boone County.
Burnthouse; post village in Ritchie County.
Burnt Ridge; mountains in Raleigh County.
Burnt Ridge; short ridge between the heads of Greenbrier and North Fork of Pocahontas River in Pocahontas County.
Burton; post village in Wetzel County on the Baltimore and Ohio Railroad. Altitude, 1,060 feet.
Bush; run, a small right-hand tributary to French Creek in Upshur County.
Buster Knob; summit in Fayette County.
Butcher; branch a small left-hand tributary to New River in Fayette County.
Butcher; fork, a left-hand branch of Sand Fork in Gilmer and Lewis counties.
Butcher; run, a small left-hand tributary to Cedar Creek in Gilmer and Braxton counties.
Butcher; run, a small left-hand tributary to Right Fork of Steer Creek in Gilmer County.
Butler; post village in Mason County.
Buzzard; branch, a small right-hand tributary to Paint Creek, a branch of Kanawha River, in Kanawha County.
Buzzard; branch, a small right-hand tributary to North Fork of Elkhorn Creek in McDowell County.
Buzzard; creek, a left-hand branch of Trace Creek in Putnam County.
Buzzard; run, a left-hand branch of Cheat River in Monongalia County.
Byrne; post village in Braxton County.

Byrnside; post village in Putnam County.

Cabell; county, situated in the western part of the State bordering on Ohio River, which, with the Guyandot, drains it. Its surface is broken, being upon the lower slopes of the plateau. Area, 261 square miles. Population, 29,252—white, 27,713; negro, 1,537; foreign born, 378; county seat, Huntington. The mean magnetic declination in 1900 was 1°. The mean annual rainfall is 40 to 50 inches, and the mean annual temperature 50° to 55°. The county is traversed by the Chesapeake and Ohio and the Ohio River railroads.

Cabell; creek, a right-hand tributary to Mud River, a branch of Guyandot River, in Cabell County.

Cabell; creek, a very small right-hand tributary to Guyandot River, a branch of Ohio River, in Cabell County.

Cabin; branch, a very small right-hand tributary to Laurel Branch, a branch of Clear Fork of Guyandot River, in Wyoming County.

Cabin; creek, a small right-hand tributary to Guyandot River in Wyoming County.

Cabin; creek, a left-hand branch of Kanawha River in Kanawha and Fayette counties.

Cabin; fork, a small indirect right-hand tributary to Pond Fork of Little Coal River, a branch of Coal River, in Boone County.

Cabin; run, a small left-hand branch of Patterson Creek, a tributary to North Branch of Potomac River, in Mineral County.

Cabin; run, a small left-hand branch of Right Fork of Holly River in Braxton County.

Cacapehon; post village in Hampshire County.

Cacapon; mountains, a short ridge in Hampshire and Morgan counties. Elevation, 2,500 feet.

Cacapon; river, a large right-hand branch of Potomac River, rising in Hardy County, and flowing in a generally northeastern direction through Hardy, Hampshire, and Morgan counties. In its upper course it is known as Lost River.

Cairo; town in Ritchie County on the Baltimore and Ohio and on the Cairo and Kanawha Valley railroads. Altitude, 658 feet. Population, 653.

Calcutta; post village in Pleasants County.

Calders Peak; one of the summits of Swoopes Knobs in Monroe County.

Caldwell; post village and railway station in Greenbrier County, located on Howards Creek; also on Chesapeake and Ohio Railway. Altitude, 1,766 feet.

Caldwell; run, a left-hand branch of Saltlick Creek in Braxton County.

Calf; run, a left-hand branch of Indian Fork of Ellis Creek in Lewis County.

Calhoun; county, situated in the western part of the State on the Alleghany Plateau. Area, 276 square miles; population, 10,266—white, 10,183; negro, 83; foreign born, 26. County seat, Grantsville. The mean magnetic declination in 1900 was 1° 10′. The mean annual rainfall is 40 to 50 inches, and the mean annual temperature 50° to 55°.

Calhoun; post village in Barbour County.

Calis; post village in Marshall County.

Calvin; post village in Nicholas County.

Camden; post village in Lewis County on the Ohio River Railroad.

Camden on Gauley; post village in Webster County on the Baltimore and Ohio Railroad.

Cameron; town in Marshall County on the Baltimore and Ohio Railroad. Altitude, 547 feet. Population, 964.

Camp; branch, a very small left-hand tributary to Loop Creek, a branch of Kanawha River, in Fayette County.

Camp; branch, a very small right-hand tributary to Dingus Run, a branch of Guyandot River, in Logan County.
Camp; branch, a small right-hand tributary to Tug River in McDowell County.
Camp; branch, a very small right-hand tributary to Dunloup Creek, a branch of New River, in Fayette County.
Camp; branch, a right-hand tributary of Beech Fork of Twelve Pole Creek in Cabell County.
Camp; creek, a very small left-hand tributary to Elk River in Clay County.
Camp; creek, a left-hand tributary to Bluestone River, a branch of New River, in Mercer County.
Camp; creek, a right-hand tributary to Little Coal River, a branch of Coal River, in Boone County.
Camp; creek, a small right-hand tributary to East Fork of Twelvepole Creek, a branch of Ohio River, in Wayne County.
Camp; creek, a very small right-hand tributary to Elk River, a large branch of Kanawha River, in Clay County.
Camp; creek, a right-hand tributary to Laurel Creek in Braxton and Webster counties.
Camp; creek, a very small right-hand branch of Tug Fork of Big Sandy River, a tributary to Ohio River, in Wayne County.
Camp; run, a left-hand branch of North Fork of Dunkard Creek in Monongalia County.
Camp; run, a right-hand tributary of Buffalo Creek in Marion County.
Camp; run, a left-hand tributary of Fishing Creek in Wetzel County.
Camp; post village in Doddridge County.
Campbell; creek, a right-hand tributary to Kanawha River in Kanawha County.
Campbell; fork, a small left-hand branch of Bell Creek, a tributary to Gauley River, in Kanawha County.
Campbell; run, a left-hand branch of Pyles Fork of Buffalo Creek in Marion County.
Campbell; post village in Calhoun County.
Campcreek; post village in Mercer County on Camp Creek.
Campus; post village in Wyoming County.
Canaan; mountain, a broken, mountainous country in Tucker and Grant counties. Elevation, 3,500 to 4,000 feet.
Canaan; post village in Upshur County.
Cane; branch, a very small right-hand tributary to Kanawha River in Fayette County.
Cane; branch, a very small right-hand tributary to Coal River, a branch of Kanawha River, in Kanawha County.
Cane; fork, a small left-hand branch of Davis Creek, a tributary to Kanawha River, in Kanawha County.
Cane; fork, a small right-hand branch of Cabin Creek, a tributary to Kanawha River, in Kanawha County.
Canebrake; branch, a very small left-hand tributary to Guyandot River, a branch of Ohio River, in Mingo County.
Canfield; post village in Braxton County.
Cannel Coal Hollow; short left-hand tributary to Elk River in Clay County.
Cannelton; post village in Kanawha County on the Ohio Central Lines. Altitude, 639 feet.
Cannoy; branch, a very small right-hand branch of Tug Fork of Big Sandy River, a tributary to Ohio River, in Logan County.
Canoe; run, a left-hand tributary to Monongahela River in Lewis County.
Canoe; run, a very small right-hand tributary to Elk River in Braxton County.
Cansada; post village in Clay County.

Canterbury; post village in Mingo County, on the Norfolk and Western Railway.
Cantikee; branch, a very small right-hand tributary to Guyandot River in Mingo County.
Canton; village in Marion County.
Cantwell; post village in Ritchie County.
Capehart; post village in Mason County.
Caperton; post village in Fayette County on New River and on the Chesapeake and Ohio Railway. Altitude, 990 feet.
Capon Bridge; post village in Hampshire County, located on Cacapon River.
Capon Iron Works; post village in Hardy County.
Capon Springs; post village in Hampshire County.
Captina; post village in Marshall County on the Baltimore and Ohio Railroad.
Carberry; run, a right-hand tributary of Buffalo Creek in Marion County.
Carbondale; post village in Fayette County.
Carder; run, a right-hand branch of Lost Run in Taylor County.
Carder; run, a left-hand branch of Husted Creek in Taylor County.
Caress; post village in Braxton County.
Carkin; post village in Kanawha County.
Carmel; post village in Preston County.
Carnes Knob; summit in Clay County.
Caro; fork, a small left-hand tributary to Joe Creek, a branch of Coal River, in Boone County.
Carpenter; creek, a small right-hand branch of Second Creek, a tributary to Greenbrier River, in Monroe and Greenbrier counties.
Carpenter; fork, a small left-hand tributary to Little Birch River in Braxton County.
Carpenter; run, a left-hand branch of Little Fishing Creek in Wetzel County.
Carrel; post village in Wayne County.
Carron Knob; summit in Nicholas County. Altitude, 2,382 feet.
Carrson; fork, a right-hand tributary of North Fork of Fishing Creek in Wetzel County.
Carter; branch, a small right-hand tributary to Loop Creek, a branch of Kanawha River, in Fayette County.
Carter; run, a right-hand branch of Wheeling Creek in Ohio County.
Carthage; post village in Jackson County.
Cartwright; branch, a small left-hand tributary to Buffalo Creek, a branch of Guyandot River, in Logan County.
Cascade; run, a right-hand branch of Buffalo Creek in Brooke County.
Cascara; post village in Doddridge County.
Casey; creek, a small left-hand tributary to Pond Fork of Little Coal River in Boone County.
Cashmere; post village in Monroe County.
Cass; post village in Pocahontas County on the Chesapeake and Ohio Railway.
Cassiday; fork a small left-hand branch of Left Fork of Middle Fork of Tygarts Valley River in Randolph County.
Cassity; post village in Randolph County.
Cassville; post village in Monongalia County.
Castle; branch, a very small right-hand tributary to Big Huff Creek, a branch of Guyandot River, in Wyoming County.
Castle; mountain, a ridge situated between South and North branches of Potomac River in Pendleton County. Elevation, 3,000 feet.
Castle; post village in Wyoming County.
Castleman; run, a left-hand branch of Buffalo Creek in Ohio and Brooke counties.
Catawba; post village in Marion County on the Baltimore and Ohio Railroad.

Cave; mountain on West and South branches of Potomac River in Pendleton and Grant counties. Elevation, 1,500 to 3,000 feet.
Cave; run, a small left-hand tributary to Little Kanawha River in Upshur County.
Cave; post village in Pendleton County.
Cavill; creek, a right-hand branch of Guyandot River in Cabell County.
Cecil; post village in Taylor County on the Baltimore and Ohio Railroad.
Cedar; branch, a very small left-hand tributary to Paint Creek, a branch of Kanawha River, in Fayette County.
Cedar; branch, a very small left-hand branch of Dunloup Creek, a tributary to New River, in Fayette County.
Cedar; branch, a very small right-hand tributary to Pinnacle Creek, a branch of Guyandot River, in Wyoming County.
Cedar; branch, a very small right-hand tributary to Beech Fork of Twelvepole Creek, a branch of Ohio River, in Wayne County.
Cedar; branch, a very small right-hand tributary to New River in Summers County.
Cedar; creek, a very small right-hand tributary to Clear Fork of Guyandot River in Wyoming County.
Cedar; creek, a small left-hand branch of Slab Fork, a tributary to Guyandot River in Wyoming County.
Cedar; creek, a large left-hand branch of Little Kanawha River in Gilmer and Braxton counties.
Cedar; run, a small right-hand tributary to Wolf Creek, a branch of Greenbrier River, in Monroe County.
Cedarburg; post village in Wyoming County.
Cedarcliff; post village in Mineral County.
Cedargrove; post village in Kanawha County.
Cedar Knob; summit in Pendleton County.
Cedarville; post village in Gilmer County, located on Cedar Creek.
Centennial; post village in Monroe County.
Center; post village in Monongalia County.
Centerpoint; post village in Doddridge County.
Centerville; town in Wayne County. Population, 156.
Central City; town in Cabell County on the Baltimore and Ohio and the Chesapeake and Ohio railroads. Population, 1,580.
Centralia; post village in Braxton County on the Baltimore and Ohio Railroad.
Central Station; post village in Doddridge County.
Century; post village in Barbour County on the Baltimore and Ohio Railroad.
Ceredo; village in Wayne County on the Baltimore and Ohio, the Chesapeake and Ohio, and the Norfolk and Western railroads. Altitude, 545 feet. Population, 1,279.
Chandler; branch, a small left-hand branch of Twomile Creek, a tributary to Kanawha River, in Kanawha County.
Channel; run, a small right-hand tributary to Valley River in Randolph County.
Chap; post village in Boone County.
Chapel; post village in Braxton County.
Chapmanville; post village in Logan County.
Chappel; branch, a very small left-hand tributary to Kanawha River in Kanawha County.
Charles Knob; summit in Grant County.
Charleston; capital of the State and county seat of Kanawha County on the Charleston, Clendennin and Sutton, the Chesapeake and Ohio, and the Ohio Central railroads. Altitude, 600 feet. Population, 1,099.
Charlestown; county seat of Jefferson County on the Baltimore and Ohio and Norfolk and Western railroads. Altitude, 514 feet. Population, 2,392.

Charley; branch, a very small left-hand tributary to Mud River, a branch of Guyandot River, in Lincoln County.
Charley; creek, a small right-hand tributary to Mud River, a branch of Guyandot River, in Cabell and Putnam counties.
Charley Ridge; summit in Pocahontas County.
Charlotte; branch, a very small left-hand branch of Right Fork of Twelvepole Creek, a tributary to Ohio River, in Wayne County.
Charlotte; post village in Monongalia County.
Cheat; mountain, a short ridge in the northern part of Pocahontas County. Elevation, 4,000 feet.
Cheat; river, a large eastern branch of the Monongahela. It drains the eastern part of the State through a number of branches and flows generally northward to its mouth near the north boundary of the State.
Cheatbridge; post village in Randolph County.
Cheat View; summit in Monongalia County. Elevation, 2,212 feet.
Chelyan; post village in Kanawha County on the Chesapeake and Ohio Railway.
Chenowith; creek, a small right-hand tributary to Valley River in Randolph County. It rises in Chenowith Knob of Cheat Mountain.
Chenowith Knob; summit in Randolph County. Altitude, 3,870 feet.
Cherry; fork, a small right-hand tributary to Little Kanawha River in Upshur and Lewis counties.
Cherry; post village in Wirt County.
Cherry; river, a large left-hand branch of Gauley River which rises in two forks, North and South, in Greenbrier County, and flows northwestward into Nicholas County to its junction with the Gauley.
Cherry; run, a right-hand tributary of Potomac River on the boundary between Morgan and Berkeley counties.
Cherry Glades; marsh at the head of Cherry River in Greenbrier and Pocahontas counties.
Cherry Pond; mountain in Boone and Raleigh counties.
Cherryrun; post village in Morgan County on the Baltimore and Ohio and the Western Maryland railroads.
Chesterville; post village in Wood County.
Chestnut; post village in Mason County.
Chestnut; run, a left-hand branch of Leading Creek in Gilmer County.
Chestnut Bottom; run, a right-hand tributary of Ellis Creek in Gilmer County.
Chestnut Knob; branch, a very small right-hand branch of Buffalo Creek, a tributary to Elk River, in Clay County.
Chestnut Lick; small left-hand branch of Left Fork of Steer Creek in Gilmer County.
Chestnut Ridge; short spur in Greenbrier County. Elevation, 2,500 to 3,000 feet.
Chestnut Ridge; short spur in Pocahontas County.
Chestnut Ridge; short spur in Monongalia and Preston counties. Elevation, 2,275 feet.
Chew; run, a small right-hand branch of Big Laurel Creek, a tributary to Cherry River, in Greenbrier County.
Chicken; run, a right-hand tributary of Right Fork of Simpson Creek in Taylor County.
Chiefton; post village in Marion County.
Childress; branch, a left-hand tributary of Buch Fork of Twelve Pole Creek in Wayne County.
Childs; post village in Wetzel County.
Chilton; post village in Kanawha County on the Kanawha and Coal River Railway.
Chimney Ridge; mountains in Monroe County.

Chimney Rock; run, a small left-hand tributary to Elk River in Randolph County.
Chrisley, fork, a small right-hand tributary to Laurel Creek, a branch of Coal River, in Boone County.
Christian; fork, a small right-hand tributary to Brush Creek, a branch of Bluestone River, in Mercer County.
Christian; post village in Logan County.
Christopher; run, a right-hand branch of Cheat River in Monongalia County.
Chub; fork, a small right-hand branch of Naul Creek in Braxton County.
Church; fork, a right-hand branch of Fish Creek in Wetzel County.
Church Knob; summit in Upshur County.
Churchville; post village in Lewis County.
Cicerone; post village in Roane County.
Circleville; post village in Pendleton County.
Cirtsville; post village in Raleigh County. Altitude, 1,640 feet.
Cisko; post village in Ritchie County.
Clapboard; run, a small left-hand tributary to Valley River in Randolph County.
Claremont; post village in Fayette County on the Chesapeake and Ohio Railway and on New River.
Clarence; post village in Roane County.
Claria; post village in Calhoun County.
Clark; branch, a very small right-hand tributary to Elkhorn Creek in McDowell County.
Clark; gap in Great Flat Top Mountain in Mercer County.
Clarksburg; county seat of Harrison County on the Baltimore and Ohio Railroad. Population, 4,050. Altitude, 1,001 feet.
Claude; post village in Taylor County.
Clawson; post village in Pocahontas County.
Clay; branch, a head fork of Big Cub Creek, a tributary to Guyandot River, in Wyoming County.
Clay; county, situated in the central part of the State, in the Alleghany Plateau; it is here deeply dissected. It is drained mainly by Elk River. Area, 348 square miles. Population, 8,248—white, 8,230; negro, 18; foreign born, 48. County seat, Clay. The mean magnetic declination in 1900 was 1° 30'. The mean annual rainfall is 40 to 50 inches, and the mean annual temperature 50° to 55°. The county is traversed by the Charleston, Clendennin and Sutton Railroad.
Clay; county seat of Clay County.
Clayton; post village in Summers County.
Clear; fork, a left-hand tributary to Tug Fork of Big Sandy River in McDowell County.
Clear; fork, a right-hand branch of Guyandot River in Wyoming County.
Clear; fork, a stream in Raleigh County uniting with Marsh Fork to form Coal River.
Clearcreek; post village in Raleigh County. Altitude, 1,520 feet.
Clear Fork; gap in Guyandot Mountain in Raleigh and Wyoming counties.
Clear Drain; a right-hand branch of Fish Creek in Wetzel County.
Clements; post village in Barbour County on the Baltimore and Ohio Railroad.
Clen; fork, a right-hand branch of Laurel Branch of Clear Fork of Guyandot River in Wyoming County.
Clen; gap in spur of Guyandot Mountains, caused by Laurel Fork, in Wyoming County.
Clendenin; post village in Kanawha County on the Charleston, Clendennin and Sutton Railroad. Altitude, 624 feet.
Cleveland; post village in Webster County.
Cleveland Knob; summit in Nicholas County.

Cliff; run, a right-hand branch of Fish Creek in Wetzel County.
Cliff Knob; summit in Webster County. Altitude, 3,012 feet.
Clifftop; post village in Fayette County.
Clifton; village in Mason County on the Baltimore and Ohio Railroad. Population, 427.
Clifton Mills; post village in Preston County.
Clifty; post village in Fayette County.
Climer; creek, a very small left-hand tributary to Trace Fork of Mud River, a branch of Guyandot River, in Putnam County.
Clint; post village in Monroe County.
Clinton; post village in Ohio County.
Clinton Furnace; post village in Monongalia County.
Clintonville; post village in Greenbrier County.
Clio; post village in Roane County.
Cloat; run, a small left-hand tributary to Salt Lick Fork of Little Kanawha River in Braxton County.
Clover; creek, a small right-hand tributary to Greenbrier River in Pocahontas County.
Clover; run, a left-hand tributary to Cheat River, in Tucker County.
Clover Creek; mountain, a short ridge in Pocahontas County. Elevation, 3,000 to 4,000 feet.
Cloverdale; post village in Monroe County.
Cloverlick; branch, a small left-hand tributary to Laurel Branch, a tributary to Clear Fork of Guyandot River, in Wyoming County.
Clover Lick; fork, a left-hand branch of Oil Creek, in Lewis County.
Cloverlick; post village in Pocahontas County on the Chesapeake and Ohio Railway.
Clower; post village in Hardy County.
Cluster; post village in Pleasants County.
Clyde; post village in Wetzel County.
Coal; branch, a very small right-hand tributary to Davis Creek, a branch of Kanawha River, in Kanawha County.
Coal; fork, a left-hand branch of Cabin Creek, a tributary to Kanawha River, in Kanawha County.
Coal; fork, a small left-hand branch of Campbell Fork, a tributary to Kanawha River, in Kanawha County.
Coal; river, a left-hand branch of Monongahela River in Marion County.
Coal; run, a large left-hand branch of Kanawha River, rising in Raleigh County, and flowing northeastward through Boone County. It forms the boundary line between a portion of Lincoln and Kanawha counties and enters Kanawha River at the town of St. Albans.
Coal; run, a small left-hand tributary to New River in Fayette County.
Coal Bank; branch, a small left-hand tributary to Elkhorn Creek, a branch of Tug Fork of Big Sandy River, in McDowell County.
Coalburg; post village in Kanawha County on the Chesapeake and Ohio Railway and on Kanawha River. Altitude, 623 feet.
Coaldale; post village and railway station in Mercer County on the Norfolk and Western Railway and on South Fork of Elkhorn Creek. Altitude, 2,345 feet.
Cobb; creek, a left-hand tributary to Little Coal River, a branch of Coal River, in Lincoln County.
Cobbs; post village in Boone County.
Coburn; post village in Wetzel County.
Cochran Knob; summit in Lewis County.
Coco; post village in Kanawha County.
Coffin; creek, a small left-hand tributary to Knapp Creek, a branch of Greenbrier River, in Pocahontas County.

Coffman; post village in Greenbrier County.
Cokeleys; village in Ritchie County.
Coketon; post village in Tucker County on the West Virginia Central and Pittsburg Railway.
Colaw Knob; summit of the Allegheny Mountains in Pocahontas County. Altitude, 4,214 feet.
Cold; fork, a small right-hand tributary to Laurel Creek, a branch of Coal River, in Boone County.
Cold Knob; fork, a small left-hand tributary to South Fork of Cherry River in Greenbrier County.
Cold Knob; summit in Greenbrier County. Elevation, 4,318 feet.
Cold Spring; run, a very small right-hand branch of Big Laurel Creek, a tributary to Cherry River, in Greenbrier County.
Coldstream; post village in Hampshire County.
Coldwater; post village in Doddridge County.
Cole; mountain, a short ridge in Greenbrier County south of Greenbrier River.
Colebank; post village in Preston County.
Coleman; creek, a right-hand branch of Guyandot River in Lincoln County.
Colemans; creek, a very small right-hand branch of Tug Fork of Big Sandy River, a tributary to Ohio River, in Logan County.
Coles; mountain, a short ridge in Greenbrier County. Elevation, 2,500 feet.
Colfax; post village in Marion County on the Baltimore and Ohio Railroad.
Colic; mountain, a short ridge west of South Fork of Potomac River in Pendleton County.
Colliers; post village in Brooke County.
Collins; branch, a very small right-hand tributary to Paint Creek, a branch of Kanawha River, in Kanawha County.
Collins; run, a right-hand branch of Stewart's Creek in Gilmer County.
Collison; creek, a small left-hand tributary to Gauley River in Nicholas County.
Columbia Sulphur Springs; post village in Greenbrier County located on Anthony Creek.
Columbus; post village in Clay County.
Comer; branch, a small right-hand tributary to Barker Creek, a branch of Guyandot River, in Wyoming County.
Comfort; post village in Boone County,
Conally; run, a small right-hand tributary to Valley River in Randolph County.
Conaway; post village in Tyler County.
Concord; post village in Hampshire County.
Concord Church; village in Mercer County. Altitude, 2,620 feet.
Confidence; post village in Putnam County.
Confluence; post village in Lewis County.
Conger; fork, a small right-hand branch of Old Lick Creek, a tributary to Holly River, in Webster County.
Congo; post village in Hancock County on the Pittsburg, Cincinnati, Chicago and St. Louis Railway.
Conings; post village in Gilmer County.
Conley; branch, a small right-hand tributary to Island Creek, a branch of Guyandot River, in Logan County.
Connelly; branch, a very small left-hand tributary to Mud River, a branch of Guyandot River, in Lincoln County.
Conyer; fork, a right-hand branch of Cedar Creek, in Gilmer and Braxton counties.
Cool; branch, a very small right-hand tributary to Huff Creek, a branch of Guyandot River, in Wyoming County.
Cool Spring Knob; Summit in Webster County.

Coon; branch, a very small left-hand branch of Coal River, a tributary to Kanawha River, in Boone County.

Coon; branch, a very small left-hand tributary to Laurel Branch, a tributary to Clear Fork of Guyandot River, in Wyoming County.

Coon; branch, a very small left-hand tributary to Clear Fork, a branch of Tug Fork of Big Sandy River, in McDowell County.

Coon; branch, a small left-hand tributary to Dry Fork, a branch of Tug Fork of Big Sandy River, in McDowell County.

Coon; creek, a very small right-hand tributary to Gauley River, in Webster County.

Coon; creek, a small left-hand branch of Meadow Creek, a tributary to New River, in Summers County.

Coon; creek, a right-hand tributary of Hurricane Creek in Putnam County.

Coon; creek, a left-hand tributary to Elk River in Braxton County.

Coon; fork, a small left-hand branch of Rock Castle Creek, a tributary to Guyandot River, in Wyoming County.

Coon; run, a right-hand branch of Cove Lick, a tributary to Sand Fork, in Lewis County.

Coon; run, a right-hand branch of West Fork River in Harrison and Marion counties.

Cooney Otter; creek, a left-hand branch of Barker Creek, a tributary to Guyandot River, in Wyoming County.

Coon Knob; summit in Braxton County. Altitude, 1,725 feet.

Coon Knob; triangulation station in Mingo County.

Coonskin; branch, a very small left-hand tributary to Elk River in Kanawha County.

Coon Tree; branch, a small left-hand tributary to Spice Creek, a branch of Tug Fork of Big Sandy River, in McDowell County.

Cooper; creek, a small right-hand tributary to Glade Creek, a branch of New River, in Raleigh County.

Cooper; creek, a right-hand tributary to Elk River in Kanawha County.

Cooper; rock, a summit in Monongalia County. Elevation, 2,000 feet.

Cooper; run, a small left-hand tributary to North Fork of Greenbrier River in Pocahontas County.

Cooper Knob; Summit of Brown Mountain in Tucker County.

Coopers; post village in Mercer County on the Norfolk and Western Railway and on Bluestone River. Altitude, 2,266 feet.

Copeland; branch, a small right-hand tributary to Big Creek, a small branch of Gauley River, in Fayette County.

Copeland; knob in Taylor County.

Copen; post village in Braxton County.

Copen; run, a small right-hand tributary to Little Kanawha River in Braxton County.

Copenhaver; fork, a small left-hand tributary to Little Sandy Creek, a small branch of Elk River, in Kanawha County.

Copenhaver; post village in Kanawha County.

Copper; run, a left-hand tributary to Little Kanawha River in Gilmer and Braxton counties.

Copperas Mine; fork, a small left-hand branch of Trace Fork of Guyandot River, a tributary to Ohio River, in Logan County.

Copperhead; branch, a very small right-hand tributary to Pinnacle Creek, a branch of Guyandot River, in Wyoming County.

Copper Snake; run, a small left-hand branch of Steer Run in Gilmer County.

Corbin; branch, a right-hand branch of Booths Creek in Taylor County.

Corcoran; post village in Randolph County.

Core; post village in Monongalia County.

Corinth; post village in Preston County on the Baltimore and Ohio Railroad.
Cork; post village in Tyler County.
Corley; post village in Braxton County.
Corliss; post village in Fayette County.
Corn; post village in Mason County.
Cornstalk; post village in Greenbrier County.
Cornwallis; post village in Ritchie County on the Baltimore and Ohio Railroad.
Cortland; post village in Tucker County.
Cos; post village in Upshur County.
Cosner Gap; height in Grant County. Elevation, 1,325 feet.
Cottageville; post village in Jackson County on the Baltimore and Ohio Railroad.
Cottle Glades; marsh in Nicholas County.
Cottle Knob; summit in Nicholas County. Altitude, 3,120 feet.
Cottonhill; post village in Fayette County on New River and on the Chesapeake and Ohio Railway. Altitude, 792 feet.
Cotton Hill; short ridge south of Kanawha River in Fayette County.
Couger; fork, tributary to Holly River.
Coulter; run, a right-hand branch of Middle Wheeling Creek in Ohio County.
Counterfeit; branch, a small left-hand branch of Witchers Creek, a tributary to Kanawha River, in Kanawha County.
Countsville; post village in Roane County.
Courtney; run, a left-hand branch of Monongahela River in Monongalia County.
Cove; creek, a small left-hand tributary to Marsh Fork of Coal River in Raleigh County.
Cove; creek, a small right-hand branch of East Fork of Twelvepole Creek, a tributary to Ohio River, in Wayne County.
Cove; mount, a summit in Lincoln County. Altitude, 1,308 feet.
Cove; mountain, a short ridge in Monroe County. Elevation, 3,000 to 3,420 feet, the latter being the height of one of its peaks.
Covecreek; post village in Wayne County.
Covegap; post village in Wayne County.
Cove Lick; right-hand branch of Sand Fork in Lewis County.
Cow; creek, a small right-hand tributary to Clear Fork, a branch of Guyandot River, in Wyoming County.
Cow; creek, a small left-hand branch of Poplar Fork of Kanawha River in Putnam County.
Cow; creek, a small left-hand branch of Pond Fork of Little Coal River in Boone County.
Cow; creek, a left-hand tributary to Island Creek, a branch of Guyandot River in Logan County.
Cow; run, a very small left-hand tributary to Buffalo Creek, a branch of Elk River, in Clay County.
Cowen; town in Webster County on the Baltimore and Ohio Railroad. Population, 257.
Cow Skin; fork, a small left-hand branch of Lower Sleith Fork, in Braxton County.
Coxs Landing; post village in Cabell County on the Baltimore and Ohio Railroad.
Coxs Mills; post village in Gilmer County.
Crabapple Knob; summit in Kanawha County. Altitude, 1,380 feet.
Crab Orchard; creek, a small left-hand tributary to Piney Creek, a branch of New River, in Raleigh County.
Craig; run, a small left-hand tributary to Williams River in Webster County.
Craigmoor; post village in Harrison County.
Craigsville; post village in Nicholas County.
Crammeys; run, a left-hand branch of Cheat River in Monongalia County.

Cranberry; creek, a small left-hand tributary to Piney Creek, a branch of New River, in Raleigh County.

Cranberry; mountain, a short ridge in Pocahontas County. Elevation, 3,500 to 4,000 feet.

Cranberry; river, a large left-hand tributary to Gauley River. It rises in Cranberry Mountain in Pocahontas County and flows northwestward through Webster and Nicholas counties to its junction with the Gauley.

Cranberry Flat; short ridge between Laurel Branch and Stone Coal Run in the central part of Randolph County.

Cranberry Glades; marsh at the head of Cranberry River in Pocahontas County.

Crane; creek, a small right-hand tributary to Dry Fork, a branch of Tug Fork of Big Sandy River, in McDowell County.

Crane; creek, a small left-hand tributary to Bluestone River in Mercer County.

Crane; fork, a small right-hand tributary to Clear Fork, a branch of Guyandot River, in Wyoming County.

Crane Camp; run, a small right-hand tributary to West Fork of Monongahela River in Lewis County.

Cranesville; post village in Preston County.

Crane Trace; branch, a small left-hand tributary to Clear Fork, a branch of Tug Fork of Big Sandy River, in McDowell County.

Crany; post village in Wyoming County.

Craven; run, a small right-hand tributary to Valley River in Randolph County.

Crawford; run, a small left-hand tributary to Gauley River in Nicholas County.

Crawford; run, a small right-hand tributary to Valley River in Randolph County.

Crawford; post village in Lewis County.

Crawley; creek, a small left-hand tributary to Guyandot River, a branch of Ohio River, in Logan County.

Crawley; post village in Greenbrier County.

Crescent; post village in Fayette County on Kanawha River and on the Chesapeake and Ohio Railway. Altitude, 638 feet.

Creston; post village in Wirt County.

Crickard; post village in Randolph County.

Crickmer; post village in Fayette County.

Crimson Springs; post village in Monroe County.

Crisp; post village in Pleasants County.

Crook; post village in Boone County.

Crooked; creek, a left-hand branch of Scary Creek, a tributary to Kanawha River, in Putnam County.

Crooked; creek, a small right-hand branch of Guyandot River, a tributary to Ohio River, in Logan County.

Crooked; creek, a small right-hand tributary to Coal River, a branch of Kanawha River, in Kanawha County.

Crooked; fork, a left-hand branch of Sand Fork in Lewis County.

Crooked; fork, a right-hand branch of Right Fork of Steer Creek in Gilmer and Braxton counties.

Crooked; fork, a right-hand tributary to the head of Big Sycamore Creek, a small branch of Elk River, in Clay County.

Crooked; run, a small left-hand tributary to North River, a branch of Cacapon River, in Hampshire County.

Crooked; run, a small left-hand branch of Cedar Creek in Gilmer County.

Crooked; run, a small left-hand branch of Wolf Creek, a tributary to New River, in Fayette County.

Crooked Ridge; short spur in Fayette County.

Crossroads; post village in Monongalia County.

Crouch Knob; summit in Randolph County.
Crow; post village in Raleigh County.
Crow; run, a left-hand branch of Fishing Creek in Wetzel County.
Crownhill; post village in Kanawha County on the Chesapeake and Ohio Railway.
Crow Summit; post village in Jackson County on the Baltimore and Ohio Railroad.
Crump; branch, a very small left-hand tributary to Cabin Creek, a branch of Kanawha River, in Kanawha County.
Crumps Bottom; post village in Summers County.
Cub; branch, a very small right-hand tributary to Run Creek, a branch of Guyandot River, in Logan County.
Cub; branch, a small right-hand tributary to Panther Creek, a branch of Tug Fork of Big Sandy River, in McDowell County.
Cub; run, a right-hand tributary of Right Fork of Steer Creek in Gilmer County.
Cuba; post village in Jackson County.
Cubana; post village in Randolph County.
Cucumber; creek, an indirect right-hand tributary to Dry Fork, a branch of Tug Fork of Big Sandy River, in McDowell County.
Culler; run, a left-hand tributary to Lost River in Hardy County.
Culloden; town in Cabell County on the Chesapeake and Ohio Railway. Population, 99.
Culverson; creek, a small creek rising and sinking in Greenbrier County.
Cummings; creek, a small left-hand branch of Knapp Creek, a tributary to Greenbrier River, in Pocahontas County.
Cunningham; fork, a left-hand branch of Big Buffalo Creek in Braxton County.
Cunningham Knob; summit of the Allegheny Mountains in Randolph County. Altitude, 4,485 feet.
Cupboard; run, a small left-hand tributary to Oil Creek in Lewis County.
Curran Knob; summit in Randolph County.
Curry; post village in Logan County.
Curry Ridge; a short spur between Plummer and Lost rivers in Taylor County.
Curtin; post village in Nicholas County on the Baltimore and Ohio Railroad.
Curtis; run, a left-hand tributary of Castleman Run in Ohio County.
Cutlip; fork, a right-hand branch of Little Otter Creek in Braxton County.
Cutlips; post village in Braxton County.
Cutwright; run, a small left-hand tributary to Buckhannon River in Upshur County.
Cuzzart; post village in Preston County.
Cyclone; post village in Logan County. Altitude, 854 feet.
Cyrus; creek, a very small left-hand tributary to Mud River, a branch of Guyandot River, in Cabell County.
Cyrus; post village in Roane County.
Daddy; run, a left-hand branch of Cedar Creek in Gilmer County.
Dahmer; post village in Pendleton County.
Dailey; village in Jefferson County on the West Virginia Central and Pittsburg Railway.
Daisy; village in Wood County.
Dakon; post village in Wetzel County.
Dale; post village in Tyler County.
Dallas; post village in Marshall County.
Dallison; post village in Wood County.
Dam; creek, a very small right-hand branch of Marrowbone Creek, a tributary to Tug Fork of Big Sandy River, in Logan County.
Dameron; post village in Raleigh County.

Dan; branch, a small left-hand tributary to Elkhorn Creek, a branch of Tug Fork of Big Sandy River, in McDowell County.
Dan Harman; branch, a small right-hand tributary to Dry Fork, a branch of Tug Fork of Big Sandy River, in McDowell County.
Daniels; post village in Raleigh County.
Danstown; post village in Jackson County.
Danville; post village in Boone County.
Darkesville; post village in Berkeley County on the Cumberland Valley Railroad.
Darnell; hollow in Monongalia County.
Dartmoor; post village in Barbour County on the West Virginia Central and Pittsburg Railway.
Daubenspeck Knob; summit in Nicholas County. Altitude, 3,020 feet.
Dave; branch, a very small left-hand tributary to Big Huff Creek, a branch of Guyandot River, in Logan and Wyoming counties.
Dave Green; branch, a small right-hand tributary to Pond Fork of Little Coal River, a branch of Coal River, in Boone County.
Daves; fork, a small right-hand branch of Brush Creek, a tributary to Bluestone River, in Mercer County.
David; branch, a very small right-hand tributary to Guyandot River in Wyoming County.
Davis; creek, a small left-hand tributary to Guyandot River, a branch of Ohio River, in Cabell County.
Davis; creek, a left-hand tributary to Kanawha River in Kanawha County.
Davis; fork, a very small right-hand tributary to Sycamore Creek, a branch of Clear Fork of Coal River, in Raleigh County.
Davis; run, a small left-hand tributary to Birch River in Braxton County.
Davis; town in Tucker County on the West Virginia Central and Pittsburg Railway. Altitude, 1,077 feet. Population, 2,391.
Davis Knob; summit in Braxton County. Altitude, 1,565 feet.
Davis, Mount; triangulation station in Cabell County. Altitude, 1,077 feet.
Davis Trace; branch, a very small right-hand tributary to Middle Fork of Mud River in Lincoln County.
Davisville; post village in Wood County, on the Baltimore and Ohio Railroad.
Davy; branch, a small right-hand tributary to Tug Fork of Big Sandy River in McDowell County.
Davy; branch, a very small left-hand tributary to Buffalo Creek, a branch of Guyandot River, in Logan County.
Davy; station in McDowell County on the Norfolk and Western Railway and on Tug Fork of Big Sandy River.
Davy Fork; creek, a right-hand branch of Buffalo Creek in Marion County.
Davy; run, a small left-hand branch of Spice Run, a tributary to Greenbrier River, in Greenbrier County.
Davy Cook; branch, a very small right-hand tributary to Toney Fork of Clear Fork, a branch of Guyandot River, in Wyoming County.
Davys; creek, a small left-hand tributary to Greenbrier River in Greenbrier County.
Dawson; post village in Greenbrier County.
Day; mountain, a short spur in Pocahontas County. Elevation, 3,000 to 3,500 feet.
Day; run, a small right-hand tributary to Williams River in Pocahontas County.
Daybrook; post village in Monongalia County.
Day Camp; branch, a small right-hand tributary to Clear Fork, a branch of Tug Fork of Big Sandy River, in McDowell County.
Dayton; post village in Harrison County. Altitude, 925 feet.
Dean; post village in Wetzel County.

Debby; post village in Mason County.
Deckers; creek, a small right-hand branch of Monongahela River in Preston and Monongalia counties.
Decota; post village in Kanawha County.
Deep; run, a small right-hand tributary to North Fork of Potomac River in Mineral County.
Deep; run, a small left-hand tributary to Elk River in Webster County.
Deep; run, a small left-hand tributary to Holly River in Webster County.
Deep Ford; branch, a very small left-hand tributary to Guyandot River, a branch of Ohio River, in Mingo County.
Deep Hole; creek, a very small right-hand branch of West Fork of Twelvepole Creek, a tributary to Ohio River, in Wayne County.
Deepvalley; post village in Tyler County.
Deepwater; post village in Fayette County on Kanawha River and on the Chesapeake and Ohio Railway. Altitude, 645 feet.
Deer; creek, a right-hand branch of North Fork of Greenbrier River in Pocahontas County.
Deer; creek, a right-hand tributary to Hominy Creek, a branch of Gauley River, in Nicholas County.
Deer; run, a small right-hand tributary to Little Birch River in Braxton County.
Deer; run, a small right-hand tributary to South Branch of Potomac River in Pendleton County.
Deer Knob; summit in Upshur County.
Deerlick; post village in Mason County.
Deerrun; post village in Pendleton County.
Deerskin; branch, a small left-hand tributary to Panther Creek, a branch of Tug Fork of Big Sandy River, in McDowell County.
Deerwalk; post village in Wood County.
Defeat; branch, a small right-hand tributary to Little Huff Creek, a branch of Guyandot River, in Wyoming County.
Deitz; post village in Fayette County.
Dekalb; post village in Gilmer County, situated on Little Kanawha River.
Delancy; post village in Wood County.
Delashmeet; creek, a very small left-hand tributary to Bluestone River in Mercer County.
Delila; post village in Webster County.
Dell; post village in Upshur County.
Dellslow; post village in Monongalia County on the Morgantown and Kingwood Railroad.
Delong; post village in Pleasants County.
Delorme; railway station in Logan County on the Norfolk and Western Railway and on Tug Fork of Big Sandy River.
Delphi; post village in Nicholas County.
Delray; post village in Hampshire County.
Delta; post village in Braxton County.
Dempsey; branch, a left-hand branch of Laurel Creek, a tributary to New River, in Fayette County.
Dempsey; mountain, a short ridge north of Greenbrier River in Summers County. Elevation, 2,500 feet.
Dempsey; post village in Fayette County.
Dennis; post village in Greenbrier County.
Dennis; run, a small right-hand branch of Laurel Creek, a tributary to Elk River, in Webster County.

Dennison; fork, a small left-hand branch of Laurel Fork, a tributary to Spruce Fork of Little Coal River, in Boone County.
Dennison; fork, a left-hand tributary of Mud River in Lincoln County.
Dent; post village in Barbour County.
Desert; branch, a small left-hand tributary to North Fork of Cherry River in Nicholas County.
Desert; fork, a right-hand head fork of Holly River in Webster County.
Deskins; fork, a small left-hand branch of Rich Creek, a tributary to East Fork of Twelvepole Creek, in Wayne County.
Deuls; run, a left-hand branch of Buffalo Creek in Marion County.
Devil; creek, a small right-hand branch of Second Creek, a tributary to Greenbrier River, in Monroe County.
Devil; run, a very small right-hand tributary to Little Kanawha River in Braxton County.
Devil; run, a small right-hand tributary to Middle Fork of Tygarts Valley River in Barbour and Randolph counties.
Devil Nose; summit in Clay County.
Devils; fork, a small left-hand tributary to Guyandot River in Raleigh County.
Devils Den; branch, a small right-hand branch of Leatherwood Creek, a tributary to Elk River, in Clay County.
Dewey; post village in Mercer County.
De Witt; post village in Wyoming County.
Dexter; post village in Roane County.
Dial; post village in Kanawha County.
Diamond; post village in Kanawha County on the Chesapeake and Ohio Railway.
Diana; post village in Webster County on the Holly River and Addison Railway.
Diatter; run, a small right-hand tributary to Birch River in Braxton County.
Dick; creek, a very small right-hand tributary to Little Coal River, a branch of Coal River and tributary to Kanawha River, in Boone County.
Dickerson; branch, a very small right-hand tributary to Kanawha River in Kanawha County.
Dick Ridge; spur in Nicholas County.
Dickson; post village in Wayne County on the Norfolk and Western Railway.
Dick Trace; small right-hand branch of Dingus Run, a tributary to Guyandot River, in Logan County.
Dicy; post village in Wayne County.
Difficult; creek, a small right-hand tributary to North Branch of Potomac River in Grant County.
Dilley; run, a small left-hand branch of Strange Creek, a tributary to Elk River, in Nicholas County.
Dilleys Mill; post village in Pocahontas County.
Dillon; branch, a small right-hand tributary to Sand Lick Creek, a branch of Marsh Fork of Coal River, in Raleigh County.
Dillon; run, a small left-hand tributary to Cacapon River in Hampshire County.
Dillons Run; post village in Hampshire County.
Dimmock; post village in Fayette County on the Chesapeake and Ohio Railway and on New River. Altitude, 1,045 feet.
Dingess; branch, a very small left-hand tributary to Buffalo Creek, a branch of Guyandot River, in Logan County.
Dingess; branch, a very small left-hand tributary to Elk Creek, a branch of Guyandot River, in Logan County.
Dingess; branch, a small right-hand tributary to Marsh Fork of Coal River in Raleigh County.

Dingess; fork, a very small left-hand branch of Big Huff Creek, a tributary to Guyandot River, in Wyoming County.

Dingess; post village in Mingo County.

Dingess; station in Logan County on the Norfolk and Western Railway and on Right Fork of Twelvepole Creek.

Dingess Trace; very small right-hand branch of Right Fork of Twelvepole Creek, a tributary to Ohio River, in Logan County.

Dingus; run, a small right-hand branch of Guyandot River in Logan County.

Divide; post village in Fayette County.

Dixie; post village in Fayette County.

Dixon; run, a right-hand branch of Pyles Fork of Buffalo Creek in Marion County.

Doak; post village in Doddridge County.

Doane; post village in Wayne County, on the Norfolk and Western Railway.

Dobbin; post village in Grant County on North Fork of Potomac River and on the West Virginia Central and Pittsburg Railway. Altitude, 2,593 feet.

Dobbin Ridge; short, broken, mountainous country in Tucker and Grant counties.

Doctor; branch, a very small right-hand tributary to Elk River, a large branch of Kanawha River, in Kanawha County.

Dodd; post village in Roane County.

Doddridge; county, situated in the northwestern part of the State on the Allegheny plateau. Area, 344 square miles. Population, 13,689—white, 13,663; negro, 25; foreign born, 129. County seat, West Union. The mean magnetic declination in 1900 was 2° 30′. The mean annual rainfall is 40 to 50 inches, and the mean annual temperature, 50° to 55°. The county is traversed by the Baltimore and Ohio Railroad.

Dodrill; post village in Calhoun County.

Dodson; run, a small right-hand tributary to Valley River in Randolph County.

Doe; branch, a small left-hand tributary to Bluestone River, a branch of New River, in Mercer County.

Doe; run, a left-hand branch of Tygarts Valley River in Taylor County.

Dogbone; branch, a small left-hand tributary to Left Fork of Mud River, a branch of Guyandot River, in Lincoln County.

Dogway; fork, a small left-hand tributary to Cranberry River in Webster and Pocahontas counties.

Dogwood; creek, a small left-hand branch of Meadow River, a tributary to Gauley River, in Fayette County.

Dola; post village in Harrison County on the Baltimore and Ohio Railroad.

Dolan Knob; summit on boundary line between Cabell and Wayne counties. Altitude, 1,090 feet.

Doman; post village in Hardy County.

Dombey; village in Wood County.

Donald; post village in Nicholas County.

Donlan; post village in Gilmer County.

Donnelly; branch, a very small left-hand tributary to Kanawha River in Kanawha County.

Donohue; post village in Ritchie County.

Dorcas; post village in Grant County.

Dority; post village in Preston County.

Dorr; post village in Monroe County.

Dorsey; branch, a very small left-hand branch of Twentymile Creek, a tributary to Gauley River, in Nicholas County.

Dorsey; knob in Monongalia County. Elevation, 1,438 feet.

Dotson; post village in McDowell County.

Double Camp; branch, a very small right-hand tributary to Guyandot River in Wyoming County.

Dougher Knob; summit in Greenbrier County. Altitude, 2,818 feet.

Doughertys; creek, a small right-hand tributary to Cheat River in Preston County.

Douglas; fork, a small right-hand tributary to Elk River in Randolph County.

Douglas; post village in Calhoun County on the West Virginia Central and Pittsburg Railway.

Dovener; post village in Lewis County.

Dowdy; creek, a very small right-hand tributary to New River in Fayette County.

Doyle; post village in Wood County.

Dragstone; creek, a very small right-hand branch of Tug Fork of Big Sandy River, a tributary to Ohio River, in Wayne County.

Drake; run, a right-hand branch of Pyles Fork of Buffalo Creek in Marion County.

Drawdy; creek, a small left-hand branch of Coal River, a tributary to Kanawha River, in Boone County.

Drews; creek, a left-hand branch of Peachtree Creek, a tributary to Marsh Fork of Coal River, in Raleigh County.

Drift; branch, a very small right-hand tributary to West Fork of Twelvepole Creek, a branch of Ohio River, in Wayne County.

Driftwood; post village in Pocahontas County.

Driscol; post village in Pocahontas County.

Droop; mountain, a short spur in Greenbrier and Pocahontas counties. One of its peaks has an altitude of 3,634 feet.

Dropping Lick; creek, a small left-hand tributary to Indian Creek, a branch of New River, in Monroe County.

Dry; branch, a very small left-hand branch of Davis Creek, a tributary to Kanawha River, in Kanawha County.

Dry; branch, a small right-hand tributary to Campbell Creek, a branch of Kanawha River, in Kanawha County.

Dry; branch, a small right-hand branch of Witchers Creek, a tributary to Kanawha River, in Kanawha County.

Dry; branch, a right-hand tributary to Cabin Creek, a branch of Kanawha River, in Kanawha County.

Dry; branch, a small right-hand tributary to Clear Fork, a branch of Guyandot River, in Wyoming County.

Dry; branch, a very small right-hand tributary to Indian Creek, a branch of Guyandot River, in Wyoming County.

Dry; branch, a very small right-hand tributary to Pond Fork of Little Coal River in Boone County.

Dry; branch, a very small right-hand tributary to Tug Fork of Big Sandy River in McDowell County.

Dry; creek, a small right-hand branch of Rich Creek, a tributary to New River, in Monroe County.

Dry; creek, a small right-hand branch of Spring Creek, a tributary to Greenbrier River, in Greenbrier County.

Dry; creek, a small right-hand tributary to Greenbrier River in Pocahontas County.

Dry; creek, a small right-hand tributary to Marsh Fork of Coal River in Raleigh County.

Dry; creek, a very small left-hand tributary to Mud River, a branch of Guyandot River, in Cabell County.

Dry; creek, a left-hand tributary to Howards Creek, a branch of Greenbrier River, in Greenbrier County. Its headwater is known locally as Tuckahoe Creek.

Dry; fork, a left-hand branch of Lower Bull Run, a small right-hand tributary to Cedar Creek, in Gilmer County.
Dry; fork, a right-hand fork of Cheat River in Tucker and Randolph counties.
Dry; fork, a small right-hand tributary to Elk River in Pocahontas County.
Dry; fork, a large right-hand tributary to Tug Fork of Big Sandy River in McDowell County.
Dry; run, a small left-hand tributary to South Branch of Potomac River in Pendleton County.
Dry; run, a small left-hand tributary to Little Kanawha River in Gilmer County.
Dry; run, a right-hand tributary to North Fork of Potomac River in Pendleton County.
Dry; run, a small right-hand tributary to Valley River in Randolph County.
Dry; run, a small right-hand tributary to Left Fork of Buckhannon River in Randolph County.
Dry; run, a small right-hand tributary to South Branch of Potomac River in Pendleton County.
Dry; run, a small right-hand branch of Second Creek, a tributary to Greenbrier River, in Monroe County.
Dry; run, a left-hand branch of Tanner Creek in Gilmer County.
Dry; run, a right-hand branch of Lost Run in Taylor County.
Drybranch; post village in Kanawha County on the Chesapeake and Ohio Railway.
Drycreek; post village in Raleigh County. Altitude, 1,342 feet.
Dryfork; post village in Randolph County on the Dry Fork Railroad.
Dryrun; hollow in Horse Ridges in Morgan County.
Dryrun; post village in Pendleton County.
Dubree; post village in Fayette County.
Duck; creek, a small left-hand tributary to Little Kanawha River in Gilmer County.
Duck; creek, a small right-hand branch of Elk River in Braxton County.
Duckworth; post village in Doddridge County on the Baltimore and Ohio Railroad.
Dudley; fork, a left-hand tributary of Pyles Fork of Buffalo Creek in Marion County.
Dudley; post village in Cabell County.
Duffields; post village in Jefferson County on the Baltimore and Ohio Railroad. Altitude, 562 feet.
Duffy; post village in Lewis County.
Dugout; post village in Raleigh County.
Duhring; post village in Mercer County on the Norfolk and Western Railway and on Bluestone River. Altitude, 2,333 feet.
Duke; post village in Kanawha County on the Baltimore and Ohio Railroad.
Dulin; post village in Wirt County.
Dull; creek, a small right-hand tributary to Elk River, a large branch of Kanawha River, in Clay County.
Dumpling; run, a small left-hand tributary to South Branch of Potomac River in Hampshire and Hardy counties.
Duncan; post village in Jackson County on the Baltimore and Ohio Railroad.
Duncan; run, a small left-hand branch of Deer Creek, a tributary to North Fork of Greenbrier River, in Pocahontas County.
Dunham Lick; run, a right-hand branch of Prichett Creek in Marion County.
Dunkard; creek, a left-hand branch of Monongahela River, heading in Monongalia County in North, South, and Middle forks.
Dunkard Mill; run, a left-hand branch of Buffalo Creek in Marion County.
Dunleith; post village in Wayne County.
Dunloup; creek, a small left-hand tributary to New River in Fayette and Raleigh counties.

Dunlow; post village in Wayne County on the Norfolk and Western Railway.
Dunmore; post village in Pocahontas County.
Dunns; post village in Mercer County.
Duo; post village in Greenbrier County.
Durbin; post village in Pocahontas County on the Chesapeake and Ohio and on the West Virginia Central and Pittsburg railways.
Dust Camp; run, a small left-hand tributary to Little Kanawha River in Gilmer County.
Dutch; fork, a very small left-hand tributary to Pocahontas River in Kanawha County.
Dyers; run, a small left-hand tributary to Elk River in Webster County.
Eads Ridge; summit in Monroe County. Altitude, 2,854 feet.
Eagle; branch, a small right-hand tributary to Greenbrier River in Summers County.
Eagle; post village in Fayette County on Kanawha River and on the Chesapeake and Ohio Railway.
Eagle Mills; post village in Doddridge County.
Earl; post village in Nicholas County.
Earnshaw; post village in Wetzel County.
East; fork, a right-hand branch of Fourteenmile Creek, a tributary to Guyandot River, in Lincoln County.
East; river, a left-hand tributary to New River in Mercer County.
East; run, a right-hand branch of Buffalo Creek in Marion County.
Eastbank; town in Kanawha County on the Chesapeake and Ohio Railway and on Kanawha River. Altitude, 623 feet. Population, 468.
East Lynn; post village in Wayne County.
Easton; post village in Monongalia County on the Baltimore and Ohio Railroad. Altitude, 967 feet.
East River; mountain, a ridge extending along boundary line between Mercer County, West Va., and Bland County, Va.
East River; station in Mercer County on the Norfolk and Western Railway and on East River.
East Sewell; station in Fayette County on the Chesapeake and Ohio Railway and on New River.
Easy; run, a small left-hand tributary to Back Fork of Elk River in Webster County.
Eatons; post village in Wood County.
Eby; post village in Taylor County.
Echart; post village in Boone County. Altitude, 1,424 feet.
Echo; post village in Wayne County on the Norfolk and Western Railway.
Eckman; post village in McDowell County on the Norfolk and Western Railway and on Elkhorn Creek.
Eden; post village in Calhoun County.
Edens; fork, a small left-hand branch of Right Fork of Twomile Creek, a tributary to Elk River, in Kanawha County.
Edgar; post village in Jackson County.
Edgarton; post village in Mingo County.
Edgington; post village in Brooke County on the Pittsburg, Cincinnati, Chicago and St. Louis Railway. Altitude, 702 feet.
Edith; post village in Wyoming County.
Edmiston; post village in Lewis County.
Edmond; post village in Fayette County.
Edmonds; branch, a small right-hand tributary to Mud River, a branch of Guyandot River, in Cabell County.
Edray; post village in Pocahontas County.
Edwin; post village in Webster County.

Efaw; knob in Monongalia County.
Effie; post village in Wayne County.
Egeria; post village in Raleigh County.
Eggleton; post village in Putnam County.
Eglon; post village in Preston County.
Egypt; post village in Wayne County.
Eighteenmile; fork, a small right-hand branch of Campbell Creek, a tributary to Kanawha River, in Kanawha County.
Eighteen Mile; small left-hand tributary to Ohio River in Putnam County.
Eldora; post village in Marion County.
Elgood; post village in Mercer County. Altitude, 2,870 feet.
Eli, post village in Wood County.
Elijah; creek, a small right-hand tributary to Big Clear Creek, a branch of Meadow River, in Greenbrier County.
Eliza; run, a left-hand tributary of Buffalo Creek in Marion County.
Elizabeth; county seat of Wirt County on the Little Kanawha Railroad. Population, 657.
Elk; creek, a small branch of Monongahela River in Harrison County.
Elk; creek, a small right-hand tributary to Guyandot River in Logan County.
Elk; fork, a small right-hand tributary to Pigeon Creek, a branch of Tug Fork of Big Sandy River, in Logan County.
Elk; mountain, a ridge between Elk and Holly rivers in Webster County. Elevation, 1,500 to 2,500 feet.
Elk; mountain, a short ridge near the head of North Fork of Potomac River.
Elk; mountain, a summit in Randolph County. Elevation, 4,000 feet.
Elk; mountain, a ridge lying east of Dry Fork of Elk River in Randolph County.
Elk; village in Tucker County.
Elk; river, a right-hand branch of Kanawha River in Webster, Braxton, Clay, and Kanawha counties.
Elk; run, a small right-hand tributary to North Branch of Potomac River in Grant County.
Elk Garden; town in Mineral County on the West Virginia Central and Pittsburg Railroad. Altitude, 2,300 feet; population, 581.
Elkhorn; creek, a right-hand tributary to Tug Fork of Big Sandy River in McDowell County.
Elkhorn; post village in McDowell County on the Norfolk and Western Railway and on South Fork of Elkhorn Creek. Altitude, 1,885 feet.
Elkhorn Rock; summit on South Fork Mountain in Hardy County.
Elkins; branch, a very small right-hand tributary to Left Fork of Mud River in Lincoln County.
Elkins; branch, a small left-hand tributary to Laurel Branch, a tributary to Clear Fork of Guyandot River, in Wyoming County.
Elkins; county seat of Randolph County on the West Virginia Central and Pittsburg Railroad. Population, 2,016.
Elkins Gap; triangulation station in Wyoming County. Elevation, 1,944 feet.
Elk Knob; post village in Summers County.
Elklick; branch, a very small left-hand tributary to Clear Fork, a branch of Guyandot River, in Wyoming County.
Elklick; branch, a very small left-hand tributary to Buffalo Creek, a branch of Guyandot River, in Logan County.
Elk Lick; branch, a small left-hand branch of Blue Creek, a tributary to Elk River, in Kanawha County.
Elk Lick; left-hand head fork of Laurel Fork of Cheat River in Randolph County.
Elk Lick; small left-hand tributary to Oil Creek in Lewis County.

Elklick; run, a small right-hand tributary to Greenbrier River in Pocahontas County.
Elk Trace; small left-hand tributary to Big Huff Creek, a branch of Guyandot River, in Logan and Wyoming counties.
Elk Trace; small right-hand branch of Big Tub Creek, a tributary to Guyandot River, in Wyoming County.
Elk Twomile; creek, a left-hand tributary to Elk River in Kanawha County.
Elk water; left-hand tributary to Valley River in Randolph County.
Elkwater; post village in Randolph County.
Ella; post village in Marshall County.
Elleber; run, a small left-hand tributary to North Fork of Greenbrier River in Pocahontas County.
Elleber Ridge; summit between Elleber Run and Tackey Fork in Pocahontas County. Elevation, 4,000 to 4,500 feet.
Ellenboro; post village in Ritchie County.
Elliot; post village in Fayette County.
Ellis; creek, a small right-hand tributary to Marsh Fork of Coal River in Raleigh County.
Ellis; creek, a right-hand branch of Sand Fork and tributary to Little Kanawha River in Gilmer County.
Ellis; post village in Gilmer County on Ellis Creek.
Ellison; post village in Summers County.
Ellsworth; post village in Ritchie County.
Elm; fork, a left-hand tributary to Buffalo Creek, a branch of Elk River, in Nicholas and Clay counties.
Elmgrove; town in Ohio County on the Baltimore and Ohio Railroad. Altitude, 681 feet; population, 768.
Elmira; post village in Braxton County.
Elmo; post village in Fayette County on the Chesapeake and Ohio Railway and on New River. Altitude, 860 feet.
Elmwood; post village in Mason County on the Chesapeake and Ohio Railway.
Eloise; post village in Wayne County.
Elton; post village in Summers County.
Elverton; post village in Fayette County.
Elwell; post village in Mason County on the Baltimore and Ohio Railroad.
Ely; fork, a small left-hand tributary to Little Coal River, a branch of Coal River, in Lincoln County.
Emanuel; hill, a summit in Fayette County. Altitude, 2,360 feet.
Emma; post village in Putnam County.
Emory; post village in Mineral County.
Endicott; post village in Wetzel County.
England; run, a small left-hand tributary to Little Kanawha River in Braxton County.
Ennis; post village in McDowell County on the Norfolk and Western Railway and on South Fork of Elkhorn Creek. Altitude, 1,990 feet.
Enoch; branch, a small left-hand tributary to Gauley River in Nicholas and Webster counties.
Enoch; post village in Clay County.
Enoch; run, a small right-hand branch of Muddlety Creek, a tributary to Gauley River, in Nicholas County.
Enon; post village in Nicholas County.
Enterprise; post village in Harrison County on the Baltimore and Ohio Railroad.
Entry; mountain, a summit in Pendleton County.
Ephraim; creek, a very small right-hand tributary to New River in Fayette County.

Erbacon; post village in Webster County on the Baltimore and Ohio Railroad.
Erie; post village in Wayne County on the Baltimore and Ohio Railroad.
Ernest; post village in Roane County.
Etam; post village in Preston County.
Ethel; post village in Boone County.
Euclid; post village in Calhoun County.
Eugene; post village in Mingo County.
Eureka; post village in Pleasants County on the Baltimore and Ohio Railroad.
Eva; post village in Ritchie County.
Evans; branch, a very small left-hand tributary to Barker Creek, a branch of Guyandot River, in Wyoming County
Evans; fork, a small left-hand branch of Falling Rock Creek, a tributary to Elk River, in Kanawha County.
Evans; post village in Jackson County on the Baltimore and Ohio Railroad.
Evans; run, a left-hand tributary of Buffalo Creek in Marion County.
Evansville; post village in Preston County.
Evelyn; post village in Wirt County.
Everett; post village in Tyler County.
Evergreen; post village in Upshur County.
Everson; post village in Marion County on the Baltimore and Ohio Railroad.
Ewing; fork, a small right-hand tributary to Clear Fork of Coal River in Raleigh County.
Extra; post village in Putnam County.
Extract; post village in Hampshire County.
Eye; post village in Nicholas County.
Eyes; run, a small right-hand tributary to Thorn Run of South Branch of Potomac River in Pendleton County.
Fabius; post village in Hardy County.
Faily; creek, a very small left-hand tributary to New River in Raleigh County.
Fairfax; post village in Mingo County on the West Virginia Central and Pittsburg Railroad.
Fairfield; post village in Kanawha County on the Chesapeake and Ohio Railway.
Fairmont; county seat of Marion County on the Baltimore and Ohio Railroad. Altitude, 888 feet. Population, 5,655.
Fairplain; post village in Jackson County.
Fairview; village in Hancock County. Population, 407.
Falkner; branch, a small right-hand branch of Muddlety Creek, a tributary to Gauley River, in Nicholas County.
Fall; creek, a small left-hand branch of Coal River, a tributary to Kanawha River, in Kanawha and Lincoln counties.
Fall; run, a right-hand branch of Little Kanawha River in Braxton County.
Fall; run, a small right-hand branch of Back Fork of Holly River in Webster County.
Fall; run, a small left-hand branch of Right Fork of Holly River in Braxton County.
Fallen Timber; run, a small right-hand tributary to Little Kanawha River in Lewis County.
Fallen Timber; short ridge in the western part of Pocahontas County. Elevation, 4,000 feet.
Falling Rock; creek, a left-hand tributary to Elk River in Kanawha and Clay counties.
Falling Spring; mountain, a short ridge north of Greenbrier River in Greenbrier County. Elevation, 2,500 feet.
Falling Spring; post village in Greenbrier County located on Greenbrier River.
Falling Spring; run, a small right-hand tributary to Elk River in Randolph County.

Falling Waters; post village in Berkeley County on the Cumberland Valley Railroad.
Fall Rock; branch, a very small left-hand tributary to Guyandot River in Wyoming County.
Falls; branch, a very small left-hand tributary to Beech Fork of Twelvepole Creek, a branch of Ohio River, in Wayne County.
Falls; creek, a small left-hand tributary to Kanawha River in Fayette County.
Falls; creek, a very small left-hand tributary to Guyandot River, a branch of Ohio River, in Lincoln County.
Falls; post village in Grant County.
Fallsmill; post village in Braxton Connty.
Fanlight; post village in Wetzel County.
Far; post village in Wetzel County.
Farley; branch, a small left-hand tributary to Cabin Creek, a branch of Guyandot River, in Wyoming County.
Farley; branch, an indirect right-hand tributary to Tommy Creek, a head fork of Guyandot River, in Raleigh County.
Farley; branch, a very small right-hand tributary to Pond Fork of Little Coal River in Boone County.
Farley; branch, a very small right-hand tributary to Mud River, a branch of Guyandot River, in Lincoln County.
Farmington; post village in Marion County on the Baltimore and Ohio Railroad.
Farnum; post village in Harrison County.
Fat; creek, a small right-hand tributary to Piney Creek, a branch of New River, in Raleigh County.
Faulkner; post village in Randolph County on the West Virginia Central and Pittsburg Railroad.
Fayette; county, situated a little south of the central part of the State on the Alleghany Plateau. It is drained by the Kanawha, New, and Gauley rivers. Area, 775 square miles. Population, 31,987—white, 26,130; negro, 5,857; foreign born, 975. County seat, Fayetteville. The mean magnetic declination in 1900 was 1° 30′. The mean annual rainfall is 50 to 60 inches, and the mean annual temperature 55° to 55°. The county is traversed by the Chesapeake and Ohio and by the Kanawha and Michigan railways.
Fayette; post village in Fayette County on New River and on the Chesapeake and Ohio Railway. Altitude, 900 feet.
Fayetteville; county seat of Fayette County about three miles west of New River. Altitude, 1,750 feet. Population, 413.
Federal; post village in Pleasants County.
Feed Trough; run, a small right-hand tributary to Birch River in Nicholas County.
Fellowsville; post village in Preston County.
Felt; run, a small left-hand tributary to Left Fork of Steer Creek in Gilmer County.
Ferguson; post village in Wayne County.
Fern; creek, a small right-hand tributary to New River in Fayette County.
Fern; post village in Pleasants County.
Ferris; post village in Fayette County.
Ferrum; village in Jefferson County.
Ferry; branch, a very small left-hand tributary to Kanawha River in Kanawha County.
Ferry; run, a right-hand tributary of Buffalo Creek in Brooke County.
Festus; village in Marion County.
Fetterman; town in Taylor County on the Baltimore and Ohio Railroad. Altitude, 984 feet. Population, 796.

Fez; creek, a very small left-hand tributary to Mud River, a branch of Guyandot River, in Lincoln County.
Fields; creek, a small left-hand tributary to Kanawha River in Kanawha County.
Fifteenmile; creek, a small left-hand tributary to Paint Creek, a branch of Kanawha River, in Fayette County.
Fifteenmile; fork, a left-hand branch of Cabin Creek, a tributary to Kanawha River, in Kanawha County.
Files; creek, a right-hand branch of Valley River in Randolph County.
Finch; post village in Ritchie County.
Finlow; post village in Fayette County.
Finney; branch, a small right-hand tributary to Kanawha River in Kanawha County.
Finster; post village in Lewis County.
Fire; creek, a very small right-hand tributary to New River in Fayette County.
Firecreek; post village in Fayette County on the Chesapeake and Ohio Railway and on New River. Altitude, 1,029 feet.
Fish; creek, a small left-hand branch of Ohio River in Marshall County.
Fisher; fork, a right-hand branch of Rocky Fork of Pocotaligo River, a tributary to Kanawha River, in Kanawha County.
Fisher Knob; summit in Braxton County. Elevation, 1,710 feet.
Fishhook; fork, a small left-hand tributary to Blake Branch of Smithers Creek, a tributary to Kanawha River, in Fayette County.
Fishing; creek, a left-hand branch of Ohio River heading in North and South Forks in Wetzel County.
Fishing Hawk; small left-hand tributary to Shavers Fork of Cheat River in Randolph County.
Fishpot; run, a right-hand branch of Little Kanawha River in Gilmer County.
Fitz; run, a small left-hand tributary to Sand Fork in Lewis County.
Fitzwater; branch, a small right-hand branch of Peter Creek, a tributary to Gauley River, in Nicholas County.
Fitzwater; run, a small right-hand branch of Buffalo Creek, a tributary to Elk River, in Clay County.
Five Lick; run, a small right-hand tributary to Laurel Fork of Cheat River in Randolph County.
Five Mile; creek, a small left-hand tributary to East River, a branch of New River, in Mercer County.
Fivemile; fork, a left-hand branch of Kelly Creek, a tributary to Kanawha River, in Kanawha County.
Fivemile; fork, a very small left-hand branch of Smithers Creek, a tributary to Kanawha River, in Fayette County.
Fivemile; fork, a small right-hand branch of Campbell Creek, a tributary to Kanawha River, in Kanawha County.
Fivemile; fork, a small right-hand branch of Cooper Creek, a tributary to Kanawha River, in Kanawha County.
Fivemile; post village in Mason County.
Flag; run, a small left-hand tributary to Cheat River in Preston County.
Flaggy Meadow; run, a right-hand branch of Buffalo Creek in Marion County.
Flat; fork, a small right-hand branch of Buffalo Creek, a tributary to Elk River, in Clay County.
Flat; run, a right-hand branch of Tygart Valley River in Taylor County.
Flat; run, a small left-hand branch of Sycamore Creek in Gilmer County.
Flat; run, a left-hand branch of Pyles Fork of Buffalo Creek in Marion County.
Flatfork; post village in Roane County.
Flatrock; post village in Mason County.

Flat Top; mountain, a ridge in Wyoming, Mercer, Raleigh, and Summers counties. Average altitude, 3,375 feet.
Flat Top; mountain, a summit in Monroe County. Altitude, 3,375 feet.
Flattop; post village in Mercer County. Altitude, 3,180 feet.
Flat Top; summit in Nicholas County.
Flatwoods; post village in Braxton County, on the Baltimore and Ohio and the West Virginia Central and Pittsburg railroads. Altitude, 1,223 feet.
Flatwoods; run, a small right-hand tributary to Elk River in Braxton County.
Flaxton; post village in Mason County.
Fleming; fork, a right-hand branch of Buffalo Creek in Marion County.
Fleming; run, a small left-hand tributary to Anthony Creek, a branch of Greenbrier River, in Greenbrier County.
Flemington; post village in Taylor County on the Baltimore and Ohio Railroad.
Fleshy; run, a small right-hand tributary to Little Kanawha River in Braxton County.
Fletcher; post village in Jackson County.
Flinn; post village in Jackson County.
Flint; post village in Doddridge County.
Flint; run, a small left-hand branch of The Creek and tributary to Back Fork of Elk River in Randolph County.
Flint; run, a small left-hand tributary to Ohio River in Doddridge County.
Flipping; creek, a small left-hand tributary to Bluestone River in Mercer County.
Flippins Ridge; mountains in Mercer County.
Floding; post village in Cabell County.
Flora; post village in Barbour County.
Floyd; branch, a very small right-hand tributary to Coal River, a branch of Kanawha River, in Boone County.
Folsom; post village in Wetzel County.
Foltz; post village in Berkeley County.
Fonda; post village in Harrison County.
Foote; post village in Mineral County.
Ford; post village in Wood County.
Ford Knob; summit of Big Sewell Mountain in Fayette County. Altitude, 3,330 feet.
Ford Knob; summit in Fayette County. Altitude, 2,860 feet.
Fore Knobs; summits in Allegheny Front in Grant County.
Foresthill; post village in Summers County.
Fork; creek, a small left-hand branch of Coal River, a tributary to Kanawha River, in Boone County.
Fork; mountain, a short ridge in Webster County.
Fork; mountain, a ridge on the south side of Cranberry River, separating it from the headwaters of the Greenbrier.
Fork; mountain, a short ridge near the head of Greenbrier River.
Fork Ridge; mountains in Mercer County.
Fork Ridge; short spur of Middle Fork Mountains.
Forksburg; village in Marion County.
Forks of Capon; post village in Hampshire County.
Forks of Little Sandy; post village in Kanawha County.
Fort: branch, a small right-hand tributary to Indian Creek, a branch of Guyandot River, in Wyoming County.
Fort Gay; post village in Wayne County.
Fort Laurel; creek, a small right-hand tributary to New River in Fayette County, called Laurel Creek at its mouth.
Fort Seybert; post village in Pendleton County.

Fort Spring; post village in Greenbrier County on Greenbrier River and on the Chesapeake and Ohio Railway. Altitude, 1,626 feet.

Forty Weight; branch, a small head tributary to Laurel Fork, a tributary to Clear Fork of Guyandot River, in Raleigh County.

Foss; post village in Summers County.

Foster; post village in Boone County.

Foster Chapel; post village in Jackson County.

Fountain Spring; post village in Wood County.

Fourmile; creek, a small left-hand branch of Lens Creek, a tributary to Kanawha River, in Kanawha County.

Fourmile; creek, a small left-hand tributary to Guyandot River, a branch of Ohio River, in Lincoln County.

Fourmile; fork, a very small left-hand branch of Smithers Creek, a tributary to Kanawha River, in Fayette County.

Fourmile; fork, a very small left-hand branch of Kelly Creek, a tributary to Kanawha River, in Kanawha County.

Fourmile; fork, a small left-hand branch of Paint Creek, a tributary to Kanawha River, in Kanawha County.

Fourmile; fork, a small right-hand branch of Whiteoak Creek, a tributary to Coal River, in Boone County.

Fourmile; fork, a right-hand branch of Cooper Creek, a tributary to Elk River, in Kanawha County.

Fourmile; run, a right-hand branch of North Fork of Fishing Creek in Wetzel County.

Four Pole; creek, a very small right-hand branch of Tug Fork of Big Sandy River in Mingo County.

Fourpole; creek, a small left-hand tributary to Ohio River in Wayne and Cabell counties.

Fourteen; post village in Lincoln County.

Fourteenmile; creek, a small left-hand branch of Guyandot River, a tributary to Ohio River, in Lincoln County.

Fowlerknob; post village in Nicholas County.

Fox; post village in Braxton County.

Fox Knob; summit in Nicholas County.

Fox Tree; run, a small left-hand tributary to Cranberry River in Webster County.

Frame; run, a left-hand branch of Strange Creek in Braxton County.

Frame Knob; summit in Braxton County. Elevation, 1,563 feet.

Frametown; post village in Braxton County.

Frances; creek, a small right-hand branch of Kiah Fork, a tributary to Twelvepole Creek, in Wayne County.

Frank; branch, a small left-hand branch of Lilly Fork of Buffalo Creek, a tributary to Elk River, in Clay County.

Frank; fork, a very small right-hand branch of Blue Creek, a tributary to Elk River, in Kanawha County.

Frank; fork, a very small right-hand branch of Laurel Fork, a tributary to Clear Fork of Guyandot River, in Wyoming and Raleigh counties.

Frank; post village in Putnam County.

Frankford; town in Greenbrier County. Population, 138.

Franklin; branch, a small right-hand branch of Twomile Creek, a tributary to Guyandot River, in Lincoln County.

Franklin; county seat of Pendleton County on the Baltimore and Ohio Railroad. Population, 205.

Frazier; run, a small left-hand tributary to Cheat River in Preston County.

Fraziers Bottom; post village in Putnam County.

Freed; post village in Calhoun County.
Freeman; post village in Mercer County, on the Norfolk and Western Railway. Altitude, 2,258 feet.
Freemansburg; post village in Lewis County.
Freeport; post village in Wirt County.
Freeze; fork, a head fork of Dingus Run, a tributary to Guyandot River, in Logan County.
French; creek, a left-hand branch of Buckhannon River in Upshur County.
Frenchcreek; post village in Upshur County.
Frenchton; post village in Upshur County.
Frew; post village in Tyler County.
Friarshill; post village in Greenbrier County.
Friendly; town in Tyler County, on the Baltimore and Ohio Railroad. Population, 253.
Friends; run, a small left-hand tributary to South Branch of Potomac River in Pendleton County.
Frisco; village in Marion County.
Front Hills; summits in Grant County.
Frost; post village in Pocahontas County.
Frozen; branch, a very small left-hand branch of Kelly Creek, a tributary to Kanawha River, in Kanawha County.
Frozencamp; post village in Jackson County.
Fry; post village in Kanawha County.
Fudge; branch, a very small left-hand tributary to Little Sandy Creek, a small branch of Elk River, in Kanawha County.
Fudger; creek, a small left-hand tributary to Mud River, a branch of Guyandot River, in Cabell County.
Fudges Creek; post village in Cabell County.
Fullen; post village in Monroe County.
Fulton; creek, a very small right-hand tributary to Clear Fork of Coal River in Raleigh County.
Fuqua; creek. a small right-hand branch of Coal River, a tributary to Kanawha River, in Lincoln County.
Furber; run, a right-hand branch of Proctor Creek in Wetzel County.
Furnace; post village in Mineral County.
Furnett; branch, a very small left-hand tributary to Big Ugly Creek, a branch of Guyandot River, in Lincoln County.
Furnett; creek, a small right-hand tributary to Guyandot River, a branch of Ohio River, in Lincoln County.
Fury Knob; summit in Nicholas County.
Gad; post village in Nicholas County.
Gaines; post village in Upshur County.
Galfred; run, a small left-hand branch of Suttleton Creek, a tributary to Greenbrier River, in Pocahontas County.
Gallatin; branch, a very small left-hand tributary to Kanawha River in Kanawha County.
Galletin; village in Marion County.
Gandeeville; post village in Roane County.
Gandy; creek, a right-hand head fork of Dry Fork of Cheat River in Randolph County.
Gandy; run, a small right-hand tributary to Red Creek in Tucker County.
Ganotown; post village in Berkeley County.
Gap; mountain in Monroe County.
Gapmills; post village in Monroe County.

Garden Gap; branch, a very small left-hand tributary to Little Huff Creek, a branch of Guyandot River, in Wyoming County.
Garden Ground; mountain in Fayette County.
Gardner; branch, a very small right-hand tributary to Clear Fork of Coal River in Raleigh County.
Garfield; post village in Jackson County.
Garland; fork, a small right-hand tributary to Spruce Fork of Little Coal River in Logan County.
Garland; post village in Barbour County.
Garnet; post village in Kanawha County.
Garrett; creek, a small left-hand branch of Twelvepole Creek, a tributary to Ohio River, in Wayne County.
Garretts Bend; post village in Lincoln County.
Garrison; run, a left-hand branch of Castleman Run in Ohio County.
Gary; post village in Webster County on the Norfolk and Western Railway.
Gashell; run, a right-hand branch of Little Wheeling Creek in Ohio County.
Gaston; post village in Lewis County on the West Virginia Central and Pittsburg Railroad. Altitude 1,040 feet.
Gate; fork, a right-hand tributary of Left Fork of Steer Creek in Braxton and Gilmer counties.
Gates; post village in Monroe County.
Gatewood; branch, a small right-hand tributary to Cabin Creek, a branch of Kanawha River, in Kanawha County.
Gatewood; post village in Fayette County.
Gath; village in Marion County.
Gauley; mountain, a ridge in Randolph and Pocahontas counties. Elevation, 4,000 feet.
Gauley; mountain, a ridge between Gauley and New rivers, forks of Kanawha River, in Fayette County. Elevation, 1,500 to 2,000 feet.
Gauley; river, a right-hand branch of Kanawha River, entering it about 20 miles above Charleston. Length, 109 miles.
Gauley Bridge; post village in Fayette County on Gauley River and on the Chesapeake and Ohio Railway.
Gay; post village in Jackson County.
Gay Knob; summit in Pocahontas County.
Gazil; post village in Kanawha County.
Geho; post village in Calhoun County.
Gem; post village in Braxton County.
Geneva; post village in Roane County.
Genoa; post village in Wayne County on the Norfolk and Western Railway.
George; branch, a small left-hand tributary to Laurel Creek, a branch of Coal River, in Boone County.
George; branch, a small right-hand tributary to Panther Creek, a branch of Tug Fork of Big Sandy River, in McDowell County.
George; branch, a very small left-hand tributary to Barker Creek, a branch of Guyandot River, in Wyoming County.
George; run, a left-hand tributary of Ohio River in Ohio County.
Georges; creek, a small right-hand tributary to Kanawha River in Kanawha County.
Georgetown; post village in Monongalia County.
Georgie; post village in Wood County.
German; post village in Braxton County.
Gerrardstown; post village in Berkeley County.
Get Out; run, a tributary to Little Kanawha River in Upshur County.
Giatto; post village in Mercer County.

Gibson; branch, a small right-hand tributary to Fifteenmile Fork of Cabin Creek, a branch of Kanawha River, in Kanawha County.
Gibson; post village in Pleasants County on the Norfolk and Western Railway.
Gibson Knob; summit in Pocahontas County. Altitude, 4,360 feet.
Gibsons Mill; post village in Fayette County.
Gilbert; creek, a left-hand tributary to Guyandot River, a branch of Ohio River, in Mingo County.
Gilbert; post village in Mingo County. Altitude, 832 feet.
Gilboa; post village in Nicholas County.
Gilkerson; post village in Wayne County.
Gilliam; post village in McDowell County on the Norfolk and Western Railway.
Gillespie; run, a left-hand branch of Middle Wheeling Creek in Ohio County.
Gilmer; county situated in the central part of the county, on the Allegheny Plateau. It is here deeply dissected. It is traversed and drained by Little Kanawha River. Area, 367 square miles. Population, 11,762—white, 11,726; negro, 36; foreign born, 18. County seat, Glenville. The mean magnetic declination in 1900 was 1° 20′. The mean annual rainfall is 40 to 50 inches, and the mean annual temperature, 50° to 55°.
Girta; post village in Ritchie County.
Girty; run, a left-hand tributary of Ohio River in Brooke County.
Given; branch, a very small right-hand tributary to Elk River in Kanawha County.
Given; post village in Jackson County.
Glade; creek, a left-hand branch of New River in Raleigh County.
Glade; creek, a small left-hand branch of Meadow River, a tributary to Gauley River, in Fayette County.
Glade; creek, a small left-hand branch of Muddlety Creek, a tributary to Gauley River, in Nicholas County.
Glade; creek, a small right-hand tributary to New River in Fayette County.
Glade; run, a left-hand tributary of Pawpaw Creek in Marion County.
Glade; run, a right-hand tributary of Cheat River in Monongalia County.
Glade; run, a small right-hand tributary to Blackwater River in Tucker County.
Glade; run, a small left-hand branch of Laurel Creek, a tributary to Elk River, in Webster County.
Glade; station in Fayette County on the Chesapeake and Ohio Railway and on New River. Altitude, 1,236 feet.
Gladefarms; post village in Preston County.
Gladesville; post village in Preston County.
Gladwin; post village in Tucker County, on the Dry Fork Railroad.
Glady; creek, a right-hand branch of Little Kanawha River in Lewis County.
Glady; creek, a right-hand branch of Tygarts Valley River in Marion County.
Glady; creek, a small right-hand tributary to Laurel Creek, a branch of Valley River, in Barbour County.
Glady; fork, a large left-hand branch of Dry Fork, one of the head forks of Cheat River, in Randolph and Tucker counties.
Glady; fork, a small left-hand tributary to Right Fork of Stone Coal Creek in Upshur County.
Glady; fork, a left-hand tributary to Brush Creek, a branch of Bluestone River, in Mercer County.
Glady; post village in Randolph County, on the West Virginia Central and Pittsburg Railway.
Glass Lick; small right-hand tributary to Beech Fork of Twelvepole Creek, a branch of Ohio River, in Wayne County.
Glebe; post village in Hampshire County.
Glenalum; post village in Mingo County on the Norfolk and Western Railway.

Glencoe; post village in Greenbrier County.
Glen Easton; post village in Marshall County.
Glen Falls; post village in Harrison County.
Glengary; post village in Berkeley County.
Glenns; run, a left-hand branch of Ohio River in Ohio County.
Glenville; county seat of Gilmer County on Little Kanawha River. Population, 398. Altitude, 738 feet.
Glenwood; post village in Mason County.
Glomera; post village in Raleigh County.
Glover; branch, a very small right-hand branch of Guyandot River, a branch of Ohio River, in Lincoln County.
Glovergap; post village in Marion County on the Baltimore and Ohio Railroad. Altitude, 1,146 feet.
Gluck; run, a very small right-hand tributary to Little Kanawha River in Gilmer County.
Gnat; run, a small right-hand tributary to Gauley River in Webster County.
Godby Knob; summit in Logan County.
Godfrey; branch, a small right-hand tributary to Wide Mouth Creek, a branch of Bluestone River, in Mercer County.
Godfrey; post village in Mercer County.
Goffs; post village in Ritchie County.
Golden; post village in Marshall County.
Goldtown; post village in Jackson County.
Gomez; post village in Calhoun County.
Goodhope; post village Harrison County.
Goodwill; post village in Mercer County on the Norfolk and Western Railway.
Goose; creek, a right-hand branch of Tygarts Valley River in Marion County.
Goosecreek; post village in Ritchie County.
Goose Lick; left-hand branch of Indian Fork in Lewis County.
Gooseneck; post village in Ritchie County.
Gordon; post village in Boone County on the Norfolk and Western Railway.
Gormania; post village in Grant County on North Branch of Potomac River and on the West Virginia Central and Pittsburg Railway.
Gough; run, a right-hand branch of Potomac River in Morgan County.
Gould; post village in Clay County.
Grace; post village in Roane County on the Baltimore and Ohio Railroad.
Grady; post village in Wood County.
Grafton; county seat of Taylor County on the Baltimore and Ohio Railroad. Altitude, 997 feet. Population, 5,650.
Graham Mines; post village in Kanawha County.
Graham Station; post village in Mason County on the Baltimore and Ohio Railroad.
Grand Camp; run, a right-hand branch of French Creek, a tributary to Buckhannon River, in Upshur County.
Grand Camp; run, a small right-hand branch of Cedar Creek in Gilmer County.
Granddaddy; run, a left-hand branch of Left Fork of Steer Creek in Braxton County.
Grandstaff; run, a right-hand branch of Wheeling Creek in Marshall County.
Grandview; post village in Raleigh County.
Grangeville; village in Marion County.
Granny; creek, a right-hand tributary to Elk River in Braxton County.
Grant; county, situated in the northeastern part of the State. Its surface consists of a close alternation of ridges and valleys. It is traversed from northeast to northwest by branches of the Potomac, by which it is drained. Area, 483 square miles. Population, 7,275—white, 7,023; negro, 252; foreign born, 95. County

seat, Petersburg. The mean magnetic declination in 1900 was 3° 45'. The mean annual rainfall is 50 to 60 inches, and the mean annual temperature 40° to 50°. The county is traversed by the West Virginia Central and Pittsburg Railway.

Grants; branch, a very small right-hand branch of Tug Fork of Big Sandy River, a tributary to Ohio River, in Logan County.

Grantsville; county seat of Calhoun County. Population, 225.

Grape Island; post village in Pleasants County, on the Baltimore and Ohio Railroad.

Grapevine; branch, a small left-hand tributary to Pond Fork of Little Coal River in Boone County.

Grapevine; branch, a small left-hand tributary to Dry Fork, a branch of Tug Fork of Big Sandy River, in McDowell County.

Grapevine; branch, a right-hand branch of Fourpole Creek in Cabell County.

Grapevine; branch, a very small right-hand tributary to Tug Fork of Big Sandy River in McDowell County.

Grapevine; creek, a small right-hand branch of Tug Fork of Big Sandy River, a tributary to Ohio River, in Logan County.

Grapevine Knob; summit in Kanawha County.

Grass; run, a left-hand branch of Little Kanawha River in Gilmer County.

Grass; run, a right-hand branch of Saltlick Creek in Braxton County.

Grasshopper; run, a right-hand branch of Potomac River in Morgan County.

Grassland; post village in Harrison County.

Grass Lick; head fork of left fork of Steer Creek in Braxton County.

Grassy; branch, a very small left-hand tributary to Bluestone River in Mercer County.

Grassy; creek, a left-hand tributary to Holly River in Webster County.

Grassy; creek, a small right-hand branch of Hominy Creek, a tributary to Gauley River, in Nicholas County.

Grassy; fork, a left-hand tributary to Big Sycamore Creek, a small branch of Elk River, in Clay County.

Grassy; fork, a small left-hand tributary to Little Coal River, a branch of Coal River, in Lincoln County.

Grassy; mountain, a summit west of North Branch of the Potomac in Pendleton County.

Grassy; run, a small right-hand tributary to Buckhannon River in Upshur County.

Grassy; run, a very small right-hand branch of Buffalo Creek, a tributary to Elk River, in Clay County.

Grassy; run, a small right-hand branch of Stewart Creek in Gilmer County.

Grassy; run, a small left-hand tributary to North River in Hampshire and Hardy counties.

Grassy; run, a left-hand branch of Prickett Run in Marion County.

Grassy Knob; summit in Greenbrier County. Elevation, 4,391 feet.

Grassy Meadows; post village in Greenbrier County.

Graux; post village in Roane County.

Grave; fork, a small right-hand branch of Slab Fork, a tributary to Guyandot River, in Raleigh County.

Gravel Lick; small right-hand branch of Morris Fork of Blue Creek, a tributary to Elk River, in Kanawha County.

Gray; run, a right-hand branch of Buffalo Creek in Marion County.

Gray; station in Logan County on the Norfolk and Western Railway and on Tug Fork of Big Sandy River.

Graydon; post village in Fayette County.

Graysflat; village in Marion County.

Gray Sulphur; springs, situated in Monroe County near Peterstown.

Graysville; post village in Marshall County on the Baltimore and Ohio Railroad.

Great Backbone; mountain, a narrow ridge in Tucker and Preston counties. Elevation, 2,500 to 3,500 feet.
Great Cacapon; post village in Morgan County on the Baltimore and Ohio Railroad.
Great Flat Top; mountain, a ridge extending along the boundary lines between McDowell, Wyoming, and Mercer counties.
Great House; branch, a very small right-hand tributary to Buffalo Creek, a branch of Elk River, in Clay County.
Great North; (*See* Shenandoah Mountains.)
Green; branch, a very small left-hand tributary to Big Huff Creek, a branch of Guyandot River, in Logan County.
Green; valley in Stony Ridge, Mercer County.
Greenbank; post village in Pocahontas County.
Green Bay; branch, a very small right-hand branch of Indian Creek, a tributary to New River, in Monroe County.
Greenbottom; post village in Cabell County.
Greenbrier; county, situated in the southeastern part of the State. Area, 1,051 square miles. Population, 20,683—white, 18,854; negro, 1,829; foreign born, 121. County seat, Lewisburg. The mean magnetic declination in 1900 was 1° 30′. The mean annual rainfall is 50 to 60 inches, and the mean annual temperature 50° to 55°. The county is traversed by the Chesapeake and Ohio Railway.
Greenbrier; creek, a small left-hand branch of West Fork of Twelvepole Creek, a tributary to Ohio River, in Wayne County.
Greenbrier; fork, a small left-hand tributary to Panther Creek, a branch of Tug Fork of Big Sandy River, in McDowell County.
Greenbrier; mountain, a ridge west of Greenbrier River in Greenbrier County. Elevation, 2,000 to 3,359 feet, the latter being the height of one peak.
Greenbrier; post village in Greenbrier County on the Chesapeake and Ohio Railway.
Greenbrier; river, a large right-hand branch of New River, entering it at Hinton.
Greencastle; post village in Wirt County.
Greenhill; post village in Wetzel County.
Green Knob; summit near the boundary line of Randolph and Pendleton counties. Elevation, 4,500 feet.
Greenland; post village in Grant County, situated on New Creek Mountain. Altitude, 1,443 feet.
Greenland Gap; height in New Creek Mountain, Grant County.
Greenmont; town in Monongalia County. Population, 349.
Greens; branch, a small right-hand tributary to Cabin Creek, a branch of Kanawha River, in Kanawha County.
Greens; run, a left-hand branch of Buffalo Creek in Brooke County.
Green Shoal; branch, a small right-hand tributary to Guyandot River, a branch of Ohio River, in Lincoln County.
Greenshoal; post village in Lincoln County.
Greenspring; post village in Hampshire County on the Baltimore and Ohio Railroad.
Green Sulphur Springs; post village in Summers County.
Greenville; post village in Monroe County.
Greenwood; post village in Doddridge County on the Baltimore and Ohio Railroad. Altitude, 880 feet.
Gregg Knob; summit in the Allegheny Mountains in Randolph County. Altitude, 4,310 feet.
Greggs; post village in Ohio County.
Griffith; branch, a very small left-hand tributary to Piney Creek, a branch of New River, in Raleigh County.
Griffith; creek, a small right-hand tributary to Greenbrier River in Summers County.

Griffithsville; post village in Lincoln County.
Grimms Landing; post village in Mason County.
Grog; run, a left-hand branch of Buffalo Creek in Brooke County.
Groomer; creek, a small left-hand tributary to Greenbrier River in Summers and Monroe counties.
Groundhog; branch, a very small right-hand tributary to Little Huff Creek, a branch of Guyandot River, in Wyoming County.
Grove; creek, a left-hand branch of Elk River in Clay County.
Grove; post village in Doddridge County.
Gulf; branch, a small left-hand tributary to Rock Castle Creek, a branch of Guyandot River, in Wyoming County.
Gunville; post village in Mason County.
Guseman; post village in Preston County.
Guy; run, a small right-hand branch of Knapp Creek, a tributary to Greenbrier River, in Pocahontas County.
Guyandot; mountain, a ridge of mountains in Raleigh and Wyoming counties.
Guyandot; river, a left-hand branch of Ohio River. It turns in the summit of the Allegheny Plateau and flows nearly northwest to its mouth at Huntington. It is navigable for 100 miles.
Guyandotte; town in Cabell County on the Baltimore and Ohio and the Chesapeake and Ohio railroads. Altitude, 558 feet. Population, 1,450.
Guyses; run, a right-hand branch of Tygarts Valley River in Marion County.
Gwin Flats; narrow summit in Webster County south of Cranberry River.
Gwinn; post village in Cabell County.
Gwins; run, a small right-hand branch of Laurel Creek, a tributary to Elk River, in Webster County.
Gypsy; post village in Harrison County on the Baltimore and Ohio Railroad.
Hacker Camp; run, a small left-hand tributary to Little Kanawha River in Lewis County.
Hacker Valley; post village in Webster County.
Haddicks; run, a small left-hand tributary to Shavers Fork of Cheat River in Tucker and Randolph counties.
Hagans; post village in Monongalia County.
Haggle; branch, a very small right-hand tributary to Coal River, a branch of Kanawha River, in Boone County.
Haines Knob; summit in the Alleghenies in Randolph County. Altitude, 4,130 feet.
Hale; branch, a very small right-hand tributary to Davis Creek, a branch of Kanawha River, in Kanawha County.
Hales; branch, a small left-hand tributary to Five Mile Creek, a branch of East River, in Mercer County.
Hall; post village in Barbour County.
Hall; run, a right-hand tributary of Middle Wheeling Creek in Ohio County.
Halleck; post village in Monongalia County.
Halls Mills; post village in Wetzel County.
Hallsville; post village in McDowell County located on or near Tug Fork of Big Sandy River.
Halltown; post village in Jefferson County on the Baltimore and Ohio Railroad.
Hambleton; post village in Tucker County on the West Virginia Central and Pittsburg Railway.
Hambleton; station in Grant County on the West Virginia Central and Pittsburg Railway and on North Branch of Potomac River.
Hamilton; branch, a very small left-hand tributary to Loop Creek, a branch of Kanawha River, in Fayette County.

Bull. 233—04——5

Hamilton; branch, a small right-hand tributary to Dunloup Creek, a branch of New River, in Fayette County.
Hamilton; creek, a small right-hand tributary to Guyandot River, a branch of Ohio River, in Lincoln County.
Hamlin; county seat of Lincoln County.
Hammer; run, a small left-hand tributary to South Branch of Potomac River in Pendleton County.
Hammick; fork, a small left-hand branch of Buffalo Creek, a tributary to Elk River, in Clay County.
Hammick Hill; summit in Kanawha County.
Hammond; post village in Marion County on the Baltimore and Ohio Railroad.
Hammond Ridge; short spur of Big Ridge in Greenbrier County.
Hampshire; county, situated in the northeastern part of the State. It is traversed by Great Cacapon and Little Cacapon rivers and the South Branch of the Potomac. The surface consists mainly of an alternation of ridges and valleys, the former of no great height. The average elevation is not far from 1,000 feet. Area, 662 square miles. Population, 11,806—white, 11,344; negro, 461; foreign born, 51. County seat, Romney. The mean magnetic declination in 1900 was 3° 45′. The mean annual rainfall is 50 to 60 inches, and the mean annual temperature 45° to 50°. The county is traversed by the Baltimore and Ohio Railroad.
Hamrick Knob; summit in Webster County.
Hamrick Ridge; short spur separating Turkey Creek and Big Run, in Webster County.
Hancock; county, situated in the Panhandle, bordering on the Ohio River. Area, 86 square miles. Population, 6,693—white, 6,646; negro, 46; foreign born, 380. County seat, New Cumberland. The mean magnetic declination in 1900 was 3° 5′. The mean annual rainfall is 30 to 40 inches, and the mean annual temperature 50° to 55°. The county is traversed by the Pittsburg, Cincinnati, Chicago and St. Louis Railway.
Handley; post village in Kanawha County on the Chesapeake and Ohio Railway. Altitude, 632 feet.
Haney Hollow; short right-hand tributary to Kanawha River, in Kanawha County.
Hanging; run, a small right-hand tributary to Middle Fork of Tygarts Valley River, in Barbour County.
Hanging Rock; branch, a small right-hand tributary to North Fork of Cherry River, in Greenbrier County.
Hanging Rock; post village in Hampshire County on the Baltimore and Ohio Railroad.
Hanging Rock; summit at the junction of Nicholas, Webster, and Granbury counties.
Hanging Rock Mills; post village in Hardy County.
Hannahsville; post village in Tucker County.
Hanover; post village in Wyoming County.
Hans; creek, a small left-hand branch of Indian Creek, a tributary to New River, in Monroe County.
Hardesty; post village in Preston County.
Harding; post village in Randolph County on the West Virginia Central and Pittsburg Railway.
Hardman; fork, a right-hand branch of Grass Run, in Gilmer County.
Hard Scrabble; summit at head of North Fork of the Potomac, in Pendleton County. Altitude, 4,500 feet.
Hardway; branch, a small left-hand branch of Twentymile Creek, a tributary to Gauley River, in Nicholas County.

Hardy; county, situated in the northeastern part of the State. It is traversed by Lost River and South Branch of Potomac River. The surface consists of alternation ridges trending northeast and southwest. The elevation ranges from 800 to 3,000 feet. Area, 594 square miles. Population, 8,449—white, 7,992; negro, 457; foreign born, 23. County seat, Moorefield. The mean magnetic declination in 1900 was 3° 15′. The mean annual rainfall is 50 to 60 inches, and the mean annual temperature 45° to 50°.

Hardy; post village in Mercer County.

Hardy; run, a small right-hand branch of Wolf Creek, a tributary to Greenbrier River in Monroe County.

Harewood; post village in Fayette County on Kanawha River and on the Kanawha and Michigan Railway.

Harker; run, a left-hand branch of Long Drain in Wetzel County.

Harless; fork, a small left-hand branch of Fourmile Creek, a tributary to Guyandot River, in Lincoln County.

Harman; branch, a small left-hand tributary to Tug Fork of Big Sandy River, in McDowell County.

Harman; post village in Randolph County on the Dry Fork Railroad.

Harmon; branch, a small left-hand tributary to East River in Mercer County.

Harmond; creek; a small right-hand branch of Pocahontas River, a tributary to Kanawha River, in Putnam County.

Harper; branch, a small right-hand tributary to Blue Creek, a branch of Elk River, in Kanawha County.

Harpers Ferry; town in Jefferson County on the Baltimore and Ohio Railroad; population, 896.

Harris; branch, a very small right-hand tributary to Tug Fork of Big Sandy River, in McDowell County.

Harrison; county, situated in the northwestern part of the State on the slope of the Alleghany Plateau, and drained northward by the Monongahela River. Area, 431 square miles. Population, 27,690—white, 26,435; negro, 1,252; foreign born, 821; county seat, Clarksburg. The mean magnetic declination in 1900 was 2° 45′. The mean annual rainfall is 40 to 50 inches, and the mean annual temperature 50°. The county is traversed by the Baltimore and Ohio Railroad.

Harrison; post village in Clay County on the West Virginia Central and Pittsburg Railway.

Harrisville; county seat of Ritchie County. Population, 472.

Harrow Knob; summit in Braxton County; elevation, 1,622 feet.

Harry; branch, a very small right-hand tributary to Guyandot River in Mingo County.

Hart; post village in Lincoln County on the Baltimore and Ohio Railroad.

Hartford; village in Mason County on the Baltimore and Ohio Railroad. Population, 515.

Hartley; post village in Ritchie County.

Hartley; run, a right-hand branch of Little Fishing Creek in Wetzel County.

Hartmonsville; post village in Mineral County.

Harts; run, a small left-hand branch of Howards Creek, a tributary to Greenbrier River, in Greenbrier County.

Harvey; creek, a right-hand branch of Trace Fork in Putnam and Lincoln counties.

Harvey; post village in Raleigh County on the Ohio Central Lines. Altitude, 2,030 feet.

Harvey; run, a left-hand branch of Paw Paw Creek in Marion and Monongalia counties.

Hatcher; post village in Mercer County.

Hateful; creek, a small left-hand tributary to Williams River, in Webster and Pocahontas counties.
Hatfield; branch, a small left-hand tributary to Big Cub Creek, a branch of Guyandot River, in Wyoming County.
Hatfield; branch, a very small right-hand tributary to Tug Fork of Big Sandy River, a branch of Ohio River, in Logan County.
Hatfield; post village in Mingo County.
Hathaway; post village in Calhoun County.
Hawes; run, a small right-hand tributary to South Fork of Potomac River in Pendleton County.
Haw Flat; run, a small right-hand tributary to North Fork of Potomac River in Pendleton County.
Hawflat Knob; summit in Randolph County.
Hawksnest; town in Fayette County on the Chesapeake and Ohio Railway and on New River. Altitude, 827 feet. Population, 109.
Haw Ridge; summit at head of Buffalo Fork of Greenbrier River in Pocahontas County.
Hayden; post village in Preston County.
Hayes; gap in Pendleton County.
Haymond; post village in Nicholas County.
Haynes; branch, a right-hand branch of Twelvepole Creek in Wayne County.
Haynes; post village in Webster County.
Hays; creek, a small left-hand tributary to Marsh Fork of Coal River in Raleigh County.
Hazel; post village in Wetzel County.
Hazelgreen; post village in Ritchie County.
Hazelton; post village in Preston County.
Hazy; gap in Raleigh County.
Headsville; post village in Mineral County.
Heaters; fork, a branch of Rocky Fork of Ellis Creek in Gilmer County.
Heaters; post village in Braxton County on the Baltimore and Ohio Railroad. Altitude, 853 feet.
Heath; creek, a small left-hand tributary to Guyandot River, a branch of Ohio River, in Cabell County.
Hebron; post village in Pleasants County.
Hecla; post village in Raleigh County.
Hedges; mountain in Berkeley County. Elevation, 1,100 feet.
Hedgesville; post village in Berkeley County. Population, 342.
Heights; post village in Mason County.
Heldreth; post village in Doddridge County.
Hell; run, a small right-hand tributary to Middle Fork of Tygarts Valley River in Barbour and Randolph counties.
Helvetia; post village in Randolph County.
Hemlock; post village in Upshur County on the Norfolk and Western Railway.
Hemp Knob; summit in Wayne County. Altitude, 1,190 feet.
Hemp Patch; run, a small left-hand branch of Fall Run, a tributary to Little Kanawha River, in Braxton County.
Henderson; village in Mason County on the Baltimore and Ohio Railroad. Population, 304.
Hendricks; creek, a small left-hand branch of Meadow River, a tributary to Gauley River, in Fayette County.
Hendricks; post village in Tucker County. Population, 317.
Henrietta; post village in Calhoun County.

Henry; post village in Grant County on the West Virginia Central and Pittsburg Railway. Population, 339.
Hensley Knob; triangulation station in McDowell County.
Herbert; post village in Wayne County.
Hereford; post village in Jackson County.
Hern; post village in Mason County.
Herndon; post village in Wyoming County.
Hernshaw; post village in Kanawha County.
Herold; post village in Braxton County.
Herring; post village in Preston County.
Hershman; run, a small right-hand branch of Buckeye Fork of Little Skin Creek in Lewis County.
Hettie; post village in Braxton County.
Hevener Knobs; summits in Pocahontas County.
Hewett; creek, a small left-hand branch of Spruce Fork of Little Coal River in Boone and Logan counties.
Hewett; post village in Boone County. Altitude, 853 feet.
Hewitt; creek, a small right-hand tributary to Little Coal River, a branch of Coal Creek, in Boone County.
Hibbs; run, a left-hand tributary of Buffalo Creek in Marion County.
Hickman; ridge in Webster County.
Hickman; run, a right-hand branch of Monongahela River in Marion County.
Hickman; run, a right-hand branch of Fish Creek in Marshall County.
Hickory; branch, a very small right-hand tributary to Pinnacle Creek, a branch of Guyandot River, in Wyoming County.
Hickory; branch, a small right-hand tributary to Dunloup Creek, a branch of New River, in Fayette County.
Hickory; fork, a small left-hand tributary to Buffalo Creek, a branch of Elk River, in Clay County.
Hickory; post village in Mason County.
Hickory Camp; branch, a very small right-hand tributary to Paint Creek, a branch of Kanawha River, in Fayette County.
Hickory Flat; run, a small right-hand tributary to Buckhannon River in Upshur County.
Hickory Knob; summit in the Allegheny Front on the boundary line between Greenbrier County, W. Va., and Alleghany County, Va. Altitude, 3,357 feet.
Hickory Knob; summit in Gilmer County. Altitude, 1,570 feet.
Hickory Knob; summit in Kanawha County. Altitude, 1,450 feet.
Hickory Knob; summit in Putnam County.
Hickory Lick; small left-hand tributary to Greenbrier River in Pocahontas County.
Hico; post village in Fayette County.
Hicumbotom; post village in Kanawha County.
Hidden Hollow; short left-hand tributary to Elk River in Kanawha County.
Higby; post village in Roane County.
Higginbotham; run, a right-hand branch of Fish Creek in Marshall County.
Higgins; run, a right-hand tributary of Potomac River in Berkeley County.
Higginsville; post village in Hampshire County.
High Knob; one of the southernmost summits of Little Middle Mountain, in the Alleghenies in Randolph County. Altitude, 4,710 feet.
High Knob; summit in Braxton County. Altitude, 1,720 feet.
High Knob; summit in Nicholas County.
High Knob; summit of Mill Creek Mountain in Hardy and Hampshire counties.
Highland; mountain ridge in Morgan County. Elevation, 990 feet.

Highland; post village in Ritchie County on the Baltimore and Ohio Railroad.
Highview; post village in Hampshire County.
Hill; creek, a small left-hand branch of Muddlety Creek, a tributary to Gauley River, in Nicholas County.
Hill; post village in Boone County.
Hillebert; post village in Doddridge County.
Hillsboro; village in Pocahontas County. Population, 204.
Hill Top; town in Fayette County. Population, 263.
Hinch; post village in Mingo County.
Hiner; post village in Pendleton County.
Hinkle; branch, a very small right-hand tributary to Gauley River in Webster and Nicholas counties.
Hinkle; post village in Upshur County.
Hinkleville; post village in Upshur County.
Hinton; county seat of Summers County on the Chesapeake and Ohio Railway. Population, 3,763. Altitude, 1,372 feet.
Hiram; post village in Taylor County.
Hite; fork, an indirect left-hand tributary to Dry Fork, a branch of Tug Fork of Big Sandy River, in McDowell County.
Hoard; post village in Monongalia County on the Baltimore and Ohio Railroad.
Hodam; mountain, a broken mountainous ridge in the central part of Webster County. Elevation, 2,000 to 2,500 feet.
Hodge Knob; summit of Paint Mountain on the boundary between Raleigh and Fayette counties.
Hodges; branch, a left-hand branch of Hurricane Creek in Putnam County.
Hodges; post village in Cabell County.
Hodom; post village in Webster County.
Hog; fork, a small right-hand branch of Tate Creek, a tributary to Elk River, in Braxton County.
Hog; run, a left-hand branch of Little Fishing Creek in Wetzel County.
Hogback; mountain ridge in Morgan County.
Hog Camp; run, a very small left-hand branch of Big Laurel Creek, a tributary to Cherry River, in Greenbrier County.
Hogg; post village in Putnam County.
Hog Hollow; small branch of Skin Creek, tributary to Monongahela River, in Lewis County.
Hog Pen; run, a small right-hand branch of Robinson Fork of Buffalo Creek, a tributary to Elk River, in Nicholas County.
Hogsett; post village in Mason County on the Baltimore and Ohio Railroad
Hogtan; run, a left-hand branch of Buffalo Creek in Brooke County.
Holbrook; post village in Ritchie County.
Holcomb; post village in Nicholas County.
Hollidays Cove; post village in Hancock County on the Pittsburg, Cincinnati, Chicago and St. Louis Railway. Altitude, 719 feet.
Holly; post village in Braxton County on the Holly River and Addison Railway.
Holly; river, a right-hand branch of Elk River in Braxton County.
Holly Bush; fork, a very small left-hand branch of Fourmile Creek, a tributary to Guyandot River, in Lincoln County.
Hollygrove; post village in Upshur County.
Hollin; branch, a very small left-hand tributary to Guyandot River, a branch of Ohio River, in Cabell County.
Hollywood; post village in Monroe County.
Holman; post village in Monongalia County.

Holmes; branch, a small left-hand branch of the Right Fork of Twomile Creek, a tributary to Kanawha River, in Kanawha County.
Holmes Knob; summit in Kanawha County. Altitude, 1,334 feet.
Holt; run, a small right-hand branch of Little Kanawha River in Gilmer County.
Holton; post village in Morgan County.
Hominy; creek, a left-hand tributary to Gauley River in Nicholas and Greenbrier counties.
Hominyfalls; post village in Nicholas County.
Honey; run, a right-hand branch of Little Fishing Creek in Wetzel County.
Honey Camp; branch, a small right-hand tributary to Spice Creek, a branch of Tug Fork of Big Sandy River, in McDowell County.
Honey Camp; run, a small right-hand tributary to Right Fork of Middle Fork of Little Kanawha River in Upshur County.
Honey Trace; creek, a small left-hand branch of Milam Creek, a tributary to East Fork of Twelvepole Creek, in Wayne County.
Honsocker; knob in Wetzel County.
Hoodsville; village in Marion County.
Hookersville; post village in Nicholas County. Altitude, 1,877 feet.
Hooks Mills; post village in Hampshire County.
Hoover; post village in Braxton County.
Hope; post village in Braxton County.
Hopeville; post village in Grant County, situated on North Fork of Potomac River.
Hopkins; branch, a very small right-hand tributary to Little Coal River, a branch of Coal River, in Boone County.
Hopkins; fork, a right-hand tributary to Laurel Creek, a branch of Coal River, in Boone County.
Hopkins; mountain in Greenbrier County. Altitude, 3,356 feet.
Horner; fork, a right-hand branch of Big Laurel Creek, a tributary to Elk River, in Clay County.
Horner; post village in Lewis County.
Horner; run, a left-hand branch of Booths Creek in Harrison County.
Horse; branch, a very small left-hand branch of Coal River, a tributary to Kanawha River, in Boone County.
Horse; creek, a left-hand tributary to Little Coal River, a branch of Coal River, in Boone County.
Horse; creek, a very small left-hand tributary to Guyandot River in Wyoming County.
Horse; creek, a small left-hand tributary to Tug Fork of Big Sandy River in McDowell County.
Horse; creek, a small right-hand tributary to Marsh Fork of Coal River in Raleigh County.
Horse; creek, a very small right-hand branch of Paint Creek, a tributary to Kanawha River, in Fayette County.
Horse; fork, a small left-hand branch of Falling Rock Creek, a tributary to Elk River, in Kanawha County.
Horse; fork, a very small left-hand tributary to New River in Summers County.
Horse; mountain ridge in Morgan County.
Horse Camp; run, a small right-hand tributary to Dry Fork of Cheat River in Randolph County.
Horse Mill; branch, a small right-hand branch of Kelly Creek, a tributary to Kanawha River, in Kanawha County.
Horseneck; post village in Pleasants County.
Horsepen; fork, a left-hand tributary to Gilbert Creek, a branch of Guyandot River, in Mingo County.

Horse Pen; ridge, mountains in Wyoming and Raleigh counties.
Horse Ridge; short spur east of Gauley River in Webster County.
Horse Ridge; short, curved spur between Cherry and Cranberry rivers in Nicholas County. Altitude, 2,500 feet.
Horse Shoe; run, a right-hand branch of Cheat River in Tucker and Preston counties.
Horseshoe Run; post village in Preston County.
Horton; post village in Randolph County on the Dry Fork Railroad.
Hoult; post village in Marion County on the Baltimore and Ohio Railroad.
Hound; fork, a very small left-hand tributary to Guyandot River in Wyoming County.
House; branch, a left-hand branch of Wolf Creek, a tributary to New River, in Fayette County.
House Place; branch, a very small left-hand tributary to Pinnacle Creek, a branch of Guyandot River, in Wyoming County.
Houston; run, a small left-hand tributary to Elk River in Braxton and Webster counties.
Hovatter; post village in Tucker County.
Howard; fork, a right-hand branch of Rocky Fork of Pocatalico River, a tributary to Kanawha River, in Kanawha County.
Howard; post village in Marshall County on the Chesapeake and Ohio Railway.
Howards; creek, a left-hand branch of Greenbrier River in Greenbrier County. It is known locally as Jericho Draft at its head.
Howards Lick; left-hand tributary to Lost River in Hardy County.
Howards Lick; post village in Hardy County.
Howell; fork, a small right-hand tributary to Right Fork of Middle Fork of Little Kanawha River in Upshur County.
Howell; post village in Cabell County.
Howell; run, a small right-hand tributary to North Branch of Potomac River in Mineral County.
Howesville; post village in Preston County on the West Virginia Northern Railroad.
Hoyt; post village in Roane County.
Hubbard; fork, a small right-hand tributary to Rock Creek, a branch of Little Coal River, in Boone County.
Hubbardstown; post village in Wayne County.
Huddleston; knob in Cabell County. Elevation, 1,021 feet.
Hudson; hollow, in Cabell County.
Hudson; post village in Preston County.
Huey; run, a right-hand branch of Buffalo Creek in Marion County.
Huff; broken mountainous country in Wyoming County, the highest peak reaching an altitude of 2,716 feet.
Huff; post village in Randolph County.
Huff; run, a right-hand branch of North Fork of Short Creek in Ohio County.
Huff Knob; summit of Flat Top Mountain on the boundary line between Mercer and Raleigh counties.
Huffman; post village in Barbour County.
Huggins; branch, a small right-hand tributary to Big Clear Creek, a branch of Meadow River, in Greenbrier County.
Hughart; post village in Greenbrier County.
Hughes; creek, a small right-hand tributary to Kanawha River in Kanawha County.
Hughes; fork, a small right-hand tributary to Salt Lick Fork of Little Kanawha River in Braxton County.
Hughes; fork, a small right-hand tributary to Skin Creek in Lewis County.

Hughes; fork, a right-hand branch of Bell Creek, a tributary to Gauley River, in Kanawha County.
Hughes; river, a left-hand tributary to Ohio River, formed by two forks—North and South—in Ritchie and Wirt counties.
Hughes; run, a small right-hand tributary to Gauley River in Webster County.
Hughes Knob; summit in Lincoln County.
Hugo; post village in Putnam County.
Hukiel; run, a left-hand branch of Buffalo Run in Brooke County.
Humphreys; run, a very small left-hand tributary to Indian Creek a branch of New River, in Monroe County.
Hundred; town in Wetzel County on the Baltimore and Ohio Railroad. Population, 261.
Hungry; creek, a right-hand branch of Trace Creek in Lincoln County.
Hunter; post village in Mingo County.
Hunters Springs; post village in Monroe County.
Huntersville; post village in Pocahontas County.
Huntsville; post village in Jackson County.
Hungards; creek, a small right-hand tributary to Greenbrier River in Summers County.
Hunter; branch, a small right-hand tributary to Spruce Fork of Little Coal River, a branch of Coal River, in Boone County.
Hunter; branch, a small right-hand tributary to North Fork of Cherry River in Nicholas County.
Hunter Place; summit in Nicholas County. Altitude, 3,738 feet.
Hunting; creek, a small right-hand tributary to Cherry River, a branch of Gauley River, in Nicholas County.
Hunting Camp; run, a left-hand tributary to Spruce Run, a small branch of Cheat River, in Preston County.
Hunting Ground; broken, mountainous country in Pendleton County west of North Fork of the Potomac.
Hunting Shirt; branch, a very small left-hand tributary to Tug Fork of Big Sandy River, in McDowell County.
Huntington; county seat of Cabell County on the Baltimore and Ohio Railroad and the Chesapeake and Ohio Railway. Altitude, 567 feet. Population, 11,923.
Hunt Road; run, a small left-hand tributary to Left Fork of Steer Creek in Gilmer County.
Hur; post village in Calhoun County.
Hurricane; branch, a small left-hand tributary to Paint Creek, a branch of Kanawha River, in Kanawha County.
Hurricane; branch, a very small left-hand branch of Kiah Fork, a tributary to Twelvepole Creek, in Wayne County.
Hurricane; branch, a small right-hand tributary to Dry Fork, a branch of Tug Fork of Big Sandy River, in McDowell County.
Hurricane; branch, a very small right-hand tributary to Laurel Branch, a tributary to Clear Fork of Guyandot River, in Wyoming County.
Hurricane; branch, a small right-hand tributary to Panther Creek, a branch of Tug Fork of Big Sandy River, in McDowell County.
Hurricane; creek, a left-hand tributary to Kanawha River in Putnam County.
Hurricane; fork, a left-hand branch of Kelly Creek, a tributary to Kanawha River, in Kanawha County.
Hurricane; village in Putnam County on the Chesapeake and Ohio Railway. Altitude, 687 feet. Population, 240.
Hurricane Ridge; mountains in Mercer County.

Hurst; post village in Lewis County.
Husted; creek, a right-hand tributary of Booths Creek in Taylor County.
Hutchinson; post village in Marion County on the Baltimore and Ohio Railroad.
Hutchison; branch, a very small right-hand branch of Peter Creek, a tributary to Gauley River, in Nicholas County.
Hutton; run, a small left-hand tributary to South Branch of Potomac River in Hardy County.
Huttons Knob; summit of Cheat Mountain in Randolph County. Altitude, 4,260 feet.
Huttonsville; post village in Randolph County on the West Virginia Central and Pittsburg Railway.
Hyar; run, a small left-hand tributary to Little Kanawha River in Braxton County.
Hyer; post village in Braxton County.
Hypes; post village in Fayette County.
Iaeger; post village in McDowell County on the Norfolk and Western Railway and on Tug Fork of Big Sandy River.
Ida; post village in Putnam County.
Ike Lick; small left-hand branch of Lilly Fork of Buffalo Creek, a tributary to Elk River, in Nicholas County.
Imans; run, a small right-hand branch of South Mill Creek, a tributary to South Branch of Potomac River, in Grant County.
Imboden; post village in Fayette County.
Improvement Lick; small left-hand tributary to Greenbrier River in Pocahontas County.
Incline; post village in McDowell County.
Independence; post village in Preston County on the Baltimore and Ohio Railroad. Altitude, 1,156 feet.
Indian; creek, a small left-hand branch of Coal River, a tributary to Kanawha River, in Boone County.
Indian; creek, a left-hand tributary to Guyandot River in Wyoming County. It rises in Indian Ridge.
Indian; creek, a small left-hand tributary to Elk River, a large branch of Kanawha River, in Kanawha County.
Indian; creek, a right-hand branch of New River in Summers and Monroe counties.
Indian; fork, a large left-hand branch of Sand Fork in Gilmer and Lewis counties.
Indian; fork, a small right-hand tributary to Mud River, a branch of Guyandot River, in Cabell and Putnam counties.
Indian; gap in Raleigh County caused by Drews Creek.
Indian; gap at head of Spice Creek in McDowell County.
Indian; triangulation station in Indian Ridge on boundary line between Wyoming and McDowell counties.
Indiancamp; post village in Upshur County.
Indian Camp; run, a small left-hand tributary to Buckhannon River, in Upshur County.
Indian Draft; small right-hand tributary to Greenbrier River in Pocahontas County.
Indian Draft; small right-hand branch of Indian Creek, a tributary to New River, in Monroe County.
Indian Grave; branch, a small right-hand tributary to Tug River in McDowell County.
Indian Mills; post village in Summers County.
Indian Ridge; mountains on boundary between Wyoming and McDowell counties.
Industry; post village in Calhoun County.
Inez; post village in Cabell County on the Chesapeake and Ohio Railway.

Ingleside; post village in Mercer County on the Norfolk and Western Railway and on East River. Altitude, 1,945 feet.

Ingram; branch, a very small left-hand tributary to Loop Creek, a branch of Kanawha River, in Fayette County.

Inkerman; post village in Hardy County.

Institute; post village in Kanawha County.

Inwood; post village in Berkeley County on the Cumberland Valley Railroad.

Iola; post village in Roane County.

Ira; post village in Clay County.

Ireland; post village in Lewis County.

Irewood; creek, a small left-hand branch of Meadow River, a tributary to Gauley River, in Fayette County.

Irona; post village in Preston County.

Irontown; post village in Taylor County.

Isaac; run, a left-hand branch of Carney Fork of Rock Run in Wetzel County.

Island; creek, a small left-hand tributary to New River in Mercer and Summers counties.

Island; creek, a small left-hand tributary to Coal Creek, a branch of Kanawha River, in Lincoln County.

Island; creek, a small left-hand tributary to Guyandot River, a branch of Ohio River, in Logan County.

Islandbranch; post village in Kanawha County.

Island Ford; run, a small left-hand tributary to Greenbrier River, in Pocahontas County.

Isners; run, a small right-hand tributary to Valley River in Randolph County.

Iuka; post village in Tyler County.

Ivanhoe; post village in Upshur County.

Ivy; creek, a small left-hand tributary to Little Coal River, a branch of Coal River, in Lincoln County.

Ivy; post village in Upshur County. Altitutde, 3,593 feet.

Ivy Knob; triangulation station on boundary line between Raleigh and Wyoming counties. Altitude, 3,693 feet.

Jack; branch, a small left-hand tributary to Pond Fork of Little Coal River in Boone County.

Jack; mountain, a short ridge in Pendleton County. Elevation, 3,500 feet.

Jack; post village in Webster County.

Jack; run, a left-hand branch of Lost Run in Taylor County.

Jackson; branch, a very small left-hand tributary to West Fork of Twelvepole Creek, a branch of Ohio River, in Wayne County.

Jackson; county, situated in the western part of the State, on the Allegheny Plateau, and bordering on the Ohio River. Area, 455 square miles. Population, 22,987— white, 22,872; negro, 115; foreign born, 91. County seat, Ripley. The mean magnetic declination in 1900 was 1° 30′. The mean annual rainfall is 40 to 50 inches, and the mean annual temperature 50° to 55°. The county is traversed by the Ohio River Railroad.

Jackson; fork, a small right-hand branch of Right Fork of Middle Fork of Tygarts Valley River in Upshur and Randolph counties.

Jackson Ridge; short spur in Pocahontas County.

Jacksonville; post village in Lewis County.

Jacky; fork, a very small right-hand tributary to Indian Creek, a branch of Guyandot River, in Wyoming County.

Jaco; post village in Monongalia County.

Jacob; fork, a right-hand tributary to Dry Fork, a branch of Tug Fork of Big Sandy River, in McDowell County.

Jacob Cook; branch, a very small right-hand tributary to Clear Fork, a branch of Guyandot River, in Wyoming County.
Jacox; post village in Pocahontas County.
Jacox Knob; summit in Pocahontas County.
Jake; branch, a very small right-hand tributary to Coal River, a branch of Kanawha River, in Boone County.
Jake; run, a small right-hand branch of Ellis Creek in Gilmer County.
Jake; run, a left-hand tributary of Wheeling Creek in Marshall County.
James; branch, a very small right-hand tributary to Pond Fork of Little Coal River in Boone County.
James; creek, a small right-hand tributary to West Fork, a branch of Pond Fork of Little Coal River, in Boone County.
James Knob; summit in Braxton County.
Janelew; post village in Lewis County on the West Virginia Central and Pittsburg Railway.
Jarrell; branch, a small right-hand tributary to West Fork, a branch of Pond Fork of Little Coal River, in Boone County.
Jarrett; branch, a very small right-hand tributary to Kanawha River in Fayette County.
Jarrett; post village in Kanawha County.
Jarrolds Valley; post village in Raleigh County.
Jarvisville; post village in Harrison County.
Jasper Workman; branch, a small left-hand tributary to Pond Fork of Little Coal River in Boone County.
Jed; branch, a small right-hand tributary to Tug Fork of Big Sandy River in McDowell County.
Jefferson; county, situated in the northeastern part of the State, limited on the east by Potomac River and the Blue Ridge. With the exception of the slopes of the Blue Ridge its surface is rolling, with an average altitude of about 500 feet. Area, 213 square miles. Population, 15,935—white, 11,994; negro, 3,941; foreign born, 96. County seat, Charlestown. The mean magnetic declination in 1900 was 4°. The mean annual rainfall is 40 to 50 inches, and the mean annual temperature 50° to 55°. The county is traversed by the Baltimore and Ohio and the Norfolk and Western railways.
Jeffery; post village in Boone County.
Jehn; branch, a small left-hand tributary to Millers Camp Branch, a fork of Marsh Fork of Coal River, in Raleigh County.
Jenk; fork, a small left-hand branch of Right Fork of Middle Fork of Tygarts Valley River in Upshur County.
Jenkins; fork, a small left-hand branch of Armstrong Creek, a tributary to Kanawha River, in Fayette County.
Jenks; post village in Lincoln County.
Jennie; creek, a small right-hand branch of Tug Fork of Big Sandy River, a tributary to Ohio River, in Wayne and Logan counties.
Jenny; gap in Guyandot Mountain, caused by Skinner Fork, in Raleigh County.
Jericho; post village in Hampshire County.
Jericho Draft; the name applied locally to the headwaters of Howards Creek, a tributary to Greenbrier River, in Greenbrier County.
Jerry; fork, a very small right-hand branch of Peter Creek, a tributary to Gauley River, in Nicholas County.
Jerry; run, a right-hand branch of Simpson Creek in Taylor County.
Jerrys Run; post village in Wood County.
Jersey; run, a small left-hand tributary to Right Fork of Middle Fork of Little Kanawha River in Webster County.

Jerseywood; run, a right-hand tributary to Ellis Creek in Gilmer County.
Jesse; post village in Wyoming County.
Jetsville; post village in Greenbrier County.
Jigly; branch, a small indirect right-hand tributary to Laurel Fork, a branch of Spruce Fork of Little Coal River, in Boone County.
Jim; branch, a very small left-hand tributary to Clear Fork, a branch of Guyandot River, in Wyoming County.
Jim; branch, a small right-hand tributary to Clear Fork, a branch of Tug Fork of Big Sandy River, in McDowell County.
Jim; branch, a very small right-hand tributary to Cooney Otter Creek, an indirect left-hand tributary to Guyandot River, in Wyoming County.
Jim; branch, a very small right-hand tributary to Guyandot River in Wyoming County.
Jim; branch, a very small right-hand tributary to Slab Fork, a branch of Guyandot River, on boundary between Raleigh and Wyoming counties.
Jimmy; fork, a right-hand branch of Wilderness Fork of Fork Creek, a tributary to Coal River, in Boone County.
Jim Spring; run, a small right-hand tributary to Gauley River in Webster County.
Jimtown; post village in Harrison County.
Job; post village in Randolph County on the Dry Fork Railroad.
Job; run, a right-hand branch of Little Kanawha River in Gilmer County.
Job Knob; fork, a small right-hand branch of South Fork of Big Clear Creek, a tributary to Meadow River, in Greenbrier County.
Job Knob; summit in Greenbrier County. Altitude, 4,359 feet.
Joblin; branch, a very small left-hand tributary to Kanawha River in Kanawha County.
Joe; branch, a very small left-hand tributary to Guyandot River in Wyoming County.
Joe; branch, a very small right-hand tributary to Coal River, a branch of Kanawha River, in Boone County.
Joe; creek, a head fork of Williams Fork, a tributary to Trace Fork of Mud River, in Lincoln County.
Joe; creek, a small right-hand tributary to Coal River, a branch of Kanawha River, in Boone County.
Joe; fork, a head fork of Right Fork of Steer Creek, in Braxton County.
Joe; run, a left-hand branch of Sand Fork in Gilmer County.
Joe; run, a right-hand branch of Buffalo Creek in Marion County.
Joebranch; post village in Wyoming County.
Joe Hollow; short left-hand tributary to Elk River in Kanawha County.
Joe Knob; summit in Greenbrier County. Altitude, 3,939 feet.
Joel; branch, a very small left-hand tributary to West Fork of Twelvepole Creek, a branch of Ohio River, in Wayne County.
Joel; run, a small right-hand tributary to Gauley River in Webster County.
Joe Ridge; mountains in Raleigh County.
Johithan; run, a small left-hand tributary to Williams River in Webster County.
John; branch, a very small right-hand tributary to Mud River, a branch of Guyandot River, in Cabell County.
John; branch, a very small indirect right-hand tributary to Dry Fork, a branch of Tug Fork of Big Sandy River, in McDowell County.
John; post village in Monongalia County.
Johnniecake; run, a left-hand branch of Pyles Fork of Buffalo Creek in Marion County.
Johnnycake; branch, a small right-hand tributary to Tug Fork of Big Sandy River in McDowell County.

John O; branch, a very small right-hand tributary to Laurel Branch, a tributary to Guyandot River, in Wyoming County.
Johnson; fork, a small left-hand branch of Falling Rock Creek, a tributary to Elk River, in Kanawha County.
Johnson; fork, a small left-hand tributary to Loop Creek, a branch of Kanawha River, in Fayette County.
Johnson; hollow in Monongalia County.
Johnson; post village in Barbour County.
Johnson; run, a small right-hand tributary to Gauley River in Webster County.
Johnson Knob; summit in Kanawha County. Altitude 2,200 feet.
Johnsons Crossroads; post village in Monroe County.
Johnstown; post village in Harrison County.
Jones; branch, a small right-hand tributary to Paint Creek, a branch of Kanawha River, in Kanawha County.
Jones; fork, a very small right-hand branch of Peter Creek, a tributary to Gauley River, in Nicholas County.
Jones; post village in Putnam County.
Jones; run, a very small left-hand branch of Big Laurel Creek, a tributary to Cherry River, in Greenbrier County.
Jones Springs; post village in Berkeley County.
Jordan; creek, a small right-hand tributary to Elk River, a branch of Kanawha River, in Kanawha County.
Jordan; post village in Kanawha County.
Jordanrun; post village in Grant County.
Joseph Mills; post village in Tyler County.
Joshua; creek, a small left-hand tributary to Greenbrier River in Pocahontas County.
Joshua; run, a very small left-hand tributary to New River in Summers County.
Josiah; post village in Tyler County.
Joy; post village in Doddridge County.
Joy; run, a left-hand tributary of North Fork of Dunkard Creek in Monongalia County.
Jud; branch, a very small left-hand tributary to Indian Creek, a branch of Guyandot River, in Wyoming County.
Judson; post village in Summers County.
Judyton; post village in Greenbrier County.
Jule Webb; fork, a head fork of Horse Creek, a tributary to Little Coal River, in Boone County.
Julia; post village in Greenbrier County.
Jumbo; post village in Webster County.
Jump; branch, a small right-hand tributary to South Fork of Tug River in McDowell County.
Jumping; branch, a left-hand tributary to Little Bluestone Creek, a branch of Bluestone River, in Summers County.
Jumping Branch; post village in Summers County.
Jumping Gut; small left-hand tributary to Elk River in Clay County.
Junction; post village in Hampshire County.
Junior; town in Barbour County on the West Virginia Central and Pittsburg Railway. Population, 335.
Kabletown; post village in Jefferson County.
Kalamazoo; post village in Barbour County.
Kanawha; county, situated in the western part of the State, on the Allegheny Plateau. It is here deeply dissected. It is traversed by Kanawha River, which, with its branches, the principal of which are Coal Creek and Elk River, drains its area. Area, 872 square miles. Population, 54,696—white, 50,711; negro,

3,983; foreign born, 744. County seat, Charleston. The mean magnetic declination in 1900 was 2°. The mean annual rainfall is 40 to 50 inches, and the mean annual temperature 50° to 55°. The county is traversed by the Charleston, Clendennin and Sutton, the Chesapeake and Ohio, the Ohio Central Lines, and the Kanawha and Michigan railways.

Kanawha; fork, a small right-hand tributary to Davis Creek, a branch of Kanawha River, in Kanawha County.

Kanawha; river, a large left-hand branch of Ohio River, heading, under the name of New River, in western North Carolina, and flowing north and northwest to its mouth opposite Gallipolis. Its chief branches are Gauley and Elk rivers, the former joining it at Kanawha Falls and the latter at Charleston. The drainage area, including New River, is 16,690 square miles. Length, 400 miles. Navigable to Kanawha Falls.

Kanawha; run, a right-hand branch of Holly River, a tributary to Elk River, in Braxton County.

Kanawha City; post village in Kanawha County on the Chesapeake and Ohio Railway.

Kanawha Falls; post village in Fayette County on Kanawha River and on the Chesapeake and Ohio and the Ohio Central railroads. Altitude, 665 feet.

Kanawha Head; post village in Upshur County.

Kanawha Station; post village in Wood County. Altitude, 611 feet.

Karn; post village in Monroe County.

Kasson; post village in Barbour County.

Kate Knob; summit in Lincoln County.

Kates; branch, a very small right-hand tributary to Glade Creek, a branch of New River, in Raleigh County.

Kates; mountain, a ridge in Greenbrier County. Altitude, 2,500 to 3,000 feet.

Katly; village in Marion County.

Katyslick; village in Harrison County.

Kausooth; post village in Marshall County.

Kearneysville; post village in Jefferson County. Altitude, 589 feet.

Kedron; post village in Upshur County.

Keenan; post village in Monroe County.

Keenan; branch, a very small left-hand branch of Peter Creek, a tributary to Gauley River, in Nicholas County.

Keeney; creek, a small right-hand tributary to New River in Fayette County.

Keeney; mountain, a ridge in Summers County north of Greenbrier River. Elevation, 2,000 to 3,500 feet.

Keeney; creek, a small right-hand tributary to New River in Fayette County.

Keeney Knob; summit of Keeney Mountain in Summers County. Altitude, 3,945 feet.

Kegley; post village in Mercer County.

Keith; fork, a small left-hand tributary to Skin Creek in Lewis County.

Keith; post village in Fayette County.

Keller; post village in Jefferson County.

Kelleys; creek, a small left-hand tributary to Greenbrier River in Summers and Monroe counties.

Kellogg; post village in Wayne County on the Chesapeake and Ohio Railway.

Kelly; creek, a very small right-hand branch of Pocotaligo River, a tributary to Kanawha River, in Putnam County.

Kelly; creek, a right-hand tributary to Kanawha River in Kanawha County.

Kelly; post village in Doddridge County.

Kelley Knob; summit in Randolph County.

Kendalia; post village in Kanawha County.

Kenna; post village in Jackson County.

Kenna Ridge; mountains in the southwestern part of Braxton County, ranging in elevation from 1,000 to 1,600 feet.

Kennison; mountain, a short ridge in the western part of Pocahontas County. Elevation, 3,500 to 4,000 feet.

Kenova; village in Wayne County on the Baltimore and Ohio, the Chesapeake and Ohio, and the Norfolk and Western railways. Altitude, 581 feet. Population, 863.

Kenton; post village in Doddridge County.

Kentuck; fork, a very small left-hand branch of Fourmile Creek, a tributary to Guyandot River, in Lincoln County.

Kentuck; post village in Jackson County.

Kerens; post village in Randolph County on the West Virginia Central and Pittsburg Railway.

Kerless Knob; summit in Greenbrier County. Altitude, 3,441 feet.

Kern; run, a small stream in Lewis County.

Keslers Crosslanes; post village in Nicholas County.

Kester; post village in Roane County.

Ketterman; post village in Grant County, located on South Branch of Potomac River.

Kettle; post village in Roane County.

Kettle; run, a small right-hand branch of Left Fork of Middle Fork of Tygarts Valley River in Randolph County.

Kueths; run, a right-hand branch of Fall Run in Braxton County.

Kewee; creek, a small left-hand tributary to Dry Fork, a branch of Tug Fork of Big Sandy River, in McDowell County.

Key; run, a small left-hand tributary to Greenbrier River in Pocahontas County.

Keyser; town and county seat of Mineral County on the Baltimore and Ohio and the West Virginia Central and Pittsburg railroads. Altitude, 802 feet. Population, 2,536.

Keystone; town in McDowell County on the Norfolk and Western Railway and on Elkhorn Creek. Population, 1,088.

Kiah; fork, a right-hand branch of East Fork of Twelvepole Creek, a tributary to Ohio River, in Wayne County.

Kiahsville; post village in Wayne County.

Kidwell; post village in Tyler County.

Kieffer; post village in Greenbrier County.

Kile Knob; summit in Pendleton County.

Kilgore; creek, a small right-hand tributary to Mud River, a branch of Guyandot River, in Cabell County.

Kimball; station in McDowell County on the Norfolk and Western Railway and on Elkhorn Creek.

Kimlin; run, a left-hand branch of Buffalo Creek in Brooke County.

Kimsey; run, a left-hand tributary to Lost River in Hardy County.

Kincaid; knob in Marion County.

Kincaid; post village in Fayette County.

Kincaid; run, a small left-hand tributary to Greenbrier River in Greenbrier County.

King; post village in Wetzel County.

Kings; run, a small right-hand tributary to Valley River in Randolph County.

Kingsbury; post village in Wood County.

King Shoal; branch, a small left-hand tributary to Guyandot River, a branch of Ohio River, in Logan County.

Kingsville; post village in Randolph County.

Kingwood; town and county seat of Preston County on the West Virginia Northern Railroad. Altitude, 1,778 feet. Population, 700.
Kirby; post village in Hampshire County.
Kirt; post village in Barbour County.
Kline; gap in New Creek Mountain caused by New Creek in Grant County.
Kline; post village in Pendleton County.
Knapp; creek, a left-hand tributary to Greenbrier River in Pocahontas County.
Knawl; post village in Braxton County.
Knight; post village in Doddridge County.
Knob; branch, a very small right-hand tributary to Paint Creek, a branch of Kanawha River, in Fayette County.
Knob; fork, a very small right-hand tributary to Clear Fork, a branch of the Guyandot River, in Wyoming County.
Knob; fork, a left-hand branch of Middle Wheeling Creek in Ohio County.
Knobley; post village in Mineral County.
Knobly; mountain, a long narrow ridge in Grant and Mineral counties. Altitude, 1,500 feet.
Knottsville; post village in Taylor County.
Knoxville; post village in Marshall County.
Kodol; post village in Wetzel County.
Krise; post village in Fayette County.
Kyger; post village in Roane County on the Baltimore and Ohio Railroad.
Kyle; post village in McDowell County on the Norfolk and Western Railway.
Lacey; branch, a small left-hand tributary to Pond Fork of Little Coal River in Boone County.
Laclede; post village in Cabell County.
Ladley; run, a left-hand branch of Middle Wheeling Creek in Ohio County.
Lahmansville; post village in Grant County.
Lake; post village in Logan County.
Lambert; branch, a small left-hand tributary to Pinnacle Creek, a branch of Guyandot River, in Wyoming County.
Lambert; creek, a very small right-hand branch of West Fork of Twelvepole Creek, a tributary to Ohio River, in Wayne County.
Lambert; branch, a small right-hand tributary to Barker Creek, a branch of Guyandot River, in Wyoming County.
Lamont; post village in Marshall County.
Lanark; post village in Raleigh County.
Landes; post village in Grant County.
Landgraff; post village in McDowell County on the Norfolk and Western Railway.
Lane; post village in Mason County.
Lanes Bottom; post village in Webster County.
Lanham; post village in Putnam County.
Lankey; mountain, a short ridge west of South Branch of Potomac River in Pendleton County.
Lansing; post village in Fayette County.
Lantz; post village in Barbour County.
Larew; post village in Taylor County.
Larkin Hollow; right-hand tributary to Kanawha River in Kanawha County.
Lashmeet; post village in Mercer County, located near Bluestone River on Delashmeet Creek. Altitude, 2,588 feet.
Latonia; post village in Gilmer County.
Lattimer; post village in Roane County.
Launa; post village in Raleigh County.

Laurel; branch, a small left-hand tributary to Marrowbone Creek, a branch of Tug Fork of Big Sandy River, in Logan County.

Laurel; branch, a small left-hand tributary to South Fork of Tug River in McDowell County.

Laurel; branch, a small left-hand tributary to Bluestone River, a branch of New River, in Mercer County.

Laurel; branch, a very small left-hand tributary to Piney Creek, a branch of New River, in Raleigh County.

Laurel; branch, a small left-hand tributary to Millers Camp Branch, a branch of Marsh Fork of Coal River, in Raleigh County.

Laurel; branch, a very small left-hand tributary to Pinnacle Creek, a branch of Guyandot River, in Wyoming County.

Laurel; branch, a left-hand tributary to Clear Fork, a branch of Guyandot River, in Wyoming County.

Laurel; branch, a left-hand branch of Left Fork of Armstrong Creek, a tributary of Kanawha River, in Fayette County.

Laurel; branch, a very small right-hand tributary to Guyandot River in Logan County.

Laurel; branch, a very small right-hand tributary to Clear Fork of Coal River in Raleigh County.

Laurel; branch, a very small right-hand tributary to Bluestone River in Mercer County.

Laurel; branch, a small right-hand tributary to Elkhorn Creek, a branch of Tug Fork of Big Sandy River, in McDowell County.

Laurel; branch, a very small right-hand branch of Tug Fork of Big Sandy River, a tributary to Ohio River, in Logan County.

Laurel; branch, a small right-hand tributary to Hominy Creek, a branch of Gauley River, in Nicholas County.

Laurel; branch, a very small right-hand tributary to Powellton Fork of Armstrong Creek, a branch of Kanawha River, in Fayette County.

Laurel; creek, a small right-hand tributary to Middle Fork of Tygarts Valley River in Randolph County.

Laurel; creek, a left-hand branch of Coal River, a tributary to Kanawha River, in Boone County.

Laurel; creek, a very small left-hand tributary to Mud River, a branch of Guyandot River, in Lincoln County.

Laurel; creek, a left-hand tributary to New River in Fayette County.

Laurel; creek, a small left-hand tributary to Greenbrier River in Greenbrier County.

Laurel; creek, a small left-hand branch of Knapp Creek, a tributary to Greenbrier River, in Pocahontas County.

Laurel; creek, a small left-hand branch of Peter Creek, a tributary to Gauley River, in Nicholas County.

Laurel; creek, a left-hand tributary to Elk River in Braxton and Webster counties.

Laurel; creek, a small right-hand tributary to New River in Summers County.

Laurel; creek, a small right-hand tributary to Williams River in Pocahontas County.

Laurel; creek, a small right-hand tributary to Gauley River in Webster County.

Laurel; creek, a small right-hand tributary to Mud River, a branch of Guyandot River, in Lincoln County.

Laurel; creek, a very small right-hand tributary to Guyandot River, a branch of Ohio River, in Lincoln County.

Laurel; creek, a right-hand branch of Big Ugly Creek, a tributary to Guyandot River, in Lincoln County.

Laurel; creek, a small right-hand branch of East Fork of Twelvepole Creek, a tributary to Ohio River, in Wayne County.

Laurel; creek, a small right-hand tributary to Gauley River, a large branch of Kanawha River, in Nicholas County.
Laurel; creek, a small right-hand branch of Second Creek, a tributary to Greenbrier River, in Monroe County.
Laurel; creek, a small right-hand branch of Meadow River, a tributary to Gauley River, in Greenbrier County.
Laurel; creek, a small right-hand branch of Brush Creek, a tributary to Bluestone River, in Mercer County.
Laurel; creek, a small right-hand tributary to New River in Fayette County.
Laurel; creek, a right-hand tributary to Valley River in Barbour County.
Laurel; creek, a right-hand tributary to Indian Creek, a branch of New River, in Monroe County.
Laurel; fork, a head fork of Holly River in Webster County.
Laurel; fork, a head fork of Williams Fork, a branch of Trace Fork of Mud River, in Lincoln County.
Laurel; fork, a left-hand branch of Horse Creek, a tributary to Little Coal River, in Lincoln County.
Laurel; fork, a small left-hand branch of Big Creek, a tributary to Mud River, in Lincoln County.
Laurel; fork, a small left-hand tributary to Elk River in Pocahontas County.
Laurel; fork, a small left-hand branch of Lilly Fork of Buffalo Creek, a tributary to Elk River, in Clay County.
Laurel; fork, a small left-hand branch of Big Sycamore Creek, a tributary to Elk River, in Clay County.
Laurel; fork, a left-hand branch of Right Fork of Peters Creek, a tributary to Gauley River, in Nicholas County.
Laurel; fork, a small left-hand branch of Witchers Creek, a tributary to Kanawha River, in Kanawha County.
Laurel; fork, a small left-hand tributary to Long Bottom Creek, a branch of Cabin Creek, in Kanawha County.
Laurel; fork, an indirect left-hand tributary to Clear Fork, a branch of Guyandot River, in Wyoming County.
Laurel; fork, a small left-hand tributary to Right Fork of Steer Creek in Gilmer County.
Laurel; fork, a small left-hand branch of Granny Creek in Braxton County.
Laurel; fork, a left-hand branch of Grove Creek in Clay County.
Laurel; fork, a large left-hand branch of Dry Fork, a head fork of Cheat River, in Randolph County.
Laurel; fork, a right-hand branch of Sand Creek, a tributary to Guyandot River, in Lincoln County.
Laurel; fork, a small right-hand branch of Little Hart Creek, a tributary to Guyandot River, in Lincoln County.
Laurel; fork, a small right-hand tributary to Twentymile Creek, a branch of Gauley River, in Nicholas County.
Laurel; fork, a small right-hand branch of Blue Creek, a tributary to Elk River, in Kanawha County.
Laurel; fork, a right-hand branch of Bell Creek, a tributary to Gauley River, in Kanawha County.
Laurel; fork, a right-hand branch of Coal Fork of Cabin Creek, a tributary to Kanawha River, in Kanawha County.
Laurel; fork, a right-hand branch of Spruce Fork of Little Coal River in Boone and Logan counties.
Laurel; fork, a small right-hand tributary to Birch River, a branch of Elk River, in Webster County.

Laurel; fork, a right-hand branch of Tanner Fork and tributary to Little Kanawha River in Gilmer County.
Laurel; fork, a small right-hand tributary to Pigeon Creek, a branch of Tug Fork of Big Sandy River, in Logan County.
Laurel; fork, a right-hand tributary to French Creek in Upshur County.
Laurel; hill, a ridge separating Cheat and Valley rivers. Altitude, 3,000 feet.
Laurel; hills, a long, narrow ridge in Preston, Barbour, and Tucker counties. Altitude, 2,000 to 2,500 feet.
Laurel; post village in Barbour County.
Laurel; run, a small left-hand tributary to Little Kanawha River in Upshur County.
Laurel; run, a small left-hand tributary to the Middle Fork of Tygarts Valley River in Upshur County.
Laurel; run, a small left-hand tributary to Left Fork of Middle Fork of Tygarts Valley River in Randolph County.
Laurel; run, a small left-hand tributary to North Fork of Potomac River in Pendleton County.
Laurel; run, a small left-hand tributary to Little Kanawha River in Braxton County.
Laurel; run, a small left-hand tributary to Meadow Creek in the western part of Greenbrier County.
Laurel; run, a small left-hand tributary to Little Birch River in Braxton County.
Laurel; run, a small right-hand branch of Duck Creek, a right-hand tributary to Elk River, in Braxton County.
Laurel; run, a small right-hand tributary to Dry Fork of Cheat River in Tucker County.
Laurel; run, a small right-hand tributary to West Fork of Monongahela River in Lewis County.
Laurel; run, a small right-hand tributary to Williams River in Webster County.
Laurel; run, a small right-hand tributary to Greenbrier River in Pocahontas County.
Laurel; run, a small branch of Youghiogheny River in Preston County.
Laurel Branch; post village in Monroe County.
Laureldale; post village in Mineral County. Altitude, 1,326 feet.
Laurel Patch; run, a right-hand branch of Left Fork of Holly River in Braxton County.
Lavalette; post village in Wayne County on the Norfolk and Western Railway.
Lavender; fork, a small right-hand tributary to Horse Creek, a branch of Little Coal River, in Boone County.
Lavinia; fork, a small left-hand branch of Hopkins Fork of Laurel Creek, tributary to Coal River, in Boone County.
Lawford; post village in Ritchie County.
Lawson; post village in Raleigh County. Altitude, 1,055 feet.
Lawton; post village in Fayette County.
Laywell; branch, a right-hand tributary to Trace Fork in Putnam County.
Lazearville; post village in Brooke County on the Pennsylvania Railroad.
Leachtown; post village in Wood County.
Leading; creek, a right-hand branch of Little Kanawha River in Gilmer County.
Leading; creek, a small right-hand tributary to Valley River in Randolph County.
Leading Creek; post village in Lewis County.
Leadmine; post village in Tucker County.
League; post village in Ritchie County.
Leander; post village in Fayette County.
Leatherbark; run, a left-hand branch of Cedar Creek in Gilmer County.
Leather Bark; run, a small right-hand tributary to Greenbrier River in Pocahontas County.

Leatherwood; creek, a left-hand tributary to Elk River in Clay, Nicholas, and Kanawha counties.
Leatherwood; creek, a small right-hand tributary to Guyandot River in Mingo County.
Leatherwood; fork, a left-hand tributary to Elk River in Webster County.
Leatherwood; town in Ohio County. Population, 123.
Lecta; post village in Wirt County.
Lee; branch, a very small left-hand tributary to Kanawha River in Fayette County.
Lee; creek, a right-hand tributary to Indian Fork of Mud River in Cabell County.
Lee; post village in Wirt County.
Leebell; post village in Randolph County.
Leetown; post village in Jefferson County.
Leewood; post village in Kanawha County.
Lefthand; post village in Roane County.
Legg; post village in Kanawha County.
Lehew; post village in Hampshire County.
Leiter; post village in Randolph County on the Roaring Creek and Belington Railroad.
Leivasy; post village in Nicholas County.
Lem; fork, a very small right-hand tributary to Sycamore Creek, a branch of Clear Fork of Coal River, in Raleigh County.
Lenox; post village in Preston County.
Lens; creek, a left-hand tributary to Kanawha River in Kanawha County.
Leo; post village in Roane County.
Leon; village in Mason County on the Ohio Central Lines. Population, 250.
Leonard; fork, a small left-hand tributary to Right Fork of Middle Fork of Tygarts Valley River in Upshur County.
Leonard; post village in Greenbrier County.
Leopard; run, a small right-hand tributary to Left Fork of Steer Creek in Braxton County.
Leopold; post village in Doddridge County.
Lerona; post village in Mercer County.
Leroy; post village in Jackson County on the Baltimore and Ohio Railroad.
Lesage; post village in Cabell County on the Baltimore and Ohio Railroad.
Leslie; branch, a small right-hand tributary to Tug Fork of Big Sandy River in McDowell County.
Lester; post village in Raleigh County.
Letart; post village in Mason County on the Baltimore and Ohio Railroad.
Letch; post village in Braxton County.
Letherbark; post village in Calhoun County.
Lettergap; post village in Gilmer County.
Levels; post village in Hampshire County.
Levisee; creek, a right-hand branch of Wolf Creek, a tributary to New River, in Fayette County.
Lewis; county, situated in the central part of the State, on the Allegheny Plateau, drained northward by tributaries of the Monongahela. Area, 414 square miles. Population, 16,980—white, 16,792; negro, 178; foreign born, 265. County seat, Weston. The mean magnetic declination in 1900 was 2° 45′. The mean annual rainfall is 40 to 50 inches, and the mean annual temperature 50° to 55°. The county is traversed by the Baltimore and Ohio Railroad.
Lewis; fork, a very small left-hand branch of Laurel Fork, a tributary to Clear Fork of Guyandot River, in Wyoming County.
Lewis; post villlage in Harrison County.
Lewis; run, a small right-hand tributary to Tygarts Valley River, in Barbour County.

Lewisburg; county seat of Greenbrier County. Population, 872.

Lewis Queen; branch, a small left-hand branch of Kiah Fork, a tributary to Twelvepole Creek, in Wayne County.

Lewiston; post village in Kanawha County.

Liberty; post village in Putnam County.

Lick; branch, a very small left-hand tributary to Beech Fork of Twelvepole Creek, a branch of Ohio River, in Wayne County.

Lick; branch, a very small left-hand tributary to Tug Fork of Big Sandy River in McDowell County.

Lick; branch, a small left-hand tributary to Fourteenmile Creek, a branch of Guyandot River, in Lincoln County.

Lick; branch, a left-hand branch of Open Fork of Bell Creek, a tributary to Gauley River, in Nicholas County.

Lick; branch, a very small left-hand tributary to Kanawha River in Kanawha County.

Lick; branch, a very small left-hand tributary to Brier Creek, a branch of Coal River, in Kanawha County.

Lick; branch, a small right-hand branch of Little Sandy Creek, a tributary to Elk River, in Kanawha County.

Lick; branch, a small right-hand tributary to Tug Fork of Big Sandy River in McDowell County.

Lick; branch, a small right-hand tributary to Pond Fork of Little Coal River in Boone County.

Lick; branch, a small right-hand tributary to Cranberry River in Webster County.

Lick; branch, a very small right-hand tributary to Paint Creek, a branch of Kanawha River, in Fayette County.

Lick; branch, a very small right-hand branch of Tug Fork of Big Sandy River, a tributary to Ohio River, in Logan County.

Lick; branch, a very small right-hand tributary to Bluestone River in Mercer County.

Lick; branch, a very small right-hand tributary to North Fork of Elkhorn Creek in McDowell County.

Lick; branch, a very small right-hand tributary to South Fork of Elkhorn Creek in McDowell County.

Lick; branch, a very small right-hand tributary to Indian Creek, a branch of Guyandot River, in Wyoming County.

Lick; creek, a small left-hand tributary to Laurel Creek in Braxton County.

Lick; creek, a small left-hand tributary to Little Coal River, a branch of Coal River, in Boone County.

Lick; creek, a small left-hand tributary to New River in Mercer and Summers counties.

Lick; creek, a small right-hand tributary to Trace Fork of Mud River, a branch of Guyandot River, in Putnam County.

Lick; creek, a small right-hand tributary to Coal River, a branch of Kanawha River, in Boone County.

Lick; creek, a small right-hand tributary to East Fork of Twelvepole Creek, a branch of Ohio River, in Wayne County.

Lick; creek, a small right-hand tributary to New River in Summers County.

Lick; fork, a very small left-hand tributary to Clear Fork of Coal River in Raleigh County.

Lick; fork, a left-hand tributary to Grass Run in Gilmer County.

Lick; fork, a small right-hand branch of Mossy Creek, a tributary to Paint Creek, in Fayette County.

Lick; fork, a small right-hand tributary to Steer Run in Gilmer County.

Lick; mountain, a short spur in Greenbrier County.

Lick; run, a small left-hand tributary to Cheat River, in Preston County.

Lick; run, a small right-hand tributary to Left Fork of Right Fork of Buckhannon River in Randolph County.

Lick; run, a right-hand tributary to South Fork of Potomac River in Pendleton County.

Lick Hollow; branch, a very small right-hand branch of Tug Fork of Big Sandy River, a tributary to Ohio River, in Logan County.

Lick Hollow; creek, a small right-hand tributary to Little Creek, a branch of Anthonys Creek, in Greenbrier County.

Licking; creek, a small left-hand tributary to Cheat River in Tucker County.

Lick Knob; triangulation station situated on Paint Mountain, on boundary line between Raleigh and Fayette counties. Altitude, 3,268 feet.

Licklog; branch, a very small right-hand tributary to West Fork of Twelvepole Creek, a branch of Ohio River, in Wayne County.

Lightburn; post village in Lewis County.

Lile; post village in Greenbrier County.

Lilly; branch, a small left-hand branch of Twentymile Creek, a tributary to Gauley River, in Nicholas County.

Lilly; fork, a left-hand branch of Buffalo Creek, a tributary to Elk River, in Clay County.

Lilly; post village in Summers County.

Lillydale; post village in Monroe County.

Lima; post village in Tyler County.

Limestone; branch, a very small right-hand tributary to Guyandot River, a branch of Ohio River, in Lincoln County.

Limestone; mountain, a short ridge in Tucker County. Altitude, 1,500 to 3,000 feet.

Limestone; post village in Marshall County.

Limestone; run, a small right-hand tributary to O'Brien Fork in Braxton County.

Lincoln; county, situated in the western part of the State on the lower slopes of the Allegheny Plateau and drained by tributaries of Guyandot River. Area, 441 square miles. Population, 15,434—white, 15,371; negro, 63; foreign born, 7. County seat, Hamlin. The mean magnetic declination in 1900 was 1°. The mean annual rainfall is 40 to 50 inches, and the mean annual temperature 50° to 55°.

Lincoln; post village in Wyoming County.

Linden; post village in Roane County.

Lindside; post village in Monroe County.

Line; creek, a small right-hand branch of Peters Creek, a tributary to Gauley River, in Nicholas County.

Link; post village in Braxton County.

Linn; post village in Gilmer County.

Linwood; post village in Pocahontas County.

Lisle; branch, a left-hand branch of Guyandot River in Cabell County.

Little; branch, a very small left-hand tributary to Clear Fork, a branch of Guyandot River, in Wyoming County.

Little; creek, a small left-hand branch of Slaughter Creek, a tributary to Kanawha River, in Kanawha County.

Little; creek, a left-hand tributary to Island Creek, a branch of Guyandot River, in Logan County.

Little; creek, a small right-hand branch of Muddlety Creek, a tributary to Gauley River, in Nicholas County.

Little; creek, a right-hand branch of Anthony Creek, a tributary to Greenbrier River, in Greenbrier County.
Little; creek, a right-hand branch of North Fork of Tug River in McDowell County.
Little; fork, a small left-hand branch of Meadow Creek, a tributary to Meadow River, in Greenbrier County.
Little; fork, a small left-hand tributary to Williams River in Webster County.
Little; fork, a small right-hand tributary to South Fork of Potomac River in Pendleton County.
Little; fork, a very small right-hand tributary to South Fork of Elkhorn Creek, in McDowell and Mercer counties.
Little; mountain, a short ridge in Monroe County. Altitude, 2,500 feet.
Little; mountain, a short ridge between North Fork of Greenbrier River and Greenbrier River in Pocahontas County. Altitude, 3,000 feet.
Little; mountain, a ridge in Monroe County.
Little; mountain, a short spur of Big Mountain, west of South Branch of Potomac River, in Pendleton County.
Little; mountain, a short spur of New Creek Mountains in Grant County. Altitude, 1,500 to 2,000 feet.
Little; mountain, a short ridge in Monroe County. Altitude, 2,000 feet.
Little; post village in Tyler County.
Little; river, a left-hand tributary to East Fork of Greenbrier River in Pocahontas County.
Little; river, a small left-hand branch of West Fork of Greenbrier River in Randolph County.
Little Beaver; creek, a right-hand tributary to Piney Creek, a branch of New River, in Raleigh County.
Little Beech; mountain, a short ridge east of Shavers Mountain, between East and West forks of Glady Fork, in Randolph County.
Little Beech Knob; summit in Greenbrier County.
Little Beechy; creek, a very small left-hand tributary to Elk River in Clay County.
Little Beechy; run, a small left-hand tributary to Williams River in Webster County.
Littlebirch; post village in Braxton County.
Little Birch; river, a right-hand branch of Birch River in Braxton and Webster counties.
Little Black; fork, a small right-hand tributary to Shavers Fork of Cheat River in Randolph County.
Little Blackwater; river, a small right-hand branch of Blackwater River in Tucker County.
Little Bluestone; creek, a small left-hand tributary to Bluestone River, a branch of New River, in Summers County.
Little Brier; creek, a small right-hand tributary to Coal River, a branch of Kanawha River, in Kanawha County.
Little Briery Knob; summit in Nicholas County.
Little Buffalo; creek, a small left-hand tributary to Elk River in Braxton County.
Little Buffalo; creek, a very small left-hand tributary to Mud River, a branch of Guyandot River, in Lincoln County.
Little Buffalo; creek, a left-hand branch of Big Buffalo River in Preston County.
Little Cabell; creek, a small right-hand tributary to Mud River, a branch of Guyandot River, in Cabell County.
Little Cacapon; river, a left-hand tributary to North Branch of Potomac River in Hampshire County.
Little Clear; creek, a right-hand branch of Meadow River in Greenbrier County.

Little Clear Creek; mountain, a ridge between Big Clear Creek and Little Clear Creek in Greenbrier County.

Little Coal; run, a large left-hand branch of Coal River, a tributary to Kanawha River, in Lincoln and Boone counties.

Little Crooked; run, a small left-hand tributary to Cedar Creek in Gilmer County.

Little Cub; branch, a very small left-hand tributary to Tug Fork of Big Sandy River in McDowell County.

Little Cub; creek, a small left-hand tributary to Guyandot River, a branch of Ohio River, in Wyoming County.

Little Day Camp; branch, a small right-hand tributary to Spice Creek, a branch of Tug Fork of Big Sandy River, in McDowell County.

Little Dents; run, a left-hand tributary of Buffalo Creek in Marion County.

Little Devil; creek, a small right-hand tributary to Second Creek, a branch of Greenbrier River, in Monroe County.

Little Dry; run, a small right-hand tributary to Left Fork of Buckhannon River in Randolph County.

Little Dunkard Mill; creek, a left-hand tributary to Buffalo Creek.

Little Elk; creek, a small right-hand tributary to Gauley River, a large branch of Kanawha River in Nicholas County.

Little Ellis; creek, a left-hand branch of Ellis Creek in Gilmer County.

Littlefalls; post village in Monongalia County on the Baltimore and Ohio Railroad.

Little Fishing; creek, a small left-hand branch of Ohio River in Wetzel County.

Little Fudger; creek, a right-hand branch of Fudger Creek, a tributary to Mud River, in Cabell County.

Little Gauley; mountains, a long, narrow, broken ridge in Kanawha and Fayette counties. Altitude 1,500 feet.

Little Hart; creek, a very small left-hand tributary to Guyandot River, a branch of Ohio River, in Lincoln County.

Little Hewitt; creek, a very small right-hand tributary to Little Coal River, a branch of Coal River, in Boone County.

Little High Knob; summit in Pocahontas County.

Little Horse; creek, a small left-hand tributary to Little Coal River, a branch of Coal River, in Boone County.

Little Huff; creek, a left-hand tributary to Guyandot River, a branch of Ohio River, in Wyoming County.

Little Hurricane; creek, a small left-hand tributary to Kanawha River in Putnam County.

Little Indian; creek, a small left-hand tributary to Tug Fork of Big Sandy River in McDowell County.

Little Jarrell; fork, a small left-hand branch of Big Jarrell Fork, a tributary to Hopkins Fork of Coal River, in Boone County.

Little Jenny; branch, a very small right-hand tributary to Tug Fork of Big Sandy River in McDowell County.

Little Jonathan; run, a small left-hand tributary to Cheat River in Tucker County.

Little Kanawha; river, a left-hand branch of Ohio River, rising in Upshur County and flowing northwest through Calhoun, Wirt, and Wood counties. It is navigable to Glenville.

Little Knob; summit in Greenbrier County.

Little Laurel; creek, a small left-hand tributary to Cherry River, a branch of Gauley River, in Nicholas and Greenbrier counties.

Little Laurel; creek, a small right-hand branch of Laurel Creek, a tributary to Coal River, in Boone County.

Little Laurel; creek, a small right-hand branch of Kiah Fork of Twelvepole Creek in Wayne County.

Little Laurel; creek, a small right-hand tributary to Williams River in Pocahontas County.
Little Laurel; creek, an indirect right-hand tributary to Hominy Creek, a branch of Gauley River, in Nicholas County.
Little Laurel; creek, a very small right-hand tributary to Brush Creek, a branch of Bluestone River, in Mercer County.
Little Laurel; run, a left-hand branch of Buffalo Creek in Marion County.
Little Laurel; run, a very small left-hand branch of Blue Creek, a tributary to Elk River, in Kanawha County.
Little Laurel; run, a left-hand tributary to Fish Creek in Wetzel and Marshall counties.
Little Locust Knob; summit in Webster County.
Little Lynn; creek, a small right-hand tributary to East Fork of Twelvepole Creek, a branch of Ohio River, in Wayne County.
Little Marsh; fork, a small right-hand branch of Marsh Fork, the left-hand head fork of Coal River, in Raleigh County.
Little Middle; mountain, a short ridge between Gandy Creek and Dry Fork of Cheat River in Randolph County.
Little Milam; creek, a small right-hand branch of Milam Creek, a tributary to East Fork of Twelvepole Creek, in Wayne County.
Little Mod; run, a right-hand branch of Buffalo Creek in Marion County.
Little Naul; creek, a left-hand branch of Naul Creek in Braxton County.
Little Ninemile; fork, a small left-hand branch of Campbell Creek, a tributary to Kanawha River, in Kanawha County.
Little Otter; creek, a small right-hand branch of Elk River in Braxton County.
Littleotter; post village in Braxton County.
Little Paw Paw; creek, left-hand tributary to Monongahela River, in Mineral County.
Little Ridge; short range of mountains in Greenbrier County.
Little Right; fork, a very small left-hand branch of Loop Creek, a tributary to Kanawha River, in Fayette County.
Little Rush; run, a right-hand tributary to Fish Creek in Wetzel County.
Little Sand; run, a small right-hand tributary to Buckhannon River in Upshur County.
Little Sandy; creek, a small right-hand branch of Elk River in Kanawha County.
Little Sandy; creek, a right-hand branch of Big Sandy Creek in Preston County.
Littlesburg; post village in Mercer County.
Little Sevenmile; creek, a small left-hand branch of Sevenmile Creek, a tributary to Ohio River, in Cabell County.
Little Sewell; creek, a small left-hand tributary to Meadow River in Greenbrier County.
Little Sewell; mountain, a short broken mountainous country in the western part of Greenbrier County. Altitude, 3,000 feet.
Little Sewell Mountain; post village in Greenbrier County.
Little Skin; creek, a right-hand branch of Skin Creek in Lewis County.
Little Slate; creek, a left-hand tributary to Dry Fork, a branch of Tug Fork of Big Sandy River, in McDowell County.
Little Spruce; summit in Pocahontas County.
Little Spruce Knob; summit in Pocahontas County. Altitude, 4,360 feet.
Little Staunch; branch, a small right-hand tributary to Dry Fork, a branch of Tug Fork of Big Sandy River, in McDowell County.
Little Stony; creek, a very small left-hand tributary to New River in Fayette County.

Little Sugar; creek, a right-hand branch of Sugar Creek, a tributary to Back Fork of Elk River, in Webster and Randolph counties.

Little Sycamore; creek, a very small left-hand tributary to Elk River in Clay County.

Little Twomile; creek, a right-hand branch of Mud River in Cabell County.

Little Ten Mile; creek, a small left-hand tributary to Monongahela River in Harrison County.

Littleton; town in Wetzel County on the Baltimore and Ohio Railroad. Altitude, 930 feet. Population, 509.

Little Twomile; creek, a small right-hand tributary to Mud River, a branch of Guyandot River, in Cabell County.

Little Ugly; creek, a very small right-hand tributary to Guyandot River, a branch of Ohio River, in Lincoln County.

Little Wheeling; creek, a right-hand branch of Wheeling Creek in Ohio County.

Little Whetstone; run, a right-hand tributary of Buffalo Creek in Marion County.

Little Whiteoak; creek, a small left-hand tributary to Pinnacle Creek, a branch of Guyandot River, in Wyoming County.

Little Whiteoak; creek, a very small right-hand tributary to Coal River, a branch of Kanawha River, in Boone County.

Little Whitestick; creek, a small left-hand tributary to Piney Creek, a branch of New River, in Raleigh County.

Little Wolf; creek, a small right-hand tributary to Cheat River in Preston County.

Liverpool; post village in Jackson County on the Baltimore and Ohio Railroad.

Lizard; branch, a very small right-hand tributary to Little Huff Creek, a branch of Guyandot River, in Wyoming County.

Lizemores; post village in Clay County.

Lizzie; post village in Jackson County.

Llewellyn; run, a left-hand tributary of Pyles Fork of Buffalo Creek in Marion County.

Lloyd; post village in Randolph County on the Baltimore and Ohio Railroad.

Lloydsville; post village in Braxton County.

Lobelia; post village in Pocahontas County.

Locke; post village in Tyler County.

Lockhart; post village in Jackson County.

Lockharts Run; post village in Wood County.

Lockney; post village in Gilmer County.

Lock Seven; post village in Kanawha County on the Ohio Central Lines.

Lockwood; post village in Nicholas County.

Locust; fork, a left-hand fork of Fork Creek, a tributary to Coal River, in Boone County.

Locust; post village in Pocahontas County.

Locust Knob; summit in Clay County. Altitude, 1,500 feet.

Locust Knob; summit in Pocahontas County. Altitude, 4,392 feet.

Locust Stump Knob; summit in Braxton County. Altitude, 1,690 feet.

Log; run, a right-hand branch of Sinking Creek, a tributary to Little Kanawha River, in Gilmer County.

Logan; county, situated in the southwestern part of the State, on the Allegheny Plateau. It is here deeply dissected, the surface being an alternation of narrow, sharp ridges and deep, narrow valleys. It is drained by Tug Fork of Big Sandy and Guyandot rivers. Area, 494 square miles. Population, 6,955—white, 6,894; negro, 61; foreign born, 8. County seat, Logan. The mean magnetic declination in 1900 was 45′. The mean annual rainfall is 50 inches, and the mean annual temperature 50° to 55°.

Logan; county seat of Logan County on the Chesapeake and Ohio Railway.

Logan; fork, a small right-hand branch of Hopkins Fork of Laurel Creek, a tributary to Coal River, in Boone County.
Logan; run, a very small right-hand tributary to Valley River in Randolph County.
Logansport; village in Marion County.
Lonecedar; post village in Jackson County on the Baltimore and Ohio Railroad.
Lonetree; post village in Tyler County. Altitude, 3,570 feet.
Lone Tree; summit of Rich Mountain in Randolph County. Altitude, 3,570 feet.
Long; branch, a very small left-hand tributary to Guyandot River in Wyoming County.
Long; branch, a left-hand tributary to Paint Creek, a branch of Kanawha River, in Kanawha County.
Long; branch, a small left-hand tributary to Middle Fork of Davis Creek, a branch of Kanawha River, in Kanawha County.
Long; branch, a small left-hand branch of Sandlick Fork of Laurel Creek, a tributary to Coal River, in Boone County.
Long; branch, an indirect right-hand tributary to Dry Fork, a branch of Tug Fork of Big Sandy River, in McDowell County.
Long; branch, a small right-hand tributary to Fifteen-mile Fork of Cabin Creek, a branch of Kanawha River, in Kanawha County.
Long; branch, a very small right-hand tributary to Clear Fork of Coal River in Raleigh County.
Long; branch, a very small right-hand tributary to Guyandot River in Wyoming County.
Long; branch, a small right-hand tributary to Big Clear Creek, a branch of Meadow River, in Greenbrier County.
Long; branch, a small right-hand tributary to Beech Fork of Twelvepole Creek, a branch of Ohio River, in Wayne County.
Long; branch, a left-hand tributary of Guyandot River in Lincoln County.
Long; branch, a very small right-hand tributary to Mill Creek, a branch of Mud River, in Cabell County.
Long; fork, a left-hand branch of Laurel Patch Run in Braxton County.
Long; post village in Randolph County.
Long; run, a very small left-hand tributary to Elk River, a large branch of Kanawha River, in Clay County.
Long; run, a left-hand branch of Left Fork of Middle Fork of Tygarts Valley River in Randolph County.
Long; run, a small left-hand tributary to Right Fork of Middle Fork of Little Kanawha River in Webster County.
Long; run, a small left-hand tributary to Cheat River in Tucker and Preston counties.
Long; run, a small left-hand branch of Pritchett Creek in Marion County.
Long; run, a small right-hand tributary to Birch River in Braxton County.
Long; run, a left-hand branch of Berkeley Run in Taylor County.
Long; run, a very small right-hand tributary to Left Fork of Buckhannon River in Randolph County.
Longacre; post village in Fayette County on the Ohio Central Lines.
Long Bottom; creek, a small left-hand branch of Cabin Creek, a tributary to Kanawha River, in Kanawha County.
Longdale; post village in Mason County on the Baltimore and Ohio Railroad.
Long Drain; left-hand branch of Fish Creek in Wetzel County.
Long Knob; summit in Braxton County. Altitude, 1,510 feet.
Long Lick; branch, a very small left-hand tributary to Big Huff Creek, a branch of Guyandot River, in Wyoming County.
Long Lick; left-hand branch of Cedar Creek in Gilmer County.

Long Pole; creek, a small right-hand tributary to Tug Fork of Big Sandy River in McDowell County.
Longreach; post village in Tyler County on the Baltimore and Ohio Railroad.
Long Ridge; short range between North and South branches of the Potomac in Pendleton County.
Longrun; post village in Doddridge County on the Baltimore and Ohio Railroad.
Long Run Hill; summit in Randolph County.
Longs; run, a left-hand branch of Castleman Run in Ohio and Brooke counties.
Long Shoal; branch, a very small right-hand tributary to Little Coal River, a branch of Coal River, in Boone County.
Long Shoal; run, a small right-hand tributary to Little Kanawha River.
Longs Ridge; short spur between Turkey and Longs runs, small left-hand branches of Elk River, in Clay County.
Lookout; post village in Fayette County.
Looneyville; post village in Roane County.
Loop; branch, a very small right-hand tributary to North Fork of Elkhorn Creek in McDowell County.
Loop; branch, a very small right-hand tributary to Tug River in McDowell County.
Loop; creek, a right-hand tributary to Kanawha River in Fayette County.
Lorentz; post village in Upshur County on the Baltimore and Ohio Railroad.
Lorton Lick; creek, a small right-hand tributary to Bluestone River in Mercer County.
Lost; branch, a very small right-hand tributary to Guyandot River in Mingo and Wyoming counties.
Lost; river, a head branch of Cacapon River, rising in Hardy County and flowing northeast into the Potomac.
Lost; run, a small left-hand tributary to Left Fork of Middle Fork of Tygarts Valley River in Randolph County.
Lost; run, a right-hand branch of Fish Creek in Wetzel County.
Lost; run, a small right-hand branch of Laurel Creek, a tributary to Elk River, in Webster County.
Lost City; post village in Hardy County.
Lostcreek; post village in Harrison County on the Baltimore and Ohio Railroad. Altitude, 1,013 feet.
Lost Flat; broad summit in Greenbrier County.
Lost River; post village in Hardy County.
Lot; post village in Wetzel County.
Lotta; post village in Wirt County.
Loudenville; post village in Marshall County on the Baltimore and Ohio Railroad.
Loudin; post village in Randolph County.
Louise; post village in Pocahontas County.
Lousecamp; run, a small left-hand tributary to Cheat River in Tucker County.
Louther; post village in Jackson County.
Loveberry; run, a right-hand branch of Sand Fork in Lewis County.
Loveridge; post village in Greenbrier County.
Lowdell; post village in Wood County.
Lowell; branch, a very small right-hand branch of Indian Creek, a tributary to New River, in Monroe and Summers counties.
Lowell; post village in Summers County on the Chesapeake and Ohio Railway. Altitude, 1,512 feet.
Lower; creek, a small right-hand tributary to Mud River, a branch of Guyandot River, in Cabell County.
Lower; gap in Wyoming County.
Lower; mountain, a summit in Pocahontas County.

Lower; run, a very small right-hand tributary to Elk River, a large branch of Kanawha River, in Clay County.
Lower; run, a right-hand branch of South Fork of Fishing Creek in Wetzel County.
Lower Big; run, a right-hand branch of Leading Creek in Gilmer County.
Lower Big; run, a small right-hand tributary to Holly River in Webster County.
Lower Birch; run, a very small left-hand tributary to Elk River in Clay County.
Lower Bull; run, a right-hand tributary to Cedar Creek in Gilmer County.
Lower Cove; head waters of Lost River in Hardy County.
Lower Frame; run, a small left-hand tributary to Elk River in Clay County.
Lower Gap; branch, a small left-hand tributary to Big Huff Creek, a branch of Guyandot River, in Wyoming County.
Lower Hensley; creek, a small right-hand tributary to Tug Fork of Big Sandy River in McDowell County.
Low Gap; branch, a small right-hand tributary to Little Marsh Fork, a branch of Coal River, in Raleigh County.
Low Gap; branch, a small right-hand tributary to Slab Fork, a branch of Guyandot River, in Raleigh County.
Low Gap; creek, a small left-hand tributary to Spruce Fork of Little Coal River, a branch of Coal River, in Boone County.
Lower Level; run, a left-hand branch of Cedar Creek in Gilmer County.
Lower Lick; small left-hand tributary to Laurel Fork, a branch of Spruce Fork of Little Coal River, in Boone County.
Lower Pond Lick; small left-hand tributary to Shavers Fork of Cheat River in Randolph County.
Lower Road; branch, a small right-hand tributary to Clear Fork, a branch of Guyandot River, in Wyoming County.
Lower Rock Camp; run, a small right-hand tributary to Elk River in Braxton County.
Lower Shannon; branch, a small right-hand tributary to Tug Fork of Big Sandy River in McDowell County.
Lower Shant; run, a small right-hand tributary to Back Fork of Elk River in Randolph County.
Lower Shaver; run, a small right-hand tributary to Left Fork of Steer Creek in Braxton County.
Lower Sleith; fork, a left-hand branch of Right Fork of Steer Creek in Braxton County.
Lower Sturgeon; branch, a small right-hand tributary to Big Cub Creek, a branch of Guyandot River, in Wyoming County.
Lower Threemile; fork, a small left-hand branch of Blue Creek, a tributary to Elk River, in Kanawha County.
Lower Tony Camp; run, a small right-hand tributary to Dry Fork of Cheat River in Randolph County.
Lower Two; run, a small left-hand tributary to Left Fork of Steer Creek in Gilmer County.
Lower Two; run, a small left-hand tributary to Cedar Creek in Gilmer County.
Lowman; post village in Wetzel County.
Lowsville; post village in Monongalia County.
Lubeck; post village in Wood County.
Lucerne; post village in Gilmer County.
Lucile; post village in Wirt County.
Lukey; fork, a small left-hand tributary to head of Mud River, a branch of Guyandot River, in Boone County.
Lumberport; post village in Harrison County on the Baltimore and Ohio Railroad.

Lunice; creek, a small left-hand tributary to South Branch of Potomac River in Grant County.
Luray; post village in Pendleton County.
Lurd; post village in Kanawha County.
Luzon; post village in Tyler County.
Lydia; post village in Clay County.
Lykins; creek, a very small right-hand tributary to Paint Creek, a branch of Kanawha River, in Fayette County.
Lynch; post village in Harrison County on the Norfolk and Western Railway.
Lynch; run, a very small right-hand tributary to Little Kanawha River in Gilmer County.
Lynn; creek, a very small left-hand branch of Twelvepole Creek, a tributary to Ohio River, in Wayne County.
Lynncamp; post village in Marshall County.
Lynn Camp; run, a small left-hand tributary to Little Kanawha River in Upshur County.
Lynn Camp; run, a left-hand branch of Fish Creek in Wetzel and Marshall counties.
Lynn Camp; run, a very small left-hand tributary to Gauley River in Webster County.
Lyuncamp; run, a right-hand tributary of Left Fork of Steer Creek in Gilmer County.
Lynn Knob; summit in Randolph County.
Lyon; post village in Doddridge County.
Lyons; branch, a right-hand branch of Buch Fork of Twelvepole Creek in Wayne and Cabell counties.
Lytton; post village in Pleasants County on the Baltimore and Ohio Railroad.
Mabie; post village in Randolph County, on the Roaring Creek and Charleston Railroad.
McAlpin; village in Harrison County.
McCauleys; run, a left-hand branch of Oil Creek in Braxton County.
McClains; post village in Jackson County.
McClung; branch, a small left-hand branch of Peter Creek, a tributary to Gauley River, in Nicholas County.
McClungs; post village in Greenbrier County.
McClure; branch, a small right-hand tributary to South Fork of Tug River in McDowell County.
McComas; branch, a very small left-hand tributary to East Fork of Twelvepole Creek, a branch of Ohio River, in Wayne County.
McComas; branch, a right-hand tributary of Mud River in Cabell County.
McComas; post village in Mercer County.
McConkey; village in Taylor County.
McCowans; mount, a spur of Shavers Mountain, between Shavers and Glady forks of Cheat River.
McCoy; run, a right-hand branch of Little Wheeling Creek in Ohio County.
McCue; post village in Upshur County.
McCurdy; post village in Cabell County.
McDonald; fork, a small left-hand branch of Big Cub Creek, a tributary to Guyandot River, in Wyoming County.
MacDonald; station in Fayette County on the Chesapeake and Ohio Railway and on Dunloup Creek, a tributary to New River.
McDonald Mill; creek, a small left-hand tributary to Clear Fork, a branch of Guyandot River, in Wyoming County.
McDowell; branch, a very small left-hand tributary to Clear Fork of Coal River in Raleigh County.

McDowell; county, situated in the southern part of the State on the Allegheny Plateau. It is deeply dissected. The surface is drained in the main by Tug Fork of Big Sandy River.
McDowell; post village in McDowell County on the Norfolk and Western Railway.
McElroy; branch, a small left-hand tributary to Ohio River in Tyler County.
McElroy; creek, a small left-hand tributary to Ohio River in Doddridge County.
MacFarlan; post village in Ritchie County.
McGee; post village in Taylor County.
McGraw; run, a right-hand branch of Little Wheeling Creek in Ohio County.
McGraws; post village in Wyoming County. Altitude, 1,802 feet.
McKee; branch, a small right-hand tributary to Gauley River in Nicholas County.
McKee; mountain, a short ridge in Nicholas County. The highest peak reaches an altitude of 2,365 feet.
McKendree; station in Fayette County on the Chesapeake and Ohio Railway and on New River. Altitude, 1,411 feet.
McKim; creek, a small left-hand tributary to Ohio River in Pleasants County.
McKim; post village in Tyler County.
Macksville; post village in Pendleton County.
McKinley; post village in Wood County.
McMechen; town in Marshall County on the Baltimore and Ohio Railroad. Population, 1,465.
McMellin; post village in Monongalia County.
McMillan; creek, a small left-hand tributary to Big Laurel Creek, a branch of Cherry River, in Greenbrier County.
McMillion; creek, a left-hand branch of Muddlety Creek, a tributary to Gauley River, in Nicholas County.
Mace Knob; summit of Cheat Mountain in Pocahontas County.
Madam; creek, a small left-hand tributary to New River in Summers County.
Madison; county seat of Boone County.
Madison; creek, a left-hand branch of Guyandot River in Cabell County.
Madison; creek, a small left-hand tributary to Guyandot River, a branch of Ohio River, in Wayne County.
Madison; run, a small right-hand tributary to Cheat River in Preston County.
Magazine; branch, a small right-hand tributary to Elk River, a branch of Kanawha River, in Kanawha County.
Maggie; post village in Mason County on the Baltimore and Ohio Railroad.
Magnolia; post village in Morgan County on the Baltimore and Ohio Railroad.
Mahan; run, a left-hand branch of Buffalo Creek in Marion County.
Mahogany; run, a left-hand branch of Muach Run in Monongalia County.
Mahone; creek, a very small left-hand tributary to Mud River, a branch of Guyandot River, in Lincoln County.
Mahone; post village in Ritchie County.
Mahoney; creek, a left-hand branch of Mud River in Lincoln County.
Maidsville; post village in Monongalia County.
Majorsville; post village in Marshall County.
Malden; post village in Kanawha County on the Chesapeake and Ohio and the Ohio Central railroads. Altitude, 606 feet.
Malta; post village in Barbour County.
Mammoth; post village in Kanawha County on the Kellys Creek Railroad.
Man; creek, a small right-hand branch of Glade Creek, a tributary to New River, in Fayette County.
Man; post village in Logan County.
Mandeville; post village in Summers County.
Manganese; post village in Wood County.

Manheim; post village in Preston County.
Manila; post village in Boone County.
Manning; branch, a very small left-hand tributary to Coal River, a branch of Kanawha River, in Kanawha County.
Manning; branch, a very small right-hand tributary to Little Coal River in Boone County.
Manning; run, a small right-hand branch of Big Laurel Creek, a tributary to Cherry River, in Greenbrier County.
Manning Knob; summit in Greenbrier County.
Mannington; town in Marion County on the Baltimore and Ohio Railroad. Altitude, 967 feet. Population, 1,681.
Mann Knob; summit in Wayne County. Altitude, 1,437 feet.
Mann Knob; summit in Greenbrier County.
Manns; creek, a small right-hand tributary to New River in Fayette County.
Manown; post village in Preston County.
Maple; fork, a small right-hand branch of Sand Fork of Paint Creek, a tributary to Kanawha River, in Raleigh County.
Maple; post village in Monongalia County.
Maple; run, a left-hand branch of Cheat River in Monongalia County.
Mapledale; post village in Greenbrier County.
Maple Meadow; creek, a small left-hand tributary to Marsh Fork of Coal River in Raleigh County.
Maplewood; post village in Fayette County.
Marary; branch, a small left-hand tributary to Laurel Creek, a branch of Coal River, in Boone County.
Marcus; post village in Webster County.
Margaret; post village in Harrison County.
Marie; post village in Summers County.
Marion; county, situated in the northern part of the State, on the Allegheny Plateau. It is drained by tributaries to the Monongahela. Area, 357 squares miles. Population, 32,430—white, 31,942; negro, 482; foreign born, 1,769. County seat, Fairmont. The mean magnetic declination in 1900 was 3° 10′. The mean annual rainfall is 40 to 50 inches, and the mean annual temperature 50° to 55°. The county is traversed by the Baltimore and Ohio Railroad.
Marion; post village in Wetzel County on the West Virginia Northern Railroad.
Mark; run, a right-hand tributary of Left Fork of Steer Creek in Gilmer County.
Market; post village in Doddridge County.
Marlin; mountain, a short ridge in Pocahontas County. The highest peak reaches an altitude of 3,198 feet.
Marlin; mountain, a short ridge between Thorny and Browns creeks in Pocahontas County.
Marlin Lick; small left-hand tributary to Greenbrier River in Pocahontas County.
Marlinton; county seat of Pocahontas County on the Chesapeake and Ohio Railway. Population, 171.
Marlowe; village in Berkeley County.
Marmet; post village in Kanawha County on the Chesapeake and Ohio Railway.
Marpleton; post village in Braxton County.
Marquess; post village in Preston County.
Marrowbone; creek, a small right-hand branch of Tug Fork of Big Sandy River, a tributary to Ohio River, in Logan County.
Marrs; branch, a very small left-hand tributary to New River in Fayette County.
Marsh; fork, a stream in Raleigh County, uniting with Clear Fork to form Coal River.

Marsh; fork, a small right-hand branch of Big Hart Creek, a tributary to Guyandot River, in Lincoln County.

Marsh; fork, a small right-hand branch of Slab Fork, a tributary to Guyandot River, in Wyoming County.

Marsh; fork, an indirect left-hand tributary to Indian Creek, a branch of Guyandot River in Wyoming County.

Marshall; county, situated at the base of the Panhandle, bordering upon the Ohio River. Area, 311 square miles. Population, 26,444—white, 25,941; negro, 499; foreign born, 1,264. County seat, Moundsville. The mean magnetic declination in 1900 was 1° 50′. The mean annual rainfall is 40 to 50 inches, and the mean annual temperature 50° to 55°. The county is traversed by the Ohio River and the Baltimore and Ohio railroads.

Marshall; post village in Jackson County.

Marshes; post village in Raleigh County.

Marshville; post village in Harrison County.

Martha; post village in Cabell County.

Marthas Ridge; short spur north of North Fork of Greenbrier River in Pocahontas County. Altitude, 3,500 to 4,000 feet.

Martin; branch, a left-hand tributary to Pocotaligo River, a branch of Kanawha River, in Kanawha County.

Martin; fork, a left-hand branch of Peachtree Creek, a tributary to Marsh Fork of Coal River, in Raleigh County.

Martin; post village in Grant County.

Martinsburg; county seat of Berkeley County on the Baltimore and Ohio and the Cumberland Valley railroads. Population, 7,564.

Marytown; post village in McDowell County.

Mash; branch, a small right-hand tributary to Dingus Run, a branch of Guyandot River, in Logan County.

Mason; county, situated in the western part of the State, bordering on Ohio River at the foot of the Allegheny Plateau. Area, 457 square miles. Population, 24,142—white, 23,604; negro, 537; foreign born, 317. County seat, Point Pleasant. The mean magnetic declination in 1900 was 0° 35′. The mean annual rainfall is 40 to 50 inches, and the mean annual temperature 50° to 55°. The county is traversed by the Ohio Central Lines and the Ohio River Railroad.

Mason; village in Mason County. Population, 904.

Masontown; post village in Preston County on the Morgantown and Kingwood Railroad.

Masonville; post village in Grant County.

Mast Knob; summit in Randolph County.

Matchless; post village in Berkeley County.

Mate; creek, a small right-hand branch of Tug Fork of Big Sandy River, a tributary to Ohio River, in Logan County.

Matewan; post village in Mingo County on the Norfolk and Western Railway.

Matewan; station in Logan County on the Norfolk and Western Railway and on Tug Fork of Chattarawha River.

Mathias; post village in Hardy County.

Mats; creek, a small right-hand tributary to West Fork, a branch of Pond Fork of little Coal River, in Boone County.

Mattie; post village in Roane County.

Matts; creek, a very small left-hand tributary to Greenbrier River in Summers and Monroe counties.

Matville; post village in Raleigh County.

Maud; post village in Wetzel County on the Baltimore and Ohio Railroad.

Maud; run, a right-hand branch of North Fork of Fishing Creek in Wetzel County.

Maxwell; post village in Pleasants County.
Maxwelton; post village in Greenbrier County.
May; post village in Doddridge County.
Maybeury; post village in McDowell County on Norfolk and Western Railway and on South Fork of Elkhorn Creek. Altitude, 2,162 feet.
Maynard; branch, a very small right-hand tributary to East Fork of Twelvepole Creek, a branch of Ohio River, in Wayne County.
Mays; gap in Little Mountain, caused by New Creek, in Grant County.
Maysville; post village in Grant County.
Mayton; post village in Webster County.
Maywood; post village in Fayette County.
Meadland; village in Taylor County.
Meadow; branch, a very small right-hand tributary to Middle Fork of Mud River, a branch of Guyandot River, in Lincoln County.
Meadow; branch, a right-hand branch of Sleepy Creek in Berkeley and Morgan counties.
Meadow; creek, a right-hand branch of Anthony Creek, a tributary to Greenbrier River, in Greenbrier County.
Meadow; creek, a small right-hand tributary to New River in Summers and Fayette counties.
Meadow; creek, a small right-hand branch of Meadow River, a tributary to Gauley River, in Greenbrier County.
Meadow; creek, a small right-hand branch of Muddlety Creek, a tributary to Gauley River, in Nicholas County.
Meadow; fork, a small left-hand branch of Devils Fork, a tributary to Guyandot River, in Raleigh County.
Meadow; fork, a small left-hand branch of Dunloup Creek, a tributary to New River, in Fayette County.
Meadow; fork, a small right-hand branch of Cabin Creek, a tributary to Guyandot River, in Wyoming County.
Meadow; fork, a small right-hand branch of Brier Creek, a tributary to Coal River, in Kanawha County.
Meadow; river, a large left-hand branch of Gauley River, rising in Greenbrier County and flowing northwestward, forming the boundary between Fayette and Nicholas counties, until it enters the Gauley at Carnifax Ferry.
Meadow; run, a right-hand branch of Oil Creek in Braxton County.
Meadow; run, a right-hand branch of Middle Wheeling Creek in Ohio County.
Meadowbluff; post village in Greenbrier County.
Meadowbrook; post village in Harrison County on the Baltimore and Ohio Railroad.
Meadow Creek; mountain, a ridge in Greenbrier County lying nearly parallel to Allegheny Mountains. Altitude, 2,500 to 3,000 feet.
Meadowcreek Station; post village in Summers County on the Chesapeake and Ohio Railway.
Meadowdale; post village in Jackson County on the Baltimore and Ohio Railroad.
Meadowville; post village in Barbour County.
Meadville; post village in Tyler County.
Measle; fork, a small right-hand branch of Slab Fork, a tributary to Guyandot River, in Wyoming County.
Medina; post village in Jackson County.
Medley; post village in Grant County.
Meethouse; branch, a small right-hand tributary to Clear Fork, a branch of Tug Fork of Big Sandy River, in McDowell County.
Meethouse; fork, a right-hand head fork of Panther Creek, a branch of Tug Fork of Big Sandy River, in McDowell County.

Meeting House; branch, a very small left-hand tributary to Elkhorn Creek, a branch of Tug Fork of Big Sandy River, in McDowell County.
Meeting House; run, a left-hand branch of Lost River in Taylor County.
Meighen; post village in Marshall County.
Melissa; post village in Cabell County.
Mentor; post village in Jackson County.
Mercer; county, situated in the southern part of the State bordering on Virginia. It lies on the Allegheny Plateau or East River Mountains, which here form the escarpment which is the southern boundary of the county. Its elevation ranges from 2,000 to 4,000 feet. It is drained by tributaries to New River. Area, 437 square miles. Population, 23,023—white, 20,119; negro, 2,902; foreign born, 269. County seat, Princeton. The mean magnetic declination in 1900 was 1°. The mean annual rainfall is 50 to 60 inches, and the mean annual temperature 50° to 55°. The county is traversed by the Norfolk and Western Railway.
Mercer; post village in Hancock County.
Mercers Bottom; post village in Mason County on the Baltimore and Ohio Railroad.
Mercers Saltworks; post village in Summers County.
Meriden; post village in Barbour County.
Merrick; branch, a small right-hand tributary to Mud River, a branch of Guyandot River, in Cabell County.
Merrick; creek, a very small left-hand tributary to Middle Fork of Mud River in Lincoln County.
Merritt; creek, a small left-hand tributary to Guyandot River, a branch of Ohio River, in Cabell County.
Messer; creek, a very small right-hand branch of Marrowbone Creek, a tributary to Tug Fork of Big Sandy River, in Logan County.
Messer; run, a left-hand tributary of Pyles Fork of Buffalo Creek in Marion County.
Metz; post village in Marion County on the Baltimore and Ohio Railroad.
Micajah Ridge; mountains in Wyoming County.
Michael; mountain, a short ridge in Pocahontas County. Altitude, 3,000 to 3,500 feet.
Middle; branch, a very small right-hand branch of Tug Fork of Big Sandy River, a tributary to Ohio River, in Logan County.
Middle; branch, a small right-hand tributary to Barker Creek, a branch of Guyandot River, in Wyoming County.
Middle; creek, a small left-hand tributary to Elk River in Clay County.
Middle; creek, a left-hand branch of Middle Fork of Mud River in Cabell County.
Middle; fork, a head fork of Back Fork of Elk River in Randolph County.
Middle; fork, a head fork of Cedar Creek in Braxton County.
Middle; fork, a small left-hand branch of Patterson Creek, a tributary to North Branch of Potomac River, in Grant County.
Middle; fork, a left-hand tributary to Williams River in Webster and Pocahontas counties.
Middle; fork, a left-hand branch of Davis Creek, a tributary to Kanawha River, in Kanawha County.
Middle; fork, a small left-hand tributary to Canoe Run in Lewis County.
Middle; fork, an indirect left-hand tributary to Dry Fork, a branch of Tug Fork of Big Sandy River, in McDowell County.
Middle; fork, a small right-hand tributary to Right Fork of Buckhannon River in Randolph County.
Middle; fork, a small right-hand branch of Trace Fork of Guyandot River, a tributary to Ohio River, in Logan County.
Middle; fork, a right-hand branch of Island Creek, a tributary to Guyandot River, in Logan County.

Middle; mountain, a narrow ridge between Gap Mountain and Cove Mountain in Monroe County. Altitude, 2,500 to 3,000 feet.
Middle; mountain, a short ridge in the northern part of Pocahontas County. Altitude, 3,500 feet.
Middle; mountain, a narrow ridge in Pocahontas and Greenbrier counties.
Middle; mountain, a short ridge in Pendleton and Grant counties. Altitude, 2,000 feet.
Middle; run, a small left-hand tributary to Little Kanawha River in Gilmer County.
Middle; run, a small left-hand tributary to Back Fork of Elk River in Webster County.
Middle; run, a small left-hand tributary to Gauley River in Nicholas County.
Middle; run, a small right-hand branch of Big Laurel Creek, a tributary to Cherry River, in Greenbrier County.
Middle; run, a small right-hand tributary to Birch River in Braxton County.
Middlebourne; county seat of Tyler County. Population, 403.
Middle Fork; mountain, a ridge in Webster and Pocahontas counties, between Cranberry and Williams rivers. Altitude, 3,500 to 4,000 feet.
Middlefork; post village in Randolph County on the Baltimore and Ohio Railroad.
Middle Island; creek, a left-hand branch of Ohio River, rising in Tyler County.
Middle Lick; fork, a small right-hand tributary to Davis Creek, a branch of Kanawha River, in Kanawha County.
Middleton; fork, a very small left-hand tributary to Bluestone River, in Mercer County.
Middleway; town in Jefferson County. Population, 466.
Middle Wheeling; creek, a left-hand branch of Little Wheeling Creek, in Ohio County.
Midkiff; post village in Lincoln County.
Midway; post village in Putnam County on the Ohio Central Lines.
Mike; run, a right-hand tributary of Ellis Creek in Gilmer County.
Mike Knob; summit of Yew Mountains in Greenbrier County. Altitude, 4,276 feet.
Milam; branch, a small right-hand tributary to South Fork of Tug River in McDowell County.
Milam; creek, a small left-hand branch of East Fork of Twelvepole Creek, a tributary to Ohio River, in Wayne County.
Milam; post village in Hardy County.
Milam Ridge; mountains in Wyoming County.
Milan; fork, a left-hand branch of Barker Creek, a tributary to Guyandot River, in Wyoming County.
Milan; fork, a left-hand branch of Laurel Fork, a tributary to Clear Fork of Guyandot River, in Wyoming County.
Milburn; branch, a small left-hand tributary to Paint Creek, a branch of Kanawha River, in Kanawha County.
Milburn; creek, a very small left-hand tributary to Paint Creek, a branch of Kanawha River, in Fayette County.
Mile; branch, a very small right-hand tributary to Kanawha River in Kanawha County.
Mile; branch, a very small right-hand tributary to Coal River, a branch of Kanawha River, in Boone County.
Mile; branch, a small right-hand tributary to Whiteoak Creek, a branch of Coal River, in Boone County.
Mile; branch, a very small right-hand tributary to Indian Creek, a branch of Guyandot River, in Wyoming County.
Mile; branch, a very small right-hand tributary to Dry Fork, a branch of Tug Fork of Big Sandy River, in McDowell County.

Mile; creek, a small right-hand tributary to Guyandot River, a branch of Ohio River, in Lincoln County.

Mile; fork, a right-hand branch of Cooper Creek, a tributary to Elk River, in Kanawha County.

Miles; post village in Pendleton County.

Miletus; post village in Doddridge County.

Mill; branch, a very small left-hand tributary to Cherry River, a branch of Gauley River, in Nicholas County.

Mill; branch, a very small left-hand tributary to Fields Creek, a branch of Kanawha River, in Kanawha County.

Mill; branch, a small right-hand tributary to Williams River in Webster County.

Mill; branch, a small right-hand tributary to Guyandot River, a branch of Ohio River, in Lincoln County.

Mill; branch, a very small right-hand tributary to Tug River in McDowell County.

Mill; branch, a small right-hand tributary to Camp Creek, a branch of Bluestone River, in Mercer County.

Mill; branch, a small right-hand tributary to Barker Creek, a branch of Guyandot River, in Wyoming County.

Mill; branch, a very small right-hand tributary to Winding Gulf, a branch of Guyandot River, in Raleigh County.

Mill; creek, a small left-hand tributary to Birch River, a branch of Elk River, in Nicholas County.

Mill; creek, a left-hand tributary to South Branch of Potomac River in Hampshire County.

Mill; creek, a small left-hand branch of Patterson Creek, a tributary to North Branch of Potomac River, in Mineral County.

Mill; creek, a very small left-hand branch of Island Creek, a tributary to Guyandot River, in Logan County.

Mill; creek, a small left-hand tributary to Bluestone River in Mercer County.

Mill; creek, a small left-hand tributary to Tug Fork of Big Sandy River in McDowell County.

Mill; creek, a very small left-hand tributary to New River in Raleigh County.

Mill; creek, a left-hand tributary to Elk River, a large branch of Kanawha River, in Kanawha County.

Mill; creek, a small left-hand branch of Ohio River in Jackson County.

Mill; creek, a left-hand tributary to Elk River in Kanawha County.

Mill; creek, a small left-hand tributary to Valley River in Randolph County.

Mill; creek, a small left-hand tributary to Elk River in Braxton County.

Mill; creek, a small left-hand tributary to Birch River, in Nicholas County.

Mill; creek, a small right-hand tributary to Mud River, a branch of Guyandot River, in Cabell County.

Mill; creek, a small right-hand tributary to Meadow River, a branch of Gauley River, in Greenbrier County.

Mill; creek, a small right-hand tributary to Tygarts Valley River in Barbour County.

Mill; creek, a very small right-hand tributary to Guyandot River, a branch of Ohio River, in Cabell County.

Mill; creek, a very small right-hand tributary to Elkhorn Creek, a branch of Tug Fork of Big Sandy River, in McDowell County.

Mill; creek, a small right-hand tributary to Dunloup Creek, a branch of New River, in Raleigh County.

Mill; creek, a very small right-hand branch of Guyandot River, a tributary to Ohio River, in Logan County.

Mill; creek, a small right-hand branch of Hurricane Creek, a tributary to Kanawha River, in Putnam County.

Mill; creek, a right-hand tributary to New River in Fayette County.
Mill; creek, a right-hand branch of Valley River in Randolph County.
Mill; gap in a spur of the South Fork Mountains, caused by Brushy Run, in Pendleton County.
Mill; mountain, a short ridge on the boundary line between Hardy County, W. Va., and Shenandoah County, Va. Altitude, 3,000 feet.
Mill; run, a small left-hand tributary to Elk River in Webster County.
Mill; run, a small left-hand tributary to Gauley River in Webster County.
Mill; run, a small left-hand tributary to North Fork of Potomac River in Pendleton County.
Mill; run, a small, left-hand tributary to Elk River in Braxton County.
Mill; run, a small right-hand branch of Knapp Creek, a tributary of Greenbrier River, in Pocahontas County.
Mill; run, a small right-hand tributary to Back Fork of Elk River in Webster County.
Mill; run, a small right-hand tributary to Gauley River in Webster County.
Mill; run, a small right-hand tributary to Williams River in Webster County.
Mill; run, a small right-hand tributary to South Branch of Potomac River in Pendleton County.
Mill; run, a small right-hand tributary to Dry Fork of Cheat River in Tucker County.
Mill; run, a small right-hand branch of Sugar Creek, a tributary to Back Fork of Elk River, in Webster and Randolph counties.
Mill; run, a small right-hand tributary to Elk River in Webster County.
Mill; run, head fork of Teter Creek, a branch of Tygarts Valley River, in Barbour County.
Millard; post village in Roane County.
Millbrook; post village in Hampshire County.
Mill Creek; mountain, a long, narrow ridge, lying parallel to the South Branch of the Potomac River, in Hardy and Hampshire counties. Altitude, 1,000 to 2,000 feet.
Mill Creek; post village in Randolph County on the West Virginia Central and Pittsburg Railway.
Miller; creek, a small right-hand branch of Meadow River, a tributary to Gauley River, in Nicholas County.
Miller; run, a left-hand branch of Miller Fork of Rock Run in Wetzel County.
Miller Knob; summit in Webster County. Altitude, 2,742 feet.
Miller Ridge; short mountainous range in Webster County, south of the Gauley River.
Millers; creek, a very small right-hand branch of Tug Fork of Big Sandy River, a tributary to Ohio River, in Logan County.
Millers; fork, a right-hand tributary to Twelvepole Creek, a tributary to Ohio River, in Wayne County.
Millers Camp; branch, a right-hand head fork of Marsh Fork of Coal River in Raleigh County.
Millers Camp Branch; post village in Raleigh County.
Millers Ridge; short spur in Greenbrier County. Altitude, 2,500 feet.
Mill Fall; run, a left-hand branch of West Fork River in Marion County.
Millhill; post village in Greenbrier County.
Mill Hill; summit in Greenbrier County.
Mill Hollow; small right-hand tributary to Kanawha River in Kanawha County.
Milligan; creek, a small right-hand tributary to Greenbrier River in Greenbrier County.
Mill Knob; summit in Nicholas County.
Millpoint; post village in Pocahontas County.

Millsboro; post village in Marshall County.

Millsite; branch, a very small right-hand tributary to Mud River, a branch of Guyandot River, in Lincoln County.

Mill Site; run, a small right-hand branch of Little Kanawha River in Gilmer County.

Mill Site; run, a small right-hand tributary to Right Fork of Buckhannon River in Upshur County.

Millstone; post village in Calhoun County.

Millstone; run, a right-hand branch of Little Kanawha River in Braxton County.

Millville; post village in Jefferson County on the Baltimore and Ohio Railroad.

Millwood; post village in Jackson County on the Baltimore and Ohio Railroad.

Milo; post village in Calhoun County.

Milroy; post village in Braxton County.

Milton; town in Cabell County on the Chesapeake and Ohio Railway. Altitude, 586 feet. Population, 582.

Mineral; county, situated in the northeastern part of the State, limited on the west and north by Potomac River. Its surface is an alternation of ridges and valleys, ranging in elevation from 800 to over 3,000 feet. Area, 332 square miles. Population, 12,883—white, 12,218; negro, 665; foreign born, 451. County seat, Keyser. The mean magnetic declination in 1900 was 2° 30'. The mean annual rainfall is 50 to 60 inches, and the mean annual temperature 45° to 50°. The county is traversed by the Baltimore and Ohio and the West Virginia Central and Pittsburg railroads.

Mineral; post village in Harrison County.

Mineralwells; post village in Wood County.

Mingo; county, situated in the southwestern part of the State, bordering on Big Sandy River, and lying on the Allegheny Plateau. It is here deeply dissected. Area, 424 square miles. Population, 11,359—white, 11,050; negro, 309; foreign born, 65. County seat, Williamson. The mean magnetic declination in 1900 was 45'. The mean annual rainfall is 50 to 60 inches, and the mean annual temperature 50° to 55°. The county is traversed by the Norfolk and Western Railway.

Mingo; post village in Randolph County.

Mingo; run, a small left-hand tributary to Valley River in Randolph County.

Mingo; run, a right-hand branch of Buffalo Creek in Brooke County.

Mingo Knob; summit in Randolph County.

Mink; post village in Kanawha County.

Minkshoal; branch, a small right-hand tributary to Elk River, a branch of Kanawha River, in Kanawha County.

Minnie; post village in Wetzel County.

Minnora; post village in Calhoun County.

Minverton; post village in Fayette County.

Mipp; post village in Wirt County.

Miracle; run, a right-hand branch of Dunkard Creek in Monongalia County.

Miracle Run; post village in Monongalia County.

Missouri; creek, a small left-hand tributary to Laurel Creek in Webster County.

Missouri; creek, a very small right-hand branch of Right Fork of Twelvepole Creek, a tributary to Ohio River, in Wayne County.

Missouri; fork, a small left-hand branch of Hewett Creek, a tributary to Little Coal River, in Boone and Logan counties.

Mitchell; branch, a very small right-hand tributary to Tug Fork of Big Sandy River in McDowell County.

Mitchell; post village in Pendleton County on the Ohio Central Lines.

Mitchell; run, a small right-hand tributary to Back Fork of Elk River in Randolph County.

Mitchell Lick; fork, a right-hand branch of Left Fork of Middle Fork of Tygarts Valley River in Randolph County.
Mitchell Ridge; mountains in Raleigh County.
Mitten Ridge; short range of mountains in Webster County. Altitude, 3,000 feet.
Mobley; post village in Wetzel County.
Moccasin; branch, a very small left-hand tributary to Guyandot River in Wyoming County.
Mod; branch, a very small left-hand tributary to Tug Fork of Big Sandy River in McDowell County.
Mod; run, a left-hand branch of Buffalo Creek in Marion County.
Modoc; post village in Greenbrier County.
Moffett Knob; summit in Pocahontas County. Altitude, 4,210 feet.
Mohr; post village in Wetzel County.
Molehill; post village in Ritchie County.
Molers; village in Jefferson County.
Moll Kelly; branch, a small left-hand tributary to Peachtree Creek, a branch of Marsh Fork of Coal River, in Raleigh County.
Molly Kincaid; branch, a very small left-hand branch of Loop Creek, a tributary to Kanawha River, in Fayette County.
Mona; post village in Monongalia County.
Monarch; post village in Kanawha County on the Ohio Central lines.
Money; run, a right-hand branch of Fishing Creek in Wetzel County.
Monitor; post village in Monroe County.
Monongah; town in Marion County on the Baltimore and Ohio Railroad. Population, 1,786.
Monongahela; river, the southernmost of the two main forks of Ohio River, the other being the Allegheny, which rises in southwestern New York. It heads in Lewis, Upshur, and Randolph counties in several large branches, West Fork, Tygart Valley, and Cheat rivers, while to the eastward heads the Youghiogheny, which flows into it near its mouth. It joins the Allegheny at Pittsburg, forming the Ohio. Length, about 190 miles; drainage area, 7,625 square miles; navigable to Morgantown.
Monongalia; county, situated in the Allegheny Plateau. It is drained by tributaries of the Monongahela. Area, 368 square miles. Population, 19,049—white, 18,747; negro, 299; foreign born, 301. County seat, Morgantown. The mean magnetic declination in 1900 was 3° 15′. The mean annual rainfall is 40 to 50 inches, and the mean annual temperature 50° to 55°. The county is traversed by the Baltimore and Ohio Railroad.
Monroe; county, situated in the southeastern part of the State. It is diversified by parallel ridges and valleys trending northeast and southwest. The western part is a plateau but little dissected and bearing numerous hills upon its surface. It is drained by tributaries of Greenbrier and New rivers. Area, 464 square miles. Population, 13,130—white, 12,300; negro, 830; foreign born, 32. County seat, Union. The mean magnetic declination in 1900 was 1° 55′. The mean annual rainfall is 50 to 60 inches, and the mean annual temperature 50° to 55°.
Monroe; post village in Randolph County.
Monroe Draft; small left-hand tributary to Howards Creek, a branch of Greenbrier River, in Greenbrier County.
Montana Mines; post village in Marion County.
Montcalm; post village in Mercer County.
Monterville; post village in Randolph County.
Montgomery; town in Fayette County on the Chesapeake and Ohio Railway and on Kanawha River. Altitude, 634 feet. Population, 1,594.

Montrose; post village in Randolph County on the West Virginia Central and Pittsburg Railway.
Moore; fork, a very small left-hand branch of Elk Creek, a tributary to Guyandot River, in Logan County.
Moore; post village in Tucker County on the West Virginia Central and Pittsburg Railway.
Moore: run, a left-hand branch of Indian Fork in Gilmer County.
Moore; run, a small left-hand tributary to Greenbrier River in Pocahontas County.
Moore Camp; branch, a small right-hand tributary to Spice Creek, a branch of Tug Fork of Big Sandy River, in McDowell County.
Moorefield; county seat of Hardy County. Population, 460.
Moorefield; river, a right-hand head branch of South Branch of the Potomac in Hardy County.
Moores; run, a left-hand branch of Rocky Fork of Ellis Creek in Gilmer County.
Mooresville; post village in Monongalia County.
Morford; post village in Roane County.
Morgan; branch, a very small right-hand tributary to Drawdy Creek, a branch of Coal River, in Boone County.
Morgan; county, situated in the northeastern part of the State, limited on the north by Potomac River. The surface consists of broad valleys alternating with narrow ridges of no great height. Area, 235 square miles. Population, 7,294—white, 7,074; negro, 220; foreign born, 68. County seat, Berkeley Springs. The mean magnetic declination in 1900 was 4°. The mean annual rainfall is 40 to 50 inches, and the mean annual temperature 45° to 50°. The county is traversed by the Baltimore and Ohio Railroad.
Morgan; run, a small left-hand tributary to Cheat River in Preston County.
Morgan Ridge; mountains in Mercer County.
Morgans Glade; post village in Preston County.
Morgansville; post village in Doddridge County on the Baltimore and Ohio Railroad.
Morgantown; county seat of Monongalia County on the Baltimore and Ohio and the Morgantown and Kingwood railroads. Population, 1,895. Altitude, 963 feet.
Morley; post village in Braxton County.
Morocco; post village in Clay County.
Morris; creek, a small left-hand tributary to Cranberry River, a branch of Gauley River, in Nicholas County.
Morris; creek, a very small left-hand tributary to Elk River in Kanawha County.
Morris; fork, a left-hand branch of Blue Creek, a tributary to Elk River, in Kanawha County.
Morris; post village in Wirt County.
Morris; run, a left-hand branch of Miller Fork of Rock Run in Wetzel County.
Morrison; fork, a very small left-hand branch of Fourmile Creek, a tributary to Guyandot River, in Lincoln County.
Morrison; fork, a left-hand branch of Little Hurricane Creek, a tributary to Kanawha River, in Putnam County.
Mosby; branch, a very small right-hand tributary to Big Cub Creek, a branch of Guyandot River, in Wyoming County.
Moscow; post village in Hancock County on the Pittsburg, Cincinnati, Chicago and St. Louis Railroad.
Moser Knob; summit in Pendleton County.
Moses; creek, a very small left-hand branch of Right Fork of Twelvepole Creek, a branch of Ohio River, in Wayne County.
Moses; run, a right-hand branch of Long Drain in Wetzel County.
Mossy; creek, a small right-hand tributary to Paint Creek, a branch of Kanawha River, in Fayette County.

Mossy; post village in Fayette County.
Mound; post village in Kanawha County.
Moundsville; county seat of Marshall County on the Baltimore and Ohio Railroad. Population, 5,362. Altitude, 640 feet.
Mountain; creek, a small left-hand tributary to Bluestone River, a branch of New River, in Mercer County.
Mountain; fork, a small indirect right-hand tributary to Dry Fork, a branch of Tug Fork of Big Sandy River, in McDowell County.
Mountain; run, a right-hand branch of Sleepy Creek in Morgan County.
Mountain Cove; post village in Fayette County.
Mountain Lick; small left-hand tributary to Williams River in Pocahontas County.
Mount Carbon; post village in Fayette County on Kanawha River and on the Chesapeake and Ohio and the Powellton and Pocahontas railways. Altitude, 639 feet.
Mount Clare; post village in Harrison County on the West Virginia Central and Pittsburg Railway. Altitude, 1,001 feet.
Mount Desert; summit in Kanawha County.
Mount Harmony; village in Marion County.
Mount Hope; town in Fayette County on Dunloup Creek, a tributary to New River. Population, 351.
Mount Lookout; post village in Nicholas County. Altitude, 2,017 feet.
Mount Nebo; post village in Nicholas County.
Mount of Seneca; post village in Pendleton County.
Mount Olive; post village in Mason County.
Mount Storm; post village in Grant County.
Mount Tell; post village in Jackson County.
Mount Zion; post village in Calhoun County.
Mouse; creek, a small left-hand branch of Hominy Creek, a tributary to Gauley River, in Nicholas County.
Moyer; gap between Sandy Ridge and Jack Mountains, caused by a small right-hand branch of South Branch of the Potomac, in Pendleton County.
Moyer; run, a small left-hand tributary to South Branch of the Potomac, in Pendleton County.
Mozelle; post village in Jackson County.
Mud; fork, a small left-hand tributary to Turtle Creek, a branch of Little Coal River, in Boone County.
Mud; fork, a small left-hand tributary to Guyandot River, a branch of Ohio River, in Logan County.
Mud; post village in Lincoln County.
Muddlety; creek, a right-hand branch of Gauley River, in Nicholas County.
Muddlety; post village in Nicholas County.
Muddy; creek, a right-hand tributary to Greenbrier River, in Greenbrier County.
Muddy; run, a small left-hand tributary to Cheat River, in Preston County.
Muddy Cove; branch, a very small right-hand tributary to Big Huff Creek, a branch of Guyandot River, in Logan County.
Muddy Creek; mountain, a ridge in Greenbrier County. Altitude, 2,000 to 2,500 feet.
Mud Hole; branch, a small right-hand tributary to Clear Fork, a branch of Tug Fork of Big Sandy River, in McDowell County.
Mud Lick; a small left-hand branch of Morris Fork of Blue Creek, a tributary to Elk River, in Kanawha County.
Mud Lick; a small right-hand tributary to Little Kanawha River, in Gilmer County.
Mudlick; branch, a small right-hand tributary to Buffalo Creek, a branch of Guyandot River, in Logan County.
Mudlick; branch, a very small right-hand tributary to Gilbert Creek, a branch of Guyandot River, in Mingo County.

Mud Lick; fork, a small left-hand branch of Leatherwood Creek, a tributary to Elk River, in Kanawha County.

Mudlick; fork, a small left-hand tributary to Laurel Creek, a branch of Coal River, in Boone County.

Mud Lick; fork, a small right-hand tributary to Blake Branch of Smithers Creek, a tributary to Kanawha River, in Fayette County.

Mudlick; run, a left-hand branch of Carney Fork of Rock Run, in Wetzel County.

Mudlick; run, a left-hand branch of Pritchett Creek, in Marion County.

Mud Lick; run, a small left-hand tributary to South Branch of the Potomac, in Hardy County.

Mulberry; fork, a left-hand branch of Jenkins Fork of Loop Creek, a tributary to Kanawha River, in Fayette County.

Mulberry; fork, a small right-hand tributary to Left Fork of Middle Fork of Tygart Valley River, in Randolph County.

Mullin; branch, a very small left-hand tributary to Winding Gap, a branch of Guyandot River, in Raleigh County.

Mulvane; post village in Fayette County.

Munday; post village in Wirt County.

Mundy Lick; small left-hand tributary to Greenbrier River, in Pocahontas County.

Mundy Lick Ridge; short mountainous range between Greenbrier River and Buckley Mountain, in Pocahontas County.

Munson; post village in Morgan County.

Murphytown; post village in Wood County.

Murraysville; post village in Jackson County, on the Baltimore and Ohio Railroad.

Muses Bottom; post village in Jackson County.

Musick; post village in Mingo County.

Mutton Run; post village in Hampshire County.

Muzzle; fork, a small left-hand branch of Little Huff Creek, a tributary to Guyandot River, in Wyoming County.

Myerstown; village in Jefferson County.

Myra; post village in Lincoln County.

Myrtle; post village in Mingo County.

Nancy; fork, a small right-hand tributary to Indian Creek, a branch of Guyandot River, in Wyoming County.

Napier; post village in Braxton County.

Napier Ridge; range of hills in Wayne County. Altitude, about 1,200 feet.

Narrow; branch, a very small right-hand tributary to Elk River, a branch of Kanawha River, in Kanawha County.

Nat; post village in Mason County.

Naul; creek, a right-hand branch of Little Kanawha River, in Braxton County.

Neal; branch, a small right-hand branch of Twentymile Creek, a tributary to Gauley River, in Nicholas County.

Nease; post village in Mason County.

Ned; branch, a very small left-hand tributary to Guyandot River, a branch of Ohio River, in Mingo County.

Needmore; post village in Hardy County.

Neel; village in Marion County.

Nelson; branch, a very small right-hand tributary to Little Huff Creek, a branch of Guyandot River, in Wyoming County.

Neponset; post village in Summers County.

Neptune; post village in Jackson County.

Nesselroad; post village in Jackson County.

Nestlow; post village in Wayne County.
Nestorville; post village in Barbour County.
Nettly; mountain, a short ridge west of Valley River, in Randolph County.
New; creek, a left-hand tributary to North Fork of Potomac River, in Grant County.
New; creek, a right-hand tributary to North Branch of Potomac River, in Grant and Mineral counties.
New; post village in Raleigh County.
New; river, a large branch of the Kanawha River, rising in Watauga County, N. C., and flowing in a peculiar course first north and thence westward to its junction with the Gauley River, where they form the Kanawha, in Fayette County, W. Va.
Newark; post village in Wirt County on the Little Kanawha Railroad.
Newberne; post village in Gilmer County.
Newburg; town in Preston County on the Baltimore and Ohio Railroad. Population, 751. Altitude, 755 feet.
Newcomb; creek, a very small left-hand branch of Twelvepole Creek, a tributary to Ohio River, in Wayne County.
Newcomb; creek, a small right-hand branch of East Fork of Twelvepole Creek, a tributary to Ohio River, in Wayne County.
New Creek; mountain, a broken, mountainous country in Grant and Mineral counties. Altitude, 2,000 to 2,500 feet.
Newcreek; post village in Mineral County.
New Cumberland; county seat of Hancock County on the Pittsburg, Cincinnati, Chicago and St. Louis Railroad. Population, 2,198.
Newdale; post village in Wetzel County.
New England; post village in Wood County.
Newfound; post village in Wyoming County.
Newhaven; post village in Mason County, on the Baltimore and Ohio Railroad.
New Hope; post village in Mercer County.
Newhouse; branch, a small right-hand tributary to Elk River, a branch of Kanawha River, in Kanawha County.
Newlands; run, a right-hand tributary of Short Creek, in Brooke County.
Newlandsville; post village in Pleasants County.
Newlonton; post village in Upshur County.
New Martinsville; county seat of Wetzel County. Population, 1,089.
New Milton; post village in Doddridge County.
Newport; post village in Wood County.
New Richmond; post village in Summers County, on the Chesapeake and Ohio Railway. Altitude, 1,289 feet.
Newson; branch, a small left-hand tributary to Spice Creek, a branch of Tug Fork of Big Sandy River, in McDowell County.
Newton; post village in Roane County, on the West Virginia Central and Pittsburg Railway. Altitude, 1,917 feet.
Newville; post village in Braxton County.
Next; post village in Tyler County.
Nicholas; county, situated in the central part of the State, on the Allegheny Plateau. It is drained by Gauley River and its tributaries. Area, 691 square miles. Population, 11,403—white, 11,384; negro, 19; foreign born, 245. County seat, Summersville. The mean magnetic declination in 1900 was 2°. The mean annual rainfall is 50 to 60 inches, and the mean annual temperature 50° to 55°.
Nickells Knob; summit in Greenbrier County. Altitude, 2,725 feet.
Nickells Mills; post village in Monroe County.
Nicklow; post village in Barbour County.
Nicolette; post village in Wood County on the Baltimore and Ohio Railroad.

Nigger; branch, a small right-hand tributary to Clear Fork, a branch of Tug Fork of Big Sandy River, in McDowell County.

Nigger Camp; run, a small right-hand branch of Old Lick Creek, a tributary to Holly River, in Webster County.

Nina; post village in Doddridge County.

Ninemile; creek, a small left-hand tributary to Ohio River in Cabell County.

Ninemile; creek, a small right-hand tributary to Guyandot River, a branch of Ohio River, in Lincoln County.

Ninemile; fork, a small left-hand branch of Campbell Creek, a tributary to Kanawha River, in Kanawha County.

Nixon; post village in Upshur County.

Nobe; post village in Calhoun County.

Nolan; post village in Mingo County.

Norman; run, a small left-hand tributary to Holly River in Webster County.

Normantown; post village in Gilmer County.

North; branch, a small right-hand tributary to Big Creek, a branch of Guyandot River, in Logan County.

North; river, a large left-hand branch of Great Cacapon River, rising in South Branch Mountain, in Hardy County.

North Fork; mountains in the eastern part of the State, lying between North and South forks of the Potomac, in Pendleton and Grant counties. Altitude, 2,000 to 4,000 feet.

North Fork; post village in McDowell County on the Norfolk and Western Railway and on Elkhorn Creek.

North Mill; creek, a right-hand tributary to South Branch of the Potomac, in Grant and Pendleton counties, known in its upper course as Brushy Run.

North Mountain; post village in Berkeley County on the Baltimore and Ohio Railroad. Altitude, 547 feet.

Northriver Mills; post village in Hampshire County.

Northspring; post village in Wyoming County.

Norwood; post village in McDowell County on Elkhorn Creek and on the Norfolk and Western Railway.

Noseman; branch, a very small right-hand tributary to Cooney Otter Creek, an indirect left-hand tributary to Guyandot River, in Wyoming County.

Notchlog; fork, a small left-hand tributary to Dry Branch of Cabin Creek, a tributary to Kanawha River, in Kanawha County.

Numan; post village in Doddridge County.

Nunly; mountain, a short ridge in Greenbrier County.

Nuttallburg; post village in Fayette County on New River and on the Chesapeake and Ohio Railway. Altitude, 944 feet.

Nutter; run, a small left-hand tributary to Little Kanawha River in Gilmer County.

Nutterfarm; post village in Ritchie County.

Nutterville; post village in Greenbrier County.

Nye; post village in Putnam County.

Oak; branch, a very small left-hand tributary to Long Pole Creek, a branch of Tug Fork of Big Sandy River, in McDowell County.

Oak; post village in Wood County.

Oakflat; post village in Pendleton County.

Oakgrove; post village in Mercer County.

Oakland; post village in Morgan County.

Oakvale; post village in Mercer County on the Norfolk and Western Railway. Altitude, 1,705 feet.

Oakville; post village in Roane County on the Norfolk and Western Railway.

O'Brien; creek, a small right-hand tributary to Elk River in Clay County.

O'Brien; fork, a left-hand branch of Salt Lick Fork of Little Kanawha River in Braxton County.
O'Brien; fork, a right-hand branch of Right Fork of Steer Creek in Gilmer and Braxton counties.
Oceana; county seat of Wyoming County. Population, 187.
Odaville; post village in Jackson County.
Odd; post village in Raleigh County.
Odell; post village in Kanawha County on the Clendennin and Spencer Railway.
Odessa; post village in Clay County on Porters Creek and Gauley Railway.
Ogdin; post village in Wood County.
Ohio; county, situated in the Panhandle, bordering on Ohio River. Area, 111 square miles. Population, 48,024—white, 46,765; negro, 1,251; foreign born, 6,140. County seat, Wheeling. The mean magnetic declination in 1900 was 1°. The mean annual rainfall is 40 to 50 inches, and the mean annual temperature 50° to 55°. The county is traversed by the Wheeling and Lake Erie, the Wheeling Terminal, the Baltimore and Ohio, the Cleveland, Lorain and Wheeling, the Ohio River, the Pittsburg, Cincinnati, Charleston and St. Louis, and the Wheeling and Elm Grove railroads.
Ohio; river, formed by the Allegheny and Monongahela rivers, which unite at Pittsburg, in Pennsylvania, where it is a navigable stream about 600 yards wide. It runs first northwestward to Beaver, and, after it has crossed the western boundary of Pennsylvania, flows southward to Wheeling. Below this point it forms the boundary between Ohio and West Virginia, and runs southwestward to the mouth of the Sandy River. It next forms the boundary between Kentucky and Ohio, and pursues a west-northwestward course to Cincinnati. After it strikes the eastern border of Indiana, it runs nearly southwestward with a very sinuous course and forms the boundary between Indiana and Illinois on the right and Kentucky on the left, until it enters the Mississippi at Cairo, in latitude 37° N., and about 1,200 miles from the mouth of the Great River. Drainage area, 201,720 square miles. Length, 963 miles. It is navigable throughout.
Oil; creek, a right-hand branch of Little Kanawha River in Braxton and Lewis counties.
Oilville; post village in Logan County.
Oka; post village in Calhoun County.
Okeeffe; post village in Mingo County.
Okonoko; post village in Hampshire County on the Baltimore and Ohio Railroad.
Old Camp; branch, a very small right-hand tributary to Pond Fork of Little Coal River in Boone County.
Old Field; fork, a left-hand head fork of Elk River in Pocahontas County.
Old Field; fork, a right-hand branch of Sand Fork in Lewis County.
Old Field; mountain, a short ridge in Greenbrier County. One of the peaks has an altitude of 4,244 feet.
Old Field Ridge; short spur between Black Run of North Fork of Greenbrier and North Fork of Pocahontas County.
Oldfields; post village in Hardy County. Altitude, 800 feet.
Old House; branch, a very small right-hand tributary to Pond Fork of Little Coal River in Boone County.
Old House; branch, a very small right-hand tributary to Spruce Fork of Little Coal River, in Logan County.
Old Lick; creek, a head fork of Left Fork of Holly River in Webster County.
Old Man; run, a small right-hand tributary to Cacapon River in Hampshire County.
Old Perryville; village, in McDowell County, located on Dry Fork, a tributary to Tug Fork of Big Sandy River.

Old Shop; branch, a very small right-hand tributary to Winding Gap, a branch of Guyandot River, in Raleigh County.
Old Slab; fork, a small right-hand branch of Slab Fork, a tributary to Guyandot River, in Wyoming County.
Oldtown; village in Mason County.
Old Woman; run, a very small right-hand tributary to Elk River in Braxton County.
Oley; post village in Raleigh County.
Olive; post village in Harrison County.
Olympia; post village in Wirt County.
Omps; post village in Morgan County.
Ona; post village in Cabell County on the Chesapeake and Ohio Railway. Altitude, 623 feet.
One; fork, a small indirect tributary to Buffalo Creek, a branch of Elk River, in Clay County.
Onego; post village in Pendleton County.
O'Neills Knob; summit in Greenbrier County.
Onemile; creek, a very small left-hand branch of East Fork of Twelvepole Creek, a tributary to Ohio River, in Wayne County.
Onemile; creek, a very small right-hand branch of Fourmile Creek, a tributary to Guyandot River, in Lincoln County.
Onemile; fork, a very small right-hand branch of Blue Creek, a tributary to Elk River, in Kanawha County.
Onoto; post village in Pocahontas County.
Oors; run, a right-hand tributary of Middle Wheeling Creek in Ohio County.
Oozley; branch, a small left-hand tributary to Dry Fork, a branch of Tug Fork of Big Sandy River, in McDowell County.
Opekiska; post village in Monongalia County on the Baltimore and Ohio Railroad.
Open; fork, a right-hand branch of Bell Creek, a tributary to Gauley River, in Nicholas and Clay counties.
Open; fork, a small right-hand tributary to Loop Creek, a branch of Kanawha River, in Fayette County.
Openmouth; branch, a very small left-hand branch of Right Fork of Twelvepole Creek, a tributary to Ohio River, in Logan County.
Ophelia; post village in Nicholas County.
Opossum; creek, a right-hand branch of Mill Creek, a tributary to New River, in Fayette County.
Oral; post village in Harrison County on the Baltimore and Ohio Railroad.
Orange; post village in Boone County.
Orchard; branch, a very small left-hand tributary to Tug Fork of Big Sandy River in McDowell County.
Orchard; branch, a very small left-hand branch of Laurel Creek, a tributary to New River, in Fayette County.
Orchard; branch, a small left-hand branch of Sandlick Fork of Laurel Creek, a tributary to Coal River, in Boone County.
Orchard; post village in Monroe County.
Orem; post village in Wood County.
Organcave; post village in Greenbrier County.
Orient; post village in Calhoun County.
Orleans Crossroads; post village in Morgan County on the Baltimore and Ohio Railroad.
Orlena; post village in Randolph County.
Orpha; post village in Barbour County.
Orr; post village in Preston County.

Osborne; creek, a right-hand branch of Mill Creek, a tributary to New River, in Fayette County.
Osbornes Mills;, post village in Roane County.
Osceola; post village in Randolph County.
Osgood; post village in Monongalia County.
Otia; post village in Mason County.
Otter; branch, a very small left-hand branch of Blue Creek, a tributary to Elk River, in Kanawha County.
Otter; creek, a small right-hand tributary to Meadow River, in Greenbrier County.
Otter; creek, a small right-hand branch of Peters Creek, a tributary to Gauley River, in Nicholas County.
Otter; creek, a left-hand branch of Tygart Valley River in Taylor County.
Otter; fork, one of the head forks of Left Fork of Steer Creek in Braxton County.
Otter; fork, a left-hand tributary to Dry Fork of Cheat River in Tucker and Randolph counties.
Otter; fork, a very small right-hand branch of Laurel Fork, a tributary to Clear Fork of Guyandot River, in Wyoming Connty.
Otter; run, a right-hand branch of Pritchett Creek in Marion County.
Otto; post village in Roane County.
Overfield; post village in Barbour County.
Overhill; post village in Upshur County.
Owen; run, a small right-hand tributary to Left Fork of Steer Creek in Gilmer County.
Oxbow; post village in Ritchie County.
Oxford; post village in Doddridge County.
Pack; branch, a very small left-hand branch of Smithers Creek, a tributary to Kanawha River, in Fayette County.
Pack; branch, a small right-hand tributary to Paint Creek, a branch of Kanawha River, in Fayette County.
Pack; fork, a small left-hand branch of Rockhouse Fork of Dingus Run, a tributary to Guyandot River, in Logan County.
Packs Ferry; post village in Summers County.
Pad; fork, a small left-hand branch of Little Huff Creek, a tributary to Guyandot River, in Wyoming County.
Pad; post village in Roane County.
Padds; run, a left-hand branch of Lost Run in Taylor County.
Paddy; branch, a very small right-hand tributary to Kanawha River in Fayette County.
Paddy; branch, a right-hand branch of Trace Fork in Cabell County.
Paddy; mountain, a short ridge in Frederick and Shenandoah counties. Altitude, 2,500 to 3,000 feet.
Paddy; run, a small left-hand branch of Cedar Creek in Gilmer County.
Paddys; run, a right-hand branch of Saltlick Creek in Braxton County.
Paddy Knob; summit in Braxton County.
Padenvalley; post village in Wetzel County on the Baltimore and Ohio Railroad.
Page; post village in Putnam County.
Paint; branch, a right-hand tributary to Cabin Creek, a branch of Kanawha River, in Kanawha County.
Paint; creek, a left-hand branch of Kanawha River in Kanawha, Fayette, and Raleigh counties.
Paint; creek, a large right-hand tributary to Kanawha River in Kanawha, Fayette, and Raleigh counties.
Paint; mountain on boundary line between Fayette and Raleigh counties.

Paintcreek; post village in Kanawha County on the Chesapeake and Ohio Railway. Altitude, 622 feet.
Palace Ridge; summit in the northern part of Randolph County.
Palace Valley; post village in Upshur County.
Palmer; post village in Braxton County on the Holly River and Addison Railway.
Palser; run, a small right-hand branch of Steer Run in Gilmer County.
Pansy; post village in Grant County.
Panther; branch, a very small left-hand tributary to Clear Fork of Coal River in Raleigh County.
Panther; branch, a small right-hand branch of Blue Creek, a tributary to Elk River, in Kanawha County.
Panther; creek, a small left-hand tributary to Gauley River in Nicholas County.
Panther; creek, a small left-hand tributary to Mud River, a branch of Guyandot River, in Lincoln County.
Panther; creek, a left-hand branch of Tug Fork of Big Sandy River in McDowell County.
Panther; creek, a small right-hand tributary to Buckhannon River in Upshur County.
Panther; post village in McDowell County on the Norfolk and Western Railway.
Panther; run, a small right-hand tributary to Left Fork of Middle Fork of Tygarts Valley River in Randolph County.
Panther; run, a small right-hand tributary to Little Kanawha River in Upshur County.
Panther Camp; fork, a small left-hand branch of Spring Creek, a tributary to Greenbrier River, in Greenbrier County.
Panther Knob; summit in Summers County.
Panther Knob; summit in Wyoming County.
Panther Knob; summit in Pendleton County.
Panther Lick; run, a small left-hand tributary to Elk River in Webster County.
Panther Lick; very small right-hand tributary to Mud River, a branch of Guyandot River, in Cabell County.
Paola; post village in Doddridge County.
Paradise; post village in Putnam County.
Parchment Valley; post village in Jackson County on the Baltimore and Ohio Railroad.
Park; gap in Fork Mountains caused by Beach Lick Run, a short branch of South Fork of Cherry River, in Greenbrier County.
Parker; creek, a small left-hand branch of Kiah Fork, a tributary to Twelvepole Creek, in Wayne County.
Parkers; post village in Doddridge County.
Parkersburg; county seat of Wood County on the Baltimore and Ohio, the Baltimore and Ohio Southwestern, and the Little Kanawha railroads. Altitude, 616 feet. Population, 11,703.
Parrish; post village in Pleasants County.
Parsner; creek, a small right-hand tributary to Mud River, a branch of Guyandot River, in Lincoln County.
Parsons; county seat of Tucker County on the West Virginia Central and Pittsburg Railway.
Pasco; post village in Roane County.
Pasture; branch, a very small left-hand tributary to Beech Fork of Twelvepole Creek, a branch of Ohio River, in Wayne County.
Patrick; creek, a small left-hand branch of West Fork of Twelvepole Creek, a tributary to Ohio River, in Wayne County.
Patrick; peak, a knob of Wolf Creek Mountain in Monroe County.

Patrick; post village in Kanawha County.
Patsey; post village in Roane County.
Patters; run, a left-hand branch of Big Creek in Lincoln County.
Patterson; creek, right-hand branch of North Branch of Potomac River in Grant and Mineral counties.
Patterson Creek; mountain, a narrow ridge along the boundary line of Grant and Hardy counties. Altitude, 2,000 to 2,500 feet.
Pattersons Depot; post village in Mineral County.
Patton; knob in Taylor County.
Patton; post village in Monroe County.
Paw Paw; creek, a small left-hand branch of Monongahela River in Monongalia County.
Pawpaw; town in Morgan County on the Baltimore and Ohio Railroad. Population, 693.
Payne Knob; summit in Fayette County. Altitude, 2,804 feet.
Payne Knob, summit in Webster County. Altitude, 3,126 feet.
Paynes; branch, a small left-hand tributary to Five Mile Creek, a branch of East River, in Mercer County.
Peabody; post village in Wetzel County.
Peach; creek, a small right-hand branch of Guyandot River, a tributary to Ohio River, in Logan County.
Peachtree; branch, a small right-hand tributary to Twentymile Creek, a branch of Gauley River, in Nicholas County.
Peachtree; creek, a left-hand branch of Marsh Fork of Coal River in Raleigh County.
Peachtree; post village in Raleigh County.
Peach Tree; run, a right-hand tributary to Steer Run in Gilmer County.
Peak Ridge; mountains in Wyoming County.
Pear; post village in Raleigh County.
Pearl; mountain ridge in bend of Tilhance Creek in Berkeley County.
Pearl; post village in Nicholas County.
Pearson; branch, a small right-hand branch of Muddlety Creek, a tributary to Gauley River, in Nicholas County.
Peck; post village in Logan County. Altitude, 653 feet.
Pecksrun; post village in Upshur County.
Peddler; run, a right-hand branch of Simpson Run in Taylor County.
Pedee; fork, a small left-hand tributary to Rock Creek, a branch of Little Coal River, in Boone County.
Pedlar; post village in Monongalia County.
Peeled Chestnut; gap in Big Stone Ridge on boundary between McDowell and Mercer counties.
Peel Tree; post village in Barbour County.
Peery Camp; branch, a small right-hand tributary to Clear Fork, a branch of Tug Fork of Big Sandy River, in McDowell County.
Peeryville; post village in McDowell County located on Dry Fork, a large left-hand tributary to Tug Fork of Big Sandy River.
Peet; post village in Randolph County.
Peewee; post village in Wirt County.
Pemberton; post village in Raleigh County.
Penbro; post village in Webster County.
Pence Springs; post village in Summers County on the Chesapeake and Ohio Railway.
Pendleton; county, situated in the eastern part of the State, against the boundary of Virginia. Its surface is mountainous, consisting of alternations of valleys and

ridges. It is drained northward by tributaries to the Potomac River. Area, 707 square miles. Population, 9,167—white, 9,044; negro, 123; foreign born, 6. County seat, Franklin. The mean magnetic declination in 1900 was 2°. The mean annual rainfall is 50 to 60 inches, and the mean annual temperature 45° to 50°. The county is traversed by the Ohio River Railroad.

Penfield; branch, a very small left-hand tributary to New River in Fayette County.
Peniel; post village in Roane County.
Pennsboro; town in Ritchie County on the Baltimore and Ohio Railroad. Population, 738.
Penrith; village in Hancock County.
Pentress; post village in Monongalia County.
Peora; village in Harrison County.
Pepper; post village in Barbour County.
Perkins; fork, a head fork of Cedar Creek in Braxton County.
Perry; branch, a small left-hand tributary to Buffalo Creek, a branch of Elk River, in Clay and Nicholas counties.
Perry; post village in Hardy County.
Perry Ridge; short spur north of Cranberry River in Nicholas County.
Persinger; post village in Nicholas County.
Persinger; run, a small right-hand tributary to Gauley River in Nicholas County.
Peru; post village in Hardy County.
Peter; run, a small left-hand tributary to South Branch of Potomac River in Pendleton County.
Peter Cove; creek, a small left-hand branch of East Fork of Twelvepole Creek, a tributary to Ohio River, in Wayne County.
Peter Johnson; run, a right-hand branch of Pritchet Creek in Marion County.
Peters; creek, a right-hand branch of Gauley River in Nicholas County.
Peters; creek, a right-hand branch of Little Wheeling Creek in Ohio County.
Peters; gap in Great Flat Top Mountain in Mercer County.
Peters; mountain, a long, narrow ridge in Monroe County, W. Va., and Alleghany County, Va.
Peters; mountain, a ridge in Monroe County.
Peters; mountain, a short ridge between North Fork and Moore Run, branches of Greenbrier River, in Pocahontas County.
Petersburg; post village and county seat of Grant County on South Branch of Potomac River.
Peters Cave; fork, a left-hand branch of Horse Creek, a tributary to Little Coal River, in Lincoln County.
Peters Creek; fork, a small left-hand branch of Hardway Branch of Twentymile Creek, a tributary to Gauley River, in Nicholas County.
Peterstown; town in Monroe County, situated on Rich Creek. Altitude, 1,745 feet. Population, 167.
Petes; fork, a very small right-hand branch of Falling Rock Creek, a tributary to Elk River, in Kanawha and Clay counties.
Petroleum; post village in Ritchie County on the Baltimore and Ohio Railroad. Altitude, 697 feet.
Pettit; post village in Randolph County.
Pewee; knob in Taylor County.
Peytona; post village in Boone County.
Pharoah; post village in Wayne County.
Phillip Camp; fork, a small tributary to Left Fork of Buckhannon River in Randolph County.
Philippi; county seat of Barbour County on the Baltimore and Ohio Railroad. Altitude, 1,192 feet. Population, 665.

Phillips; branch, a very small right-hand branch of Tug Fork of Chattarawha River, a tributary to Ohio River, in Logan County.

Phillips; run, a small left-hand tributary to Muddlety Creek, a branch of Gauley River, in Nicholas County.

Philoah; post village in Putnam County.

Pickaway; post village in Monroe County.

Pickens; post village in Randolph County on the Baltimore and Ohio Railroad.

Pickle; mountain, a short ridge west of the South Branch of the Potomac in Pendleton County. Altitude, 2,500 to 3,000 feet.

Pickles; fork, a small right-hand tributary to Salt Lick Fork of Little Kanawha River in Braxton County.

Piedmont; town in Mineral County on the Baltimore and Ohio and on the Cumberland and Pennsylvania railroads. Altitude, 933 feet. Population, 2,115.

Piercy; post village in Jackson County.

Pigeon; creek, a right-hand branch of Tug Fork of Big Sandy River, a tributary to Ohio River, in Logan County.

Pigeon; creek, a very small right-hand tributary to Guyandot River in Wyoming County.

Pigeon; fork, a left-hand branch of Naul Creek in Braxton County.

Pigeon; post village in Roane County.

Pigeon; run, a right-hand branch of left fork of Steer Creek in Gilmer County.

Pigeon; run, a right-hand branch of Stony Creek, tributary to Greenbrier River, in Pocahontas County.

Pigeon; station in Logan County on the Norfolk and Western Railway and at junction of Pigeon Creek with Tug Fork of Big Sandy River. Altitude, 1,299 feet.

Pigeon Knob; summit in Lincoln County. Altitude, 1,354 feet.

Pigeon Roost; a summit in Wayne County. Altitude, 1,105 feet.

Pigeon Roost; branch, a small right-hand tributary to Spruce Fork of Little Coal River in Logan County.

Pigeon Roost; creek, a left-hand branch of Big Ugly Creek, a tributary to Guyandot River in Lincoln County.

Pigeon Roost; fork, a small left-hand branch of Lower Sleith Fork in Braxton County.

Pigeon Roost; fork, a small left-hand branch of Right Fork of Stone Coal Creek in Upshur County.

Pigeon Roost; fork, a small, indirect left-hand tributary to Blue Creek, a branch of Elk River, in Kanawha County.

Pigeon Roost; fork, a right-hand branch of Lick Creek, a tributary to Little Coal River, in Boone County.

Pike; post village in Ritchie County.

Pilot; triangulation station on Great Flat Top Mountain on boundary line between Wyoming and Mercer counties.

Pinch; creek, a small left-hand tributary to Elk River in Kanawha County.

Pinch Gut; creek, a small right-hand tributary to Glade Creek, a branch of New River, in Raleigh County.

Pine; creek, a left-hand tributary to Island Creek, a branch of Guyandot River, in Logan County.

Pine; run, a right-hand branch of Indian Fork in Gilmer County.

Pine; run, a small right-hand tributary to Peter Creek, a branch of Gauley River, in Nicholas County.

Pinebluff; village in Harrison County.

Pine Glade; run, a small right-hand tributary to Gauley River in Webster County.

Pinegrove; post village in Wetzel County on the Baltimore and Ohio Railroad.

Pine Grove; run, a small right-hand tributary to Williams River in Webster County.
Pineville; post village in Wyoming County.
Piney; creek, a left-hand branch of New River in Raleigh County.
Piney; creek, a small right-hand branch of Meadow River, a tributary to Gauley River, in Greenbrier and Nicholas counties.
Piney; fork, a left-hand branch of Fishing Creek in Wetzel County.
Piney; post village in Wetzel County on the Ohio Central Lines. Altitude, 1,120 feet.
Piney; run, a right-hand branch of Pritchett Creek in Marion County.
Piney Mount; triangulation station in Cabell County. Altitude, 1,115 feet.
Piney Swamp; run, a small right-hand tributary to North Branch of Potomac River in Mineral County.
Pink; post village in Calhoun County.
Pinkerton; knob in Third Hill Mountain in Berkeley County. Elevation, 1,700 feet.
Pinnacle; creek, a left-hand branch of Guyandot River in Wyoming County.
Pinnacle; hill in Mercer County.
Pinnacle; triangulation station in Allegheny Front in Mineral County. Altitude, 3,827 feet.
Pinoak; post village in Mercer County.
Pioneer; post village in Marshall County.
Pious; mountain ridge in Morgan County. Elevation, 800 feet.
Piper; fork, a small right-hand tributary to Crooked Fork in Braxton County.
Pipestem; creek, a small left-hand tributary to New River in Summers County.
Pipestem; post village in Summers County.
Pipestem Knob; summit in Mercer County.
Pisgah; mount, a summit in Clay County. Altitude, 1,683 feet.
Pisgah; post village in Preston County.
Pisgah; run, a very small left-hand tributary to Elk River, a branch of Kanawha River, in Clay County.
Pittman; post village in Fayette County.
Plankcabin; creek, a small left-hand branch of Second Creek, a tributary to Greenbrier River, in Monroe County.
Plant; post village in Lewis County.
Plantation; fork, a left-hand tributary to O'Brien Fork in Braxton County.
Plantation; fork, a head fork of Right Fork of Steer Creek in Braxton County.
Pleasant; creek, a left-hand branch of Tygart Valley River in Taylor County.
Pleasant; run, a small left-hand tributary to Left Fork of Middle Fork of Tygart Valley River in Randolph County.
Pleasant; run, a small left-hand tributary to Shavers Fork of Cheat River in Randolph County.
Pleasantdale; post village in Hampshire County.
Pleasanthill; post village in Preston County.
Pleasant Retreat; post village in Clay County.
Pleasantrun; post village in Tucker County.
Pleasants; county, situated in the northwestern part of the State, bordering on the Ohio River. Area, 142 square miles. Population, 9,341—white, 9,335; negro, 6; foreign born, 83. County seat, Saint Marys. The mean magnetic declination in 1900 was 2°. The mean annual rainfall is 40 to 50 inches, and the mean annual temperature 50° to 55°. The county is traversed by the Ohio River Railroad.
Pleasants; post village in Pleasants County.
Pleasant Valley; town and post village in Marshall County. Population, 180.
Pleasantview; post village in Jackson County on the Baltimore and Ohio Railroad.

Pliny; post village in Putnam County.
Plum; fork, a right-hand branch of Grove Creek in Clay County.
Plum; post village in Tyler County.
Plum; run, a left-hand branch of Buffalo Creek in Marion County.
Plum; run, a right-hand branch of Tygart Valley River in Taylor County.
Plum Orchard; creek, a small right-hand branch of Paint Creek, a tributary to Kanawha River, in Fayette County.
Plummer; knob in Taylor County. Elevation, 1,500 feet.
Plummer; run, a right-hand branch of Booths Creek in Taylor County.
Pluto; post village in Raleigh County.
Plymah; branch, a right-hand branch of Twelvepole Creek in Wayne County.
Plymouth; post village in Putnam County on the Ohio Central Lines.
Poca; post village in Putnam County on the Ohio Central Lines. Altitude, 573 feet.
Poca; river, a small left-hand tributary to Ohio River rising in Roane County.
Pocahontas; county, situated in the eastern part of the State. Its surface is mountainous, consisting of a broken plateau, deeply dissected. It is drained by Greenbrier River. Area, 858 square miles. Population, 8,572—white, 7,947; negro, 625; foreign born, 345. County seat, Marlington. The mean magnetic declination in 1900 was 2° 5′. The mean annual rainfall is 50 to 60 inches, and the mean annual temperature 45° to 50°.
Pocotaligo; post village in Kanawha County.
Pocotaligo; river, a right-hand branch of Kanawha River in Putnam, Kanawha, and Roane counties.
Pocosin; fork, a small right-hand branch of Rich Creek, a tributary to Bluestone River.
Poindexter; branch, a small left-hand tributary to Hurricane Creek, a branch of Kanawha River, in Putnam County.
Point; mountain, a short ridge in Greenbrier County. Altitude, 3,500 feet.
Point; mountain, a broken, mountainous range in Webster and Randolph counties.
Point; mountain, a short ridge in Greenbrier and Pocahontas counties.
Point; mountain, a short ridge between Back Fork of Elk River and Elk River in Webster County.
Point; run, a left-hand branch of Little Wheeling Creek in Ohio County.
Point Lick; fork, a left-hand branch of Campbell Creek, a tributary to Kanawha River, in Kanawha County.
Point Mountain; run, a small left-hand tributary to Back Fork of Elk River in Webster County.
Point Pleasant; county seat of Mason County on the Baltimore and Ohio and the Ohio Central railroads. Altitude, 563 feet. Population, 1,934.
Points; post village in Hampshire County.
Pointy Knob; summit in Tucker County. Altitude, 4,286 feet.
Polandale; post village in Wood County.
Polard; post village in Tyler County.
Polemic; run, a small left-hand tributary to Little Birch River in Braxton County.
Poley Ridge; short spur west of Greenbrier River in Greenbrier County. Altitude, 2,500 feet.
Pollock; mountain, a summit in Greenbrier County. Altitude, 3,900 feet.
Pompeys Knob; summit in Webster County north of Gauley River.
Pond; fork, a small left-hand branch of Middle Fork of Blue Creek, a tributary to Elk River, in Kanawha County.
Pond; fork, a right-hand head fork of Little Coal River, a branch of Coal River, in Boone County.
Pond Gap; height in Kanawha County.
Pondgap; post village in Kanawha County.

Pond Lick; creek, a small left-hand tributary to Howards Creek, a branch of Greenbrier River, in Greenbrier County.
Pondlick; post village in Mason County on the West Virginia Central and Pittsburg Railway.
Pond Mill; run, a small left-hand tributary to North Fork of Potomac River in Pendleton County.
Pond Range; short ridge in the central part of Pendleton County. Altitude, 2,500 to 3,000 feet.
Pond Trace; branch, a very small left-hand branch of Right Fork of Twelvepole Creek, a tributary to Ohio River, in Logan County.
Pool; post village in Nicholas County.
Poplar; creek, a small left-hand tributary to Birch River, a branch of Elk River, in Nicholas County.
Poplar; fork, a small left-hand tributary to Kanawha River in Putnam County.
Poplar; post village in Webster County on the Baltimore and Ohio Railroad.
Poplar Lick; small left-hand tributary to Left Fork of Steer Creek in Gilmer County.
Poppa; post village in Wayne County.
Porter; post village in Clay County on the Charleston, Clendennin and Sutton and the Porters Creek and Gauley railroads.
Porter Knob; summit in Cabell County. Altitude, 1,252 feet.
Porter Knob; summit in Wayne County. Altitude, 1,407 feet.
Porters; branch, a very small left-hand tributary to Kanawha River in Kanawha County.
Porters; creek, a left-hand tributary to Elk River in Clay County.
Porters Falls; post village in Wetzel County on the Baltimore and Ohio Railroad.
Portersville; post village in Lincoln County.
Porterwood; post village in Tucker County on the West Virginia Central and Pittsburg Railway.
Posey; run, a small right-hand branch of Oil Creek in Braxton County.
Pot; branch, a small left-hand tributary to Trace Fork of Davis Creek, a branch of Kanawha River, in Kanawha County.
Potato; branch, a very small right-hand tributary to Laurel Creek, a branch of Coal River, in Boone County.
Potato; hill, a summit on boundary line between Raleigh and Fayette counties. Altitude, 3,256 feet.
Potato; hill, a summit in Webster County.
Potato Hill; run, a small left-hand tributary to Back Fork of Elk River in Webster County.
Potato Hole Knob; summit in Webster County.
Potomac; river, heading in the northeastern part of the State, in two branches, North and South. North Branch heads near Fairfax Stone and flows northeast, forming a part of the north boundary of the State. After its junction with South Branch, some miles below Cumberland, it continues along the north boundary to Harpers Ferry, the easternmost point of the State.
Potomac; village in Ohio County.
Pound; fork, a very small right-hand branch of Fourmile Creek, a tributary to Guyandot River, in Lincoln County.
Pound Mill; branch, a very small right-hand tributary to Big Huff Creek, a branch of Guyandot River, in Logan County.
Pound Mill; run, a small left-hand tributary to Valley River in Randolph County.
Powell; branch, a small left-hand tributary to Spruce Fork of Little Coal River, a branch of Coal River, in Boone County.

Powell; creek, a small left-hand tributary to Birch River, a branch of Elk River, in Nicholas County.
Powell; fork, a small left-hand tributary to Leatherwood Fork of Elk River in Webster County.
Powell; mountains, a short ridge in Nicholas County. Its highest peak is 2,316 feet.
Powell Knob; summit in Gilmer County. Altitude, 1,460 feet.
Powells; post village in Marion County on the Baltimore and Ohio Railroad.
Powellton; fork, a right-hand branch of Armstrong Creek, a tributary to Kanawha River, in Fayette County.
Powellton; town in Fayette County on the Powellton and Pocahontas Railway and on Powellton Fork of Kanawha River. Population, 503. Altitude, 904 feet.
Powers; post village in Wood County.
Powhatan; post village in McDowell County on the Norfolk and Western Railway and on South Fork of Elkhorn Creek.
Powley; creek, a small right-hand tributary to Greenbrier River in Summers County.
Pratt; post village in Kanawha County, on the Chesapeake and Ohio Railway.
Press Kincaid; branch, a very small right-hand branch of Loop Creek, a tributary to Kanawha River, in Fayette County.
Preston; county, situated in the northern part of the State on the Allegheny Plateau, here not greatly dissected, and having an average elevation of about 3,000 feet. Area, 671 square miles. Population, 22,727—white, 22,565; negro, 162; foreign born, 482. County seat, Kingwood. The mean magnetic declination in 1900 was 3° 30′. The mean annual rainfall is 40 to 50 inches, and the mean annual temperature 45° to 50°. The county is traversed by the West Virginia Northern and the Baltimore and Ohio railroads.
Preston; post village in Wayne County.
Prestonia; post village in Webster County.
Pretty Ridge; mountains in Wyoming County.
Pretty Ridge; short spur of North Fork Mountain in Pendleton County. Elevation, 2,000 feet.
Price; branch, a very small right-hand tributary to Little Coal River, a branch of Coal River, in Boone County.
Price; branch, a very small right-hand tributary to Beech Fork of Twelvepole Creek, a branch of Ohio River, in Wayne County.
Price; fork, a small left-hand tributary to Hominy Creek, a branch of Gauley River, in Nicholas and Greenbrier counties.
Pride; post village in Mercer County.
Priestly; post village in Lincoln County.
Prince; post village in Fayette County on the Chesapeake and Ohio Railway and on New River. Altitude, 1,188 feet.
Princeton; county seat of Mercer County. Altitude, 2,450 feet.
Pringle; fork, a small left-hand tributary to Right Fork of Stone Coal Creek in Upshur County.
Pringle; run, a small left-hand tributary to Cheat River in Preston County.
Pritchard; post village in Ritchie County.
Procious; post village in Clay County.
Proctor; post village in Wetzel County on the Baltimore and Ohio Railroad.
Proctors; creek, a small left-hand branch of Ohio River in Wetzel County.
Progress; post village in Braxton County.
Props; gap in Long Ridge, caused by a small right-hand branch of the South Branch of Potomac River, in Pendleton County.
Prospect Valley; village in Harrison County.

Prosperity; post village in Raleigh County.
Providence; post village in Jackson County.
Pruett; branch, a very small right-hand tributary to Dry Fork, a branch of Tug Fork of Big Sandy River, in McDowell County.
Pruntytown; village in Taylor County.
Pugh; post village in Webster County.
Pullman; post village in Ritchie County.
Puncheon Camp; branch, a very small right-hand branch of Blue Creek, a tributary to Elk River, in Kanawha County.
Purgitsville; post village in Hampshire County.
Pursley; post village in Tyler County.
Push; post village in Doddridge County.
Putnam; county situated in the western part of the State on the lower slopes of the Allegheny Plateau; it is traversed by Kanawha River, which drains it. Area, 353 square miles. Population, 17,330—white, 16,951; negro, 379; foreign born, 107. County seat near Winfield. The mean magnetic declination in 1900 was 1° 15'. The mean annual rainfall is 40 to 50 inches, and the mean annual temperature 50° to 55°. The county is traversed by the Kanawha and Michigan and the Chesapeake and Ohio railways.
Pyle; mountain, a short ridge west of Greenbrier River in Pocahontas County. Altitude, 2,500 to 3,275 feet, the latter being the height of one peak.
Pyles; fork, a small left-hand branch of Monongahela River in Monongalia County.
Quaker Knob; summit in Webster County. Altitude, 2,722 feet.
Queens; post village in Upshur County.
Queens Camp; fork, a small left-hand branch of Milam Creek, a tributary to East Fork of Twelvepole Creek, in Wayne County.
Queen Shoal; creek, a small left-hand tributary to Elk River in Clay County.
Queens Ridge; post village in Wayne County.
Queer; branch, a small left-hand tributary to Cranberry River in Webster County.
Quiet Dell; post village in Harrison County.
Quincy; post village in Kanawha County.
Quinnimont; post village in Fayette County on the Chesapeake and Ohio Railway and on New River. Altitude, 1,195 feet.
Racine; post village in Boone County. Altitude, 665 feet.
Racoon; creek, a small right-hand tributary to Teter Creek, a branch of Tygarts Valley River, in Barbour County.
Racoon; creek, a right-hand tributary to Valley River in Preston County.
Raccoon; creek, a small right-hand branch of Beech Fork of Twelvepole Creek, a tributary to Ohio River, in Wayne County.
Racy; post village in Ritchie County.
Radnor; post village in Wayne County on the Norfolk and Western Railway.
Rafe; run, a very small left-hand tributary to Valley River in Randolph County.
Ragland; post village in Mingo County.
Raider; fork, a small left-hand tributary to Twenty Mile Creek in Nicholas County.
Raines; fork, a very small left-hand branch of Sycamore Creek, a tributary to Clear Fork of Coal River, in Raleigh County.
Raleigh; county, situated in the southern part of the State, on the Allegheny Plateau, here having an average elevation of 2,500 feet, and is not greatly dissected. It is drained by tributaries of the Kanawha and New rivers. Area, 560 square miles. Population, 12,436—white, 12,076; negro, 360; foreign born, 33. County seat, Beckley. The mean magnetic declination in 1900 was 1° 15'. The mean annual rainfall is 50 to 60 inches, and the mean annual temperature 50° to 55°.
Raleigh; post village of Raleigh County on the Chesapeake and Ohio Railway. Altitude, 2,440 feet.

Raleman; mountain, a short ridge in Pendleton County. Altitude, 3,000 feet.
Ralph; branch, a very small right-hand tributary to Clear Fork, a branch of Guyandot River, in Wyoming County.
Ralston; run, a small left-hand tributary to Valley River in Randolph County.
Ramsey; post village in Fayette County.
Rams Horn; spur of Allegheny Front in Pocahontas County.
Randall; post village in Monongalia County on the Baltimore and Ohio Railroad.
Randolph; county, situated in the eastern part of the State. The surface is entirely mountainous, the western part lying on the Allegheny Plateau, and the eastern part consisting of heavy parallel ridges, trending northeast and southwest, separated by limestone valleys. It is drained by tributaries to the North Branch of the Potomac and to the Monongahela River. Area, 1,086 square miles. Population, 17,670—white, 17,149; negro, 519; foreign born, 698. County seat, Elkins. The mean magnetic declination in 1900 was 2° 30′. The mean annual rainfall is 50 to 60 inches, and the mean annual temperature 45° to 50°. The county is traversed by the West Virginia Central and Pittsburg Railway.
Ranger; post village in Lincoln County.
Ranger; run, a left-hand branch of West Virginia Fork of Dunkard Creek in Monongalia County.
Ratcliff; run, a small left-hand tributary to Buckhannon River in Upshur County.
Rattlesnake Draft; very small right-hand tributary to Paint Creek, a branch of Kanawha River, in Fayette County.
Ravenrock; post village in Pleasants County on the Baltimore and Ohio Railroad.
Ravens Eye; post village in Fayette County.
Ravenswood; town in Jackson County. Population, 1,074. Altitude, 544 feet.
Raymond; run, a right-hand tributary of North Fork of Fishing Creek in Wetzel County.
Raymond City; post village in Putnam County on the Ohio Central Lines.
Read; fork, a left-hand tributary to Grass Run in Gilmer County.
Reader; creek, a right-hand branch of Fishing Creek in Wetzel County.
Reader; post village in Wetzel County on the Baltimore and Ohio Railroad.
Real Gap; height in Little Mountain in Grant County.
Red; creek, a right-hand tributary to Dry Fork of Cheat River in Tucker and Randolph counties.
Redbird; post village in Raleigh County.
Red Bridge; run, a small left-hand tributary to Shavers Fork of Cheat River in Randolph County.
Redcreek; post village in Tucker County.
Redhill; post village in Wood County.
Redhouse Shoals; post village in Putnam County on the Ohio Central Lines.
Redknob; post village in Roane County.
Red Lick; mountain, a short ridge in Pocahontas County. The altitude of one peak is 4,671 feet.
Red Lick; small left-hand tributary to Oil Creek in Lewis County.
Redmud; post village in Mason County.
Red Oak; creek, a small right-hand tributary to North Branch of Potomac River in Grant County.
Red Oak Knob; summit in Webster County. Altitude, 3,750 feet.
Red Oak Ridge; mountains in Mercer County.
Red River; fork, a small left-hand branch of Fourmile Creek, a tributary to Guyandot River, in Lincoln County.
Redstar; station in Fayette County on the Chesapeake and Ohio Railway and on Dunloup Creek, a tributary to New River.
Red Sulpher Springs; post village in Monroe County.

Reed; creek, a left-hand tributary to South Branch of Potomac River in Pendleton County.
Reeds; creek, a small left-hand tributary to North Fork of Potomac River in Pendleton County.
Reedsville; post village in Preston County.
Reedy; branch, a very small right-hand tributary to Guyandot River in Wyoming County.
Reedy; branch, a small right-hand tributary to Clear Fork, a branch of Guyandot River, in Wyoming County.
Reedy; town in Roane County on the Baltimore and Ohio Railroad. Population, 300.
Reedyripple; post village in Wirt County.
Reedyville; post village in Roane County.
Reeses Mill; post village in Mineral County.
Reid; post village in Cabell County.
Removal; post village in Webster County.
Rena; post village in Putnam County.
Rend; post village in Fayette County.
Renicks Valley; post village in Greenbrier County, on the Chesapeake and Ohio Railway.
Renius; post village in Wood County.
Replete; post village in Webster County.
Reuben; right-hand branch of Pritchett Creek in Marion County.
Revel; post village in Gilmer County.
Revere; post village in Gilmer County.
Rex; post village in Putnam County.
Rezrode; post village in Pendleton County.
Reynolds; branch, a very small right-hand tributary to Kanawha River in Kanawha County.
Reynoldsville; post village in Harrison County.
Rhine; fork, a head tributary to Youghiogheny River in Preston County.
Rice; post village in Wayne County.
Rices; run, a left-hand branch of Garrison Run in Ohio County.
Rich; branch, a small left-hand tributary to Pond Fork of Little Coal River in Boone County.
Rich; creek, a very small left-hand tributary to Guyandot River in Wyoming County.
Rich; creek, a small left-hand tributary to Guyandot River, a branch of Ohio River, in Logan County.
Rich; creek, a left-hand tributary to Bluestone River in Mercer County.
Rich; creek, a small left-hand branch of East Fork of Twelvepole Creek, a tributary to Ohio River, in Wayne County.
Rich; creek, a small right-hand tributary to New River in Monroe County.
Rich; knob in Cabell County. Altitude, 1,047 feet.
Rich; mountain, a ridge lying west of Valley River in the northwestern part of Randolph County.
Rich; mountain, a ridge lying east of Laurel Fork of Cheat River in the eastern part of Randolph County.
Rich; post village in Logan County.
Richardson; post village in Calhoun County.
Rich Knob; summit in Greenbrier County. Altitude, 3,848 feet.
Richlands; post village in Greenbrier County.
Rich Mountain; post village in Randolph County.
Rich Patch; creek, a small left-hand tributary to Howards Creek, a branch of Greenbrier River, in Greenbrier County.

Richwood; post village in Nicholas County, on the Baltimore and Ohio Railroad.
Richwood; run, a right-hand branch of South Fork of Fishing Creek in Wetzel County.
Riddle; branch, a very small right-hand tributary to Big Huff Creek, a branch of Guyandot River, in Logan County.
Riddleboch; run, a small right-hand tributary to South Fork of Potomac River in Hardy County.
Ridersville; post village in Morgan County.
Ridge; post village in Morgan County.
Ridgedale; post village in Monongalia County on the Baltimore and Ohio Railroad.
Ridgeley; post village in Mineral County on the West Virginia Central and Pittsburg Railway.
Ridgeville; post village in Mineral County.
Ridgeway; village in Berkeley County on the Cumberland Valley Railroad.
Riffle; branch, an indirect right-hand tributary to Tommy Creek, a head fork of Guyandot River, in Raleigh County.
Riffle; run, a small right-hand tributary to Little Kanawha River in Braxton County.
Riffles; creek, a small right-hand tributary to Valley River in Randolph County.
Riggs; branch, a very small right-hand tributary to Kanawha River in Fayette County.
Rilla; post village in Calhoun County.
Rinehart; post village in Harrison County.
Riney; mountain in Cabell County. Altitude, 1,107 feet.
Ring; branch, a small right-hand tributary to Dry Fork, a branch of Tug Fork of Big Sandy River, in McDowell County.
Rio; post village in Hampshire County.
Ripley; county seat of Jackson County on the Baltimore and Ohio Railroad. Population, 579.
Rippon; post village in Jefferson County on the Norfolk and Western Railway. Altitude, 516 feet.
Rising Sun; branch, a small left-hand tributary to Little Bluestone Creek, a branch of Bluestone River, in Summers County.
Ritchie; county, situated in the western part of the State, near the foot of the Alleghany Plateau. Area, 457 square miles. Population, 18,901—white, 18,875; negro, 26; foreign born, 120; county seat, Harrisville. The mean magnetic declination in 1900 was 2°. The mean annual rainfall is 40 to 50 inches, and the mean annual temperature 50° to 55°. The county is traversed by the Baltimore and Ohio Railroad.
Ritter; post village in McDowell County at junction of upper Shannon Branch with Tug Fork of Big Sandy River.
River; fork, a left-hand tributary to Coal River in Boone County.
River; run, a left-hand branch of Tygart Valley River in Marion County.
River Laurel; branch, a very small left-hand tributary to Tug Fork of Big Sandy River in McDowell County.
River Road; run, a very small right-hand tributary to Greenbrier River in Summers County.
Riverside; post village in Kanawha County.
Riverton; post village in Pendleton County.
Rivesville; town in Marion County. Population, 164.
Roach; branch, a small left-hand tributary to West Fork, a branch of Pond Fork of Little Coal Creek, in Boone County.
Roach; post village in Cabell County.
Road; branch, a very small left-hand tributary to Big Ugly Creek, a branch of Guyandot River, in Lincoln County.

Road; branch, a small right-hand tributary to Cranberry River in Webster County.

Road; branch, a very small right-hand tributary to Little Huff Creek, a branch of Guyandot River, in Wyoming County.

Road; fork, a small left-hand tributary to Twentymile Creek, a branch of Gauley River, in Nicholas County.

Road; fork, a small left-hand branch of Peters Cave Fork of Horse Creek, a tributary to Little Coal River, in Lincoln County.

Road; fork, a left-hand tributary to Trace Fork of Mud River, a branch of Guyandot River, in Lincoln County.

Road; fork, a small left-hand branch of Big Huff Creek, a tributary to Guyandot River, in Wyoming County.

Road; fork, a small left-hand tributary to Tug Fork of Big Sandy River in McDowell County.

Road; fork, a small left-hand tributary to Buffalo Creek, a branch of Elk River, in Clay and Nicholas counties.

Road; fork, a small right-hand branch of Seng Camp Creek, a tributary to Spruce Fork of Little Coal River, in Logan County.

Road; fork, a small right-hand branch of Fuqua Creek, a tributary to Coal River, in Lincoln County.

Road; fork, a small right-hand branch of Rock Camp Fork of Twentymile Creek, a tributary to Gauley River, in Nicholas and Clay counties.

Road; fork, a small right-hand branch of Left Fork of Witchers Creek, a tributary to Kanawha River, in Kanawha County.

Road; fork, a right-hand branch of Grove Creek in Clay County.

Road; run, a small left-hand branch of Oil Creek in Braxton County.

Road; run, a small right-hand tributary to Little Birch River in Braxton County.

Roane; county, situated in the western part of the State near the foot of the Alleghany Plateau. Area, 547 square miles. Population, 19,852—white, 19,820; negro, 32; foreign born, 52. County seat, Spencer. The mean magnetic declination in 1900 was 1° 30′. The mean annual rainfall is 40 to 50 inches, and the mean annual temperature 50° to 55°. The county is traversed by the Ohio River Railroad.

Roanoke; post village in Lewis County on the Baltimore and Ohio Railroad. Altitude, 1,053 feet.

Roaring; creek, a small left-hand tributary to Seneca Creek, a branch of North Fork of Potomac River, in Pendleton County.

Roaring; creek, a small right-hand branch of Valley River in Randolph County.

Roaring; plains, summit near the Allegheny Front, lying on the boundary line between Randolph and Pendleton counties.

Robbins; fork, a small left-hand branch of Spring Creek, a tributary to Greenbrier River, in Greenbrier County.

Roberts; post village in Doddridge County.

Roberts; run, a left-hand branch of Long Drain in Wetzel County.

Robertsburg; post village in Putnam County on the Ohio Central Lines.

Robertson; right-hand branch of Tygarts Valley River in Marion County.

Robinette; branch, a very small left-hand tributary to Guyandot River in Wyoming County.

Robinette; branch, a very small left-hand tributary to Buffalo Creek, a branch of Guyandot River, in Logan County.

Robinson; branch, a very small left-hand branch of Loop Creek, a tributary to Kanawha River, in Fayette County.

Robinson; creek, a small right-hand tributary to Pond Fork of Little Coal River, a branch of Coal River, in Boone County.

Robinson; fork, a left-hand tributary to Buffalo Creek, a branch of Elk River, in Nicholas and Clay counties.

Robinson; fork, a small left-hand tributary to Twentymile Creek, a branch of Gauley River, in Nicholas County.

Robinson; run, a left-hand branch of Monongahela River in Monongalia County.

Robinson; run, a small left-hand branch of the Right Fork of Holly River in Braxton County.

Robinson; run, a right-hand branch of Lunice Creek, a tributary to South Branch of Potomac River, in Grant County.

Robinson Gap; height in Grant County.

Robinsons Mill; post village in Wetzel County.

Robson; post village in Fayette County.

Rock; branch, a very small left-hand tributary to Piney Creek, a branch of New River, in Raleigh County.

Rock; branch, a small left-hand tributary to Beaver Creek, a branch of Piney Creek, in Raleigh County.

Rock; creek, a small right-hand tributary to Marsh Fork of Coal River in Raleigh County.

Rock; creek, a right-hand tributary to Little Coal River, a branch of Coal River, in Boone County.

Rock; post village in Mercer County.

Rock; run, a small left-hand tributary to Greenbrier River in Pocahontas County.

Rock; run, a right-hand branch of Sand Fork in Lewis County.

Rock Camp; branch, a small left-hand branch of Peter Creek, a tributary to Gauley River, in Nicholas County.

Rock Camp; creek, a small, indirect left-hand tributary to Indian Creek in Monroe County.

Rock Camp; fork, a right-hand branch of Twentymile Creek, a tributary to Gauley River, in Nicholas and Clay counties.

Rock Camp; fork, a right-hand branch of Bell Creek, a tributary to Gauley River, in Clay County.

Rock Camp; fork, a small right-hand branch of Blue Creek, a tributary to Elk River, in Kanawha County.

Rock Camp; mountain, a short ridge in Greenbrier County.

Rockcamp; post village in Monroe County.

Rock Camp; run, a small left-hand branch of Spring Creek, a tributary to Greenbrier River, in Greenbrier County.

Rock Camp; run, a small right-hand tributary to Elk River in Braxton County.

Rock Camp; run, a very small right-hand tributary to Gauley River in Nicholas County.

Rock Camp; run, a left-hand branch of Tanner Creek in Gilmer County.

Rock Camp Knob; summit in Greenbrier County.

Rock Castle; creek, a small right-hand branch of Guyandot River in Wyoming County.

Rockcastle; post village in Jackson County.

Rockcave; post village in Upshur County.

Rockford; post village in Harrison County.

Rockgap; post village in Morgan County.

Rock House; branch, a very small left-hand tributary to Gauley River in Webster County.

Rockhouse; branch, a small left-hand tributary to Tug River in McDowell County.

Rockhouse; branch, a very small left-hand tributary to Guyandot River in Wyoming County.

Rockhouse; branch, a small left-hand branch of Road Fork, a tributary to Trace Fork of Mud River, in Lincoln County.

Rockhouse; branch, a small left-hand tributary to Guyandot River, a branch of Ohio River, in Logan County.

Rockhouse; branch, a small right-hand tributary to Elkhorn Creek in McDowell County.

Rockhouse; branch, a very small right-hand tributary to Island Creek, a branch of Guyandot River, in Logan County.

Rockhouse; creek, a small left-hand branch of Mud Fork of Guyandot River, a tributary to Ohio River, in Logan County.

Rockhouse; creek, a very small left-hand tributary to Spruce Fork of Little Coal River in Logan County.

Rockhouse; creek, a small right-hand branch of Clear Fork, a tributary to Coal River, in Raleigh County.

Rockhouse; fork, a small left-hand branch of Big Hart Creek, a tributary to Guyandot River, in Logan County.

Rockhouse; fork, a small left-hand tributary to Clear Fork of Guyandot River in Wyoming County.

Rockhouse; fork, a small left-hand tributary to Marsh Fork of Coal River in Raleigh County.

Rockhouse; fork, a right-hand tributary to Pigeon Creek, a branch of Tug Fork of Big Sandy River, in Logan County.

Rockhouse; fork, a head fork of Dingus Run, a tributary to Guyandot River, in Logan County.

Rockland; post village in Hardy County on the Chesapeake and Ohio Railway.

Rocklick; branch, a very small right-hand tributary to Pond Fork of Little Coal River in Boone County.

Rock Lick; a small left-hand branch of Arbuckle Creek, a tributary to New River, in Fayette County.

Rock Lick; a small right-hand tributary to Williams River in Webster County.

Rocklick; fork; a small left-hand tributary to Leatherwood Creek, a small branch of Elk River, in Clay County.

Rocklick; post village in Marshall County.

Rocklick; run, a right-hand branch of Buffalo Creek in Marion County.

Rock Narrow; branch, a very small left-hand tributary to Tug Fork of Big Sandy River in McDowell County.

Rockoak; post village in Hardy County.

Rockport; post village in Wood County.

Rockruffle; run, a right-hand tributary of Little Kanawha River in Gilmer County.

Rocksdale; post village in Calhoun County.

Rockview; post village in Wyoming County.

Rockville; post village in Preston County.

Rocky; fork, a left-hand branch of Pocotaligo River, a tributary to Kanawha River, in Kanawha County.

Rocky; fork, a left-hand tributary to Indian Fork in Gilmer and Lewis counties.

Rocky; run, a very small left-hand branch of Big Laurel Creek, a tributary to Cherry River, in Greenbrier County.

Rocky; run, a small left-hand tributary to Buckhannon River in Upshur County.

Rocky; run, a small right-hand tributary to Williams River in Webster County.

Rocky; run, a small right-hand branch of Thorn Run, a tributary to South Branch of Potomac River, in Pendleton County.

Rockyfork; post village in Kanawha County.

Rocky Knob; summit in Putnam County. Altitude, 1,170 feet.

Rodamers; post village in Preston County.

Roderfield; post village in McDowell County on the Norfork and Western Railway and on Tug Fork of Big Sandy River.
Rodgers; mountain, a summit in Pocahontas County. Altitude, 3,176 feet.
Roe; post village in Kanawha County.
Rohr; post village in Preston County.
Roller; fork, a small right-hand branch of Kiah Fork, a tributary to Twelvepole Creek, in Wayne County.
Rollins; post village in Mason County.
Rome; post village in Kanawha County.
Romines Mills; post village in Harrison County.
Romney; county seat of Hampshire County on the Baltimore and Ohio Railroad. Population, 580.
Romont; post village in Fayette County.
Ronceverte; town in Greenbrier County on Greenbrier River and on the Chesapeake and Ohio Railway. Population, 968. Altitude, 1,663 feet.
Ronda; post village in Kanawha County.
Roneyspoint; post village in Ohio County on the Baltimore and Ohio Railroad. Altitude, 829 feet.
Roneyspoint; run, a right-hand branch of Little Wheeling Creek in Ohio County.
Rook; branch, a very small right-hand tributary to Left Fork of Mud River in Lincoln County.
Roose; creek, a very small left-hand tributary to Mud River, a branch of Guyandot River, in Cabell County.
Rorebagh; run, a small right-hand tributary to South Fork of Potomac River in Hardy County.
Rosbysrock; post village in Marshall County. Altitude, 787 feet.
Rose; branch, a very small right-hand tributary to Little Huff Creek, a branch of Guyandot River, in Wyoming County.
Rosedale; post village in Braxton County.
Rosen; creek, a small left-hand tributary to North Fork of Greenbrier River in Pocahontas County.
Roseville; post village in Fayette County.
Rosina; post village in Kanawha County.
Ross; post village in Wetzel County.
Ross; run, a small right-hand tributary to Salt Lick Fork of Little Kanawha River in Braxton County.
Rough; run, a small right-hand tributary to Cranberry River in Webster County.
Rough; run, a small right-hand tributary to South Fork of Potomac River in Pendleton County.
Rough; run, a small right-hand tributary to Left Fork of Middle Fork of Valley River in Randolph County.
Rough Gap; run, a very small right-hand tributary to Elk River in Randolph County.
Round Bottom; branch, a very small right-hand tributary to Coal River, a branch of Kanawha River, in Boone County.
Roundbottom; post village in Wayne County on the Baltimore and Ohio Railroad.
Roundknob; post village in Putnam County.
Round Knob; summit in Pocahontas County.
Round Knob; summit in Raleigh County.
Round Knob; summit in Randolph County.
Rover; post village in Wirt County.
Rowlesburg; town in Preston County on the Baltimore and Ohio Railroad. Altitude, 1,402 feet. Population, 652.

Roxalana; post village in Roane County.
Roy; post village in Roane County.
Rubens; branch, a left-hand branch of Buck Fork of Twelvepole Creek in Wayne County.
Rucker; branch, a very small right-hand tributary to Little Coal River, a branch of Coal River, in Boone County.
Ruckman; post village in Hampshire County.
Ruddle; post village in Pendleton County.
Ruffner; branch, a small left-hand tributary to Little Sandy Creek, a small branch of Elk River, in Kanawha County.
Ruffner; branch, a very small right-hand tributary to Kanawha River in Kanawha County.
Rugger; run, a small left-hand tributary to Right Fork of Buckhannon River in Upshur County.
Rum; creek, a small right-hand tributary to Guyandot River in Logan County.
Rupert; post village in Greenbrier County.
Ruraldale; post village in Upshur County.
Rush; creek, a very small left-hand tributary to Kanawha River in Kanawha County.
Rush; fork, a small right-hand tributary to Elk River in Braxton County.
Rush; run, a small left-hand tributary to Monongahela River in Lewis County.
Rush; run, a very small left-hand tributary to New River in Fayette County.
Rush Knob; summit in Lewis County. Altitude, 1,642 feet.
Rushrun; post village in Fayette County on the Chesapeake and Ohio Railway and on New River.
Rushville; post village in Roane County.
Rusk; post village in Ritchie County.
Russell; creek, a very small left-hand tributary to Guyandot River, a branch of Ohio River, in Cabell County.
Russellville; post village in Fayette County. Altitude, 1,092 feet.
Russet; post village in Calhoun County.
Ruth; post village in Kanawha County.
Rutherford; post village in Ritchie County on the Cairo and Kanawha Valley Railroad.
Ryan; post village in Roane County.
Rye; post village in Wood County.
Rymer; village in Marion County.
Sago; post village in Upshur County on the Baltimore and Ohio Railroad. Altitude, 1,425 feet.
Saint Albans; town in Kanawha County on the Chesapeake and Ohio Railroad. Population, 816. Altitude, 593 feet.
Saint Clara; post village in Doddridge County.
Saint Cloud; post village in Monongalia County.
Saint George; town in Tucker County. Population, 152.
Saint Joseph; post village in Marshall County.
Saint Leo; post village in Monongalia County.
Saint Marys; county seat of Pleasants County on the Baltimore and Ohio Railroad. Population, 825.
Salama; post village in Pleasants County on the Baltimore and Ohio Railroad.
Salem; town in Harrison County on the Baltimore and Ohio Railroad. Population, 746.
Sally; run, a small right-hand tributary to Gauley River in Webster County.
Salt Block; run, a small right-hand tributary to Left Fork of Right Fork of Buckhannon River in Randolph County.

Salt Lick; branch, a very small left-hand tributary to New River in Fayette County.
Salt Lick; fork, a left-hand branch of Little Kanawha River in Braxton County.
Salt Lick; run, a small left-hand tributary to Leading Creek in Randolph County.
Saltlick Bridge; post village in Braxton County.
Salt Rock; post village in Cabell County on the Chesapeake and Ohio Railway.
Salt Sulphur; branch, a very small left-hand tributary to Guyandot River, a branch of Ohio River, in Lincoln County.
Salt Sulphur Springs; post village in Monroe County.
Saltwell; village in Harrison County.
Sam; branch, a very small right-hand tributary to Guyandot River in Wyoming County.
Sam; branch, a small right-hand branch of Big Clear Creek, a tributary to Meadow River, in Greenbrier County.
Samaria; post village in Marion County.
Sammy; run, a left-hand branch of Sand Fork in Lewis County.
Samp; post village in Webster County.
Sam Ridge; short spur between Big Clear Creek and its branch, Sam Creek, in Greenbrier County.
Sancho; post village in Tyler County.
Sand; branch, a very small left-hand tributary to Big Huff Creek, a branch of Guyandot River, in Logan County.
Sand; creek, a very small right-hand tributary to Guyandot River, a branch of Ohio River, in Lincoln County.
Sand; fork, a small left-hand tributary to Middle Fork of Mud River, a branch of Guyandot River, in Lincoln County.
Sand; fork, a small right-hand branch of Paint Creek, a tributary to Kanawha River, in Raleigh County.
Sand; fork, a right-hand branch of West Fork of Monongahela River in Lewis County.
Sand; fork, a small right-hand branch of Buffalo Creek, a tributary to Elk River, in Clay County.
Sand; fork, a right-hand branch of Little Kanawha River in Lewis and Gilmer counties. It rises in Lewis County and flows southwestward to its junction with Sand Fork in Gilmer County.
Sand; river, a small right-hand tributary to Gauley River in Webster County.
Sand; run, a very small right-hand tributary to Elk River, a large branch of Kanawha River, in Kanawha County.
Sand; run, a small right-hand tributary to French Creek in Upshur County.
Sand; run, a right-hand head fork of Laurel Fork of French Creek in Upshur County.
Sanders; post village in Wyoming County.
Sandfork; post village in Gilmer County situated on Little Kanawha River.
Sandhill; post village in Marshall County.
Sand Lick; branch, a small left-hand tributary to Big Huff Creek, a branch of Guyandot River, in Logan County.
Sandlick; branch, a very small left-hand tributary to Guyandot River, a branch of Ohio River, in Logan County.
Sand Lick; branch, a very small right-hand branch of Blue Creek, a tributary to Elk River, in Kanawha County.
Sand Lick; branch, a very small right-hand tributary to Bluestone River in Mercer County.
Sand Lick; creek, a right-hand branch of Marsh Fork of Coal River in Raleigh County.

Sand Lick; creek, a small left-hand tributary to Tug Fork of Big Sandy River in McDowell County.
Sandlick; fork, a left-hand branch of Laurel Creek, a tributary to Coal River, in Boone County.
Sandlick; run, a right-hand branch of Right Fork of Simpson Creek in Taylor County.
Sand Ridge; hill west of the South Branch of Potomac River in Pendleton County.
Sandrun; post village in Upshur County.
Sandusky; post village in Tyler County.
Sandy; creek, a small left-hand branch of Ohio River in Jackson County.
Sandy; creek, a right-hand branch of Valley River formed by two forks, Little and Big Sandy creeks, forming boundary line between Taylor and Barbour and between Barbour and Preston counties.
Sandy; post village in Monongalia County on the Baltimore and Ohio Railroad.
Sandy Huff; branch, a small right-hand tributary to Tug Fork of Big Sandy River in McDowell County.
Sandy Huff; post village in McDowell County.
Sandy Ridge; short ridge in Pendleton County. Altitude, 2,500 to 3,000 feet.
Sandy Ridge; mountains in Hampshire County.
Sandy Ridge; short range east of Greenbrier River in Pocahontas County.
Sandyville; post village in Jackson County, on the Baltimore and Ohio Railroad.
Sang; run, a left-hand head fork of Laurel Fork of French Creek in Upshur County.
Sangamore; fork, a small right-hand branch of Open Fork of Bell Creek, a tributary to Gauley River, in Clay County.
Sanoma; post village in Wirt County.
Santifee; post village in Summers County.
Sapp; run, a right-hand branch of Booths Creek in Marion County.
Sarah; post village in Cabell County.
Sardis; post village in Harrison County.
Sassafras; post village in Mason County.
Sattes; post village in Kanawha County on the Ohio Central Lines.
Saulsbury; post village in Wood County.
Saulsbury; run, a small left-hand branch of Deer Creek, a tributary to North Fork of Greenbrier River, in Pocahontas County.
Saulsville; post village in Wyoming County.
Saunders; creek, a very small left-hand tributary to Mud River, a branch of Guyandot River, in Cabell County.
Savage; post village in Mineral County.
Savanah; post village in Greenbrier County.
Saw Mill; run, a small left-hand tributary to Buckhannon River in Upshur County.
Sawyer; run, a small left-hand tributary to Back Fork of Elk River in Webster County.
Saxon; post village in Raleigh County.
Scab; run, a right-hand branch of Tygarts Valley River in Taylor County.
Scary; creek, a very small left-hand tributary to Middle Fork of Mud River in Lincoln County.
Scary; creek, a small left-hand tributary to Kanawha River in Putnam County.
Scary; post village in Putnam County on the Chesapeake and Ohio Railway. Altitude, 591 feet.
Scheidler; run, a right-hand branch of Little Fishing Creek in Wetzel County.
Scherr; post village in Grant County.
Schilling; post village in Roane County.
Schoolcraft; run, a small left-hand tributary to Left Fork of Middle Fork of Tygarts Valley River, in Randolph County.

Schoolhouse; branch, a very small right-hand tributary to Pocotaligo River, a branch of Kanawha River, in Kanawha County.
Schoolhouse; branch, a small right-hand tributary to Twomile Creek, a branch of Guyandot River, in Lincoln County.
Schoolhouse; branch, a very small left-hand tributary to Clear Fork, a branch of Guyandot River, in Wyoming County.
Schoolhouse; fork, a small, indirect left-hand tributary to Blue Creek, a branch of Elk River, in Kanawha County.
Schoolhouse; post village in Jackson County on the Baltimore and Ohio Railroad.
Schoolhouse; run, a left-hand tributary to Indian Fork in Gilmer County.
Schoonover Knob; summit in Clay County. Altitude, 1,595 feet.
Schultz; post village in Pleasants County.
Scidmore; run, a very small left-hand tributary to Elk River in Braxton County.
Scott; branch, a very small left-hand tributary to Fields Creek, a branch of Kanawha River, in Kanawha County.
Scott; branch, a very small left-hand tributary to Glade Creek, a branch of New River, in Raleigh County.
Scott; fork, a left-hand fork of Westfall Fork of Cedar Creek in Braxton County.
Scott; post village in Wood County on the Chesapeake and Ohio Railway. Altitude, 694 feet.
Scott; run, a left-hand branch of Buffalo Creek in Brooke County.
Scottdale; post village in Marion County.
Scott Depot; post village in Putnam County.
Scotts; branch, a small left-hand tributary to Rich Creek, a branch of New River, in Monroe County.
Scotts; run, a left-hand branch of Miracle Run in Monongalia County.
Scrabble; creek, a small right-hand tributary to Gauley River in Fayette County.
Scrafford; post village in Monongalia County.
Scratchers; run, a left-hand branch of Prickett Run in Marion County.
Seaman; post village in Roane County on the Baltimore and Ohio Railroad.
Second; branch, a left-hand branch of Hurricane Creek in Putnam County.
Second; creek, a left-hand branch of Greenbrier River in Monroe and Greenbrier counties.
Second Big; run, a small right-hand tributary to Oil Creek in Lewis County.
Secondcreek; post village in Monroe County.
Sedalia; post village in Doddridge County.
Sedan; post village in Hampshire County.
See All; summit in Pocahontas County.
Seebert; post village in Pocahontas County, on the Chesapeake and Ohio Railway.
See Camp; gap in hills caused by Schoolcraft Run, a small tributary to Monongahela River, in Randolph County.
Seemly; post village in Grant County.
Selbyville; post village in Upshur County.
Sell; post village in Preston County.
Senate; branch, a right-hand branch of Lilly Fork of Buffalo Creek, a tributary to Elk River, in Clay County.
Seneca; creek, a left-hand tributary to North Fork of Potomac River in Pendleton County.
Seneca; creek, a right-hand branch of North Fork of Potomac River in Pendleton County.
Seneca; town in Monongalia County. Population, 723.
Seng; branch, a very small left-hand tributary to Mulberry Fork of Loop Creek, a branch of Kanawha River, in Fayette County.
Seng; creek, a very small right-hand tributary to Coal River in Boone County.

Seng; fork, a small right-hand tributary to Hopkins Fork of Laurel Creek, a branch of Coal River, in Boone County.
Seng; post village in Logan County.
Seng Camp; creek, a small right-hand tributary to Spruce Fork of Little Coal River in Logan County.
Serena; post village in Clay County.
Servia; post village in Braxton County.
Seth; post village in Boone County.
Settle; post village in Mason County.
Sevenmile; creek, a small left-hand tributary to Ohio River in Cabell County.
Sevenpines; village in Marion County.
Sewell; creek, a small left-hand tributary to Meadow River in Greenbrier County.
Sewell; post village in Fayette County on New River and on the Chesapeake and Ohio Railway. Altitude, 1,003 feet.
Seymourville; post village in Grant County.
Shabby Room; branch, a very small right-hand tributary to Spice Creek, a branch of Tug Fork of Big Sandy River, in McDowell County.
Shad; post village in Roane County.
Shadrick; fork, a right-hand branch of Hughes Creek, a tributary to Kanawha River, in Kanawha County.
Shadyspring; post village in Raleigh County.
Shafter; post village in Pendleton County.
Shamblings Mills; post village in Roane County.
Shanghai; post village in Berkeley County.
Shanks; post village in Hampshire County.
Shannon; post village in Ohio County.
Shannon Mill; creek, a very small right-hand tributary to Guyandot River in Wyoming County.
Sharp Knob; summit in Pocahontas County. Altitude, 4,545 feet.
Shaver; fork, a right fork of Westfall Fork of Cedar Creek in Braxton County.
Shavers; mountain, a ridge east of Shavers Fork of Cheat River in Randolph County.
Shavers; run, a small right-hand tributary to Valley River in Randolph County.
Shaw; post village in Mineral County on the West Virginia Central and Pittsburg Railway. Altitude, 1,290 feet.
Shawnee; post village in Pleasants County.
Sheep; run, a left-hand branch of North Fork of Fishing Creek in Wetzel County.
Shelby; run, a left-hand branch of Berkeley Run in Taylor County.
Shell Camp Ridge; narrow, broken mountains between Big Clear Creek and Smokehouse Branch, a fork of Big Clear Creek, in Greenbrier County. Altitude, 4,000 feet.
Shelley; post village in Clay County.
Shelton; post village in Clay County on the Charleston, Clendennin and Sutton Railroad.
Shenandoah; mountain, a broken range of mountains originating in Bath County, Virginia, and extending northeasterly through Hardy and Hampshire counties, West Virginia. Altitude, 1,500 to 3,000 feet.
Shenandoah Junction; post village in Jefferson County on the Baltimore and Ohio and Norfolk and Western railroads. Altitude, 512 feet.
Shenango; creek, a right-hand branch of Fishing Creek in Wetzel County.
Shepherd Spring; branch, a small right-hand tributary to Dunloup Creek, a branch of New River, in Raleigh County.
Shepherdstown; town in Jefferson County on the Norfolk and Western Railway. Population, 1,184.
Sheppard; post village in Mingo County.

Sheridan; post village in Lincoln County on the Chesapeake and Ohio Railway.
Sherman; post village in Jackson County on the Baltimore and Ohio Railroad.
Sherrard; post village in Marshall County.
Shiloh; post village in Tyler County.
Shinnston; town in Harrison County. Population, 535.
Shirkey; branch, a small right-hand branch of Blue Creek, a tributary to Elk River, in Kanawha County.
Shirley; post village in Tyler County.
Shoal; branch, a very small right-hand tributary to Twelvepole Creek, a branch of Ohio River, in Wayne County.
Shoals; post village in Wayne County, on the Norfolk and Western Railway.
Shock; post village in Braxton County.
Shock; run, a small left-hand branch of Suttleton Creek, a tributary to Greenbrier River, in Pocahontas County.
Shockley; branch, a small left-hand tributary to Millers Camp Branch of Marsh Fork of Coal River in Raleigh County.
Shock Mill; fork, a small left-hand tributary to Right Fork of Steer Creek in Braxton County.
Shooks; run, a small right-hand tributary to Moorefield River in Hardy County.
Shoomaker Knob; summit in Greenbrier County.
Shop; branch, a very small right-hand tributary to Indian Creek, a branch of Guyandot River, in Wyoming County.
Shops; post village in Putnam County.
Short; branch, a small right-hand tributary to Fifteenmile Fork of Cabin Creek, a branch of Kanawha River, in Kanawha County.
Short; branch, a small left-hand tributary to Davis Creek, a branch of Kanawha River, in Kanawha County.
Short; branch, a very small left-hand tributary to Tug Fork of Big Sandy River in McDowell County.
Short; creek, a left-hand branch of Ohio River in Ohio County.
Short; creek, a very small right-hand branch of Wolf Creek, a tributary to New River, in Fayette County.
Short; creek, a very small right-hand tributary to Coal River, a branch of Kanawha River, in Boone County.
Short; mountain, a summit in Greenbrier County.
Short; mountain in Morgan County. Elevation, 1,388 feet.
Short; run, a small right-hand tributary to Middle Fork of Tygarts Valley River in Randolph County.
Short; run, a very small right-hand tributary to Left Fork of Buckhannon River in Randolph County.
Short Bend; creek, a small right-hand branch of Little Hart Creek, a tributary to Guyandot River, in Lincoln County.
Short Bend; fork, a small right-hand branch of Fourteenmile Creek, a tributary to Guyandot River, in Lincoln County.
Shortcreek; post village in Brooke County on the Pittsburg, Cincinnati, Chicago and St. Louis Railway.
Short Pole; branch, a very small right-hand tributary to Tug Fork of Big Sandy River in McDowell County.
Shreeve; run, a very small left-hand tributary to Little Kanawha River in Braxton County.
Shrewsbury; post village in Kanawha County.
Shriner; run, a left-hand branch of West Virginia Fork of Dunkard Creek in Monongalia County.
Shryock; post village in Greenbrier County.

Shumate; branch, a small left-hand tributary to Marsh Fork of Coal River in Raleigh County.
Siberia; post village in Mercer County.
Sidney; post village in Wayne County.
Sigman; post village in Putnam County.
Siloam; post village in Mason County.
Silverhill; post village in Wetzel County.
Silverton; post village in Jackson County, on the Baltimore and Ohio Railroad.
Simmon; creek, a small left-hand tributary to Bluestone River in Mercer County.
Simmon; run, a small left-hand tributary to Right Fork of Buckhannon River in Upshur County.
Simmons; branch, a very small left-hand tributary to Clear Fork, a branch of Guyandot River, in Wyoming County.
Simmons; creek, a small right-hand tributary to Kanawha River in Kanawha County.
Simmons; creek, a small right-hand tributary to Kanawha River in Kanawha County.
Simmons; mountain, a short ridge between Dry Run and Hammer Run, left-hand branches of South Branch of the Potomac, in Pendleton County.
Simoda; post village in Pendleton County.
Simon; branch, a very small right-hand tributary to Middle Fork of Mud River in Lincoln County.
Simons; post village in Barbour County.
Simpson; post village in Taylor County, on the Baltimore and Ohio Railroad.
Simpson; run, a small right-hand branch of Little Sandy Creek in Preston County.
Sims; branch, a very small right-hand tributary to Paint Creek, a branch of Kanawha River, in Raleigh County.
Sincerity; post village in Wetzel County.
Sinclair; post village in Preston County.
Sinking; creek, a right-hand branch of Little Kanawha River in Gilmer County.
Sinking; creek, a small stream in Greenbrier County, rising in Big Clear Mountain. It flows southward a short distance and sinks.
Sinks Grove; post village in Monroe County.
Sioto; post village in Lincoln County.
Sir Johns; run, a right-hand branch of Potomac River in Morgan County.
Sir Johns Run; post village in Morgan County, on the Baltimore and Ohio Railroad.
Sissonville; post village in Kanawha County.
Sistersville; city in Tyler County. Population, 2,979.
Sixmile; creek, a small left-hand branch of Lens Creek, a tributary to Kanawha River, in Kanawha County.
Sixmile; creek, a small left-hand tributary to Spruce Fork of Little Coal River in Boone County.
Sixmile; creek, a small right-hand tributary to Guyandot River, a branch of Ohio River, in Lincoln County.
Sixmile; post village in Boone County.
Skelt; post village in Webster County.
Skidmore; post village in Jackson County.
Skidmore; run, a small right-hand branch of Little Kanawha River in Gilmer County.
Skillet; creek, a very small right-hand tributary to Gilbert Creek, a branch of Guyandot River, in Mingo County.
Skin; creek, a right-hand tributary to West Fork of Monongahela River in Lewis County.

Skin; fork, a small left-hand tributary to Pond Fork of Little Coal River in Boone County.

Skin; fork, a very small right-hand tributary to Guyandot River in Wyoming County.

Skinner; fork, a small left-hand tributary to Surveyor Fork, a branch of Marsh Fork of Coal River, in Raleigh County.

Skin Poplar; branch, a small right-hand tributary to Laurel Fork, a branch of Spruce Fork of Little Coal River, in Boone County.

Skin Poplar; gap, a height in Guyandot Mountain in Raleigh County. Altitude, 2,360 feet.

Skitter; creek, a very small left-hand tributary to Paint Creek, a branch of Kanawha River, in Fayette County.

Skull Run; post village in Jackson County.

Skyle; creek, a small right-hand tributary to Birch River in Webster County.

Skyles; post village in Webster County.

Slab; creek, a very small left-hand tributary to Mud River, a branch of Guyandot River, in Lincoln County.

Slab; fork, a right-hand tributary to Guyandot River in Raleigh and Wyoming counties.

Slab Camp; creek, a small left-hand tributary to Greenbrier River in Greenbrier County.

Slab Camp; fork, a left-hand branch of French Creek, a tributary to Buckhannon River, in Upshur County.

Slab Camp; mountain, a short ridge in Greenbrier County. Altitude, 3,000 to 3,050 feet.

Slab Camp; run, a small right-hand tributary to Williams River in Webster County.

Slab Creek; run, a small right-hand branch of Cedar Creek in Braxton County.

Slack; branch, a small left-hand tributary to Blue Creek, a branch of Elk River, in Kanawha County.

Slanesville; post village in Hampshire County.

Slap Camp; run, a right-hand tributary of Right Fork of Skin Creek in Gilmer County.

Slash Lick; creek, a small left-hand tributary to Howards Creek, a branch of Greenbrier River, in Greenbrier County.

Slate; post village in Wood County.

Slate Lick; small right-hand branch of Campbell Creek, a tributary to Kanawha River, in Kanawha County.

Slate Lick Knob; summit in Pocahontas County.

Slater; branch, a very small right-hand tributary to Kanawha River in Kanawha County.

Slater; creek, a very small right-hand tributary to New River in Fayette County.

Slater; station in Fayette County on the Chesapeake and Ohio Railway and at junction of Slater Creek and New River. Altitude, 1,108 feet.

Slaty; fork, a small right-hand branch of Old Field Fork of Elk River in Pocahontas County.

Slatyfork; post village in Pocahontas County.

Slaty Ridge; broken mountainous country in Pocahontas County.

Slaughter; creek, a small left-hand tributary to Kanawha River in Kanawha County.

Slaunch; fork, a left-hand head fork of Panther Creek, a branch of Tug Fork of Big Sandy River, in McDowell County.

Sleepy; creek, a small left-hand tributary to Hurricane Creek, a branch of Kanawha River, in Putnam County.

Sleepy; creek, a right-hand branch of Potomac River in Morgan County.

Sleepy Creek; mountain in Berkeley and Morgan counties. Elevation, 1,800 feet.

Sleith; post village in Braxton County.
Sleps; branch, a very small right-hand tributary to Elk River in Webster County.
Slick Rock; branch, a very small left-hand tributary to Big Huff Creek, a branch of Guyandot River, in Wyoming County.
Slick Rock; branch, a small right-hand tributary to Tug Fork of Big Sandy River in McDowell County.
Sliding Hill; run, a small right-hand branch of Little Kanawha River in Gilmer County.
Slipcamp; run, a right-hand branch of Indian Fork Run in Gilmer County.
Slippery Gut; branch, a small left-hand tributary to Little Coal River, a branch of Coal River and indirect tributary to Kanawha River, in Boone County.
Sloan; post village in Wood County.
Slowers; branch, a very small left-hand tributary to Beech Fork of Twelvepole Creek, a branch of Ohio River, in Wayne County.
Smith; branch, a small right-hand branch of Bell Creek, a tributary to Gauley River, in Fayette County.
Smith; branch, a very small left-hand branch of Dunloup Creek, a tributary to New River, in Fayette County.
Smith; branch, a very small left-hand tributary to Pinnacle Creek, a branch of Guyandot River, in Wyoming County.
Smith; branch, a very small left-hand tributary to New River in Mercer County.
Smith; creek, a small right-hand tributary to Coal River, a branch of Kanawha River, in Kanawha County.
Smith; creek, a left-hand tributary to South Branch of Potomac River in Pendleton County.
Smith; creek, a small left-hand tributary to Guyandot River, a branch of Ohio River, in Cabell County.
Smithers; creek, a small right-hand tributary to Kanawha River in Kanawha and Fayette counties.
Smithfield; post village in Wetzel County on the Baltimore and Ohio Railroad.
Smithton; post village in Doddridge County on the Baltimore and Ohio Railroad. Altitude, 795 feet.
Smithville; post village in Ritchie County.
Smoke Camp Knob; summit in Pocahontas County.
Smoke Hole Settlement; neighborhood at the base of the South Fork of the Potomac at the east base of North Fork Mountains, in Pendleton and Grant counties.
Smokehouse; branch, a small right-hand branch of South Fork of Big Clear Creek, a tributary to Meadow River, in Greenbrier County.
Smokehouse; fork, a small right-hand branch of Big Heart Creek, a tributary to Guyandot River, in Logan County.
Smoot; post village in Greenbrier County on the Baltimore and Ohio Railroad.
Snake; fork, a small right-hand tributary to Elk River in Clay County.
Snake; run, a small right-hand tributary to Muddy Creek, a branch of Greenbrier River, in Greenbrier County.
Snake Root; branch, a small right-hand tributary to Clear Fork, a branch of Tug Fork of Big Sandy River, in McDowell County.
Snap; branch, a small left-hand tributary to Guyandot River, a branch of Ohio River, in Logan County.
Snow; mount in Pendleton County. Altitude, 4,500 feet.
Snowden; post village in Lincoln County.
Snowhill; post village in Nicholas County on the Ohio Central Lines.
Snowy; creek, a left-hand tributary to Youghiogheny River in Preston County.
Snyder Knob; summit in Randolph County.
Snyders Mills; village in Jefferson County.

Soab; branch, a very small right-hand branch of Tug Fork of Big Sandy River, a tributary to Ohio River, in Logan County.

Soak; creek, a small left-hand tributary to Piney Creek, a branch of New River, in Raleigh County.

Soak; post village in Raleigh County.

South; fork, a small head tributary to Left Fork of Buckhannon River in Randolph County.

South; fork, a right-hand head tributary to Snowy Creek, a branch of Youghiogheny River, in Preston County.

South Branch; mountain, a narrow ridge in Hardy and Hampshire counties. Altitude, 1,500 to 3,000 feet.

Southbranch Depot; post village in Hampshire County.

South Elkins; town in Randolph County. Population, 206.

South Fork; mountain, broken range in the eastern part of the State. Altitude, 1,500 to 3,000 feet.

South Mill; creek, a right-hand tributary to South Branch of Potomac River in Grant and Pendleton counties.

South Millcreek; post village in Pendleton County.

South Morgantown; town in Monongalia County. Population, 405.

Southside; post village in Mason County.

Souttell; run, a left-hand branch of Short Creek in Ohio County.

Sow; branch, a very small right-hand tributary to Laurel Branch, a tributary to Clear Fork of Guyandot River, in Wyoming County.

Spangler; branch, a very small left-hand tributary to Winding Gulf, a branch of Guyandot River, in Raleigh County.

Spangler; fork, a small left-hand branch of Middle Fork of Blue Creek, a tributary to Elk River, in Kanawha County.

Spangler; post village in Kanawha County.

Spanishburg; post village in Mercer County, located on Bluestone River. Altitude, 2,074 feet.

Spanker; branch, a very small right-hand tributary to Marsh Fork of Coal River in Raleigh County.

Sparrow; creek, a small left-hand tributary to Spruce Fork of Little Coal River, a branch of Coal River, in Boone County.

Sparrow; run, a small left-hand tributary to Holly River in Braxton County.

Spaulding; post village in Mingo County.

Speed; branch, a very small left-hand tributary to Sycamore Creek, a branch of Clear Fork of Coal River, in Raleigh County.

Speed; post village in Roane County.

Spencer; branch, a small right-hand tributary to Boyer Fork of Piney Creek, a branch of New River, in Raleigh County.

Spencer; county seat of Roane County on the Baltimore and Ohio Railroad. Population, 737.

Spice; creek, a very small right-hand tributary to Guyandot River in Mingo County.

Spice; creek, a small left-hand tributary to Tug Fork of Big Sandy River in McDowell County.

Spice; creek, a small left-hand tributary to South Forth of Tug River in McDowell County.

Spice; run, a small left-hand tributary to Greenbrier River on boundary line between Pocahontas and Greenbrier counties.

Spice; run, a small right-hand tributary to Williams River in Webster County.

Spice; run, a very small right-hand tributary to Gauley River in Nicholas County.

Spice Laurel; branch, a small left-hand tributary to Spice Creek, a branch of Tug Fork of Big Sandy River, in McDowell County.

Spicelick; fork, a head fork of Joe Creek, a tributary to Coal River, in Boone County.
Spider; creek, a right-hand branch of Pinnacle Creek, a tributary to Guyandot River, in Wyoming County.
Spider Ridge; mountains in Wyoming County.
Spilman; post village in Mason County on the Baltimore and Ohio Railroad.
Spottswood; post village in Logan County.
Spread Bend; mountain, a short ridge north of Elk River in Clay County. Altitude, 1,000 feet.
Spring; branch, a very small right-hand tributary to Twelvepole Creek, a branch of Ohio River, in Wayne County.
Spring; branch, a small right-hand branch of Rock Camp Fork of Twentymile Creek, a tributary to Gauley River, in Nicholas County.
Spring; creek, a small right-hand tributary to Greenbrier River in Greenbrier County.
Spring; creek, a right-hand branch of Grass Run in Gilmer County.
Spring; creek, a small left-hand tributary to Ohio River, rising in Roane County.
Spring; fork, a left-hand branch of Ben Creek, a tributary to Tug Fork of Big Sandy River, in Mingo County.
Spring; fork, a small left-hand branch of Campbell Creek, a tributary to Kanawha River, in Kanawha County.
Spring Creek; post village in Greenbrier County on the Chesapeake and Ohio Railway.
Springdale; post village in Fayette County.
Springfield; town in Hampshire County on the Baltimore and Ohio Railroad. Population, 143.
Springgap; post village in Hampshire County.
Springgarden; post village in Roane County.
Springhill; post village in Kanawha County on the Chesapeake and Ohio, the Kanawha and Coal River, and the Ohio Central Lines railroads. Altitude, 597 feet.
Sprive; run, a small right-hand tributary to Left Fork of Steer Creek in Braxton County.
Spruce; branch, a very small left-hand branch of Right Fork of Twelvepole Creek, a tributary to Ohio River, in Wayne County.
Spruce; fork, a stream in Logan and Boone counties, uniting with Pond Fork to form Little Coal River.
Spruce; fork, a small left-hand tributary to Right Fork of Middle Fork of Little Kanawha River in Webster County.
Spruce; fork, a small left-hand tributary to Horse Creek, a branch of Little Coal River, in Boone County.
Spruce; fork, a left-hand head fork of Little Coal River, a branch of Coal River, in Boone and Logan counties.
Spruce; fork, a small right-hand tributary to Right Fork of Stone Coal Creek in Upshur County.
Spruce; fork, a small right-hand branch of Brier Creek, a tributary to Coal River, in Kanawha Count .
Spruce; fork, a small right-hand branch of Blue Creek, a tributary to Elk River, in Kanawha County.
Spruce; fork, a small right-hand tributary to Birch River, a branch of Elk River, in Webster County.
Spruce; fork, a very small right-hand tributary to Clear Fork of Coal River in Raleigh County.
Spruce; fork, a right-hand tributary to Wolf Creek in Braxton County.
Spruce; run, a small right-hand tributary to Cedar Creek in Gilmer County.

Spruce; run, a right-hand tributary to Cheat River in Preston County.
Spruce; run, a small right-hand branch of Brushy Fork of Muddlety Creek, a tributary to Gauley River, in Nicholas County.
Spruce; run, a small right-hand branch of Dry Creek, a tributary to Howards Creek, in Greenbrier County.
Spruce; mountain, a short ridge lying west of the North Fork of the Potomac, parallel to the Timber Ridge, in Pendleton County.
Spruce Knob; summit in Pocahontas County. Altitude, 4,730 feet.
Spruce Knob; summit of Spruce Mountain in Pendleton County. Altitude, 4,860 feet.
Spruce Low; gap caused by Spruce Fork of Blue Creek.
Spruce Pine Hollow; small right-hand tributary to Kanawha River in Kanawha County.
Spurlock; branch, a very small left-hand tributary to Beech Fork of Twelvepole Creek, a branch of Ohio River, in Wayne County.
Spurlockville; post village in Lincoln County.
Squealer Knob; summit in Raleigh County.
Squirejim; post village in McDowell County.
Stafford; branch, a very small right-hand tributary to Guayandot River in Mingo County.
Stafford; post village in Mingo County.
Stags; run, a small left-hand branch of Patterson Creek, a tributary to North Branch of Potomac River, in Mineral County.
Stalnaker; post village in Lewis County.
Stamping; creek, a small right-hand tributary to Greenbrier River in Pocahontas County.
Stanaford; branch, a small left-hand tributary to Piney Creek, a branch of New River, in Raleigh County.
Stanley; fork, a very small right-hand tributary to Mud River, a branch of Guyandot River, in Boone County.
Stanley; post village in Ritchie County.
Starkey; run, a left-hand tributary of Buffalo Creek in Marion County.
State; fork, a right-hand branch of Pyles Fork of Buffalo Creek in Marion County.
Staten; post village in Calhoun County.
Staten; run, a very small right-hand tributary to Kanawha River in Kanawha County.
State Road; run, a left-hand branch of Paw Paw Creek in Marion County.
Statler Run; post village in Monongalia County.
Statts Mills; post village in Jackson County.
Steel; post village in Wood County.
Steel; run, a right-hand branch of Little Fishing Run in Wetzel County.
Steel Trap; branch, a very small left-hand tributary to Tug Fork of Big Sandy River in McDowell County.
Steener; fork, a left-hand tributary of Lynn Camp Run in Wetzel County.
Steep; run, a small right-hand tributary to Wolf Creek in Braxton County.
Steep Gut; branch, a very small right-hand branch of Tug Fork of Big Sandy River, a tributary to Ohio River, in Logan County.
Steer; creek, a small left-hand tributary to Ohio River in Calhoun County.
Steer; run, a right-hand branch of Left Fork of Steer Creek in Gilmer County.
Stevens; branch, a small right-hand tributary to Marsh Fork of Coal River in Raleigh County.
Stevens; post village in Mason County on the Baltimore and Ohio Railroad.
Stewart; creek, a small left-hand tributary to Little Bluestone Creek in Summers County.

Stewart; creek, a right-hand branch of Little Kanawha River in Gilmer County.
Stewart; run, a small right-hand tributary to Valley River in Randolph County.
Stewartstown; post village in Monongalia County.
Still; run, a small right-hand tributary to Guyandot River in Wyoming County.
Stillhouse; branch, a small right-hand tributary to Twentymile Creek, a branch of Gauley River, in Nicholas County.
Stillhouse; branch, a very small right-hand tributary to Peters Creek, a branch of Gauley River, in Nicholas County.
Still House; branch, a small left-hand tributary to Leatherwood Fork of Elk River in Webster County.
Stillhouse; run, a small left-hand tributary to Birch River, a branch of Elk River, in Nicholas County.
Stillman; post village in Upshur County.
Stillwell; post village in Wood County.
Stinking Lick; creek, a very small right-hand tributary to New River in Summers and Monroe counties.
Stinson; branch, a small left-hand tributary to Left Fork of Mud River, a branch of Guyandot River, in Lincoln County.
Stinson; post village in Calhoun County.
Stitt; branch, a very small right-hand tributary to Davis Creek, a branch of Kanawha River, in Kanawha County.
Stockerts; post village in Upshur County.
Stockton; post village in Mason County.
Stockton; station in Fayette County on the Kanawha and Michigan Railway and on Kanawha River. Altitude, 618 feet.
Stockton Knob; summit in Fayette County. Altitude, 3,252 feet.
Stolling; fork, a small left-hand tributary to Laurel Creek, a branch of Coal River, in Boone County.
Stone; fork, a very small left-hand tributary to Beech Fork of Twelvepole Creek, a branch of Ohio River, in Wayne County.
Stone; run, a small right-hand tributary to Valley River in Barbour County.
Stonecliff; post village in Fayette County on New River and on the Chesapeake and Ohio Railway. Altitude, 1,076 feet.
Stone Coal; branch, a very small right-hand tributary to Clear Fork of Coal River in Raleigh County.
Stonecoal; branch, a very small right-hand tributary to Mud River, a branch of Guyandot River, in Lincoln County.
Stone Coal; branch, a small right-hand tributary to Spice Creek, a branch of Tug Fork of Big Sandy River, in McDowell County.
Stone Coal; creek, a right-hand branch of Tommy Creek, a head fork of Guyandot River, in Raleigh County.
Stonecoal; post village in Wayne County.
Stone Coal; run, a small right-hand tributary to Left Fork of Middle Fork of Tygarts Valley River in Randolph County.
Stonewall; post village in Raleigh County on the Chesapeake and Ohio Railway.
Stony; creek, a small left-hand tributary to Elk River in Braxton County.
Stony; creek, a small left-hand tributary to Greenbrier River in Summers County.
Stony; creek, a small right-hand tributary to Greenbrier River in Pocahontas County.
Stony; post village in Hampshire County.
Stony; river, a large right-hand tributary to North Branch of Potomac River in Grant County.
Stony; run, a small left-hand tributary to Elk Water in Randolph County.
Stony; run, a small left-hand branch of Suttleton Creek, a tributary to Greenbrier River, in Pocahontas County.

Stony; run, a small right-hand tributary to South Fork of Potomac River in Pendleton County.
Stony Creek; mountain, a short ridge north of Greenbrier River, in Pocahontas County. Altitude, 2,500 to 3,500 feet.
Stony Ridge; mountains in Mercer County.
Stotlers Crossroads; post village in Morgan County.
Stout; creek; a very small left-hand tributary to Guyandot River, a branch of Ohio River, in Lincoln County.
Stouts Mills; post village in Gilmer County situated on Little Kanawha River.
Stover; branch, a very small right-hand tributary to Coal River, a branch of Kanawha River, in Boone County.
Stover; fork, a small left-hand tributary to Clear Fork of Coal River in Raleigh County.
Stover; fork, a small left-hand tributary to Piney Creek, a branch of New River, in Raleigh County.
Stover; fork, a very small right-hand tributary to Sycamore Creek, a branch of Clear Fork of Coal River, in Raleigh County.
Stover; post village in Tucker County on the Dry Fork Railroad.
Straight; creek, a small left-hand tributary to Gauley River in Webster County.
Straight; fork, a head fork of Little Skin Creek in Lewis County.
Straight; fork; a small left-hand tributary to West Fork of Monongahela River in Lewis County.
Straight; fork, a very small left-hand tributary to Huff Creek, a branch of Guyandot River, in Wyoming County.
Straight; fork, a left-hand tributary to Middle Fork of Mud River, a branch of Guyandot River, in Lincoln County.
Straight Creek; mountain, a short ridge north of Williams River in Webster County.
Strange; creek, a small left-hand tributary to Elk River in Nicholas and Braxton countries.
Strangecreek; post village in Braxton County.
Streeter; post village in Summers County.
Stroud; creek, a small right-hand tributary to Gauley River, in Nicholas and Webster counties.
Stroud Knobs; summit in Nicholas County.
Strouds; post village in Webster County.
Stump; run, a small right-hand tributary to South Fork of Potomac River in Hardy County.
Stumptown; post village in Gilmer County.
Stumpy; creek, a very small left-hand tributary to Mud River, a branch of Guyandot River, in Lincoln County.
Sturms Mill; village in Marion County.
Styles; run, a left-hand branch of Long Drain in Wetzel County.
Suck; creek, a small right-hand branch of Little Bluestone Creek, a tributary to Bluestone River, in Summers County.
Sue; post village in Greenbrier County.
Sugar; branch, a very small left-hand tributary to Hominy Creek, a branch of Gauley River, in Nicholas County.
Sugar; creek, a right fork of Laurel Creek, a tributary to Valley River, in Barbour County.
Sugar; creek, a right-hand branch of Back Fork of Elk River in Webster and Randolph counties.
Sugar; creek, a very small right-hand tributary to Big Huff Creek, a branch of Guyandot River, in Logan and Wyoming counties.

Sugar; creek, a small left-hand branch of Twomile Creek, a tributary to Kanawha River, in Kanawha County.

Sugar; creek, a very small left-hand branch of Dunloup Creek, a tributary to New River, in Fayette County.

Sugar; creek, a small left-hand tributary to Williams River in Pocahontas County.

Sugar; run, a left-hand branch of Fish Creek in Wetzel County.

Sugar; run, a very small right-hand tributary to Guyandot River in Wyoming County.

Sugar; run, a left-hand branch of Paw Paw Creek in Marion County.

Sugar; run, a small right-hand tributary to Left Fork of Middle Fork of Tygarts Valley River in Randolph County.

Sugar; ran, a left-hand branch of West Virginia Fork of Dunkard Creek in Monongalia County.

Sugar Camp; branch, a very small left-hand tributary to Mulberry Fork of Loop Creek, a branch of Kanawha River, in Fayette County.

Sugar Camp; branch, a small left-hand branch of Twentymile Creek, a tributary to Gauley River, in Nicholas County.

Sugar Camp; branch, a small right-hand tributary to Paint Creek, a branch of Kanawha River, in Kanawha County.

Sugar Camp; branch, a very small right-hand branch of Hughes Creek, a tributary to Kanawha River, in Kanawha County.

Sugar Camp; branch, a very small right-hand branch of Kelly Creek, a tributary to Kanawha River, in Kanawha County.

Sugarcamp; branch, a very small right-hand tributary to Davis Creek, a branch of Kanawha River, in Kanawha County.

Sugar Camp; branch, a very small right-hand tributary to Guyandot River in Wyoming County.

Sugarcamp; creek, a very small right-hand branch of Davis Creek, a tributary to Kanawha River, in Kanawha County.

Sugarcamp; post village in Doddridge County.

Sugar Camp; run, a small right-hand tributary to Elk River in Braxton County.

Sugar Camp; run, a left-hand tributary of Booths Creek in Harrison County.

Sugar Camp; run, a small left-hand tributary to Knapp Creek, a branch of Greenbrier River, in Pocahontas County.

Sugar Camp Knob; summit in Greenbrier County.

Sugarcamp Knob; summit in Lincoln County.

Sugar Creek; mountain, a short ridge between Williams River and Williams River Mountain in Pocahontas County.

Sugargrove; post village in Pendleton County.

Sugar Grove Knob; summit in Nicholas County. Altitude, 3,028 feet.

Sugar Knob; summit in Braxton County. Altitude, 1,630 feet.

Sugar Knob; summit in Greenbrier County.

Sugar Run; branch, a small left-hand tributary to Rich Creek, a branch of New River, in Monroe County.

Sugartree; branch, a very small right-hand tributary to Mud River, a branch of Guyandot River, in Boone County.

Sugar Tree; branch, a very small right-hand branch of Tug Fork of Big Sandy River, a tributary to Ohio River, in Logan County.

Sugar Tree; branch, a small left-hand tributary to Tug Fork of Big Sandy River in McDowell County.

Sugartree; fork, a left-hand tributary to Middle Fork of Mud River, a branch of Guyandot River, in Lincoln County.

Sugar Tree Bench; mountains, a short spur of Yew Mountains in Greenbrier and Pocahontas counties.

Sugar Valley; post village in Pleasants County.
Suke; creek, a small left-hand branch of Little Huff Creek, a tributary to Guyandot River, in Wyoming County.
Sulphur; post village in Mineral County.
Sulphur; run, a small right-hand branch of Hughes Fork, in Braxton County.
Sulphur Spring; fork, a small right-hand branch of Fourteenmile Creek, a tributary to Guyandot River, in Lincoln County.
Sulphur Spring; fork, a small left-hand branch of Fourmile Creek, a tributary to Guyandot River, in Lincoln County.
Sulphur Spring; fork, a small left-hand branch of Peters Cave Fork of Horse Creek, a tributary to Little Coal River, in Lincoln County.
Summers; county, situated in the southern part of the State on the summit of the Allegheny Plateau, which here presents the broken, mountainous surface with numerous high points, the highest 3,945 feet, Keeney Knob. Area, 368 square miles. Population, 16,265—white, 15,149; negro, 1,115; foreign born, 64. County seat, Hinton. The mean magnetic declination in 1900 was 1° 30′. The mean annual rainfall is 50 to 60 inches, and the mean annual temperature 50° to 55°. The county is traversed by the Chesapeake and Ohio Railway.
Summers; post village in Doddridge County.
Summersville; county seat of Nicholas County. Population, 223.
Summersville; mountain in Nicholas County. Altitude, 2,584 feet.
Summit Point; post village in Jefferson County on the Baltimore and Ohio Railroad. Altitude, 623 feet.
Sunhill; post village in Wyoming County.
Sunlight; post village in Greenbrier County.
Sunnyside; post village in Fayette County on the Chesapeake and Ohio Railway and on New River. Altitude, 842 feet.
Sunrise; branch, a small right-hand branch of Trace Creek, a tributary to Middle Fork of Mud River, in Lincoln County.
Sunset; branch, a small left-hand tributary to Trace Creek, a branch of Middle Fork of Mud River, in Lincoln County.
Sunset; post village in Pocahontas County.
Surveyor; fork, a left-hand head fork of Marsh Fork of Coal River, in Raleigh County.
Sutherland; post village in Kanawha County.
Sutphin; branch, a very small left-hand tributary to Piney Creek, a branch of New River, in Raleigh County.
Suttleton; creek, a small left-hand tributary to Greenbrier River in Pocahontas County.
Sutton; county seat of Braxton County on the Baltimore and Ohio Railroad. Population, 864. Altitude, 823 feet.
Sutton; run, a small left-hand tributary to North Fork of Greenbrier River in Pocahontas County.
Sutton; run, a small right-hand tributary to Birch River in Nicholas County.
Swago; creek, a small right-hand tributary to Greenbrier River in Pocahontas County.
Swago; mountain, a short ridge in central part of Pocahontas County. Altitude, 3,500 to 4,000 feet.
Swamp; branch, a very small left-hand tributary to Guyandot River, a branch of Ohio River, in Cabell County.
Swamp; run, a small right-hand tributary to Valley River in Barbour County.
Swamprun; post village in Upshur County.
Swann; post village in Cabell County.

Sweedlin Hill; short ridge lying east of South Fork of the Potomac in Pendleton County.
Sweep; run, a left-hand branch of Booths Creek in Harrison and Morgan counties.
Sweetland; post village in Lincoln County.
Sweetsprings; post village in Monroe County.
Sweet Water; branch, a very small right-hand branch of Right Fork of Twelvepole Creek, a tributary to Ohio River, in Wayne County.
Swell Knob; summit in Fayette County.
Swift; run, a small right-hand tributary to Greenbrier River, in Summers County.
Swoopes Knobs; group of summits in Monroe County.
Sycamore; branch, a small right-hand tributary to Big Huff Creek, a branch of Guyandot River, in Wyoming County.
Sycamore; branch, a small right-hand tributary to Big Cub Creek, a branch of Guyandot River, in Wyoming County.
Sycamore; branch, a very small right-hand tributary to West Fork of Twelvepole Creek, a branch of Ohio River, in Wayne County.
Sycamore; branch, a small right-hand tributary to Paint Creek, a branch of Kanawha River, in Kanawha and Fayette counties.
Sycamore; creek, a very small right-hand branch of Tug Fork of Big Sandy River, a tributary to Ohio River, in Logan County.
Sycamore; creek, a small right-hand branch of Little Kanawha River in Gilmer County.
Sycamore; creek, a small left-hand branch of Clear Fork of Coal River in Raleigh County.
Sycamore; creek, a right hand branch of Trace Fork in Putnam County.
Sycamore; fork, a small right-hand tributary to Laurel Fork, a branch of Spruce Fork of Little Coal River, in Boone County.
Sycamore; fork, a small right-hand tributary to Left Fork of Mud River, a branch of Guyandot River, in Lincoln County.
Sycamore; fork, a left-hand tributary to Middle Fork of Mud River, a branch of Guyandot River, in Lincoln County.
Sycamore; post village in Calhoun County.
Sycamore Dale; village in Harrison County.
Sylvia; branch, a very small left-hand tributary to Guyandot River, a branch of Ohio River, in Mingo County.
Tabler; post village in Berkeley County on the Cumberland Valley Railroad.
Tablerock; post village in Raleigh County.
Table Rock; summit in Kanawha County. Altitude, 1,756 feet.
Tackett; creek, a small left-hand branch of Coal River, a tributary to Kanawha River, in Kanawha County.
Tackey; fork, a small left-hand tributary to North Fork of Greenbrier River in Pocahontas County.
Tacy; post village in Barbour County.
Tague; fork, a small right-hand tributary to Right Fork of Steer Creek in Braxton County.
Takein; creek, a very small right-hand tributary to Piney Creek, a branch of New River, in Raleigh County.
Talcott; post village in Summers County on the Chesapeake and Ohio Railway. Altitude, 1,512 feet.
Tallmansville; post village in Upshur County.
Tallow Knob; summit in Pocahontas County.
Tallyho; post village in Wood County.
Tank; branch, a very small right-hand tributary to Piney Creek, a branch of New River, in Raleigh County.

Tanner; fork, a right-hand branch of Little Kanawha River in Gilmer County.
Tanner; fork, a small left-hand tributary to Right Fork of Steer Creek in Gilmer County.
Tanner; post village in Gilmer County.
Tantrough; branch, a very small right-hand tributary to Guyandot River, a branch of Ohio River, in Lincoln County.
Tantrough; run, a right-hand branch of Fish Creek in Wetzel County.
Tappan; post village in Taylor County.
Tarcoat; creek, a left-hand tributary to North River in Hampshire County.
Tariff; post village in Roane County.
Tate; creek, a small right-hand branch of Elk River in Braxton County.
Tate; post village in Braxton County.
Tate; run, a small right-hand branch of Peters Creek, a tributary to Gauley River, in Nicholas County.
Tater Knob; run, a small right-hand tributary to Back Fork of Holly River in Webster County.
Taylor; branch, a small left-hand tributary to Gauley River in Nicholas County.
Taylor; county, situated on the Allegheny Plateau. Drained by tributaries to the Monongahela River. Area, 132 square miles. Population, 14,978—white, 14,553; negro, 423; foreign born, 384. County seat, Grafton. The mean magnetic declination in 1900 was 4° 5'. The mean annual rainfall is 40 to 50 inches, and the mean annual temperature 45 to 50°. The county is traversed by the Baltimore and Ohio Railroad.
Taylor; fork, a left-hand tributary to Buffalo Creek, a branch of Elk River, in Nicholas and Clay counties.
Taylor; fork, a left-hand branch of Jenkins Fork of Loop Creek, a tributary to Kanawha River, in Fayette County.
Taylor; run, a very small right-hand tributary to Elk River in Braxton County.
Tea; branch, a small right-hand tributary to South Fork of Tug River in McDowell County.
Tea; creek, a small right-hand tributary to Williams River in Pocahontas County.
Tea Creek; mountain, a short ridge at foot of Gauley Mountain in Pocahontas County. Altitude, 3,500 to 4,000 feet.
Tearcoat Hill; town between North Fork of Lunice Creek and Brushy Run in Grant County.
Teays; post village in Putnam County.
Teddy; post village in Clay County.
Teeny Knob; summit in Braxton County.
Ten Mile; creek, a small right-hand tributary to Buckhannon River in Upshur County.
Tenmile; creek, a small left-hand branch of Guyandot River, a tributary to Ohio River, in Lincoln County.
Tenmile; fork, a small left-hand branch of Campbell Creek, a tributary to Kanawha River, in Kanawha County.
Tenmile; fork, a left-hand branch of Cabin Creek, a tributary to Kanawha River, in Kanawha County.
Tenmile; fork, a left-hand tributary to Paint Creek, a branch of Kanawha River, in Kanawha County.
Tenmile; post village in Upshur County on the Baltimore and Ohio Railroad. Altitude, 1,608 feet.
Terra Alta; town in Preston County on the Baltimore and Ohio Railroad. Population, 616.
Tesla; post village in Braxton County.
Teter; creek, a right-hand tributary to Valley River in Barbour County.

Texas; post village in Tucker County on the Baltimore and Ohio Railroad. Altitude, 883 feet.

Texel; post village in Randolph County.

Thacker; creek, a small right-hand branch of Tug Fork of Big Sandy River, a tributary to Ohio River, in Logan County.

Thacker; post village in Mingo County on the Norfolk and Western Railway.

Thayer; post village in Fayette County.

The; creek, a small left-hand tributary to Back Fork of Elk River in Randolph County.

The Big Bend; a portion of Greenbrier River, forming a big bend, in Summers County.

The Loop; a bend in Meadow River, a branch of Gauley River.

The Pond; summit in Raleigh County.

The Roughs; hills in Mingo County.

The Sinks; valley at the head of Gandy Creek in Randolph County.

Third; run, a small right-hand branch of Little Kanawha River in Gilmer County.

Thoburn; village in Marion County.

Thomas; creek, a small left-hand tributary to Greenbrier River in Pocahontas County.

Thomas; mountain, a short ridge between Laurel and Moore runs, branches of Greenbrier River, in Pocahontas County.

Thomas; town in Tucker County, on the West Virginia Central and Pittsburg Railway. Population, 2,126.

Thompson; post village in Marshall County on the Baltimore and Ohio Railroad.

Thompson; run, a small right-hand tributary to Valley River in Randolph County.

Thorn; post village in Pendleton County.

Thorn; run, a small left-hand tributary to Patterson Creek, a branch of North Branch of Potomac River, in Grant County.

Thorn; run, a right-hand tributary to South Branch of Potomac River in Pendleton County.

Thornton; post village in Taylor County on the Baltimore and Ohio Railroad. Altitude, 1,038 feet.

Thorny; creek, a small left-hand tributary to Greenbrier River in Pocahontas County.

Thorny Bottom; right-hand tributary to Cacapon River in Hardy County.

Thorny Creek; mountain, a short ridge between Thorny Creek and Greenbrier River in Pocahontas County. Altitude, 3,000 feet.

Thorny Flat; summit of Back Alleghany Mountains in Pocahontas County.

Thoroughfare; branch, a small right-hand tributary to Paint Creek, a branch of Kanawha River, in Kanawha County.

Three Churches; post village in Hampshire County.

Three Fork; creek, a right-hand tributary to Valley River in Taylor County.

Three Forks; run, a small left-hand tributary to Left Fork of Middle Fork of Tygarts Valley River in Randolph County.

Three Forks; very small left-hand tributary to Buffalo Creek, a branch of Guyandot River, in Logan County.

Three Lick; small right-hand branch of Oil Creek in Lewis County.

Three Lick; small right-hand branch of Little Skin Creek in Lewis County.

Three Lick; run, a right-hand branch of Oil Creek in Gilmer County.

Threemile; creek, a left-hand branch of Ohio River in Cabell County.

Threemile; fork, a small right-hand tributary to Whiteoak Creek, a branch of Coal River, in Boone County.

Threemile; fork, a very small left-hand branch of Smithers Creek, a tributary to Kanawha River, in Fayette County.

Three Springs; branch, a small left-hand tributary to Big Huff Creek, a branch of Guyandot River, in Logan County.
Third Heel; mountain in Berkeley County. Elevation, 1,777 feet.
Thurmond; post village in Fayette County on New River and on the Chesapeake and Ohio Railway. Altitude, 1,056 feet.
Tichenal; post village in Harrison county.
Tigarts Valley; river, a right-hand branch of the Monongahela, joining it at Fairmont.
Tilhance; creek, a right-hand tributary of Potomac River in Berkeley County.
Timber Ridge; mountains lying parallel with Spruce Mountains, west of the North Fork of the Potomac, in Pendleton County. Altitude, 2,000 to 4,000 feet.
Timothy; run, a small right-hand branch of Clover Lick Fork in Lewis County.
Tincture; fork, a left-hand tributary of Middle Fork of Mud River in Lincoln County.
Tiney; creek, a small left-hand tributary to Little Coal River, a branch of Coal River, in Lincoln County.
Tipton; post village in Nicholas county.
Tobacco; run, a small left-hand tributary to Little Kanawha River in Lewis County.
Todd; run, a right-hand branch of Middle Wheeling Run in Ohio County.
Tollgate; post village in Ritchie County on the Baltimore and Ohio Railroad.
Tom; branch, a small right-hand tributary to Paint Creek, a branch of Kanawha River, in Kanawha and Fayette counties.
Tom; branch, a very small right-hand tributary to Coal River in Raleigh County.
Tom; branch, a very small right-hand tributary to North Fork of Elkhorn Creek in McDowell County.
Tom; creek, a very small right-hand tributary to Guyandot River, a branch of Ohio River, in Cabell County.
Tom; creek, a very small left-hand branch of Twelvepole Creek, a tributary to Ohio River, in Wayne County.
Tom; creek, a small right-hand tributary to Meadow River, a branch of Gauley River, in Greenbrier County.
Tom; fork, a small left-hand tributary to Coal River, a branch of Kanawha River, in Lincoln County.
Tom; run, a small left-hand branch of Cedar Creek in Braxton County.
Tom; run, a very small left-hand tributary to New River in Summers County.
Tom; run, a small right-hand tributary to Sand Fork in Lewis County.
Tomahawk; village in Berkeley County.
Tomahawk; run, a left-hand branch of Indian Fork in Lewis County.
Tom Bailey; branch, a small right-hand tributary to Glen Fork, a branch of Laurel Branch of Clear Fork of Guyandot River, in Wyoming County.
Tommy; creek, a left-hand head fork of Guyandot River in Raleigh County.
Tommy Ridge; mountains in Raleigh County.
Toney; creek, a very small right-hand tributary to Coal River, a branch of Kanawha River, in Boone County.
Toney; fork, a small right-hand tributary to Clear Fork of Coal River in Raleigh County.
Toney; fork, a right-hand branch of Clear Fork of Guyandot River in Wyoming County.
Toney; fork, a small right-hand branch of Buffalo Creek, a tributary to Guyandot River, in Logan County.
Toney; fork, a small right-hand branch of Big Huff Creek, a tributary to Guyandot River, in Wyoming County.
Tony; branch, a small left-hand tributary to Right Fork of Lower Creek, a branch of Mud River, in Cabell County.

Tony; branch, a very small left-hand tributary to Big Ugly Creek, a branch of Guyandot River, in Lincoln County.
Tooley; post village in Wayne County.
Tophet; post village in Summers County.
Topins Grove; post village in Jackson County.
Top of Alleghany; post village in Pocahontas County.
Tornado; post village in Kanawha County. Altitude, 608 feet.
Town; branch, a very small right-hand tributary to Guyandot River, a branch of Ohio River, in Logan County.
Town; creek, a very small left-hand tributary to Paint Creek, a branch of Kanawha River, in Fayette County.
Town; mountain, a summit in Pendleton County near Franklin.
Town Creek Knob; summit of Paint Mountain on boundary line between Raleigh and Fayette counties. Altitude, 3,088 feet.
Trace; branch, a very small left-hand tributary to Horse Creek, a branch of Little Coal River, in Lincoln County.
Trace; branch, a left-hand head fork of Elk Creek, a tributary to Guyandot River, in Logan County.
Trace; branch, a small right-hand tributary of Slab Fork, a branch of Guyandot River, in Wyoming County.
Trace; branch, a very small right-hand tributary to South Fork of Elkhorn Creek in McDowell County.
Trace; creek, a small left-hand tributary to Mud River, a branch of Guyandot River, in Cabell County.
Trace; creek, a small left-hand tributary to Middle Fork of Mud River in Lincoln County.
Trace; creek, a very small right-hand tributary to Guyandot River, a branch of Ohio River, in Cabell County.
Trace; fork, a head fork of Strange Creek in Nicholas County.
Trace; fork, a small left-hand branch of Big Hart Creek, a tributary to Guyandot River, in Logan County.
Trace; fork, a small left-hand tributary to Panther Creek, a branch of Tug Fork of Big Sandy River, in McDowell County.
Trace; fork, a small left-hand branch of Hurricane Creek, a tributary to Kanawha River, in Putnam County.
Trace; fork, a small left-hand branch of Fourmile Creek, a tributary to Guyandot River, in Lincoln County.
Trace; fork, a small left-hand branch of Huff Creek, a tributary to Guyandot River, in Wyoming County.
Trace; fork, an indirect left-hand tributary to Indian Creek, a branch of Guyandot River, in Wyoming County.
Trace; fork, a left-hand branch of Davis Creek, a tributary to Kanawha River, in Kanawha County.
Trace; fork, a right-hand branch of Pigeon Creek, a tributary to Tug Fork of Big Sandy River, in Logan County.
Trace; fork, a right-hand branch of Tanner Fork, and tributary to Little Kanawha River, in Gilmer County.
Trace; fork, a small right-hand branch of Joe Creek, a tributary to Coal River, in Boone County.
Trace; fork, a large right-hand branch of Mud River in Lincoln and Putnam counties.
Trace; run, a small left-hand tributary to Little Kanawha River in Lewis and Upshur counties.
Trace; run, a small left-hand branch of Cedar Creek in Braxton County.

Trace Fork; branch, a small left-hand branch of Sandlick Fork of Laurel Creek, a tributary to Coal River, in Boone County.

Tract Hill; short ridge in the central part of Pendleton County. Altitude, 2,000 to 2,500 feet.

Trail; fork, a right-hand branch of Long Drain River in Wetzel County.

Travellers Repose; post village in Pocahontas County.

Tressel; post village in Pendleton County.

Triadelphia; town in Ohio County on the Baltimore and Ohio Railroad. Altitude, 735 feet. Population, 287.

Tribble; post village in Mason County.

Trilby; post village in Ritchie County.

Triplets; run, a right-hand branch of Little Kanawha River in Braxton County.

Triplett; fork, a right-hand branch of O'Brien Fork in Braxton County.

Triplett; post village in Roane County.

Tristan; post village in Roane County.

Triune; post village in Monongalia County.

Trough; creek, a right-hand branch of Kiah Fork of Twelvepole Creek in Wayne County.

Trough; fork, a small right-hand branch of Laurel Fork, a tributary to Clear Fork of Guyandot River, in Wyoming County.

Trough; fork, a small left-hand tributary to Laurel Fork, a branch of Spruce Fork of Little Coal River, in Boone County.

Trout; post village in Greenbrier County.

Trout; run, a small left-hand tributary to Left Fork of Right Fork of Buckhannon River in Randolph County.

Trout; run, a small right-hand tributary to South Branch of Potomac River in Pendleton and Hampshire counties.

Trout; run, a right-hand tributary to Cacapon River in Hardy County.

Trout; run, a small right-hand tributary to Left Fork of Right Fork of Buckhannon River in Randolph County.

Troy; town in Gilmer County. Population, 148.

Trubie; run, a small right-hand tributary to Buckhannon River in Upshur County.

True; post village in Summers County.

Truebada; post village in Gilmer County, situated on Little Kanawha River.

Tuckahoe; post village in Greenbrier County on the Chesapeake and Ohio Railway and on Dry Creek. Altitude, 2,035 feet.

Tucker; county, situated in the northern part of the State on the Allegheny Plateau. The average elevation is not far from 3,000 feet. Area, 440 square miles. Population, 13,433—white, 13,077; negro, 353; foreign born, 1,508. County seat, Parsons. The mean magnetic declination in 1900 was 3°. The mean annual rainfall is 50 inches, and the mean annual temperature 45° to 50°. The county is traversed by the West Virginia Central and Pittsburg Railway.

Tucker; post village in Wirt County.

Tucker; run, a right-hand branch of Lost Creek in Taylor County.

Tuckers; run, a small right-hand tributary to South Branch of Potomac River in Hardy County.

Tudell; post village in Wayne County.

Tug; fork, a small left-hand tributary to Birch River, a branch of Elk River, in Nicholas County.

Tug Fork of Big Sandy; fork, large branch of Big Sandy River, heading in McDowell County; it flows northwest, forming a portion of the western boundary of the State and joining Levisa Fork at Louisa.

Tugg; creek, a very small right-hand tributary to New River in Summers County.

Tug River; post village in McDowell County, located on Tug Fork of Big Sandy River.

Tunnelton; town in Preston County on the Baltimore and Ohio and the West Virginia Northern railroads. Altitude, 1,820 feet. Population, 479.

Turkey; branch, a very small left-hand branch of Right Fork of Twelvepole Creek, a tributary to Ohio River, in Wayne County.

Turkey; branch, a very small left-hand tributary to Piney Creek, a branch of New River, in Raleigh County.

Turkey; creek, a very small right-hand tributary to Guyandot River in Wyoming County.

Turkey; creek, a very small right-hand branch of Tug Fork of Big Sandy River in Mingo County.

Turkey; creek, a very small right-hand tributary to New River in Fayette County.

Turkey; creek, a small left-hand tributary to Trace Fork of Mud River, a branch of Guyandot River, in Putnam and Lincoln counties.

Turkey; creek, a small left-hand branch of Indian Creek, a tributary to New River, in Monroe County.

Turkey; creek, a small left-hand tributary to Gauley River in Webster County.

Turkey; fork, a left-hand tributary to Buffalo Creek, a branch of Elk River, in Nicholas County.

Turkey; mountain, a short ridge north of Williams River in Webster County. Altitude, 3,500 to 3,887 feet, the latter being the height of one of its peaks.

Turkey; post village in Mingo County.

Turkey; run, a small right-hand tributary to Right Fork of Middle Fork of Little Kanawha River in Upshur County.

Turkey; run, a right-hand branch of Plummer Run in Taylor County.

Turkey Bone; mountain, a short ridge in the western part of Randolph County. Altitude, 3,000 to 3,500 feet.

Turkey Camp Knob; summit in Wayne County.

Turkey Gap; branch, a very small right-hand tributary to South Fork of Elkhorn Creek in McDowell County.

Turkey Knob; branch, a very small right-hand tributary to Dunloup Creek, a branch of New River, in Fayette County.

Turkeylick; run, a right-hand branch of Tanner Creek in Gilmer County.

Turkey Ridge; mountains in Wyoming County.

Turkey Ridge; short spur between Taylor Ridge and Turkey Creek in Nicholas County.

Turkey Wallow; branch, a very small left-hand tributary to Indian Creek, a branch of Guyandot River, in Wyoming County.

Turley; branch, a small right-hand tributary to Dunloup Creek, a branch of New River, in Fayette County.

Turnhole; branch, a very small right-hand tributary to Tug Fork of Big Sandy River in McDowell County.

Turnrow; branch, a very small right-hand tributary to Indian Creek, a branch of Guyandot River, in Wyoming County.

Turtle; creek, a left-hand tributary to Little Coal River, a branch of Coal River, in Boone County.

Turtlecreek; post village in Boone County.

Twelve Mile; creek, a small left-hand tributary to East River, a branch of New River, in Mercer County.

Twelvepole; creek, a left-hand branch of Ohio River, formed by two forks, east and west, which rise in Wayne County.

Twelvepole; creek, a left-hand tributary to Ohio River in Wayne County.

Twentymile; creek, a right-hand tributary to Gauley River, a large branch of Kanawha River, in Nicholas County.
Twiggs; post village in Pleasants County.
Twilight; village in Ohio County.
Twin; branch, a small right-hand tributary to Tug Fork of Big Sandy River in McDowell County.
Twin; branches, small right-hand tributaries to Cranberry River, in Webster County.
Twin Sugars; summit in Greenbrier County.
Twisted Gun Gap; height in Mingo County. Altitude, 1,422 feet.
Twistville; post village in Braxton County.
Two; run, a small right-hand tributary to Crooked Fork of Steer Creek in Gilmer County.
Two and Three Quarters Mile; creek, a small left-hand tributary to Kanawha River in Kanawha County.
Two Lick; small right-hand tributary to Oil Creek in Lewis County.
Two Lick; run, a right-hand tributary to Little Birch River in Braxton County.
Twomile; branch, a small left-hand branch of Twentymile Creek, a tributary to Gauley River, in Nicholas County.
Twomile; branch, a very small left-hand branch of Dunloup Creek, a tributary to New River, in Fayette County.
Twomile; branch, a very small right-hand tributary to Glade Creek, a branch of New River, in Raleigh County.
Twomile; creek, a small right-hand tributary to Guyandot River, a branch of Ohio River, in Lincoln County.
Twomile; creek, a small right-hand tributary to Kanawha River in Kanawha County.
Twomile; creek, a very small left-hand branch of East Fork of Twelvepole Creek, a tributary to Ohio River, in Wayne County.
Twomile; fork, a small left-hand branch of Whiteoak Creek, a tributary to Coal River, in Boone County.
Tygart; creek, a small left-hand tributary to Ohio River in Wood County.
Tygart; post village in Randolph County on the Baltimore and Ohio Railroad.
Tygarts Valley; large branch of Monongahela River, heading in Randolph County. Its course is generally north through Barbour and Taylor counties to its mouth at Fairmont in Marion County.
Tyler; county, situated in the northwestern part of the State, bordering on Ohio River; situated at the foot of the slope of the Allegheny Plateau. Area, 269 square miles. Population, 18,252—white, 18,153; negro, 94; foreign born, 295. County seat, Middlebourne. The mean magnetic declination in 1900 was 2° 30′. The mean annual rainfall is 40 to 50 inches, and the mean annual temperature 50° to 55°. The county is traversed by the Ohio River Railroad.
Tyler; creek, a very small right-hand tributary to Guyandot River, a branch of Ohio River, in Cabell County.
Tyler; creek, a small right-hand tributary to Kanawha River in Kanawha County.
Tyner; post village in Wood County.
Tyrconnell Mines; post village in Taylor County.
Tyrone; post village in Monongalia County.
Uffington; post village in Monongalia County on the Baltimore and Ohio Railroad.
Ugly; branch, a small right-hand tributary to Marsh Fork of Coal River in Raleigh County.
Uler; post village in Roane County.
Ungers Store, post village in Morgan County.
Union; county seat of Monroe County. Population, 256.

Union Mills; post village in Pleasants County.
Unionridge; post village in Cabell County.
Uniontown; post village in Wetzel County.
Unknown; branch, a very small right-hand tributary to Paint Creek, a branch of Kanawha River, in Fayette County.
Uno; post village in Wyoming County.
Unus; post village in Greenbrier County.
Upland; post village in Mason County.
Upper; gap, height of Huff Mountain in Wyoming County.
Upper; creek, a very small right-hand tributary to Elk River, a large branch of Kanawha River, in Clay County.
Upper; mountain, a summit between two forks of Moore Run, a left-hand branch of Greenbrier River, in Pocahontas County.
Upper; run, a right-hand branch of South Fork of Fishing Creek in Wetzel County.
Upper Bee Tree; run, a small left-hand tributary to Back Fork of Elk River in Randolph County.
Upper Belcher; branch, a small left-hand tributary to Elkhorn Creek, a branch of Tug Fork of Big Sandy River, in McDowell County.
Upper Birch; run, a very small left-hand tributary to Elk River in Clay County.
Upper Cove; headwaters of Lost River in Hardy County.
Upperglade; post village in Webster County.
Upper Hensley; creek, a small right-hand tributary to Tug Fork of Big Sandy River in McDowell River.
Upper Level; run, a left-hand branch of Cedar Creek in Gilmer County.
Upper Lick; small left-hand tributary to Laurel Fork, a branch of Spruce Fork of Little Coal River, in Boone County.
Upper Mill; creek, a small left-hand tributary to Elk River in Braxton County.
Upper Pond Lick; small left-hand tributary to Shavers Fork of Cheat River in Randolph County.
Upper Road; branch, a small right-hand tributary to Clear Fork, a branch of Guyandot River, in Wyoming County.
Upper Shannon; branch, a small right-hand tributary to Tug Fork of Big Sandy River in McDowell County.
Upper Shant; run, a small right-hand tributary to Back Fork of Elk River in Randolph County.
Upper Shaver; run, a small left-hand tributary to Left Fork of Steer Creek in Braxton County.
Upper Sleith; fork, a small left-hand tributary to Right Fork of Steer Creek in Braxton County.
Upper Sturgeon; branch, a head fork of Big Cub Creek, a tributary to Guyandot River, in Wyoming County.
Upper Threemile; fork, a small right-hand branch of Blue Creek, a tributary to Elk River, in Kanawha County.
Upper Tony Camp; run, a small right-hand tributary to Dry Fork of Cheat River in Randolph County.
Uppertract; post village in Pendleton County.
Upper Two; run, a small left-hand tributary to Left Fork of Steer Creek in Gilmer County.
Upshur; county situated in the central part of the State. It is drained northward by Buckhannon River. Area, 326 square miles. Population, 14,696—white, 14,473; negro, 221; foreign born, 106. County seat, Buckhannon. The mean magnetic declination in 1900 was 2° 30′. The mean annual rainfall is 50 inches, and the mean annual temperature 45° to 50°. The county is traversed by the Baltimore and Ohio Railroad.

GAZETTEER OF WEST VIRGINIA. 155

Upton; branch, a very small left-hand tributary to Mud River, a branch of Guyandot River, in Lincoln County.
Upton; creek, a very small left-hand tributary to Kanawha River in Kanawha County.
Upton; village in Marion County.
Utica; post village in Jackson County.
Uvilla; post village in Jefferson County.
Vadis; post village in Lewis County.
Vall; creek, a small left-hand tributary to Dry Fork, a branch of Tug Fork of Big Sandy Creek, in McDowell County.
Valley; fork, a left-hand branch of Middle Fork of Mud River, a tributary to Guyandot River, in Lincoln County.
Valley; fork, a right-hand branch of Elk River in Randolph County.
Valley; mount, a summit in Pocahontas County. Altitude, 3,500 feet.
Valley; river, a tributary to Monongahela River.
Valleybend; post village in Randolph County on the West Virginia Central and Pittsburg Railway.
Valleydale; post village in Greenbrier County.
Valleyfalls; post village in Marion County, on the Baltimore and Ohio Railroad. Altitude, 969 feet.
Valleyfork; post village in Clay County.
Valley Furnace; post village in Barbour County.
Valley Grove; branch, a small right-hand branch of Elk Twomile Creek, a tributary to Elk River, in Kanawha County.
Valleygrove; post village in Ohio County on the Baltimore and Ohio Railroad.
Valleyhead; post village in Randolph County.
Valley Mills; post village in Wood County.
Valleypoint; post village in Preston County.
Van; post village in Boone County.
Vancamp; post village in Wetzel County.
Van Clevesville; post village in Berkeley County on the Baltimore and Ohio Railroad. Altitude, 500 feet.
Vandalia; post village in Lewis County.
Vandegrift; post village in Randolph County.
Vanetta; creek, a very small right-hand tributary to Guyandot River, a branch of Ohio River, in Lincoln County.
Vannoys Mill; post village in Barbour County.
Vanvoorhis; post village in Monongalia County on the Baltimore and Ohio Railroad.
Varney; post village in Mingo County.
Vaughan; post village in Nicholas County on the Chesapeake and Ohio Railway.
Vegan; post village in Upshur County.
Venable; branch, a very small left-hand tributary to Kanawha River in Kanawha County.
Venison; fork, a right-hand branch of Perkins Fork in Braxton County.
Venus; post village in Gilmer County.
Veranda; post village in Mason County.
Victor; post village in Fayette County.
Victoria; post village in Preston County.
Vienna; post village in Wood County on the Baltimore and Ohio Railroad.
View; village in Greenbrier County.
Vilas; post village in Ritchie County.
Villa; post village in Kanawha County.
Vincen; post village in Wetzel County.

Viney; mountain, a ridge in Pocahontas County.
Vinton; post village in Nicholas County.
Viola; post village in Marshall County.
Virgie; post village in Clay County.
Viropa; post village in Harrison County on the Baltimore and Ohio Railroad.
Vista; post village in Raleigh County.
Vivian; post village in McDowell County on the Norfolk and Western Railway and on Elkhorn Creek. Altitude, 1,502 feet.
Volcano; post village in Wood County on the Baltimore and Ohio Railroad.
Volga; post village in Barbour County on the Baltimore and Ohio Railroad.
Waddles; run, a right-hand branch of Short Creek in Ohio County.
Wade; fork, a left-hand branch of Little Sycamore Creek, a tributary to Elk River, in Clay County.
Wade; post village in Wetzel County.
Wadestown; post village in Monongalia County.
Wagner Knob; summit in Pendleton County.
Wainville; post village in Webster County.
Waites; run, a small right-hand tributary to Cacapon River in Hardy County.
Waiteville; post village in Monroe County.
Waldo; post village in Putnam County.
Walker; fork, a right-hand branch of Conyer Fork, a tributary to Cedar Creek, in Braxton County.
Walker; post village in Wood County on the Baltimore and Ohio Railroad.
Walker Ridge; short spur in Grant County.
Walkers; creek, a small left-hand branch of Ohio River in western Virginia.
Walkersville; post village in Lewis County.
Wall; branch, a very small right-hand tributary to Clear Fork, a branch of Guyandot River, in Wyoming County.
Wallace; branch, a very small left-hand tributary to Guyandot River, in Wyoming County.
Wallace; post village in Harrison County on the Baltimore and Ohio Railroad.
Wallow Hole; fork, a small left-hand tributary to Buffalo Creek, a branch of Elk River, in Clay County.
Wallow Hole; mountain, a short spur east of Greenbrier River in Greenbrier County. Altitude, 2,000 to 2,500 feet.
Wallow Hole Knob; summit in Clay County.
Walnut; creek, a very small left-hand tributary to Elk River in Kanawha County.
Walnut; fork, a small right-hand tributary to Elk River in Braxton County.
Walnut; gap, a height in Wyoming County. Altitude, 2,716 feet.
Walnut; post village in Calhoun County.
Walnut; run, a small right-hand tributary to Left Fork of Steer Creek in Braxton County.
Walnutgrove; post village in Roane County on the Charleston, Clendennin and Sutton Railroad.
Walnut Knob; summit in Clay County.
Walton; post village in Roane County on the Chesapeake and Ohio Railway.
Wanless; post village in Pocahontas County on the Cairo and Kanawha Valley Railroad.
Wappocomo; post village in Hampshire County.
War; branch, a very small right-hand tributary to Tug Fork of Big Sandy River in McDowell County.
War; creek, a small left-hand tributary to Dry Fork, a branch of Tug Fork of Big Sandy River, in McDowell County.
Warden; post village in Raleigh County.

Warden; run, a right-hand tributary of Little Wheeling Creek in Ohio County.
Wardensville; town and post village in Hardy County. Population, 152.
Ward Knob; summit in Randolph County.
Wards; run, a small right-hand tributary to Valley River in Randolph County.
Warfield; post village in Clay County on the Porters Creek and Gauley Railroad.
Warford; post village in Summers County.
Warm Hollow; branch, a very small right-hand branch of Tug Fork of Big Sandy River, a tributary to Ohio River, in Logan County.
Warren; post village in Jackson County on the Baltimore and Ohio Railroad.
Warrior; fork, a left-hand branch of Buffalo Creek in Marion County.
Washburn; post village in Ritchie County.
Wash Hill; fork, a left-hand tributary to Horse Creek, a branch of Little Coal River, in Boone County.
Washington; post village in Wood County on the Baltimore and Ohio Railroad.
Wasp; post village in Pleasants County.
Watering Pond; small left-hand tributary to North Fork of Greenbrier River in Pocahontas County.
Watering Pond Knob; summit in Pocahontas County.
Waterloo; post village in Mason County.
Watkins; post village in Tyler County.
Watson; branch, a very small right-hand tributary to Kanawha River in Kanawha County.
Watson; island in Kanawha River in Kanawha County.
Watson (Capon Springs); town in Marion County. Population, 18.
Watts; branch, a very small left-hand tributary to West Fork of Twelvepole Creek, a branch of Ohio River, in Wayne County.
Wattsville; post village in Clay County.
Waverly; post village in Wood County on the Baltimore and Ohio Railroad.
Way; run, a left-hand branch of South Fork of Fishing Creek in Wetzel County.
Wayne; county, situated in the southwestern part of the State on the lower slopes of the Allegheny Plateau. It is drained mainly by Twelvepole Creek. Area, 545 square miles. Population, 23,619—white, 23,298; negro, 321; foreign born, 51. County seat, Wayne. The mean magnetic declination in 1900 was 30'. The mean annual rainfall is 40 to 50 inches, and the mean annual temperature 50° to 55°. The county is traversed by the Norfolk and Western and the Chesapeake and Ohio railways.
Wayne; county seat of Wayne county on the Norfolk and Western Railway.
Wayside; post village in Monroe County.
Weaver; post village in Randolph County on the Belington and Beaver Creek Railroad.
Weavers Knob; summit in Greenbrier County. Altitude, 2,931 feet.
Webster; county, situated in the central part of the State, on the Allegheny Plateau, and drained by tributaries to Little Kanawha River. Area, 590 square miles. Population, 8,862—white, 8,850; negro, 12; foreign born, 74. County seat, Addison. The mean magnetic declination in 1900 was 2° 10'. The mean annual rainfall is 50 to 60 inches, and the mean annual temperature 45° to 50°. The county is traversed by the Baltimore and Ohio Railroad.
Webster; post village in Taylor County on the Baltimore and Ohio Railroad. Altitude, 1,022 feet.
Webster Springs; county seat of Webster County. Population, 297.
Weiss Knob; summit of Canaan Mountain in Tucker County. Altitude, 4,490 feet.
Welch; county seat of McDowell County at junction of Elkhorn Creek with Tug Fork of Big Sandy River and on the Norfolk and Western Railway. Altitude, 1,297 feet. Population, 442.

Welcome; post village in Marshall County.
Wellford; post village in Kanawha County.
Wellington; post village in Roane County.
Wells; post village in Marshall County on the Baltimore and Ohio Railroad.
Wells; run, a right-hand branch of Buffalo Creek in Brooke County.
Wellsburg; county seat of Brooke County on the Pittsburg, Cincinnati, Chicago and St. Louis Railroad. Population, 2,588. Altitude, 635 feet.
Welsh Glade; summit in Webster County on the Pittsburg, Cincinnati, Chicago and St. Louis Railway. Altitude, 2,222 feet.
Wesley; post village in Wood County.
West; fork, a large right-hand branch of Pond Fork of Little Coal River in Boone County.
West; post village in Wetzel County.
West; run, a right-hand branch of Monongahela River in Monongalia County.
West Columbia; village in Mason County on the Baltimore and Ohio Railroad. Population, 205.
West End; post village in Preston County on the Baltimore and Ohio Railroad. Altitude, 945 feet.
Westfall; fork, a small right-hand branch of Cedar Creek in Braxton County.
West Liberty; post village in Ohio County.
West Milford; town in Harrison County. Population, 187.
Weston; county seat of Lewis County on the Baltimore and Ohio Railroad. Altitude, 824 feet.
West Union; county seat of Doddridge County on the Baltimore and Ohio Railroad. Population, 623. Altitude, 800 feet.
Wet; branch, a left-hand tributary to Cabin Creek, a branch of Kanawha River, in Kanawha County.
Wetzel; county, situated in the northwestern part of the State, bordering on Ohio River and lying at the foot of the slope of the Allegheny Plateau. Area, 365 square miles. Population, 22,880—white, 22,440; negro, 439; foreign born, 393. County seat, New Martinsville. The mean magnetic declination in 1900 was 2° 30′. The mean annual rainfall is 40 to 50 inches, and the mean annual temperature 50° to 55°. The county is traversed by the Ohio River and the Baltimore and Ohio railroads.
Wharncliffe; post village in Mingo County on the Norfolk and Western Railway. Altitude, 822 feet.
Wheatland; post village in Jefferson County on the Norfolk and Western Railway.
Wheeler; fork, a small right-hand tributary to Skin Creek in Lewis County.
Wheeler; small islands in Kanawha River in Fayette County.
Wheeling; creek, a small left-hand branch of Ohio River, rising in Pennsylvania and flowing west into Ohio River.
Wheeling; county seat of Ohio County on the Baltimore and Ohio, the Pittsburg, Cincinnati, Chicago and St. Louis, and the Wheeling and Lake Erie railroads. Altitude, 645 feet.
Whetstone; creek, a left-hand branch of Fish Creek in Wetzel County.
Whetstone; post village in Clay County.
Whetstone; run, a small left-hand tributary to South Branch of Potomac River in Pendleton County.
Whetstone; run, a right-hand branch of Buffalo Creek in Marion County.
Whisler; run, a left-hand branch of Dunkard Creek in Monongalia County.
Whitcomb; post village in Greenbrier County on the Chesapeake and Ohio Railway.
White; post village in Preston County.
White; run, a right-hand tributary of Potomac River in Berkeley County.
Whiteday; post village in Monongalia County.

Whiteman; branch, a small right-hand branch of Aaron Fork of Little Sandy Creek, a tributary to Elk River, in Kanawha County.

Whiteoak; branch, a very small right-hand tributary to East Fork of Twelvepole Creek, a branch of Ohio River, in Wayne County.

Whiteoak; branch, a very small right-hand branch of Laurel Fork, a tributary to Clear Fork of Guyandot River, in Wyoming County.

Whiteoak; branch, a small right-hand tributary to Laurel Fork, a branch of Spruce Fork of Little Coal River, in Boone County.

Whiteoak; branch, a very small right-hand tributary to Indian Creek, a branch of Guyandot River, in Wyoming County.

Whiteoak; branch, a small left-hand tributary to Panther Creek, a branch of Tug Fork of Big Sandy River, in McDowell County.

Whiteoak; branch, a very small left-hand tributary to Coal River, a branch of Kanawha River, in Boone County.

Whiteoak; creek, a left-hand branch of Dunloup Creek, a tributary to New River, in Fayette County.

Whiteoak; creek, a very small left-hand tributary to Guyandot River, a branch of Ohio River, in Mingo County.

Whiteoak; creek, a small right-hand tributary to Clear Fork of Coal River in Raleigh County.

Whiteoak; creek, a small right-hand tributary to Coal River, a branch of Kanawha River, in Boone County.

White Oak; fork, a small indirect left-hand tributary to Blue Creek, a branch of Elk River, in Kanawha County.

White Oak; fork, a small right-hand tributary to Williams River in Webster County.

Whiteoak; fork, a small right-hand branch of Loop Creek, a tributary to Kanawha River, in Fayette County.

White Oak; mountain, a short ridge north of Williams River, in Webster County. Altitude, 3,500 feet.

White Oak; mountain, a broken mountainous range, forming the boundary between Raleigh and Summers counties. Altitude, 3,418 feet.

Whiteoak; post village in Ritchie County.

White Oak; run, a small right-hand tributary to Left Fork of Steer Creek in Gilmer County.

Whitepine; post village in Calhoun County.

White Rock; mountain, a short ridge east of Greenbrier River in Greenbrier County. Altitude, 2,500 to 3,212 feet, the latter the height of one peak.

Whites; branch, a small right-hand tributary to West Fork, a branch of Pond Fork of Little Coal River, in Boone County.

Whites; run, a left-hand branch of Cheat River in Monongalia County.

Whites Creek; post village in Wayne County.

Whites Draft; small left-hand tributary to Anthony Creek, a branch of Greenbrier River, in Greenbrier County.

Whites Trace; very small left-hand tributary to Spruce Fork of Little Coal River in Logan County.

White Sulphur Springs; post village in Greenbrier County on Howards Creek and on the Chesapeake and Ohio Railway. Altitude, 2,000 feet.

Whitewater; small left-hand branch of Peter Creek, a tributary to Gauley River, in Nicholas County.

Whitfield; post village in Ohio County.

Whitman; run, a small left-hand tributary to Valley River in Randolph County.

Whitman Flats; summit in Randolph County.

Whitman Knob; summit in Randolph County.

Whitmans; run, a small left-hand tributary to Anthony Creek, a branch of Greenbrier River, in Greenbrier County.
Wick; post village in Tyler County.
Wickwire; run, a right-hand branch of Tygarts Valley River in Taylor County.
Wide Mouth; creek, a left-hand tributary to Bluestone River in Mercer County.
Wiggins; post village in Summers County on the Chesapeake and Ohio Railway.
Wikel; post village in Monroe County.
Wilbur; post village in Tyler County.
Wildcat; post village in Lewis County.
Wild Cat; run, a small left-hand tributary to Skin Creek in Lewis County.
Wild Cat Knob; summit in Nicholas County. Altitude, 2,837 feet.
Wilderness; fork, a middle fork of Fork Creek, a tributary to Coal River, in Boone County.
Wilding; post village in Jackson County.
Wiley; fork, a right-hand branch of North Fork of Fishing Creek in Wetzel County.
Wiley Spring; branch, a small left-hand tributary to Devils Fork, a branch of Guyandot River, in Raleigh County.
Wileyville; post village in Wetzel County.
Wilkerson; branch, a very small left-hand tributary to Pocotaligo River, a branch of Kanawha River, in Kanawha County.
Willey; fork, a right-hand branch of North Fork of Fishing Creek in Wetzel County.
Willey; post village in Monongalia County.
William; post village in Tucker County on the West Virginia Central and Pittsburg Railway.
William Camp; run, a small right-hand tributary to Gauley River in Webster County.
Williams; fork, a left-hand tributary to Trace Fork of Mud River, a branch of Guyandot River, in Lincoln County.
Williams; river, a large left-hand branch of Gauley River, rising in Pocahontas County, and flowing northwesterly through Webster County to its mouth.
Williamsburg; post village in Greenbrier County.
Williamson; branch, a very small right-hand branch of Tug Fork of Big Sandy River, a tributary to Ohio River, in Logan County.
Williamson; branch, a very small right-hand tributary to Guyandot River in Wyoming County.
Williamson; county seat of Mingo County on the Norfolk and Western Railway.
Williamson; station in Logan County on the Norfolk and Western Railway and on Tug Fork of Big Sandy River.
Williamsport; post village in Grant County, situated on Patterson Creek. Altitude, 988 feet.
Williams River; mountain, a ridge extending from Webster County into Pocahontas. Altitude, 3,000 to 4,000 feet.
Williamstown; post village in Wood County.
Willis; branch, a very small left-hand tributary to Paint Creek, a branch of Kanawha River, in Fayette County.
Willow; post village in Pleasants County.
Willowbend; post village in Monroe County.
Willowdale; post village in Jackson County.
Willowgrove; post village in Jackson County, on the Baltimore and Ohio Railroad.
Willowton; post village in Mercer County.
Willowtree; post village in Jackson County.
Wills; creek, a left-hand branch of Little Sandy Creek, a tributary to Elk River, in Kanawha County.

Wilmore; station in McDowell County on the Norfolk and Western Railway and on Tug Fork of Big Sandy River.

Wilmoth; run, a small right-hand tributary to Valley River in Randolph County.

Wilson; branch, a small left-hand branch of Laurel Creek, a tributary to New River, in Fayette County.

Wilson; branch, a very small right-hand tributary to Kanawha River in Kanawha County.

Wilson; creek, a small right-hand branch of Twelvepole Creek, a tributary to Ohio River, in Wayne County.

Wilson; fork, a small left-hand branch of Laurel Patch Run in Braxton County.

Wilson; post village in Grant County on North Fork of Potomac River and on the West Virginia Central and Pittsburg Railway. Altitude, 2,512 feet.

Wilson; run, a small right-hand tributary to South Fork of Potomac River in Hardy and Pendleton counties.

Wilson; run, a right-hand branch of South Fork of Fishing Creek in Wetzel County.

Wilsonburg; post village in Harrison County, on the Baltimore and Ohio Railroad.

Wilsondale; post village in Wayne County on the Chesapeake and Ohio Railway and on the Right Fork of Twelvepole Creek.

Wilsonia; post village and railway station in Grant county, situated on North Branch of Potomac River, also on West Virginia Central and Pittsburgh Railway. Altitude, 2,747 feet.

Wilson Knob; summit in Upshur County.

Winding Gulf; right-hand head fork of Guyandot River in Raleigh County.

Wind Mill; gap, in Great Flat Top Mountain in Mercer County.

Windmill Gap; branch, a right-hand tributary to North Fork of Elkhorn Creek in McDowell County.

Windom; post village in Wyoming County on the West Virginia Central and Pittsburg Railway.

Windy; post village in Wirt County.

Windy; run, a small right-hand tributary to Little Birch River in Braxton County.

Windy; run, a small right-hand tributary to Valley River in Randolph County.

Winfield; county seat of Putnam County. Population, 338.

Wingrove; branch, a small right-hand tributary to Sand Lick Creek, a branch of Marsh Fork of Coal River, in Raleigh County.

Winifrede; post village in Kanawha County on the Chesapeake and Ohio Railway and the Winifrede Railroad.

Winnie; village in Wirt County.

Winona; post village in Fayette County.

Winters; run, a right-hand tributary of Wheeling Creek in Marshall County.

Wirt; county, situated in the western part of the State on the lower slope of the Alleghany Plateau. Area, 254 square miles. Population, 10,284—white, 10,220; negro, 64; foreign born, 19. County seat, Elizabeth. The mean magnetic declination in 1900 was 3°. The mean annual rainfall is 40 to 50 inches, and the mean annual temperature 50° to 55°. The county is traversed by the Little Kanawha Railroad.

Wise; post village in Monongalia County.

Wise; run, a left-hand branch of West Virginia Fork of Dunkard Creek in Monongalia County.

Wiseburg; post village in Jackson County.

Witchers; creek, a left-hand tributary to Kanawha River in Kanawha County.

Wolf; creek, a small left-hand tributary to Greenbrier River in Summers County, joining it at The Big Bend.

Wolf; creek, a small left-hand tributary to Greenbrier River in Monroe County.
Wolf; creek, a small left-hand tributary to Bluestone River in Mercer County.
Wolf; a left-hand tributary to New River in Fayette County.
Wolf; creek, a left-hand branch of Skin Creek, a tributary to West Fork of Monongahela River, in Lewis County.
Wolf; creek, a left-hand tributary to Elk River in Braxton County.
Wolf; creek, a small right-hand tributary to Cheat River in Preston County.
Wolf; gap in Pretty Ridge in Wyoming County.
Wolf; hill in Morgan County. Elevation, 900 feet.
Wolf; run, a small right-hand tributary to Skin Creek in Lewis County.
Wolf; run, a right-hand branch of Fish Creek in Wetzel County.
Wolf Creek: mountain, a short ridge in Monroe County. Altitude, 2,500 to 2,810 feet, the highest point the height of one peak.
Wolf Creek; mountain, a short, curved ridge in Summers County. Altitude, 2,000 to 2,500 feet.
Wolfcreek; post village in Monroe County on the Chesapeake and Ohio Railway.
Wolf Fork; mountain, a short ridge in Lewis County.
Wolfpen; branch, a very small right-hand branch of Big Sycamore Creek, a tributary to Elk River, in Clay County.
Wolf Pen; branch, a small right-hand tributary to Clear Fork, a branch of Tug Fork of Big Sandy River, in McDowell County.
Wolfpen; branch, a very small right-hand tributary to Beech Fork of Twelvepole Creek, a branch of Ohio River, in Wayne County.
Wolfpen; branch, a small right-hand tributary to Indian Creek, a branch of Guyandot River, in Wyoming County.
Wolfpen; branch, a small right-hand branch of Little Sandy Creek, a tributary to Elk River, in Kanawha County.
Wolfpen; branch, a very small left-hand tributary to Guyandot River in Wyoming County.
Wolfpen; branch, a very small left-hand tributary to Clear Fork of Guyandot River in Wyoming County.
Wolf Pen; run, a small left-hand tributary to Birch River in Braxton County.
Wolf Pen; run, a small left-hand tributary to West Fork of Monongahela River in Lewis County.
Wolf Pen; run, a right-hand branch of Sand Fork in Lewis County.
Wolf Pen; run, a small right-hand branch of Stewart Creek in Gilmer County.
Wolf Pen; run, a small right-hand tributary to Right Fork of Steer Creek in Braxton County.
Wolf Pen Ridge; short range in the central part of Pocahontas County.
Wolfpit; fork, a small left-hand tributary to Little Coal River, a branch of Coal River, in Lincoln County.
Wolfrun; post village in Marshall County.
Wolf Summit; post village in Harrison County on the Baltimore and Ohio Railroad.
Womelsdorf; post village in Randolph County.
Wood; county, situated in the western part of the State on the Ohio River and lying at the foot of the Allegheny Plateau. Area, 357 square miles. Population, 34,452—white, 33,528; negro, 922; foreign born, 925. County seat, Parkersburg. The mean magnetic declination in 1900 was 1° 10'. The mean annual rainfall is 40 to 50 inches, and the temperature 50° to 55°. The county is traversed by the Baltimore and Ohio, the Baltimore and Ohio Southwestern, the Little Kanawha, and Ohio River railroads.
Woodbine; post village in Nicholas County.

GAZETTEER OF WEST VIRGINIA.

Woodlands; post village in Marshall County.
Woodrow; post village in Morgan County on the West Virginia Central and Pittsburg Railway.
Woodruff; post village in Marshall County on the Baltimore and Ohio Railroad.
Woodrum; branch, a very small right-hand branch of Powellton Fork of Armstrong Creek, a tributary to Kanawha River, in Fayette County.
Woods; run, a small right-hand tributary to Greenbrier River in Pocahontas County.
Woods; run, a right-hand branch of Wheeling Creek in Ohio County.
Woodward; branch, a small right-hand branch of Twomile Creek, a tributary to Kanawha River, in Kanawha County.
Woodyard; post village in Roane County.
Woodzell; post village in Webster County.
Woosley; post village in Wyoming County.
Workman; branch, a small right-hand tributary to Pond Fork of Little Coal River, a branch of Coal River, in Boone County.
Workman; branch, a very small right-hand tributary to Pinnacle Creek, a branch of Guyandot River, in Wyoming County.
Workman; creek, a small left-hand tributary to Clear Fork of Coal River in Raleigh County.
Workman Knob; summit in Boone County.
Worley; post village in Monongalia County on the Chesapeake and Ohio Railway.
Worth; post village in McDowell County.
Worthington; post village in Marion County on the Baltimore and Ohio Railroad.
Wrack Timber; run, a small right-hand tributary to Holly River in Webster County.
Wright; post village in Raleigh County on the Chesapeake and Ohio Railway.
Wyant; fork, a right-hand branch of Grass Run in Gilmer County.
Wyatt; post village in Harrison County.
Wyatt; run, a left-hand branch of Left Fork of Steep Creek in Braxton County.
Wylies; falls in New River on boundary between Mercer and Summers counties.
Wyoma; post village in Mason County.
Wyoming; county, situated in the southern part of the State and drained by Guyandot River. The Allegheny Plateau is here deeply dissected. Area, 526 square miles. Population, 8,380—white, 8,286; negro, 94; foreign born, 5. County seat, Oceana. The mean magnetic declination in 1900 was 1°. The mean annual rainfall is 50 to 60 inches, and the mean annual temperature 50° to 55°.
Yankeedam; post village in Clay County on the Charleston, Clendennin and Sutton Railroad.
Yeager; post village in Mason County.
Yeager; run, a left-hand branch of West Virginia Fork of Dunkard Creek in Monongalia County.
Yelk; post village in Pocahontas County.
Yellow; creek, a small right-hand tributary to Blackwater River in Tucker County.
Yellowspring; post village in Hampshire County.
Yellow Spring; run, a left-hand branch of Sleepy Creek in Morgan County.
Yew; mountains, a broken mountainous range extending into Greenbrier and Webster counties. Altitude, 3,000 to 4,000 feet.
Yokum; post village in Upshur County.
Yokums Knob; summit in the Allegheny Mountains in Randolph County. Altitude, 4,330 feet.
Yorkville; post village in Wayne County.
Youngs; mountain, a summit in Day Mountain in Pocahontas County.

Youngs Knob; summit in Kanawha County.
Zackville; post village in Wirt County.
Zar; post village in Preston County.
Zebs; creek, a small left-hand tributary to Valley River in Barbour and Randolph counties.
Zela; post village in Nicholas County.
Zenith; post village in Monroe County.
Zinnia; post village in Doddridge County.
Zona; post village in Roane County.
Zypho; post village in Harrison County.

O

www.ingramcontent.com/pod-product-compliance
Lightning Source LLC
Chambersburg PA
CBHW050620300426
44112CB00012B/1589